ECONOMIC ANALYSIS AND POLICY

Background Readings for Current Issues

ECONOMIC ANALYSIS AND POLICY

PRENTICE-HALL, INC., Englewood Cliffs, New Jersey

Myron L. Joseph

*Professor of Economics
and Head, Department of Industrial Management
Carnegie Institute of Technology*

Norton C. Seeber

*Assistant Professor of Economics
Carnegie Institute of Technology*

George Leland Bach

*Maurice Falk Professor of Economics and Social Science
Carnegie Institute of Technology*

BACKGROUND READINGS

FOR CURRENT ISSUES

SECOND EDITION

ECONOMIC ANALYSIS
AND POLICY

Background Readings for Current Issues

SECOND EDITION

Myron L. Joseph,
Norton C. Seeber,
and George Leland Bach

© 1963, 1966 by PRENTICE-HALL, INC.
Englewood Cliffs, N.J.

LIBRARY OF CONGRESS
CATALOG CARD NUMBER: 66-13946

Current Printing (last digit):
10   9   8   7   6   5   4   3   2   1

Printed in the UNITED STATES OF AMERICA
C-22288

PRENTICE-HALL INTERNATIONAL, INC., *London*
PRENTICE-HALL OF AUSTRALIA, PTY. LTD., *Sydney*
PRENTICE-HALL OF CANADA, LTD., *Toronto*
PRENTICE-HALL OF INDIA (PRIVATE) LTD., *New Delhi*
PRENTICE-HALL OF JAPAN, INC., *Tokyo*

Preface

This volume of readings is designed for instructors who want their students to apply economic theory to the big public policy issues of the day. It selects a relatively small number of major economic problems (poverty, growth, unemployment, gold and international payments, and the like) and provides readings *in depth* as materials to which students may *apply the relevant micro and macro theory* taken from the text *to reach their own conclusions.*

We believe that economics can be a lively science to students when they can see its relevance to important issues of concern to them. The selections provide a rich source of material on the crucial economic problems of our time and will give students vital problem-solving experience. If students become involved and interested in using their economics to analyze important problems, the likelihood is that they will remember and use their economics five or ten years later after the threat of the final examination is long past.

The readings are not brief paragraphs or excerpts. Each is long enough to convey the "substance and feel" of the position being stated by the author, and can really be understood and analyzed by the student. Thus, students can achieve thoroughness and depth of understanding without having to purchase a paperback for each problem area studied.

The volume was designed to accomplish its objectives in the following ways:

1. The selections are especially chosen to provide the materials for independent student problem-solving on prominent, relatively unstructured economic problems, such as "automation," inflation, and poverty. In this revision, we have included completely new or substantially revised sections on economic growth, unemployment and manpower problems, big business and government policy, labor markets, poverty and insecurity, monetary policy and debt, and international finance and gold. In general, we have increased the focus on economic analysis and the discussion of specific policy alternatives.

2. To illuminate and clarify the outstanding public policy issues of today, we have included directly conflicting statements by economists, political leaders, and other observers. These are intended not only to sharpen the economic issues, but also to help students understand the deep cross currents often involved in economics, how economic analysis is used by different people, and the interactions

of economic and non-economic forces in the policy-making process. Some examples are:

(a) The public disagreement of William Martin, Chairman of the Federal Reserve Board, and Professor James Tobin, former member of the Council of Economic Advisers.
(b) The opposing views of J. K. Galbraith and of Ernest van den Haag—a strong conservative—on the expansion of the range of social services provided by government.
(c) The conflicting interpretations of the Council of Economic Advisers and the minority members of the Joint Economic Committee on the role of fiscal policy in the 1961-1964 recovery.
(d) The opinions of structuralist Professor Charles Killingsworth contrasting with those of Professor Robert Solow on the causes of unemployment.

3. There are several selections on the political, sociological, and organizational aspects of the world within which solutions to economic problems must be reached. For example:

(a) Selections on the plight of the unemployed worker and the aged poor.
(b) President Kennedy's account of the pressures facing a legislator in his consideration of economic legislation.
(c) Accounts of Alfred Hayes, President of the Federal Reserve Bank of New York, and by two other economists on the actual process of monetary policy formation and the considerations taken into account in this process.

4. Several selections provide concrete historical background for current economic problems, enabling students to consider current issues against the events and the attitudes that have produced them. For example:

(a) The sit-down strikes and picket lines of the 1930's, which still help to explain the attitudes and behavior of many union leaders and members today.
(b) The unemployment and desperation of the great depression of the 1930's, which were crucial in shaping modern attitudes toward economic stabilization and social security policies.
(c) The financial panic and bank holiday of the depression days, which provide a vivid backdrop for current monetary and financial problems.

We have included historical readings on all of these subjects, covering both the economic and non-economic forces at work.

We believe this volume will be a significant aid to teachers who want to supplement a solid, analytically-oriented text with readings that offer a wealth of materials for a sample of major policy problems. These readings should help to crystallize the issues with which the student must grapple if, by applying economic analysis, he is to reach his own solutions to complex, real-world issues.

We are greatly indebted to our secretaries, Francis Gibson and Thelma Johnson, for services far beyond the call of their duty; and to Ruth Corrigan in the Carnegie Institute of Technology Library for her invaluable aid in helping us do the library research underlying this volume.

M. L. J.
N. C. S.
G. L. B.

Contents

x   *Contents*

PART ONE

The Foundations of Economic Analysis

What is economics about? How should it be studied? Is it a science in the same sense that the natural sciences are? The famous English economist Alfred Marshall presents the classical view that "economics is a study of mankind in the ordinary business of life," and discusses its relation to other scientific fields.

Alfred Marshall was perhaps the most influential economist in the world during the last part of the nineteenth and early part of the twentieth century. He was Professor of Economics at Cambridge University.

1

Economic Generalizations or Laws

ALFRED MARSHALL

Political Economy or Economics is a study of mankind in the ordinary business of life; it examines that part of individual and social action which is most closely connected with the attainment and with the use of the material requisites of wellbeing.

Thus it is on the one side a study of wealth; and on the other, and more important side, a part of the study of man. For man's character has been moulded by his every-day work, and the material resources which he thereby procures, more than by any other influence unless it be that of his religious ideals; and the two great forming agencies of the world's history have been the religious and the economic. Here and there the ardour of the military or the artistic spirit has been for a while predominant: but religious and economic influences have nowhere been displaced from the front rank even for a time; and they have nearly always been more important than all others put together. Religious motives are more intense than economic, but their direct action seldom extends over so large a part of life. For the business by which a person earns his livelihood generally fills his thoughts during by far the greater part of those hours in which his mind is at its best; during them his character is being formed by the way in which he uses his faculties in his work, by the thoughts and the feelings which it suggests, and by his relations to his associates in work, his employers or his employees.

*　　*　　*

The advantage which economics has over other branches of social sci-

From *Principles of Economics,* 8th ed. (New York: The Macmillan Co., 1920), pp. 1–2, 15, 31–33, 36–37. Reprinted by permission.

ence appears then to arise from the fact that its special field of work gives rather larger opportunities for exact methods than any other branch. It concerns itself chiefly with those desires, aspirations and other affections of human nature, the outward manifestations of which appear as incentives to action in such a form that the force or quantity of the incentives can be estimated and measured with some approach to accuracy; and which therefore are in some degree amenable to treatment by scientific machinery. An opening is made for the methods and the tests of science as soon as the force of a person's motives—*not* the motives themselves—can be approximately measured by the sum of money, which he will just give up in order to secure a desired satisfaction; or again by the sum which is just required to induce him to undergo a certain fatigue.

It is essential to note that the economist does not claim to measure any affection of the mind in itself, or directly; but only indirectly through its effect. No one can compare and measure accurately against one another even his own mental states at different times; and no one can measure the mental states of another at all except indirectly and conjecturally by their effects.

*   *   *

It is the business of economics, as of almost every other science, to collect facts, to arrange and interpret them, and to draw inferences from them. "Observation and description, definition and classification are the preparatory activities. But what we desire to reach thereby is a knowledge of the interdependence of economic phenomena. . . . Induction and deduction are both needed for scientific thought as the right and left foot are both needed for walking." The methods required for this twofold work are not peculiar to economics; they are the common property of all sciences.

*   *   *

Let us then consider more closely the nature of economic laws, and their limitations. Every cause has a tendency to produce some definite result if nothing occurs to hinder it. Thus gravitation tends to make things fall to the ground: but when a balloon is full of gas lighter than air, the pressure of the air will make it rise in spite of the tendency of gravitation to make it fall. The law of gravitation states how any two things attract one another; how they tend to move towards one another, and will move towards one another if nothing interferes to prevent them. The law of gravitation is therefore a statement of tendencies.

It is a very exact statement—so exact that mathematicians can calculate a Nautical Almanac, which will show the moments at which each satellite of Jupiter will hide itself behind Jupiter. They make this calculation for many years beforehand; and navigators take it to sea, and use it in finding out where they are. Now there are no economic tendencies which act as steadily and can be measured as exactly as gravitation can: and consequently there are no laws of economics which can be compared for precision with the law of gravitation.

But let us look at a science less exact than astronomy. The science of the tides explains how the tide rises and falls twice a day under the action of the sun and the moon: how there are strong tides at new and full moon, and weak tides at the moon's first and third quarter; and how the tide running up into a closed channel, like that of the Severn, will be very high; and so on. Thus, having studied the lie of the land and the water all round the British isles, people can calculate beforehand when the tide will *probably* be at its highest on any day at London Bridge or at Gloucester; and how high it will be there. They have to use the word *probably*, which the astronomers do not need to use when talking about the eclipses of Jupiter's satellites. For, though many forces act upon Jupiter and his satellites, each one of them acts in a definite manner which can be predicted beforehand: but no one knows enough about the weather to be able to say beforehand how it will act. A heavy downpour of rain in the upper Thames valley, or a strong north-east wind in the German Ocean, may make the tides at London Bridge differ a good deal from what had been expected.

The laws of economics are to be compared with the laws of the tides, rather than with the simple and exact law of gravitation. For the actions of men are so various and uncertain, that the best statement of tendencies, which we can make in a science of human conduct, must needs be inexact and faulty. This might be urged as a reason against making any statements at all on the subject; but that would be almost to abandon life. Life is human conduct, and the thoughts and emotions that grow up around it. By the fundamental impulses of our nature we all—high and low, learned and unlearned—are in our several degrees constantly striving to understand the courses of human action, and to shape them for our purposes, whether selfish or unselfish, whether noble or ignoble. And since we *must* form to ourselves some notions of the tendencies of human action, our choice is between forming those notions carelessly and forming them carefully. The harder the task, the greater the need for steady patient inquiry; for turning to account the experience, that has been reaped by the more advanced physical sciences; and for framing as best we can well thought-out estimates, or provisional laws, of the tendencies of human action.

*   *   *

Economic laws, or statements of economic tendencies, are those social laws which relate to branches of conduct in which the strength of the motives chiefly concerned can be measured by a money price.

There is thus no hard and sharp line of division between those social laws which are, and those which are not, to be regarded also as economic laws. For there is a continuous gradation from social laws concerned almost exclusively with motives that can be measured by price, to social laws in which such motives have little place; and which are therefore generally as much less precise and exact than economic laws, as those are than the laws of the more exact physical sciences.

*   *   *

It is sometimes said that the laws of economics are "hypothetical." Of course, like every other science, it undertakes to study the effects which will be produced by certain causes, not absolutely, but subject to the condition that *other things are equal,* and that the causes are able to work out their effects undisturbed. Almost every scientific doctrine, when carefully and formally stated, will be found to contain some proviso to the effect that other things are equal: the action of the causes in question is supposed to be isolated; certain effects are attributed to them, but only *on the hypothesis* that no cause is permitted to enter except those distinctly allowed for. It is true however that the condition that time must be allowed for causes to produce their effects is a source of great difficulty in economics. For meanwhile the material on which they work, and perhaps even the causes themselves, may have changed; and the tendencies which are being described will not have a sufficiently "long run" in which to work themselves out fully.

*   *   *

Though economic analysis and general reasoning are of wide application, yet every age and every country has its own problems; and every change in social conditions is likely to require a new development of economic doctrines.

2

The Methodology of Positive Economics

In the previous selection Alfred Marshall gave one view on the nature and role of economics. Here a noted contemporary American economist argues that economics must be a "positive" science; it should be objective in the same sense other sciences are, and the real test of a good economic theory is its ability to predict actual economic behavior.

Milton Friedman is Professor of Economics at the University of Chicago.

MILTON FRIEDMAN

In his admirable book on *The Scope and Method of Political Economy* John Neville Keynes distinguishes among "a *positive science* . . . [,] a body of systematized knowledge concerning what is; a *normative* or *regulative science* . . . [,] a body of systematized knowledge discussing criteria of what ought to be . . . ; an *art* . . . [,] a system of rules for the attainment of a given end"; comments that "confusion between them is common and has been the source of many mischievous errors"; and urges the importance of "recognizing a distinct positive science of political economy."

$$*\qquad *\qquad *$$

Positive economics is in principle independent of any particular ethical position or normative judgments. As Keynes says, it deals with "what is," not with "what ought to be." Its task is to provide a system of generalizations that can be used to make correct predictions about the consequences of any change in circumstances. Its performance is to be judged by the precision, scope, and conformity with experience of the predictions it yields. In short, positive economics is, or can be, an "objective" science, in precisely the same sense as any of the physical sciences. Of course, the fact that economics deals with the interrelations of human beings, and that the investigator is himself part of the subject matter being investigated in a more intimate sense than in the physical sciences, raises special difficulties in achieving objectivity at the same time that it provides the social sci-

Excerpts reprinted from *Essays in Positive Economics* by Milton Friedman, by permission of the University of Chicago Press; copyright 1953 by the University of Chicago.

entist with a class of data not available to the physical scientist. But neither the one nor the other is, in my view, a fundamental distinction between the two groups of sciences.

Normative economics and the art of economics, on the other hand, cannot be independent of positive economics. Any policy conclusion necessarily rests on a prediction about the consequences of doing one thing rather than another, a prediction that must be based—implicitly or explicitly—on positive economics. There is not, of course, a one-to-one relation between policy conclusions and the conclusions of positive economics; if there were, there would be no separate normative science. Two individuals may agree on the consequences of a particular piece of legislation. One may regard them as desirable on balance and so favor the legislation; the other as undesirable and so oppose the legislation.

The ultimate goal of a positive science is the development of a "theory" or "hypothesis" that yields valid and meaningful (i.e., not truistic) predictions about phenomena not yet observed. Such a theory is, in general, a complex intermixture of two elements. In part, it is a "language" designed to promote "systematic and organized methods of reasoning." In part, it is a body of substantive hypotheses designed to abstract essential features of complex reality.

Viewed as a language, theory has no substantive content; it is a set of tautologies. Its function is to serve as a filing system for organizing empirical material and facilitating our understanding of it; and the criteria by which it is to be judged are those appropriate to a filing system. Are the categories clearly and precisely defined? Are they exhaustive? Do we know where to file each individual item, or is there considerable ambiguity? Is the system of headings and subheadings so designed that we can quickly find an item we want, or must we hunt from place to place? Are the items we shall want to consider jointly filed together? Does the filing system avoid elaborate cross-references?

*   *   *

Viewed as a body of substantive hypotheses, theory is to be judged by its predictive power for the class of phenomena which it is intended to "explain." Only factual evidence can show whether it is "right" or "wrong" or, better, tentatively "accepted" as valid or "rejected." As I shall argue at greater length below, the only relevant test of the *validity* of a hypothesis is comparison of its predictions with experience. The hypothesis is rejected if its predictions are contradicted ("frequently" or more often than predictions from an alternative hypothesis); it is accepted if its predictions are not contradicted; great confidence is attached to it if it has survived many opportunities for contradiction. Factual evidence can never "prove" a hypothesis; it can only fail to disprove it, which is what we generally mean when we say, somewhat inexactly, that the hypothesis has been "confirmed" by experience.

To avoid confusion, it should perhaps be noted explicitly that the "predictions" by which the validity of a hypothesis is tested need not be about phenomena that have not yet occurred, that is, need not be forecasts of future events; they may be about phenomena that have occurred but observations on which have not yet been made or are not known to the person making the prediction. For example, a hypothesis may imply that such and such must have happened in 1906, given some other known circumstances. If a search of the records reveals that such and such did happen, the prediction is confirmed; if it reveals that such and such did not happen, the prediction is contradicted.

The validity of a hypothesis in this sense is not by itself a sufficient criterion for choosing among alternative hypotheses. Observed facts are necessarily finite in number; possible hypotheses, infinite. If there is one hypothesis that is consistent with the available evidence, there are always an infinite number that are. . . . The choice among alternative hypotheses equally consistent with the available evidence must to some extent be arbitrary, though there is general agreement that relevant considerations are suggested by the criteria "simplicity" and "fruitfulness," themselves notions that defy completely objective specification. A theory is "simpler" the less the initial knowledge needed to make a prediction within a given field of phenomena; it is more "fruitful" the more precise the resulting prediction, the wider the area within which the theory yields predictions, and the more additional lines for further research it suggests.

*   *   *

Unfortunately, we can seldom test particular predictions in the social sciences by experiments explicitly designed to eliminate what are judged to be the most important disturbing influences. Generally, we must rely on evidence cast up by the "experiments" that happen to occur. The inability to conduct so-called "controlled experiments" does not, in my view, reflect a basic difference between the social and physical sciences both because it is not peculiar to the social sciences—witness astronomy—and because the distinction between a controlled experiment and uncontrolled experience is at best one of degree. No experiment can be completely controlled, and every experience is partly controlled, in the sense that some disturbing influences are relatively constant in the course of it.

*   *   *

A [. . .] serious effect of the difficulty of testing economic hypotheses by their predictions is to foster misunderstanding of the role of empirical evidence in theoretical work. Empirical evidence is vital at two different, though closely related, stages: in constructing hypotheses and in testing their validity. Full and comprehensive evidence on the phenomena to be generalized or "explained" by a hypothesis, besides its obvious value in suggesting new hypotheses, is needed to assure that a hypothesis explains what it sets out to explain—that its implications for such phenomena are not contradicted in advance by experience that has already been observed. Given that the hypothesis is consistent with the evidence at hand, its further testing involves deducing from it new facts capable of being observed but not previously known and checking these deduced facts against additional empirical evidence. For this test to be relevant, the deduced facts must be about the class of phenomena the hypothesis is designed to explain; and they must be well enough defined so that observation can show them to be wrong.

*   *   *

Misunderstanding about this apparently straightforward process centers on the phrase "the class of phenomena the hypothesis is designed to explain." The difficulty in the social sciences of getting new evidence for this class of phenomena and of judging its conformity with the implications of the hypothesis makes it tempting to suppose that other, more readily available, evidence is equally relevant to the validity of the hypothesis—to suppose that hypotheses have not only "implications" but also "assumptions" and that the conformity of these "assumptions" to "reality" is a test of the validity of the hypothesis *different from* or *additional to* the test by implications. This widely held view is fundamentally wrong and productive of much mischief. Far from providing an easier means for sifting valid from invalid hypotheses, it only confuses the issue, promotes misunderstanding about the significance of empirical evidence for economic theory, produces a misdirection of much intellectual effort devoted to the development of positive economics, and impedes the attainment of consensus on tentative hypotheses in positive economics.

In so far as a theory can be said to have "assumptions" at all, and in so far as their "realism" can be judged independently of the validity of predictions, the relation between the significance of a theory and the "realism" of its "assumptions" is almost the opposite of that suggested by the view under criticism. Truly important and significant hypotheses will be found to have "assumptions" that are wildly inaccurate descriptive representations of reality, and, in general, the more significant the theory, the more unrealistic the assumptions (in this sense).[1] The reason is simple. A hypothesis is important if it "explains" much by little, that is, if it abstracts the common and crucial elements from the mass of complex and detailed circumstances surrounding the phenomena to be explained and permits valid predictions on the basis of them alone. To be important, therefore, a hypothesis must be descriptively false in its assumptions; it takes account of, and accounts for, none of the many other attendant circumstances, since its very success shows them to be irrelevant for the phenomena to be explained.

To put this point less paradoxically, the relevant question to ask about the "assumptions" of a theory is not whether they are descriptively "realistic," for they never are, but whether they are sufficiently good approximations for the purpose in hand. And this question can be answered only by seeing whether the theory works, which means whether it yields sufficiently accurate predictions. The two supposedly independent tests thus reduce to one test.

*   *   *

Economics as a positive science is a body of tentatively accepted generalizations about economic phenomena that can be used to predict the consequences of changes in circumstances. Progress in expanding this body of generalizations, strengthening our confidence in their validity, and improving the accuracy of the predictions they yield is hindered not only by the limitations of human ability that impede all search for knowledge but also by obstacles that are especially important for the social sciences in general and economics in particular, though by no means peculiar to them. Familiarity with the subject matter of economics breeds contempt for special knowledge about it. The importance of its subject matter to everyday life and to major issues of public policy impedes objectivity and promotes confusion between scientific analysis and normative judgment. The necessity of relying on uncontrolled experience rather than on controlled experiment makes it difficult to produce dramatic and clear-cut evidence to justify the acceptance of tentative hypotheses. Reliance on uncontrolled experience does not affect the fundamental methodological principle that a hypothesis can be tested only by the conformity of its implications or predictions with observable phenomena; but it does render the task of testing hypotheses more difficult and gives greater scope for confusion about the methodological principles involved. More than other scientists, social scientists need to be self-conscious about their methodology.

One confusion that has been particularly rife and has done much damage is confusion about the role of "assumptions" in economic analysis. A meaningful

---

[1] The converse of the proposition does not of course hold: assumptions that are unrealistic (in this sense) do not guarantee a significant theory.

scientific hypothesis or theory typically asserts that certain forces are, and other forces are not, important in understanding a particular class of phenomena. It is frequently convenient to present such a hypothesis by stating that the phenomena it is desired to predict behave in the world of observation *as if* they occurred in a hypothetical and highly simplified world containing only the forces that the hypothesis asserts to be important. In general, there is more than one way to formulate such a description—more than one set of "assumptions" in terms of which the theory can be presented. The choice among such alternative assumptions is made on the grounds of the resulting economy, clarity, and precision in presenting the hypothesis; their capacity to bring indirect evidence to bear on the validity of the hypothesis by suggesting some of its implications that can be readily checked with observation or by bringing out its connection with other hypotheses dealing with related phenomena; and similar considerations.

Such a theory cannot be tested by comparing its "assumptions" directly with "reality." Indeed, there is no meaningful way in which this can be done. Complete "realism" is clearly unattainable, and the question whether a theory is realistic "enough" can be settled only by seeing whether it yields predictions that are good enough for the purpose in hand or that are better than predictions from alternative theories. Yet the belief that a theory can be tested by the realism of its assumptions independently of the accuracy of its predictions is widespread and the source of much of the perennial criticism of economic theory as unrealistic. Such criticism is largely irrelevant, and, in consequence, most attempts to reform economic theory that it has stimulated have been unsuccessful.

*   *   *

What to produce and how to divide up the goods and services produced—these are the key economic questions faced by all societies. Professor Heilbroner describes three broad approaches to the allocation of resources and distribution of products.

Robert L. Heilbroner is a member of the faculty at the New School for Social Research and a well-known free-lance writer.

3

The Three Solutions to the Economic Problem

ROBERT HEILBRONER

THE THREE SOLUTIONS TO THE ECONOMIC PROBLEM

Thus to the economist, society presents itself in an unaccustomed aspect. He sees it essentially as an elaborate mechanism for survival, a mechanism for accomplishing the complicated tasks of production and distribution necessary for social continuity.

But the economist sees something else as well, something which at first seems quite astonishing. Looking not only over the diversity of contemporary societies, but back over the sweep of all history, he sees that man has succeeded in solving the production and distribution problems in but three ways. That is, within the enormous diversity of the actual social institutions which guide and shape the economic process, the economist divines but three over-arching *types* of systems which separately or in combination enable human-kind to solve its economic challenge. These great systemic types can be called economies run by Tradition, economies run by Command, and economies run by the Market. Let us briefly see what is characteristic of each.

Tradition

Perhaps the oldest and, until a very few years, by far the most generally prevalent way of solving the economic challenge has been tradition. It has been a mode of social organization in which both production and distribution were based on procedures devised in the distant past and rigidified as the outcome of a long process of historic trial and error.

From Robert L. Heilbroner, *The Making of Economic Society,* copyright 1962 by R. L. Heilbroner, pp. 9–17. Reprinted by permission of Prentice-Hall, Inc., publisher.

Societies based on tradition solve the economic problems very manageably. First, they deal with the production problem—the problem of assuring that the needful tasks will be done—by assigning the jobs of fathers to their sons. Thus a hereditary chain assures that skills will be passed along and that the on-going jobs will be staffed from generation to generation. In ancient Egypt, wrote Adam Smith, the first great economist, "every man was bound by a principle of religion to follow the occupation of his father and was supposed to commit the most horrible sacrilege if he changed it for another."[1] And it was not merely in antiquity that tradition preserved a productive orderliness within society. In our own Western culture, until the fifteenth or sixteenth centuries, the hereditary allocation of tasks was also the main stabilizing force within society. Although there was some movement from country to town and from occupation to occupation, birth usually determined one's role in life. One was born to the soil or to a trade; and on the soil or within the trade, one followed in the footsteps of one's forebears.

Thus tradition has been the stabilizing and impelling force behind a great repetitive cycle of society, assuring that society's work would be done each day very much as it had been done in the past. Even today, among the less industrialized nations of the world, tradition continues to play this immense organizing role. In India, until very recently at least, one was born to a caste which had its own occupation. "Better thine own work is, though done with fault," preached the Bhagavad-Gita, the great philosophic moral poem of India, "than doing other's work, even excellently."

Tradition not only provides a solution to the production problem of society, but it also regulates the distribution problem. Take, for example, the Bushmen of the Kalahari Desert in South Africa who depend for their livelihood on hunting prowess. Elizabeth Marshall Thomas, a sensitive observer of these peoples, reports on the manner in which tradition solves the problem of distributing their kill.

> The gemsbok has vanished . . . Gai owned two hind legs and a front leg, Tsetchwe had meat from the back, Ukwane had the other front leg, his wife had one of the feet and the stomach, the young boys had lengths of intestine. Twikwe had received the head and Dasina the udder.

It seems very unequal when you watch Bushmen divide the kill, yet it is their system, and in the end no person eats more than any other. That day Ukwane gave Gai still another piece because Gai was his relation, Gai gave meat to Dasina because she was his wife's mother. . . . No one, of course, contested Gai's large share, because he had been the hunter and by their law that much belonged to him. No one doubted that he would share his large amount with others, and they were not wrong, of course; he did.[2]

The manner in which tradition can divide a social product may be, as the illustration shows, very subtle and ingenious. It may also be very crude and, by our standards, harsh. Tradition has often allocated to women, in nonindustrial societies, the most meager portion of the social product. But however much tradition may accord with or depart from our accustomed moral views, we must see that it is a workable method of dividing society's production.

Traditional solutions to the economic problems of production and distribution are most commonly encountered in primitive agrarian or nonindustrial societies,

---

[1] *The Wealth of Nations* (New York: Modern Library, Inc., 1937), p. 62.
[2] *The Harmless People* (New York: Alfred A. Knopf, Inc., 1959), pp. 49–50.

where in addition to serving an economic function, the unquestioning acceptance of the past provides the necessary perseverance and endurance to confront harsh destinies. Yet even in our own society, tradition continues to play a role in solving the economic problem. It plays its smallest role in determining the distribution of our own social output, although the persistence of such traditional payments as tips to waiters, allowances to minors, or bonuses based on length of service are all vestiges of old traditional ways of distributing goods, as is the differential between men's and women's pay for equal work.

More important is the place which tradition continues to hold, even in America, as a means of solving the production problem—that is, in allocating the performance of tasks. Much of the actual process of selecting an employment in our society is heavily influenced by tradition. We are all familiar with families in which sons follow their fathers into a profession or a business. On a somewhat broader scale, tradition also dissuades us from certain employments. Sons of American middle-class families, for example, do not usually seek factory work, even though factory jobs may pay better than office jobs, because "bluecollar employment" is not in the middle-class tradition.

Even in our society, which is clearly not a "traditional" one, custom provides an important mechanism for solving the economic problem. But now we must note one very important consequence of the mechanism of tradition. *Its solution to production and distribution is a static one.* A society which follows the path of tradition in its reegulation of economic affairs does so at the expense of large-scale rapid social and economic change.

Thus the economy of a Bedouin tribe or a Burmese village is in few essential respects changed today from what it was a hundred or even a thousand years ago. The bulk of the peoples living in tradition-bound societies repeat, in the daily patterns of their economic life, much of the routines which characterized them in the distant past. Such societies may rise and fall, wax and wane, but external events—war, climate, political adventures and misadventures—are mainly responsible for their changing fortunes. Internal, self-generated economic change is but a small factor in the history of most tradition-bound states. Tradition solves the economic problem, but it does so at the cost of economic progress.

Command

A second manner of solving the problem of economic continuity also displays an ancient lineage. This is the method of imposed authority, of economic command. It is a solution based not so much on the perpetuation of a viable system by the changeless reproduction of its ways, as on the organization of a system according to the orders of an economic commander-in-chief.

Not infrequently we find this authoritarian method of economic control superimposed upon a traditional social base. Thus the Pharaohs of Egypt exerted their economic dictates above the timeless cycle of traditional agricultural practice on which the Egyptian economy was based. By their orders, the supreme rulers of Egypt brought into being the enormous economic effort which built the pyramids, the temples, the roads. Herodotus, the Greek historian, tells us how the Pharaoh Cheops organized the task.

> [He] ordered all Egyptians to work for himself. Some, accordingly, were appointed to draw stones from the quarries in the Arabian mountains down to the Nile, others he ordered to receive the stones when transported in vessels across the river. . . . And they worked to the number of a hundred thousand men at a

time, each party during three months. The time during which the people were thus harassed by toil lasted ten years on the road which they constructed, and along which they drew the stones; a work, in my opinion, not much less than the Pyramid.[3]

The mode of authoritarian economic organization was by no means confined to ancient Egypt. We encounter it in the despotisms of medieval and classical China which produced, among other things, the colossal Great Wall or in the slave labor by which many of the great public works of ancient Rome were built. Of course, we find it today in the dictates of the communist economic authorities. In less drastic form, we find it also in our own society, for example, in the form of *taxes*—that is, in the preemption of part of our income by the public authorities for public purposes.

Economic command, like tradition, offers solutions to the twin problems of production and distribution. In times of crises, such as war or famine, it may be the only way in which a society can organize its manpower or distribute its goods effectively. Even in America, we commonly declare martial law when an area has been devastated by a great natural disaster. On such occasions we may press people into service, requisition homes, impose curbs on the use of private property such as cars, or even limit the amount of food a family may consume.

Quite aside from its obvious utility in meeting emergencies, command has a further usefulness in solving the economic problem. Unlike tradition, the exercise of command has no inherent effect of slowing down economic change. Indeed, the exercise of authority is the most powerful instrument society has for *enforcing economic change*. One example is, of course, the radical alterations in the systems of production and distribution which authority has effected in modern China or Russia. But again, even in our own society, it is sometimes necessary for economic authority to intervene into the normal flow of economic life to speed up or bring about change. The government may, for instance, utilize its tax receipts to lay down a network of roads which brings a backwater community into the flux of active economic life. It may undertake an irrigation system which will dramatically change the economic life of a vast region. It may very considerably affect the distribution of income among social classes.

To be sure, economic command which is exercised within the framework of a democratic political process is very different from that which is exercised by strong-arm methods: there is an immense social distance between a tax system controlled by Congress and outright expropriation or labor impressment by a supreme and unchallengeable ruler. Yet whilst the means may be much milder, the *mechanism* is the same. In both cases, command diverts economic effort toward goals chosen by a higher authority. In both cases it interferes with the existing order of production and distribution, to create a new order ordained from "above."

This does not in itself serve to commend or condemn the exercise of command. The new order imposed by the authorities may offend or please our sense of social justice, just as it may improve or lessen the economic efficiency of society. Clearly, command can be an instrument of a democratic as well as of a totalitarian will. There is no implicit moral judgment to be passed on this second of the great mechanisms of economic control. Rather, it is important to note that no society —certainly no modern society—is without its elements of command, just as none is devoid of the influence of tradition. If tradition is the great brake on social and

[3] *Histories,* trans. Cary (London: 1901), Book II, p. 124.

economic change, so economic command can be the great spur to change. As mechanisms for assuring the successful solution to the economic problem, both serve their purposes, both have their uses and their drawbacks. Between them, tradition and command have accounted for most of the long history of man's economic efforts to cope with his environment and with himself. The fact that human society *has* survived is testimony to their effectiveness.

The Market

There is also a third solution to the economic problem—that is, a third solution to the problem of maintaining socially viable patterns of production and distribution. This is the *market organization of society,* an organization which, in truly remarkable fashion, allows society to insure its own provisioning with a minimum of recourse either to tradition or command.

Because we live in a market-run society, we are apt to take for granted the puzzling—indeed, almost paradoxical—nature of the market solution to the economic problem. But assume for a moment that we could act as economic advisers to a society which had not yet decided on its mode of economic organization. Suppose, for instance, that we were called on to act as consultants to one of the new nations emerging from the continent of Africa.

We could imagine the leaders of such a nation saying, "We have always experienced a highly tradition-bound way of life. Our men hunt and cultivate the fields and perform their tasks as they are brought up to do by the force of example and the instruction of their elders. We know, too, something of what can be done by economic command. We are prepared, if necessary, to sign an edict making it compulsory for many of our men to work on community projects for our national development. Tell us, is there any other way we can organize our society so that it will function successfully—or better yet, more successfully?"

Suppose we answered, "Yes, there is another way. Organize your society along the lines of a market economy."

"Very well," say the leaders. "What do we then tell people to do? How do we assign them to their various tasks?"

"That's the very point," we would answer. "In a market economy no one is assigned to any task. The very idea of a market society is that each person is allowed to decide for himself what to do."

There is consternation among the leaders. "You mean there is *no* assignment of some men to mining and others to cattle raising? No manner of selecting some for transportation and others for cloth weaving? You leave this to people to decide for themselves? But what happens if they do not decide correctly? What happens if no one volunteers to go into the mines, or if no one offers himself as a railway engineer?"

"You may rest assured," we tell the leaders, "none of that will happen. In a market society, all the jobs will be filled because it will be to people's advantage to fill them."

Our respondents accept this with uncertain expressions. "Now look," one of them finally says, "let us suppose that we take your advice and let our people do as they please. Now let's talk about something important, like cloth production. Just how do we fix the right level of cloth output in this 'market society' of yours?"

"But you don't," we reply.

"We don't! Then how do we know there will be enough cloth produced?"

"There will be," we tell him. "The market will see to that."

"Then how do we know there won't be *too much* cloth produced?" he asks triumphantly.

"Ah, but the market will see to that too!"

"But what *is* this market that will do all these wonderful things? Who runs it?"

"Oh, nobody runs the market," we answer. "It runs itself. In fact there really isn't any such *thing* as 'the market.' It's just a word we use to describe the way people behave."

"But I thought people behaved the way they wanted to!"

"And so they do," we say. "But never fear. They will want to behave the way you want them to behave."

"I am afraid," says the chief of the delegation, "that we are wasting our time. We thought you had in mind a serious proposal. But what you suggest is madness. It is inconceivable. Good day, sir." And with great dignity the delegation takes its leave.

Could we seriously suggest to such an emergent nation that it entrust itself to a market solution of the economic problem? That will be a problem to which we shall return. But the very perplexity which the market idea would rouse in the mind of someone unacquainted with it may serve to increase our own wonderment at this most sophisticated and interesting of all economic mechanisms. How *does* the market system assure us that our mines will find miners, our factories workers? How does it take care of cloth production? How does it happen that in a market-run nation each person can indeed do as he wishes and, withal, fulfill the needs which society as a whole presents?

Economics and the Market System

Economics, as we commonly conceive it and as we shall study it in much of this book, is primarily concerned with these very problems. Societies which rely primarily on tradition to solve their economic problems are of less interest to the professional economist than to the cultural anthropologist or the sociologist. Societies which solve their economic problems primarily by the exercise of command present interesting economic questions, but here the study of economics is necessarily subservient to the study of politics and the exercise of power.

It is a society which solves its economic problems by the market process that presents an aspect especially interesting to the economist. For here, as we shall see, economics truly plays a unique role. Unlike the case with tradition and command, where we quickly grasp the nature of the economic mechanism of society, when we turn to a market society we are lost without a knowledge of economics. For in a market society it is not at all clear that the problems of production and distribution will be solved by the free interplay of individuals without guidance from tradition or command.

. . . But . . . there is a problem which has surely occurred to the reader. As our hypothetical interview with the leaders of an emergent nation must have suggested, the market solution appears very strange to someone brought up in the ways of tradition or command. Hence the question arises: how did the market solution itself evolve? Was it imposed, full-blown, on our society at some earlier date? Or did it arise spontaneously and without forethought? These are the questions to which we must first turn, as we retrace the evolution of our own market system out of the tradition- and authority-dominated societies of the past.

PART TWO

National Income, Employment, and Economic Growth

The following four articles deal with
the recurring problem of inflation, its
measurement and its effects. Dr. Jaffe
provides an authoritative description of the
widely-used Bureau of Labor Statistics
consumer price index and how it is
constructed.

*Sidney A. Jaffe, Bureau of Labor
Statistics, U. S. Department of Labor.*

4

Consumer
Price Index

SIDNEY A. JAFFE

INTRODUCTION

The daily flow of correspondence received by the Bureau asking for information on our procedures, criticizing the Consumer Price Index, demanding explanations of its movements and questioning its accuracy is a continual reminder of the public interest in our work and of the importance of the statistics we produce. When the index starts to rise, the retailers challenge us to prove it because, they insist, their prices have not gone up. When we report lower food prices and the index falls, the housewives scoff at us for not knowing the facts of family living.

At the same time, we are subjected to a continuous crossfire from the experts, the statisticians, economists, market researchers, and others who use the index in various ways for analytical purposes. One of the surprising aspects of our critical audience is that so many of them have no conception of what the CPI really is. And this misunderstanding is not confined to the statistically uninitiated—housewives, retired military officers, and retail store proprietors. Some members of our own statistical profession have revealed a remarkable lack of knowledge about the figures they criticize. Or when they do have that knowledge they sometimes criticize the index because they differ with us about what the index should measure.

In this paper I shall attempt to answer some of the questions, technical and otherwise, most frequently raised about the Consumer Price Index. My answers will of course be limited by the fact that we haven't found

From *Hearings Before the Subcommittee on Economic Statistics of the Joint Economic Committee,* Congress of the United States, May 1–5, 1961, pp. 603–611.

solutions to all the questions raised both within and outside the Bureau. Needless to say we welcome all the help we can get in finding practical answers to our problems.

It is a well-known principle in the index field that every index number is related to a specific question or problem. There is no index number that serves all purposes and answers all questions. The CPI is designed to measure only one thing—the change in prices of goods and services paid by families of urban wage earners and clerical workers to maintain their level of living. Many of the questions about the index arise from a misunderstanding of the index and an attempt to interpret it as something that it is not supposed to be. At the start, therefore, it might be well to explain what the CPI is and also explain what it is not.

DEFINITION OF THE CONSUMER PRICE INDEX

The title, "Consumer Price Index" was adopted in 1945 as a substitute for the more popular term "The Cost of Living Index." This was done at the suggestion of a special committee of the American Statistical Association appointed at the request of the Bureau of Labor Statistics to review and evaluate the index. In testimony before a committee of Congress, Ewan Clague, Commissioner of Labor Statistics, explained the rationale of the name change and described the index in the following words:

"A cost-of-living index, as defined in contemporary economic thinking, is an index of the change in the cost of maintaining the same or an equivalent standard of living from one time to another, or from one place to another. The key to this concept is in the word 'equivalent.' Properly speaking, what distinguishes a cost-of-living index from the more narrowly defined price index is that in a cost-of-living index we would try to measure the changes in the cost of an equivalent market basket of goods and services whereas in a price index we try to measure the same market basket."

But the term "cost-of-living" is very commonly interpreted even more broadly to comprise what one newsman has called the cost of better living. At another point in his testimony Mr. Clague noted that the error in this reasoning "is the notion that either a price index or a cost-of-living index is intended to measure changes in costs of living that arise from changes in standards of living. Usually when people live better, when they buy more or better goods and services, it costs more. This kind of change would be reflected in an index of family expenditures, but not in a price index or a cost-of-living index." "Furthermore," Mr. Clague continued, "while it would be possible to make an index of family expenditures, the use of such an index to adjust wages would lead to the circular absurdity of saying, 'The more I spend the more the index will go up, and the more the index goes up, the more I'll have to spend.'"

It requires only a few additional sentences to describe the fundamental character of the Consumer Price Index. The population group to which the index refers is the aggregate of families of city wage earners and clerical workers. In structure the index is of the Laspeyres type with weights representing typical expenditures of the defined population group in a base period. The prices entering into the index calculation are transaction prices corresponding to types of transactions which actually take place in the markets patronized by the index population.

*   *   *

Statisticians who ask how well the CPI measures the price movements of the wage-earner's basket of purchases often have in mind the precision of the index in terms of its sampling error. I must regretfully answer them that while we believe the CPI provides a measurement of price change sufficiently accurate for practical uses, we are unable to supply a statistical measure of its precision. Before going on with the reasons for this, I would like to state further that I don't consider this lack terribly important. The idiosyncrasies of the price data are far more significant in determining the character and accuracy of a price index. I am afraid that a measure of sampling error that ignored the problems of price measurement and comparison would, by giving a wrong impression of accuracy, defeat its own purpose.

The CPI is built upon a series of samples. The primary sampling units are the cities in which we sample households for determination of weights and measurement of rents, or outlets for collection of prices. The selection of items, and of varieties and qualities of items, is still another mode of sampling. Completing the index structure is a sampling in time, since we collect prices in different cities and for different items at different intervals. Aside from the selection of the cities there are few features of the index where the Bureau has been able to apply systematic sampling. The principal exception[s] where probability sampling is applied are in the selection of households for the consumer expenditure surveys which supply the index weights and in the sample of rents for which we use a probability cross section of households for our data.

The selection of outlets in which we price, in particular, presents difficulties to a probability approach. Except for foods we are able to obtain only a relatively few quotations per item. Yet we would like these to be representative of different kinds of stores in the various locations (central city, neighborhood, suburban) in which index families shop. We have had to achieve these objectives largely by a judgment selection.

Since the probability sampling is so generally accepted as desirable, its honoring in the breach calls for some explanation. Given unlimited resources it would probably be possible to establish probability sampling procedures for all components of the Consumer Price Index. However, because of the wide scope of the index, the diversity of elements that must be sampled, and the complexity of the marketing situations in which prices must be gathered, there is no practical probability sampling approach that can be applied with present resources. This does not mean that we at the Bureau ignore the statistical principles of sampling. They are applied to the extent that is practical and are always held forth as guides to our day-to-day sampling decisions.

Another question often raised is how much of what people buy is covered in the index and how the items for pricing are selected. The typical family may buy 3,000 or more items in the course of a year; we obtain prices on a sample of about 300 specific commodities and services. The selection of the item for pricing was made in two stages. First, all items which accounted for 1 per cent or more of consumer expenditures as determined in the BLS benchmark surveys were considered for pricing. Then, on the basis of the Consumer Expenditures Survey results and special price studies all expenditure items were grouped into families of related commodities or services which had similar price trend characteristics. The most important item in each price family was then included in the index sample. The value weights of the unpriced items were imputed to the items selected as representative. The weights and imputations have remained relatively unchanged since the latest revision of the CPI completed in 1952. Obviously changes in spending patterns, market practices, and products during the past eight years have altered these relationships somewhat. A complete review of the sample and the imputation system will be made as part of the major revision program which we will undertake during the next four years.

In the meantime, how have changes in products and expenditures affected the validity of the index? Critics of the index often exaggerate the importance of items and weights because they forget that the index is a measure of change, not levels. Insertion of new products or shifts in weights does not necessarily affect the index to any marked extent. Currently, for example, we are being questioned about the new compact automobiles. If they are not included in the sample, it is argued, the index will fail to reflect the true price situation. They are lower in price, it is true, but they are a different item and we have no reason to believe that the price trends for the small cars will not conform to the trends shown by the standard models.

There is, of course, another aspect of this problem. If buyers generally shift from high-priced big cars to lower-priced small cars a change occurs in the basic structure of expenditures. But such changes in spending patterns are constantly occurring in some degree. Here we face a dilemma. If we revise the items and their weights frequently it is difficult to define what the index means. As a practical matter, therefore, we use what is essentially a fixed market basket over the period of years between the general index revisions. This provides a meaningful measure of price trends over relatively short periods of time, perhaps ten years or so. Over very long periods, however, the whole complex of products and services changes to such an extent that a fixed base price comparison is obviously impossible. There is nothing today comparable in all respects to the wheat, oil and wine which formed the basis for the first price index, and there's nothing we can do about it.

*   *   *

PROBLEMS OF QUALITY CHANGE

Quality can be defined in several ways. It may be described in physical terms: type of material, size, color, flavor, weight, calorie content, etc. Variations in quality may be indicated by performance: miles per gallon, speed, or length of life, ease and/or expense of repairs. In addition, buyers apply many purely subjecitve tests in judging quality, such as style, prestige value, etc. In a sense, of course, the ultimate measure of quality lies in the consumer's subjective evaluation. He assesses the value of the good in terms of the satisfaction it provides. And this is the crux of our problem.

Collection of data for the CPI is based upon the principles of specification pricing. In order to insure that we are pricing the comparable items from month to month and from city to city, a list of the significant characteristics of each item is set forth for the guidance of our pricing agents. The quality determining elements of the specification are established in discussions with manufacturers, merchandisers, and buyers. Generally the specifications include more information pertaining to the quality or intrinsic value of an item that our field agents can in practice apply in selecting items in the stores for pricing. Our experience has often been that the store owners and buyers are not sufficiently acquainted with their merchandise to answer our detailed questions on specifications. Nor can our agents, well trained though they are, uncover all the facts regarding quality and conformance to specification by a personal inspection of the merchandise; e.g., the "innards" of a TV set.

Our greatest difficulties with specification pricing arise primarily from product changes and the failure of our specification mechanism to provide a measurement of the dollar worth of new items as compared with the items they replace. This has led to criticisms somewhat along the lines of the following syllogism: (*a*) with technology on an upward trend, this year's products are better than last year's; (*b*) the BLS compares prices of this year's products against last year's; (*c*) therefore the BLS price index is biased upward. The missing link in this logic is the BLS price index mechanism.

There are varying practices employed in the Consumer Price Index for the comparison of prices when products change. For example, in the case of automobiles our practice has been to substitute the new model car for the previous model, assuming no quality change except for those features which affect some easily observed difference in operational characteristics and for which a value can be determined. Usually such changes involve the incorporation in the standard model of some feature which had formely been offered as an extra. Thus, for example, if backup lights had been offered as an extra-cost feature at $25 on last year's model but are included in the quoted price for the new model, we would assume a quality improvement worth $25 in the new model. If last year's model was introduced at $2,500 retail, without the backup lights, and the new model with backup lights comes in at $2,600, we would show a price increase of $75, unless there were other added features similar to the backup lights. In such a comparison we would make no allowances for such changes as greater length or more wrap in the windshield, because we have no objective standard by which to determine the relationship between quality and price for such features.

The practice of making direct price comparison between new items and their counterpart old items would seem to lead to some bias, as in the automobile component of the index. Among the many changes in automobiles, however, not all, certainly, can be considered unqualified improvements. Some "improvements" have been abandoned because they were found to be unworkable, too costly to maintain, or not of sufficient appeal to the car buyer.

Where information on the effect of quality changes on prices or costs is available, the Bureau attempts to adjust the prices being compared to an equivalent quality basis. The use of cost information in this context is considered an expedient of not much more than minimum acceptability for approximating the market value of a quality change. In the absence of information on price and cost differences due to quality, the BLS uses either direct comparison procedures, as in the automobile example, or linking procedures. The first procedure, on the assumption of higher quality, introduces an upward bias in the index. The linking procedure on the other hand, by introducing a new item at the index level of the old item which it replaces can be presumed to cause a downward bias when the price trend is upward.

*   *   *

My remarks may have implied that quality is conceptually measurable, even if in practice measurement is difficult or impossible. This is not the case. Quality is often something subjective or personal, as in the case of women's hats, or taste in foods and drinks. No objective standards are available, for example, to determine just what constitutes a premium beer, unless one wished perhaps to use advertising outlays as a criterion. Are the differences between the various cola drinks a matter of quality or a matter of taste? Since the formulas are kept secret, the objective criterion of manufacturing cost is not available, and would it be appropriate even if it were? What the BLS generally does in these cases is to price by brand name and not make price comparisons across brands. This is all right until there is a switch of brands; then, in the absence of a basis for price comparison, the new brand price is linked in at the former index level. When prices are on the upgrade such a procedure has a downward bias, but no other available method seems preferable.

Is the BLS consumer price index an accurate barometer of changes in the cost of living? Many economists believe that the index overstates the actual rise in prices because it fails to take into account adequately improvements in the quality of the products included. Professor Ruggles examines this important problem.

Richard Ruggles is Professor of Economics at Yale University.

5

Measuring the Cost of Quality

RICHARD RUGGLES

The bogy of inflation is with us again. This cry, which was chronic during the Fifties, has been a major factor in determining our monetary and fiscal policies. Since these policies are based on the movements in the price indexes, it is time to consider whether our confidence in these indexes is justified.

Since 1948 the Consumer Price Index has increased by approximately 25 per cent. A large part of this increase—about one-third of it—occurred in the brief space of one year, at the beginning of the Korean war. The other two-thirds was spread more or less evenly over the other 12 years— an average increase of about one and a half per cent a year.

In view of these statistics, policy makers might have concluded that we had relative price stability in the Fifties, except at the beginning of the Korean war when scare buying forced prices up. Instead, we hear much about a continual and insidious price creep. When price indexes continued to rise during periods of recession, such as in 1958, many policy makers concluded that rising prices stemmed from increasing costs due to excessive wage demands and administered prices of monopolies.

To understand what has *really* been happening to prices, we must first examine the factors responsible for the rises in the index. For this purpose let us take a look at the 12 per cent increase in the Consumer Price Index that has occurred since the Korean war. There are major segments of consumer purchases for which prices have not risen at all since that time. The price index for consumer durables, for example, shows a decline of ap-

Reprinted from *Challenge, the Magazine of Economic Affairs* (New York: 475 Fifth Avenue, 10017), Vol. X, No. 2, November 1961, pp. 6–9.

proximately three per cent. On the other hand, the index for medical care rose by more than 30 per cent. On the average, the prices of services rose a substantial 23 per cent, while those of commodities rose only six per cent.

This difference in behavior largely reflects the fact that the price of a service is generally the rate of compensation of those performing it. And these wages naturally rise as per capita income rises. In the last 50 years the prices of services relative to those of commodities have risen continually as a consequence of such general rises in living standards. Commodity prices, on the other hand, can sometimes reflect increased productivity. If the increase in output per man-hour is greater than the increase in the wage rate, the cost of production may actually fall, thus permitting lower commodity prices despite higher wages.

The identification of price indexes with rates of pay in the service industries involves the implicit assumption that the productivity of the service industries has remained unchanged. In some instances, this assumption may be correct, but in others quite wide of the mark.

In the case of medical care, for example, the apparent 30 per cent price increase of the last eight years must be qualified by considering the increase in medical knowledge, better drugs, and the new preventive medicines. Certainly the Salk vaccine was a tremendous medical advance which, in addition to sparing many lives, will save consumer dollars that would have gone for the treatment of polio.

Basically, then, the measurement of price changes comes down to a question of whether one gets more or less for his money. In the field of medical care it can be argued that most people would rather pay today's prices for today's medical care than yesterday's prices for yesterday's medical care. The fact that diseases were treated more cheaply in yesterday's world is more than offset by the increased knowledge and new drugs available for curing disease today. Although it is difficult to measure improvement in the *quality* of medicine in quantitative terms, there is no justification for ignoring it—which is what our present method of computing price indexes does.

The problem of measuring changes in quality also rises in the commodity components of the Consumer Price Index. In the Congressional hearings on government price statistics conducted early this year, Prof. Zvi Griliches of the University of Chicago reported on the effect that changes in specifications had upon automobile prices. Dr. Griliches computed the value of specifications such as size, automatic transmission, horsepower, etc., by taking the price differences for a given year among cars with these varying specifications. Automobile prices were then adjusted to take into account the different features included as standard equipment in each year.

On this basis, using the value of specifications given by the 1954 price schedule, the prices of the "low-priced three" dropped 27 per cent from 1954 to 1960, although their unadjusted list price rose 34 per cent, and the Consumer Price Index for these automobiles reported a rise of 11 per cent. The significance of this study is not that the Consumer Price Index for automobiles needs some minor adjustment to reflect the true price situation, but rather that the overemphasis on price change is itself in question. Instead of an 11 per cent price increase over this period, there may have been a price reduction of as much as 27 per cent.

This same kind of analysis could, of course, be applied to other major kinds of consumer durables, such as home laundry equipment, refrigerators and freezers, portable radios, cameras, and hi-fi equipment. Almost all of these have shown considerable change in recent years. If the change in *quality* were taken into account the price index for consumer durables would have fallen far more than the three per cent now reported.

Besides the quality change in existing goods, we should also take into account the effect of the introduction of totally new commodities upon the consumer's purchasing power. The index of consumer prices is purposely designed so that the introduction of new goods or the dropping of old ones will have no effect. Thus the introduction of such things as television, synthetic fibers, and plastic products has had no effect upon the index.

But the introduction of new products obviously *does* have an influence upon consumers' standards of living, just as do quality improvements in existing products. It is quite possible to imagine an economic system which obtains its higher standard of living through the introduction of new products which are superior to the old ones they replace. In such a system, the consumer might continuously get more value for his dollar, even though the prices of the old products rose steadily due to rising wage and material costs. Yet conventional price indexes would show this situation as one in which prices are rising and consumers are getting less for their dollars. Although, of course, in our economy not all of the improvement in the standard of living comes about through the substitution of new products for old, it does seem clear that much of it has been achieved in this way, despite the systematic exclusion of this factor from price indexes.

Innovations and new products are not restricted to the durable goods field. They have, for instance, been highly significant in the food industry over the last decade. Meals are much easier to get and the choice available to the housewife is much greater. There will be those who claim that the additional packaging and processing now common is an undesirable element of cost, and that the personal contact between the individual proprietor and the customer has been lost. Conversely, it can be argued that increased attention to packaging not only standardizes the merchandise, but it raises the level of sanitation and grading. In addition, the freedom to examine goods allows the customer to make comparisons before buying in a way that would not have been possible before.

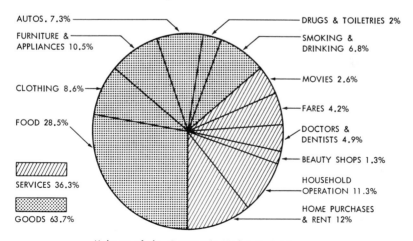

Make-up of the Consumer's Market Basket *

* Relative weights of goods and services used by Bureau of Labor Statistics to Prepare the Consumer Price Index.

It is, of course, not possible to measure accurately the dimensions of quality and product change. Nevertheless, one can safely suggest that, given the size of the average yearly increase in the Consumer Price Index since Korea, quality and product improvements may well have been much greater, so that we may actually have had declining rather than rising prices.

This does not mean that price indexes are completely invalid. Price indexes are useful in that they can show the relative differences in price behavior over time or between countries. For example, the eight per cent increase in the price index at the beginning of the Korean war indicates that prices were rising more rapidly in this period than at any other time in the decade of the Fifties.

In periods of hyperinflation, such as have been experienced by some Latin American countries in recent years, where the price index may rise by as much as 80 per cent in a single year, the indexes give a good indication of what is happening since such large increases cannot be offset by quality change. It is only in periods when price changes are relatively small that it becomes a serious error to use the indexes as an exact measure of what is taking place in the economy. In such periods the systematic biases of the price index may well be greater than the reported price change.

The defects of the Consumer Price Index are also inherent in the other price indexes which are used to deflate the gross national product to measure the change in real output. Two major categories of goods are produced by the economy besides consumer goods. These are goods and services purchased by the government, ranging from school teaching to missiles, and plant and equipment purchased by producers for use in later production. To measure the quantity of output in these categories, we need price indexes to calculate it in noninflationary terms.

In measuring the output of government, it is assumed—as it is throughout the service sector—that the productivity of civil servants never changes. The price indexes for this area are merely based on the changes in pay of government employees. While one may be tempted to agree with this evaluation of civil servants, the fact is that the introduction of computers, office machines and other automatic equipment has greatly increased the effectiveness of the individual worker. For example, the 1960 census data were processed by microfilming the original schedules and automatically producing magnetic tape for the electronic computers. Automatic equipment performed jobs which took thousands of clerks in previous censuses. Not only was the payroll reduced, but far more information was made available in a much shorter space of time. Output per census employee thus rose very considerably.

Similar examples of the increased output of government employees can be cited at the local level. For example, policemen have been provided with radio-equipped patrol cars and, more recently, transistorized walkie-talkies. Street cleaners have been given mechanized equipment. In some areas—education, for instance—progress is more difficult to measure. Yet most of us would be unwilling to have our children given the same education as we received, especially in the areas of sciences and mathematics.

In producers' durable equipment, once again, the price indexes leave out quality change and new products. But there are probably very few industries in which producers in 1960 would have been willing to buy 1950 models of machines even if they could get them at the 1950 prices. According to the Wholesale Price Index the 1960 price of producers' durable equipment was 23 per cent above the 1950 price; if producers' durable equipment showed as much quality change as was shown in the study referred to above for automobiles, it seems probable that in fact prices actually fell.

For construction, both industrial and residential, the index is computed on the basis of wage rates and material cost. Thus again it is assumed that productivity does not change. While the construction industry is notorious for its lack of progressiveness, if we consider the new methods of off-the-site fabrication of components it is obvious that this assumption is not entirely valid. Once again, it seems that price indexes have greatly exaggerated the actual price rise.

Thus, we see that for almost every category of goods, whether purchased by consumers for household consumption, by government for public services or by producers for plant and equipment, the conventional price indexes do not reflect the effects of the introduction of new products and the improvement of existing products, or the increased productivity of those performing services. These omissions mean that the price indexes are higher than they should be. And since the indexes are used to deflate the value of current output and calculate its worth in noninflationary terms, our rate of growth is thus considerably understated.

The fact that our growth rate has probably been higher than we thought does not mean, however, that we should be any happier vis-à-vis the Russians. These elements would also have at least as much effect upon the Russian figures. As we well know, the Soviet rate of technological progress in some areas has exceeded ours, but even in the areas where they are still well behind us, the *rate* at which they introduce new technology might be faster than ours.

A half-century ago many more industries were producing the kind of output that could be measured quite satisfactorily in quantity terms. Today new major industries such as electronics, chemicals, machinery, and household appliances account for an increasingly important share of our output. In all these industries the changes in prices and output are very difficult to measure, since the nature of the products is continually changing. It may mean, therefore, that the national concern over a sagging economic growth rate is really not warranted. The problem may be our inability to measure growth represented by product changes and increased productivity in the service industries. The inadequacy of the price indexes will become even more glaring in the years ahead.

It is interesting to speculate on what will happen to our measurement of output when further growth does not take the form of additional consumption of identical items, but rather of the consumption of goods of improved quality, the substitution of new products for old, and the consumption of higher quality services. In such a world, our conventional price indexes would fail to catch the quality improvement; they would not recognize that the substitution of new products for old was any increase in the standard of living; and they would report the continued increase in the use of services solely in terms of the rates of remuneration. Thus they might show an economy with constant output and rising prices, even though the standard of living was increasing rapidly. What is perhaps more serious, the conventional price and output indexes would fail completely to distinguish between a dynamic economy and one that was truly stagnant.

The single-minded pursuit of price stability, coupled with the false soundings given by our present price indicators, is likely to lead our economy policy makers astray. The tragedy of the postwar period is not so much the low rate of growth (which we cannot measure anyway), but rather the underutilization of our resources and the low level of investment to which the continuous existence of excess capacity leads.

At the quiver of a decimal point in the Consumer Price Index, the government has instituted restrictive monetary and fiscal policies. Its objective has been to restrain demand so that producers would find themselves with excess capacity and thus would not raise prices; and labor unions would be deterred by the existence of unemployment from seeking wage increases. The economy has been either in a depressed state or under restraining monetary and fiscal policies throughout almost the entire period since Korea. It is small wonder that in such an environment the rate of investment is low. In an economy where a false fear of inflation continually holds demand in check, even a low level of investment creates capacity which cannot be fully utilized.

With this in mind, it is appropriate to inquire what a faster rate of growth and better utilization of our capacity would do to our price indexes. Historically, if we look at any period of upward change in the general level of activity, we find that the price indexes rise. Thus, for example, in the recovery from the depression of the 1930s, prices in certain sectors responded sharply to the increase in demand. Farm prices rose by about 85 per cent in the five years from 1932 to 1937. Even in the metals industry, prices went up about 30 per cent. At the same time, unemployment dropped from 25 per cent to about 14 per cent. It cannot very well be argued that these price rises were the result of excess demand pressing on fully employed resources.

In other words, growth and the increase in real income tend to produce price increases in certain sectors irrespective of the pressure on resources. If the price index is to remain stable, the increases in such sectors would have to be balanced by lower prices in other sectors, where productivity increases would permit prices to fall. Given the imperfections of our price indexes, however, economic growth will almost inevitably result in an upward movement of the price index irrespective of the pressure of demand.

Despite the relatively high unemployment rate of close to seven per cent, there is a tendency to minimize the underutilization of our resources which has resulted from too much concern with small movements in the price index. It is argued that at least four per cent of this is frictional unemployment, and thus that we are operating at 97 per cent of full employment—a high level in anybody's vocabulary. Such a computation, however, is very misleading. The unemployment rate is not very closely related to the economy's excess capacity. The spread of automation and the increase in the number of white-collar employees means that many industries can expand their output considerably without hiring many more workers. Thus, a steel company operating at 50 per cent capacity might be able to double its output by adding 10 or 20 per cent more employees. This is even more true in such sectors of the economy as electric power, communications, finance, insurance, and retail trade—all sectors whose activity (and thus output) increases with an increase in the general level of activity of the economy without requiring any substantial increase in manpower.

This relationship between the increase in man-hours employed and the increase in output shows up clearly in the over-all statistics. In the recoveries from all of our past recessions output has risen much faster than man-hours employed. On average, output tends to rise during economic recoveries about three times as fast as the man-hours required to produce it. In the first six months of the present recovery, if we are to believe the figures, an increase in output of approximately 5 per cent has been accompanied by an increase in man-hours of less than one per cent.

Much of the increase in manpower that is needed, furthermore, does not come from the reservoir of the unemployed. Unutilized manpower within firms is drawn upon, and cuts in the workweek which may have been put into effect during the recession are restored. With increasing employment opportunities, the labor force itself tends to expand, thus providing additional resources. Even allowing for frictional unemployment, it seems reasonable that there could be an increase of 10 or 12 per cent in man-hours.

The Council of Economic Advisers has estimated that in early 1961 the economy was operating at a level some 10 per cent below full capacity. This figure seems far too conservative when one takes into account the additional man-hours available and their relation to potential output. If past performance is a guide, it would not seem unreasonable to suppose that the 10 or 12 per cent additional man-hours which were available in the spring of 1961 could have been utilized to produce 25 per cent more output. This seems all the more likely since, by late summer of 1961, output had risen by about five per cent and unemployment had not fallen at all.

It is true, of course, that an increase in real output of 25 per cent, even though it created no pressure on resources, would cause our price indexes to rise. Under present anti-inflation policy we would then move quickly to prevent such real output increases from occurring. In fact, that is exactly what we are doing, even though the increase in real output has been far less than this. The price indexes have quivered, and there is talk of putting the brakes on. Those wishing to restrict demand have labeled the unemployment "structural," and thereby have succeeded in removing it from their own consciences. This rationalization may satisfy them, but it is not much help for the unemployed—since it is obvious that the only cure for unemployment, whether structural or any other kind, is more jobs, and you don't get more jobs by restricting demand, no matter how much retraining you do.

The loss in potential output may not seem to be very impressive when expressed in percentage of total output, but, in fact, we waste through underutilization an amount equal in size to two or three times what we now spend on defense, or 20 to 25 times as much as we now are giving in foreign aid. These wasted resources could rebuild our cities and automate our factories within a few short years; they could raise our rate of growth to equal or surpass that of any other nation.

This then is the cost of taking our price indexes too seriously. We inhibit real growth, because growth by its very nature must lead to increases in the price indexes. And because this inhibited growth in output does not keep up with the growth in our capacity to produce, we have ever-present excess capacity. The excess in machines is self-limiting; producers soon learn when investment is unprofitable. But the excess in manpower is harder to dispose of—the unemployed are there, and you can't really make the problem go away by saying that they don't exist.

The German experience following World War I provides a vivid picture of what happens when a great inflation breaks loose and runs wild. This account emphasizes the close ties of most such inflations to major wars and their aftermath.

Donald B. Woodward is an economist with wide experience in government. Marc A. Rose was a newspaper and magazine editor, and served as a senior editor of Reader's Digest.

6

The German Nightmare

DONALD B. WOODWARD

MARC A. ROSE

Wildest of all the inflations the world ever has seen, the German orgy after the war is the horrible example held up in solemn warning before the eyes of anyone who ventures to suggest that money might be managed to avert, or at least to soften, the impact of violent price upheavals.

Indeed, it was a nightmare. Large classes of the population paid bitterly for it. But the candid historian must record that there were some compensations to the nation at large. At least it wiped out internal debt, albeit by the brutality of complete repudiation.

Before the war, the German mark was firmly based on gold, with a parity of 23 cents. Germany, in fact, was the nation which broke up bimetallism in Europe. Demanding a $1,000,000,000 gold indemnity from France at the close of the Franco-Prussian war, she seized the opportunity to use the gold as a base for a single-standard currency.

The war put a severe strain on the German economy, but the depreciation of the mark was not beyond recovery; after the armistice, the mark was quoted at about 12 cents.

Then came the peace negotiations. When the full weight of the terms imposed under the Treaty of Versailles became apparent, the Germans felt their situation hopeless—and so did financiers in other countries. The new government's financial difficulties kept increasing. The nation's debt was heavy, and much of it was not funded. It was necessary to resort to the expedient of printing marks, mere fiat money, to pay the government's expenses. By early 1920, the mark was worth about one cent, gold. The decline was checked at that point, and there was even some improvement; but late in 1921, the mark began to sink again in terms of foreign exchange. Reparations had been fixed at 132,000,000,000 gold marks, or some $33,000,000,000. More and more, Germany was completely discouraged at the outlook; financial recovery looked impossible, and the occupation of the Ruhr in January, 1923, seemed to show that the harder the Germans tried to beat their way upward the more the demands that would be made upon them.

The Treasury proceeded to issue bills to the Reichsbank at an accelerating rate, discounting them for paper money. The printing presses ran more and more rapidly; pieces of currency were issued in denominations of millions of marks. Prices, of course, kept rising, which steadily increased the government's expenses and made it necessary to print more currency. The spiral was started; nothing, it seemed, could break it. Under the conditions, there was little incentive to try.

The banks, which had participated very little at the outset, began to discount bills at the Reichsbank and to increase their loans and deposits. Ultimately, the municipalities began to issue money, also the railroads, and many other institutions. Metal coins previously used for small change disappeared into hoarding or were converted into paper, the bullion content being worth vastly more than the stamped value of the coins.

Before the war, the total money in circulation in Germany had averaged about 6,000,000,000 marks. At the end of 1923, the authorized circulation was 518,000,-000,000,000,000,000—518 billions of billions. No estimate ever has been attempted of the amount of other currencies in circulation. Conditions were utterly chaotic.

In November, 1923, the situation was taken in hand. A new currency unit, the rentenmark, was established, its value put at 1,000,000,000,000—a million million—of the marks it was to supersede. The new rentenmark was fixed at parity with the prewar mark—that is, at 23 cents. Incidentally, it was pure fiat money, but its value was successfully controlled in terms of gold.

The Dawes plan was made effective in 1924, fixing Germany's obligations to the outside world at a point more nearly within reason. With that encouragement, the reichsmark was established on a gold basis, also at 23 cents.

That was the end of inflation. Behind this bare story of the course of events are a million human comedies and tragedies. No one ever will record even a small part of them. But some of the most fantastic and absurd incidents are remembered.

As this one: the total German mortgage debt before the war was about 40,000,-000,000 marks. At the peak of the inflation, 40,000,000,000 marks were worth less than a cent. All the mortgages in Germany could have been paid off for one cent, American. A box of matches sold for more than 6,000,000,000 marks, which it will be remembered was the total amount of money in circulation in Germany in prewar years.

Things happened as in a fever-ridden dream. Prices changed by the hour. Before the summit was reached, a ham sandwich was quoted at 14,000 marks one day and 24,000 marks the next. An article in a retail store priced at 5,000,000,000 marks in the morning had increased to 12,000,000,000 by afternoon. A sheet of writing paper cost 120 marks—$30 at prewar exchange—while yet the inflation was young. Interest rates rose to 900 per cent, and even then lenders at times were not protected, because by the time they were paid—even tenfold—the sum they received was worth less than the sum they lent.

What this meant in terms of human hardship can easily be imagined. Savings patiently built up by a lifetime of thrift might buy as much as a package of cigarettes. Life insurance policies matured—and the proceeds would not buy a handkerchief. It might be cheaper to light a cigar with a bond than to buy a match. The thrifty were penalized; the only wise folk were the spendthrifts. The nation became a spendthrift one, of course; everyone who received money rushed madly to convert it into goods. Things would be worth more tomorrow, perhaps this very afternoon. Money would be worth less. Debts were wiped out; farm mortgages were paid off with a sack of potatoes.

Translated into economic jargon, the creditor class was ruined; debtors were freed. People who had lived on investments were paupers.

The government tried to protect its citizens but could not do much. Prices of necessities were fixed from time to time to assure people of food and a roof over their heads, but fixing prices at a reasonable level one day did not solve the problem the next. Wages were moved up frequently—in the early stages, every month, then every ten days, but they always lagged behind the cost of living. The principle of fixing wages on a sliding scale geared to the cost of living was adopted, but it never was very popular with labor, because most workingmen did not understand its complexities, and those who did protested that the scale was inadequate. Labor troubles were widespread.

While great classes were being pauperized, other skillful manipulators were becoming fabulously wealthy. The speculators' method was to borrow money, buy goods or real estate or factories, then pay off the debt in worthless money. Then they could either keep the tangibles or sell them and repeat the operation.

Business of course boomed, for everyone was buying goods. A great boom developed in the stock market, from the scramble to buy shares in tangible properties.

Toward the close of the era, many localities began to quote prices of foreign currencies, usually dollars. Various institutions issued scrip redeemable in goods—rye, barley, coal, wood, and even kilowatt hours.

It was impossible, obviously to plan ahead in terms of paper money. Construction and similar industries languished.

After monetary stabilization, there was a brief depression, but business did not for long stay inordinately dull, since there had been an accumulation of demands for goods and services that could not be supplied during the inflation—demands for new homes and improved factories, for example. So recovery progressed with reasonable rapidity.

But profound changes had been made in the social structure. There were new rich and new poor. The middle class, by and large, suffered most. The very poor had had little to lose; many of the wealthy had known how to protect themselves. Businesses emerged with most of their debts wiped out.

7

Inflation
in Perspective

The problem of inflation in the United
States today differs widely from the
post-war hyperinflation in Germany.
Professor Bach examines the nature of
modern "creeping" inflation and the ways
it affects the behavior of the economy.

G. L. Bach is Maurice Falk Professor of
Economics at Carnegie Institute of
Technology.

G. L. BACH

Recently many economists and businessmen have argued that we face a
new type of "cost-push" and "administered-price" inflation substantially
unlike the traditional "excess-demand" or "demand-pull" inflation. From
this argument they draw major new public policy implications that cast
serious doubt on the efficacy of traditional monetary and fiscal policies
against inflation. At the same time, and for many of the same reasons, they
argue that we have entered a new period of long-run secular inflationary
drift that will be difficult if not impossible to avoid. But for every claim
there is a counterclaim—that the new inflation is no different, that long-
run inflation is not inevitable.

In the midst of all this controversy, almost everyone is against inflation,
at least in principle. Even Sumner H. Slichter now states that he is not for
inflation but just accepts it as the lesser of two evils. Recent debate has
begun to clarify the issues and to probe under the earlier superficial
diatribes against "inflation"—which is often undefined. Yet little attention
has been given to spelling out carefully and systematically just what the results of "creeping" (i.e., moderate) long-range inflation are, and which of
these results we should try to prevent or encourage. In this article I
propose:

1. To argue that the distinction between the new "cost-push, administered-
price" inflation and the traditional "excess-demand" inflation, although real, is
less substantial than is often argued, and is of much less significance for the

From the *Harvard Business Review*, January–February, 1958, pp. 99–110. Reprinted by permission.

conduct of governmental monetary-fiscal policy against inflation than is commonly supposed.

2. To summarize briefly the major economic effects of recent "moderate" American inflation, together with some comments on comparable recent inflations abroad, in the hope of throwing some light on the effects of continuing inflation.

3. To suggest, in the light of these facts, some of the public policy implications for the present and foreseeable future.

WHAT IS IT?

One reason why so many arguments about inflation get nowhere is that the disputants too often fail to define the term. This is especially unfortunate because there is no one "best" definition of inflation on which all the experts agree. Some speak of rising prices themselves as inflation. Others think of inflation in terms of the cause, often cited as excess monetary demand, and describe rising prices as merely a symptom. Still others, combining these definitions, define inflation as a situation of excess monetary demand which forces up prices after full employment has been reached.

By inflation I shall mean a rise in the price level or, what is the same thing, a fall in the purchasing power of the monetary unit. To measure changes in the price level, I shall generally use the well-known United States Bureau of Labor Statistics Index of Consumer Prices or Index of Wholesale Prices. But for most of what I say the precise index used is not of crucial importance, so long as it is a broadly based one and represents many prices in the economy.

*　　*　　*

Under the proposed definition, rising prices are inflation whether they rise rapidly or slowly (a small rise in prices is a little inflation, and a big rise a large inflation), and whether there is full employment or not. The likelihood of rising prices is, of course, greater after full employment has been reached, but history shows us that prices may rise substantially before resources are fully employed. And there is some reason to suppose this phenomenon of rising prices together with some unemployment may become increasingly common. It occurred last year, and it may well occur again this year if present moderate recession tendencies persist.

THE NEW INFLATION

In the new inflation, it is argued, powerful labor unions push wages upward faster than productivity increases. Then the leading firms in oligopolistic industries (where one or a few firms dominate the field and substantially establish prices, as in the automobile industry) raise their prices at least enough to cover the increase in costs, and often more. When total demand is strong, this wage-price spiral may rise rapidly. Even when the aggregate demand is relatively weak, some economists argue, union wages and administered prices will continue their upward push. Appreciable unemployment is no sure check to this "sellers' inflation."

The new inflation, according to this view, does not necessarily depend upon excess total monetary demand for its existence. Though wages and prices in highly competitive sectors of the economy may not rise rapidly or at all, unionized wages and administered prices—both widespread in our economy—mean persistent secular inflation.

By contrast, the traditional view of inflation is that prices in the aggregate rise when there is too much money chasing too few goods—that is, when there is excess total demand for goods and services offered for sale at prevailing prices. This is "demand-pull" inflation. Such a view looks on markets as competitive to a substantial degree. Prices rise when demand runs ahead of supply, and only then to any significant degree. Where individual firms or unions set wages or prices, they cannot get far out of line with what the demand side of the market will bear. If they do, surplus labor and surplus goods will exert a heavy drag on further price advances or even bring price reductions. Persistent long-run inflation will occur only if for some reason excess total demand prevails. And the traditional view suggests that excess demand can prevail for long only if the money supply (demand deposits and currency) increases more rapidly than total output of goods and services.

How Different?

In extreme cases the new and the old inflations may be quite different. If inflation is generated by a large increase in the money supply (say by huge government expenditures financed by bank borrowing), it is clear that we have traditional excess-demand inflation. Whether the wage-price structure is highly competitive or not, both wages and prices will be bid up rapidly as the new money is spent.

In most cases, however, the difference between the new and the old is plainly one of degree. The economy has never been perfectly competitive with prices and wages responding only to impersonal market forces of supply and demand. Both wages and prices have long been administered to varying degrees in different markets. And with nearly all administered wages and prices there is a margin, large or small, within which the price is set mainly according to the judgment of the price setter. If competitive pressures are strong, this discretionary margin is small; but if the seller has a substantial monopoly position, it may be quite large.

But no seller, no matter how administered his prices, can long escape the test of the market. He can raise his wage or price; but if his price moves far beyond customers' willingness or ability to buy, he will lose sales. If many prices are moving up at the same time, widespread sales losses may occur as prices across the board begin to outrun consumer incomes.

How Far?

The important thing is that a cost-push, administered-price inflation cannot continue long unless there is growing total demand in the economy. Costs may "push" upward on prices, but, unless total demand is growing, the resultant price increases will not go very far. Thus there is a limit—the cold hand of lack of demand—which every seller must ultimately face unless the demand side of the market is rising too.

If the new and the old inflations are different only in degree, what of the argument that a long-run inflationary drift is inevitable because of the union wage push and the administered-price structure of our economy? The answer is: it is inevitable only if excess demand is provided to support the inflation. Organized labor is much stronger now than over past decades; moreover, there are many administrative price setters. But this is clearly not enough to guarantee long-run inflation. Indeed, we may have intermittent periods of some deflation.

As Peter L. Bernstein pointed out in the July 1957 issue of this magazine, the past decade has seen several circumstances especially conducive to inflation (shortage of labor, strong postwar demand, and high postwar liquidity), and these may well vanish in the near future. But, to argue, as Bernstein does, that because these special forces vanish the likelihood of long-range inflation also vanishes, seems to me to miss the main point: whether there will be excess demand. Neither do the arguments of Jacoby or Slichter really emphasize this key condition of continuing inflation.

There will be persistent excess total demand if governmental policy, as made by the Federal Reserve Board, Congress, and the executive branch in budget making, assures the excess total demand—whether in response to excessive wage-price policies or to more traditional pressures like defense spending needs. If the policy of the Federal Reserve Board and of the rest of the government denies excess total demand, then there will not be any substantial amount of long-range inflation.

This brings us squarely to the issue of governmental monetary-fiscal policy in assessing the likelihood of long-range inflation. But first let us consider what some of the major economic effects of inflation have been in America over the past two decades.

WHAT ARE ITS EFFECTS?

What are the major economic effects of moderate inflation? From a casual reading of the daily papers and a sampling of the history books and campaign speeches of recent years:

> It bleeds the little fellow and the laborer.
> It increases profits at the expense of wages—or it transfers profits to the wage earner.
> It lowers the national standard of living.
> It leads inevitably to boom and bust.
> It transfers income and wealth from the poor to the rich—or from the rich to the poor.
> It wipes out the value of savings.
> It induces waste and dissolution.

Clearly, not all of these allegations can be true, at least not of any one inflation at any one time. What are the real effects? To get an answer, we must break the question down into two more specific parts: (1) What effect does inflation have on the *total volume* of goods and services being produced—that is, on the "real gross national product" or "real national income"? (2) What effect does it have on the *distribution* of those goods and services among the various individuals and groups in society?

The logical approach would seem to be to look at the American inflation at the past two decades, supplemented by experience in other countries. Helpful as this information may be, though it does not provide a thoroughly satisfactory basis for predicting the future. One trouble is that we can never be sure in the complex interplay of forces just what conditions inflation actually *caused* during the past two decades. Even though changes occurred together with or just after inflation, we cannot be sure that other forces were not the causes. Secondly, even if we could identify precisely cause and effect in the past, we could never be sure that the future would be just like the past.

Accordingly, in analyzing the effects of inflation, we need to supplement historical observation by economic theory. The problems of accurate interpretation and evaluation are difficult, but, by combining history and theory, we can get some idea of the main lessons to be drawn from the welter of evidence, argument, and counterargument.

Remember throughout that we are considering moderate, relatively slow inflations like that in America recently, not the great hyperinflations of postwar Central Europe.

Total Economic Output

Consider first the effect of inflation on the economy's total output. Imagine this total output, the real gross national product, as a huge pie of real goods and services. The question is: Does inflation either increase or decrease significantly the total size of the pie? Of course, the money value of any year's pie can be raised by bidding up prices, but this would merely raise the *money* gross national product, not the nation's *real* output and income.

Inflation may increase or decrease the nation's total output now or in the future, or it may have no effect at all. For simplicity, let us consider the *current* effects of inflation as being those which occur within, say, the next year or so, and the *future* effect as being those which show up over a longer period.

Does inflation reduce current real output? There is little a priori reason to suppose that moderate inflation reduces the size of the current national output. The evidence of history is flatly against this claim, *except* in cases of runaway, or hyper-, inflation. The common belief that inflation disrupts the economy and reduces its total output apparently goes back largely to the massive hyperinflations of Central Europe following World War I. At that time the currency became substantially worthless; a wheelbarrow full of money was needed to buy one meal; and speculative activity became more rewarding than productive work. By 1923 in Germany, for example, shortly before the collapse, this diversion of energy from normal productive work had become a vast drag on the output of real goods and services.

But in milder inflations history shows output generally rising. In the United States since 1937, for example, prices have roughly doubled, but the money value of our national output has risen to over 400% of 1937. Total real output has more than doubled. A similar picture has prevailed in most other countries over this same period—for example, in almost all of non-Communist Europe, where the inflation has far exceeded ours in some cases.

To be sure, it was easy to increase real output in the late 1930's, since there was so much unemployment. But the growth in total output, paralleling inflation, has been a persistent one both here and abroad, even in full-employment conditions. Conversely, cases of appreciable inflation accompanied by an appreciable drop in total real output have been rare indeed.

Output, of course, reflects managerial decision making. Jacoby and Slichter have argued vigorously as to whether the recent American inflation has disrupted managerial decision making and lowered the quality of managerial performance. But, boiled down, their argument is largely of a "'tis, 'taint" variety. The answer seems to me clear: we just do not know, and cannot tell unambiguously from the limited evidence. But, as Slichter points out, the economy has, over-all, done very well indeed over these inflation decades; managerial decision making cannot have been too greatly upset.

These historical facts do not prove that inflation has not exerted a downward pressure on output. It is possible, of course, that other expansive forces have overcome any downward pressure that inflation has exerted. The evidence indicates, however, that if this has been the case, the depressive impact of inflation has generally been a weak one.

Does inflation increase current real output? Some scholars have claimed that inflation stimulates output and employment, especially in periods of widespread unemployment. There is no doubt that output has generally risen in periods of inflation. But this does not necessarily mean that inflation has generally, or ever, *caused* the rising output, or has even been *necessary* to it. It should be borne in mind that output has also risen in periods of stable, or even slightly declining, prices; the 1920's in the United States provide a leading example. Thus, to see inflation and increased output together by no means automatically indicates that rising prices are the cause.

We are thrown back, then, to a considerable extent on theory. The main arguments are that inflation increases current output by:

  1. Pushing up prices faster than costs (especially wages) rise, thereby increasing profits and stimulating investment and output.
  2. Inducing lagging income groups to work harder and longer.
  3. Stimulating buying and output now because the expectation of continued inflation puts a premium on early purchases.

It is generally agreed that arguments #1 and #3 hold only when substantial unemployment exists; the second argument may apply even in high-employment periods. Let us see.

Price-cost differentials. The wage lag has apparently played a major role in many past inflations. But, as is shown below, wages have not lagged appreciably behind prices. Indeed, wages throughout the Western industrialized world seem to be increasingly mobile in an upward direction, in many instances linked to rising prices through built-in escalator clauses.

Some other costs may lag in inflation, even though wages do not. Interest charges, rents, many salaries, and other costs are temporarily fixed in dollar terms as selling prices of business products rise. But these lags can easily be overcome by only a modest wage lead.

Inflation does lead to substantial overstatement of profits under prevailing accounting practices, because depreciation and inventory replacement costs are understated. This overstatement of profits may induce businesses to invest and to produce more than they otherwise would. Partial estimates suggest that this understatement of replacement costs approached one-third of corporate profits during the decade of the 1940's. While most businessmen surely recognize the phantom nature of part of their inflation-period profits, it may be that the figures nevertheless stimulate them to increase their investment spending beyond what the "real" profit figures warrant.

Lagging income groups. How valid is the argument that inflation drives lagging income groups, especially nonworkers, to work more and harder in order to protect their real incomes? Casual observation turns up numerous cases where this effect seems to apply—retired men driven back to part-time work, wives of college professors working to supplement their husbands' lagging salaries, school teachers driving taxis or working in industry during summer vacations. But it is doubtful that the effect is a major one, at least for creeping inflation, for two reasons.

(a) The largest groups whose incomes are pinched by inflation are old folks and employees of nonprofit organizations, neither likely sources of major increases in productive power. (b) The ratio of the labor force (i.e., people in and looking for jobs) to the number of people of labor-force age has shown no significant growth tendency during inflation, except during the war period. While the proportion of women holding jobs has risen steadily over the past 25 years, outside of the war period there has been no significant relationship between the rate of increase and the rate of inflation. So it seems doubtful that inflation has had much do with the *number* of people working today.

Speculation. Will the expectation of continuing inflation lead to increased current real output? This is an obviously short-run argument. Inflation fears may temporarily stimulate buying, but people and businesses cannot pile up inventories indefinitely on speculation that prices tomorrow will be higher than today. Except as a "shot in the arm," this can hardly be a major effect.

Slichter has properly emphasized one other factor. When prices are rising generally, resources are bid into growing industries from mature or declining industries by higher wages and prices. Without inflation, prices in declining industries would have to fall. This would be painful, and resources might be reluctant to leave. But the real difficulty is the need to move, either way. Chalk up a small credit to inflation as a social lubricant, therefore. Whether it significantly increases total output is a more dubious matter.

Does inflation reduce future real output? There are two major arguments that inflation reduces future real output: (a) the boom-and-bust argument that inflation causes a speculative situation that is necessarily followed by a bust and depression; and (b) the much longer-run argument that inflation discourages saving and thus decreases the rate of capital accumulation, which holds down the economy's long-run growth rate.

What is the evidence for the boom-and-bust argument? History both supports the argument and contradicts it. Thus it is clearly wrong to say that inflation *must* be followed directly by collapse and depression. For example, in the United States, the United Kingdom, France, and most of Western Europe substantial inflation more or less continuously over the past two decades has been paralleled by a persistent growth in real national output. In Brazil inflation averaging over 10% per year has continued since the 1930's with rising real output. In Japan the postwar picture is similar.

On the other hand, examples of inflation-induced collapse do exist. The post-World War I slump of the early 1920's in the United States may be an example. Certainly the massive hyperinflations have led to major economic collapse. Conclusion: a Scotch verdict, neither case proven. Rapid inflation may lead to economic collapse, but milder inflation certainly may not.

How about the argument that inflation discourages saving and retards capital accumulation? Proponents claim that inflation erodes the value of accumulated saving and thus encourages current consumption.. This theory sounds convincing, but here again there is a counterargument—that inflation shifts income to the rich and to corporate profits and thereby increases saving relative to consumption.

The historical evidence is mixed. Everyone knows of individual cases where friends have said they might as well spend their money now as to save it and lose its value through inflation. In hyperinflation this effect is obviously dominant. But counterexamples are easy to find, too; for instance, in almost all the post-World War II inflations of the Western world, capital accumulation has proceeded

Table 1

*Inflation, Production, and Employment
From 1952 to 1955 (1952 = 100)*

	United States	Belgium	France	Germany	Italy	Nether- lands	Sweden	United Kingdom
Cost of living:								
1953	101	100	99	98	102	100	101	103
1954	101	102	99	98	105	104	102	105
1955	101	101	100	100	108	106	105	110
Industrial production:								
1953	108	100	97	109	110	110	100	106
1954	100	106	106	122	120	120	104	114
1955	112	114	117	141	130	128	110	119
Employment:								
1953	103	99	98	104	100	103	97	101
1954	100	99	99	109	101	107	98	104
1955	102	101	100	118	103	109	100	107

Source: Data are from J. Herbert Furth, "Indicators of Inflation in Western Europe, 1952–1955," *Review of Economics and Statistics*, August 1956, pp. 336–337.

rapidly. In the recent American inflation, to complicate matters, the traditional pattern of income redistribution toward profits and the rich has been shaken.

Until recently, it seemed clear that moderate inflation increased saving and capital goods accumulation relative to consumption, and thus increased long-run total output. This occurred as inflation shifted income from the poor to the rich and from workers to businessmen. But certainly recent American experience does not support this interpretation. On balance, the wage share has risen appreciably relative to property income during the past two decades, and the share of the rich has declined a little.

In summary, there is no very strong case that inflation of *modest* proportions either increases or decreases substantially the rate of capital accumulation. Inflation militates against saving in most forms, but the motives for saving are many and mixed, and modern society provides some effective investment channels to escape the erosion of inflation.

Some Recent Evidence

Table 1, outlining the experience of European countries plus the United States over the mild inflationary period of 1952 through 1955, shows no consistent relationship at all between inflation and changes in production:

> The largest increase in output and employment occurred in West Germany, which had no inflation at all; the smallest in Sweden, which had an intermediate amount of inflation.
>
> Italy, with a slightly smaller price increase than Sweden and the United Kingdom, had a much larger increase in output than either.
>
> The United States and Belgium, with almost no inflation, had a bigger increase in output than inflationary Sweden but less than noninflationary Germany and the mildly inflationary Netherlands.

The figures cannot be explained away by such differences between countries as varying increases in the supply of money, varying money wage rates relative to prices, or varying positions on international trade account.

Distribution of Output

We have found that the effect of moderate inflation on total real output appears to be slight under most circumstances and not a priori predictable. But what effect does it have on the relative size of the pieces of the national income pie going to different individuals and economic groups? If we can judge from the American inflation of the past two decades, it does have an impact, but not as much as is often claimed. And the redistribution that does take place does not correspond very well to some of the common preconceptions about inflation.

How are different income groups affected? Since 1939 every broad functional economic group in the United States has gained substantially in real income. Within the rapidly growing total, however, wages and salaries did *not* lag behind profits as a share of the national income. On the contrary, the wage share grew appreciably over the period. Moreover:

> Farmers, who are commonly supposed to gain most from inflation, saw their share of the national income decline persistently, perhaps in spite of inflation, but decline nevertheless.
>
> The share represented by corporation profits held stable or declined slightly.
>
> Unincorporated businesses, usually thought to be gainers from inflation, also took a cut in their share of the total.
>
> The interest share dropped drastically during World War II, as interest rates were held down by government policy, but has since grown moderately back toward its earlier level.
>
> The rent share has changed little.
>
> There is no evidence that inflation has shifted income from the poor to the rich; if anything, the effect may have been the other way.

The most significant thing about Figure 1, which shows these changes, is the lack of dramatic functional income shifts over two decades of inflation. Thus, it is not to the effect on major income groups, but rather to the effect on particular segments and individuals within these major groupings, that we must look for the major redistributional effects of inflation, although the basic shift to the wage and salary share is pronounced.

Because inflation penalizes primarily those whose incomes rise more slowly than the incomes of their fellows, it has been those with fixed incomes who lost relatively, whether rich or poor, young or old, farmer or city dweller. Above all, it appears that older people's piece of the national income pie suffered most. Their share of the national income dropped substantially as inflation ate away at their largely fixed incomes.

Here it appears that inflation has discriminated against the middle incomes and the poor. Well-to-do retired individuals can afford to diversify the investments which underlie their retirement incomes and to include substantial amounts of such variable income assets as common stocks and real estate, whose dollar yields increase with inflation. But to the lower income families and widows this alternative is hardly open. To be sure, Slichter has properly emphasized that there are some offsets; for instance, Social Security payments have increased greatly, and many older people have jobs. But this does not eliminate the basic fact that inflation is a major blow to this group, which lives considerably on past savings.

The other most important lagging income group appears to have been employees of nonprofit organizations—of governments and of other nonprofit institutions, especially teachers. In some cases, teachers' salaries have lagged so greatly that their real incomes have actually declined during the greatest boom of our history.

More generally, it is the "passive" economic groups—those who sell no products on which they can raise the price or who work under arrangements where their output cannot readily be raised in price—who have suffered at the expense of the "active" groups in society. The major economic groups, on the other hand, especially wage and salary earners, appear to be increasingly effective in protecting their own income shares during slow inflation.

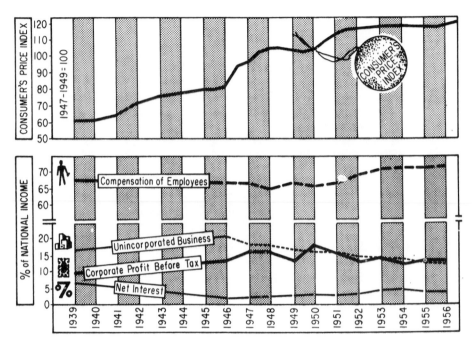

Fig. 1.   Shares of National Income in Inflation, 1939–1956.

Debtors and Creditors

It is well recognized that inflation transfers wealth (future purchasing power) from creditors to debtors. This is because the debtor who borrows $100 and repays the same $100 later when prices are twice as high repays only half as much real purchasing power.

The American inflation since 1939 has wiped out in this way over half a trillion dollars of creditors' claims on debtors (in 1957 prices). All fixed-dollar-value intangible assets (such as bank deposits, currency, mortgages, government and corporation bonds, life insurance reserves, and pension and retirement funds) are debts owed to creditors and are susceptible to this erosion by inflation. In 1939 all such assets totaled about $320 billion. If we calculate the loss of purchasing power on these debts up to the present and make a similar calculation for the additional debts of each following year, we obtain the very rough estimate of over $500 billion inflationary erosion of the real purchasing power of creditors over this period.

Who gained this huge sum of purchasing power? To answer this question, we need a sectorial picture of the economy showing main net debtor and net creditor groups (Table 2). Unfortunately, the most recent complete data we have are those for 1949, but the relative position of different groups in the picture does not appear to have changed greatly since then.

In summary, Table 2 shows that "households" (families and individuals) were massive net creditors, and that their creditor position was substantially offset by the massive net debtor position of government, especially the federal government.

Table 2

Net Debtors and Creditors in the American Economy From 1939 to 1949 (In billions of dollars)

	1939	1949
Households	+$87	+$249
Unincorporated businesses	+ 3	+ 16
Nonfinancial corporations	− 25	− 17
Financial corporations	− 3	+ 17
Governments	− 68	− 263

Source: Data are computed from Raymond Goldsmith, *A Study of Saving in the United States* (Princeton, Princeton University Press, 1955), Vol. III, Tables W-14, 15, and 16. Plus figures show net creditor status; minus figures show net debtor status.

Thus, the figures also show that inflation has caused a huge transfer of purchasing power from households to the federal government. But this is clearly not the end of the matter, since the government is not some separate entity but is an agency for all of us. We must look *through* the government to see who the actual beneficiaries of this inflation-induced levy on creditors are.

At first glance, it would appear that taxpayers (that is, all of us in our capacities as taxpayers) are the gainers. We now need to give up less purchasing power in taxes to meet payments on interest and principal on the government debt. Since government bondholders and taxpayers are not identical, there is a real shift of wealth from creditors to taxpayers.

It is highly unlikely, however, that the federal debt will be paid off through taxation in the foreseeable future. Who, then, is the gainer of the purchasing power confiscated from government creditors by inflation? The buying public as a whole gains *in proportion to its expenditures*. Bondholders' real purchasing power is reduced, thus increasing the share of total current output that the rest of the buying public can command as their incomes rise with inflation.

Put in common-sense language, government bondholders and moneyholders are partially expropriated by inflation, and the benefit is distributed over the whole population, with the biggest benefits to those who buy the most. Although government creditors and spenders are the same people to some extent, on balance savers *in fixed dollar value assets* subsidize spenders. There is no clear evidence that in moderate inflation this effect transfers real income from the poor to the rich or, in a fully employed economy, from rich to poor.

How are different creditors groups affected? Since all of us are parts of households, more information on particular types of households is needed if we are to see clearly the impact of inflation on us as creditors. Some relevant information is summarized in Table 3.

All households combined hold about 3 per cent of their total wealth in the form of fixed dollar value assets. By contrast, they are in debt up to only a little over 10 per cent of their total wealth. The difference is a measure of their net creditor position. Nearly every major group of households is a substantial net creditor.

Table 3
Assets and Debts of Households in Early 1950

	Per cent of all households	Total assets (in billions)	Per cent of total assets:		
			Monetary assets	Variable price assets	Debts
All households	100%	$613	24%	76%	11%
By 1949 money income before taxes:					
Under $1,000	14%	$ 39	19%	81%	12%
1,000–2,999	40	119	26	74	13
3,000–4,999	29	150	27	73	16
5,000–7,499	11	107	25	75	12
75,000 and over	5	188	19	81	5
By occupation:					
Professional and semiprofessional	7%	$ 61	32%	68%	10%
Managerial	4	40	27	73	12
Self-employed	8	155	16	84	6
Clerical and skilled	41	136	29	71	18
Unskilled	12	23	31	69	14
Farm operators	9	97	13	87	12
Retired	5	55	31	69	2
All other	14	46	28	72	8
By net worth in 1950:					
Negative net worth	5%	$ 2	30%	70%	490%
$0– 1,999	33	17	46	54	33
2,000– 9,999	34	117	29	71	20
10,000–24,999	18	162	24	76	9
25,000–59,999	7	135	22	78	6
60,000 and over	3	180	17	83	3
By age of head of household:					
18–24	10%	$ 9	23%	77%	20%
25–34	23	69	22	78	27
35–54	40	285	24	76	12
55 and over	26	244	23	77	4

Source: Data are from Raymond Goldsmith, op. cit., Tables W-46, 47, 48, 49, based in turn primarily on Federal Reserve—Michigan Survey Research Center survey of consumer finances for early 1950. Columns may not add to totals because of minor unascertained items and rounding.

The extent to which different groups are net creditors varies a good deal, however. Thus:

> The heaviest net creditors, relative to their incomes, are older people, especially those who are retired. They hold a larger proportion of their wealth in fixed dollar value assets than any other major group, largely because of the importance to them of insurance and pension and other retirement funds. It is they who, relative to their total wealth, stand to lose most as creditors when inflation comes. Moreover, they are least in debt and do not reap offsetting benefits on that score.
>
> At the other extreme, the very penurious or injudicious who are so heavily in debt as to have a negative net worth and younger families in the 25–34 age range are the least susceptible to "creditor" loss from inflation. They are substantially in debt, which is, other things being equal, a good state to be in during inflation.

The very well-to-do families are slightly higher net creditors than the average, relative to their total wealth, and their debts are small. Thus, they appear quite vulnerable to inflation. On the other hand, they hold an exceptionally large proportion of their total assets in "variable price" form (common stock, real estate, and so on), which serves as a partial offset to their exposure as net creditors.

Interestingly, most American households appear to have made comparatively little effort during the long period of persistent inflation to switch from their position as heavy net creditors. While the data are inadequate, they suggest only a mild attempt by most households to shift to more "inflation-proof" assets, even in periods of rapidly rising prices.

COPING WITH IT

The real danger of creeping inflation is that it will pick up steam and grow beyond a creep. While there is little evidence that creeping inflation is disastrous, there is overwhelming evidence that a hyperinflation is. Just where the costs of inflation mount to major proportions is hard to specify. It is clear, though, that the more rapid the rise in prices is, the more inequitable and disruptive shifts in income and wealth may become, and also the greater the danger that productive activity may be shifted into unproductive lines to "beat the inflation."

Creep or Gallop?

Is the danger that creeping inflation will turn into galloping inflation a real one for the United States if we do not check it in the creeping stage? I believe that real hyperinflation is extremely unlikely. On the other hand, I am concerned that the creep may become a little faster during the next five years, even though it may possibly be interrupted by a business recession.

My prediction is that excess income claims of labor, business, and agriculture will persist—and probably mount. Our democratic government, essentially committed to maintaining high-level employment, will find it extremely difficult not to provide the additional purchasing power needed to support employment at higher cost and price levels as wages and prices of strong income groups are pushed up. This it can do either through deficit financing or by providing additional bank reserves to finance private loans.

Once people understand this process and trust government underwriting of high-level employment, there is logically no limit to the rate of inflation which might develop. But, as a practical matter, the inflation is not likely to be a rapid one (outside of war periods) because income groups are not yet confident enough of government policy to put aside caution in their income claims, because widespread competition slows price increases, and because public fear of inflation is strong enough to restrain private and public action that conspicuously produces rapid price increases.

This is the long-run peacetime inflation danger. It arises from the fact that we are a society of powerful economic and political groups, and that, as such, we place top priority on the maintenance of a high level of employment and are willing to use federal monetary and fiscal policies to achieve this. Without these two interacting factors of powerful excess income claims and governmental high-employment policy, there is little reason to expect persistent secular inflation in America—in the absence of war.

Accordingly, a fundamental approach to limit inflation must either blunt the excess income claims or prevent the provision of additional purchasing power through the banking system.

Checks on Income Claims

The first approach does not seem promising. President Eisenhower has repeatedly exhorted labor and management to moderate their wage and price claims, but with little success. A few economists have suggested drastic action to break up the monopolistic powers of large unions and large corporations, but action sufficiently strong to eliminate the problem this way seems unrealistic on the modern scene. Others have suggested countervailing power—making businesses and other groups even stronger to resist the pressures of the unions. But it will still be tempting for management to give in to the unions and merely pass the cost along in the form of higher prices, which is by all odds the easier solution when two powerful giants meet.

A more sophisticated suggestion is that we improve the inducements to businesses to hold down costs, perhaps by lowering the corporation income tax rate and thereby reducing the extent to which the government itself indirectly bears the cost of any wage increase granted. Some have suggested imposition of direct governmental controls over wages and prices. Still other writers have emphasized that the ultimate solution must lie in an increased sense of responsibility on the part both of unions and of management in moderating their claims for higher wages and prices.

Each of these ideas has merit. But none of them provides a very reliable basis for giving up a search for effective inflation hedges.

Monetary-Fiscal Policy

In the last analysis, almost everyone comes back to federal monetary-fiscal policy—if the job is to be done. Monetary-fiscal policy has a harder time in an economy of administered prices and wages since its impact may be slower and less predictable in any short period. The credit squeeze of tight money falls unequally on different firms and different industries; in general, the least credit-worthy (often the smaller, highly competitive firms) feel the pinch of monetary restriction first. Slower though the check may be, however, shortage of total monetary demand is one sure way of checking inflation.

But if, as Slichter has argued, it is extremely difficult in times of moderate inflation to generate large federal surpluses to fight inflation, and if a really tight money policy can work only by generating unemployment, is this approach a *realistic* solution? My answer is that monetary policy against inflation is workable if it has the support of the public—and only if it does!

By limiting the supply of money the Federal Reserve Board can check inflation. Without more money, total expenditures will not long continue to grow.

No seller, no matter how powerful, will continue to raise prices if the consumer cannot continue to buy at the higher prices; and, with a fixed money supply, consumers can continue to buy at higher prices only if they spend the existing money supply faster—only if there is an increase for V in the old textbook equation $MV = PT$ (where M represents money, V, the velocity of turnover of money, P, the price, T, the number of units sold). It is true that V may increase to a moderate extent. For example, over the past two years the money supply has increased by only 1% per year while total expenditures have risen 5% per year. History shows, though, that no *major* inflation will occur without an increase in the money supply. While a federal policy that holds the money supply constant may not work precisely and completely, it will certainly shut off any substantial inflationary sweep within a moderate amount of time. Perhaps selective controls, like consumer credit, can help to pinpoint monetary restraint where inflationary rises are strongest, but they can do only a small part of the job.

The real issue, thus, is whether the Federal Reserve Board (and the federal government) will stand firm and refuse to increase the money supply when the pressure for higher prices and wages necessitates more total spending power to prevent falling sales and unemployment.

Pressure To Be Resisted

Tight money that checks inflation may cause unemployment, and the Federal Reserve authorities do not want that particular result. Slichter and Jacoby have argued vigorously about just how much unemployment would be required to hold down inflationary wage demands if tight money pressure were applied. Argument of this sort is helpful in exposing the issues, but it seems to me quite illusory to suppose that we can answer this question accurately now.

Critics of tight money argue that only large-scale unemployment can be counted on to check inflationary wage and price policies. This seems overly pessimistic to me, and I suspect we may be seeing now a rather effective demonstration of the way tight money can slow down inflation without inducing a major recession. Our post-World War II experience has provided encouraging evidence, as has that of other countries. Whatever the weight of these arguments, the crucial point is that, to avoid inflation in an economy of major power groups, the government must convince the public and the major economic groups within the public, by temporary unemployment or otherwise, that we *will* act to check inflation, even at the cost of some temporary unemployment and unsold goods.

If we do not convince them, we will have inflation and probably as much unemployment too in the long run. For, however fast a government pumps in money, the wage and price demands of the powerful groups can readily be raised more rapidly. The 1958 wage demands of the major unions may well be eye openers on this score. *Thus, we face the same temporary unemployment issue whether we draw the line against power-group inflation at the creeping or at some more advanced stage.*

The basic issue is not, then, whether we shall have inflation with full employment, or stable prices with unemployment. It is likelier to be whether we shall have stable prices or inflation, with some temporary unemployment in either case. Viewed in this way, the case for creeping inflation becomes a good deal less appealing than Slichter has made it seem.

Where shall we take our stand against ever-rising income claims? A stable price level policy is not necessarily better than others, such as a slowly rising price level policy, but it seems to me to present by all odds the strongest rallying point for public support. It is the most equitable position, given the general presumption in our habits and economic mores that the value of the monetary unit is roughly stable. We can all agree that high-level employment is our first objective, but we must still face the fact that inflation is not necessarily, or even probably, the road to maintaining high-level employment

*   *   *

Words are inadequate to convey the human misery, the despair, the baffled uncertainty and hopelessness in the great depression of the 1930's. The long bread lines, the silent factories, the wandering "Okies," the "dust bowl," the evicted hungry families huddled in cardboard shacks—these were the desperate reality of the depression behind the statistics. These pages should convey a little of this reality to a generation for whom the great depression is increasingly far away and unreal.

Frederick Lewis Allen has been editor of Harper's *magazine, and has written several popular books describing different periods of American history.*

8

Black Depression

FREDERICK LEWIS ALLEN

*   *   *

Statistics are bloodless things.

To say that during the year 1932, the cruelest year of the Depression, the average number of unemployed people in the country was 12½ million by the estimates of the National Industrial Conference Board, a little over 13 million by the estimates of the American Federation of Labor, and by other estimates (differently arrived at, and defining unemployment in various ways) anywhere from 8½ to 17 million—to say this is to give no living impression of the jobless men going from office to office or from factory gate to factory gate; of the disheartening inevitability of the phrase, "We'll let you know if anything shows up"; of men thumbing the want ads in cold tenements, spending fruitless hours, day after day and week after week, in the sidewalk crowds before the employment offices; using up the money in the savings bank, borrowing on their life insurance, selling whatever possessions could be sold, borrowing from relatives less and less able to lend, tasting the bitterness of inadequacy, and at last swallowing their pride and going to apply for relief—if there was any to be got. (Relief money was scarce, for charitable organizations were hard beset and cities and towns had either used up their available funds or were on the point of doing so.)

A few statistical facts and estimates are necessary, however, to an understanding of the scope and impact of the Depression. For example:—

Although the amount of money paid out in interest during the year 1932 was only 3.5 per cent less than in 1929, according to the computations of Dr. Simon Kuznets for the National Bureau of Economic Research, on the other hand the amount of money paid out in salaries had dropped 40 per cent, dividends had dropped 56.6 per cent, and wages had dropped 60 per cent. (Thus had the debt structure remained comparatively rigid while other elements in the economy were subjected to fierce deflation.)

Do not imagine, however, that the continuation of interest payments and the partial continuation of dividend payments meant that business as a whole was making money. Business as a whole lost between five and six billion dollars in 1932. (The government figure for all the corporations in the country—451,800 of them—was a net deficit of $5,640,000,000.) To be sure, most of the larger and better-managed companies did much better than that. E. D. Kennedy's figures for the 960 concerns whose earnings were tabulated by Standard Statistics—mostly big ones whose stock was active on the Stock Exchange—show that these 960 leaders had a collective profit of over a third of a billion. Yet one must add that "better managed" is here used in a special sense. Not only had labor-saving devices and speed-ups increased the output per man-hour in manufacturing industries by an estimated 18 per cent since 1929, but employees had been laid off in quantity. Every time one of the giants of industry, to keep its financial head above water, threw off a new group of workers, many little corporations roundabout sank further into the red.

While existing businesses shrank, new ones were not being undertaken. The total of domestic corporate issues—issues of securities floated to provide capital for American corporations—had dropped in 1932 to just about *one twenty-fourth* of the 1929 figure.

But these cold statistics give us little sense of the human realities of the economic paralysis of 1932. Let us try another approach.

Walking through an American city, you might find few signs of the Depression visible—or at least conspicuous—to the casual eye. You might notice that a great many shops were untenanted, with dusty plate-glass windows and signs indicating that they were ready to lease; that few factory chimneys were smoking; that the streets were not so crowded with trucks as in earlier years, that there was no uproar of riveters to assail the ear, that beggars and panhandlers were on the sidewalks in unprecedented numbers (in the Park Avenue district of New York a man might be asked for money four or five times in a ten-block walk). Traveling by railroad, you might notice that the trains were shorter, the Pullman cars fewer—and that fewer freight trains were on the line. Traveling overnight, you might find only two or three other passengers in your sleeping car. (By contrast, there were more filling stations by the motor highways than ever before, and of all the retail businesses in "Middletown" only the filling stations showed no large drop in business during the black years; for although few new automobiles were being bought, those which would still stand up were being used more than ever —to the dismay of the railroads.)

Otherwise things might seem to you to be going on much as usual. The major phenomena of the Depression were mostly negative and did not assail the eye.

But if you knew where to look, some of them would begin to appear. First, the breadlines in the poorer districts. Second, those bleak settlements ironically known as "Hoovervilles" in the outskirts of the cities and on vacant lots—groups of makeshift shacks constructed out of packing boxes, scrap iron, anything that could be picked up free in a diligent combing of the city dumps: shacks in which men and sometimes whole families of evicted people were sleeping on automobile seats carried from auto-graveyards, warming themselves before fires of rubbish in grease drums. Third, the homeless people sleeping in doorways or on park benches, and going the rounds of the restaurants for leftover half-eaten biscuits, piecrusts, anything to keep the fires of life burning. Fourth, the vastly increased number of thumbers on the highways, and particularly of freight-car transients on the railroads: a huge army of drifters ever on the move, searching half-aimlessly for a place where there might be a job. According to Jonathan Norton Leonard, the Missouri Pacific Railroad in 1929 had "taken official cognizance" of 13,745 migrants; by 1931 the figure had already jumped to 186,028. It was estimated that by the beginning of 1933, the country over, there were a million of these transients on the move. Forty-five thousand had passed through El Paso in the space of six months; 1,500 were passing through Kansas City every day. Among them were large numbers of young boys, and girls disguised as boys. According to the Children's Bureau, there were 200,000 children thus drifting about the United States. So huge was the number of freight-car hoppers in the Southwest that in a number of places the railroad police simply had to give up trying to remove them from the trains: there were far too many of them.

Among the comparatively well-to-do people of the country (those, let us say, whose pre-Depression incomes had been over $5,000 a year) the great majority were living on a reduced scale, for salary cuts had been extensive, especially since 1931, and dividends were dwindling. These people were discharging servants, or cutting servants' wages to a minimum, or in some cases "letting" a servant stay on without other compensation than board and lodging. In many pretty houses, wives who had never before—in the revealing current phrase—"done their own work" were cooking and scrubbing. Husbands were wearing the old suit longer, resigning from the golf club, deciding, perhaps, that this year the family couldn't afford to go to the beach for the summer, paying seventy-five cents for lunch instead of a dollar at the restaurant or thirty-five instead of fifty at the lunch counter. When those who had flown high with the stock market in 1929 looked at the stock-market page of the newspapers nowadays their only consoling thought (if they still had any stock left) was that a judicious sale or two would result in such a capital loss that they need pay no income tax at all this year.

Alongside these men and women of the well-to-do classes whose fortunes had been merely reduced by the Depression were others whose fortunes had been shattered. The crowd of men waiting for the 8:14 train at the prosperous suburb included many who had lost their jobs, and were going to town as usual not merely to look stubbornly and almost hopelessly for other work but also to keep up a bold front of activity. (In this latter effort they usually succeeded: one would never have guessed, seeing them chatting with their friends as train-time approached, how close to desperation some of them had come.) There were architects and engineers bound for offices to which no clients had come in weeks. There were doctors who thought themselves lucky when a patient paid a bill. Mrs. Jones, who went daily to her stenographic job, was now the economic mainstay of her family, for Mr. Jones was jobless and was doing the cooking and looking after the children (with singular distaste and inefficiency). Next door to the Joneses lived Mrs. Smith, the widow of a successful lawyer: she had always had a comfortable income, she prided herself on her "nice things," she was pathetically unfitted to earn a dollar even if jobs were to be had; her capital had been invested in South American bonds and United Founders stock and other similarly misnamed "securities," and now she was completely dependent upon hand-outs from her relatives, and didn't even have carfare in her imported pocket-book.

The Browns had retreated to their "farmhouse" in the country and were trying to raise crops on its stony acres; they talked warmly about primal simplicities but couldn't help longing sometimes for electric light and running hot water, and couldn't cope with the potato bugs. (Large numbers of city dwellers thus moved to the country, but not enough of them engaged in real farming to do more than partially check the long-term movement from the farms of America to the cities and towns.) It was being whispered about the community that the Robinson family, though they lived in a $40,000 house and had always spent money freely, were in desperate straits: Mr. Robinson had lost his job, the house could not be sold, they had realized on every asset at their command, and now they were actually going hungry—though their house still looked like the abode of affluence.

Further down in the economic scale, particularly in those industrial communities in which the factories were running at twenty per cent of capacity or had closed down altogether, conditions were infinitely worse. Frederick E. Croxton's figures, taken in Buffalo, show what was happening in such communities: out of 14,909 persons of both sexes willing and able to work, his house-to-house canvassers found in November, 1932, that 46.3 per cent were fully employed, 22.5 per cent were working part time, and as many as 31.2 per cent were unable to find jobs. In every American city, quantities of families were being evicted from their inadequate apartments; moving in with other families till ten or twelve people would be sharing three or four rooms; or shivering through the winter in heatless houses because they could afford no coal, eating meat once a week or not at all. If employers sometimes found that former employees who had been discharged did not seem eager for re-employment ("They won't take a job if you offer them one!"), often the reason was panic: a dreadful fear of inadequacy which was one of the Depression's commonest psycho-pathological results. A woman clerk, offered piecework after being jobless for a year, confessed that she almost had not dared to come to the office, she had been in such terror lest she wouldn't know where to hang her coat, wouldn't know how to find the washroom, wouldn't understand the boss's directions for her job.

For perhaps the worst thing about this Depression was its inexorable continuance year after year. Men who have been sturdy and self-respecting workers can take unemployment without flinching for a few weeks, a few months, even if they have to see their families suffer; but it is different after a year . . . two years . . . three years. . . . Among the miserable creatures curled up on park benches or standing in dreary lines before the soup kitchens in 1932 were men who had been jobless since the end of 1929.

At the very bottom of the economic scale the conditions may perhaps best be suggested by two brief quotations. The first, from Jonathan Norton Leonard's *Three Years Down*, describes the plight of Pennsylvania miners who had been put out of company villages after a blind and hopeless strike in 1931: "Reporters from the more liberal metropolitan papers found thousands of them huddled on the mountainsides, crowded three or four families together in one-room shacks, living on dandelions and wild weed-roots. Half of them were sick, but no local doctor would care for the evicted strikers. All of them were hungry and many were dying of those providential diseases which enable welfare authorities to claim that no one has starved." The other quotation is from Louise V. Armstrong's *We Too Are the People,* and the scene is Chicago in the late spring of 1932:—

"One vivid, gruesome moment of those dark days we shall never forget. We saw a crowd of some fifty men fighting over a barrel of garbage which had been set outside the back door of a restaurant. American citizens fighting for scraps of food like animals!"

Human behavior under unaccustomed conditions is always various. One thinks of the corporation executive to whom was delegated the job of discharging several hundred men: he insisted on seeing every one of them personally and taking an interest in each man's predicament, and at the end of a few months his hair had turned prematurely gray. . . . The Junior League girl who reported with pride a Depression economy: she had cut a piece out of an old fur coat in the attic and bound it to serve as a bathmat. . . . The banker who had been plunged deeply into debt by the collapse of his bank: he got a $30,000 job with another bank, lived on $3,000 a year, and honorably paid $27,000 a year to his creditors. . . . The wealthy family who lost most of their money but announced bravely that they had "solved their Depression problem" by discharging fifteen of their twenty servants, and showed no signs of curiosity as to what would happen to these fifteen. . . . The little knot of corporation officials in a magnificent sky-scraper office doctoring the books of the company to dodge bankruptcy. . . . The crowd of Chicago Negroes standing tight-packed before a tenement-house door to prevent the landlord's agents from evicting a neighbor family: as they stood there, hour by hour, they sang hymns. . . . The one-time clerk carefully cutting out pieces of cardboard to put inside his shoes before setting out on his endless job-hunting round, and telling his wife the shoes were now better than ever. . . . The man in the little apartment next door who had given up hunting for jobs, given up all interest, all activity, and sat hour by hour in staring apathy. . . .

*   *   *

No only were ideas boiling; the country was losing patience with adversity. That instinct of desperate men to rebel which was swelling the radical parties in a dozen Depression-hit countries and was gathering stormily behind Hitler in Germany was working in the United States also. It was anything but unified, it was as yet little organized, and only in scattered places did it assume the customary European shape of communism. It had been slow to develop—partly because Americans had been used to prosperity and had expected it to return automatically, partly because when jobs were vanishing those men who were still employed were too scared to be rebellious, and simply hung on to what they had and waited and hoped. (It is not usually during a collapse that men rebel, but after it.) There had been riots and hunger-marches here and there but on the whole the orderliness of the country had been striking, all things considered. Yet men could not be expected to sit still forever in the expectation that an economic system which they did not understand would right itself. The ferment of dissatisfaction was working in many places and taking many forms, and here and there it was beginning to break sharply through the orderly surface of society.

In the summer of 1932 the city of Washington was to see an exciting example of this ferment—and a spectacular demonstration of how not to deal with it.

All through June thousands of war veterans had been streaming into Washington, coming from all over the country by boxcar and by truck. These veterans wanted the government to pay them now the "adjusted compensation" which Congress had already voted to pay them in 1945. They set up a camp—a shanty-town, a sort of big-scale "Hooverville"—on the Anacostia flats near the city, and they occupied some vacant land with disused buildings on it on Pennsylvania Avenue just below the Capitol. More and more of them straggled to Washington until their number had reached fifteen or twenty thousand.

Among such a great crowd there were inevitably men of many sorts. The Hoover Administration later charged that many had had criminal records, or were communists. But unquestionably the great majority of them were genuine veterans; though there was one small communist group, it was regarded with hostility by the rest; in the main this "Bonus Expeditionary Force" consisted of ordinary Americans out of luck. They were under at least a semblance of military discipline and were on the whole well-behaved. Many brought their wives and children along, and as time went on the Anacostia camp took on an air half military and half domestic, with the family wash hanging on the line outside the miserable shacks, and entertainers getting up impromptu vaudeville shows.

General Pelham D. Glassford, the Washington superintendent of police, sensibly regarded these invaders as citizens who had every right to petition the government for a redress of grievances. He helped them to get equipment for their camp and treated them with unfailing consideration. But to some Washingtonians their presence was ominous. A group of the veterans—under a leader who wore a steel neckbrace and a helmet with straps under the chin, to support a broken back—picketed the Capitol for days while the Bonus bill was being considered; and on the evening when the bill was to come to a vote, the great plaza before the Capitol was packed with veterans. The Senate voted No. What would the men do? There were people looking out the windows of the brightly lighted Senate wing who wondered breathlessly if those thousands of ragged men would try to rush the building. But when their leader announced the news, a band struck up "America" and the men dispersed quietly. So far, so good.

Some of them left Washington during the next few days, but several thousand stayed on, hopelessly, obstinately. (Where had they to go?) Officialdom became more and more uneasy. The White House was put under guard, its gates closed and chained, the streets about it cleared, as if the man there did not dare face the unrest among the least fortunate of the citizenry. It was decided to clear the veterans out of the disused buildings below the Capitol (to make way for the government's building program); and on the morning of July 28, 1932, General Glassford was told that the evacuation must be immediate. He set about his task.

It began peacefully, but at noon somebody threw a brick and there was a scuffle between the veterans and the police, which quickly subsided. Two hours later there was more serious trouble as a policeman at whom the veterans had thrown stones pulled his gun; two veterans were killed before Glassford could get the police to stop shooting. Even this battle subsided. All Glassford wanted was time to complete the evacuation peacefully and without needless affront. But he was not to get it.

Earlier in the day he had told the District Commissioners that if the evacuation was to be carried out speedily, troops would be required. This statement had been needlessly interpreted as a request for military aid, which Glassford did not want at all. President Hoover had ordered the United States Army to the rescue.

Down Pennsylvania Avenue, late that hot afternoon, came an impressive parade—four troops of cavalry, four companies of infantry, a machine-gun squadron, and several tanks. As they approached the disputed area they were met with cheers from the veterans sitting on the curb and from the large crowd which had assembled. Then suddenly there was chaos: cavalrymen were riding into the crowd, infantrymen were throwing tear-gas bombs, women and children were being trampled and were choking from the gas; a crowd of three thousand or more spectators who had gathered in a vacant lot across the way were being pursued by the cavalry and were running wildly, pell-mell across the uneven ground, screaming as they stumbled and fell.

The troops moved slowly on, scattering before them veterans and homegoing government clerks alike. When they reached the other end of the Anacostia bridge and met a crowd of spectators who booed them and were slow to "move on," they threw more gas bombs. They began burning the shacks of the Anacostia camp—a task which the veterans themselves helped them accomplish. That evening the Washington sky glowed with fire. Even after midnight the troops were still on their way with bayonets and tear-gas bombs, driving people ahead of them into the streets of Anacostia.

The Bonus Expeditionary Force had been dispersed, to merge itself with that greater army of homeless people who were drifting about the country in search of an ever-retreating fortune. The United States Army had completed its operation "successfully" without killing anybody—though the list of injured was long. The incident was over. But it had left a bitter taste in the mouth. Bayonets drawn in Washington to rout the dispossessed—was this the best that American statesmanship could offer hungry citizens?

The farmers were rebellious—and no wonder. For the gross income of American agriculture had declined from nearly 12 billion dollars in 1929—when it had already for years been suffering from a decline in export sales—to only $5\frac{1}{4}$ billions in 1932. While most manufacturing businesses dropped their prices only a little and met slackened demand with slackened production, the farmer could not do this, and the prices he got went right down to the cellar. Men who found themselves utterly unable to meet their costs of production could not all be expected to be philosophical about it.

Angry Iowans, organized by Milo Reno into a Farmers' Holiday Association, were refusing to bring food into Sioux City for thirty days or "until the cost of production had been obtained"; they blockaded the highway with spiked telegraph poles and logs, stopped milk trucks and emptied the milk into roadside ditches. Said an elderly Iowa farmer with a white mustache to Mary Heaton Vorse, "They say blockading the highway's illegal. I says, 'Seems to me there was a Tea Party in Boston that was illegal too.'"

Elsewhere farmers were taking the obvious direct means to stop the tidal wave of mortgage foreclosure sales. All through the prairie country there were quantities of farmers who not only had heavy mortgages on their property but had gone deeply into debt for the purchase of farm machinery or to meet the emergencies of years of falling prices; when their corn and wheat brought to even the most industrious of them not enough money to meet their obligations, they lost patience with the laws of bankruptcy. If a man sees a neighbor of his, a formerly successful farmer, a substantial, hard-working citizen with a family, coming out of the office of the referee in bankruptcy stripped of everything but an old team of horses, a wagon, a few dogs and hogs, and a few sticks of furniture, he is likely to see red. Marching to the scene of the next foreclosure sale, these farmers would drive off prospective bidders, gather densely about the auctioneer, bid in horses at 25 cents apiece, cows at 10 cents, fat hogs at a nickel—and the next morning would return their purchases to the former owner.

In a quiet county seat, handbills would appear: "Farmers and workers! Help protect your neighbors from being driven off their property. Now is the time to act. For the past three and a half years we have waited for our masters, who are responsible for the situation, to find a way out. . . . On Friday the property of _____ is to be sold at a forced auction at the courthouse. . . . The Farmers Committee has called a mass protest meeting to stop the above-mentioned sale." And on Friday the trucks would drive up to the courthouse and men by the hundreds, quiet, grim-faced, would fill the corridors outside the sheriff's office while their leaders demanded that the sale be not held.

They threatened judges in bankruptcy cases; in one case a mob dragged a judge from his courtroom, beat him, hanged him by the neck till he fainted—and all because he was carrying out the law.

These farmers were not revolutionists. On the contrary, most of them were by habit conservative men. They were simply striking back in rage at the impersonal forces which had brought them to their present pass.

*   *   *

But it was during 1934 and 1935—the years when Roosevelt was pushing through his financial reforms, and Huey Long was a national portent, and the languishing NRA was put out of its misery by the Supreme Court—that the thermometer in Kansas stayed week after week at 108 or above and the black storms raged again and again. The drought continued acute during much of 1936. Oklahoma farms became great dunes of shifting sand (so like seashore dunes, said one observer, that one almost expected to smell the salt). Housewives in the drought belt kept oiled cloths on the window sills and between the upper and lower sashes of the windows, and some of them tried to seal up every aperture in their houses with the gummed paper strips used in wrapping parcels, yet still the choking dust filtered in and lay in ripples on the kitchen floor, while outside it blew blindingly across a No Man's Land; roads and farm buildings and once green thickets half-buried in the sand. It was in those days that a farmer, sitting at his window during a dust storm, remarked that he was counting the Kansas farms as they came by.

Retribution for the very human error of breaking the sod of the Plains had come in full measure. And, as often happens, it was visited upon the innocent as well as upon the guilty—if indeed one could single out any individuals as guilty of so pervasive an error as social shortsightedness.

Westward fled the refugees from this new Sahara, as if obedient to the old American tradition that westward lies the land of promise. In 1934 and 1935 Californians became aware of an increasing influx into their state of families and groups of families of "Okies," traveling in ancient family jalopies; but for years the streams of humanity continued to run. They came along U. S. Highway 30 through the Idaho hills, along Highway 66 across New Mexico and Arizona, along the Old Spanish Trail through El Paso, along all the other westward trails. They came in decrepit, square-shouldered 1925 Dodges and 1927 La Salles; in battered 1923 Model-T Fords that looked like relics of some antique culture; in trucks piled high with mattresses and cooking utensils and children, with suitcases, jugs, and sacks strapped to the running boards. "They roll westward like a parade," wrote Richard L. Neuberger. "In a single hour from a grassy meadow near an Idaho road I counted 34 automobiles with the license plates of states between Chicago and the mountains."

They left behind them a half-depopulated countryside. A survey of the farmhouses in seven counties of southeastern Colorado, made in 1936, showed 2,878 houses still occupied, 2,811 abandoned; and there were also, in that area, 1,522 abandoned homesites. The total number of drought refugees who took the westward trek over the mountains was variously estimated in 1939 at from 200,000 upwards—with more coming all the time.

As these wanderers moved along the highways they became a part of a vast and confused migratory movement. When they camped by the wayside, they might find themselves next to a family of evicted white Alabama sharecroppers who had been on the move for four years, snatching seasonal farm-labor jobs wherever they could through the Southwest; or next to tenant families from the Arkansas Delta who had been "tractored off" their land—expelled in order that the owner might consolidate two or three farms and operate them with tractors and day labor; or next to lone wanderers who had once held industrial jobs and had now for years been on relief or on the road—jumping freights, hitchhiking, panhandling, shunting back and forth across the countryside in the faint hope of a durable job. And when these varied streams of migrants reached the Coast they found themselves in desperate competition for jobs with individuals or families who for years had been "fruit tramps," moving northward each year with the harvests from the Imperial Valley in southern California to the Sacramento Valley or even to the apple-picking in the Yakima Valley in Washington.

Here in the land of promise, agriculture had long been partly industrialized. Huge farms were in the control of absentee owners or banks or corporations, and were accustomed to depend upon the labor of migratory "fruit tramps," who had formerly been mostly Mexicans, Japanese, and other foreigners, but now were increasingly Americans. Those laborers who were lucky enough to get jobs picking cotton or peas or fruit would be sheltered temporarily in camps consisting typically of frame cabins in rows, with a water line between every two rows; they were very likely to find in their cabin no stove, no cots, no water pail. Even the best of the camps offered a way of life strikingly different from that of the ruggedly individualist farmer of the American tradition, who owned his farm or else was preparing, by working as a resident "hired man," or by renting a farm, for the chance of ultimate ownership. These pickers were homeless, voteless nomads, unwanted anywhere save at the harvest season.

When wave after wave of the new migrants reached California, the labor market became glutted, earnings were low, and jobs became so scarce that groups of poverty-stricken families would be found squatting in makeshift Hoovervilles or bunking miserably in their awkward old Fords by the roadside. Being Americans of native stock and accustomed to independence, they took the meager wages and the humiliation bitterly, sought to organize, talked of striking, sometimes struck. At every such threat, something like panic seized the growers. If this new proletariat were permitted to organize, and were to strike at picking time, they might ruin the whole season's output of a perishable crop. There followed antipicketing ordinances; the spectacle of armed deputies dislodging the migrants from their pitiful camps; violence by bands of vigilantes, to whom these ragged families were not fellow-citizens who had suffered in a great American disaster but dirty, ignorant, superstitious outlanders, failures at life, easy dupes for "red" agitators. This engulfing tide of discontent must be kept moving.

Farther north the refugees were likely to be received with more sympathy, especially in regions where the farms were small and not industrialized; here and there one heard of instances of real hospitality, such as that of the Oregon town which held a canning festival for the benefit of the drought victims in the neighborhood. The well-managed camps set up by the Farm Security Administration were havens of human decency. But to the vast majority of the refugees the promised land proved to be a place of new and cruel tragedy.

＊   ＊   ＊

What it means to look for a job when
there aren't any jobs is the picture
conveyed by this diary of a few weeks in
the life of an unemployed job hunter
in 1933. The creeping, deadening
impact of week after week of such job
hunting was the human side of
unemployment for millions of men.

9
Job Hunters

*E. Wight Bakke is Sterling Professor of
Economics, and Director of the Labor
and Management Center, Yale
University.*

E. WiGHT BAKKE

The foreman tapped Joseph Torrio on the shoulder as he pulled the
switch on his machine. "Clapham wants to see you, Joe."

"You mean—I'm getting my time, Jim?"

"Just temporary, I hope, and you know what I think of your work, old
man. It won't be long—unless—but why worry about it? Clapham will give
you the dope."

With a slow step Joe headed for the front office where Clapham, the
company's personnel department, was already telling some of his mates
what Joe knew to be "the bad news." He sat down on a bench in the outer
office. His turn had come! Here he was an eighteen-year man. Others had
been laid off one by one, but he had thought his job was safe. Why, he
had been a foreman in the night shift during the War, and now Clapham
was going to tell him the bad news! It wouldn't be easy for Clapham,
for in spite of the fact that the workers dubbed the personnel department,
"the worse-n-hell department," Clapham was a good egg. He knew most
of the men by sight if not by name.

"Torrio," called the office boy.

As he walked out the front gate he could hardly remember what Clapham had said. He had been thinking his own thoughts. A phrase or two
penetrated his preoccupation. "Tough break . . . no new orders . . .
maybe only a short time . . . but better look around, no telling when
. . . call you if things pick up."

Reprinted from *The Unemployed Worker*, by E. Wight Bakke (Yale University
Press, 1940), by permission of the publisher.

This was not the first time he had been laid off, but this time the ugly rumors that "the company was slipping," that "the whole damned country is on the rocks," had created a fear he had not felt before. He'd lay off a couple of weeks —he deserved a vacation after eight years of steady work. But if he didn't get called back in that time, he'd start hunting another job.

Joseph Torrio in 1933 had about 18,000 companions in the city who joined him in this search for work. What kind of job is looking for a job, and how did these workers who had been "told the bad news" go about that task? They came to unemployment with an economic equipment which we have attempted to describe in some detail. We have suggested that they are motivated in their economic activity by the desire: to play one or more socially respected roles, to obtain the measure of economic security deemed possible by their associates, to gain an increasing degree of control over their own affairs, to understand the casual forces in their problems of self-maintenance. We have surveyed the essential controlling conditions of their economic environment and the effect of these in furthering or frustrating their progress toward these goals. We have recorded the normal adjustments made in the face of these conditions, which adjustments provide them with a stock of habitual practices available as suggestive alternatives in meeting the problem of unemployment.

How did they use this equipment in effecting the new economic adjustments made necessary by the loss of their jobs? In the following chapters we shall try to share the experience of Torrio and his mates as they set about bridging the gap between jobs.

THE JOB OF JOB HUNTING

In a factory town the great majority of workers are accustomed to assume that factory employment is the major, if not the only, possibility of making a living. Joseph Torrio after his two weeks' vacation "pounded pavements" for an additional four weeks. We need not go with him to every gate, but a sample of his experiences taken from his diary kept for us during that time will help us to understand why he left off searching for that kind of job six weeks after his layoff.

April 19, 1934.

Decided to have a go at the State Employment Office. Got there at eight. Fellow I knew sitting on steps. Big sign there "No loitering in the doorway." Janitor or someone came down and asked him to move.

"Are you going upstairs?" he asked. "If you are, go, but don't sit here." The fellow jumped; not looking at the janitor, he began a loud bluster about his father paying taxes to support the place and he could sit on the steps if he wanted to. When the janitor left, he returned to the steps for a moment. Meanwhile a group of people had gathered to see what was going on.

Asked the janitor when the manager would be in. He said, "Nine o'clock." Decided to come back. When I got back, a line had formed clear out into the street. I took my place. Officials and clerks kept coming and had a good cheery word for us as they passed. But after they had gone, many sarcastic remarks followed them like, "Gives you a nice smile, but that's all."

The manager himself drove up before the office a little past nine—appeared sore that there was no parking space in front of the office. The fellows standing outside purposely raised their voices so he could hear and made remarks such as, "Not much use coming here, they never do anything but tell you to come back in sixty days"; "What'd they ever do for me?—Nothing"; "First it was April 1st, then it was the 15th, and now it will be God knows when."

One of the young fellows asked an official of the Bureau as he entered the building if there was anything in his line available—stated he was a soda jerker or plumber's helper—or he'd "take anything." The official smiled and wanted to know if the fellow was following the ads in the newspaper. The fellow returned to the group, swore a moment, and asked, "Who ever got a job from the ads in a paper?"

Fellow next to me was apparently an electrician. He was sore because he couldn't get a P.W.A. job. He said, "All these contractors have their own men and when this Employment Office tries to do the hiring for the P.W.A. jobs, it doesn't know where to get off. The P.W.A. provision reads that the contractor must take men from the State Employment Bureau where they are able to do the work. Well, the Bureau sends its men out. They work for a day, and then they are let go as not fit for the job; then the contractor has fulfilled the specifications and hires his own men."

I register, but they say not much chance today; maybe a week from today. I go out. Tony grabs my arm. He says, "Work?—there is no work. I go to the Employment Office. I stand and wait. Soon—my turn. I give the girl my card. She takes it, turns it over and over in her hand. Bluff—just to take up time. By and by, she gives it back. 'Sorry, nothing today.' I say, 'But I no work in three years, with seven children, what do I eat?' She reply, 'Come back again, maybe soon there will be something.' It is the big bluff."

Jim joins us at the foot of the stairs. He's mad too. "God, I'm disgusted with this place, and everybody else is that I know. Some fine day a mob's going to drop down on this place and tear it apart. I'm telling you, these fellows from down around Wooster Street aren't going to take this tomorrow business forever."

Looks as though I'd be better off to depend on the grapevine. Word gets around plenty fast if they're taking men on any place.

April 27.

Up at seven, cup of coffee, and off to Sargent's. Like to be there when the gang comes to work, the lucky devils. Employment manager not in. Waited in his outer office fitted with six benches and about thirty nearly worn out chairs. Took a bench—looked more likely to stay up. Three others waiting, two reporting for compensation. Other one laid off two weeks ago and said he called at office every day. He inquired what I was doing and when I said "looking for work" he laughed. "You never work here? No? What chance you think you got when 400 like me who belong here out?" Employment manager showed up at 9:30. I had waited two hours. My time has no value. A pleasant fellow; told me in a kind but snappy way business was very bad. What about the future, would he take my name? Said he referred only to the present. Nothing more for me to say, so left. Two more had drifted into office. Suppose they got the same story. Must be a lot of men in New Haven that have heard it by now.

Down Chestnut Street to Peck Brothers. Thought something might be going there. Since beer bill they have been calling back old employees, might have use for another hand. No real employment office here. From street into a long hall with two offices both with clerks on each side of hall. Picked the wrong one. Smart flapper didn't even speak just tossed her head and thumb in the direction of across the hall. Went across and another girl at an information desk asked if I had ever worked there before. Told her "No." She said no immediate chance then, but I could file an application; but added, "It won't do you no good as there is plenty of our own men to fill the jobs for some time to come." Guess I won't get a job till they've skimmed the cream from their own men. That's proper of course and a good break for them. But if it's like this all over, what's the point in applying for jobs? Filled out application anyway—might as well, didn't have any better way to spend my time. No one else here looking for work.

No heart for any more so dropped into Jake's for a doughnut and a glass of milk and then went home.

April 28.

To New Haven Clock Company. Met a company "dick" who said plant was shut down till Monday. Gave me an application blank and said, "You look all right, fill this out in ink. Do it neatly, and they may give you a break. Do you know anybody inside?" I said, "No." Then he shrugs his shoulders and says, "Well, I don't know if there is much use you sending this in then, but you might try."

In the afternoon went to the park and talked with men trying to find out what luck they had had. No good news.

May 2.

Started out at seven for New Haven Clock Shop. No one in employment office. Lady at information desk asked, "What do you want?" I told her. She wanted to know if I had worked there before and when I said "No," she didn't even ask if I had any experience in clockmaking (which I have). And when I started to tell her so, she cut me off with, "No use—sorry." Suppose she gets tired too.

From Clock Shop to E. Cowells and Co. who make auto equipment. If they want to have old men, well, I worked here in 1916 and 1917. Didn't get to see anyone here because just as you get to the hall there is a big sign "No Help Wanted." You can't miss it, and I find it kind of hard to disregard a sign of that type. I assume it means what it says or they wouldn't have gone to the trouble and expense to have it painted. I'll have to see a fellow I know who works there. He may know some way to get me on the call list, seeing how I once worked there.

Having heard Seamless Rubber was working quite steady I went down there. Regular employment office furnished with one bench. Another chap, a foreigner, waiting also. In about ten minutes a fellow asked us our business and told us very politely they had no jobs even for skilled men, let alone laborers. No use to tell him I wasn't always a laborer for I never had done the skilled jobs on rubber.

Saw a sign hanging out of one place in gilt letters, "No Help Wanted." In guilt, mind you, as if to make it more permanent.

Then to Bradley-Smith candymakers, where I had also worked before. The first few days I hadn't had the heart for more than a couple of tries a morning. I'm getting hardened to the word "No" now, though, and can stick it out most of the morning. Bradley-Smith has no employment office. The telephone switchboard operator is apparently instructed to switch off anyone looking for work, as she made quick work of my question. I notice no one seems to be instructed to find out if we know anything about the business or work. Firms might be passing up some good bets for their force. But apparently that isn't important now.

Walking away, met two friends out going the rounds too. They said it was useless and that they were only looking through force of habit. That's going to be me before long. Even if they hadn't said so. I'm thinking it is useless to run around like this; you just appear ridiculous, and that gets your goat—or would if you kept it up too long. Wish I had some drag with someone on the inside of one of those gates. I expect it's that everyone knows they have to know someone that keeps me from having more company at the employment offices. This is what a former pal of mine who is up at Yale calls "competition in the labor market," I guess. Well, it's a funny competition and with guys you never see.

*   *   *

Our banking system rests on the confidence
of the people. Marriner Eccles, later
head of the Federal Reserve System, tells
what the bank panic of 1932–33 meant to
an individual banker, and how he tried
to deal with it.

*Marriner S. Eccles has been Chairman
of the Board of Governors of the Federal
Reserve System. He is now President
of the First Security Corp., President of
the Eccles Investment Co., and director of
a number of corporations.*

10

The Pit

MARRINER S. ECCLES

During 1930 I awoke to find myself at the bottom of a pit without any
known means of scaling its sheer sides.

Since the crash of 1929, men I respected assured me that the economic
crisis was only temporary and that soon all the things that had pulled the
country out of previous depressions would operate to that same end once
again. But the weeks turned to months. The months turned to a year or
more. Instead of easing, the economic crisis worsened. The pit grew deeper
and I found myself in it.

On the morning of the awakening, I saw for the first time that though
I'd been active in the world of finance and production for seventeen years
and knew its techniques, I knew less than nothing about its economic
and social effects. Yet, by itself a confession of ignorance led nowhere.
Friends whose estates I managed, my family, whose interests I represented, and the community at large, in whose economic life I played a
sensitive role, all expected me to find the way out of the pit. Yet all I
could find within myself was despair. Having been reared by my father
to accept the responsibilities of wealth and having been placed by circumstances at the helm of many enterprises, there were times when I felt the
whole depression was a personal affront.

Wherein had I been at fault?

Night after night following that head-splitting awakening I would return home exhausted by the pretensions of knowledge I was forced to wear
in a daytime masquerade. I would slump forward on a table and pray that

by a supreme act of will the answers would somehow be revealed. As an individual I felt myself helpless to do anything. I heard grass-roots talk that "the government ought to do something." But why the government? Wherein is the government different from the individual? Is it not just a sum of all individuals? Or, granting there is a difference, what specifically should the government do?

For instance:

What should be done in a situation where the dollar was so painfully sound when measured by its power to buy goods and services that when prices fell and unemployment increased, the dollar somehow got "sounder"?

What was to be done in a situation such as I faced in our lumber mills, where we would operate at a loss even if men worked without pay?

What was to be done by our banks when loans on homes, farms, livestock, and securities or to business and industrial enterprises could not be paid because values had drastically declined?

What was to be done when the pressure on the banks to "get liquid" so as to meet depositor claims caused a situation where the liquidation of debts made it impossible to pay off debts?

What was to be done when men on the farms and in the cities, who needed each other's goods, were stranded on opposite river banks without the consumer purchasing power by which they could navigate a crossing for trading?

These were not academic questions. They were intimately connected with day-to-day dangers, and particularly the danger of a sudden run on the banks. It didn't matter where the run started. A weak bank that closed its doors could create community tensions of a sort that could close the doors of sound banks as well.

Fortunately, the banks of the First Security Corporation kept their doors open throughout the depression. No depositor lost one penny. But time after time the life of our organization was imperiled by failures or imminent failures in neighboring banks. Physical nearness alone tended to involve all banks in the fate of any one of them. I still grow weak when I think of the runs or threatened runs with which we had to deal.

The first one occurred in 1931 in Ogden. Here one of the most highly regarded and oldest banks in the entire state was the Ogden State Bank. Under the management of the Bigelow family it had served the community well for over forty years. In size it was only slightly smaller than our Ogden banks. But the officers of our banks were, like myself, young men or men relatively new to the community. We didn't have the sort of public confidence enjoyed by the Ogden State Bank. If it got into trouble, what could the community expect of a bank managed by much younger and less experienced men?

I had advance warning of trouble when Archie Bigelow, the president of the Ogden State Bank, revealed to Bennett and me that his bank was facing great losses on its loans due to the deflation, that its capital and surplus were impaired, and that it was losing deposits. But Bigelow felt his bank could be saved if it was merged with our Ogden banks.

Examination of the imperiled bank showed that it was so far gone it would pull down our banks if they were linked to it as a lifesaver. Came the week-end in the late summer of 1931 when doom could no longer be staved off. Word reached us that the Ogden State Bank would not open its doors on the coming Monday.

We knew we could expect a severe run on our Ogden banks; we also knew that when word of it got around, the effect would extend to other areas where the First Security Corporation owned banks. These others had to be alerted and prepared for imminent developments, and because our Ogden banks were the central institutions in our banking complex, it was imperative that they break the run as quickly as possible and stay open at all costs.

The Sunday preceding the Monday when the Ogden State Bank did not open, I called together all the officers and directors of the First National and the First Savings banks. Having a list of all the important commercial accounts held by the Ogden State Bank, I pointed out to the directors and officers of our banks that the firms represented on the list would be without banking facilities on Monday morning when the Ogden State Bank remained closed. Yet they would need to make deposits, get currency, borrow money, and issue checks. The directors of our banks were to pick out the firms on the list with whom they had close personal or business dealings. Then on Monday morning they were to call the heads of these firms, invite them to deposit their funds on hand with our banks, and say that if they needed a loan or currency we would be glad to take care of their pressing needs. I wanted not only to gain an inflow of deposits but to develop confidence among the employees of those firms. They would be paid in checks drawn on our banks, and the combined incoming traffic would help reverse the current of the outgoing traffic we knew was to be expected on the next day.

The officers and directors went at this job with zeal and set in motion what it was hoped would happen.

While this plan was formed to stabilize our commercial accounts held locally, we had cause to fear a concealed run on our commercial and bank accounts that could start at distant points. Specifically, like other city banks, we held balances of many outside corporations as well as of independent country banks in the area. We knew that if the officials of these outside concerns heard of a run on our banks, they would take precautionary measures to avoid getting caught short. They would either ask for a direct transfer of funds or they would make a draft or checks on our banks and deposit them with other banks.

I'd seen this happen many times. I'd also seen its aftermath. The process by which large corporations, for instance, withdrew funds from the hinterland and concentrated them in New York and other large cities hastened the collapse of countless country banks. Having this danger in mind, we felt we had a fighting chance to overcome it if, first, our outside accounts were warned in advance of an imminent run, and, second, if they heard the news directly from us and not from press reports or from some other source. That Sunday night a telegram was drafted for delivery the first thing Monday morning to each of our outside accounts.

The telegram read:

THE OGDEN STATE BANK WILL NOT OPEN ITS DOORS THIS MONDAY MORNING. THIS WILL CAUSE SOME DEMANDS FOR WITHDRAWAL OF FUNDS ON OUR OWN BANKS. WE HAVE ANTICIPATED THIS FOR SOME TIME AND ARE FULLY PREPARED TO MEET ANY AND ALL DEMANDS WHICH ARE MADE UPON US. WE FELT IT DESIRABLE THAT YOU SHOULD GET THIS INFORMATION FIRST HAND.

Fortunately, there was not a single transfer of funds from among the accounts that received these telegrams.

While we made this bid to shore up the confidence of our commercial accounts, we realized that the greatest potential danger lay with the savings group.

If they were thrown into panic by a run on our savings bank, the effect would not be self-limiting. Our national bank shared the same premises with our savings bank; a run on the latter would certainly be duplicated in a run on the former. In view of this, all officers and employees of the national and savings banks were contacted that Sunday and asked to be at work the next morning at eight o'clock.

When they assembled the next morning, I told them what they would have to face in a few hours. "If you want to keep this bank open," I said, "you must do your part. Go about your business as though nothing unusual was happening. Smile, be pleasant, talk about the weather, show no signs of panic. The main burden is going to fall on you boys in the savings department. Instead of the three windows we normally use, we are going to use all four of them today. They must be manned at all times because if any teller's or clerk's window in this bank closes for even a short time, that will stir up more panic. We'll have sandwiches brought in; no one can go out to lunch. We can't break this run today. The best we can do is slow it down. People are going to come here to close out their savings accounts. You are going to pay them. But you are going to pay them very slowly. It's the only chance we have to deal with the panic. You know a lot of depositors by sight, and in the past you did not have to look up their signatures, but today when they come here with their deposit books to close out their accounts, you are going to look up every signature card. And take your time about it. And one other thing: when you pay out, don't use any big bills. Pay out in fives and tens, and count slowly. Our object is to pay out a minimum today."

The tellers and clerks ably carried out their part of the act despite the crowd that surged through the doors of the bank the moment they were opened. Some-one with an objective turn of mind could have learned much that day about the degree to which banking is understood by the community at large. I recall one depositor, for instance, who in great anxiety closed his savings account and with the currency given him promptly bought a cashier's check. He did not know that if the bank closed, his check would be worth no more than his deposit. But amidst the pushing and shoving inside the bank there was little time to reflect on matters of this sort.

At two o'clock that afternoon Bennett, my brother George, and I met to de-cide what should be done when the regular three-o'clock closing hour was reached. The crowd in the bank was as taut as it was dense. Some people had been waiting for hours to draw out their money. If we tried to close at three, there was no telling what might happen. But, as in all other things, a poverty of alternatives made us adopt the boldest one. We decided to make an exception of this one day and to re-main open so long as there were people who wanted to get their money.

In the meantime a call had been put through to the Federal Reserve Bank in Salt Lake City to send currency to our Ogden banks as well as to all others in the First Security Corporation. The armored car that brought funds to us in Ogden arrived on the scene as in the movies when the Union cavalry charges in to save all from the Indians. The guards strode through the crush inside the bank, and all made way before them.

Of equal importance in the events of the day, Morgan Craft, the deputy man-ager of the Federal Reserve Bank in Salt Lake City, had been a passenger in the armored car that raced to Ogden. When he entered our bank, I grabbed his arm and led him through the crowd to a black and gold marble counter in the officers' section of the savings bank. Mounting the counter, I raised my hand and called for attention:

"Just a minute!"

There was instant silence.

"Just a minute!" I repeated. "I want to make an announcement. It appears that we are having some difficulty handling our depositors with the speed to which you are accustomed. Many of you have been in line for a considerable time. I notice a lot of pushing and shoving and irritation. I just wanted to tell you that instead of closing at the usual hour of three o'clock, we have decided to stay open just as long as there is anyone who desires to withdraw his deposit or make one. Therefore, you people who have just come in can return later this afternoon or evening if you wish. There is no justification for the excitement or the apparent panicky attitude on the part of some depositors. As all of you have seen, we have just had brought up from Salt Lake City a large amount of currency that will take care of all your requirements. There is plenty more where that came from." (This was true enough—but I didn't say we could get it.)

"And if you don't believe me," I continued, "I have here Mr. Morgan Craft, one of the officers of the Federal Reserve Bank, who has just come up in an armored car. Mr. Craft, say a few words to the folks."

I pulled him up to the top of the counter. He not only said a few words, but threw in one or two for extra measure.

"I just want to verify what Mr. Eccles has told you," he said. "I want to assure you that we have brought up a lot of currency and there is plenty more where that came from."

This, again, was perfectly true. But he didn't say the currency belonged to us. Nevertheless, the mood of the day was so unreasoning that men were heartened by words as meaningless as those which caused them fright. In a split instant the faces before me relaxed in relief. The edge in all voices seemed to vanish. Some people stepped out of line and left the bank. And a happy buzz replaced the waspish one heard earlier. The word was passed to the crowd outside the bank: "They are going to stay open. They are going to stay open."

*   *   *

11

The Operation of the Open Market Committee

The President of the Federal Reserve
Bank of New York presents an
authoritative statement on the way
monetary policy is formulated in the
Federal Open Market Committee, stressing
the continuous consultative process used
by the substantial number of Federal
Reserve officials involved. Compare this
with the following selection.

*Alfred Hayes is President of the Federal
Reserve Bank of New York.*

ALFRED HAYES

*　　*　　*

It goes without saying that the Federal Reserve Bank of New York,
of which I have the privilege of being the chief executive officer, undertakes a great variety of important activities, most of which are related
in some degree to the operations of the Federal Open Market Committee. I am thinking of such things as handling the reserve and borrowing
accounts of the member banks, the provision of currency, the processing
and crediting of checks received for collection, the expediting of wire transfers of deposit balances among banks and of Government securities among
investors, the calling and disbursement of funds for the United States
Treasury, the handling of transactions for foreign central bank and government accounts representing settlement of the United States balance
of payments with other countries, and the supervision of member banks.
These activities, most of which we undertake in common with the 11 other
Federal Reserve Banks, have a great deal to do with the System's major
responsibility of contributing to an efficient and adequate money and credit
mechanism for the Nation. But they are sometimes referred to as "de-
fensive" or "passive" operations, in contrast with the three "dynamic"
or "active" instruments—reserve requirements, discount rates, and open
market operations—which are employed in our efforts to minimize both
inflation and deflation and to facilitate sturdy economic growth.

To discuss the Federal Open Market Committee's activities without

Statement by Alfred Hayes, reprinted from *Hearings Before the Subcommittee
on Economic Stabilization of the Joint Economic Committee,* Congress of the United
States, December 10 and 11, 1956, pp. 142–150.

66

referring to all three of these instruments would be quite misleading. For while it is true that the Board of Governors alone has the responsibility for determining reserve requirements, and while discount rates are established by the individual Reserve banks—subject to review and determination by the Board of Governors— in practice the Federal Open Market Committee has become the principal forum in which these two instruments, as well as that of open market operations, are discussed and weighed by representatives of the entire System in arriving at a systemwide consensus as to what should be done at any given time in the field of general credit control. The emergence of the Federal Open Market Committee as the meeting place where representatives of all parts of the System's complex structure can be brought together, for joint discussion of interrelated responsibilities, is one of the most interesting, and also probably one of the most constructive developments in Federal Reserve history.

Meetings of the Federal Open Market Committee are generally held every 2 or 3 weeks in Washington, so that I have been privileged to attend some 6 or 7 times since I became associated with the New York Reserve Bank. As you know, the Committee consists of 12 members, including the 7 members of the Board of Governors and 5 of the Reserve bank presidents. The president of the New York Reserve Bank is continuously a member, while the other four presidents are appointed in rotation. The 12 members of the Committee which was established by statute, sit and reach decisions as responsible individuals, not as representatives of any constituency. Each must find the answer, in the light of all the facts and his own conscience, to the question: "What policy of credit control would be the best policy under present conditions for the economy of the United States?" Naturally each member brings to the Committee the full benefit of any special information available to him, including—in the case of the Reserve bank presidents—information concerning economic conditions in the various districts and the views concerning them held by businessmen and others; but each member also gives careful consideration to nationwide conditions and makes his final judgment on that basis.

The 7 presidents who are not, at the time, members of the Federal Open Market Committee nevertheless attend these meetings regularly by invitation and participate in the discussions on the same basis as the 12 Committee members, with the sole exception that they have no vote on matters requiring a vote. Thus the Committee obtains a first hand report on conditions in each of the 12 Federal Reserve districts. During the periods between meetings, the 7 Governors and the 12 Presidents are of course pursuing their various other duties, but they are also preparing for the coming deliberations of the Federal Open Market Committee by observing the results of policies established at previous meetings, gathering new economic data, and continually reviewing their judgments of past decisions and current events. In New York, for example, our senior officers gather at least once each week to review important developments, and we have another special meeting of officers a few days in advance of each Federal Open Market Committee meeting for the special purpose of discussing the current state of business and credit conditions, Treasury finance, and related matters, and what type of credit policy seems best suited to this state of affairs.

At each Federal Open Market Committee meeting the procedure is to have the Manager of the System Account, who is also vice-president in charge of the securities function at the New York Reserve Bank, lead off with any observations he may wish to make on what has actually happened in the Account and in financial markets in general since the last meeting. He will already have furnished each member of the Board of Governors and each president with special written reports that are complete through the close of business on the preceding day. Thereafter two of the senior staff members of the Board of Governors present a comprehensive and detailed summary of current business and credit conditions in the country as a whole. After this the Chairman, following such introductory remarks as he considers appropriate on domestic or foreign developments, calls on each president and each governor, in turn, to give his appraisal of the current situation and to state his views concerning appropriate policy in the circumstances. Customarily the president of the New York Reserve Bank is called on first, and, because of the location of the bank in the country's money center, I usually talk of business and credit developments and expectations in national terms, and of the open market and other Federal Reserve policies I would consider appropriate in the light of those developments. The other presidents usually start off with comments on conditions in their particular districts and they, too, give their views as to credit policy. Likewise each member of the Board of Governors states his opinion concerning the appropriate policy after discussing any particular developments in the country's economy which appear to him pertinent. Generally the last man to comment is the Chairman of the Federal Open Market Committee, who is of course also Chairman of the Board of Governors. He summarizes his own appraisal of the situation and then undertakes the difficult task of pulling together the threads of all the preceding discussion and expressing the consensus of the meeting in terms of, first, how the directive to the New York Reserve Bank should be worded and, second, what specific actions are called for in the way of open market purchases or sales or other credit control measures—perhaps mentioning, for example, the possibility that consideration may be given to discount rate changes by the various Reserve banks, or to changes in reserve requirements by the Board of Governors. The Chairman then gives all present a chance to state whether they agree with his understanding of the consensus. The Manager of the System Account is asked whether the instructions are sufficiently explicit to enable him to carry out the Committee's wishes effectively, and at this point the Committee has an opportunity to convey to the Manager any nuances of policy which they think should be kept in mind.

I have been greatly impressed by the effectiveness of this whole procedure in bringing together a variety of disinterested and objective views on our country's economic conditions and problems, and then in deriving from these a reasoned consensus as to monetary and credit policy. Often the opinion of any one member is not yet crystallized when he arrives at the meeting, and it may well be modified during the meeting by this process of give-and-take. On the other hand, I think it is pretty clear that with 19 well-informed people having a full opportunity to present their views, on the basis of data assembled by able staffs throughout the System, it would be quite impossible for any one man holding an extreme position to dominate the Committee and dictate the Committee's conclusions. Indeed, the thinking of any one man may not be fully in accord with the consensus; the consensus is acceptable because it is a fusing of all the views, and it provides a workable basis for operations. Over time, such a consensus is bound to be far more reliable than the occasional flash of insight that a single individual might produce.

I have been struck by the degree of harmony which has been achieved in this whole procedure. It has almost always been possible, without even the formality of a vote, to reach a consensus through the give-and-take of reasoned discussions.

As I have already indicated, the general conclusions of the Committee as to credit policy are set forth in the directive issued to the Federal Reserve Bank of New York. The directive is amplified by the statement of the consensus and by the full discussion, all of which are of course noted in the Committee's minutes. From this point on, and until the next Federal Open Market Committee meeting, the primary responsibility for conducting open market operations is in the hands of the Federal Reserve Bank of New York, acting in accordance with the instructions of the Committee. With the country's money market and securities markets centered in New York, most open market operations must necessarily be executed there, but I would like to stress that the New York bank is acting at all times for the System as a whole on the instructions of the Committee and is at all times responsive to the Committee's wishes. In my capacity as a member and Vice Chairman of the Federal Open Market Committee, I am in a position to help interpret the Committee's wishes to the Manager, and he himself has of course been present at the last meeting when he was specifically instructed on the varied detailed considerations which the Committee wishes him to keep in mind. He knows, for example, approximately what member bank reserve position the Committee believes appropriate, or he may have been told to give only secondary consideration to this factor and for a time to be guided primarily by such factors as the tightness of the banking structure in the money centers, the degree of market pressure suggested by United States Treasury bill rates and other money market rates, the impact of a large Treasury borrowing operation, and even more broadly by that on-the-spot appraisal of current attitudes and actions which is described as the "feel" of the market.

A comprehensive procedure has been worked out for keeping the Board of Governors and the other members of the Federal Open Market Committee promptly and fully informed on market conditions and all actual transactions for the System account, as well as on contemplated transactions. One of the most effective tools to this end is the so-called daily conference call at 11 A.M., each business day, when the manager of the account or his assistant talks by telephone with the economic adviser and a senior economist of the Board of Governors. The presidents of those Federal Reserve banks outside of New York who are currently serving on the Committee also participate by long-distance telephone in these discussions on a rotating basis, one President sharing in the call for a period of two or three weeks. At the New York Reserve Bank, the first vice-president or I often "sit in" on the telephone call and many times both of us are present. (The first vice-president is, in conformity with the statute, my alternate as a member of the Federal Open Market Committee.) The manager of the account summarizes conditions in the money and capital markets, the various reports or comments received from the dealers in United States Government securities, the reserve position of the principal New York banks, and the reserve position of the country's member banks as a whole—together with the New York Reserve Bank's expectations as to changes in this national reserve position day by day for the next few weeks. The manager then indicates whether these available data and expected developments point to a need for open market operations in order to fulfill the Federal Open Market Committee's instructions, i.e., whether Treasury bills should be purchased or sold, whether repurchase agreements should be made with dealers, whether holdings of acceptances should be increased or run down, and in approximately what amount any or all of these might be considered. Participation in the call provides the economic adviser to the Board of Governors and the other president who is taking part in the call, the opportunity and responsibility of contributing their views as to existing conditions and the proposed course of action, particularly as these relate to the policy set at the most recent Federal Open Market Committee meeting. Usually there is immediate agreement, but suggestions may be made which result in some modification of the manager's program. Immediately following this conversation, a full summary is prepared at the Board and distributed to all of the Governors in Washington; the same summary is sent by wire to the various Reserve bank presidents.

The staff of the Board of Governors is advised periodically during the day by telephone on all details concerning actual operations and market developments. In addition, a written report is submitted daily to the Board of Governors by the New York Reserve Bank with copies to the interested officers of the other Federal Reserve banks and branches. At the end of each statement week a full written report is submitted by the manager to the members of the Federal Open Market Committee and to the other presidents. These reports not only provide a complete statement of all actions taken but they also give a full running record of conditions in the money and capital markets, with emphasis on interest rate changes and on the behavior of United States Government and other security prices. Prior to each Federal Open Market Committee meeting, as I have mentioned earlier, a detailed recapitulation of all major market developments and all transactions since the last previous meeting is prepared for submission to all Committee members and the other presidents.

Questions may occur to the account manager between Federal Open Market Committee meetings, perhaps as a result of some unforeseen development at home or abroad, which appear to call for an interpretation of some policy decision reached at the last meeting. If it is a minor matter, the question may be settled by discussion with the president or first vice-president of the New York bank, but if it involves a major policy consideration, we may decide to consult by telephone with the Chairman, or, in his absence, with the Vice-Chairman of the Board of Governors or some other member of the Committee. Or the initiative may come from Washington; i.e., Chairman Martin or Vice-Chairman Balderston may telephone me and raise some question or make some suggestion having to do with interpretation of the current Federal Open Market Committee policy. If very urgent questions arise, it is possible to arrange on short notice for a telephone meeting of the Federal Open Market Committee to deal with whatever emergency may exist.

We in the New York Reserve Bank encourage the governors and the other Reserve bank presidents, as well as senior members of the staffs of the Board of Governors and of the other Reserve banks, to spend as much time as they can spare visiting our trading desk, observing the manager and his assistants carry out open-market operations, and familiarizing themselves with the actual market atmosphere in which these operations are conducted. I am happy to say that we have had fine visits of this kind recently from the chairman and several of the governors and presidents.

The chief point which I would like to emphasize is the high degree of close contact and close cooperation existing between the Federal Open Market Committee as the originator of all open-market policy and the Federal Reserve Bank of New York as the executor of this policy. In my brief experience with the System I have felt that this whole mechanism works very effectively in the public interest.

*   *   *

These observers, one a former economist for the Federal Reserve, argue that the elaborate board and committee arrangements of the Federal Reserve in actual operation contribute little to arriving at sound economic policy, and that we would be better off with a simpler organizational structure and more focused responsibility.

Delbert C. Hastings is Professor of Statistics, University of Minnesota; Ross M. Robertson is Professor of Business Economics at the University of Indiana and was formerly an economist for the Federal Reserve Board.

12

The Mysterious World of the FED

DELBERT C. HASTINGS
ROSS M. ROBERTSON

First-time visitors to the lovely Washington building that houses the Board of Governors of the Federal Reserve System are invariably struck by its lofty tone. Federal Reserve personnel and guests alike move decorously through marble halls and amber-lit, carpeted rooms that epitomize the vast dignity of the monetary authority. Highly placed staff members approach the offices of Board members with deference; lesser functionaries enter with an obsequious respect that makes onlookers uncomfortable. Indeed, an almost religious aura pervades the place, and the uninitiated expect momentarily to catch a whiff of incense or the chant of choirboys not far off.

The physical atmosphere is simply an extension of a carefully nurtured public image of trustworthiness and high morality. Because of the technicality of its operations and the obscurity of its statements of purpose, the Federal Reserve has avoided evaluation and criticism of its actions by the public at large. Instead, explicit comment has been left to academicians, highly placed financial managers, and a few members of Congress. Thus, the public trusts the Fed without fully understanding it; with the possible exception of the Federal Bureau of Investigation, no other government agency enjoys such high repute and splendid public relations.

To be sure, much of the System's prestige is merited. It performs its vast service roles—collectors of checks, fiscal agent for the U. S. government, and issuer of currency—with accuracy and dispatch. At both board and bank levels, the Federal Reserve can boast a research organization

From *Business Horizons,* Spring, 1962, pp. 97–104. Reprinted by permission of the authors, *Business Horizons,* and the University of Indiana.

second to none. Yet it is by no means certain that the Fed has managed the money supply better than the money supply would have managed itself, nor is it clear that Federal Reserve influence on growth, stability, and price levels has been as beneficial as the Fed's reputation would suggest.

In a word, the Federal Reserve System has nobly performed its service functions. On the other hand, it is by no means certain that the control functions have been discharged with the imagination and vigor that modern central-bank action requires. Painfully sensitive to criticism, which invariably evokes defense reactions, the monetary authority gives continual evidence of an eroding self-consciousness. Indeed, System acceptance of responsibility for stability of prices and output seems to vary from time to time. The Fed certainly wants no competitors; whenever it has been suggested that an Administration economic policy group be formed, there is immediate central-bank resistance to the proposal. Yet System authorities occasionally come close to admitting their inability to stabilize the economy, and, whenever the Congressional heat is on, central-bank spokesmen are at pains to explain that they can only nudge the economy in one direction or another, that there are too many variables to be controlled by any one institution. System attitude seems to be, "We will use the tools we choose in the way we choose, and if they don't do the job, we deny responsibility in the matter. But we don't want anyone else interfering." To understand the Fed, we must apprehend this deep-rooted instinct for self-preservation that manifests itself in insistence upon insulation from "political" interference.

The mysterious world of the Fed is really known only to its employees and its alumni—the insiders, as it were. No amount of examination, no amount of Congressional testimony, no amount of study by scholars temporarily connected with the System can reveal the inner workings of Fed mentality. Only years of participation in the charismatic effort of central-bank policy provide the sense of System motivation so essential to an interpretation of Fed dogma, facetiously referred to, internally, as the "party line." As alumni, now a decent interval away from System activity, we herewith set forth our observations about (1) the nodes of power in the System and (2) the tenuous lines of communication that carry power impulses from one node to another.

THE NODES OF POWER

Although its major structural outlines were laid down by the original Federal Reserve Act, the Federal Reserve System has evolved in a way clearly not foreseen by its founders. As in every organization that must act, there are important nodes of power within the System; the relative standing of these power centers depends somewhat on law, somewhat on custom, and somewhat on the economic facts of life, such as the size and wealth of the different Federal Reserve districts. In roughly descending order of power, the major nodes are as follows: 1. the chairman of the Board of Governors; 2. the other governors; 3. the staff of the board, in particular the senior advisers; 4. the Federal Open Market Committee; 5. the trading desk of the New York Federal Reserve Bank; 6. the president of the New York Federal Reserve Bank; 7. other Federal Reserve bank presidents; 8. boards of directors of the twelve banks; 9. System-wide committees, standing and ad hoc; and 10. the Federal Advisory Council.

This listing will doubtless raise eyebrows both inside and outside the System, but we consider it, nonetheless, a fair appraisal of the current order of power loci in the System. It is impossible to understand the operations of today's central bank without knowing the relative importance of these power centers.

It is common knowledge, of course, that the Banking Act of 1935 made a drastic switch in the seat of System power. Under the aegis of Benjamin Strong, fair-haired boy of J. Pierpont Morgan and the 1913 New York banking community, real authority in the System lodged in the hands of the chief executive officers of the several Reserve banks. Indeed, the quick seizure of the term "governor" by the executive heads of the twelve banks revealed their own assessment of their authority. Until Strong's death in 1928, the Federal Reserve Board made nearly futile efforts to seize the power it never had, and the terrible failure of the Federal Reserve to arrest the deflation of 1929–32 gave positive proof, if proof were needed, that board authority had been emasculated in practice. The designation in the Banking Act of 1935 of the "Board of Governors" signified the intent of Congress to make it the "board of bosses."

Even so, no one could have foreseen a generation ago the gradual settling of vast power in the person of the chairman of the board. The tradition of chairman domination was, of course, started during the reign of Marriner S. Eccles, but it has reached a new high under Chairman William McChesney Martin, Jr., able son of one-time Governor Martin of the St. Louis Reserve bank.

This is not to say that other board members are without authority. Yet the position of each one depends upon his intellectual quality and personal force. A board member not deemed a contributor to the welfare of the System is likely to be shunted aside and given assignments that keep him away from inner councils. On the other hand, a particularly knowledgeable governor may be given heavy responsibilities, especially if he has a bent for economic or legal analysis.

The fact remains that the chairman of the board is in a position to exercise a great measure of control over the board and thus over the entire System. His is the final word on appointments at both board and bank levels. He is the System spokesman in its relationships with Congress, other executive branches of the government, the President, and even with foreign governments. Within the law, his powers are circumscribed only by the personal qualities of the other governors and by the five-year term of his appointment to the chair. When, as in the case of Martin, the chairman possesses an uncommon singleness of purpose and great political ability, he will work by persuasion rather than by ukase. He nevertheless operates as a dominant political figure in the best and highest sense of the word.

The staff of the Board of Governors, particularly the senior advisers, are a frequently overlooked power center. To be sure, their influence is derived from that of the governors. But their proximity to the governors, their long service, and their familiarity with Fed history give them a more than considerable influence on policy matters. Old pros like Woodlief Thomas and Ralph A. Young command enormous prestige. Younger men like Guy E. Noyes, Director of Research and Statistics, exert their influence through control of research activities at both board and bank levels; all publications of the several banks as well as reports of System-wide committees must receive the approval of the board staff before release, and directives sent by staff members to the banks are accepted as bearing the authority of the Board of Governors.

Because it nominally determines the magnitude and direction of the most important monetary weapon—purchases and sales of government securities—the Federal Open Market Committee is the next most powerful organization within the System. Since it is the official forum as well as the administrative body for monetary policy actions, the FOMC has a key place in System councils. As late as 1953, the Open Market Committee met only quarterly, with an executive committee meeting more frequently to perform the significant policy-making functions. Since that time, however, the full committee has met at intervals of approximately three weeks. Although the official membership consists of the seven governors and five of the twelve bank presidents, all the presidents try to attend regularly.[1]

Resisting the inexorable erosion of authority at the bank level, the Federal Reserve Bank of New York always poses something of a threat to board authority in Washington. The trading desk, which administers the open market account upon receipt of FOMC directives, is the very nerve center of the System. Since, as we shall see, orders of the Open Market Committee are always ambiguous and often nebulous, the account manager, a vice-president of the New York Reserve bank, must have great latitude in making judgments. And though he may have many masters, not excluding the senior staff member of the board who advises with him each day, it goes without saying that the account manager's immediate boss, the president of the New York Reserve bank, will not be without influence. Indeed, a strong New York president can be a source of great annoyance and even friction in Federal Reserve councils. It is no secret that many officers in the System heaved a collective sigh of relief when Allan Sproul, one-time chief officer of the New York bank and in some respects the most artistic of all American central bankers, went into retirement. But no matter what the attitude of a New York president toward Washington may be, the counsels of that officer are bound to have weight as they reflect the opinions of the New York financial community.

It is no depreciation of the abilities and prestige of the other eleven bank presidents to say that they rank well down the list of System power centers. The presidents are in general gifted and articulate men, and their views will always be weighed by the board and its chairman. Nevertheless, the last remaining power of the banks vanished when the original tool of monetary management—changes in the discount rate—lost its money-market effectiveness. And since the appointments of presidents and first vice-presidents are subject to board approval, really serious resistance to board decisions is not to be expected at bank, to say nothing of branch, levels. It is probably not unfair to say that the boards of directors of the twelve banks have had their power reduced to that of nominating committees, which on occasion submit to the Board of Governors the names of possible president and first vice-president candidates. Like the boards of directors of the Reserve bank branches, their positions are largely honorific; and though the board expresses public gratitude for the "economic intelligence" furnished by bank and branch directors, the plain fact is that their monthly meetings are simply genteel bull sessions.[2]

Indeed, it is probably a fair generalization that the Reserve banks, at least outside New York City, exert their remaining vestiges of influence by placing their talented officers and economists on System committees. Thus, a System Committee

---

[1] The president of the Federal Reserve Bank of New York is a permanent member and vice-chairman of the committee. Membership rotates among the other bank presidents as follows: Boston, Philadelphia, and Richmond; Chicago and Cleveland; St. Louis, Atlanta, Dallas; and Minneapolis, Kansas City, and San Francisco.

[2] Branches of Federal Reserve banks are an historic anomaly, originally established to salve the feelings of citizens disappointed at their failure to get a Reserve bank in their city. For this story see Ross M. Robertson, "Branches of Federal Reserve Banks," *Monthly Review,* Federal Reserve Bank of St. Louis, XXXVIII (August, 1956), pp. 90–97.

to Study Consumer Credit unquestionably affected board and Administration thinking with its multivolume 1957 report; more recently, a System committee has produced an influential report on the Federal Funds market. Furthermore, articulate individuals like Robert V. Roosa and George Garvy of New York, Clay J. Anderson of Philadelphia, and Homer Jones of St. Louis, through their writings and oral presentations, are likely to have an earnest and respectful hearing by the policy makers in Washington. They are nevertheless a long way from the seat of power.

The Conference of Presidents, once the vehicle of dominance over System policy, is now regarded largely as a forum for administrative and operating problems of the several banks. The presidents advise with each other on such matters as check collection, currency and coin issue, agency functions for the Treasury, and personnel classifications. The Federal Advisory Council, never even ostensibly a part of the formal power structure, is clearly an honorific group. Although their advice is presumably weighed by the Board of Governors, council members, like directors of banks and branches, bring personal prestige and orthodox witness as their chief contribution.

TRANSMISSION LINES OF POWER

Few Federal Reserve insiders would make a major rearrangement of the order in which we have listed the nodes of power, but many would express the honest conviction that we have underestimated the democratic processes by which System decisions are made. A look at these procedures may be helpful to a clear comprehension of them.

As a prerequisite to understanding, we must divest ourselves of a good bit of textbook foolishness about how monetary policy is effected. Although it is customary to speak of the instruments of monetary control, there is really only one— the extension and absorption of central-bank credit. The *means* by which central-bank credit is manipulated are irrelevant. Changes in reserve requirements, though still employed, are an anachronistic inheritance from the excess-reserve problem of the 1930's; any sensible person knows that required reserve ratios can be set at any level with consequent central-bank and commercial-bank adjustment to them. Changing the discount rate, though originally conceived to be the *only* weapon of monetary control, has long since lost its effectiveness; the discount rate is no longer a true money-market rate but serves simply as a Fed signal of reaffirmation of a policy in being or a change in monetary policy. In practice, the only demonstrable effect of the discount rate is to set an upper limit to the Federal Funds rate—that is, the rate charged one bank by another for the short-term loan of deposits with a Reserve bank. So we are left with one important instrument of monetary control—open market operations. System intervention in the government securities market is a day-to-day, hour-to-hour, minute-to-minute activity that intimately affects the lives of us all.

We have suggested that the chairman of the Board of Governors is by all odds the most powerful person in the System. But power is synonymous with substantial control over Federal Reserve credit. How, then, does the chairman exercise his great influence? Largely by being the mouthpiece and deciding vote of the Federal Open Market Committee.

In the conduct of FOMC meetings, a formality is observed that requires each governor and president in attendance, whether currently a member of the committee or not, to give a brief economic analysis and state his policy recommendations. By custom each member, together with the board secretary, the senior advisers, and the manager of the Open Market Account, occupies a fixed position around the great oval table in the committee room. After a brief business and financial analysis by the senior staff members, the account manager reports on his activities since the last meeting. Next, the governors and presidents take turns in order of their seating at the table, the circuit being made in one direction at one meeting and in the opposite direction at the next. The chairman speaks last, customarily framing his closing remarks in the form of a consensus of the preceding recommendations. Often, however, there is less than complete agreement among committee members; less often, but not infrequently, the chairman may wish to give stronger than usual direction to current policy. In such circumstances, the "Martin consensus" has emerged, this consensus being largely the view of the chairman himself, whether or not it coincides with that of the majority. Rarely—if then—are policy recommendations put into a motion and voted upon.

The account manager listens to the discussion and at its conclusion is asked by the chairman if he comprehends the wishes of the committee. He almost always answers in the affirmative. But though the account manager listens with great care, even tabulating the recommendations of each speaker, FOMC members frequently complain that they cannot communicate precisely with the manager. This problem has several dimensions. First, each committee member, being a rugged individualist, would probably be satisfied with little less than complete direction of current policy. Second, because the FOMC does not make a precise statement of its wishes, the account manager must consider nineteen sets of recommendations, some of them rambling discourses on the state of the Union. Third, the three-week interval between meetings is long enough to require adaptations on the part of the manager, and these cannot possibly coincide with all nineteen committee opinions. Fourth, policy recommendations of FOMC members are stated in terms that are at best ambiguous—"a little tighter," or "about the same degree of ease," or "shoot for net free reserves between $500 million and $600 million." Committee members frequently disavow the free reserves target, pointing out that it lacks sufficient connection with the complex of economic variables to be useful as a measure of the effectiveness of policy. It is little wonder then that communication between the FOMC and the trading desk is poor. Nor is it any wonder that Chairman Martin, for better or worse, must determine a consensus that would lead only to endless argument if it were brought to a vote.

A more basic difficulty of communication arises from the unwillingness of the committee to state its economic outlook in precise terms. There exists in the Federal Reserve System an unwritten rule against explicit forecasting of business conditions; even modest attempts at prognosis are blue-penciled if written and ignored if expressed verbally. Members of the FOMC often remark that "we are making policy only for the next three weeks," the implication being that inaction or wrong action can be reviewed or corrected at the next meeting. Now it is manifestly impossible to frame an intelligent monetary policy without at least implicit forecasting; and since a major objective of monetary policy is cyclical amelioration, the forecast period must be a major portion of a cycle. Fortunately, many FOMC members have their own unstated projections. But the emphasis on the short term, the avoidance of a solid, common forecast, and the frequency of FOMC meetings all lead to erratic action, lagged responses, and policy more often than not based on correction of past errors rather than on anticipation of future events.

But whatever the difficulties and ambiguities of communicating with the trading desk, transmissions *are* made and received. However, the man in charge of the desk, no matter how dedicated, has a rough, tough job. If, as is frequently true, the FOMC has set some range of free reserves as its most precise measure of policy direction, the account manager ideally tries to achieve this goal in his day-to-day operations. But the goal is elusive, simply because some of the money-market factors affecting reserves cannot be predicted at all and others can be estimated only with difficulty. (Actual figures may become available only two or three weeks later.) Actions taken by the desk on the basis of the daily predictions of the money-market factors frequently turn out to have been perverse—in the wrong direction. The chief upsetting factor, of course, is Federal Reserve float, which is extremely volatile and almost completely unpredictable on a daily basis. Float could be safely ignored on a daily basis and dealt with only on a weekly average basis, Federal Reserve studies having shown that commercial banks do not alter their short-term investment positions on the basis of changing float levels. Yet fear of commercial-bank response ostensibly forms the basis for the frequency of a Fed's float-offsetting action, with consequent uncertainty in the money markets when desk action is in the wrong direction.

Another major influence on the administration of the trading desk is the solicitude of the Fed for the government security dealers, particularly for the nonbank dealers. The basic premises of this solicitude are that a "broad, deep, and resilient" market for government securities is necessary for successful Federal Reserve action and that such a market can be made only by financially impregnable dealers who can obtain financing on favorable terms. A "negative carry"—that is, a yield on any security held in inventory smaller than the rate paid on funds borrowed by the dealer—is taken as conclusive evidence that financing terms for the dealers are not favorable. The same concern is not felt for bank dealers, since they are assumed to have a ready internal source of funds to finance their positions.

Solicitude for the dealers is expressed in several ways. For example, the FOMC has approved and the desk has made frequent use of the repurchase agreement. Although this instrument is a means by which the desk can make bank reserves available for a short time with automatic withdrawal, it is also a means by which short-term credit is extended to a dealer. The timing is usually to the advantage of the dealer, because the desk makes the privilege available when there is a real pinch in the money market. The repurchase agreement is in reality a fully secured loan; the desk purchases securities (bills) from the dealer, who agrees to repurchase them within a definite period (maximum, fifteen days). Interest is computed on the basis of amount and term of loan rather than by reckoning the difference between purchase and sale price of the bills, as would be true in the case of a true purchase and repurchase.

Fed concern for the government securities dealer is further demonstrated by the expressed opinion that the money-market banks ought to favor the securities dealers in financing arrangements, particularly during tight-money periods. The money-market banks have protested that no group ought to be favored merely because of its function. Although the interest of the Fed authorities in maintaining a facilitating market organization is understandable, it is doubtful that financing favoritism is essential to a strong dealer organization. A hands-off attitude, requiring dealers to stand the market test of services rendered, charges made, and competition for custom, seems more likely to achieve ultimate Federal Reserve aims.

Nor is arranging Fed intervention in the government securities market to suit the convenience of nonbank dealers likely to inspire public confidence. Federal Reserve acceptance of the notion that System entry into the government securities market should be in short issues, preferably bills, had its philosophical basis in a weird principle of "minimum effective interference," a mystical idea that the limitless authority of the central bank could somehow be softened by dealing in securities "closest to money" in the spectrum of financial assets. But a careful reading of the famed *Ad Hoc Subcommittee Report* of 1952 makes it clear that strong support for the "bills only" dogma came from the dealers, who would avoid, for obvious reasons, "capricious" System purchases and sales throughout the maturity range of the Treasury list. Dealers with positions in bonds naturally want to be warned of fluctuations in bond prices by preliminary changes in the prices of bills.

RETURN TO REGIONALISM?

Knowledgeable men know perfectly well that the informal power structure of an institution—whether a Christian denomination, a great corporation, or a university —may well be more important than its formal one. So long as the distinction is clear, so long as people are aware of what is really going on, it makes little difference whether the formal or informal power centers are operative. But it makes a great deal of difference if the people in a democracy, unaware of the arbitrary nature of the actual decision making, go on believing that the money power, like all other sovereign power, is responsive to democratic processes. For plainly it is not.

We do not for one moment question either the integrity or the sincerity of the money managers. If government at all levels were staffed by men of the competence and dedication of those found in the Federal Reserve System, the American political system would be upgraded tremendously.

We do believe, however, that a realistic appraisal of System structure in terms of its genuine power centers leads to only one conclusion—that the regional structure, adopted by the framers of the Federal Reserve Act two generations ago, is presently outmoded and has become an expensive anachronism. We may as well face up to the fact that Federal Reserve banks have become only operating offices with responsibility for service functions and not, in any real sense, for monetary policy.

In our view a workable regional system *could* be devised. A return to regional structure would require, as a very minimum, restoration of the discount rate as an instrument of monetary control. Such a restoration implies the rescinding of Regulation A, the complex and meddlesome set of rules by which the twelve discount windows are presently administered. It further implies free access to discount windows at whatever rates the regional banks prescribe.

Ostensibly, the discount rates of the several banks are set by their boards of directors. In practice, they are raised and lowered at the wish of the board. When Chairman Martin senses the strategic moment has arrived for a discount-rate change, he initiates action via a discreet telephone call to one or more bank presidents out in the provinces. Once a Reserve bank president (at St. Louis, Kansas City, Atlanta, or Dallas, for example) has the word, it is up to him to get his board of directors, or the executive committee of his board, to do what the Reserve board wants. When the change is made, the business press ordinarily announces it as the simultaneous decision of two or more banks. Within ten days or so, all the other banks fall in line—not by mere chance, you may be sure.

There is much to be said for operating the discount window on a rate basis rather than on an administered basis. To be sure, Federal Reserve credit must be injected partly with regard to grand strategic considerations, as determined by the board and the New York bank. But much of the hour-to-hour and day-to-day intervention by the trading desk could be avoided by letting the commercial banks tell the Fed when they need reserves. It sounds a little old-fashioned to suggest that the private banking community may on occasion know what's best for it, but we'd like to return some of the reserve-injection initiative to the commercial banks.

There are reasons why it may be impossible to go back to a regional system. For one thing, the American economy has lost most of the provincial characteristics that marked it as late as the eve of World War II. For another, our understanding of monetary (stabilization) theory has changed since the formation of a geographically decentralized central bank, placing emphasis on unified control of the economy rather than on patchwork assistance to parts of it.

Yet there would be a demonstrable gain from making central-bank control less authoritarian. Moreover, continued centralization of the money power leads logically to the ultimate in a centralized power structure—combination of the central bank and the Treasury under a single head. Those who feel that such an arrangement bodes no good would do well to reflect on the possibility of greater reliance on markets in the implementation of central-bank policy.

A long-time Congressional critic of the Federal Reserve asserts that the Fed exerts great power over the economy, from a position beyond the control of the President or the elected representatives of the people; and that, moreover, the Fed is banker dominated.

13

Views of
Chairman Patman

Representative Wright Patman (Texas) is Chairman of the powerful House Banking and Currency Committee, and has been a member of that committee since the 1930's.

WRIGHT PATMAN

The policies of the U.S. Government for full employment, international stability, equitable taxation, and domestic prosperity can never be sound or dependable while the most important part of the Nation's economic powers is in the hands of a private group which exists as a separate government. We have two governments in the District of Columbia. One consists of the Congress and the President—the elected representatives of the people. The other is the Federal Reserve, operating as a self-appointed money trust, far removed from the will of the people.

This shocking state of affairs has been brought home bluntly to the American public by the assertion of the Federal Reserve that it is independent of the executive branch and that it can operate contrary to the President's wishes. It is an open and defiant proclamation that the Nation's gold and money printing press have been seized by a private group and are now being used by them in utter disregard of the principles of democratic government.

The Constitution clearly vests the monetary power in Congress, and with good reason. History has repeatedly demonstrated that possession of the monetary power gives its holder a life and death power over a society. But in spite of our Constitution, Chairman Martin left no doubt as to his views when he told this committee, on February 26, that "the Federal Reserve Board has the authority to act independently of the President," even "despite the President."

Excerpted from the *Report of the Joint Economic Committee on the January, 1965 Economic Report of the President,* March 17, 1965, pp. 35–37.

FEDERAL RESERVE SYSTEM IS BANKER DOMINATED

What makes these claims even more appalling is the fact that our Federal Reserve System, as it functions at the present time, is a banker-dominated, banker-oriented autocracy. The fact of the matter is that there has been a struggle over control of the Federal Reserve System for 50 years, ever since it was founded. It is a struggle that the bankers have been winning, and it is clear now from Mr. Martin's statement that they have come out in the open defiantly. Savings and loan associations, cooperatives, credit unions, and other financial institutions not within the privileged banking circle should take notice that this usurpation of monetary authority places them in jeopardy.

*   *   *

OPEN MARKET COMMITTEE EXERCISES TREMENDOUS POWER

The fundamental monetary powers of the Nation are exercised by the Open Market Committee which is made up, on the record, of five Federal Reserve bank presidents and the seven members of the Board. In practice, however, all 12 presidents participate in the deliberations which, of course, are conducted in secret every three weeks. Thus, the basic power for good or ill in our economy is exercised by a group closely identified with the banking community and operating willfully and knowingly outside the pale of Government. This extralegal power is so great that the banker-controlled group can create prosperity, or, by turning the financial screws, can create recession, depression, or even panic. That this power can be abused to the advantage of a particular political party or candidate is too obvious to need elaboration.

The $36.8 billion portfolio of the Federal Reserve System is a fund that could be considered a recession fund, or a depression fund, and if its masters so choose, a panic fund. There is nothing to prevent them, in an election year, from letting a candidate President know that if he didn't manage to see eye to eye with them for the next four years his November election might be endangered.

14
The Federal Reserve System After Fifty Years

Differing with Representative Patman, many observers conclude that the "independence" of the Fed is a complex issue, and that the present arrangement represents a good compromise between the need for Federal Reserve responsibility to the public and freedom from day-to-day political pressures.

G. L. Bach is Maurice Falk Professor of Economics at Carnegie Institute of Technology.

G. L. BACH

The Commission on Money and Credit, in a temperate analysis of governmental operations and Federal Reserve responsibilities, drew these conclusions concerning Federal Reserve independence:

1. The President must bear the central responsibility for governmental economic policy recommendations and execution.

2. Federal Reserve responsibilities for national economic policy are closely intertwined with those of other Government agencies, especially the Executive Office of the President and the Treasury.

3. Federal Reserve independence is now adequately protected, and Federal Reserve influence could be increased by closer participation in governmental policy determination.

4. To the end of closer and more informal working relationships between the Federal Reserve and the White House, the Federal Reserve Board Chairman and Vice-Chairman should be designated by the President from among the Board's membership, with four-year terms coterminous with the President's.

5. To improve efficiency and attract more able members, the Federal Reserve Board should be reduced from seven to five members, and all major Federal Reserve monetary powers should be centered in the Board.

6. To improve national economic policy formulation and coordination, the President should establish a cabinet-level "Advisory Board on Economic Growth and Stability," including the Chairman of the Federal Reserve Board.

From *Hearings Before the Subcommittee on Domestic Finance of the Committee of Banking and Currency House of Representatives,* 88th Congress, 2nd Session, February, March, 1964.

These proposals have been widely criticized by conservatives on the ground that they would undermine the independence of the Federal Reserve. The critics suggest that the "liberals" on the Commission somehow outflanked the "conservatives" in bringing about this stab in the back for financial soundness (a neat trick if indeed it occurred, since two-thirds of the 20 Commission members were highly successful businessmen and bankers, only two were labor leaders, and the other five were independent professional men). On such a vital issue of monetary arrangements as this, it is well to take a closer look.

CASE FOR INDEPENDENCE

Stated bluntly, the traditional argument for Federal Reserve independence is that, if independent, the Fed will stand against inflation and financial irresponsibility in the Government. History tells of many treasuries which have turned to money issue to pay their bills when taxes were inadequate. The modern world's major inflations have all come with large governmental deficits, covered by the issue of new money (currency or bank deposits). While legislatures vote the expenditures, treasuries must pay the bills. Thus, it is argued that treasuries have a predictable inflationary bias, however well intentioned their secretaries may be. Against this bias, central bankers are alleged to be basically conservative; they can be counted on to look out for the stability of the monetary unit.

Another variant is based on the presumption that the entire political process is inherently inflationary. It is always easier for Congress to spend money than to raise taxes; "politicians" are inherently financially irresponsible. Thus, an independent Federal Reserve is needed to call a halt to the overspending tendencies of the politicians, and to the tendency of the politicians to plump too readily for good times for the economy as a whole, even though these good times may generate some inflation.

Lastly, there is an argument that the President, the politician par excellence, is not to be trusted on financial matters, and that an independent Federal Reserve is needed to see that he does not go too far with expansionary, inflationary economic policies.

MEANING OF INDEPENDENCE

These arguments suggest that we need to examine the meaning of the term "independence." Independence from whom? A Federal Reserve independent of the U.S. Treasury rests squarely on the realistic assessment of history. Treasuries have been inflationary in their biases, and we therefore need a powerful agency in governmental economic circles to stand against these inflationary biases when they threaten the soundness of our economic structure.

But Federal Reserve independence from the Congress is hardly meaningful in our governmental system. Congress established the Federal Reserve. It can change it any time it wishes, or call it to account for any of its actions. Federal Reserve officials readily acknowledge their responsibility to Congress—though the Fed need not go to Congress for appropriations to conduct its affairs and though, in practice, Congress, happily, is reluctant to intervene directly in Federal Reserve policymaking.

The really difficult question is this: Should, or can, the Federal Reserve be independent from the President? The Constitution clearly allots to the Federal Government the power to create money and regulate the value thereof. In our society, where bank deposits comprise some 80 per cent of our total money supply and currency only 20 per cent, control over the supply of bank deposits is control over the volume of money. Federal Reserve officials have consistently recognized the basically governmental nature of their function, though they value the close relationships they have with private bankers.

Furthermore, control over the money supply of the Nation is a vital operating responsibility. Monetary policy is inextricably intermingled with fiscal policy and debt management policy, if the Nation's economic goals are to be achieved effectively. The President must ultimately be responsible for recommendation and execution of the Nation's basic economic policy. This logic leads clearly to the conclusion that the Federal Reserve must work closely with other agencies under the general responsibility of the President for executing national economic policy.

To give an independent Federal Reserve the power to negate the basic policies arrived at by the executive and legislative branches of the Federal Government would be intolerable for any administration, Republican or Democratic. But independence, looked at practically, is a matter of degree, not of black and white. The real question, thus, is the terms on which the Federal Reserve participates in governmental policymaking and execution.

NEED FOR COOPERATION

To be most effective, the Federal Reserve needs to be in a position to work closely with the other major Government agencies responsible for national economic policy—especially the Treasury, the Budget Bureau, and the Council of Economic Advisers. No Federal Reserve Chairman has ever claimed that the Board should disregard the debt management problems of the Treasury, or that the Government's financial needs should be given no weight.

On the contrary, all major Federal Reserve officials have agreed on the need for close working relationships with the Treasury on monetary, fiscal, and debt policy. The times when the Federal Reserve has been least effective have been the times when it has been most isolated from the President and from effective, coequal working relationships with the Secretary of the Treasury and other high-level Government officials. This was substantially the case throughout the much-discussed decade of the 1940's when the Federal Reserve was most subservient to Treasury debt management needs. Secretaries Morgenthau and Snyder were close personal confidants of Presidents Roosevelt and Truman; but Federal Reserve officials seldom saw either President.

An effective Federal Reserve voice for the stable-money point of view can best be assured if the Fed is an active, continuous participant in the day-to-day process of governmental economic policy formation. Seldom indeed does a central bank undertake a major war with the Congress and the administration in a showdown on economic policy. Federal Reserve participation in policymaking will generally be a more effective device for presenting the sound-money point of view than will spectacular defiance of the Government's policies. Extreme independence is, unfortunately, likely to mean splendid isolation from the decisions that matter.

ON BALANCE

The need is for recognized Federal Reserve independence from the Treasury and for coequal voice with other major agencies in the economic policy councils of the Government. In other words, the need is to maintain a strong and substantially independent voice for a stable-money point of view without placing Federal Reserve officials in an untenably isolated position, where to use their independence involves major intragovernmental conflict and divided national economic policy. Budgetary and monetary matters call for the best efforts of wise men. But we must not fall into the trap of supposing that all wisdom will reside in appointed Federal Reserve officials, rather than in other Government officials appointed by the same President and approved by the same Senate. The President, the Secretary of the Treasury, and other high governmental officials also seek to advance the national welfare, as they see it. How best to mesh the judgments and reponsibilities of these various public officials is the problem, not simply to set up an independent nongovernmental board with a legal (but seldom practical) power to say no to the U.S. Government.

RECOMMENDED CHANGES

To improve the coordination of overall economic policy and to increase the influence of the Federal Reserve while maintaining its special quasi-independent status, the Commission recommended, primarily, two modest changes:

> 1. The President should establish a cabinet-level Advisory Board on Economic Growth and Stability which would include the Chairman of the Federal Reserve Board.
> 2. The term of office of the Chairman (and Vice-Chairman) of the Federal Reserve Board should be made coterminous with that of the President, to eliminate the possibility that a Federal Reserve Chairman would be personally unacceptable to a President.

A new President could (as now) immediately appoint one new Board member, and could name him Chairman; or he could name a new chairman from among existing Board members. The staggered-term membership of the Board would remain unchanged, except that it would be reduced from seven to five members. While further centralization of System authority in the Board would increase somewhat the President's power over the Fed, overlapping 10-year terms would go far to protect the stability and independence of the Board members from short-run political pressures.

These two recommendations might help substantially to assure effective working relationships between the Fed, the Presidency, and the rest of the administrative branch of the Government. To insist that a new president accept a Federal Reserve Chairman to whom he objected strongly would probably serve little purpose, and would be more likely to decrease the effectiveness of the Fed than to increase it. As a practical matter, the Chairman must represent the System in its most important contacts with the President, as well as with the Treasury and in most cases with Congress. Making the chairmanship coterminous with the President's term, though it might have little importance in most instances, makes practical administrative sense. It is significant that both William

M. Martin, the present Chairman of the Fed, and Marriner S. Eccles, Chairman for longer than any other man and the individual who was most responsible for the restored independence of the Fed in 1951, concur in the recommendation to make the chairmanship coterminous with the President's term.

Appointment by the President of an Advisory Board on Economic Growth and Stability would be one device for assuring closer coordination among the governmental agencies (including the Fed) responsible for national economic policy. Whether such a special advisory board would be effective would depend heavily on whether the President wanted to use it. Some such device is obviously necessary. The Commission wisely avoided a recommendation to make such an advisory board mandatory by legislation, while stressing the importance of coordinated national policy formation in which the Federal Reserve has a strong voice.

Critics have labeled these recommendations a stab in the back for Federal Reserve independence. This appears to be a serious exaggeration. They reflect operating realities, and are modest proposals indeed when viewed in the light of the experience of most other nations, where central banks have been completely subordinated to treasuries or to governments.

15

Money Supply and Stable Economic Growth

A leading economist reviews our monetary history and concludes that a simple policy of increasing the money stock at a stable rate annually, without trying to counter each business fluctuation, would make the greatest contribution to stable economic growth.

EDWARD S. SHAW

Edward S. Shaw is Professor of Economics at Stanford University.

DEFINITIONS OF MONEY

Everyone Rolls His Own

It is almost true that everyone rolls his own definition of money and has his own rules for measurement of the money supply. Federal Reserve people are noncommittal, and in the representative *Federal Reserve Bulletin* offer no tabulations headed *Money* or *Supply of Money*. Their essays about money coat the term with a film of adjectives—"active" money, "relatively active" money, "inactive" money. Our central bank cultivates uncertainty even in monetary semantics.

The rest of us have been no more incisive. Here is a list of items from which we concoct now one, now another definition of money with measurements to match. The figures apply to a date chosen at random, February 26, 1958.

MONEY OR NOT?

Item	Amount ($ billions)
Currency outside banks	$ 27.3
Demand deposits adjusted	105.5
United States Government balances in banks	4.2
Treasury cash holdings	.7
Time deposits of commercial banks	57.5
Other time deposits	33.4

From *United States Monetary Policy;* The American Assembly, 1958, pp. 49–71. Reprinted by permission.

"Money," as the composite of some items above, increased in amount over the year before the date of measurement. "Money" comprising a different combination of these items decreased over the year. If you suspect that there was monetary expansion, you can tailor a definition to your suspicion. If you prefer to think that there was monetary contraction, you can be right again—with a different definition.

There is good fundamentalist authority for counting as money only the hard core of legal tender, the first item in our Table. There is equally reputable reformist authority for counting items that are not mentioned in the Table, for counting anything called a "deposit" in any institution called a "bank." I can cite no authority for including "shares" of savings and loan associations or credit unions, though authority may not be lacking when and if the associations win their battle of nomenclature and become "banks" owing "deposits."

A Personal Preference

The definition that strikes the writer's fancy begins with the dictum *A dollar is a dollar*. A unit of money bearing the price, or face value, of $1 today bears the same price tomorrow and next year. It discharges a debt for $1 anytime, and it always buys something else with a price tag of $1. No one haggles over money's price.

This definition is not quite as rigorous as it may seem, because one would count in money not merely legal-tender pocket money but checking balances as well. The latter do depreciate a little in price, subject as they are to service charges. And they would appreciate a little, if Congress once again permitted interest credits on demand accounts. This definition is flexible enough to admit anything that people use as money—as a means of payment: money is as money does!

Modern money is a debt, differing from other forms of debt in that its price does not vary. It is a debt of the monetary system—the commercial banks, the Federal Reserve Banks, and the Treasury monetary accounts. It is issued to other sectors of the economy in payment by the monetary system for purchases principally of nonmonetary securities and monetary metals. Textbooks classify our money as "token" money, to distinguish it from fragments of one commodity or another that people have used, in other times and places, as fixed-price means of payment.

THE SUPPLY OF MONEY

At any moment the supply or quantity of money is the monetary system's dollar aggregate of fixed-price debt. It is the sum of all legal tender in pockets and tills together with the sum of all unused credits to checking accounts. The "quantity of money" that economists talk about is this simple statistic doctored in various ways.

An observation at a moment of time does not give as accurate a "fix" as is necessary for precision in relating the supply of money to, say, national income for a year. Instead of a momentary measurement, one needs an average figure for money outstanding.

An average supply or quantity of money may be outrageously inflationary if it is spread over a small community, grossly deflationary if the community is much larger. Especially in a growth context, it is often the money supply *per capita* that one needs for analytical purposes. This is not a datum regularly accessible in official tabulations or elsewhere, possibly because most of us are preoccupied with the behavior or misbehavior of money in the short run, too few of us with monetary phenomena in periods long enough for significant change in the population of money-users.

The money we are discussing is *nominal* money—the face value of the monetary system's debt. Economists usually suppose that it is *real* money, rather than nominal money, that affects levels and patterns of economic activity and economic welfare. Real money is the purchasing power of nominal money. The supply of real money is the supply of nominal money deflated by some one or other index of prices for things that money buys. Old hands at monetary analysis are ruefully aware that no price index is quite right for measurement of the real money supply and of changes in it.

As one puts the quantity of money into one statistical disguise after another, he can get very different impressions of its behavior. The sum of currency outside banks and demand deposits adjusted, without statistical frills, was nearly $140 billions on December 31, 1956, and nearly $138 billions on December 25, 1957. Obviously the supply of money was reduced about 1.4 per cent. But was it? In real terms, *per capita* of our noninstitutional population, the supply of money fell from $1,177 to $1,103. This is a decline of 6.3 per cent. In its policy of restraint for 1957, was the Federal Reserve aiming at the target of 1.4 per cent or at the target of 6.3 per cent?

The "supply of money" that central banks manipulate, that people hold most of the time and spend once in a while, that economists investigate, is not, then, a simple concept. It is a figure so transformed by its visit to the statistical beauty parlor as hardly to be recognizable by its closest friends. Laymen take warning; there may be more than meets the eye in any measurement of the supply or quantity of money!

GROWTH IN THE SUPPLY OF MONEY: FIRST THE THROTTLE, THEN THE BRAKES

It was a common complaint, before passage of the Federal Reserve Act in late 1913, that our monetary system was inelastic. The Federal Reserve Act and its amendments, and administration of the Act, have quashed that complaint. Partly out of conviction and partly to arouse discussion, we are going to argue that the Act and its administrators have put far too much elasticity into our monetary system. Switching metaphors, our point will be that it was a mistake to demolish the old Model T monetary system of the pre-1914 era. The juggernaut that has replaced it is not designed, nor is it driven, on principles that are compatible with monetary stability in a growing economy. These are fighting words that call for adequate documentation.

The Statistical Record (Stop and Go in Monetary Policy)

The Table which follows is a rough tracery of our monetary experience during 1896–1957. It measures growth in nominal money over the entire period and during seven sub-periods. The sub-periods begin with 1896–1914, when the old monetary system was running out its last miles under critical inspection by a bevy of monetary commissions, public and private. In four of the remaining six sub-periods, policies of the new monetary system were stipulated primarily by the Treasury Department. In the other two sub-periods, monetary policy was stipulated by the Federal Reserve Board, *alias* the Board of Governors of the Federal Reserve System.

The four "Treasury" intervals were:

1914–1919
1933–1941
1941–1945
1945–1951

In two of these intervals the monetary system was conscripted for war finance. For the greater part of 1933–1941 any "independent" monetary policy was subordinated to the broad objective of restoring liquidity to an economic system that had been parched and seared by deflation. The Treasury's parental concern with the viability of its debt distinguished the years 1945–1951.

The two interludes of "Board" tenure were:

1919–1933
1951–1957

Both interludes opened with a palace revolution, within the federal executive, against the Treasury's excessive concern with its debt. The first closed in the disaster of a monetary moratorium. The second continued, but once again—as in the two decades before 1914—the vigilantes were gathering into monetary commissions.

In 1896 the nominal supply of money was at the near-microscopic level of $3.8 billions. At the close of 1957, the nominal supply of money was thirty-six times larger, or $137.7 billions. The average annual compound rate of growth

Stop and Go in Monetary Policy

Period	Change in Nominal Money ($ billions)	Annual Rate of Change (%)
1896–1914	$ 7.5	6
1914–1919	11.4	15
1919–1933	−3.5	−1
1933–1941	27.7	14
1941–1945	55.5	21
1945–1951	22.2	3
1951–1957	13.2	2
(1896–1957)	134.0	6

was approximately 6 per cent. One had no need for a microscope to see the money supply at the end of last year.

Six Decades in Review

For perspective, the growth rate of 6 per cent in nominal money may be compared with the more modest growth rate of about 3.75 per cent in real value of money. Evidently prices rose at the average annual rate of 2.25 per cent. It may come as a mild surprise that this degree of price inflation has been our method of repudiating about $100 billions of growth in nominal money: nominal money increased by $134 billions; real money by perhaps $30–35 billions in 1896–1957. Our textiles may have been shrink-proof, but our dollar has not. (See accompanying table and chart, which show annual values of real output, money supply, price level and real money in the United States over the period 1900–1957.)

The Model-T Period

Consider the pre-Federal Reserve years 1896–1914 a little more closely. In correspondence with accelerating growth in physical production and in the nation's real income, the money stock grew at the average rate of 9 per cent in 1896–1906. From year to year there was relatively little variation in the rate of growth. After 1906 the tempo of growth slackened throughout the economy, the annual rate of growth in money falling to a little less than 3 per cent. The money supply declined in one year (1907); and it rose in each year of depression, including the dismal year of 1908. During 1906–1914 variation in annual rates of growth was narrow.

Waving aside the seasonal stresses of the old monetary system, which were amenable to treatment on the principle of the Aldrich-Vreeland Act, one is tempted to shed a nostalgic tear for our monetary experience in the two decades prior to the Federal Reserve Act. The monetary system was Model T, but it was not too much for us to handle.

Drag-racing the Monetary System

The Federal Reserve Act multiplied both horsepower and brakepower in the monetary system. Since 1914 effective control of the system has alternated between Treasury and Reserve Board. The Treasury takes out its aggressions on the throttle of the new machine. The Board reaches for the brakes. And the money supply lurches along a sawtooth course of growth.

In 1914–1919 the annual rate of growth in nominal money was accelerated from 3 to 15 per cent. Then the brakes! Over the next fourteen years, there was a net decline in the money supply. To be sure, there was growth in money balances of 1 per cent annually to 1929; but then deceleration set in at the average annual rate of 6 per cent. This is not a profile of monetary stability.

Twice during its tenure of control in 1919–1933, the Reserve Board presided over a decline of nearly 10 per cent in nominal money. In both years, 1921 and 1930, the monetary brakes were applied to an economic system that was already on the skids of deflation. In eight of the fourteen years there was net monetary contraction, and in six of these eight years monetary contraction was superimposed on other depressing circumstances. In two years of cyclic recession, 1924 and 1927, it is true that the Reserve Board followed the precedent of the old monetary system in increasing liquidity. But these were years when such a stimulus was less necessary than in four of the six years in which the Board departed from pre-1914 tradition.

The Board's license to drive the monetary system was, in effect, suspended in 1933, when the Treasury took over the controls. Probation was granted in 1936–1937, but once more the Board applied the brakes too hard. The United States economy slid into the recession of 1937–1938, and again the Board's license to drive was lifted.

Over fourteen years, 1919–1933, the Board had subjected the economy to a negligible rate of growth in money. In the next eight years, apart from the interlude of 1936–1937, the Treasury chauffeur reversed monetary policy and subjected the economic system to an absurdly high rate of monetary expansion. By 1941 the prestige of monetary policy was, properly, very low indeed.

Gross National Product, Money Supply, and Price Level of the United States, 1900–1957

The shaded areas are periods of economic recession. Dates at the base of the chart are at year-ends. The straight trend lines joining the initial and terminal points on the four curves give the average annual rate of growth in each series, compounded annually.

1. $\frac{M}{P}$ (Real Money).

2. Price Level (implicit deflator for gross national product).
   $1929 = 100 \, (= P)$
   1900–1949: Raymond W. Goldsmith, *A Study of Saving in the United States*, I, p. 377.
   1949–1957: *Survey of Current Business*, June, 1957, adjusted from 1947 base to 1929 base.

3. Gross national product, 1929 prices $(= T)$
   1900–1949: Raymond W. Goldsmith, *A Study of Saving in the United States*, III, p. 429.
   1949–1957: *Survey of Current Business*. Deflator adjusted to 1929 base.

4. Adjusted demand deposits plus currency outside banks, year-end figures $(= M)$.
   1900–1949: Raymond W. Goldsmith, *A Study of Saving in the United States*, pp. 382–3.
   1949–1957: *Federal Reserve Bulletin*.

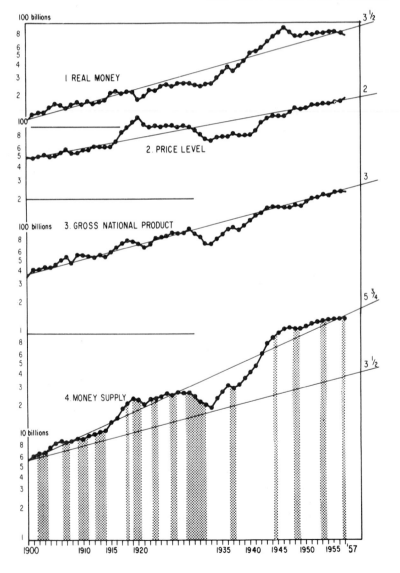

In reaction to the monetary experience of 1919–1933, the Congress added to the monetary system's capacity for both acceleration and deceleration in the series of reforms that appeared during 1933–1945. Retrospectively, it seems that the rational thing to do was to put the system on automatic pilot after 1914–1933 and disengage manual controls. Important statutory restraints on monetary expansion were eased or eliminated, and powerful new discretionary restraints were added.

Gross National Product, Money Supply,
and Price Level of the United States,
1900–1957

	M *	P **	M/P †	T ‡
1900	$ 5,934	50	$11,868	$37,442
1901	6,536	50	13,072	40,901
1902	6,994	51	13,714	41,495
1903	7,167	52	13,783	43,641
1904	7,827	51	15,347	43,190
1905	8,730	52	16,790	45,869
1906	9,159	56	16,356	50,940
1907	8,889	59	15,066	52,353
1908	9,086	55	16,520	48,700
1909	9,576	56	17,100	56,279
1910	9,674	59	16,400	56,158
1911	10,371	60	17,285	55,161
1912	10,665	64	16,664	55,468
1913	11,105	64	17,351	57,815
1914	11,565	64	18,070	55,532
1915	13,812	65	21,250	60,635
1916	16,015	72	22,243	67,300
1917	18,408	87	21,159	74,187
1918	21,171	98	21,603	78,875
1919	23,799	110	21,635	77,418
1920	22,812	125	18,248	73,298
1921	20,601	105	19,620	68,700
1922	22,804	99	23,034	72,775
1923	23,284	102	22,824	83,980
1924	24,797	101	24,551	85,427
1925	26,096	102	25,584	87,970
1926	25,510	103	24,748	93,833
1927	26,447	100	26,447	95,092
1928	26,784	101	26,519	96,136
1929	26,518	100	26,518	103,800
1930	24,669	96	25,697	94,400
1931	21,780	87	25,034	87,400
1932	20,343	78	26,081	74,800
1933	19,771	75	26,361	74,300
1934	23,178	79	29,340	82,000
1935	27,043	81	33,383	89,300
1936	31,010	81	38,284	101,400
1937	29,625	85	34,853	106,200
1938	31,739	83	38,240	101,500
1939	36,181	83	43,592	110,300
1940	42,274	84	50,326	120,800
1941	48,607	91	53,414	139,600
1942	62,865	110	57,150	146,866
1943	79,619	121	65,801	160,601
1944	90,455	127	71,224	168,258
1945	102,341	128	79,953	169,144

Gross National Product, Money Supply,
and Price Level of the United States,
1900–1957—(Continued)

	M *	P **	M/P †	T ‡
1946	110,044	126	87,336	167,558
1947	113,597	139	81,725	167,500
1948	111,599	150	74,399	172,900
1949	111,165	149	74,608	172,000
1950	117,670	151	77,927	189,000
1951	124,549	162	76,882	203,000
1952	129,002	165	78,183	209,000
1953	130,542	167	78,169	218,000
1954	134,402	168	80,001	215,000
1955	137,900	170	81,118	230,000
1956	139,726	175	79,840	236,000
1957	137,700	184	74,837	236,000

Sources:
  * Adjusted demand deposits *plus* currency outside banks for end-year dates.
1900–1949, Raymond W. Goldsmith, *A Study of Saving in the United States,* I, pp. 382–3.
1950–1957, *Federal Reserve Bulletin.*
  ** Deflator of gross national product.
1900–1949, Goldsmith, *ibid.,* I, p. 377. 1929 = 100.
1950–1957, based on series by U.S. Department of Commerce, *Survey of Current Business* as adjusted
from 1947 base to 1929 base.
  † Column 1 divided by column 2.
  ‡ Gross national product in 1929 prices.
1900–1949, Goldsmith, *ibid.,* III, p. 429.
1950–1957, current figures in *Survey of Current Business,* divided by column 2.

This is the kind of reform one might have expected if the post-1914 monetary mechanism had been driven skillfully. Yet bad driving was rewarded by placing a new and still more powerful machine in the driver's hands!

This is not the occasion to debate wartime economic controls. One may simply offer the opinion that the rate of growth in money during 1941–1945, on the order of 21 per cent annually, is a blemish on our record that no amount of rationalization can erase. We expanded the money supply at a rate surpassing by a wide margin even the requirements for rapid real growth in wartime; then deputized thousands of price policemen in OPA and WPB to patrol the channels of moneyflow. The money accelerator was pushed to the floorboard, and policemen were deployed in droves to keep the public out of the way of the money juggernaut. The new monetary system was not the cause but the instrument of our folly.

The Board's fight for repossession of the monetary system was not won until 1951. The foot, shackled since 1936–1937, was freed and instinctively stepped on the monetary brakes again. The ensuing screech of complaint in the security markets, in the Spring of 1953, still echoes in our ears.

Since the Reserve Board settled back on the brakeman's seat in 1951, real national income has grown at approximately 4 per cent annually, real money a little over 1 per cent annually, nominal money 2 per cent. After five years of reckless acceleration in 1914–1919, fourteen years of excessive deceleration in 1919–1933, eighteen years of reckless acceleration in 1933–1951, we are again in the deceleration phase of our monetary drag-race. The economy's spinal column has not snapped as it has been whipped back and forth by alternating pressure on throttle and brake; but no credit is due to our "elastic" monetary system for our survival. Safety belts, sometimes known as built-in stabilizers, take up some of the strain, as OPA and WPB did in wartime. It is a pity that some of the ingenuity spent in contriving nonmonetary stabilizers has not been spent instead on stabilizing growth of the money supply.

In its twenty years of brakesmanship, the Board has permitted an average annual increase in the money supply of $440 millions. This rate of nominal growth is almost identical with the rate of nominal growth in 1896–1914, but in real terms it can hardly be half as rapid. It is a small fraction of the economy's rate of growth in real income. In its twenty-three years the Treasury has permitted an average annual increase in the money supply of $4,880 millions. It has added $11 to the money supply for every $1 permitted by the Board. Neither rate of expansion is close to an appropriate target rate.

In its twenty years of control, the Board has presided over an absolute decrease in nominal money during nine years. There has been price deflation in eleven of its twenty years. There have been no more than six years in which the Board has permitted nominal money to increase at a rate comparable with growth in the nation's productive capacity. The Treasury team that took over monetary control when the Board moved out has inflated money in all but three of its twenty-three years, a record that may be saluted at least for its consistency.

Neither driver of the monetary system has demonstrated sensitive reflexes to cyclical turning points along our road of growth. The old Model T was more maneuverable on the curves. With its predilection for restraint, the Board has characteristically punished a cyclical boom past its prime, aggravating ensuing depression. The notorious instances are 1919–1921 and 1929–1933, but the cyclical turning points of 1953 and 1957 are not exceptions to the rule.

A Robot at the Wheel

There are numerous alternative designs for a monetary system. The design that this country has hit upon builds into the monetary system an enormous capacity for both inflation and deflation. In successive trips back to the Congressional fix-it shop, the system's elasticity has been increased. As it is now put together, the United States monetary system is a brilliant solution for short-period instability in some security markets. But it has financed long-period inflation on the commodity markets, interrupted by painful episodes of excessive deceleration in monetary growth and declines in price levels. In its first half-century, the system has not created the temperate monetary environment that is most congenial to stable growth in real terms.

Now that the monetary system is undergoing revaluation, fundamental changes in its design should at least be discussed. The writer's own feeling is that, on balance, there would be improvement in its performance if the monetary system were put on automatic pilot. This suggestion is not a new one. The Reserve Board had to contend thirty years ago with proposals for automatized monetary control and turned them down in favor of "judgment in matters of credit administration."

What instructions are to be fed into an automatic monetary pilot? From the long list of alternatives that have been proposed in the history of monetary thought, one of the simplest appears most feasible. It is that, year in and year out, the nominal supply of money should increase by the *average* rate of growth in demand for nominal money at a stable level of commodity prices. According to usual estimates, which should be refined, the appropriate annual growth rate would be on the order of 3–4 per cent.

For any good other than money, no eyebrows would rise over the premise that it is right to balance supply with demand. But "demand for money" is not a concept in popular use. There is no mention of it in the Federal Reserve Act. Only one small tabulation remotely akin to it is published in the *Federal Reserve Bulletin*. If the demand for money is to be considered as the standard for regulation for money supply, a moment spent in probing demand may not be amiss.

THE "DEMAND STANDARD" FOR MONETARY CONTROL

The pure gold standard is an automatic rule of monetary control. And so is pure bimetallism. The automatic rule that I am reviving for consideration may be termed the "demand standard" of monetary control. What it means can be worked out very simply with the help of a familiar expression:

$$MV = PT$$

The Money Equation

All symbol-scarred veterans of Elementary Economics will recall that M is the average nominal supply of money during a period of time. V stands for the average frequency in turnover for a unit of money against the flow of goods and services from the community's productive facilities. P is the price level of goods and services, and T is their physical quantity—the national real income.

The money equation is a better tool for our use if it is twisted a little:

$$M = (1/V) \, (P) \, (T)$$

A second twist replaces the inconvenient expression $1/V$ with k and changes the order of terms:

$$M = P \, (kT)$$

Now we have the nominal supply of money M counterpoised against the community's demand for nominal money $P(kT)$. The community's demand for money in real measure—for money balances in terms of their purchasing power is kT alone. And k is simply a proportion, a desired proportion, between the community's real balances in money and the community's real income.

With its seasonal and cyclical wrinkles ironed out, k is a remarkably stable relationship. In this country, k increased through the nineteenth century and apparently changed very little after 1900 in trend measurements. For present purposes, it may be stipulated that real money is a commodity, demand for which now grows at the same rate as real national income. Demand for money, of course, is motivated both by the utility of money as a means of payment and by the safety of money as a fixed-price asset.

Equality between M and $P(kT)$ is probably rare and fleeting. When it happens, there is monetary equilibrium. At all other times there is monetary disequilibrium. During most of the Treasury's tenure in monetary control, disequilibrium has been in the inflationary direction. Then M has exceeded $P(kT)$ at a stable level of prices P, so that money has been in excess supply. During approximately one-half of the Board's tenure, disequilibrium has been in the deflationary direction. Then M has been depressed below $P(kT)$ at a stable level of prices, so that money has been in excess demand.

Under the Demand Standard of monetary control, the automatic pilot would be instructed to increase M in step with the long-run growth rate of T. On the evidence that k is disposed to stability and on the judgment that a constant P is optimal for our economy and our social structure, the automatic pilot would link growth in money to growth in output of goods and services. Better evidence may turn up that k rises a little as we produce more goods *per capita,* and the view may win out that a little price inflation is good for us. Then the automatic pilot would be instructed to be a little more generous with the supply of nominal money. In effect, the pilot would be told to aim for the spot where monetary equilibrium should be, and not to worry about missing its target in the short run.

Missing the Turns in Monetary Control

Responsibility for monetary control other than by a fixed and simple rule, is too heavy a cross to thrust upon Treasury officials or upon a small group of men in an independent agency. A quick glance over possible disturbances to monetary equilibrium may indicate why some monetary technicians do conclude that automation is overdue in monetary control.

Economic systems must grow—in effective labor force, in productive capital, in output T. According to the money equation, growth in output increases demand for money. Other things equal, it creates excess demand for money. But other things do not long remain equal. If the community has less money than it wants, it reduces demand for goods. Then growth in output implies unwanted growth in inventories. Inventories full to overflowing may be cleared by price reductions, but prices reduced in an unbalanced way cannot be relied upon to dispel excess supply of goods and excess demand for money. Price deflation is painful, and it can cumulate out of all proportion to its initial cause.

Excess demand for money is not cured by economy in demand for money k. Instead k may rise, as deflation threatens, and accentuate excess demand for money. The sensible solution for a shortage in money balances is simply creation of more money balances, in nominal amount, by the monetary system.

Consider a second source of monetary instability. The k in the money equation is stable in longer periods, not seasonally and not cyclically. Business recession is initiated by an increase in k that precedes the cyclical turning point apparently by a variable interval. Demand for money rises at the expense of demand for goods. Excess demand for money eventually is satisfied, but its costs mount up in the forms of falling prices, falling output, and falling employment.

In every recession popular attention focuses on a villain. The latest villain is the "cost-price push," the rise in price that imperfectly competitive sellers force upon their markets not in response to current demand but in anticipation of demand. The cost-price push is characteristic of endemic inflation, but its first consequence is deflationary. It generates excess demand for money so that there is pressure brought to bear upon a monetary authority to underwrite advancing prices with increasing supplies of nominal money. If the monetary authority accedes to pressure, the cost-price push intensifies. If the monetary authority defies pressure, excess demand for money at inflated prices punishes output and employment.

Awkward manipulation of nominal money is the final source of monetary instability. Any monetary authority makes its decisions on the basis of information that is incomplete and not altogether accurate or timely. The authority in our monetary system is handicapped by technically imperfect controls. The authority cannot see clearly the road that the monetary system should travel and, in comparison with ideal designs, the steering devices are primitive. We do not have fingertip control of money, with the result that the best-laid plans for management of *M* can miscarry, and widen the supply-demand gap of monetary disequilibrium.

In the light of monetary experience, it appears that many of us have romanticized monetary control. It is an illusion that the money supply can be manipulated, according to the daily flux of economic statistics and their translation by men of refined intuition, into continuous equilibrium. The limit of feasibility is to ascertain the trend rate of growth in demand for money at a given price level and to set the money supply automatically on the same course. Some may ask: In a serious economic recession, should not the monetary authorities be required to augment the money supply even *more* than this rule would call for? The answer is "no." When the *nominal* supply of money is growing at a stable rate, a serious recession would itself generate a very large increase in *real* money. If the door is opened even slightly to discretionary monetary management, there is no point at which it can be closed.

Money vs. Credit

The essential characteristic of a monetary system is that it produces money: it creates the money supply. The essential function of a monetary system is to adapt the money supply to the community's demand for money. The adaptation is most felicitious for real economic growth when nominal money expands along the same trend line as demand for money at a stable level of commodity prices.

Money has purchasing power. When the monetary system creates money for the rest of us to hold in money balances, the monetary system can obtain something of value in exchange. That something may be gold or silver. According to some students, that something should be composite bundles of raw materials, or foreign bills of exchange, or even bricks. The monetary authority need not be instructed to buy something with the money it creates. It could give away the purchasing power its money-creation commands, perhaps in remission of taxes.

How the monetary system does dispose of this purchasing power is incidental to the primary job of creating money. Any social benefits that result from its disposal of purchasing power are a by-product of the money industry. Any monetary system must have a technique for getting rid of the money that it produces, but there are innumerable techniques, and their relative merits should be a matter of secondary concern.

Our monetary system takes gold and silver from the community, but these purchases exhaust only a fraction of the purchasing power that creation of money puts at the system's disposal. A much larger fraction is spent on securities —in "making loans" and "granting credits." The by-product of our monetary system is credit.

I cannot emphasize too strongly that "credit" is a by-product. I cannot emphasize too strongly that it is an optional by-product. Congress willing, our monetary system need not be an investor in consumer credit, business loans, mortgages, and Treasury debt. It need not be staffed with loan and investment committees. It could be staffed with commodity specialists who would fill warehouses with goods rather than portfolios with bonds and notes.

The Congress, the Federal Reserve Board, and the Treasury have been preoccupied with the by-product of our monetary system. Their correct course would have been to prescribe and administer rules of growth in the amount of money balances, then to tackle the lesser issue of what to do with the fallout of purchasing power. The course they have chosen, and still pursue, is to prescribe and administer rules for disposition of purchasing power on securities. As they see it, the money supply is the by-product of their operations, and the monetary system should create as much or as little as is necessary for "accommodating commerce and business" with credit and for maintaining "sound credit conditions." Our monetary management has been credit-minded, not money-minded.

The Federal Reserve Act bristles with injunctions upon the monetary system to grant this kind of credit and not that kind. Be open-handed with agriculture and starve the stock market. The Board concerns itself with proliferating details of *credit* granted to government, business, and consumers. Quality and quantity of credit are its operating criteria. During its tenure in monetary management, the Treasury falls in line with the same tradition, fitting policy to the alleged requirements of government as borrower rather than to the requirements of the community as holders and users of money. When Board and Treasury disagree, the points of contention are the quantity, quality, and terms of credit.

The Federal Reserve Act is not the constitution of a monetary system. A new Act should be prepared, in two sections. Section I would declare the rule of growth in money balances. Section II would specify disposition of the purchasing power that growth in money balances provides to the monetary system, and its preamble would state unambiguously that Section II is subsidiary to Section I.

Laymen often suspect some perversity in monetary affairs, and rightly so. The goal of a monetary system should be literally to create the right amount of money balances. What the system does with the money is secondary. For the rest of us, coming into possession of purchasing power is presumably a means, and the end we work for is the intelligent use of purchasing power. The monetary system is on the other side of the Looking Glass.

The Demand Standard in Action

By the rule of the Demand Standard, the nominal supply of money would be increased at a constant rate compounded annually. The rate would be adjusted only with Congressional assent, since full and free debate on the matter of long-run price inflation or deflation is no less important than full and free debate on such issues as tax burdens or labor policy or foreign aid.

The technical procedures of adding to the stock of money should be no more difficult to establish than the procedures of extracting tax payments from the community for subsequent spending under the government budget. Monetary expansion could be a daily, weekly, or monthly "spending" by the monetary system. It could be adapted to seasonal instabilities in demand for money balances.

Demand for money would grow parallel with the money supply in the long run, but its growth line would rise and fall in shorter periods. In each recession, the combination of an increasing money supply and a decreasing demand for money would generate excess supply of money. In each cyclic boom, the combination of increasing money supply and still more rapidly increasing demand for money would generate a shortage in money. Both recession and boom would call forth automatically the kind of imbalance between supply of and demand for money that is cyclically corrective. No one has a principle for doing any better by discretionary means.

On various pretexts, each important user of "credit" would be able to make an eloquent case for some expansion of the money supply in his behalf. The Treasury would request support of new issues. Agriculture would expect credit accommodation for crop movements. Business, large or small, would cry out its need for "capital," and consumers would remember when banks courted their demands for loan funds to spend on cars, houses, and appliances. No sympathy should be wasted on any of these complaints, because giving in to it would mean a demonstrably inflationary acceleration in the growth rate of money.

It is no more difficult to administer orderly growth in money than disorderly growth. Every banker is more than a little proud of his ability to turn down credit applications. The automaton of the Demand Standard can be taught to say "no" to any demand upon the monetary system that would violate the basic rule of growth in means of payment.

ANOTHER BUILT-IN STABILIZER

This country takes pride in its built-in stabilizers, the economic balance-wheels that automatically limit our deviations from normal growth. The stabilizers are automatically sensitized to economic instability and go into action against it without forethought, plan, or discretion. It is not a radical proposal that monetary control should be added to the list of self-activating countermeasures against disturbances in the growth process. Two lines of argument favor the proposal. One is that discretionary control of money supply has done badly. The other is that stable growth in money contributes to stable growth in other economic dimensions.

Discretionary Monetary Management Has Had Its Day

On the evidence of our monetary experience since 1914, American money management has not been a success. Over the long period, the money supply M has been inefficiently balanced against money demand $P(kT)$ at relatively stable prices. The long run casts its shadow over shorter periods. In the 1930's the long run had been deflationary, and the mood of deflation restrained short-run recoveries. As we see it now, the long run has been inflationary, and the mood of inflation permeates short-run expectations. There is an hypothesis that chronic inflation is partly to blame for one paradox of the 1957–1958 recession. The paradox is that prices have run uphill against the gravity of deflation. Perhaps the gravity of long-run inflation has exerted the stronger pull.

Our monetary managers have not succeeded in the cyclical short run. Students of business cycles fail to find convincing evidence that business cycles have shortened in duration since 1914. They find considerable evidence that cycles have become more violent, with amplitude of movement increased. I indicated earlier that monetary management has not been delicately attuned to cyclical turning points. It has missed the turns when monetary policy might have been most effective in damping instability.

Our monetary managers have not sensed the need of a growing economy for stability of monetary expectations. The deeds of management have cultivated alternately expectations of inflation and expectations of deflation. As for words, the notion has developed somehow that the monetary authority is privileged to behave as a benevolent despot; that the authority may mask its plans and policies and neglect to advise the community of its plans and intentions; that the community's prospect concerning the balance of supply and demand for money should be confused and uncertain.

If any form of policy should be explicit, out in the open for all to see, it is monetary policy. There should be certainty of price inflation or certainty of price deflation rather than doubt concerning the monetary atmosphere in which economic plans will materialize. Uncertainty is an impediment to growth. It depresses rational investment, defers gains in productivity, and contributes to the scarcities that policy is supposed to remedy.

The Positive Case for Automatic Monetary Control

The case for automatic control does not rest solely on disillusionment with discretionary control. There are six principal ways in which continuous and stable growth in money can increase the probability of growth in real output at a relatively high rate with minimal perturbations.

1. Stable growth in money lays the foundation for a solvent and efficient payments mechanism. In recurrent inflation, bank capital is sharply reduced relative to bank assets and deposits. Each deflation undermines bank capital through deterioration in asset quality. Our own banking system is propped upright, at public expense, by various devices that are presumed to be adequate substitutes for private investment in banking. Each of these devices has originated during violent movements in the money supply.

2. Stable growth in money supplied and demanded removes one hazard of private or governmental economic planning. That is uncertainty about the length of the monetary yardstick that planners use to measure prospective costs and revenues. Our own monetary system provides us with a yardstick, the value of the dollar, that has been shrinking for sixty years. Steady shrinkage at a constant rate is tolerable and certainly not as damaging to the planning process as shrinkage by fits and starts. Our yardstick has been rubberized, stretching out in each deflation and snapping back in each bout we have with inflation.

3. Stable growth in money avoids the inflations that distort the form of real capital accumulation, and it relieves the economic system of the interruptions in capital formation that result when deflation is applied as the remedy for inflation. Deflation does not undo damage done by inflation: it compounds the damage. During inflation savings are used wastefully on capital projects that are made to seem worthwhile by advancing prices. During deflation savings are destroyed by underemployment of men and resources. Savings misapplied or lost are never recoverable.

4. Stable growth in money and stability in the price level create a favorable environment for flexible individual prices and price relationships. General price deflation results in specific price rigidities, usually in the form of price floors. It invites combination in restraint of price adjustments downward. General price inflation produces its own crop of controlled or administered prices. The controls may be ceilings imposed by buyers or escalators dictated by sellers. Flexibility of the price level promotes rigidity of price relationships. Since a private-enterprise society relies upon flexible price relationships to allocate resources and guide demands, flexible price levels reduce its growth potential.

5. Stable growth of money and stability in the price level diminish social conflict. Deflation in the last century was politically and socially divisive. Infla-

tion in this century has helped to cleave the population into pressure groups. Any pronounced swing in the price level incites an organized March on Washington and concessions to noisy claimants for special advantage. When price levels are on the move, rational competition of the market place loses out to passionate competition for political leverage.

6. Steady growth in money contributes to development of orderly financial arrangements throughout the community. Deflation creates its distinctive pattern of debt, financial assets, and financial institutions. Inflation gives rise to a different pattern. Debtors are affected by a consideration that should not occur to them— the chance of windfall gain by inflation, of windfall loss by deflation. Creditors pick and choose their financial assets not solely according to debtors' real productivity but also according to debtors' vulnerability to unstable price levels. Loanable funds are allocated inefficiently among borrowers through a financial mechanism that is unduly intricate and expensive.

Stable growth in money minimizes financial distractions in the growth process. Stop-and-go growth in money, dignified as "monetary management," is a nervous tic in the economic system that diverts to finance attention and resources that should be spent on real aspects of development. Money is at its best when it is unobtrusive, its supply increasing according to a firm rule that is known to everyone.

AN INNING FOR THE OPPOSITION

It is not too partisan to say much less about the con's of automatic money than about the pro's. The principle of "look-Ma-no-hands" in money management has been debated so often that the critics have their brief well in hand. I shall tip off a few of their points simply to warn readers that there are two sides of the issue.

Objection 1

There is no one infallible rule of monetary growth. Since any single standard will not do, we must entrust our monetary fate to authority. It will deduce, in frequent conclave of its experts, the community's need for money and turn the money tap to just the right volume. Money is a mystery, and the layman should delegate its management to the expert.

Rejoinder

There is no expert in money management. Neither of our money-management teams, the Treasury or the Board, has earned the accolade of public confidence. Both teams have *expertise* in credit-management, but that is a different matter.

No one can measure the community's "need for money"—the quantity demanded at a stable price level in a growing economy—on a day-to-day or even month-to-month basis. There is no clear channel of communication from public to monetary authority that reports growth in demand for money $P(kT)$ so that growth in supply can be in continuous balance with it. The balance of supply with demand for *money* is not improved when it is the practice of the authority to study demand for the wrong thing—for *credit*.

Objection 2

The first half-century of our experiences with discretionary management has not been a fair test. It has been distorted by two world wars and their aftermath of crisis and disaster. The Treasury and the Board have done remarkably well under the circumstances. In a tranquil world the Federal Reserve Act would be an effective charter for sound money.

Rejoinder

Peace and tranquility are not on the horizon of the next half-century. It is just as well to take the pessimistic stand that temptations to misuse the monetary system will not diminish. There will be occasions when the Treasury will want to borrow cheaply in disregard of monetary stability. There will be occasions when the Board will think it wise to disillusion the inflationary expectations that Treasury policy has generated.

If there were clear sailing ahead, discretionary management would be good enough. With trouble in prospect, it is more important to put monetary control on automatic pilot so that mistakes in policy will not aggravate our misfortunes. When inflationary forces are rampant, we will not want them intensified by monetary expansion in behalf of cheap credit for the Treasury. When deflation is the hazard, we will not want it accelerated by the Board's precautions against the next inflation. In rough weather the wheel of the monetary system should be lashed down.

Objection 3

A growing economy has a changing pattern of credit requirements. Legitimate demands for credit rise and fall, and they come from different sectors of the community in an unpredictable rotation. There must be a flexible program of credit control, and a central management of credit that is alert to satisfy legitimate demands while discouraging speculation, to segregate credit of high quality from credit of low quality, to smooth out discontinuities on credit markets, and to encourage development of credit facilities.

Rejoinder

Granted that credit management by the banking system is an important resource-allocation function in the United States economy, the linkage of money with credit is an historical accident. Credit is one of various possible uses for the purchasing power that the monetary system commands as it increases the money supply. Whatever the use may be, disposing of the monetary system's purchasing power is incidental to the process of creating money.

The Credit Standard of money management, written into the Federal Reserve Act and administered by Treasury and Board, is a built-in destabilizer of economic activity. The community's demands upon the monetary system for credit grow quantitatively and improve qualitatively in each cyclic boom. They shrink in volume and deteriorate in quality during each cyclic relapse. The effect of linking the money supply to the cyclic yo-yo of credit demand is to intensify cycles.

Real growth is measured in terms of goods. It is not measured in terms of credit. In guiding real growth, monetary expansion should have the direct impact on markets for goods that fiscal policy has. Monetary policy is not committed by any Law of Nature to work its effects upon goods only after a detour through the markets for credit. Monetary policy yields perverse results on markets for goods when the impression develops, as it has in this country, that the credit detour is the end of the line for monetary policy.

In earlier phases of American economic growth, credit markets were embryonic. Then the banking system necessarily wore two hats, as supplier of money and as supplier of credit. Now the credit markets have matured, and there are efficient channels outside of the banking system for the flow of funds from saving to investment in real capital. Now the monetary system can attend to its essential function of supplying money.

Objection 4

The Demand Standard is provincial. It would isolate the American economy from world markets, raising a domestic rule of monetary growth to a pedestal above the principle of international economic cooperation. In view of this country's responsibility for stable growth internationally, self-interest in monetary policy is a luxury we cannot afford.

Rejoinder

American monetary policy has not abided by the rules of an international standard since 1914. The national gold stock has been a buffer between money here and money abroad. On the record the Credit Standard has been autarchic.

Sawtooth growth in the money supply of this country indicates our immaturity as London's successor to the role of international central bank. If a stable dollar is to be the anchor of a stable pound, peso, franc, yen, or piastre, rates of growth in the supply of dollars must vary no more between such extremes as *plus* 20 per cent and *minus* 10 per cent. Under our present rules of monetary management, we are announcing that we do not choose to run for the job that was London's for a century. Under an automatic rule, there would be less incentive for our allies to work out their own regional monetary coalitions.

IN CONCLUSION

Monetary economics has been dormant for two decades. Other aspects of economic analysis have left it far behind. It is so becalmed in an intellectual doldrum that no gentle breeze of inquiry can stir it. A lively storm of controversy may raise the prestige of monetary economics as an intellectual discipline, and it can do no harm to the prestige of the Federal Reserve as an instrument of social welfare if its prestige is deserved. The present paper is a bid for the active interchange of views that may restore vitality to thinking about money.

16

The Channels
of Monetary Policy

This statement presents a brief, but
careful, analysis of the channels of effect
of monetary policy on the economy.
Note the complex issues involved and
the uncertainty which exists as to the size
and timing of some of the effects.

*Franco Modigliani is Professor of Finance
and Economics at Massachusetts
Institute of Technology.*

FRANCO MODIGLIANI

EFFECTS ON AGGREGATE DEMAND

Monetary policy may be expected to influence directly certain components of aggregate demand through two main mechanisms which we
may label respectively the "inducement" and the "availability" mechanism.

By changing interest rates and other terms on which funds are available, such as length of loan and provision of security, monetary policy
increases or decreases the rate at which the public wishes to acquire
funds—by borrowing, new equity issues, or liquidation of the portfolio of
intangible assets—to be spent on the acquisition of newly produced fiscal
assets. The main types of expenditures that one would expect to be affected
are: investments in plant and equipment, and inventories, residential
construction, capital outlays of state and local government, and consumers' expenditures for major durables. The sum of these items—which
may be labeled domestic capital formation—constitute a very large fraction of aggregate demand, and this fraction in turn affects the remaining
major components of GNP, other consumers' expenditures, via the income
they generate.

There are considerable divergences of views between economists as to
the quantitative effects of variations in the terms on which funds are
available on the rate of spending and about the stability of these effects;
and views have also tended to change over time. Nor is this an issue on
which evidence can be easily brought to bear, as is obvious from the

Reprinted by permission of the author.

fact that the crude association between interest rates and the rate of investment tends to be positive rather than negative: both interest rates and investments tend to be high at high rates of activity and low in depression. This positive association does not imply of course that a high cost of funds stimulates, and a low cost retards, investments spending, but reflects instead the fact that, over time, there occur substantial changes in the prospective profitability of investment in physical assets, and hence in the demand schedule relating the desired rate of investment to the cost of funds. Hence, even though this schedule may have a negative slope, shifts over time in the position of the schedule, coupled with an inelastic supply of investible funds, will cause interest rates and the rate of investment to tend to move in the same direction. In order to isolate the effect, if any, of the cost of funds on investment activity it is necessary to isolate and control the other forces causing shift in the profitability of investments.

Despite these difficulties a good many careful empirical studies carried out in recent years have seemed, by and large, to agree on the following two conclusions: (1) that domestic capital formation is strongly affected by factors other than the cost of funds, such as the relation between prospective demand for output and available capacity, but (2) that, given these other factors, the rate of investment is also significantly affected by interest rates, the only dimension of the cost of capital which can be readily measured from available data. Thus, just to cite a few of the most recent studies, Solow and Kareken in a study for the Commission on Money and Credit have found that the rate of new orders for machinery responds to variations in bond yields, a fall of 10 per cent in yields tending to result in an increase of orders of about 4 per cent, and that similarly the rate of investment in manufacturers' inventories tends to increase with a fall in the loan rate. Maisel, among others, has shown a similar effect of interest rates on residential construction. DeLeeuw has found an appreciable effect of long-term interest rates on investment in fixed plant and equipment. His results have been confirmed by a more recent study of Resek, carried out under the auspices of the Social Science Research Council with financial support of the Board of Governors, which finds clear indication of at least some interest rates effects on the rate of investment of twelve out of thirteen individual manufacturing industries studied. In the majority of industries a 10 per cent reduction in the interest rate appears to generate an expansion of the rate of investment larger than 10 per cent, in some instances as large as 30 per cent to 40 per cent. Resek also finds a positive association between the rate of investment and stock prices, though the precise interpretation of this result still remains to be clarified.

However, in every instance, the effects on the level of output tend to occur with non-negligible lags. Thus Maisel finds that housing starts respond to changes in short-term interest rates six to twelve months earlier, an average lag of nine months. And, though Solow and Kareken find that new orders for machinery respond fairly promptly to changes in bond yields, the effect of new orders on the rate of machinery production occurs only rather gradually. Similarly, Resek's results suggest that changes in the bond yields exert their maximum influence on the rate of investment about one year later. To this expenditure lag one must add the lag intervening between changes in the policy variables directly controlled by the monetary authority, such as bank reserves, and to some extent short-term market rates and changes in the long-term rates or in rates charged by banks on business loans, a lag on which little systematic information is presently available. There is also a dearth of studies concerning the quantitative effect of cost of funds on state and local expenditures or the order of magnitude of the lags involved.

In summary the fragmentary evidence available seems to confirm the existence of significant inducement effects of variation in the cost of funds, but also indicates that these effects tend to occur but gradually in time. The lag intervening before the levers controlled by monetary policy have exercised most of their effects may be substantial, extending perhaps even beyond one year.

The other route through which monetary policy is likely to affect aggregate demand is "availability," or direct credit rationing. At least to some extent banks and other financial intermediaries may endeavor to achieve a balance between the demand for credit and the flow of funds available to them for credit extension by recourse to some form of direct rationing, rather than by endeavoring to change the demand for credit by appropriate changes in its cost. Through this route a reduction in bank reserves—or in the rate of expansion of reserves—may result in a corresponding reduction in the flow of bank credit without significant changes in interest rate or other terms and hence in the demand for credit—and conversely for an expansion of reserves. In general, of course, a contraction of reserves in the face of an unchanged demand (or failure to expand reserves in the face of a growing demand) is likely to be accompanied by some rise in market rates as some demanders of funds attempt to tap directly credit markets and as banks and other intermediaries endeavor to liquidate part of their portfolio of marketable securities to increase loans to customers. However, such increases are to a large extent an effect and symptom rather than the direct cause of the reduced flow of credit. Similarly an expansion of reserves in the face of an unchanged demand may result in part in a larger flow of loans to customers as banks tend to satisfy a larger share of the existing demand, even without a significant change in interest rates; though, once more, some fall in interest rates is likely to occur as banks also expand their demand for marketable securities. Note further that the initial expansion by banks, by increasing capital formation and hence income, will in turn tend to expand the flow of saving to other financial institutions enabling them in turn to reduce credit rationing.

It must be readily acknowledged that our inferences about the modus operandi of the availability mechanism is largely based on speculation, casual observation of behavior, and more or less informed guesses, as quantitative evidence amenable to systematic analysis and tests is largely non-existent and extremely hard to assemble and use. For one thing, it is extremely hard to draw the line between refusal of credit (formal or informal) arising from true credit rationing and that arising from failure of customers to meet justified standard of credit-worthiness. One would conjecture, however, that in so far as this type of mechanism is operating, the lags involved would be appreciably smaller than those connected with the inducement mechanism; and also that the credit rationing might be more effective in holding down effective demand in the face of a strong potential demand than in expanding demand in the face of a dwindling potential demand. Indeed, it is quite conceivable that, beyond some point, further expansion of reserves may produce little direct availability effects and may largely spend itself in pressing down market rates, which of course can still eventually lead to expansive inducement effects.

17

A New Era
for the Economy

This brief statement presents data on
the state of the national economy in early
1965, the time of the controversy
reported in the following two statements.

**FIRST NATIONAL CITY BANK
OF NEW YORK**

A "NEW ERA" FOR THE ECONOMY?

The strength and longevity of the advance led the Council of Economic
Advisers last month to term this the beginning of "a new era" in the
economic annals of the United States—not unmindful of the echoes of
the Twenties which that phrase evokes. Nevertheless, two facts stand out:
postwar cycles have been appreciably milder than those before World
War II, and the latest expansion has been remarkably durable.

The upper panel of the first chart illustrates how the fluctuations in
the past twenty years have been much smaller than the severe swings between World War I and World War II. Since 1946, annual figures on
the gross national product in current prices have registered a year-to-year
decline only twice—in 1949 and in 1954. Both times the dip was less than
one per cent. (Quarterly data have, of course, shown additional and somewhat greater fluctuations.) In contrast, during the interwar period the
economy suffered not only the 46 per cent drop in GNP during the Great
Depression but also contractions of 24 per cent in 1921 and 6 per cent in
1938, as well as several lesser setbacks.

The lower panel, in constant 1964 prices, shows that fluctuations in
GNP during the interwar period appear less abrupt when adjusted for
the wide swings in prices. But the cycles were still more pronounced than
those during the last two decades. Both panels demonstrate clearly the

From *Monthly Economic Letter,* June 1965, published by First National City Bank.
Reprinted by permission.

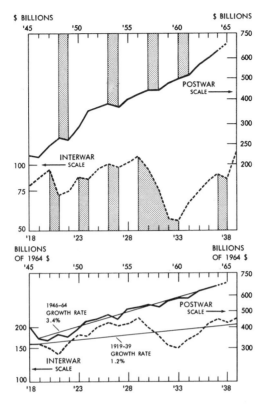

Gross National Product in Current and Constant Prices Postwar Period vs. Interwar Period

Note: Ratio scales to show proportionate changes. Shaded areas represent periods of business contraction. Growth trends fitted to data for 1919–39 and 1946–64.

greater rate of growth in the twenty years since World War II than in the corresponding period after the First World War.

One factor in this better showing is fairly obvious. Between Armistice Day in 1918 and the German invasion of Poland in 1939, a period of 250 months, the economy was on the down grade—in the contraction phase of the cycle—for 106 months or 42 per cent of the time. Since V-J Day, in contrast, only 44 of the 238 months have been characterized by contraction; in 82 per cent of the postwar period we have experienced expansion.

In a much more detailed comparison of cyclical patterns,[1] Julius Shiskin, Chief Economic Statistician of the Bureau of the Census, finds:

> There has been a dramatic improvement in economic stability during the post-World War II period. . . . The recorded history of business cycles does not show an earlier sequence of four or even three business cycles with such small average monthly changes.

[1] "The Current Expansion in Historical Perspective," *Business Cycle Developments*, Bureau of the Census, U. S. Department of Commerce, January 1965, pp. 55–79.

This improvement in stability has been accomplished "with, at worst, no change in the rate of long-term economic growth."

Economic performance from the end of the war through the early 1950s was largely influenced by the filling of postponed wants of consumers. This factor was extended through the mid-1950s by the Korean War. Apart from this influence, the better performance of the economy in the past 20 years is often attributed to Federal Government actions under the mandate of the Employment Act of 1946 and to the automatic stabilizers contained in social insurance programs and the tax structure. Because these governmental influences are easily visible and usually in the right direction, there is a tendency to overstress their importance while neglecting other basic influences. Accordingly, whenever a pause or slackening in economic activity is expected, it is feared that unless some new form of governmental stimulus is found and applied without delay the economy will slide into recession. This view underestimates the strength of the inherent stability and growth tendencies of the economy.

In June, 1965, the Chairman of the
Federal Reserve Board warned about
"disquieting similarities between our
present prosperity and the fabulous '20's,"
and explained his warning at length.
This speech set off a major controversy
over the soundness of the prosperity and
its similarities to conditions just before
the great depression of the 1930's.

18

Does Monetary
History Repeat Itself?

*William McChesney Martin has been
Chairman of the Federal Reserve Board
since 1952.*

WILLIAM McCHESNEY MARTIN

When economic prospects are at their brightest, the dangers of com-
placency and recklessness are greatest. As our prosperity proceeds on its
record-breaking path, it behooves every one of us to scan the horizon of
our national and international economy for danger signals so as to be ready
for any storm.

Some eminent observers have recently compared the present with the
period preceding the breakdown of the interwar economy, and have
warned us of the threats of another Great Depression. We should take
these warnings seriously enough to inquire into their merits and to try
to profit in the future from the lessons of the past.

And indeed, we find disquieting similarities between our present prosperity and the fabulous twenties.

Then, as now, there had been virtually uninterrupted progress for seven
years. And if we disregard some relatively short though severe fluctuations,
expansion had been underway for more than a generation—the two
longest stretches of that kind since the advent of the industrial age; and
each period had been distorted in its passage by an inflationary war and
post-war boom.

Then, as now, prosperity had been concentrated in the fully developed
countries, and within most of these countries, in the industrialized sectors
of the economy.

Then, as now, these was a large increase in private domestic debt; in
fact, the expansion in consumer debt arising out of both residential mort-

Address before the Commencement Day Luncheon of the Alumni Federation of
Columbia University, June 1, 1965.

gages and instalment purchases has recently been much faster than in the twenties.

Then, as now, the supply of money and bank credit and the turnover of demand deposits had been continuously growing; and while in the late twenties this growth had occurred with little over-all change in gold reserves, this time monetary expansion has been superimposed upon a dwindling gold reserve.

Then, as now, the Federal Reserve had been accused of lack of flexibility in its monetary policy: of insufficient ease in times of economic weakness and of insufficient firmness in times of economic strength.

Then, as now, the world had recovered from the wartime disruption of international trade and finance, and convertibility of the major world currencies at fixed par values had been restored for a number of years.

Then, as now, international indebtedness had risen as fast as domestic debt; recently, in fact, American bank credits to foreigners and foreign holdings of short-term dollar assets have increased faster than in the closing years of the earlier period.

Then, as now, the payments position of the main reserve center—Britain then and the United States now—was uneasy, to say the least; but again, our recent cumulative payments deficits have far exceeded Britain's deficits of the late twenties.

Then, as now, some countries had large and persistent payments surpluses and used their net receipts to increase their short-term reserves rather than to invest in foreign countries.

Then, as now, the most important surplus country, France, had just decided to convert its official holdings of foreign exchange into gold, regardless of the effects of its actions on international liquidity.

Then, as now, there were serious doubts about the appropriate levels of some existing exchange rate relationships, leading periodically to speculative movements of volatile short-term funds.

And most importantly, then as now, many government officials, scholars, and businessmen were convinced that a new economic era had opened, an era in which business fluctuations had become a thing of the past, in which poverty was about to be abolished, and in which perennial economic progress and expansion were assured.

If some of these likenesses seem menacing, we may take comfort in important differences between the present and the interwar situation.

The distribution of our national income now shows less disparity than in the earlier period; in particular, personal incomes, and especially wages and salaries, have kept pace with corporate profits, and this has reduced the danger of investment expanding in excess of consumption needs.

Perhaps related to that better balance, the increase in stock market credit now has been much smaller.

Instead of a gradual decline in wholesale prices and stability in consumer prices, there has now been stability in wholesale prices though consumer prices have been creeping up.

The worst defects in the structure of commercial and investment banking and of business seem to have been corrected—although we are time and again reminded of our failure to eliminate all abuses.

The potentialities of monetary and fiscal policies are, we hope, better understood—although the rise in government expenditures even in times of advancing prosperity threatens to make it difficult to be still more expansionary should a serious decline in private business activity require it.

In spite of the rise in the international flow of public and private credit and investment, business abroad appears in general to be less dependent upon American funds. The recent restraint on the outflow of United States capital has had little effect on business activity abroad, in contrast to the paralyzing effect of the cessation of United States capital outflows in the late twenties.

While the cold war makes for sources of friction absent in the twenties, we are no longer suffering from the cancer of reparations and war debts.

We have learned the lessons taught by the failure of trade and exchange restrictions, and of beggar-my-neighbor policies in general, although the temptation to backslide is ever present.

We have become aware of our responsibility for helping those less developed countries that seem willing and able to develop their economies—although the poor countries still are not becoming rich as fast as the rich countries are becoming richer.

The International Monetary Fund has proved to be a valuable aid to a better working of the international payments system.

A network of international, regional, and bilateral institutions and arrangements has reduced the danger of lack of international financial communication.

And finally, the experience of the twenties has strengthened the resolution of all responsible leaders, businessmen and statesmen alike, never again to permit a repetition of the disasters of the Great Depression.

But while the spirit is willing, the flesh, in the form of concrete policies, has remained weak. With the best intentions, some experts seem resolved to ignore the lessons of the past.

Economic and political scientists still argue about the factors that converted a stock-exchange crash into the worst depression in our history. But on one point they are agreed: the disastrous impact of the destruction of the international payments system that followed the British decision to devalue sterling in September 1931. At that time, sterling was the kingpin of the world payments system, exactly as the dollar is today. While changes in the par values of other peripheral currencies affected mainly or sorely the devaluing countries themselves, the fate of sterling shook the entire world.

This is not wisdom of hindsight. Only a few weeks before the fateful decision was taken, the most eminent economist of the day stated that "for a country in the special circumstances of Great Britain the disadvantages [of devaluation] would greatly outweigh the advantages," and he concurred with his colleagues in rejecting the idea. His name was John Maynard Keynes.

And soon afterwards, another great British economist, Lionel Robbins, declared that "no really impartial observer of world events can do other than regard the abandonment of the Gold Standard by Great Britain as a catastrophe of the first order of magnitude." This was long before the final consequences of that step had become apparent—the political weakening of the West which followed its economic breakdown and which contributed to the success of the Nazi revolution in Germany, and thus eventually to the outbreak of the Second World War and to the emergence of Communism as an imminent threat to world order.

As if neither Keynes, the founder of the anti-classical school of economics, nor Robbins, the leader of the neo-classical school, ever had spoken, some Keynesian and neo-classicist economists—fortunately with little support at home but with encouragement from a few foreign observers—are urging us to follow the British example of 1931 and to act once more in a way that would destroy a payments system based on the fixed gold value of the world's leading currency. In doing so, they not only show that they have not learned from monetary history; they also impute to our generation even less wisdom than was shown in the interwar period.

The British Government in 1931, and the U. S. Administration in 1933, can rightly be accused of underestimating the adverse international effects of the devaluation of the pound and the dollar. But at least they had some plausible domestic grounds for their actions. They were confronted with a degree of unemployment that has hardly ever been experienced either before or after. They were confronted with disastrously falling prices, which made all fixed-interest obligations an intolerable burden on domestic and international commerce. They were confronted with a decline in international liquidity, which seemed to make recovery impossible.

Neither Keynes nor Robbins have denied that, from a purely domestic point of view, there was some sense in devaluation. In the United States of 1933, one worker out of four was unemployed; industrial production was little more than half of normal; farm prices had fallen to less than half of their 1929 level; exports and imports stood at one-third of their 1929 value; capital issues had practically ceased. In such a situation, any remedy, however questionable, seemed better than inaction.

In the Britain of 1931, things were not quite as bleak as in the United States of 1933; but fundamentally, the economic problems were similar. Ever since 1925, the British economy had failed to grow, and by 1931, one out of five workers had become unemployed, exports—far more important for the British economy than for our own—had declined by nearly one-half, and most observers believed that over-valuation of the British pound was largely responsible for all these ills. Can anybody in good faith find any similarity between our position of today and our position of 1933, or even the British position of 1931?

In 1931 and 1933, an increase in the price of gold was recommended in order to raise commodity prices. Today, a gold price increase is recommended as a means to provide the monetary support for world price stability. In 1931 and 1933, an increase in the price of gold was recommended in order to combat deflation; today it is recommended in effect as a means to combat inflation. In 1931 and 1933, an increase in the price of gold was recommended as a desperate cure for national ills regardless of its disintegrating effect on world commerce; today it is recommended as a means to improve integration of international trade and finance. Can there be worse confusion?

True, most advocates of an increase in the price of gold today would prefer action by some international agency or conference to unilateral action of individual countries. But no international agency or conference could prevent gold hoarders from getting windfall profits; could prevent those who hold a devalued currency from suffering corresponding losses; could prevent central banks from feeling defrauded if they had trusted in the repeated declarations of the President of the United States and of the spokesmen of United States monetary authorities and kept their reserves in dollars rather than in gold. To this day, the French, Belgian, and Netherlands central banks have not forgotten that the 1931 devaluation of sterling wiped out their capital; and much of the antagonism of those countries against the use of the dollar as an international reserve asset should be traced to the experience of 1931 rather than to anti-American feelings or mere adherence to outdated monetary theories.

But most importantly, no international agency or conference could prevent a sudden large increase in the gold price from having inflationary consequences for those countries that hoarded gold, and deflationary consequences for those that did not. And the gold-holding countries are precisely those whose economies are least in need of an inflationary stimulus since they are most prosperous—not prosperous because they are holding gold, but holding gold because they are prosperous; in contrast, those that do not hold gold are most in need of further expansion. Hence the inflationary and deflationary effects of an increase in the price of gold would be most inequitably and most uneconomically distributed among nations.

If we were to accept another sort of advice given by some experts, we might repeat not the mistakes of 1931–33 but those of earlier years. We are told that a repetition of the disaster of the Great Depression could be averted only, or at least best, by returning to the principles of the so-called classical gold standard. Not only should all settlements in international transactions between central banks be made in gold; but also the domestic monetary policy of central banks should be oriented exclusively to the payments balance, which means to changes in gold reserves. Whenever gold flows out, monetary policy should be tightened; whenever it flows in, it should be eased.

This is not the place to discuss whether this pure form of gold-standard theory has ever been translated into practice. I doubt that any central bank has ever completely neglected domestic considerations in its monetary policy. And conversely, we do not need to adhere to an idealized version of the gold standard in order to agree that considerations of international payments balance need to play a large role in monetary policy decisions. But even strict adherence to gold-standard principles would not guarantee international payments equilibrium. As a great American economist, John H. Williams, put it in 1937:

> For capital movements, the gold standard is not a reliable corrective mechanism. . . . With capital the most volatile item in the balance of payments, it is apt to dominate and to nullify any corrective effects which might otherwise result from the gold standard process of adjustment. . . . It is surely not a coincidence that most booms and depressions, in the nineteenth century as well as in the twentieth, had international capital movements as one of their most prominent features.

Even countries that advocate a return to gold-standard practices do not practice what they preach. Gold reserves of some Continental European countries have been rising strongly and continuously for many years, and according to the rules, these countries should follow a clearly expansionary policy. But in order to offset inflationary pressures, they have done exactly the opposite—and who is there to blame a country that wishes to assure domestic financial stability even at the expense of endangering equilibrium in international payments?

But obviously, if we permit one country to violate the rules of the gold standard in order to avert domestic inflation, we must also permit another country to violate those rules in order to avert domestic deflation and unemployment. In other words, we must agree that a country may be justified in avoiding or at least modifying a tightening of monetary policy even though its gold reserves are declining, if otherwise it were to risk precipitating or magnifying a business recession.

True, this deviation from gold-standard rules could be carried too far. Domestic developments might be taken as a pretext to avoid an unpopular monetary move, although the payments situation would seem to demand it and although the action would be unlikely to be damaging to the domestic economy. But the possibility of abuse and error is inherent in all human decision, and just as no sane observer would ascribe infallibility to the decisions of central bankers, neither should he ascribe infallibility to a set of rules. Few experts today would want to argue that it was right for the German Reichsbank in 1931, in the middle of the greatest depression that ever hit Germany, to follow the gold-standard rules by raising its discount rate to 7 per cent merely in order to stem an outflow of gold; or that it was right for our own Federal Reserve to take similar restrictive action, for the same reason, in the fall of 1931.

And just as the success of monetary policy cannot be guaranteed by an abdication of discretion in favor of preconceived gold-standard rules, it cannot be guaranteed by following the advice of those who would shift the focus of policy from national agencies to an international institution. Surely, international cooperation should be encouraged and improved whenever possible. And the functions of the International Monetary Fund might well be enlarged so as to reinforce its ability to act as an international lender of last resort and as an arbiter of international good behavior.

But no institutional change can exclude the possibility of conflicts between national and international interests in specific circumstances. Moreover, there is no reason to believe that such conflicts would necessarily be resolved more wisely, more speedily, and with less rancor and dissent if they were fought out in the governing body of some supranational bank of issue rather than by discussion and negotiation among national authorities.

It is true that such discussion and negotiation may prove fruitless and that inconsistent decisions may be taken on the national level. But similarly, lack of consensus within a supranational agency may result in a paralysis of its functions, and the effects of such paralysis could well be worse than those of inconsistent national actions.

If then we doubt the wisdom of the three most fashionable recent proposals—to increase the dollar price of gold, to return to pure gold-standard principles, or to delegate monetary policy to an international agency—what should be our position? And what is the outlook for solving present and future difficulties in international monetary relations, and thus for avoiding a repetition of the disasters of 1929–33?

In my judgment, it is less fruitful to look for institutional changes or for a semiautomatic mechanism that would guarantee perennial prosperity than to draw from interwar experience some simple lessons that could save us from repeating our worst mistakes.

First, most observers agree that to a large extent the disaster of 1929–33 was a consequence of maladjustments born of the boom of the twenties. Hence, we must continuously be on the alert to prevent a recurrence of maladjustments—even at the risk of being falsely accused of failing to realize the benefits of unbounded expansion. Actually, those of us who warn against speculative and inflationary dangers should return the charge: our common goals of maximum production, employment, and purchasing power can be realized only if we are willing and able to prevent orderly expansion from turning into disorderly boom.

Second, most observers agree that the severity of the Great Depression was largely due to the absence of prompt anti-recession measures. In part, the necessary tools for this were not then available nor were their potentialities fully understood. Today it is easy to understand where observers went wrong 35 years ago. But it is less easy to avoid a repetition of the same mistake; we always prefer to believe what we want to be true rather than what we should know to be true. Here again, we need most of all eternal vigilance. But we must also be ready to admit errors in past judgments and forecasts, and have the courage to express dissenting even though unpopular views, and to advocate necessary remedies.

Third, and most importantly, most observers agree that the severity of the Great Depression was due largely to the lack of understanding of the international implications of national events and policies. Even today, we are more apt to judge and condemn the worldwide implications of nationalistic actions taken by others than to apply the same criteria to our own decisions.

Recognition of the close ties among the individual economies of the free world leads to recognition of the need to maintain freedom of international commerce. This means not only that we must avoid the direct controls of trade and exchange that were characteristic of the time of the Great Depression. It means also that we must avoid any impairment of the value and status of the dollar, which today acts—just as sterling did until its devaluation in 1931—as a universal means of international payment between central banks as well as among individual merchants, bankers, and investors.

If the dollar is to continue to play its role in international commerce, world confidence in its stability must be fully maintained; the world must be convinced that we are resolved to eliminate the long-persistent deficit in our balance of international payments. The measures taken in accordance with the President's program of February 10, 1965, have so far been highly successful. But some of these measures are of a temporary character, and these include the efforts of the financial community to restrain voluntarily the expansion of credit to foreigners. We should not permit the initial success of these efforts to blind us against the need of permanent cure.

Some observers believe that our responsibility for maintaining the international function of the dollar puts an intolerably heavy burden on our monetary policy; that this responsibility prevents us from taking monetary measures which might be considered appropriate for solving domestic problems. I happen to disagree with that view. I believe that the interests of our national economy are in harmony with those of the international community. A stable dollar is indeed the keystone of international trade and finance; but it is also, in my judgment, the keystone of economic growth and prosperity at home.

Yet even if I were wrong in this judgment, and if indeed an occasion arose when we could preserve the international role of the dollar only at the expense of modifying our favored domestic policies—even then we would need to pay attention to the international repercussions of our actions. We must consider these international effects not because of devotion to the ideal of human brotherhood, not because we value the well-being of our neighbors more than our own. We must do so because any harm that would come to international commerce and hence to the rest of the world as a result of the displacement of the dollar would fall back on our own heads. In the present stage of economic development we could not preserve our own prosperity if the rest of the world were caught in the web of depression. Recognition of this inter-dependence gave rise to the Marshall Plan —in my judgment the greatest achievement of our post-war economic policy.

It should not have taken the Great Depression to bring these simple truths home to us. Today, as we approach the goal of the "Great Society"—to make each of our citizens a self-reliant and productive member of a healthy and progressive economic system—we can disregard these truths even less than we could a generation ago. By heeding them instead, we will have a good chance to avoid another such disaster. If monetary history were to repeat itself, it would be nobody's fault but our own.

Here a leading academic economist
challenges Chairman Martin's implied
parallel between 1965 and 1929, stressing
the major changes that have occurred
which, in his judgment, makes a
repetition of the collapse of 1929 very
unlikely. Above all, he argues that
government policy can and should help
to avoid another 1929–33.

*James Tobin is Sterling Professor of
Economics at Yale University, and was a
member of President Kennedy's Council
of Economic Advisers in 1961–63.*

19

What Is the
Lesson of 1929?

JAMES TOBIN

William McChesney Martin Jr., chairman of the Federal Reserve System since 1951, has suffered professorial attacks longer and more patiently than most officials. On June 1, he counterattacked at Columbia.

His main message—somewhat veiled but well enough understood in Wall Street—was that the country may need, soon if not now, tighter money and higher interest rates to protect its domestic economic health and its balance of payments. Here Chairman Martin takes issue with a host of critics, mainly academics, some of whom may even have infiltrated Washington. Many think that the current expansion needs further stimulus rather than sterner discipline and that the dollar's prestige abroad already receives too high priority in United States policy.

Chairman Martin reads the critics lessons from the history of the 'twenties and the Great Depression. The irony is that before 1933 Chairman Martin's intellectual and official precursors were firmly in the saddle here and in Europe. Unlike him, they did not have to accommodate or even answer heretical financial views. The mistakes they made were all their own.

A boom is a trying period for a central banker who believes, like Chairman Martin, that recesssions and depressions are inescapable retribution for the "maladjustments" of prosperity. Should he let such "excesses" develop? Or should he administer a dose of tight money? This medicine itself may turn prosperity into recession. But the doctor will always assure

From *The New Republic*, June 19, 1965, pp. 11–12. © 1965, Harrison-Blaine of New Jersey, Inc. Reprinted by permission.

his perplexed and involuntary patients that they needed it to forestall much worse suffering later.

The current expansion is especially trying. It has been proceeding for 52 months without the degree of monetary discipline the Federal Reserve became accustomed to administer in the 'fifties. Yet it is hard even for the hypersensitive antennae of the central bank to detect any maladjustments or excesses. Since February, 1961, a $150 billion expansion in total annual public and private spending has reduced unemployment from 7 to 4.5 per cent, without noticeably raising prices. In the spring of 1961 Chairman Martin told Congress that unemployment was structural, that it could not be reduced by more spending except at serious risk of bottlenecks and inflation. Similar warnings, similarly unfounded, have been repeated in orthodox financial circles at every step of the recovery. Had they been heeded, the country would have lost millions of jobs and billions of dollars in production and income.

Chairman Martin views economic expansion as a potentially explosive chain reaction, which only the tightest control prevents from running away. Some booms may merit this metaphor. But the current one seems in more danger of ending with a whimper than with a bang. To keep it going has required a succession of carefully timed and gauged stimuli—increases in federal spending, income tax cuts, and now excise reductions. "Leaning against the wind," the favorite posture of the Federal Reserve, is not an appropriate stance when the problem is to keep the wind blowing.

What is the lesson of 1929? Chairman Martin says, "to a large extent the disaster of 1929–33 was a consequence of maladjustments born of the boom of the 'twenties." More likely, the expansion of the 'twenties—non-inflationary like the present expansion—simply ran out of steam. Instead of taking action to prolong it, Chairman Martin's predecessors tightened credit and raised interest rates. Like many contemporary observers and historians, they paid too much attention to a sideshow, stock market speculation, and too little to the main ring, the real economy.

Certainly no maladjustments or overindulgences occurred in the 'twenties which preordained that a routine recession in 1929–30 should become a worldwide economic and political catastrophe. That took incredible sins of omission and commission, all justified in the name of fiscal and financial orthodoxy. In the monetary area, the worst overt sins were *raising* the discount rate in September-October, 1931 (Chairman Martin agrees this was a mistake) and in February, 1933. On both occasions, the Federal Reserve's purpose was to protect the international gold value of the dollar. Chairman Martin was telling history upside down at Columbia when he blamed the severity of the depression on *in*sufficient concern for the external status of the dollar. Recovery did not begin in the United States until Roosevelt gave recovery higher priority than the gold standard.

It is true that the position of the dollar as an international reserve currency today is analogous to the role of the pound sterling from 1925 to 1931. But the lesson of the analogy is the opposite of the one Chairman Martin draws. In 1925, through an excess of orthodox zeal and a Colonel Blimp conception of imperial prestige, Britain returned to the gold standard at the 1914 parity of sterling with gold and the dollar. This made British exports too expensive. The result, foreseen by J. M. Keynes, was unemployment, civil strife, and depression. Nor did the sacrifices imposed on the British people and their trading partners overseas save for long the gold value of the pound or London's financial prestige. Britain was forced to devalue in 1931, and then British recovery began.

Chairman Martin deplores the ensuing destruction of the international gold standard. But this was the result of the depression, not its cause. And the depression itself owed much of its severity to the British government's previous determination to give the prestige of the pound sterling absolute priority over domestic prosperity.

It is worth noting in passing that then as now France had a "strong" currency because of previous devaluations, that then as now French threats to take gold forced deflationary policies on the United States and Britain, and that then as now France took gold anyway.

This is the history to which Chairman Martin appeals in asking us to place the international "value and status of the dollar" above all other considerations of economic policy. He excoriates "some Keynesian and neo-classical economists" for wishing the United States to follow the British 1931 example. But the issue is not really devaluation. The exchange value of the dollar in the 'sixties is by no means as unrealistically high as that of the pound in the late 'twenties. The issue is whether the maintenance of gold-dollar convertibility at the present rate has an absolute priority over all other objectives of United States domestic and foreign policy. Is "going off gold" such an ultimate catastrophe, like nuclear war, that we must avoid at all costs the slightest risk of its occurrence? And if, as Chairman Martin dubiously argues, the result would be worldwide depression, should we not expect more cooperation and forbearance from our allies than we are likely to receive so long as we define the problem, as he does, as a strictly American responsibility?

Both America and the world have more to gain from steady economic progress and sustained full employment in the United States than from timid obsession with foreign confidence in the dollar. Gratifying as it is, our long economic expansion has not yet restored full employment. The social costs of a persistent shortage of jobs can be observed daily in the streets of our cities and in the demoralization of those groups, notably Negroes and teen-agers, who get jobs only when labor markets are tight. In a real sense these people—and the mayors, social workers, police and anti-poverty warriors who must struggle with their problems—are the victims of the shortcomings of fiscal and monetary policy.

The identification of prosperity with imprudent self-indulgence may have an appealing Puritan ring. But it is wholly a vicarious Puritanism, like the austerity of the international financiers who in 1931 forced the Labor government to cut the dole of the unemployed and the salaries of teachers in a vain attempt to "save" the pound. It would be criminal folly to endanger our current economic growth either by an attack on conjectural maladjustments and imagined excesses or by subservience to gold-hungry foreign central banks. As Chairman Martin says, "If monetary history were to repeat itself, it would be nobody's fault but our own."

20

The New Look in Tax and Fiscal Policy

Conflicting policy goals confront the government's economic policy makers at every turn. A leading economist suggests how we may be able to achieve apparently conflicting ends by using a proper "mix" of fiscal and monetary policies.

Paul A. Samuelson is Professor of Economics at Massachusetts Institute of Technology.

PAUL A. SAMUELSON

I

There is much talk about taxes. When I flick on the dial of my radio in the morning, I hear a Congressman quoted on how our high level of taxes is ruining the Nation or a Senator's tape-recorded alarm over the unfair burden the poor man has to carry because the administration has been favoring big business. My morning paper at breakfast brings me the view of its editor that the United States has been pursuing unsound fiscal policy for the last 25 years. Scratch the barber who cuts my hair and you find a philosopher ready to prescribe for the Nation's monetary ills.

This is as it should be. We expect sweeping statements in a democracy. We hope that out of the conflict of extreme views there will somehow emerge a desirable compromise. Yet such sweeping statements have almost no validity from a scientific, or even from a leisurely commonsense point of view: spend as little as a year going over the factual experience of American history and of other economies, devote as little as a month to calm analysis of probable cause and effect, or even spend a weekend in a good economics library—and what will you find? Will you find that there breathes anywhere in the world an expert so wise that he can tell you which of a dozen major directions of policy is unquestionably the best? You will not. Campaign oratory aside, the more assuredly a man asserts the direction along which salvation is alone to be found, the

From *Federal Tax Policy for Economic Growth and Stability:* Papers submitted by Panelists Appearing Before the Subcommittee on Tax Policy, Joint Economic Committee on the Economic Report, November 9, 1955, pp. 229–234.

more patently he advertises himself as an incompetent or a charlatan.

The plain truth is this, and it is known to anyone who has looked into the matter: The science of economics does not provide simple answers to complex social problems. It does not validate the view of the man who thinks the world is going to hell, nor the view of his fellow idiot that ours is the best of all possible tax systems.

I do not wish to be misunderstood. When I assert that economic science cannot give unequivocal answers to the big questions of policy, I do not for a moment imply that economists are useless citizens. Quite the contrary. They would indeed be useless if any sensible man could quickly infer for himself simple answers to the big policy questions of fiscal policy. No need then to feed economists while they make learned studies of the obvious. It is precisely because public policy in the tax and expenditure area is so complex that we find it absolutely indispensable to invest thousands of man-years of scholarly time in scholarly economic research in these areas.

Make no mistake about it. The arguments that we all hear every day of our lives on the burning partisan issues have in every case been shaped by economists —by economists in universities, in business, in Government, and by that rarest of all birds, the shrewd self-made economist. What economists do not know about fiscal policy turns out, on simple examination, not to be known by anyone.

II

With this necessary preamble out of the way, let me record the general views that studies have led me to, about the current state of our fiscal system. This will clear the way for a more detailed analysis of taxes and growth, taxes and stable full employment, taxes and equity, taxes and the level of public expenditure programs.

Here then are the major facts about our system as I see them.

(1) The postwar American economy is in good shape. There is nothing artificial or unsound about its underpinnings. For more than a decade we have had generally high employment opportunities. Our production efficiency has been growing at a steady rate that compares well with anything in our history or in the history of countries abroad. For all this we must, in our present-day mixed economy, be grateful to both public and private institutions.

(2) The existing structure of Federal, state, and local taxes is in its broad features highly satisfactory. Repeatedly at the polls and through all the legitimate processes of government the citizens of this Republic have indicated that they want our present type of fiscal structure—its substantial dependence at the Federal level on personal and corporate income taxes, its eclectic dependence on selective excises, on payroll levies for social security, on property and sales taxes at the local levels. If the consensus of citizens in our democracy were to be other than it is— toward less or more equalitarianism, toward less or more local autonomy—there is no reason that the careful analytic economist can see why our fiscal system is not capable of being altered in the desired direction. In other words, there is nothing in the mechanics of a modern economy which makes it impossible or difficult for the citizenry to get the kind of a tax system that they want; our tax system has plenty of give, plenty of room for adaptation and change.

All the above does not imply that we are living in a new era of perfection. The American economy now faces, and will continue to face, many tough problems, many hard decisions. And, to be sure, there are numerous imperfections, inconsistencies, and loopholes in the present tax structure; these do need improving.

What the optimistic diagnosis of the modern-day economist does contradict is the following:

(1) The view that America has long since departed from an orthodox fiscal policy and that it is only a matter of time until a grim Mother Nature exacts retribution from us for our folly in departing from the narrow line of fiscal rectitude. (This is a philosophical position that any dissenter from current trends is free to assume; but it is not a factually verifiable view about reality that dispassionate study of statistics and facts can substantiate.)

(2) The view, shared in by the extremes of both left and right wings, that our economy generally is moving in unsound directions so that we must ultimately end up in some unnamed disaster or convulsion. (In terms of business-cycle stability and efficient growth, the United States has in the last dozen years dramatically refuted the sour expectations both of those who look back on a fictitious past golden age and of collectivists who look forward to a golden age that only a revolution can usher in.)

III

Turning now to the goals of any tax system, we can ask: What tax structure will give us the most rapid rate of growth? What tax system will give us the highest current standard of living? What tax structure will make our system most immune to the ups and downs in employment and prices that make American families insecure? What tax structure will realize most closely the community's sense of fairness and equity? What tax structure will have the least distorting effects on our use of economic resources, instead of maximizing the efficiency with which we produce what our citizens most want?

Upon careful thought it will be obvious that there cannot exist a tax system which will simultaneously maximize these five quite different goals of social life.

It is easy to see that high current living standards and rapid growth of our ability to produce are conflicting ends: you have only to look at a collectivized society like the Soviet Union, which decides to sacrifice consumption levels of the current generation in favor of a crash program of industrialization; you have only to reflect that historically in the slums of Manchester working families might have lived longer in the 19th century if England and the other nations had during the industrial revolution slowed down their rates of material progress; you have only to consider the problem of conserving scarce exhaustible natural resources to realize that every society must all the time be giving up higher future resource potentials in favor of keeping current generation consumption as high as it is.

You can imagine a society that decides to devote its income in excess of the bare physiological existence level 100 per cent to capital formation. You can imagine it—but there never has been such a society. Nor would any of us want to live in such a one. It should be obvious, therefore, that no sane person would ever seek a tax program which literally maximized our rate of economic growth. (Yet how many times over the chicken a la king have we all heard speakers reiterate this nonsensical goal.) It is just as obvious that no sane person would want to maximize present living levels if this meant eating up all our capital on a consumption bender that would leave us an impoverished Nation.

There is no need to go through all the other pairs of the five listed goals to show their partial incompatibility. If we are willing to frame a tax system that strongly favors thrifty men of wealth, we may thereby be able to add to our rate of current growth; if we encourage a gentle rate of inflation, we may be able to increase the profits in the hands of the quick-reacting businessman, perhaps thereby stepping up our rate of growth. So it goes, and one could easily work through the other permutations and combinations.

But not all of our five goals are necessarily competing. Some, when you realize them, help you to realize the others. If we succeed in doing away with the great depressions that have dogged the economic record, we may thereby add to our rate of growth. If we shape a graduated-tax system that enables lower income groups to maintain minimum standards of life, we may ease the task of stabilizing business activity. If we replace distorting taxes by less distorting alternatives, the fruits of the resulting more efficient production can add to our current consumption and to our rate of progress in capital formation.

I shall not prolong the discussion of the degree to which the diverse goals of tax policy are competing or complementary. For it will turn out that we can formulate proper policies without having to measure these important, but complicated, relationships.

IV

Upon being told by the economist that it is absurd for Congress to aim at the most rapid rate of growth possible and that it is equally absurd for Congress to aim at the highest possible current level of consumption, the policymaker may be tempted to say: "I understand that. Won't you therefore as an economist advise us as to just what is the best possible compromise between these extremes?"

A good question but, unfortunately, not one that the expert economist can pretend to give a unique answer to. If he is honest, he must reply: "The American people must look into their own hearts and decide on what they consider to be the best compromise rate of growth."

Just because I have advanced degrees in economics and have written numerous esoteric works in the field, I am not thereby empowered to let my personal feelings, as to how much the present generation ought to sacrifice in favor of generations to come, become a prescription for society. It would be as presumptuous for me to offer such specific advice as to let my family's notions about dental care determine how much the typical American family ought to spend on toothpaste. But it is legitimate for me as an economist to say this: "Whatever rate of capital formation the American people want to have, the American system can, by proper choice of fiscal and monetary programs, contrive to do." This can be shown by an example.

Suppose the vast majority of the American people look into the future or across the Iron Curtain at the rate of progress of others. Suppose they decide that we ought to have a more rapid rate of capital formation and technological development than we have been having recently. Then the economist knows this can be brought into being (*a*) by means of an expansionary monetary policy that makes investment funds cheaper and easier to get. Admittedly, such an expanded investment program will tend, if it impinges on an employment situation that is already full and on a price level that is already stationary, to create inflationary price pressures and overfull employment—unless something is done about it. What would have to be done about this inflationary pressure? Clearly (*b*) a tight fiscal policy would be needed to offset the expansionary monetary policy: By raising taxes relative to expenditure, we would reduce the share of consumption out of our full employment income, releasing in this way the real resources needed for investment. (It should be unnecessary to go through the reverse programs which would be called for if the national decision were to slow down the rate of capital formation as compared to that of recent years.)

From these remarks it will be clear that economic science is not only neutral as to the question of the desired rate of capital accumulation—it is also neutral as to the ability of the economy to realize any decided-on rate of capital formation.

I repeat: With proper fiscal and monetary policies, our economy can have full employment and whatever rate of capital formation and growth it wants.

V

The optimistic doctrine that our economy can have stability and the rate of growth it wants may seem rather novel. Perhaps even a little shocking. But there are worse surprises yet to come.

The reader may think that my argument rests on something like the following reasoning:

Suppose that political party R is more concerned with progress than political party D, which shows a greater concern for the little man, with security, and with current consumption. Then if the Nation gives its approval to the general policy goals of R, the Government will have to change its emphasis away from reducing taxes on individuals—particularly rapid-spending lower-income people; and it will have to change its emphasis toward reducing taxes on business, in an attempt to bolster the incentives toward investment. In short, it is by changing the qualitative pattern of taxation, by sacrificing equity to incentive, that the community succeeds in getting higher levels of capital formation when it desires such higher levels.

I predict that much of the testimony before this subcommittee will proceed along these lines. Certainly much of the political discussion of the last three years, when it has had the courage to be frank, has been along these lines.

But this is not at all the train of thought that I wish to emphasize in my testimony. I want to cap the daring doctrine that an economy can have the rate of capital information it wants with a doctrine that may seem even more shocking. Naturally, I cannot here develop all of the underlying reasoning, nor give all the needed qualifications. But I do in advance want to stress the earnestness with which I put it forward, and to underline that it does spring from careful use of the best modern analyses of economics that scholars here and abroad have over the years been able to attain. The doctrine goes as follows:

A community can have full employment, can at the same time have the rate of capital formation it wants, and can accomplish all this compatibly with the degree of income-redistributing taxation it ethically desires.

This is not the place to give a detailed proof of the correctness of this general proposition. It will suffice to illustrate it with two extreme examples.

In the first, suppose that we desire a much higher rate of capital formation but stipulate that it is to be achieved by a tax structure that favors low-income families rather than high-income. How can this be accomplished? It requires us to have an active expansionary policy (open-market operations, lowering of reserve requirements, lowered rediscount rates, governmental credit agencies of the FHA and RFC type if desired) which will stimulate investment spending. However, with our taxes bearing realtively lightly on the ready-spending poor, consumption will tend to be high at the same time that investment is high. To obviate the resulting inflationary pressure, an increase in the overall tax take with an overly balanced budget would be needed.

Alternatively, suppose the community wants a higher level of current consumption and has no wish to make significant redistributions away from the relatively well-to-do and toward the lower income groups. Then a tighter money policy that holds down investment would have to be combined with a fiscal policy of light taxation relative to expenditure. But note that in this case, as in the one just above, any qualitative mix of the tax structure can be offset in its effects by appropriate changes in the overall budget level and in the accompanying monetary policy.

21

United States and Western Europe Differ on Budget Deficits

Although many observers criticize the large budget deficits in the United States since the 1920's, European economists and businessmen increasingly suggest that undue concern for a balanced federal budget may account for the United States' lagging growth rate in recent years. In fact, the Western European nations have used much more expansionary budget policies than we have.

Edwin L. Dale, Jr., is a specialist on economic affairs for The New York Times.

EDWIN L. DALE, JR.

Paris, May 10. The remarkably successful performances of Western Europe in recent years, contrasted with chronic unemployment and slow growth in the United States, has prompted a profound examination on both sides of the Atlantic.

With the evidence of five or six years of contrasting performance in hand, conclusions are being reached by government officials, economists, and others. Some of the conclusions clash with widely held beliefs in the United States on such matters as the budget. However, the conclusions arrived at by various analysts appear to show a wide amount of agreement.

By every generally accepted test of economic performance except one, it is agreed, Western Europe as a whole has done better than the United States since about 1956. Economic growth has been twice as rapid in Europe as in the United States. This means total production has risen twice as fast.

Europe has had almost uninterrupted full employment and now has a labor shortage. Unemployment in the United States has mounted with each successive business cycle and is now just under 4,000,000. The standard of living, as measured by the income of the average citizen, has been rising faster in Western Europe, though the United States remains well ahead.

Investment in new plant and equipment and other assets, in relation to the total output of the economy, has been nearly half again higher in

Western Europe than in the United States, most of it financed by rising business profits.

Europe's international balance of payments, the relationship between total payments to foreigners and total receipts from foreigners, has shown consistent surpluses. That of the United States has been in chronic deficit, with a consequent loss of gold.

The one exception—the one economic test by which the United States has had a better record—is in the effort to check the slow rise in prices that has afflicted all nations. Prices have risen slightly less in the United States in the last four or five years than in most European countries, though the rise has been small on both sides of the Atlantic.

Governments in Europe do a number of things differently from what is normal practice in the United States, ranging from different tax systems to tariff-cutting in the European Economic Community, or Common Market. Thus few students of the recent economic record attribute the differing performances on the two sides entirely to one cause.

However, one cause is receiving the heaviest stress in analyses and comments. This is the contrast between American and European financial policies: government budget policy (spending and taxation) and monetary policy. There are the policies that strongly influence the total level of demand, or spending power in the economy. Demand has been consistently stronger in Europe, which means simply that business has been better most of the time.

In the United States the financial actions of the government, for varying reasons, have normally been designed to check demand—mainly through budget decisions aimed at a surplus and frequent use of "tight money." (High interest rates.)

Budget deficits have often occurred, despite original decisions aiming at a surplus, because tax receipts failed to come up to expectations as the economy lagged. But, according to most current analysis, this has not altered the restrictive effects of the original decisions.

In Europe, governments have almost never aimed at budget surpluses, by United States budget definitions. With demand already strong and tending to perpetuate itself, budget policy has normally been approximately "neutral," with most countries regularly running small deficits. When demand in the economy weakened, deficits were quickly increased on purpose, but this was seldom necessary.

An economist describes the contrast in these terms:

> The rule in Europe has been never to restrict demand by budget surpluses or tight money unless the economy reached the stage of being badly overheated, with a serious labor shortage and full-capacity operation by business. Even then, the restrictive policy has been maintained for as brief a period as possible. This is true of all countries.
>
> In the United States, partly because of a certain mythology about balanced budgets and partly for more plausible reasons, the rule has been to restrict demand, mainly by aiming at a budget surplus, each time the economy showed the slightest sign of rising, long before there was full employment or overheating.
>
> This fundamental difference has been at work since the middle of the last decade. In my opinion and that of many others, it accounts for most of the difference on the two sides.

A government official expresses a common viewpoint:

> Quite frankly, I fear you will continue to do rather badly in the United

States until you become more modern in the matter of the Federal budget and its use as an economic weapon. We have all learned the lesson in Europe some years ago. You never hear anyone talking about the "national debt," for example. We approve of deficits and they don't have to be inflationary.

If your Government had aimed at one or two sizeable deficits at the right times over the past six years, instead of always trying to balance the budget and getting deficits by mistake, I will warrant you there wouldn't be half as many people out of work in West Virginia today. We have coal trouble, too, but we have no unemployment.

A businessman adds:

Do not blame your troubles on automation. We have been investing in new machines in Europe faster than you have. The difference here is that Governments have pursued a policy of expansion, which means that demand has risen so fast and production with it that few people have been put out of work by mechanization. Those that have were able to find other jobs almost at once.

Demand is natural. It has risen here without interruption because our Government helped it to do so. You could follow a policy of expansion too.

Western European governments have averted budget surpluses mainly by compensating for a rapid rise in tax revenues. The compensation has been a rapid rise in spending—on schools, roads, agriculture, civil service pay, and other things. Although spending has not been allowed to "run away," the increase in expenditures in nearly all countries has been considerably faster than in the United States. In addition, government spending of all kinds in Europe represents a higher portion of the national income.

A few countries, notably Britain, have used tax cuts as an alternative to a rapid rise in spending. The net effect of European government financial policies has not been inflationary, but more important, neither has it been restrictive.

A major reason for restrictive budget and monetary policy in Washington has been the unsatisfactory state of the United States' balance of international payments. Checking demand and spending has the aim of killing inflation and thus making a nation more competitive.

Economists and others in the United States and Europe differ on whether the balance of payments situation in the United States warranted a restrictive policy and whether the policy helped.

However, there is agreement, based on European experience, that a policy of expansion need not hold back exports. Western Europe's export performance has been outstanding.

There is also increasing agreement that modern "creeping inflation" is often the result, not of excess demand but of other causes, such as overly large wage increases. In such conditions, Western European governments appear to believe, holding back demand brings on unemployment without helping much to reduce prices.

22

Fiscal Policy
1961-1964

The Council of Economic Advisers
analyzes the effects of recent federal
expenditure and tax policies on the
economy in terms of the "full employment
surplus." They argue that the big tax
cut of 1964 was highly successful in
stimulating economic expansion.

COUNCIL OF ECONOMIC ADVISERS

FISCAL POLICY, 1961–64

The instruments of fiscal policy—purchases of goods and services, transfer payments, subsidies, grants-in-aid, and taxes—are the Government's most powerful tools for expanding or restraining over-all demand. Federal purchases of goods and services are directly part of market demand, and—through their impact on production, employment, and income—encourage further private consumption and investment expenditures. Taxes, transfers, subsidies, and grants-in-aid affect consumption and investment through their influence on disposable personal income, after-tax profits, incentives, and state and local expenditures.

The basic task of Federal fiscal policy is to help to provide a total market demand for goods and services that neither exceeds nor falls short of the economy's productive capacity at full employment. Maintaining this continuous balance between demand and capacity normally involves two basic requirements. First, since total productive capacity grows steadily over time, total demand also must grow. Second, since fluctuations in private demand occur independently of Federal policy, these fluctuations must be offset in order to avoid dips or surges that could touch off recession or inflation.

Since 1960, a third requirement has been added as the result of earlier failures to meet the first two: the need to eliminate the large gap that developed in the late 1950's between potential output and demand. Thus, in the last four years the main challenge to United States policy has been to

From *Economic Report of the President,* January 1965, pp. 62–66.

stimulate a massive growth in total demand, sufficient not merely to *keep up* but to *catch up* with the growth of productive capacity. During the past four years, fiscal policy has been dominated by this purpose. In addition to a growth of $21 billion in Federal expenditures (first quarter 1961 to fourth quarter 1964), reductions in tax liabilities now in effect leave about $16 billion more a year in private hands than would be the case under 1960 tax rates.

As previous Annual Reports have shown, the stimulus provided by a given budget cannot be measured by the realized surplus or deficit. Since tax revenues and some expenditures automatically vary with economic activity, the realized surplus or deficit reflects the automatic effect of these variations, as well as discretionary actions on the part of the Federal Government. To distinguish the two effects, revenues and expenditures are calculated at a fixed level of economic activity—usually the full-employment level. At any given time, the larger the surplus at full employment, the more restrictive is fiscal policy; changes in the full-employment surplus or deficit indicate whether fiscal policy has, on balance, moved in an expansionary or a restrictive direction. This concept cannot measure perfectly the effect of a given budgetary change because it does not reflect changes in the composition of the budget. Moreover, a rise in the level of the budget may have a stimulating effect even with no change in the full-employment surplus. But the full-employment surplus is the best simple measure available and is a useful tool of analysis.

For the calendar year 1960, the Federal budget, on a national income and product account basis, showed an actual surplus of $3.5 billion, but the full-employment surplus was about $13 billion (see chart). Given the extent of the unutilized human and material resources, this surplus obviously needed to be reduced.

During 1961 a sharp increase in expenditures had an expansionary impact on the economy. As this increase was in excess of built-in gains in revenue at full employment, a first step was taken toward reducing the full-employment surplus. After the initial increase, the growth of expenditures continued at a substantial though slowing pace through the following two years. From the first quarter of 1961 to the fourth quarter of 1963, total Federal expenditures, which include transfer payments, subsidies, interest, and grants-in-aid, as well as purchases of goods and services, increased by $17 billion, or roughly 17 per cent. These expenditures, undertaken primarily to strengthen defense and space programs but also to provide for unmet civilian needs, directly raised the level of aggregate demand and were highly stimulating to the rest of the economy.

The stimulus of fiscal policy was not limited to the expenditure side of the budget. Two tax-reducing measures were adopted to provide a needed long-run stimulus to lagging private investment. New depreciation guidelines were announced in July 1962, and an investment tax credit was enacted by Congress in the Revenue Act of 1962. The net effect of these two measures was to increase by $2½ billion the annual cash flow to corporations and to increase appreciably the after-tax rate of return on new investment projects, thus providing a needed long-range stimulus to investment. Through a combination of expenditure increases and tax reductions, the full-employment surplus was reduced to about $6½ billion in 1962.

Although it had been hoped that these measures, together with an accommodating monetary policy, might stimulate sufficient recovery of private spending to bring total demand to full-employment levels, events proved otherwise. Unemployment fell to 5.6 per cent by the beginning of 1962 but then held close to that

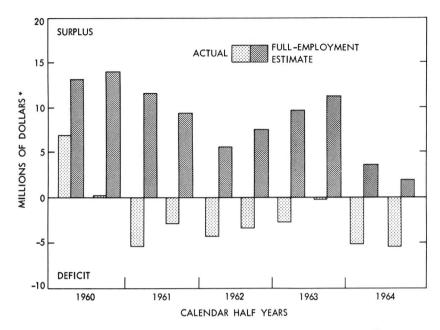

Federal Surplus or Deficit: Actual and Full-Employment Estimates
National Income Accounts Basis

Sources: Department of Commerce, Bureau of the Budget, and Council of Economic Advisers.

unsatisfactory level. Major expansionary fiscal action was needed to strengthen and sustain the upswing.

Thus in August 1962, President Kennedy reported to the Nation that a major tax reduction would be proposed to accelerate the economy's progress toward full employment. This recommendation constituted a milestone in the use of fiscal policy to meet the requirements of the Employment Act, as well as a dramatic innovation in the choice of fiscal instruments.

However, Congressional action on the proposal was not completed in 1963. Since Federal expenditures were not rising as rapidly as in the two preceding years, the full-employment surplus began to rise again. Thus the Federal Government provided no further stimulus to the economy as full-employment revenues rose (because of the normal trend growth of full-employment GNP) more rapidly than expenditures.

By the fourth quarter of 1963, the full-employment surplus reached $11 billion, and even the realized budget, on a national income and product account basis showed a surplus. At the same time, output remained about $30 billion short of potential and the unemployment rate at 5.6 per cent.

The aggregate demand generated by business, consumers, and governments had not been adequate to move the economy even close to full employment. The future course of the expansion was in doubt, and enactment of President Kennedy's tax cut recommendation had become increasingly urgent.

REVENUE ACT OF 1964 AND ITS EFFECTS

Under the vigorous leadership of President Johnson, the tax-reduction bill was enacted early in 1964. At 1964 levels of income, personal income tax liabilities were cut by $6.7 billion and corporate profits tax liabilities by $1.7 billion. With further reductions in rates taking effect in 1965, the cuts in liabilities will be $11 billion for individuals and $3 billion for corporations. Withholding rates on wages and salaries were reduced from 18 per cent to 14 per cent in one stage in early March 1964, rather than in two stages. This meant that most of the tax reduction was immediately reflected in consumers' disposable incomes.

The Council's 1964 Annual Report estimated that a personal tax cut of nearly $9 billion would result in a direct increase of more than $8 billion in consumption. Subsequent rounds of spending and respending would add another $10 billion to consumption—producing a tax cut "multiplier" of about two. Thus, through increased consumption alone, GNP would ultimately be raised by more than $18 billion above what it would have been in the absence of the tax cut.

The evidence to date indicates that this expectation is being borne out. After rising to 7.9 per cent in the second quarter of 1964, the ratio of personal saving to disposable income had fallen back to a relatively normal 7.1 per cent in the third quarter, suggesting that the gains of disposable income resulting from tax reduction were already being largely spent for the purchase of consumer goods and services. (A jump in the saving rate in the fourth quarter appears to be attributable to delayed deliveries of automobiles as a result of strikes.) The tax cut directly added $7.7 billion to disposable income in 1964, and the addition was running at an annual rate of $9½ billion by the end of the year. The Council estimates that the total increase in consumer spending alone resulting from the tax cut's impact was $9 billion in 1964, and had reached an annual rate of $13 billion by the end of the year. Subsequent rounds of spending and respending will bring the full impact on consumption in 1965 and beyond.

From 1963 to 1964, GNP grew 4.5 per cent after adjustment for price changes. The above calculations suggest that, in the absence of the tax cut, the growth would have been only 3.0 per cent, even if it is assumed that without the tax cut all expenditures other than consumption would have been just what they in fact were.

These figures, however, underestimate the full beneficial effects of the cut. Tax policies were also prominent among the factors that helped to generate a $5.0 billion advance (current prices) in business fixed investment between the fourth quarters of 1963 and 1964. The depreciation reform and the investment credit of 1962 continued to provide added strength to capital spending. The Revenue Act of 1964 reduced the basic rates of corporation taxes and, by increasing consumer demand, gave businessmen added assurance of sustained expansion and expanded markets. This assurance was a stimulating factor, even before tax cuts added to sales or cash flow. As the tax cut raised cash flows and operating rates during the year, business investment plans were revised upward.

Since the full effects on business investment of greater sales, improved profits, and larger cash flow are accomplished only after a substantial lag, and since part of the tax cut becomes effective in 1965, much of the rise in investment stimulated by the 1964 tax cut is still ahead of us. This extra investment will have multiplied effects on total production through the route of expanded incomes and larger consumer spending.

23

1965 Joint Economic Report— Minority View

The Republican minority of the Joint Economic Committee criticizes the Administration for placing sole reliance on fiscal policy to stimulate aggregate demand, and for failing to recognize that large budget deficits can interfere with the effective use of monetary policy. They are not convinced that discretionary fiscal policy can be trusted to promote economic stability.

JOINT ECONOMIC COMMITTEE

A MORE "FLEXIBLE" FISCAL POLICY

Not yet having reached its full employment target and once more concerned about the possibility of recession late this year or next year, the administration now seeks methods by which it can more flexibly and forcibly bring fiscal policy to bear on the economy.

Implicit in this approach is the belief that only fiscal policy can exert a major and effective influence in generating increases in aggregate demand. Monetary policy is generally accorded a relatively inactive role, except that a less easy money policy is claimed to lead almost automatically to recession, even in as vigorous and healthy an economy as the administration now says exists.

It is now, of course, generally recognized that for either restraining or stimulating total demand in the economy fiscal policy and monetary policy are both substitutes and complements. When this is recognized, discussion can proceed critically on the advantages and disadvantages of each policy tool. This sort of discussion is absent from the economic report, and the noninformed reader will be misled into thinking that budget deficits are a necessary condition for demand-stimulating action and that monetary policy cannot serve this function alone. Fiscal policy and monetary policy are much closer substitutes than the Council wants to recognize. An expansionary fiscal policy will get us in trouble with balance of payments just as will expansionary monetary policy. It is dangerous to assume otherwise.

Excerpted from the *Report of the Joint Economic Committee on the January, 1965 Economic Report of the President,* March 17, 1965, pp. 65–67.

135

It should also be noted that a fiscal policy leading to large budget deficits may impair the effective use of monetary policy because of the problems of managing the growing Federal debt. The existence of the debt and the considerations of the cost of debt servicing have affected Federal Reserve monetary policy in the past and are likely to do so again in the future. The Federal debt can also impair economic growth. Federal borrowing in the long-term market will withdraw funds that would otherwise be used for private, growth-creating investment unless monetization of debt with the likelihood of accompanying inflation is the route followed.

More careful examination is needed on how much we can expect discretionary tax and spending changes to promote economic stability. The danger always exists that political pressures will lead to the unwise and unsound use of such powers. More importantly, many economists are skeptical about whether the state of knowledge is sufficiently advanced to result in the proper amount and timing of fiscal policy medicine. The record of the past is not reassuring about the ability of the economic managers to use the weapons at their command in such a way as to promote stability. In fact, the opposite has sometimes been the case. Economic forecasts eventually depend on the psychological reactions of people, and these are not accurately predictable.

One wonders what would have happened in the past four years if the administration had had discretionary powers to implement tax and spending decisions based upon its appraisal of the state of the economy. For example, just as the economy was beginning to recover in late 1961, the Kennedy-Johnson administration was taking a highly pessimistic view of the future. It implemented a number of its expansionary policies, but they actually did not take effect until the natural forces of recovery in the economy had already been at work for some time. Optimism early in 1962 changed to gloom by midyear, and there was talk of the need for an emergency tax cut. However, the economy gathered steam and proceeded upward before the administration had time to propose any new actions. Then administration economists turned gloomy again in 1963 and urged a quick tax reduction in order to prevent a recession. What happened, ultimately, was that the economy grew more without the tax cut than the administration predicted it would grow with the tax cut.

In the postwar period there were tax cuts in 1948, 1954, and 1964. These tax cuts were approximately the same size in relation to the size of the economy. However, the 1948 tax cut was shortly followed by a recession. Although the last two tax cuts were followed by a strong upturn in economic activity, it is still impossible to say how much of the recent upturn was due to the tax cut, how much to the restraint on Federal spending, and how much to monetary policy. As Federal Reserve Board Chairman Martin told the committee: "Even with the benefit of hindsight, it is very difficult to say how much of the expansion in activity last year flowed directly from the stimulus of tax reduction. It is equally difficult to say what part monetary policy played in last year's economic advance."

Careful research is needed to reveal how much tax cut medicine can be relied upon to cure our economic ills. It would certainly be incorrect to regard tax cuts as a panacea without, at the same time, considering the economic effects of the level and composition of Federal spending and the direction of monetary and debt management policies.

The extent to which Federal expenditures can and should be manipulated to stabilize the economy also is open to question. The basic policy issue involved is whether government spending should be altered in response to changes in the economy or whether it should serve as a reasonably firm and predictable part of the economic structure within which other public policies operate.

In discussing the difficulties of trying to use discretionary *ad hoc* shifts in government expenditures as an economic balance wheel, Prof. Walter D. Fackler, assistant dean of the Graduate School of Business Administration of the University of Chicago, notes three serious timelags which plague the policymaker. The first is the information lag. The policymaker never knows where the economy is at the moment because of the lag in statistical indicators. As a result, considerable time elapses before the need for policy action is clearly perceived.

Second is a decision lag. Even after the need for action is noted, decisions take time and often a great deal of time. These two factors alone mean that by the time any sufficient fiscal shifts take place, the need has often passed, and the effects are often perverse. The third lag is the time required for the economic adjustments themselves to take place. The effects of any policy spread only gradually through the economy, some more slowly than others.

LAGS LIMIT POLICY SCOPE

As Professor Fackler notes, these three lags severely limit the scope for stabilizing expenditure policies. They pose an ever-present danger that fiscal manipulations may accentuate the swings of the business cycle rather than moderate them. Stabilizing expenditure policies are also wasteful since it is highly likely that "whipsawing" government expenditures back and forth is likely to lead to spending decisions that are even less rational than are those made under present procedures.

Our automatic fiscal stabilizers have worked well, particularly when compared with the uncertain results of discretionary stabilizing fiscal policy. We should rely primarily on the automatic stabilizers—taxes and expenditures—and upon monetary policy to promote economic stability. However, we believe the automatic stabilizers can be strengthened, and we recommend that the Fiscal Policy Subcommittee of the Joint Economic Committee give attention to this subject.

24
Debt in the New
Economic
Environment

A prominent banker examines the "mythology" that growing debt must bring disaster. He analyzes the size and rate of growth of public and private debt in the United States, and concludes that debt must grow in order for our economy to prosper.

RUDOLPH A. PETERSON

Rudolph A. Peterson is President of the Bank of America.

> *Neither a borrower, nor a lender be;*
> *For loan oft loses both itself and friend,*
> *And borrowing dulls the edge of husbandry . . .*

The above lines are from Shakespeare's *Hamlet*, spoken by Polonius as he bids farewell to his son Laertes. It is clear that Polonius was neither a banker nor a Californian. If he had been a banker, he might have said something more favorable about lending, or at least commented on the merits of good collateral as compared to the possible loss of a few friends. And if he had been a Californian, caught in the vigor of a growth economy, the idea of not being a borrower would never have occurred to him. Therefore, it should not be surprising that a California banker has something to say on behalf of debt.

I am not under any illusion that the myths about debt have never been exposed, but somehow fears of further debt extension live on. This seems to be the case even when there is no problem of deterioration in the quality of credit. These fears may not have done particular damage a century and a half ago, when most of our forebears were a pretty independent lot. Today, however, in the new environment of essential interdependence of people, the proper extension of debt performs a vital function.

Nor is this new environment of interdependence something our nation can escape. The progress of the world is irreversible. We cannot undo the discoveries that have shrunk the globe and made the survival of all nations dependent on one another. We cannot depopulate our cities and scatter their

Reprinted from *Challenge*, The Magazine of Economic Affairs, 475 Fifth Avenue, New York, N.Y. 10017, December, 1964, pp. 15–19.

inhabitants sparsely at the edge of the vast geographical frontier that was once part of our land. These changes that have taken place are permanent. The environment in which most of us will have to live is one in which our daily sustenance depends on the performance of our fellowmen as well as of ourselves. In our society, this means dependence on the smooth and continuous functioning of a sensitive market mechanism that responds to money expenditure. In order to keep in healthy operation the delicate interplay of millions of independent economic decisions, balancing actions by society are needed. In addition, this new environment continually requires gigantic investment of capital to provide a rising level of living for an increasing population. Savings need to be generated in great volume and efficiently converted into investment.

There would, of course, be no need for debt today if everyone's "wants" coincided identically with the supplies of goods available, and if individuals were self-sufficient or at least provided for their purchases and investments out of their own individual savings. But neither is the case. The efficient transfer of funds from savers to investors in our complex economy involves extensive use of financial intermediaries. And, in some cases, more than one financial intermediary is interposed. This situation gives rise to a growth in debt claims greater than the expansion of real savings and investment. With the increased size and complexity of our financial system, this divergence increases.

Thus, debt is an essential element of the modern world. True, it can grow too fast or too slowly. Its uses can be badly distributed, or its quality impaired, with sad consequences for the nation. Basically, however, under the conditions which prevail today, debt must grow in order for the economy to prosper.

There is a special reason for the growth of debt in the new environment of overwhelming market interdependence. In this kind of economy, total income cannot be allowed to fall over any long period of time without disrupting the markets. This means that total money expenditures cannot be allowed to decline more rapidly than prices fall. But prices do not readily move downward. Therefore, when some elements in the economy spend less than their incomes, other elements must spend more than their incomes to keep the markets balanced. Some of this balance is provided by spending funds previously saved; much of it is provided by new debt extensions. Most of the borrowing is undertaken without any thought of its economic effects. If the economy is working properly, however, the borrowing will provide a necessary balance.

It is particularly important in today's new environment that leaders of thought and action appreciate the *positive* role that debt can and does play. If the necessary balancing actions of society are to be effective, quick and adequate response of debt to changes in savings is required. If this response is not forthcoming from original savers and from final borrowers, it should come from commercial banks and other private financial intermediaries. If it does not come from those private institutions, it must come from the Federal Reserve System or the public treasuries. In any event, when debt extension is needed for the health of the economy, there should be no time-consuming hesitations as a result of false fears concerning debt.

Setting aside the question of debt quality, which I shall not discuss today, let us look specifically at four of these fears—the mythology of debt in the United States. These fears are expounded over and over again at banquet tables. The speaker warns of the dire results of reckless spending and heedless prodigality. He hints at the awful day of reckoning when we shall have to repay. He righteously denounces the burden we are leaving to our children. He castigates the federal government as the prime source of this hideous evil of debt. And, finally, he urges us to mend our ways, get out of debt, and be saved. The speech has a moral ring to it. It has some of the elements of a revival meeting in its fervor.

None of us will argue that the incurring of debt should be done without prudence and caution. Most of us are continually concerned about safeguarding the quality of credit. In the cold light of banking experience, I can testify that there *are* moral issues involved in debt, and ethical aspects, the preservation of which is basic to our society. But these proper considerations tend often to be glossed over in the enthusiastic denunciations of debt as such. The banquet speech is wrong, not because there are no seeds of truth in the general concern about debt, but because so much of the sermon is devoted to aspects which are not true. Today, I want to look at four of these questionable propositions or myths.

Myth Number One: Debt in the United States is too high. There is no question about the fact that total net debt in this nation is huge. It passed the trillion-dollar mark near the end of 1962. But absolute figures are deceptive. Bigness is not badness per se. One cannot say that debt is too high except in relation to the *effects* of debt and in light of reasonable criteria as to when the negative effects become unbearable.

One of the most serious results of an "excessive" volume of outstanding debt is the reduced ability to expand debt further. This causes trouble for the economy, paradoxically, not because of the absolute size of the debt outstanding, but because of the *insufficient* size of the new debt flotations.

In this sense, total net debt in the United States is not excessive. The change in outstandings last year was at an all-time high—$76 billion—following the previous high in 1962 of $73 billion. These changes in outstandings substantially exceeded the records posted during World War II.

Based upon this fact, I would say that there is no apparent dearth of credit in this country. Nor are there any signs that credit as a whole is approaching a breakdown. There is every expectation that we can continue a reasonable expansion of our debt if the proceeds are used productively.

Myth Number Two: Debt in the United States has grown many times more rapidly than our nation's ability to pay it off. There is certainly no question that net debt in the United States has grown rapidly. The present level of debt is six times what it was in 1929 and has grown by $687 billion just since the end of World War II. This represents a compound growth rate of about 5.7 per cent from 1945.

But the country has also grown tremendously since 1929 and since the end of World War II. The United States has 67 million more people than it had at the start of the Great Depression, and some 50 million more than at the end of the war. Therefore, while total debt grew at a rate of 5.7 per cent, net per capita debt has grown since 1945 at a compound rate of 3.9 per cent.

Per capita figures, of course, like all averages, mask the unequal distribution of the obligations to repay the debt. The same is true when we combine all types of debt for total debt figures. Corporate debt is not the same as personal debt, nor is the debt of states and municipalities spread in the same pattern as the obligations of the federal government. Nevertheless, it is instructive to see how these totals and averages have changed over time.

When we talk about "the ability to pay off the current total debt," we are dealing with still another distortion. Implicit in the prospect of "paying off total current debt" is the idea that the total debt could suddenly be called, and that there would be an immediate shift of real assets from debtors to creditors. There are at least three flaws in this concept.

• First, we have no comparative spreads of maturities of our existing previous debt. It is clear, however, that total debt does not require immediate repayment, but, rather, prolonged periods for settling these obligations.

• Second, if the past is any indication of the future, a large but unknown part of current net debt will be extended or renewed, thus further prolonging the period in which debt would have to be paid off. It is indeed possible to maintain perpetual debt as the refunding operations of some of our most prudently managed corporations prove.

• Third, any dramatic effort to shift resources suddenly and burdensomely from debtors to creditors would surely run into popular and political obstacles which would probably make it impossible to effect such a sudden shift.

Moreover, in recent years the average American citizen has increased his capacity to pay a dollar of maturing debt in two respects, and one of these changes has grown more rapidly since 1929 than has total net debt.

First is the increase in the "paying power" of goods and services. This has been caused by the increase in prices—inflation, in other words—which, in turn, reflects the gradual decline in the purchasing power of money. Over the years total net debt in the United States has grown at just about the same rate as current dollar gross national product—a little more since 1929, a little less than World War II. There is no really adequate measure of changes in all the relevant market values so that it is virtually impossible to "deflate" the debt accurately. Using the widest measure of price change, however—the so-called GNP deflator—it was twice as costly in terms of goods to repay a dollar of debt in 1929 as it is today. In other words, the physical volume of the things we would have to do without in order to pay off a dollar of debt in 1964 is only about half what it was at the 1929 peak of prosperity. While inflation may raise legitimate ethical and economic questions about redistribution of real assets between creditors and debtors, it nonetheless clearly reduces the real cost to the individual debtor of repaying existing debt. Total net debt per person expressed as an index of the volume of goods and services required to pay it off has grown since 1945 at a compound rate of seven-tenths of one per cent. This is substantially less than our economy's growth rate.

There is a second and even more relevant concept of the cost of repaying individual money obligations. This is the cost in terms of human effort. Since 1929 tremendous strides have been made in the productivity of the U.S. economy. Man-hours required to pay off a dollar of debt have been reduced considerably. It is roughly estimated that total man-hours worked in the recession year 1960 were about 25 per cent greater than during the prosperity year 1929, while real output was nearly 150 per cent greater. Real output per man-hour worked, therefore, has probably at least doubled since 1929. If this is the case, the human effort cost of repaying the debt in 1963 would be about half as great as the "paying power" figures show. This would indicate that the real per capita cost of repaying total net debt is lower today than it was in 1929, and that the number of man-hours required has dropped by more than 25 per cent since 1945.

Myth Number Three: The recent high growth of the federal debt is a major problem. A basic difficulty here is that some critics of federal debt look at it out of context, with no reference to total net debt—or they fail to differentiate between the two. Between 1929 and 1945 the bulk of the changes in total net debt were, indeed, accounted for by the growth in federal debt. During those years there was some justification for confusing the two or considering them as one.

However, net federal debt outstanding at the end of 1963 was little higher than at the end of 1945, which was, of course, one of the peak years in history. Federal debt grew by only $9 billion during this period, while the rest of the total net debt grew by $679 billion. Clearly, the federal government is far from leading the debt extension parade.

Debt of state and local governments has contributed about eight times as much to the growth of total net debt since the war as has federal government debt. The main contributor, however, has been the private sector of our economy—corporations and individuals. Altogether, governmental entities added $74 billion to the total of net debt in the postwar period, compared with $613 billion added by the private sector. Certainly, the growth of federal debt since the war has been minor compared with the growth of private debt.

From the standpoint of taxable income, which represents a rough estimate of the potential for paying off the federal debt, we are in a far easier position today than we were at the end of World War II. At that time, net federal debt was nearly one-third higher than total personal and corporate income combined. Last year, net federal debt was barely half as large as personal and corporate income in the United States. Except for three recession years, the annual growth of this "tax base" since 1945 has been several times as great as the growth in net federal debt. Moreover, the extensive assets under federal ownership could well be considered as an offset to federal debt in calculating whether that debt has grown too high to be managed. In view of these facts, can we properly consider the existence, the magnitude or the rate of growth of federal debt a serious problem for the United States?

Myth Number Four: Federal debt must be reduced, or, at the very least, cannot be allowed to expand further. It is little wonder that this is a popular myth. A gross federal debt of well over $300 billion is awesome to contemplate. Yet we must come to grips with the fact that $1 billion or $300 billion are units of counting with which we measure our economic universe in much the same way we use light years to measure the physical universe. Our economic universe is already immense and is growing with each passing day. Our annual output of goods and services is well over half a trillion dollars, and our national wealth can be conservatively estimated in the neighborhood of $1.5 trillion. Both figures could double in a generation or so.

It is against these astronomical figures that the federal debt should be considered. And when so considered, it becomes a good deal less frightening. Hence, all of the arguments I have previously stated relative to debt—its relation to GNP; its relation to taxable income; its relation to the real cost of repayment—are all applicable to the concern that federal debt must be reduced.

There are other reasons why this is not an acceptable proposition. In the first place, we must never forget that government obligations are an asset to their holders. Indeed, under ordinary circumstances, the purchasers of government bonds, notes, certificates, or bills consider these investments more valuable than the money they give up for them. As long as this valuation holds good, does the economy as a whole necessarily gain by wiping out these assets through debt liquidation?

Moreover, some debt possesses a liquidity which facilitates private business transactions. Millions of individuals have achieved some sense of financial security through their holdings of "E" bonds, for example. Increased flotations of Treasury bills have been partly responsible for holding some corporate funds in this country rather than adding to the deficit in our balance of international payments. Federal National Mortgage Association issues—included in the previous figures on federal debt along with the obligations of other federal agencies—have provided a flexibility which the mortgage market would not otherwise have had. It is misleading to look upon federal debt instruments as unmitigated evils.

Finally, there is no more reason for extinguishing federal debt than for forbidding corporate debt, for example, to be renewed. Many corporations of great stature and financial strength operate with substantial volumes of outstanding debt on a seemingly perpetual basis. Provided the funds obtained from investors or lenders are productively invested by the borrower, there is no cause for them to be deleted from the financial structure of the businesses. Similarly with federal debt. It will often be desirable and economic for a maturing federal issue to be rolled over rather than paid off. The wisdom of such action cannot be judged sweepingly in advance, but only in the light of circumstances prevailing at the moment.

The sum and substance of these arguments is that the question of reducing federal debt or of expanding it further should not be determined by absolute size of the debt, but by the economic impact that will result. It is the functioning of the economy that counts.

Here the new environment bears most directly on the problem of debt. The overwhelming dependence of the men, women and children of this nation on the stable functioning of markets means that the preservation of the order and efficiency of these markets is vital to the preservation of the society itself. The proper rate and direction of extension of total net debt is basic to the smooth functioning of our markets. And net federal debt operations can form a key catalytic element in the expansion of total debt.

This does not mean that federal debt expansion need be a large part of the whole, but it must occur when needed. It does not mean that Treasury financing operations are crucial, independent of the Federal Reserve actions which determine the *net* impact of federal debt on the economy. Nor does it mean that the financing flows themselves are the most important part of the federal contribution; the tax and expenditure impacts which federal debt flotations make possible may be even more important. What it does mean is that federal expenditure and tax policy is a stout staff on which our economy must lean from time to time, and emotional attitudes toward debt should not be allowed to interfere with that support when the necessity arises. Unrealistic limitations to the quick expansion of federal debt when required for the health of the total economy, and unreasoning pressures to reduce federal debt regardless of the economic impact of such action, seem out of place in a sound, modern economy.

These, then, are the principal elements of the mythology of debt. I hope I have succeeded in placing a cloud of suspicion over their intellectual sanctity, because these myths may bar the door to the possibilities of wiser and more flexible use of federal debt as an instrument of economic policy.

*   *   *

Using debt as an instrument of a nation's economic policy is not new, of course.

It is a far cry, however, from the simple attitudes toward debt that once fit an earlier environment and that still serve a useful purpose in disciplining household budgets.

Who can fail to grasp the elementary and irrefutable logic of Charles Dickens' Mr. Micawber when he postulates: "Annual income—20 pounds; annual expenditure—19 pounds, 19 shillings and sixpence: result, happiness. Annual income —20 pounds; annual expenditure—20 pounds, no shillings and sixpence: result, misery."

But even in Dickens' day there might have been less need for almshouses—less human misery arising out of bleak, desperate poverty—if the English society had recognized that Micawber's dictum failed to apply to governments. And in today's environment, Ben Franklin's homely epigram "Who goeth aborrowing, goeth asorrowing" is even less an adage to which we must all adhere at all times.

The federal government is not a household, and it is not a business. It is an entity with special responsibilities to society for keeping the economy moving smoothly ahead. It is charged with initiating balancing actions to avoid extremes both of inflation and of deflation—to minimize the waste of resources from either misuse or nonuse. This responsibility was assumed by the Congress of the United States a generation ago and has been a cornerstone of its policy ever since. A large part of this responsibility has been exercised through the monetary policy implementations of the Federal Reserve System—a responsibility carried out, on the whole, both faithfully and well. Indeed, however one may differ on details of monetary policy formulation and execution, on this 50th anniversary the Federal Reserve System deserves our respect and salutes. In recent years, however, it has become increasingly clear that monetary policy cannot be asked to carry the full weight of responsibility for the economic health of our nation. Fiscal policy—the control of governmental receipts and expenditures in the interest of the best performance of the total economy—has been utilized in the past, but not to its full potential. Perhaps it is time to think of making more effective use of its powerful tools, including the controlled extension, contraction, and placement of federal debt.

25

The Evils
of Deficit Spending

Senator Byrd, perhaps the best-known
critic of government deficits and debt,
presents his summary of the evils of an
unbalanced budget. He argues that
taxes should be reduced only when
government spending is reduced first.

HARRY F. BYRD

*Harry F. Byrd has been a United States
Senator from Virginia since 1933.*

As I see it, balancing the budget without resorting to legerdemain or
unsound bookkeeping methods is certainly in the category of our No. 1
problems.

Beginning with 1792, the first fiscal year of our Federal Government,
and through 1916, Federal deficits were casual and usually paid off in
succeeding years. In this 124-year period there were 43 deficit years and 81
surplus years. As late as July 1, 1914, the interest-bearing debt was less
than $1 billion.

In Andrew Jackson's administration the public debt was paid off in toto,
an achievement in which President Jackson expressed great pride.

It can be said for this first 124 years in the life of our Republic we were
on a pay-as-you-go basis. In that period I think it can be accurately said that
we laid the foundation for our strength today as the greatest nation in all
the world.

It is disturbing these days to hear some economists argue the budget
should not be balanced and that we should not begin to pay on the debt
because, they allege, it will adversely affect business conditions. Have we
yielded so far to the blandishments of Federal subsidies and Government
support that we have forgotten our Nation is great because of individual
effort as contrasted to state paternalism?

From a speech by Senator Harry F. Byrd reprinted in *Congressional Record,* Vol.
101, pt. 4, 84th Congress, 1st Session, May 4, 1965, pp. 5693–5695.

EVILS OF DEFICIT SPENDING

Here are some of the evils of deficit spending:

The debt today is the debt incurred by this generation, but tomorrow it will be debt on our children and grandchildren, and it will be for them to pay, both the interest and the principal.

It is possible and in fact probable that before this astronomical debt is paid off, if it ever is, the interest charge will exceed the principal.

Protracted deficit spending means cheapening the dollar. Cheapened money is inflation. Inflation is a dangerous game. It robs creditors, it steals pensions, wages, and fixed income. Once started, it is exceedingly difficult to control. This inflation has been partially checked but the value of the dollar dropped slightly again in the past year. It would not take much to start up this dangerous inflation again.

Public debt is not like private debt. If private debt is not paid off, it can be ended by liquidation, but if public debt is not paid off with taxes, liquidation takes the form of disastrous inflation or national repudiation. Either is destructive of our form of government.

Today the interest on the Federal debt takes more than 10 per cent of our total Federal tax revenue. Without the tremendous cost of this debt our annual tax bill could be reduced 10 per cent across the board.

*   *   *

A TAX CUT?

No one favors a reduction of our present burdensome taxes more than I do. I sit on both sides of the table. As an individual, I pay substantial taxes on my business operations. As a member of the Senate Finance Committee I have the opportunity to hear testimony of those who protest exorbitant taxation.

But as anxious as I am as an individual for tax reduction, I am opposed patriotically to tax reduction which requires us to borrow and add to the public debt. It seems to me to be a certain road to financial suicide to continue to reduce taxes and then to borrow the money to make good this loss in revenue.

As things are now shaping up, there will be keen competition between the two political parties for tax reduction. If we reduce expenditures, this is all well and good but, under political pressure, we should not yield to reducing taxes and still further unbalance the budget. Tax reduction should never be made a political football.

To borrow money to reduce taxes is not, in fact, a tax reduction. It is merely a postponement of the collection of taxes as, sooner or later, the taxes thus reduced will have to be paid with interest. There is only one sound way to reduce taxes and that is to reduce spending first.

At home we can get along without Federal usurpation of individual, local, and State responsibilities, and we can get along without Federal competition in business whether it be hotels, furs, rum, clothing, fertilizer, or other things.

The Bible says if thine eye offend thee pluck it out. I say if the Federal Government should not engage in such activities, we should first stop new invasions and then gradually, if not abruptly, eliminate the old intrusions. When we do these things we shall balance the budget, lower taxes, and reduce debt. There will be no further need for trick budgets and debt-ceiling evasions and hiding taxes. The Government will be honest in itself, and honest with the people.

26

The Manpower Report of the President

In this 1965 Manpower Report, the President focused attention on what he considered to be the most important manpower problems facing the nation: unemployment, the special difficulties of young workers, problems created by technological and economic change, and the inadequacy of our manpower resources.

PRESIDENT LYNDON B. JOHNSON

To the Congress of the United States:

I report on a year of progress toward an active manpower policy.

We have raised employment and lowered unemployment through programs

—to stimulate more employment opportunities.
—to upgrade the skills and adaptability of our work force.
—and to link the two—jobs and men—more effectively.

Much remains to be done. We are still far from the goals of the Great Society.

Each individual must have a fair chance to develop his abilities and to engage in productive and rewarding activity. In the Great Society, all men must have the self-respect and economic security that flow from full use of their talents.

Remarkable advances of science must be directed to permit increasing freedom of choice in shaping the character and quality of our world. We have the potential in terms of manpower and material resources to apply new knowledge and techniques to insure that the life of all Americans —at home and at work—can be more creative, more productive, and more satisfying. Although we may not fully realize our goal of "human work for human beings" in our lifetime, we can make dramatic progress toward that goal in this generation.

From *The Manpower Report* of the President, transmitted to the Congress by President Lyndon B. Johnson, March 5, 1965, pp. IX–XII.

Manpower problems are many and everchanging. But several are paramount —and call for the highest priorities in manpower policy.

The number one problem is still unemployment. Despite recent improvements, unemployment and underemployment are intolerably high, particularly for those lacking education, skills, or opportunity because of poverty and discrimination.

A second problem relates to the needs of the great number of new young job-seekers. An unprecedented increase is occurring at a time when the rate of youth unemployment is already three times greater than adult unemployment.

A third major problem concerns rapid change that burdens many workers and communities, even while benefiting the economy generally. Technological change can be the key to ever-greater prosperity and individual opportunity. But it also brings the growth of new demands and the decline of old ones, readjustments in government programs, migration of people from rural to urban areas, and other changes that require difficult adjustments.

A fourth problem concerns jobs that remain undeveloped. Despite high levels of unemployment and vast numbers of new workers and workers being released from outmoded work, the desires and needs of many consumers, businesses, and communities for additional services are not being adequately met.

These are the immediate challenges for an affirmative manpower policy:

—to open the way to employment for the undereducated and poverty-stricken.
—to provide our young people with opportunities for education, training, and constructive work experience needed for satisfying adult worklife.
—to ease the sting of change for displaced workers and disrupted communities.
—to develop and fill jobs, especially in the service occupations, to satisfy unmet needs in business, at home, and in the community.

We can and shall meet these challenges. But while I focus here on Federal Government activities, success can come only through cooperation and hard work at all levels of government and by all sectors of our society.

Many policies are involved. Economic policy will have to promote necessary overall economic growth. Policy making related to scientific, social welfare, health, education, and other fields will have to recognize manpower implications and objectives.

THE CHALLENGES

Some of these challenges are not new. And we have responded to them already. Our progress to date provides a firm foundation for an increased effort in the future.

In 1964—as reflected in the accompanying manpower report from the Secretary of Labor—more men were working, producing greater abundance at higher wages and profits, than ever before in history. Employment was up more than a million and one half over the previous year, the largest increase since the 1959 recovery from recession. There are now more than 70 million Americans engaged in civilian work.

Last year we also cut into the waste of our manpower. Unemployment was reduced by 300,000, to the lowest percentage of our work force during the last seven years. Long-term unemployment also decreased, as did the number of people working part time who wished to work full time.

Unemployment

But these lower unemployment levels do not indicate that we have eliminated waste of manpower and the hardship that accompanies such waste. In an average week during 1964, almost 3.9 million jobless persons sought and failed to find employment. Another 2.5 million who wanted full-time jobs could only find part-time work.

Many of our men and women on farms, though technically classified as employed, are underemployed. They are working at unacceptably low incomes, as are millions of other workers throughout the economy.

In 1964, the unemployment rate was reduced to 5.2 per cent of the labor force; at the beginning of 1965, it stood at just under five per cent. But it still is considerably higher than it had been in earlier post-World War II years.

The major problems of unemployment do not show up in these aggregate national figures. They show up in the sharp differences in unemployment rates between the undereducated and the highly educated, the unskilled and the skilled, the nonwhite and the white, and the young and the adult workers.

Workers who did not complete high school have unemployment rates nearly twice as high as those with more education, and five times as high as those who have gone through college.

Laborers and many types of semiskilled manual workers are unemployed at rates of two to three times the average for skilled and technical groups.

Unemployment of nonwhites, at nearly 10 percent, is more than twice as prevalent as for whites.

The unemployment rate for teenagers is almost 15 per cent—over three times that for all adults and over five times as high as for married men. Nonwhite teenagers are unemployed at a shocking rate of over 25 per cent.

Other concentrations of unemployment provide cause for alarm:

> —jobless workers over the age of 45 remain unemployed far longer than do younger persons; more than 35 per cent of the jobless in this age group remain unemployed 15 or more weeks.
> —in some areas, joblessness and gross underemployment blight the lives of a quarter of the residents.

There is no simple solution, no single means of providing employment opportunities for all these disadvantaged Americans. For many, greater economic growth will create new opportunities. For many others who are chronically unemployed, or underemployed, there must be special assistance to overcome handicaps barring the way to employment.

Young Workers

A recent study has indicated some of the handicaps compounding employment difficulties for young people out of school.

The first handicap is lack of a basic education. There are about seven million young people between the ages of 16 and 21 who are out of school. Of these, three million dropped out before finishing high school; one million completed only elementary school or less.

One out of every four dropouts in the labor force could not find employment—twice the unemployment rate of the high school graduates.

A second handicap is lack of skills or work experience. About 65 per cent of the dropouts and 40 per cent of the graduates had no work experience during the years they were in school. Nine dropouts out of every ten reported no job training after leaving school. High school graduates, on the other hand, were three times as likely to enter an occupational training program.

A third handicap is poverty: four dropouts out of every 10 still living at home were in families with less than $3,000 annual income; only two high school graduates of every 10 came from such low-income families.

A fourth handicap is lack of knowledge of training and jobs that are available. Of every 10 high school dropouts, eight reported that they had never been counseled by a school official or by a public employment office about job training or the kind of work to look for. Even among high school graduates, less than half reported that they had received occupational guidance.

A final handicap is the sharp increase in the number of new young jobseekers —crowding into a work force already containing high teenage unemployment.

Change: Manpower Resources

In 1965, the number of 18- and 19-year-old workers is expected to increase by 500,000—twice the increase of last year. Succeeding waves of new young workers will swell the 18-to-24-year-old work force by more than three million in the next five years, an increase two-thirds higher than in the past five years.

But the increase in the size of the work force will not be confined to young ages alone. Overall, the labor force is expected to grow by 7½ million workers in the next five years—50 per cent greater than in the last five years.

There will be many more workers in those categories confronted by major employment difficulties—particularly nonwhites and older workers.

Negroes presently constitute only 10 per cent of the work-age population, but they may account for 18 per cent of the coming manpower increase. In the next five years, almost a million and a half nonwhites will be added to the work force; less than 800,000 were added during the last five years. The marked increase of nonwhites in the labor force will intensify the need for eliminating discrimination in employment, training, and education opportunities.

The increase of men age 55 or older in the labor force will require more attention to solving problems of discrimination against older workers. It will raise the importance of retraining and reemploying those with substantial but outmoded skills.

Change: Requirements

In our dynamic economy, occupational demands change continually: New skills are needed; old ones become outmoded; individual companies and industries often contract or expand rapidly. As a result, there are always some workers seeking new employment and some employers seeking new workers. Fluctuations in area growth rates and patterns often lead workers to relocate in order to find or fill job needs.

Too often this change requires workers to undergo dislocation, joblessness, or underemployment. It requires employers to experience unfilled job needs. These burdens and wastes can be minimized substantially by improving the mechanisms for anticipating and aiding needed adjustment to change.

We cannot pinpoint the timing, magnitude, and location of specific changes, but we can interpret broad underlying trends. We can do much to prepare to meet these trends more effectively.

We know that the growth of technology will change the content of many jobs and intensify the need for adaptation and retraining. But the impact of technology on total employment is not foreordained. That remains for us to shape and determine. New technology will not soon curtail need for human labor. Its impact varies by industry, expanding manpower requirements in many industries even while contracting in others.

We know too that we must have large quantities of highly trained manpower in many professional and technical fields if we are to obtain the rate and types of growth we seek for the future. We are now giving more attention to preparing for manpower requirements that will result from major public programs recommended this year.

In the long run, the need for semiskilled production workers and for many types of unskilled workers will continue to shrink in relation to demand in other occupational fields.

Here, we can learn from the experience of 1964. This was the best year for economic and employment growth in this decade; there was a marked increase in the employment of semiskilled production workers and even a small increase in employment of laborers.

But this upturn did not change the long-term trend: most of the employment rise and the greatest rates of increase in 1964 were not in goods-production industries, but in trade, services, and State and local government activities. The sharpest upturns in demand continued to be in clerical, professional, and technical occupations.

Demand for agricultural workers will continue to decline, releasing farm manpower for other sectors of the economy. During World War II, one worker of every six in the Nation was employed on the farm. Today only one worker in 16 is so employed. The skills required for farm employment are becoming less manual and more mechanical, scientific, technical, and managerial.

In many service fields, there is high and rising demand as consumers spend a growing proportion of rising incomes for various services. But this demand often remains unfulfilled for lack of qualified workers.

Demand for repair services, home maintenance, and hospital and other community services, for example, often goes unmet because trained workers and efficient firms to provide these services are in short supply.

The service industries provide new challenges for the development of new business enterprises and jobs to put to rewarding use more of the manpower no longer needed for industrial and farm production.

Here a leading academic "structuralist"
argues that the persistently high
unemployment rates we have experienced
since 1957 result primarily from a
growing imbalance between the structure
of labor demand and the labor force.
He concludes that manpower bottlenecks
will prevent growing aggregate demand
from reducing unemployment much
below the five per cent level.

*Charles Killingsworth is Professor of
Economics at Michigan State University.*

27

Automation, Jobs,
and Manpower

CHARLES KILLINGSWORTH

. . . The President's Council of Economic Advisers has repeatedly
declared that automation and "structural unemployment" are not responsible for the gradual creep of unemployment above the 4-per cent level
of 1957. For example, the 1963 report of the Council includes the following pasage (p. 25):

> The problems of structural unemployment—of imperfect adaptation of
> jobs and workers—are persistent and serious, and they are thrown into
> bold relief by the prolonged lack of sufficient job opportunities over the
> past five years. *But these problems of adaptation have not constituted a
> greater cause of unemployment in recent years than in earlier periods.*
> The source of the high unemployment rates in recent years, even in
> periods of cyclical expansion, lies not in labor market imbalance, but in
> the markets for goods and services. [Emphasis not in original.]

This analysis of the unemployment problem—that it is caused primarily
by a lagging growth rate—is the basis for the administration's emphasis on
a large tax cut as the top-priority item in the program to "get the economy
moving again." Chairman Walter Heller of the CEA has repeatedly said
that there is a "good prospect" that the tax cut would reduce unemployment to the 4-per cent level. (See, for example, "Employment and Aggregate Demand," address delivered in Berkeley, Calif., April 19, 1963.)
I think that it can be demonstrated that the Council is the victim of a

From *Hearings before the Subcommittee on Employment and Manpower,* United
States Senate, Eighty-Eighth Congress, 1st Session, September 20, 1963, Part 5,
pp. 1475–1479.

half-truth. The lagging growth rate is only a part of the problem, and it may not be the most important part. I think that it is extremely unlikely that the proposed tax cut, desirable though it is as a part of a program, will prove to be sufficient to reduce unemployment to the 4-per cent level. Perhaps it is true that in politics you can't get everything all at once. But I feel compelled to say that my analysis leads me to the conclusion that the administration's economic program is seriously incomplete. It gives woefully inadequate attention to what I regard as a key aspect of the unemployment problem of the 1960's: namely, labor market imbalance.

The Council's position on labor market imbalance, quoted above, rests on meticulous and extensive statistical studies. I am sure that the members of the Council, who are scholars of the highest competence and integrity, are willing to go where the facts lead them. The trouble is that their staff studies have not analyzed the figures which, in my judgment, clearly show a growing problem of labor market imbalance.

Let me preface my own analysis of those figures with a brief restatement of my argument to this point. The fundamental effect of automation on the labor market is to "twist" the pattern of demand—that is, it pushes down the demand for workers with little training while pushing up the demand for workers with large amounts of training.

The shift from goods to services is a second major factor which twists the labor market in the same way. There are some low-skilled, blue-collar jobs in service-producing industries; but the most rapidly growing parts of the service sector are health care and education, both of which require a heavy preponderance of highly trained people.

I have already presented some figures showing the changing patterns of demand for labor. These changing patterns of demand would not create labor market imbalance, however, unless changes in the supply of labor lagged behind. We turn now to the figures which show that such a lag has in fact developed.

Table 16 shows the relationship between rates of unemployment and levels of education of males 18 and over in two years—1950 and 1962.

Table 16

Education and Unemployment, April 1950 and March 1962
(males, 18 and over)

Years of school completed	Unemployment rates		Percentage change, 1950 to 1962
	1950	1962	
0 to 7	8.4	9.2	+ 9.5
8	6.6	7.5	+13.6
9 to 11	6.9	7.8	+13.0
12	4.6	4.8	+ 4.3
13 to 15	4.1	4.0	− 2.4
16 or more	2.2	1.4	−36.4
All groups	6.2	6.0	− 3.2

The overall unemployment rate was substantially the same in both years—6.2 in 1950, and 6.0 in 1962. But there was a redistribution of unemployment between these two years. The unemployment rates at the top of the educational attainment ladder went down, while the rates at the middle and lower rungs of the ladder went up substantially. The most significant figure in this table, I think, is the one showing the very large decrease in the unemployment rate of college graduates.

In a sense, these unemployment figures are only the part of the iceberg that is above the water. For a better understanding of their significance, we must consider also the changes in demand and supply that took place at the various educational levels between 1950 and 1962. Figure 8 shows (for males 18 and over) the percentage changes in the supply of labor (labor force), in the demand for labor (employment), and in unemployment rates at various levels of educational attainment between 1950 and 1962. The left-hand bars show labor force changes, the center bars show employment changes, and the right-hand bars show unemployment rate changes. . . . The three bars at the far right of the chart show these changes for all groups combined; these aggregates obviously conceal some differences between educational levels which are of cardinal importance.

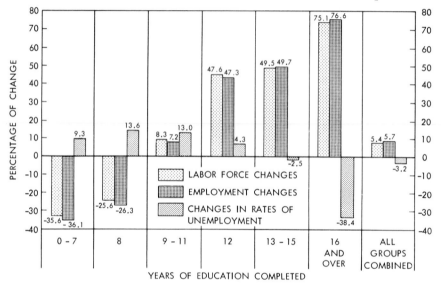

Source: U.S. Department of Labor

Fig. 8. The Changing Structure of Labor Force, Employment and Unemployment, 1950 to 1962. (Males, 18 and Older)

The bars for the 0 to 7 years of education group show that the number of this group in the labor force declined very greatly from 1950 to 1962; but the jobs held by this group declined even more, so that its unemployment rate went up. The supply of labor with 8 years of education also decreased, and the demand for this group decreased even more, and its unemployment rate increased by more than the increase in rate for the 0 to 7 classification. We see a different relationship between supply and demand in the 9 to 11 years of education group. Supply increased; demand also increased, but by less than the increase in supply, so that a higher unemployment rate resulted here too. The high school graduates (12 years of education) fared somewhat better. There was a substantial increase in supply in this group, and demand also kept pace, so that this group's unemployment rate went up by less than the rates of the less educated groups. The groups with college training were quite fortunate, especially those with at least four years of college. The supply of men with 13 to 15 years of education increased by almost 50 per cent, but the jobs for them increased by slightly more, so that their unemployment rate (which was already low) went down slightly. The experience of the group with 16 or more years of education was particularly striking. The supply of men in this group increased by 75 per cent, but the jobs for them increased even more than that, so that their unemployment rate went down by more than a third.

It is important to note that all of the improvement in the unemployment situation in 1962, as compared with 1950, was concentrated in the elite group of our labor force—the approximately 20 per cent with college training. In all of the other categories, which have about 80 per cent of the labor force, unemployment rates were substantially higher in 1962 than in 1950. These figures, I contend, substantiate the thesis that the patterns of demand for labor have been twisted faster than the patterns of supply have changed, and that as a result we had a substantially greater degree of labor market imbalance in 1962 than in 1950.

But these figures do not fully reveal the power of the labor market twist. The "labor force" enumeration includes (with minor exceptions) only those who say that they have jobs or that they have actively sought work in the week preceding the survey. Those who have been out of work so long that they have given up hope and are no longer "actively seeking" work—but who would take a job if one were available—are simply not counted either as unemployed or as a member of the labor force. The percentage of a given category of the total population that is "in the labor force" (under the foregoing definition) is expressed as the "labor force participation rate." It seems probable that worsening employment prospects for a particular group over a long period would force down the labor force participation rate—i.e., would squeeze a number of people out of the labor market altogether, in the sense that they would give up the continuing, active search for jobs. Conversely, it seems probable that improving employment prospects would tend to pull more people into the labor market and thus to raise the labor force participation rate. These two trends are indeed observable since 1950. The squeezing out of people at the lower end of the educational ladder and the pulling in of people at the upper end is another manifestation of the labor market twist. Table 17 presents the pertinent figures for males.

Table 17

Labor Force Participation Rates and Educational Attainment,
April 1950 and March 1962
(males, 18 and over)

Years of school completed	Labor force participation rates		Percentage change in rate, 1950–62
	1950	1962	
0 to 4	74.6	58.2	−22.0
5 to 7	85.0	74.6	−14.4
8	88.1	78.2	−12.7
9 to 11	92.1	88.8	− 3.9
12	94.0	90.7	− 3.7
13 to 15	79.6	83.0	+ 5.4
16 or more	92.1	92.3	+ .2
All groups	87.6	83.5	− 4.7

This table tells us that the participation rates at the lower end of the educational scale, which were already relatively low in 1950, had gone much lower by 1962. At the other end of the scale, participation rates had gone up by 1962. (The reason why the increase for college graduates was so small is that even in 1950 their participation rates in the prime age groups—especially 25 to 54—were already quite high, in some categories 98 or 99 per cent.) Some of the decline in participation rates at the lower end of the scale is due to higher averages ages, with a larger proportion in this group (as compared with upper groups) attaining age 65 and voluntarily retiring. But that is by no means the whole story. A detailed comparison by age group as well as by educational level shows that declines occurred at almost every age level in the noncollege category, while there was a rise in participation rates for a majority of the age groups of men with college training.

The important point that I want to make with these figures is that in all likelihood the official unemployment statistics substantially understate the size of the labor surplus of men with limited education. If we found jobs for most of those now officially reported as unemployed, the news of improving opportunities would undoubtedly bring back into the labor force many men who are not now counted as members of it. Unfortunately, we cannot count on the same flexibility of supply at the top of the educational scale. Even the most extreme pressures of demand cannot pull the participation rate much above 98 or 99 per cent, which (as just stated) is the current rate in some college-trained age groups.

Our overall unemployment rate has now been above 5 per cent for more than 5 years, and we cannot be sure what effects a substantial increase in spending by consumers, businesses, and Government (i.e., an increase in aggregate demand) would have on the patterns of employment, unemployment, and labor force participation just discussed. Many respected economists believe, as one of them once put it, that the hard core of unemployment is made of ice, not rock, and that it would melt away if overall demand rose high enough. As already noted, the Council of Economic Advisers has virtually guaranteed that the administration's tax-cut program—which in its current version would put about $11 billion in the hands of consumers and businesses—would reduce unemployment to an "interim target" rate of 4 per cent by 1966. This line of reasoning assumes (either implicitly or sometimes explicitly) that no serious bottlenecks of labor supply would appear before the achievement of the overall unemployment rate of 4 per cent. I seriously question the validity of this critically important assumption under the labor market conditions of today and the foreseeable future.

The benefits of a decline in the overall rate of unemployment appear to be quite unevenly distributed among the educational attainment groups that we have been considering. The year 1957 was the last one in which we had an unemployment rate as low as 4 per cent. It is instructive to see how the patterns of unemployment changed from 1950, when the overall rate was above 6 per cent, to 1957, and then again to 1962, which had about the same overall rate as 1950. This comparison is made in two forms in table 18. This table shows the actual unemployment rates for the various educational attainment groups in those 3 years, and it also expresses the unemployment rate for each group in each of the 3 years as a ratio of the rate for all of the other groups combined. (Thus, the 0 to 7 years of education group had an unemployment rate about 50 per cent higher than all other groups combined in 1950; its rate was more than double the rate for all other groups in 1957; and its rate was 70 per cent higher in 1962.)

Table 18

Actual and Relative Unemployment Rates
by Educational Attainment, April 1950,
March 1957, and March 1962
(males, 18 and over)

Years of school completed	Unemployment rates					
	Actual percentages			Relative [1]		
	1950	1957	1962	1950	1957	1962
0 to 7	8.4	6.9	9.2	154	203	170
8	6.6	4.4	7.5	108	110	132
9 to 11	6.9	4.7	7.3	115	120	142
12	4.6	3.0	4.8	70	67	75
13 to 15	4.1	2.7	4.0	64	64	65
16 or more	2.2	.6	1.4	34	14	21
All groups	6.2	4.1	6.0	(1)	(1)	(1)

[1] The relative unemployment rate is the ratio between the percentage unemployment rate for a given educational attainment group and the percentage unemployment rate for all other groups at the same point in time.

Clearly, unemployment at the bottom of the educational scale was relatively unresponsive to general increases in the demand for labor, while there was very strong responsiveness at the top of the educational scale. The percentage unemployment rate for college graduates in 1957 merits close attention. It was an almost incredible 0.6 per cent. I have queried the experts in the Bureau of Labor Statistics on this figure, and they assure me that they have no less confidence in it than in the other 1957 figures. Surely a figure as low as that represents what is sometimes called "overfull" employment—i.e., demand which seriously exceeds supply.

Bear in mind that the unemployment rates for the lower educational attainment groups (those with 80 per cent of the men) are now higher than in 1950, and that the unemployment rate for college graduates is now substantially lower than in 1950. Also bear in mind that the labor force participation rate figures strongly suggest a large and growing "reserve army"—which is not counted among the unemployed—at the lower educational levels, and that there is no evidence of any such reserve of college-trained men. Finally, bear in mind the differences between the lower end of the educational scale and the upper end in responsiveness to overall decreases in the unemployment rate.

When you put all of these considerations together, I believe that you are ineluctably led to the conclusion that long before we could get down to an overall unemployment rate as low as four per cent, we would have a severe shortage of workers at the top of the educational ladder. This shortage would be a bottleneck to further expansion of employment. I cannot pinpoint the level at which the bottleneck would begin to seriously impede expansion; but, on the basis of the relationships revealed by Table 18, it seems reasonable to believe that we could not get very far below a five-per cent overall unemployment level without hitting that bottleneck.

28

The Nature and Source of Unemployment in the United States

Contrary to the preceding argument, this analysis finds that the amount of structural unemployment has not increased substantially. The author specifically rejects the view that a shortage of highly educated people will keep us from reducing unemployment to four per cent or lower.

Robert M. Solow is Professor of Economics at Massachusetts Institute of Technology.

ROBERT SOLOW

The broad picture can be quickly traced because it is widely known. From 1947 to 1953, from the first full year after reconversion from a war economy to the year in which the Korean war ended and a minor recession began, the unemployment rate averaged 4.0 per cent. From 1954 through 1963, the average was 5.5 per cent. Naturally one can argue whether this is a fair or meaningful comparison. From some points of view it would be better to include the recession year 1954 in the first half of the period, or even to divide the postwar period in 1957. Then the comparison would be less sharp, but the contrast would still be there. On the other side, one can argue that more inclusive measures of unemployment would show an even sharper contrast. If some account is taken of the loss of work through part-time unemployment, and of the probable number of disappearances from the measured labor force because of the lack of jobs, the difference between the tight early years and the soft later years appears more marked. Allowance for the first of these adjustments gives an average unemployment rate of 5.2 per cent for 1956–1957 and 7.1 per cent for 1958–63. A more conjectural adjustment for the second factor alone (for which I am indebted to Professor Thomas Dernburg of Oberlin College) suggests an increase in the unemployment rate from 4.8 per cent in 1953 to 9.5 per cent in 1962, with every year from 1958 on showing a higher rate than the recession year 1954. It is obvious there is something here to be explained. The explanation would be easy if one could show that the first half of the period represented predominantly high phases of the business cycle and

Excerpted from *The Nature and Sources of Unemployment in the United States* (Uppsala, Almquist, and Wiksells, 1962).

the second half low phases. But the fact is that even at business cycle peaks the unemployment rate is higher in recent years than earlier. And today, after more than three years of expansion from the low point at the beginning of 1961, the seasonally adjusted unemployment rate stood at 5.4 per cent in February and March 1964 and has barely fallen since the spring of 1962.

THE STRUCTURAL UNEMPLOYMENT THESIS

It is therefore hardly surprising that in the United States, as in Australia and Denmark, the hypothesis has arisen that the economy suffers primarily from "structural" unemployment that will not yield to—and would indeed frustrate— the standard recipe of expansionary fiscal and monetary policy. This view of the situation has become commonplace among journalists, including those writing for foreign readers. Here is an example that came to hand just as I was preparing this lecture: "American society has been so transformed by the new technology and demographic trends that, under present conditions, the private sector of the economy is no longer capable of providing jobs for our burgeoning work force. The tremendous increase in productivity or output per man-hour over the last four years simply means that increased consumer demand—say, the result of the proposed tax-cut—could be satisfied with little if any increase in payrolls." [1] It would be easy to collect many such statements from the serious press, from Congressional debates, and from trade union and business executives.

In fact, as you will have guessed, I believe this analysis of the problem to be wrong. The evidence, as I hope to show, suggests overwhelmingly that the pace of structural change in the United States has not accelerated recently, and that the chronically high unemployment rate is the sign of chronically weak demand and not of a progressively worse mismatching of the knowledge and skills of the labor force with the requirements of a modern economy. Even so, I might not have used this occasion to argue against the "structuralist" view if it had not recently been adopted by so acute and justly respected an observer of the American scene as Professor Gunnar Myrdal. In his California lectures of exactly a year ago, extended and published in a new book *Challenge to Affluence*, Professor Myrdal lends his prestige as economist and plain-talker to the "structuralist" explanation of American unemployment. He says:

> American unemployment is . . . increasingly structural. . . . This structural character of unemployment in America means, first, that already at the present low rate of economic growth and at the present high and rising level of unemployment there is a scarcity of educated and skilled labor which shows up in the high figures for overtime among employees belonging to this elite. A rising trend of business activity would very soon be bottlenecked by a lack of this type of worker, long before the hard core of unemployed—those of an inferior quality— had become absorbed. Expansion simply cannot proceed very far before it meets this physical limitation, which must also have inflationary effects since wages must tend to rise. A balanced employment situation cannot be achieved purely by business expansion. [2]

*   *   *

[1] Arnold Beichman in the *Spectator*, January 31, 1964, p. 135.
[2] *Challenge to Affluence*, pp. 29–30.

Suppose that, as output expands from below-capacity level in response to increased demand, the supply of highly-skilled and perfectly-trained labor in some narrow category approaches exhaustion. Textbook economics does not argue that production must stop expanding. Textbook economics says instead that the wages of skilled workers will rise compared with those of unskilled workers and that the prices of goods and services heavily-weighted with the services of highly-skilled workers will rise relative to those of goods and services produced more with unskilled workers. We know that it is always or almost always possible to make marginal substitutions of somewhat less-skilled for somewhat more-skilled labor here and there in the production process. This is not without cost; but the change in relative wages is supposed, in the textbooks, to make the cost worth incurring. And the change in relative prices is supposed, in the textbooks, both to cover the additional cost and to induce consumers to ease their pressure on those goods and services which have become more costly to produce, and to substitute instead those whose supply is more easily expanded.

Now I am not so naive as to believe that the labor and commodity markets in any advanced economy behave exactly like textbook markets. But I should be very surprised if there were not some of this kind of flexibility to be observed in real-life markets. . . . But what I find so amusing is that the American defenders of the virtues of free enterprise against the encroachment of perfectly ordinary compensatory fiscal and monetary policy should be prepared to abandon so lightly one of the chief virtues of the system they claim to be defending. One must be quite clear: the claim that American unemployment is increasingly structural is equivalent to a statement that the labor market (and to some extent commodity markets too) is becoming less and less efficient in its operations.

Of course, if this were a true description of the state of affairs, then the fact that it is used as an argument against strong compensatory fiscal and monetary policy would be beside the point—though perhaps interesting to the student of politics. I propose now to argue that it is, in fact, not true.

THE "STRUCTURALIST HYPOTHESIS" PRECISELY STATED

The proposition I want to establish is not that there is no structural unemployment in the United States, nor even that there is only a little. It is that there has been no substantial *increase* in the amount of structural unemployment. I have already granted that there is some casual evidence that there may be more structural unemployment in the United States than in some European countries—by which I mean roughly that when, by any reasonable measure, the pressure of general demand is about equally high in the U.S. and in Europe, the unemployment rate will be somewhat higher in the U.S. I think there is little to be gained by trying very hard to define precisely what is to be meant by "full employment" or "structural unemployment." The important thing is to say something about how employment and unemployment will respond to an increase in the general pressure of demand. If an increase in demand results in a reduction of unemployment, then evidently at least that much unemployment was not "structural" in character. If an increase in general demand fails to reduce unemployment, then one may say that such unemployment as remains is "structural." (I don't think one can simply ask whether an increase in demand will begin to generate inflationary wage increases. That is an interesting and important question in itself, but it is not what people have in mind when they speak of structural unemployment, unless the wage increases are a symptom of important bottlenecks. But in that case there will be little increase in employment, and the criterion I have suggested will suffice.)

It may be thought, however, that I am seriously begging the question when I speak casually of "the general pressure of demand." There is no such thing as general demand; there are only particular expenditures. Some kinds of expenditures may avoid pressing on the bottleneck resources; they will be able to generate increases in employment. Other expenditures may not do so. Thus Professor Myrdal proposes that the United States Government should launch a massive program of civil public works construction, which will be able to absorb masses of unskilled labor, as a temporary expedient until the structural bottlenecks can be removed by a slow process of education and training. I would be delighted to see the program of public works construction, but primarily because I would like to see the public works. While I am prepared to grant the point about "general demand" in principle, I think that for empirical analysis the concept is quite good enough and one can apply it to this problem.

In the first place, under current American conditions, the short-run multiplier is about two. So given any billion dollars of government purchases, whatever their composition within reason, the total amount of output and income generated will be about two billion dollars. Moreover, if one makes allowances for the investment outlays generated by any primary increase in demand, it is possible that a good estimate of the longer-run multiplier would be about three. Thus somewhere between a half and two-thirds of the income and output generated by, say, a public works program, comes from the multiplier-chain of spending and re-spending. It is, therefore, more or less independent of the precise direction of the initial or primary expenditure.

This proposition is strengthened by a second point. A large part of the employment and productive activity that goes on in an industrial economy goes on in the production of intermediate goods: semi-finished materials, fuels and power, transportation, trade and financial services, and the like. The steel beams in public buildings are, at a certain stage of their career, indistinguishable from the steel plates in a refrigerator. The fuel that heated the furnace to make glass for windows in hospitals might instead have made glass for whiskey bottles. For both the reasons I have mentioned, the particular aspects of particular expenditures are rather less significant than they seem. For ordinary purposes, I think we will not go far wrong if we speak simply of the general pressure of demand. The most important exception to what I have just been saying is probably the regional distribution of expenditures; and even there, leakage begins pretty soon.

The hallmark of rising structural unemployment is a tendency for unemployment to become *more* concentrated in certain groups of the labor force or sectors of the economy. This comes about because the demand for certain kinds of labor (unskilled labor, manufacturing labor, West Virginia labor) falls, compared with the demand for labor generally, while the supply of those kinds of labor fails to fall, or rises, in relative terms. In a sense, structural unemployment is the symptom of a failure of labor mobility. It is a sign of something else as well. Given the circumstances I have just mentioned—falling demand for one category of labor, even at a constant general level of demand, but without fast enough net migration to other parts of the labor market—the result might be not the emergence of concentrated unemployment but falling relative wages. One would expect both consequences to occur in fact. Wage structures are sticky but not completely immovable, even in organized labor markets. They will give at least a little in the fact of growing excess supply. But they may not give enough to provide employment for all those who have not, or not yet, left this weak sector of the labor market. (I hope it is clear that I am not suggesting that cuts in the real wage are a solution for general unemployment, but that a lower relative real wage may mop up some relative unemployment, a quite different matter.) So a rising level of structural unemployment is a sign of some combination of insufficiently rapid labor mobility and insufficiently flexible wage structures. It goes without saying that I would not regard the problem as "solved" if incipient structural unemployment could be converted into chronically low wages in some sectors of the labor market. It is not much better to have people trapped in low-wage employment than in structural unemployment. The solution in either case is to open up new routes of mobility. But for analytical purposes one must see all the dimensions of the problem.

To put the structuralist hypothesis to a test one must try to find—by direct observation or by some kind of statistical adjustment—two or more periods of time when the general pressure of demand was about the same. If it then turns out that in the more recent period the level of unemployment was higher, or more strongly concentrated in certain skill categories or industries or regions, then the conclusion is that there has been an increase in structural unemployment. If the general level of unemployment and its incidence on different groups, or its dispersion among the various groups in the labor force, is about the same in the two periods, then there is evidence that the volume of structural unemployment has not significantly changed. The difficult thing is to know when the general pressure of demand is about the same in two separate years. About all anyone can do is to exercise some statistical ingenuity, and this has been done in various ways by the several students of the problem whose results I would like to describe.

*   *   *

REGIONAL UNEMPLOYMENT DIFFERENCES

My job now is to see whether there has been in the past decade or two any tendency for unemployment to become *more* concentrated in particular sectors of the labor market. There are various ways of dividing the labor market into sectors: by industry, by skill or occupation, by age or other demographic characteristics, by region, or by other broad or narrow categories. Apart from color—which is a special though not independent problem in the United States—I think most people would expect the regional division of the labor market to be the one with the sharpest barriers. Most countries have a "problem of the North" or a "problem of the South," and the United States is so large in land area that one might expect the barriers to geographical mobility to be especially high. Even the inter-regional flow of information about employment opportunities might be limited. So I will review some recent evidence on the regional incidence of unemployment and its changes during the postwar period.

The most clearcut study is one made by Edward F. Denison for the Committee for Economic Development. He is able to work with a very detailed geographical breakdown because he uses not the regular unemployment statistics, but the Censuses of 1950 and 1960. The recorded national unemployment rate was 4.8 per cent in April 1950 and 5.1 per cent in April 1960, when the Censuses were taken. These rates are in fact essentially identical, because a change in definitions that was made in 1957 had the effect of raising the measured unemployment rate by exactly 0.3 per cent. Thus the economist is in the rare but lucky circumstance of having had history perform an experiment for him. With the overall unemployment rate the same at two dates ten years apart, we can observe how uneven the incidence of unemployment was and how the unevenness changed.

If one looks at the unemployment rates for the 48 states (Alaska and Hawaii offer special problems and are omitted), there is a wide range: in 1950, Maine had 9.1 per cent and Iowa 2.1 per cent (I have added 0.3 per cent to make these comparable with the 1960 data); in 1960, the highest rate was 8.3 per cent in West Virginia, and the lowest 3.1 per cent in Nebraska. Some of the interstate differences in unemployment rates are easy to understand. It is no accident that the low states were Iowa and Nebraska; they are heavily agricultural and agricultural populations have a low risk of unemployment. There is a tendency for states which had above-average unemployment in 1950 to have it in 1960 too, though this is not universal. But the most remarkable of Denison's findings, and the one that bears directly on the structuralist hypothesis, is that "there was a general and pronounced tendency for regional and state unemployment rates to be closer to the national rate in 1960 than in 1950." That is, the incidence of unemployment by geographic areas became more even between 1950 and 1960, not more uneven. This finding contradicts both the hypothesis of increasing structural unemployment and common gossip, and it suggests how unreliable casual impressions of complex statistical facts can be.

Denison has repeated his calculation using, instead of state boundaries, so-called "standard metropolitan areas" of which there are 149. This confines the analysis to the urban, generally non-agricultural, labor force. The conclusion, however, remains the same: between 1950 and 1960 the dispersion of unemployment rates decreased and did not increase. Metropolitan areas became more alike, not less alike in this respect in the course of the decade.

*   *   *

It is so easy to misunderstand what I am saying that I will run the risk of repeating myself. I am not asserting that there is no "regional problem" in the United States. I have already said that there are persistent differences in unemployment rates. There are also substantial differences in personal income per head. In 1960, personal income per capita was 64 per cent higher in the Far West than in the Southeast. Differentials among smaller areas are even more striking. But the structuralist hypothesis requires that the differentials be increasing over time, and they are not. If anything, they are decreasing. In 1948, the Far West region also had the highest personal income per head and the Southeast region the lowest. But in 1948 the differential was 77 per cent rather than 64 per cent. Moreover, it seems to me highly likely that if the general level of economic activity had been higher in the last few years, the interregional differentials would have fallen even faster than they have done. One of the best ways to promote geographical mobility is to have some expanding centers of activity where jobs are easily available and a strong demand for labor keeps wages high. People are pulled into moving much easily than they are pushed. But that attraction to mobility, and that incentive for manufacturers to move to pools of unemployed labor, has been lacking in the United States since the end of 1957. The adjustment mechanism appears to be working as well as it used to, but the fuel to run it has been wanting.

AGE AND EDUCATION

I turn briefly now to two other categories according to which the global un-employment totals can be broken down, age and education. We have rather good figures on unemployment by age group and much less satisfactory figures on unemployment by educational status. In consequence, one can be fairly definite about the implications of recent changes in the age structure of the labor force, and much less definite about changes in the demand for and the supply of people of different educational attainments.

It is perfectly clear that different age groups have characteristically different unemployment rates, and there are analogous differences between the incidence of unemployment on men and women. The main source of these differences is probably different mobility patterns. Young people, in particular, are less firmly attached to any given job than are more experienced workers, and so they have always suffered higher unemployment rates. Something similar is true, to a lesser extent, about women. There are, no doubt, other reasons for the differentially high unemployment of young workers, and there is evidence that the pattern may have been changing for the worse recently. Professor Albert Rees of the University of Chicago points out that the unemployment rate of teenagers has been rising relative to the rate for adults. In 1963, 15.6 per cent of those in the labor force between 14 and 19 years old were unemployed. Moreover, within that age group the incidence of unemployment is highest for those with the least education: Rees gives figures for October 1961 when the unemployment rate for June high school graduates not attending college was 17.9 per cent, and for those who had dropped out of school before graduation was 26.8 per cent. Whatever the cause of this shift, it is clear that changes in the demographic composition of the labor force can change the unemployment rate associated with any given volume of effective demand.

It is possible to show, however, that up to now this demographic factor has not been the cause of the upward drift in overall unemployment. I made a study of this for 1960, and Rees has recently reported a similar study for 1962. The re-sults are the same and so I will quote Rees's more up-to-date analysis. The method is to apply the 1962 unemployment rates for detailed age-sex categories to the demographic composition of the labor force as it existed in 1955, when the un-employment rate was 4 per cent. If that is done, one calculates that the overall unemployment rate in 1962 would have been 5.5 per cent; in fact it was 5.6 per cent. The difference of 0.1 per cent is all that can be attributed to changes in the composition of the labor force since 1955. It is worth underlining that, even if this source of increased unemployment has been negligible in the past seven years, it does not follow that it will be negligible in the future. It simply means that demographic shifts have so far been slight. More radical shifts in the composition of the labor force can be expected in the next half-dozen years; unless age differ-entials are reduced, this will be a force making for higher unemployment rates in the future. Fortunately, young workers are the most flexible and mobile part of the labor force; it should be possible to improve their adaptability to the de-mands of the labor market, but not without devoting public resources to the effort.

The current high rate of unemployment is not the result either of relatively worsening unemployment rates among special age groups nor of a shift in the composition of the labor force toward age groups with higher specific unemployment rates. This much is proved by Rees's figures and my own earlier ones. Nevertheless there has been an increase in unemployment rates among young people, aged 14–19. This is an important enough social fact to be worth some comment.

The fact itself is easy to see. One need only compare the years 1954, 1959, and 1963, when the overall unemployment rates were 5.6, 5.5, and 5.7 per cent. In 1954, the unemployment rate among male teenagers was 11.4 per cent (after adjustment for a change in definition that took place in 1957); in 1959 it was 13.8 per cent; in 1963 it was 15.5 per cent. It appears that the change was not smooth; there was a small deterioration in 1957 and a major deterioration in 1963. One can say that there are now about 200,000 more unemployed teenagers than the 1948–1957 experience would have predicted for this year. This is less than one-third of one per cent of the labor force, but it is a number one doesn't like to contemplate, especially since it may get worse.

One cannot be dogmatic about the causes of higher unemployment among young people. By no means all of the young unemployed are premature school-leavers, and the others may well be better educated than their opposite numbers a decade or more ago. One hypothesis makes even this component of unemployment a result of the years of stagnation of demand since 1957. Imagine that young people are in some ways "inferior" employees, because they are inexperienced, or more likely to change jobs frequently, or interested in part-time employment. All these things may well be true. Then during a prolonged period of stagnation, with the supply of labor exceeding the demand, it may well happen that employers succeed in gradually exchanging "inferior" workers for superior ones. Then teenagers will come to suffer abnormally high unemployment rates for the given level of general unemployment simply because the high unemployment is prolonged rather than occasional. Moreover, if the weak growth of demand shows itself not in a high rate of layoffs or discharges (as in fact it has not), but in a slow growth of new job opportunities, then it is natural to expect unemployment to become abnormally concentrated on new members of the labor force.

I find these arguments fairly plausible. They do not mean that one can afford to ignore increasing unemployment among young people, but they suggest that adequate growth of demand over several years might correct even this aspect of the unemployment problem.

On the relation between unemployment and educational attainment, Professor Charles Killingsworth of Michigan State University has produced some figures which suggest a kind of imbalance. They show that between April 1950 and March 1962, the unemployment rates for males with amounts of schooling ranging between none and 12 years had increased, while the rate was about constant for those with 13–15 years of school completed, and fell sharply, from 2.2 per cent to 1.4 per cent for college graduates. From this and some other analysis he concludes:

> . . . that long before we could get down to an overall unemployment rate as low as 4 per cent, we would have a severe shortage of workers at the top of the educational ladder. This shortage would be a bottleneck to further expansion of employment. . . . We could not get very far below a 5 per cent overall unemployment level without hitting that bottleneck.

This is a rather different argument from the one we have been considering so far. The structural unemployment thesis is usually applied to what Myrdal calls the "underclass" of unskilled, low-productivity, often even illiterate members of the labor force. Here we are being told that it is in effect the tail of college graduates that wags the dog of unemployment. I find this new line of argument implausible. In the first place, it would be peculiar if the United States, with its very large proportion of university-trained people, should be unable to reduce its unemployment rate to 4 per cent because it does not have even more, while the other major industrial countries of the world should be able to maintain much lower rates with little difficulty despite a smaller diffusion of university education. In the second place, as Rees has commented, it is natural that when labor markets are generally soft, employers should insist and be able to insist on hiring college graduates for positions which do not really require so much education. A tightening of the labor market would involve a reshuffling of the educated labor force to other kinds of jobs without generating any real bottleneck.

Moreover, there are some difficulties with the figures themselves. I will not bore you with the details, but it may be that the 1950 figures are not directly comparable with the later ones, which come from a different source. But even taking the figures as they stand, they may require a different interpretation. Between April 1950 and March 1957, while the overall unemployment rate was falling by one-third, from 6.2 to 4.1 per cent, the rate for college graduates fell by almost three-quarters, from 2.2 to 0.6 per cent. Between March 1957 and March 1962, while the overall unemployment rate rose back to 6.0 per cent, the rate for college graduates actually rose more rapidly to 1.4 per cent. Thus it appears that while the balance of supply and demand may have favored highly-educated workers to an unusual extent in 1957, it may actually have been shifting against them slightly in the past 5 years. This interpretation is confirmed by the figures for unemployment among professional and technical workers, an occupational category which is not identical to the group of college graduates. In the years 1948–51, unemployment in this category was rather higher than one would have expected it to be, given the general economic situation. Since then, speaking roughly, the normal situation seems to have been restored. You can imagine that I do not like to say a word against higher education; but I cannot honestly attribute the high unemployment rates in the United States to a shortage of my own product. Unless it results from the apparent inability of university courses in elementary economics to produce any impact on the ideas of those who sit through them.

*   *   *

. . . Of course I am not opposed to labor market policy. I am strongly in favor of it for a number of reasons. In the first place, I am in favor of it because anything that improves the efficiency of the labor market is good for the economy, because the personal and economic benefits from more and better information and more and better vocational training seem certain far to outweigh their costs, and because there are good reasons to believe that these services are likely to be insufficiently provided unless the government provides them. In the second place, I favor labor market policy because even if the United States has not been suffering from increased structural unemployment, it does suffer from too much structural unemployment, and there remains a real possibility that demographic and technological trends will cause the problem to worsen in the next decade. In the third place—and most important to my mind—I favor labor market policy as a way of getting greater equality in the distribution of employment, income, and opportunity. I have already remarked that high levels of unemployment are easier to bear if unemployment compensation and free social services are full in coverage and generous in amount. But they are not, especially not in proportion to the wealth of the American economy. I applaud Myrdal's insistence on the paradox that in the United States public services seem perversely designed to skip over the very neediest claimants in favor of some middle group. As an example I need only mention that unemployment compensation benefits usually become exhausted after 26 weeks, presumably just at the moment that they become most urgently needed. In a generally rich economy, extremes of very great wealth may be merely unaesthetic, but extreme and self-perpetuating poverty is or should be intolerable.

What I have been trying to say in these lectures is that among the reasons for favoring extensive labor market policy one can not legitimately count a belief that the American economy has behaved badly in recent years because of a creeping failure of adjustment to new technology and new demands. That plausible-sounding analysis simply will not stand up under close examination. The corollary to this conclusion is that to set up labor market policy as an alternative to expansionary fiscal and monetary policy is a double mistake. It is a mistake, first, because the immediate problem to be faced—the weak economic performance of the last seven years—is primarily a reflection of insufficient aggregate demand and needs to be attacked in the obvious way. It is a mistake, second, because as Bertil Olsson [3] and others have pointed out, it is hopeless to expect labor market policy to work successfully in a climate of general underemployment. Even the motivations to try it are lacking: employers see little advantage in using resources to improve the supply of labor when labor is not a bottleneck to production and profit; and employed workers can not be expected to press very hard for training programs which will merely generate more competition for already scarce jobs. And the essential driving force is lacking: it is like clearing the fuel lines in an automobile which has run out of gas.

. . . My conclusion has been that the developments of the past five or ten years require no very new or unconventional explanation. The economy has been suffering from a period of chronically insufficient demand. What it needs is a policy of determined expansion.

[3] See for example his contribution to *Adjusting to Technological Change*, Somers, Cushman, and Weinberg, eds. (New York: Harper & Row, Publishers, 1963), pp. 190–205.

Teenage unemployment has become a matter of national concern. But the unemployment rates must be understood in the light of the changing role of the teenager in our economy. The author concludes that teenage unemployment has not risen because of inadequate educational preparation or because "entry jobs" for teenagers have disappeared.

Charles E. Silberman is a member of the Board of Editors of Fortune *magazine and a Fellow of the National Association of Business Economists.*

29

What Hit
the Teenagers

CHARLES E. SILBERMAN

In the U.S., Eric Larrabee has remarked, childhood "is not only admired; it is looked upon as a national asset, somewhat on a par with the Declaration of Independence or the Mississippi River." But while childhood is regarded as a national asset, adolescence seems more and more to be regarded as a national problem, like traffic congestion, water pollution, or slums. Specifically, the current problem of teenagers is unemployment. Dr. James B. Conant, who helped direct national attention to the problem, has described it as "social dynamite"; President Kennedy called it "one of the most expensive and explosive social and economic problems now facing this country"; and Lyndon Johnson has given expansion of teenage employment top priority on the road to the Great Society. For teenagers, who represent just 8 per cent of the labor force, account for 22 per cent of total unemployment and about 35 per cent of the *increase* in unemployment since the middle 1950's. All told, nearly 850,000 teenagers—14 per cent of those in the labor force—are currently looking for work; another 300,000 teenage boys are, for various reasons, neither in school nor in the labor force. (Some are waiting to go into the Army, some are juvenile delinquents, some are unable to work, and some are just drifting.) And unemployed teenagers could very well increase this year, with a record number—500,000 or thereabouts—expected to pour into the labor force.

There is a certain irony, of course, in the fact that providing more jobs for teenagers has become a major concern of statesmen and of social re-

Reprinted from the April 1965 issue of *Fortune Magazine* by special permission; copyright, 1965, Time, Inc.

168

formers; for during most of this century and part of the last, reformers' zeal was devoted to the *elimination* of child labor. In 1904 the National Child Labor Committee was organized to further that cause. In 1959, after voting down several suggestions that the organization be dissolved, since its original goal had long since been achieved, the trustees instead established the National Committee on Employment of Youth. *Its* objective is "to create greater job opportunities for America's youth." At first, the new committee (technically, a division of the old) felt the need to persuade people that a shortage of teenage jobs really was a problem. "With all the headlines about delinquency," the committee's publicity director told the readers of the *New York Times,* in a somewhat plaintive letter to the editor, "it is important to remember that this is only one of many juvenile problems . . . teenagers need help in planning for, choosing, and getting suitable jobs. . . ."

It didn't require a new organization, however, to bring teenage unemployment to the forefront of public consciousness. The recent increases in the number of teenagers wanting to work have created a labor-market situation without precedent in the last half-century. One would have to go back to around 1900 to find another peacetime period when the teenage labor force was growing so rapidly. But the teenage labor market then was an entirely different proposition. A third of the population was living on the farm, only 15 per cent of the high-school-age youngsters were actually attending school, and fewer than 10 per cent of them finished. The great majority went to work after the sixth or eighth grade. In the cities, working-class families depended on the children's earnings to supplement the father's meager wage; and farm families were even more dependent on child labor.

But the growth of free and compulsory education signaled a new trend—and the end of any large expansion of the teenage labor force. Between 1910 and 1940 the proportion of fourteen-to-seventeen-year-olds attending high school went up from 15 per cent to more than 70 per cent; the proportion graduating from high school went up from under 10 per cent to over 50 per cent. This change was accompanied (and to a considerable degree caused) by the enormous migration of Americans from the farm, where teenage labor was particularly valuable, to the city. In 1910 teenagers had been about 15 per cent of the labor force; by 1940 they were 7.5 per cent of it.

This long-run contraction of teenage employment was temporarily reversed during World War II, when every available hand was put to work. But it resumed as soon as the war ended; between 1947 and 1955 the number of teenagers in the labor force declined by 200,000 as the teenage "participation rate"— i.e., the proportion who were either at work or looking for work—continued to fall.

The participation rate is still declining, as the proportion of teenagers completing high school and attending college continues to rise. But the teenage population has been growing so rapidly that this declining percentage now represents a growing number. Between 1955 and 1960 the teenage labor force increased by 900,000, and it grew almost as much again between 1960 and 1964. It is now about six million. . . .

A SEARCH FOR SOMETHING

Adolescence, as Professor Edgar Z. Friedenberg of the University of California has defined it, "is the period during which a young person learns who he is, and what he really feels." In the phrase of psychiatrist Erik H. Erikson, of Harvard, it is "the search for something and somebody to be true to." It is difficult for a youngster to learn who he is under the best of circumstances. It is even harder if he is unemployed, for unemployment can make the most secure man feel useless and unwanted. It is particularly hard for an unemployed adolescent to feel true to the society he lives in if he has an impoverished background. Indeed, the slum youngster's unemployment seems only to confirm his well-grounded suspicion that he can't "make it"—that decent jobs are not available to young people of his color, or his nationality, or his social class. The gates of life seem to clang shut when he is still at a remarkably early age.

Thus the concern now being expressed about teenage unemployment is amply justified. But the explanations of how the problem has come about, and what it portends, are inadequate. In the most common view, a high level of teenage unemployment is a symptom of far-reaching technological and economic changes. Technological change is said to be destroying unskilled jobs, most especially the traditional "entry jobs" through which teenagers used to make their way into the labor force—i.e., jobs that could be filled by youngsters with little education and no particular skill or training, but that might lead to more skilled and better-paying jobs later on. Eli E. Cohen, executive secretary of the National Committee on Employment of Youth, has estimated that some 250,000 "entry jobs" a year are disappearing as a result of technological change. Meanwhile—the argument continues—new technology is constantly increasing the educational requirements of jobs. "The machine," Secretary of Labor Willard Wirtz contends, "now has a high-school education in the sense that it can do most jobs that a high-school graduate can do, so machines will get the jobs because they work for less than a living wage. A person needs fourteen years of education to compete with machines."

In short, Wirtz, Cohen, and others see the teenage unemployment problem as rooted in the dwindling opportunities for the uneducated and untrained. In contrast to the 1920's or 1930's, they also believe, formal education and training have become young people's only reliable means of entry into the world of work. That is why Wirtz has proposed that an additional two years of school attendance be made compulsory. "Boys and girls simply have to be trained to fit into an economy which no longer includes the unskilled work they could get before. Anybody who drops out of school may very well be committing economic suicide." In a 1963 address Wirtz recalled that thirty years previously, when he taught high-school literature and grammar, very little of *Macbeth* or English syntax got through to the students. "But it didn't matter," he went on, for this was "a town where most of the boys were going into the boiler works, and if the girls didn't get married, they would probably get work at the glove factory." (The town, which Wirtz did not name, was Kewanee, Illinois.)

WHY CAN'T JOHNNY WORK?

Plausible as it sounds, this diagnosis both oversimplifies and overcomplicates the current situation, and contrasts it with a past that never was. In general, as *Fortune* demonstrated in the first two articles in this series, it is simply not true that new technology is eliminating the demand for relatively unskilled or poorly educated blue-collar workers; nor is technology raising the demand for people with a great deal of education and professional or technical training as rapidly as Wirtz

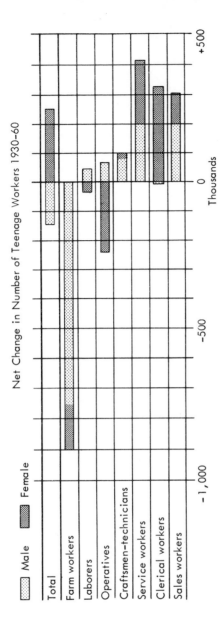

Chart 1. Net Change in Number of Teenage Workers 1930-60.

The teenage unemployment crisis has not arisen only because there are more teenagers than ever. Actually, there are not many more in the labor force than there were in 1930. What *has* changed is that most are now in the competitive labor market, whereas in 1930 a large proportion were "unpaid family workers"—typically helping around the farm. The number of teenage farm workers declined by 900,000 between 1930 and 1960. Meanwhile, the number of nonfarm workers increased by 1,020,000 or one-third. The biggest increase, evenly divided between boys and girls, was in the form of 420,000 more "service workers," e.g., waiters and waitresses, hospital attendants.

suggests. (See "The Real News about Automation," January, 1965, and "The Comeback of the Blue-Collar Worker," February, 1965.) In particular, the much-discussed disappearance of "entry jobs" is a myth, based upon some fanciful reconstruction of the kinds of jobs teenagers used to get, and how they used to get them. Actually, those "entry jobs" that have been disappearing—e.g., bowling-alley pin boy, Western Union messenger, elevator operator—have typically been deadend jobs, not jobs that led to something. And meanwhile a great many new jobs that teenagers can fill have been created, especially in trade and service industries.

Most important of all, the official diagnosis blurs the real problem about the dropouts. The problem is indeed a critical one for our society; but it is not, we shall see below, simply a matter of persuading potential dropouts to stay in school.

Why, then, *are* there so many unemployed teenagers? The answer, stripped to its essentials, is that the sudden expansion of the teenage population happened to coincide with a slowdown in the economy between 1957 and 1961. Teenagers had the bad luck to begin pouring into the labor force at a time when there was an oversupply of adult workers. Given a choice between experienced or, in any case, comparatively stable adults and inexperienced and relatively unstable teenagers, employers naturally hired the adults.

Typically, the adults in question were women; working wives often seek—and get—the kind of unskilled and part-time jobs that are most suitable for teenagers. To a degree that has not generally been appreciated, teenagers have been competing for jobs with their mothers. One of the major difficulties about finding jobs for teenagers has been the enormous, and completely unanticipated, increase in the proportion of married women who are in the labor force: from 20 per cent in 1947 to 26 per cent in 1953 and 34 per cent in 1964. Had their participation rate stayed at the 1947 level, there would have been nearly six million fewer women working last year.

WHY THE STANDARDS ARE UP

Not surprisingly, the labor surplus has led to a stiffening of hiring standards all along the line. Thus adults without any previous work experience—for example, married women looking for part-time jobs while their children are in school—have also had difficulty finding jobs; when there is a choice, employers prefer an experienced to an inexperienced adult. *People seeking their first jobs constitute twice as large a proportion of the unemployed today as they did a decade ago.*

A distinction is in order at this point. Employers have raised the educational requirements for new employees—but not necessarily because the technical requirements of the jobs have changed. A great many employers have made a high-school diploma a prerequisite for employment simply as a screening device, to cut down the number of people who have to be interviewed or to ensure "a better class of workers." To some degree, publicity campaigns to persuade youngsters to stay in school, or to return if they've already dropped out, may make it harder for those who do drop out to find a job; if enough people are persuaded that dropouts are unemployable, they will insist on hiring only high-school graduates (or teenagers clearly determined to finish school) even for dead-end jobs.

Some companies are now discovering that they have overdone this upgrading. They are even learning that for some jobs the unambitious or not-too-bright dropout may be preferable to the high-school graduate. In staffing two plants, for example, Ford hired many young high-school graduates, expecting that this would raise productivity. Instead, the policy lowered productivity and increased absenteeism; the new workers tended to find the assembly line oppressive. In any case, Ford has substituted a literacy test administered by the U.S. Employment Service for formal credentials like high-school diplomas.

LIFE ON THE MARGIN

Teenage unemployment today is too high, not because the relatively unskilled and the poorly educated are unemployable, but because the aggregate demand for labor has been weak—which is to say, because the economy has not grown rapidly enough. Professor Stanley Lebergott of Wesleyan University, a profound academic student of the labor force, is one of the few who have argued persuasively against the notion that the unemployed are victims of under-education. This notion, he says, "misapprehends at least one fundamental characteristic of the unemployed"—the fact that they "are marginal in the existing state of offer and demand in the labor market. If all workers in the labor force had their education improved," Lebergott argues, "some would still be marginal," but "their marginality would then appear to be associated with some other simple single characteristic."

To be sure, the educational level of the entire labor force (i.e., including the unemployed) is rising rapidly; the median number of years of schooling went from 9.1 in 1940 to 11.1 in 1952 and 12.2 last year, and the proportion of workers aged eighteen to sixty-four with a high-school education or better has risen from 32 per cent in 1940 and 44 per cent in 1952 to 57 per cent last year. But this change is the result of a great many things having nothing whatever to do with the amount of education people need for the job. The educational attainment of the labor force has risen because of the shift of population from rural to urban areas (a much larger proportion of youngsters finish high school in urban areas); the expansion of facilities for public education throughout the country; the rise in average income (which enables young people to stay in school longer); and a radical change in public attitudes toward education. Thus even the average laborer, household domestic, or service worker—as well as the craftsman, technician, or clerk—has more education than he had ten years ago.

In any case, there is no evidence of any decline in the number of "entry jobs." A detailed manpower survey by the New York State Department of Labor, for example, revealed that approximately two-thirds of all the jobs in existence in that state involve such simple skills that they can be—and are—learned in a few days, weeks, or at most months of on-the-job training. And the fact is that nearly half the Americans holding jobs today did not finish high school. Indeed, studies by Dr. A. J. Jaffee of Columbia University's Bureau of Applied Social Research indicate that even in industries experiencing the most rapid technological change and the highest rate of productivity growth half or more of the male production workers did not finish high school, i.e., they are "dropouts."

It is also a fact that in 1962, when output expanded by 6.3 per cent, and again last year, when output increased by 4.6 per cent, the economy was able to provide enough jobs to offset the entire increase in the teenage labor force. Indeed, teenagers accounted for 17 per cent of the increase in employment last year and about the same in 1962. In 1963, on the other hand, when the growth rate slowed down to 3.4 per cent, the number of jobs filled by teenagers actually declined.

THE TURN TO COMPETITION

At the same time, the structure of teenage employment has changed substantially in the last thirty years or so, as Chart I demonstrates. The chart is based on a detailed analysis of changes in teenage occupations between 1930 and 1960, and was developed for *Fortune* by industrial economist Alan Greenspan, president of Townsend-Greenspan & Co. (Only the decennial censuses provide the kind of detailed data necessary for such an anlaysis. Nineteen-thirty was chosen as the base year because it is about the closest that one can come to a "normal" pre-World War II year.) The most striking change, as the chart indicates, is the decline of 900,000 in the number of teenage agricultural workers. One-third of the teenage workers were on the farm in 1930, most of them classified as "unpaid family workers"—hence outside the operation of the competitive labor market; by 1960 the ratio was down to 10 per cent. The change is even greater for teen-age boys: 50 per cent of the fourteen-to-seventeen-year-old boys, and 30 per cent of the eighteen-to-nineteen-year-olds, were farm laborers in 1930. Most of the boys, in short, did not go directly into the boiler works when they abandoned *Macbeth*; only 27 per cent of the teenage workers in 1930, in fact, were employed in manufacturing industries.

For all the talk about the disappearing "entry jobs," the number of unskilled

The School-Age Population, 1964
(School year averages, in thousands)

Age:	14–17	18–19	20–21	22–24
TOTAL	13,864	5,164	5,181	6,831
NOT IN SCHOOL:				
In labor force:	593	2,116	2,925	4,425
Employed	474	1,816	2,635	4,137
Unemployed	119	300	290	288
Not in labor force:	619	771	1,137	1,909
Total	1,212	2,887	4,062	6,334
IN SCHOOL:				
In labor force:	2,515	655	336	168
Employed	2,203	550	290	142
Unemployed	312	105	*	*
Not in labor force:	10,137	1,622	783	329
Total	12,652	2,277	1,119	497

* Less than 100,000

It is natural to think of teenagers as being either in school or at work, but many are both. Among fourteen-to-seventeen-year-olds, for example, 91 percent, or 12,652,000, were in school; 2,203,000 of these were also working (mostly part time) and 312,000 were looking for work. Of the 1,212,000 out-of-school fourteen-to-seventeen-year-olds, 474,000 were working and 119,000 were unemployed. In the ages between twenty and twenty-four, almost a third of those in school were in the labor force. Those not in school or the labor force are predominantly girls. (Figures refer to the civilian population only.)

and semiskilled teenage jobs outside of agriculture has increased twice as fast as the teenage population. Between 1930 and 1960 the number of teenage boys who were laborers and semiskilled blue-collar workers increased by 115,000, or 12 per cent. It is true that teenage employment in manufacturing declined in these years; and Secretary Wirtz is right in suggesting that not many boys go into the boiler works nowadays. But plenty of them do go to work in the local supermarket, gas station, or parking lot. Or they become ushers, hospital attendants, busboys, and waiters; the number of such teenage "service workers" went up by 200,000, a threefold increase since 1930. The number of "sales workers" also increased by 200,000, but about three-quarters of that increase represents an expansion in the number of newspaper delivery boys.

Some traditional teenage jobs have virtually disappeared, of course, e.g., Western Union messenger, elevator operator, bowling-alley pinboy. But these jobs were never very important: there were just 5,000 to 6,000 male teenage elevator operators in 1930 (there are fewer than 2,000 now) and the number of teenage Western Union messengers never exceeded 13,000, compared to 2,500 or thereabouts now. And despite the displacement of bowling-alley pinboys by automatic pinsetting machines, more teenage boys work in bowling alleys today than in 1930—e.g., as cashiers, porters, and "pinchasers" (unjamming jammed automatic pinsetters).

Many of the jobs teenagers hold—perhaps even the majority—are essentially dead-end jobs. They *always* were; much of the current discussion about youth employment is based on nostalgia for a past that never existed—on what might be called "the sweatshops were fun" view of the case. Thus the U.S. Employment Service officially laments the fact that "the time has passed when a young worker can begin an occupation with assurance that he has entered a lifetime vocation." Whenever that time was, it is not within the memory of anyone now alive.

Half or more of the teenagers in the labor market, moreover, have no particular desire to begin "a lifetime vocation"; they simply want a job that won't interfere too much with their studies. Some 3,200,000 teenagers—55 per cent of those in the labor force—are also students, most of them holding or looking for jobs after school or during summer vacations. *All the increase in the teenage labor force in recent years—and all the increase in teenage unemployment—has occurred among teenagers attending school.* Since 1962 the number of students in the labor force has gone up by 450,000, or 17 per cent. In the same period the number of unemployed students has increased by 150,000, or 54 per cent. More than half the unemployed teenage boys are now students.

The student workers represent an extraordinary new phenomenon. "This youthful work economy," the sociologist Reuel Denney of the University of Hawaii, has written, "is not, by and large, vocationally directed, even though it may serve as a way of trying out possible occupations. It is rather a form of paid sociability combined with study, an existence in which the student-waiter brings some of the campus to the resort and uses the pool after hours."

Not every student works as a waiter or a lifeguard in a summer resort, of course; many depend on year-round jobs to keep them in school. But for most, the earnings from a job are only one of several sources of income: parental support, private scholarships, public scholarships, and wages are all mingled together. For working after school or during vacations is no longer the mark of respectable poverty; on the contrary, students from middle-income families are more likely to be in the labor force than students from low-income families—perhaps because it is easier for the former to find jobs.

The real teenage employment problem involves the *out*-of-school youngsters. Contrary to the general impression, the out-of-school teenage labor force has not been growing in the last several years. The number of unemployed out-of-school teenage boys has actually declined slightly—from 243,000 in 1962 to 223,000 last year. It is these boys, three-fifths of them dropouts—plus another 300,000, 100,000 to 150,000 of whom could have been in the labor force but weren't—who constitute what Wirtz calls the "outlaw pack." [1] Many of them appear to be unemployable: they are—or seem to be—uninterested in working, unwilling or unable to adjust to the routine and discipline of a job, and generally apathetic, sullen, or hostile. Others seem willing enough to work, but have trouble following any task through to completion.

It is understandable that adults view these nonworking teenagers with deep misgivings, and are confounded by the story Wirtz tells, of asking an unemployed Harlem teenager whether he was looking for a job, and the youngster's replying, "Why?" To an adult, the answer seems obvious: men work because they have to. And thirty or forty years ago teenagers worked for the same reason—because of economic necessity, their own or their parents'. The children's earnings were depended upon to supplement the father's; the mother stayed home to raise the children. It was simply taken for granted that youngsters went to work when they left school; that was, in fact, why they left.

WHY WON'T JOHNNY WORK?

Today's teenagers, even those in slums, are in a quite different situation. If the family is intact, it is now the mother who is supplementing the father's wage. If the family is not intact, the Welfare Department or the federal Aid to Dependent Children program provides the supplement.

Teenagers also lack the psychological pressures that make the great majority of adult men prefer work to idleness. In adult society, as Professor David Riesman has put it, "holding down a job is necessary to a sense of responsible and respectable adulthood." Not only do most working-class men believe that it is a man's duty to "bring home the bacon"; a sizable minority, Riesman argues, "believe that marriage is important because it provides a man with a family for whom he may work"— a paradoxical reversal of the comic-strip stereotype of male resentment at having been trapped by marriage into a life of servitude.

But these social and cultural pressures to work don't operate very effectively in teenage society; holding down a job is not necessarily a source of status, as in adult society, nor is unemployment a source of shame. On the contrary, in at least some city slums, teenage society displays a certain disdain for legitimate work. The kinds of menial jobs that are available are regarded as "slaving"; status and prestige attach, rather, to "the tough guy" who affects a show of bravado, or to "the hustler" who earns his living through petty criminality—e.g., as a runner for a numbers game.

And to the extent that work *is* a value to teenagers, the kind of work that is valued may not be the kind that is available—and certainly not the kind that leads to middle-class status. There is, in lower-class culture, a respect for manual or outdoor labor, especially labor having to do with *things,* and a corresponding disdain for many white-collar and service jobs; more precisely, there is a fear that holding such a job may diminish the teenager's virility. "We're outdoor types;" "we like to fiddle with engines," young men interviewed by *Fortune* re-

---

[1] Some economists define "the youth employment problem" as involving sixteen- to twenty-one-year-olds. In this age group there are 386,000 unemployed out-of-school males and 309,000 out of school and out of the labor force; perhaps 100,000 to 150,000 could be in the labor force.

marked, in explaining why they were reluctant to go back to school to qualify for white-collar jobs. "Only finks do I.B.M."

But if there is a disdain for white-collar work, so is there, quite often, a resentment of unskilled or semiskilled service jobs as too servile or degrading. Americans, and particularly young Americans, balk at accepting the role implied or required in such jobs as waiter, hospital attendant, household domestic; we do not have the British tradition of service without servility. Yet these jobs—not those for which a high-school diploma is really necessary—are the ones for which there is an unfilled and rapidly growing demand. (On the Labor Department's own calculations, the supply of high-school graduates over the next ten years will be "adequate to meet the demand for workers with this amount of education.")

*   *   *

30

Retraining Programs— At Home and Abroad

We have a great deal to learn from European manpower programs. Professor Gordon does not give government training programs much credit for maintaining full employment in Europe, but rates them higher in terms of efficiency and broader social objectives.

Margaret S. Gordon is Professor of Economics at the University of California, Berkeley.

MARGARET GORDON

INTRODUCTION

When Congress adopted the Manpower Development and Training Act of 1962, it was authorizing a type of government program which had been in effect in most Western European countries throughout the postwar period. Provisions for the retraining of the unemployed were also included in the Area Redevelopment Act of 1961, the Trade Expansion Act of 1962, and, more recently, in the Economic Opportunity Act of 1964.

What lessons, if any, can be learned from European experience with government retraining programs that may be of value in the development of our own retraining policies? This paper is based on a study designed to answer this question and conducted over the course of the last two years. My research included field work in Belgium, France, West Germany, Italy, The Netherlands, Sweden, and the United Kingdom.

The term "retraining" will be used as a convenient catchall for programs which may actually include: (a) vocational training for unskilled adults, (b) retraining for persons with an obsolescent skill, and (c) refresher or further training courses for those whose skills have become rusty or require adaptation to technological change. My study has not been concerned with traditional vocational training programs for young people, nor with employer-sponsored on-the-job training, except insofar as such training has been subsidized by public agencies as part of a policy of combatting unemployment.

From *Proceedings of the Seventeenth Annual Meeting of the Industrial Relations Research Association*, December 1964, pp. 128–138. Reprinted by permission.

POSTWAR DEVELOPMENT OF EUROPEAN RETRAINING

European retraining programs for the unemployed have gone through a process of evolution during the postwar period. They were originally designed: (1) to increase the employability of the unemployed, (2) to facilitate the return of war veterans to civilian employment, and (3) to relieve expected shortages of skilled labor in the postwar reconstruction period.

Everywhere it was anticipated that there would be unemployment problems from time to time, at least in recession periods, and toward the end of the War or early in the postwar period many European countries adopted full employment policies. However, as American economists are now well aware, unemployment has ceased to be much of a problem in most of Western Europe since about 1955, and some countries, such as France and Sweden, have largely escaped an unemployment problem throughout the postwar period. Whether this happy state of affairs will continue is, of course, debatable and, fortunately, beyond the scope of this paper.

In the tight labor markets which have generally prevailed in Western Europe in the last ten years or so, the need for retraining programs to increase the employability of the unemployed has markedly diminished. Nevertheless, government retraining programs have remained in effect and in some countries have been expanded.

The emphasis on rapid growth in Western Europe has had much to do with the desire to expand retraining and other labor market adjustment policies. Particularly where the labor force is increasing slowly or not at all, rapid growth tends to be dependent to a considerable extent on achieving a high rate of increase in productivity. The Swedes have been particularly effective in articulating the superiority of emphasis on labor market adjustment policies rather than relying on the "expansion-hampering and inflationary method of changing wage differentials," in order to induce the necessary occupational and geographic shifts to encourage the most effective use of the labor force. Moreover, under the influence of the reduction of trade barriers occurring in the Common Market and the Outer Seven, keeping pace in the growth and productivity race has come to be regarded as essential for economic survival.

Clearly, however, there is a basic dilemma involved in an attempt to expand retraining in a tight labor market, stemming from the drying up of the supply of retrainable unemployed persons. But appropriate measures can be developed to induce employed persons to enter retraining programs, and trainees may also be drawn from the ranks of the under-employed, married women, young men emerging from military training, the disabled, and seasonal workers. Much of the training for the building trades, in fact, is conducted in the winter when construction activity is slack.

The policy changes which have been adopted to meet these changing conditions have included liberalization of eligibility requirements, greater variety in course offerings and in the duration of courses, increases in training allowances, and greater emphasis on policies designed to encourage retraining for workers *threatened* with labor displacement. Some of the changes, moreover, have been deliberately designed to encourage training for such occupations as technician, engineering aide, and draftsman, in which acute shortages have developed under the impact of technological change.

Thus there are significant differences between European and American retraining policies, which are associated with the contrasting labor market settings in which the programs are being conducted. This has complicated my search for lessons to be drawn from European experience. Nevertheless, I believe that we have much to learn from European experience with retraining, and it is to my findings in this regard that I now turn.

A PERMANENT RETRAINING PROGRAM

The most important lesson to be drawn from an examination of the postwar development of retraining programs in Western Europe is that government retraining programs have come to be viewed as a permanent instrument of manpower policy, as valuable in a period of full employment as in a period of unemployment. I believe we should move toward official acceptance of this view of retraining in the United States and that we should not wait until the Manpower Development and Training Act is about to expire (in mid-1966) before reaching this decision. There is increasing agreement among labor market experts that we shall have a difficult residual problem of structural unemployment even if we succeed in reducing the overall unemployment rate to four per cent or below. Moreover, retraining should properly be looked upon as a method of encouraging adaptation to structural changes in employment, *whether or not* those changes are accompanied by any appreciable unemployment problem. And it should hardly be necessary to add that we can expect a continuation of structural changes in employment for many decades to come.

In addition, it should be abundantly clear that the job of eliminating the problem of an abysmally low level of education from sectors of our adult labor force is not going to be accomplished in a few short years or even, perhaps, in a whole generation. Many of the children who are growing up in urban slum areas or in backward rural areas today will contribute their share to a problem of inadequate preparation for the labor market a decade or two hence. And labor displacement is hardly likely to disappear. Indeed, it could well become more serious, particularly if automation in the office begins to result in a more difficult problem of displacement of white-collar workers, along with continuation of the more familiar problem of displacement of blue-collar workers.

The development of a large retraining program requires expansion of the number of vocational training instructors and, particularly in the case of special programs for disadvantaged groups, the training of counsellors and other types of personnel equipped to deal with such groups. In many situations, it requires the acquisition of specialized equipment and the rental, purchase, or construction of buildings to house training classes. In the light of these needs it is scarcely surprising that our MDTA program was slow to get under way in the first year or two. Examination of the European experience certainly seems to suggest that we would have been far better off if we had developed this type of program earlier in the postwar period. Moreover, once we have an adequate staff and facilities for a large-scale retraining program, it would seem a great mistake to discontinue their use.

THE ROLE OF RETRAINING IN INDUSTRY

Some may argue that, in periods of relatively full employment, employers can be relied on to provide all the training and retraining required, and thus there is no need for a permanent government program. Very briefly, I believe there are three main reasons why employer-sponsored training will not suffice.

In the first place, it is primarily the large firms that provide training, and, at least until very recently, there has been very little employer-sponsored retraining.

Secondly, we are not likely to do away altogether with recessions in the future, and it has been apparent in the last few recessions that a good many workers who are laid off during the downswing, especially from firms experiencing rapid increases in productivity, are not rehired in the recovery period. To the extent that such cases can be identified reasonably promptly, government retraining can be made available for the individuals concerned during the recession or the early part of the upswing, when opportunities for other jobs are limited. Then, when the recovery is well under way, these retrained workers are likely to stand a good chance of being placed in the type of work for which they have been trained.

Thirdly, the workers who will be hired and trained by employers are those who can meet employer selection standards. Not only is discrimination on the basis of age, race, and sex unlikely to disappear altogether, but there are many unemployed persons who are not hired because of poor performance on aptitude tests, poor grooming, or other individual problems. Those who are subject to discrimination may in some cases be placed more readily if they have received appropriate training, and at least some types of government retraining courses can be designed to provide practice in taking aptitude tests, suggestions on applying for jobs, and the like.

Undoubtedly we should continue to provide for a certain amount of subsidized on-the-job training under MDTA and other programs, particularly where highly specialized equipment is needed. But European experience does not suggest that this approach will remove the need for public institutional retraining. Various types of provisions for subsidized employer-sponsored retraining are found in all the countries included in my study, but there is a good deal of evidence that many employers are reluctant to participate in this type of program. The subsidies may not be large enough to overcome employer resistance to getting involved in government "red tape," and firms often prefer to recruit workers through a variety of channels rather than commit themselves to hiring unemployed workers through the public employment service for the sake of receiving a training or retraining subsidy. When the subsidy is designed to encourage firms to provide retraining for their own employees who are threatened with permanent layoff, employers frequently prefer to remain free to dismiss groups of workers as they choose rather than become involved in a program under which the government may be in a position to influence their manpower decisions. The Swedish Employers' Confederation has successfully resisted extension of eligibility for retraining allowances to employed workers and the payment of subsidies for retraining in situations of threatened redundancy (except in areas with special unemployment problems) because of fears that such policies would lead to increasing interference by the National Labor Market Board with their manpower decisions.

Nevertheless, one of the most interesting trends in manpower policy in Western Europe is increasing concern with devising policies to deal with redundancy. The Swedish "early warning" system, under which employers' organizations have voluntarily entered into agreements with the National Labor Market Board to give advance notice of impending layoffs has been much publicized in this country. The program of adjustment assistance in the European Coal and Steel Community has also received a good deal of attention. But some of the national programs aimed at providing subsidized retraining, relocation, adjustment assistance, early retirement benefits, and other types of aid in situations of labor displacement are less well known. Probably the most interesting legislation of this type is the French law of December 18, 1963, establishing the National Employment Fund. Its interest lies particularly in its attempt to provide for collaboration among government agencies, employers, unions, and the private collectively bargained unemployment insurance system in meeting such situations in local communities.

These policies deserve careful study and consideration in the United States, although European experience in this area tends to be more recent and less adequately reported than the experience with government retraining programs.

THE RELATIVE ROLE OF RETRAINING

There is much debate going on in the United States over the relative role of retraining versus other methods of combatting unemployment—a debate which is, of course, associated with the controversy over whether our unemployment problem is attributable primarily to structural changes or to a deficiency of aggregate demand. In Western Europe retraining has played a significant, but distinctly minor, role in combatting unemployment. As comparative studies like those of Maddison and Lamfalussy show, national economic policies aimed at maintaining a high and expanding level of aggregate demand, along with the mutually stimulating effects of expanding markets for exports, have been mainly responsible for European success in maintaining full employment and achieving rapid growth. Even in those situations involving a prolonged problem of heavy unemployment—in Belgium, Italy, and West Germany, particularly in the early 1950's—underlying economic factors and policy measures aimed at stimulating demand largely accounted for the decline in the unemployment rate, although manpower policies played a role. And, among manpower policies, such measures as the resettlement of the expellees and refugees in West Germany, public works in Belgium, and a combination of public works and assisted emigration in Italy tended to play a more important role than retraining.

Moreover, the number of workers involved in European government retraining programs has generally been quite small, although efforts are currently being made in a number of countries to expand the scope of these programs. The country which has had the greatest success in bringing about a sharp increase in enrollment in recent years is Sweden, where the present policy of the government aims at retraining 35,000 workers, or about one per cent of the labor force, every year. The latest available statistics indicate that this goal is being approached although it has not yet been reached. In the United States, one per cent of the labor force would amount to some 700,000 to 750,000 workers, or a vastly greater number than the 103,000 trainees who were admitted to MDTA training in 1963.

EFFICIENCY VERSUS BROADER SOCIAL OBJECTIVES

Comparison of retraining policies in Western Europe reveals marked contrasts between those countries in which efficiency appears to be the predominant objective—France and The Netherlands—and those countries which have placed at least *some* emphasis on broader social objectives—West Germany and Sweden. (Belgium, Italy, and the United Kingdom are not quite so clearly classifiable.)

In the countries which appear to emphasize efficiency, policies are geared to selecting young and highly qualified male trainees, training largely for occupations in which labor shortages are most acute, achieving a high rate of placement, and thereby, presumably, making a maximum contribution to increasing productivity. In West Germany and Sweden, on the other hand, at least some degree of emphasis is placed on providing retraining opportunities for women, as well as older persons and other relatively disadvantaged groups.

The choice between these two types of policies clearly involves the problem of the relative values attached to conflicting social and economic goals. Some of the differences in policy, moreover, appear to be associated with variations in the pattern of differentials in unemployment rates by age and sex, as well as differences in the availability of various types of income maintenance programs for displaced older persons.

In the MDTA program, the emphasis was largely on efficiency in the sense defined above in the first year or so of the program. More recently, however, there has been a gradual shift toward at least some degree of emphasis on developing training programs especially designed to meet the needs of the more disadvantaged among the unemployed—a shift which was encouraged by the 1963 MDTA amendments.

Both in this country and abroad, there has been a tendency to measure the efficiency of retraining programs in terms of the rate of placement of trainees immediately or within a very short time after the completion of training. European countries whose programs emphasize efficiency achieve placement rates of the order of 90 to 100 per cent, whereas the overall placement rate in Sweden is about 80 per cent, and in West Germany about 80–90 per cent, with lower rates prevailing for some of the more disadvantaged groups. In the United States, with its higher unemployment rate, 70 per cent of those who completed training during 1963 were employed by the end of the year—88 per cent of them in training-related jobs.

There are, however, alternative methods of measuring efficiency, some of which are beginning to be applied by American economists in studies using various techniques of cost-benefit analysis. The relative gains in earnings of those completing training over a period of months or years, for example, as compared with the earnings experience of control groups of unemployed workers who did not participate in training programs, can be measured for trainees of varying age, sex, and other characteristics, completing different types of programs. Such data should eventually be extremely helpful as a guide to decisions with respect to the relative emphasis to be placed on training for the most highly qualified versus the more disadvantaged among the unemployed, although they should not be the only factor in such decisions.

In the meantime, acceptance of retraining as a permanent instrument of manpower policy should enable us to distinguish more clearly between short-run and long-run objectives of retraining programs.

OTHER ASPECTS OF RETRAINING

There are a number of other aspects of retraining programs which are considered at some length in the full report on my study but which will have to be discussed extremely briefly here.

When I undertook this project, I hoped to develop useful suggestions from European experience on the occupations for which workers should be retrained. I soon concluded that the contrast in labor market settings was so great that data relating to the occupations for which workers were being retrained in Europe could, in general, provide very little guidance in relation to American programs. It is clear, however, that where emphasis is placed on granting a good deal of responsibility to local employment offices in the initial formulation of training proposals, as in West Germany and Sweden, a much greater variety of course offerings appears to result than in countries where the planning of retraining programs is more centralized. In this respect, our procedures seem generally sound, but the long delays involved in review procedures in the MDTA program are a decided disadvantage. In West Germany, a *Landesarbeitsamt* (state labor office) has authority for final approval of retraining proposals except where the program will cut across several *Länder* or where unusual costs are involved, while in Sweden the county labor boards must seek approval of the National Labor Market Board *only* in the case of new courses, but not for continuation of courses that are already being given. As experience with our MDTA program develops, I believe we should seriously consider granting greater autonomy to state agencies, particularly if Congress carries out its intention of requiring matching state funds after the middle of 1965. Moreover, our present practices may over-emphasize identification of labor shortages in local communities and under-emphasize regional and national occupational trends.

There are many other issues relating to the geographical aspects of retraining programs on which European experience sheds interesting light. The whole question of the relationship between retraining, relocation, and regional economic policies deserves careful consideration. Suffice it to say here that there has been a decided trend toward increasing emphasis on policies aimed at moving the job to the worker rather than moving the worker to the job in Western European countries during the course of the postwar period. Relocation allowances are available in most countries, but governments have come increasingly to recognize, among other things, that out-migration from depressed or underdeveloped regions tends to be selective and that those who remain in such areas are frequently not the individuals best equipped to combat a cumulative process of economic deterioration or a condition of stagnation. Regional economic policies have come to place increasing emphasis on regional *planning* and, in some cases, on the selection of growth zones *within* depressed or underdeveloped regions, for programs of intensified development measures. Such an approach would appear to increase the likelihood that unemployed or underemployed workers living in such regions, and reluctant to leave them, might be provided with retraining and re-employment opportunities within the region.

In this connection, it is particularly interesting to note that Sweden, which has placed more emphasis on liberal relocation allowances than any other country in recent years, and has resisted adoption of a vigorous program of regional economic development, has recently taken steps toward inauguration of a large-scale program of development in the North. A 1962 follow-up survey of persons who had received relocation allowances, which showed, among other things, that 40 per cent of those who had been granted such assistance in October 1959 had moved back to their home counties by the end of 1961, may have played a role in the government's decision.

Finally, the training allowances available under our MDTA and ARA programs are seriously inadequate by European standards, if the relationship between allowances and prevailing wage rates is used as the basis of comparison. Since our training allowances are geared to unemployment insurance benefits, which average only about 35 per cent of earnings for the country as a whole, adoption of more adequate unemployment benefit standards would result in a corresponding increase in training allowances.

CONCLUSIONS

The main thesis of this paper has been concerned with the need for adoption of a permanent government retraining program in the United States. Such a step would be consistent with the growing realization that we should move toward a permanent and continuous program of manpower policies. Nevertheless, as I have argued elsewhere, we must be careful not to put too many of our eggs into the basket of retraining, lest we fail to provide enough jobs for those who have been retrained. At a time when cutbacks are taking place in defense spending, the case for increased government spending on job creation and anti-poverty programs is exceedingly strong.

31
How to Raise the High-Employment Growth Rate by One Percentage Point

The rate of economic growth depends on many factors. A noted economist offers a program for raising our growth rate, including estimates of how much might be achieved through different concrete measures—and he suggests that speeding up the long-term growth rate by even one per cent is a tough job.

Edward Denison is a senior member of the research staff of The Brookings Institute in Washington.

EDWARD F. DENISON

My assignment is to devise a package of proposals that can raise the growth rate over the next twenty years by one percentage point. The package was put together for this session, but my estimate of the contribution each ingredient of the package would make to growth rests upon a study which is about to be published by the Committee for Economic Development.

I was asked to talk about ways of altering the growth of the economy's productive potential, when success in maintaining fairly full utilization of labor and other resources is assumed. We must also find ways to validate the high-employment assumption, but that is outside the present discussion.

Next, I shall be concerned with ways to raise the growth rate of real national income or product as defined and measured by the Department of Commerce. Certain characteristics of these output measures somewhat limit the ways available to raise their growth rate. They preclude raising the growth rate by shifting resources so as to produce things that are more urgently wanted; for example, by eliminating distortions in the pattern of output introduced by excise taxes, monopoly, or farm programs. Again, the treatment of quality change in the price indexes bars raising the future high-employment growth rate of measured output by developing new or better final products more rapidly.

I omit from my discussion steps that would increase the satisfactions derived from output without changing its amount as measured. However, I shall not consider shifts of resources that would increase measured output

From the *American Economic Review*, May, 1962, pp. 67–75. Reprinted by permission.

while leaving unchanged or reducing a "truer" output measure. Real national income or product may be thought of as an index with certain biases that may be fairly uniform over time so long as steps are not taken deliberately to "rig" the index.

The specific series I shall use to measure economic growth is the index of real national income, which is the same thing as the index of real net national product except that components are weighted by factor cost rather than market price. It is *net* income or product, not GNP, that economic policy properly seeks to maximize. Factor cost valuation is more appropriate and convenient than market price valuation for examination of changes in productivity or inputs. However, the conclusions I shall reach would be little changed if reference were to net or even gross national product.

Next, the assigned topic concerns means of changing the growth rate over a twenty-year period. This is a reasonable period to consider, but it should be understood that the length of the period greatly affects my results. Because most ways of changing output, and hence affecting the growth rate, are in the one-shot category, it is easier to raise the growth rate by a given amount for twenty years than for a hundred. Suppose, for example, some obstacle to efficient production costs us 1 per cent of the national income. If the obstacle were eliminated, which could be done only once, the level of national income thereafter would be 1 per cent higher than if the obstacle remained. The effect on the growth rate is approximately 1 per cent divided by the number of years over which the growth rate is computed. Thus elimination of the obstacle would raise the growth rate computed over a twenty-year period by one-twentieth of a percentage point, and the growth rate computed over a hundred-year period by one-hundredth of a percentage point. Some measures, on the other hand, would not have their maximum effect in a period as short as twenty years. Provision of additional education to the young and an increase in the saving rate are examples.

I shall use 1960 to 1980 as my twenty-year period, as if it were now 1960, because the calculations I draw on were based on those twenty years. But nothing would be changed materially by substituting 1961 to 1981, or 1962 to 1982.

Next, this paper is not directed to the question of how we can raise the growth rate from what it was in the past. The question posed for this session by Edward Mason is how the growth rate can be raised by one percentage point from "whatever the speaker thinks it will be" if unemployment is low, and in other respects we continue existing policies. I project a 1960–80 growth rate of $3\frac{1}{3}$ per cent in potential national income, starting from a 1960 high-employment level. The amount by which this projected rate exceeds the actual rate in the past is not part of the one percentage point increment my prescription must provide. My task is to indicate how to raise the high-employment growth rate from $3\frac{1}{3}$ per cent to $4\frac{1}{3}$ per cent. Let me also stress that the topic is not whether $3\frac{1}{3}$ per cent is a correct projection given existing policies, but how the rate can be raised one percentage point from whatever it would be if we do nothing special to affect it.

So much for ground rules. Now for some general observations. First, the difference between a $3\frac{1}{3}$ per cent rate and a $4\frac{1}{3}$ per cent rate is big. One implies an increase in per capita income from 1960 to 1980 of 33 per cent, the other of 61 per cent. Thus, a prescription to raise the growth rate of total income by one percentage point must be powerful enough to nearly double the anticipated increase in per capita real income. This conclusion must be modified insofar as the growth rate is to be stimulated by more immigration.

Second, I can hardly stress enough that, as I use the term, economic growth refers only to output. Quite aside from defects in measures of output, aggregate output is anything but a complete measure of economic welfare or economic progress, even less of total welfare or progress. To talk about changing even economic welfare, we would have also to consider, at the very least, real costs of production and the distribution of income and output.

In the present context this is no small caveat. It is the heart of the matter. The output we get, aside from involuntary underuse of resources, is determined by individual and collective decisions as to what is or is not worth doing.

I stress that to accelerate growth requires that someone act differently than he would otherwise, that this action usually means higher costs as well as higher output, and that more output is never the only effect of any action we might take. To decide whether steps to accelerate growth are sensible requires comparison of costs, the size of the effect on growth, and side effects.

This leads to the first of two conditions I deem essential for any program to stimulate growth a great deal beyond what it will be if we have no such objective. It is that the public be persuaded that acceleration of growth must be made an overriding national goal. Moreover, it must probably be persuaded of this for reasons other than the increase in individual welfare—probably reasons related to the external situation facing the country. This is necessary because there is a presumption that the more important steps required impose costs that exceed the income benefits and thus reduce welfare. Otherwise they presumably would be taken anyway. Even where the benefits may exceed the costs for the country as a whole, we are usually dealing with some deep-seated condition, often of long standing, that is likely to be changed only for some new and overpowering reason.

The presumption that the costs of a proposed change exceed the benefits may be refuted in specific instances. We need not suppose that we now act rationally on the basis of full information in reaching all of our individual and collective decisions, so we need not assume that every step that would increase growth would reduce individual welfare. In putting together my own package of proposals, I try to stress those where I think the possibility is greatest—I do not mean that it is necessarily great—that present practices derive from ignorance and would be changed by greater knowledge and understanding. This may imply a certain arrogance on my part, but without some such approach this paper could not be written.

The second condition necessary for any large effort to stimulate growth is full utilization of resources. It will hardly be possible to obtain support for a broad program to increase our productive potential unless we use rather fully the potential that we do have. Indeed, if unemployment is persistently high, we can look forward to actions that will reduce growth, including greater public and private restrictions on efficient production, and reduction of hours intended to spread employment rather than to increase leisure.

To add one percentage point to the growth rate I shall suggest a thirteen-part program that seems to me to combine feasibility, in the sense of avoiding things no one knows how to do, with minimization of sacrifice. The expected contribution from each proposal to the growth rate over twenty years will be stated in hundredths of a percentage point. Thus we need means of adding 100 hundredths of a percentage point to the growth rate.

Let me now indicate the general approach I use to assess the effect of each proposal on the growth rate. To raise the growth rate over twenty years by one hundredth of a percentage point requires some action not now in prospect that would make the 1980 national income .2 per cent, or nearly 2 billion dollars, larger than it would be in the absence of that action. The action must serve either to increase the quantity or quality of labor, land, or capital going into the productive system, or else to increase their productivity.

Because of the presence of economies of scale, an increment of slightly less than .2 per cent to total factor input in 1980 would probably suffice to raise the 1980 national income .2 per cent. I assume the addition to output would exceed that in total input by one-eleventh. Hence an increase in total input of slightly over .18 per cent would raise output by .2 per cent. This could, in principle, be accomplished by increasing all kinds of input by .18 per cent or only one kind of input by a larger percentage. From national income data I estimate that labor comprises 77 per cent of total input, capital 20 per cent, and land 3 per cent. Hence we could raise total input by slightly over .18 per cent in 1980 if we could raise labor input alone by .24 per cent over what it would otherwise be, or capital input alone by .93 per cent, or land input alone by 6.10 per cent. My proposals would not change the ratio of capital to labor input very much, so the problem of diminishing returns is not acute.

I shall first suggest some ways to increase inputs, indicating the contribution expected from each and sketching the basis of the estimate, and then turn to ways of raising productivity.

1. Yearly net immigration currently equals .2 per cent of our population. As recently as 1911–15 it averaged .6 per cent. Immigration could be increased simply by changing the law. I assume the additional immigrants would make a per capita contribution of labor two-thirds as large, after adjustment for quality differences, as does the existing population. On this assumption, doubling the present immigration rate would raise labor input in 1980 by about 2½ per cent, enough to add .10 to the growth rate of national income. Extra immigration probably would not lower the per capita income of the existing population, but it would impose some other costs. It would also benefit our international relations. More immigration seems to me among the most sensible means of stimulating growth.

2. By working three hours a week, or about 8½ per cent, longer than we otherwise would in 1980, we could add .28 to the growth rate.

My projection of a 3⅓ per cent growth rate assumed that normal annual working hours will drop the equivalent of four hours a week from 1960 to 1980. This is about the rate at which they dropped during the fifties and much less than they dropped during the thirties and forties. Had I assumed a drop of only one hour instead of four, my projected growth rate would have been .28 higher. The calculation that we could add .28 to the growth rate by working three hours a week longer assumes that, in the range within which we will then be operating, more than three-fourths of the impact of shorter hours falls on output rather than being offset in labor efficiency. A decline of only one hour a week in twenty years would allow some leveling down where hours are especially long and some additional holidays, vacations, or coffee breaks, but no change in the standard forty-hour week.

Longer hours are in my list partly because it would be hard to obtain the desired total effect on the growth rate without them. But it is at least possible that we tend to arrive at a level of hours too short to maximize welfare. I say this partly because so little is known about the amount of income that actually is sacrificed for more leisure, and partly because hours have sometimes been shortened in order to spread employment.

Acceptance of this proposal requires employment opportunities so abundant that work spreading disappears as a reason for shortening standard hours, no reduction in legal standards for hours, and probably general acceptance by labor and employers of the need to maintain present hours. Since the AFL-CIO has already established the thirty-five hour week as an objective, this means a change in the present policy of labor.

3. I call upon additional education to raise the quality of labor enough to add .07 to the growth rate. I estimate that this requires addition of one year to the average amount of schooling that would otherwise be received by everyone leaving school between now and 1980. This estimate is derived from existing income differentials among groups with different amounts of education, and the assumption that three-fifths of these differentials result from more education rather than reflect associated variables such as natural ability. It allows for the loss of work by those who will be in school in 1980 rather than working, on the assumption that if they were working their labor would be of half the average quality. Provision of the extra schooling would absorb .3 or .4 per cent of the national income.

My national income projection already assumes a considerable increase from the present age at which young people leave school. This trend can be confidently anticipated. To add still another year, without adversely affecting the quality of education, would place great strain on educational resources and require a major effort to secure teachers and facilities. Noneconomic benefits of extra schooling seem to me large, and this is another case where we might do more than we will be doing if the public had complete information on which to base decisions.

4. I estimate that we could add .03 to the twenty-year growth rate if we could cut in half structural unemployment and underemployment that results from long-term declines in labor requirements in individual areas and industries, including agriculture.

To contribute to growth in any real sense this must be done by speeding re-employment in expanding industries and areas, not by curtailing the displacement of workers that results from demand shifts or technological progress. If we have a bouyant economy in which unfilled jobs at least match the number unemployed, there ought to be ways to cut these types of structural unemployment in half. Swedish experience can be drawn upon in devising means.

5. I look to increased capital input for a contribution of .20 to the growth rate. This requires capital input in 1980 to be 19 per cent larger than it would be otherwise. Whereas my projection assumes a 64 per cent increase in capital input from 1960 to 1980, capital input must nearly double in the same period to provide this additional contribution to growth.

I look for this to be made possible by the other measures proposed to raise growth. I assume here that the crucial difficulty in accelerating growth by increasing the rate of capital formation concerns the possibility of providing attractive investment opportunities rather than of changing saving propensities. Hopefully, the other means of accelerating growth that I am suggesting would bring about the required broadening of investment opportunities. The capital-output ratio will be the same in 1980 if real national income increases $4\frac{1}{3}$ per cent a year and capital input doubles or if national income increases $3\frac{1}{3}$ per cent a year and capital input increases 64 per cent.

To raise capital formation this much requires a higher fraction of national income to be saved during the next twenty years, even though income would itself be larger with a higher growth rate. Hence it would require the sacrifice of consumption that could otherwise be made. If net private saving proves inadequate for so high a rate of net investment, as it may, additional saving could be provided by a surplus in the federal budget.

These five ways of increasing labor and capital input would provide 68 of the required 100 hundredths of a point in the growth rate. For the remaining 32 hundredths, I turn to ways of increasing output per unit of input.

6. From estimates by Gary S. Becker, it can be inferred that employment discrimination against Negroes, taking their qualifications as given, costs us .8 per cent of the national income. If discrimination could be abolished within twenty years by a concerted national effort, this would add .04 to the growth rate. To the extent that progress will be made anyway the economic costs of discrimination twenty years hence will be less than now, and the opportunity for further growth stimulation is overstated.

7. For nearly two centuries most economists have held that restrictions on international trade reduce output and living standards while most [of] the public has believed the exact opposite to be true. The economists are right, but I am not sure how they can become more persuasive in the future than in the past. The cost to us of misallocation of resources resulting from barriers to international trade is not easy to estimate, but I have put it at about 1½ per cent of the national income. My projection assumes this percentage will not change. A serious program to stimulate growth would sweep away all barriers to imports and use our willingness to do so as leverage to get foreign nations to eliminate barriers to our exports. If we could eliminate all barriers far enough in advance of our twenty-year deadline to allow basic readjustments in production and trading patterns to be made throughout the world, this would add .07 to the growth rate.

8. Resale price maintenance laws result in the use of more resources in trade than are required to perform the function. Their cost is very hard to estimate, but I believe it to be large. If, as I have guessed, fair trade costs us 1 per cent of the national income, repeal of fair-trade laws could add .05 to the growth rate.

9. Formal obstacles imposed by labor unions in some industries against the most efficient use of resources costs us output, although again it is very difficult to say how much. My guess is that the cost here might also be 1 per cent of the national income. It seems to me possible that a determined program to adopt better ways of meeting labor's needs might cut this cost in half. This would add .02 to the growth rate.

10. The effectiveness of labor incentives is important to productivity. Close correspondence between each employee's individual contribution to production and his individual reward, and employee awareness of the correspondence, are crucial. Shifts from time rates to piecework have sometimes been accompanied by large increases in productivity. Greater use of incentive pay systems where they are or can be made feasible is the obvious way to obtain substantial improvement. Better evaluation of individual performance for use in setting pay differentials among salaried employees and others paid by time, and in promotion, and more honest letters of recommendation would be helpful. Certain changes in the tax laws might also help. It strikes me as possible that an intensive effort to improve incentives along these lines could contribute .05 to the growth rate. This

could be done, for example, if the efficiency of one-tenth of the work force could be raised 11 per cent.

11. We could add to output by permitting consolidation in the regulated industries where this would mean greater efficiency. If claims that as many as 200,000 employees could be eliminated by railroad consolidation are correct and some minor economies are possible in other regulated industries, consolidation could add about .02 to the growth rate.

12. We could increase output by shortening the lag of average business practice behind the best known. My projection assumes that knowledge will be advancing fast enough to contribute .8 percentage points to the growth rate of real product, as measured, in the next twenty years. This exceeds my estimate of its rate of advance in the past. If we could shorten the lag of average practice behind the best known by nine months, which I consider a large reduction for the whole economy, output in 1980 would therefore be .6 per cent larger than otherwise and the twenty-year growth rate .03 higher. My projection of national product already assumes a reduction of nine months in the lag; thus I am calling for an additional nine-months reduction.

Sweeping away all barriers to international trade, aside from the benefits previously taken into account, would put pressure for modernization upon protected industries that are not now highly competitive, and some of the other steps I have suggested would be slightly helpful in this respect. For the rest, we should have to look to better means of disseminating information and alertness in adopting it. I may note in passing that there is nothing to be added on this account to the contribution of additional investment to growth that I have already computed.

13. For the final .04 required to reach my goal of a full point in the growth rate I look to the advance of knowledge itself. This requires that the state of knowledge in 1980 be where it would otherwise be in 1981. I would be uncomfortable in looking for a large contribution because we know too little about how to alter the rate at which knowledge relevant to production advances to feel sure we know how to get much more out of this source of growth. There is little evidence that the big postwar increase in research and development expenditures has had much effect on the rate of increase in measured productivity. Moreover, present prospects are that we shall absorb into research and development all the qualified personnel that will be available and be expanding these human resources as fast as is likely to be fruitful. But something can probably be done about the distribution of effort. There is extreme concentration of research expenditures in a few product lines and industries. In 1956, industries accounting for only 31 per cent of the national income made 96 per cent of research and development expenditures. Moreover, most of the effort, by far, is devoted to development of new and better products rather than cost reduction. It seems likely that greater dispersion of research effort might get us ahead faster, and it is to steps to bring this about that I would look for the additional contribution to growth.

I suspect there are important possibilities of raising productivity in research. But in the absence of agreement even on whether we should move toward more or less organization and planning of research, I cannot very well recommend what should be done that would not otherwise be done.

This completes my prescription for raising the growth rate by one percentage point. The contributions to be obtained from the individual elements obviously are crude estimates, but with any luck overestimates will be offset by under-estimates and the package should achieve the assigned target.

Many alternative packages of proposals could be put together to arrive at the same effect on the growth rate. The study from which this list is drawn tries to provide a rather complete menu of the choices available to stimulate growth. From that list anyone can make his own combination. This particular package is fairly concrete and practical in the sense that the principal steps required do not exceed our knowledge. I have tried to put together as attractive a package as I could. In my view it would not impose intolerable burdens. But this does not mean I am advocating it or think the country would necessarily be better off for adopting it. This depends mainly on a judgment as to how important it is to raise the rate at which output grows, and why.

Investment in "human capital" through education and training has clearly been a major factor in our persistent, rapid economic growth. In this selection one of America's leading economists argues that we ought to do more to encourage such investment, and examines some of the issues involved.

Theodore W. Schultz is Professor of Economics and Chairman of the Department of Economics at the University of Chicago.

32

Investment in Human Capital

THEODORE W. SCHULTZ

. . . One proceeds at his own peril in discussing social implications and policy. The conventional hedge is to camouflage one's values and to wear the mantle of academic innocence. Let me proceed unprotected!

1. Our tax laws everywhere discriminate against human capital. Although the stock of such capital has become large and even though it is obvious that human capital, like other forms of reproducible capital, depreciates, becomes obsolete, and entails maintenance, our tax laws are all but blind on these matters.

2. Human capital deteriorates when it is idle because unemployment impairs the skills that workers have acquired. Losses in earnings can be cushioned by appropriate payments but these do not keep idleness from taking its toll from human capital.

3. There are many hindrances to the free choice of professions. Racial discrimination and religious discrimination are still widespread. Professional associations and governmental bodies also hinder entry; for example, into medicine. Such purposeful interference keeps the investment in this form of human capital substantially below its optimum.

4. It is indeed elementary to stress the greater imperfections of the capital market in providing funds for investment in human beings than for investment in physical goods. Much could be done to reduce these imperfections by reforms in tax and banking laws and by changes in banking practices. Long-term private and public loans to students are warranted.

Excerpted from "Investment in Human Capital," *American Economic Review*, March, 1961, pp. 13–16. Reprinted by permission.

5. Internal migration, notably the movement of farm people into industry, made necessary by the dynamics of our economic progress, requires substantial investments. In general, families in which the husbands and wives are already in the late thirties cannot afford to make these investments because the remaining payoff period for them is too short. Yet society would gain if more of them would pull stakes and move because, in addition to the increase in productivity currently, the children of these families would be better located for employment when they were ready to enter the labor market. The case for making some of these investments on public account is by no means weak. Our farm programs have failed miserably these many years in not coming to grips with the costs and returns from off-farm migration.

6. The low earnings of particular people have long been a matter of public concern. Policy all too frequently concentrates only on the effects, ignoring the causes. No small part of the low earnings of many Negroes, Puerto Ricans, Mexican nationals, indigenous migratory farm workers, poor farm people and some of our older workers, reflects the failure to have invested in their health and education. Past mistakes are, of course, bygones, but for the sake of the next generation we can ill afford to continue making the same mistakes over again.

7. Is there a substantial underinvestment in human beings other than in these depressed groups? This is an important question for economists. The evidence at hand is fragmentary. Nor will the answer be easily won. There undoubtedly have been overinvestments in some skills, for example, too many locomotive firemen and engineers, too many people trained to be farmers, and too many agricultural economists! Our schools are not free of loafers and some students lack the necessary talents. Nevertheless, underinvestment in knowledge and skill, relative to the amounts invested in nonhuman capital would appear to be the rule and not the exception for a number of reasons. The strong and increasing demands for this knowledge and skill in laborers are of fairly recent origin and it takes time to respond to them. In responding to these demands, we are heavily dependent upon cultural and political processes, and these are slow and the lags are long compared to the behavior of markets serving the formation of nonhuman capital. Where the capital market does serve human investments, it is subject to more imperfections than in financing physical capital. I have already stressed the fact that our tax laws discriminate in favor of nonhuman capital. Then, too, many individuals face serious uncertainty in assessing their innate talents when it comes to investing in themselves, especially through higher education. Nor is it easy either for public decisions or private behavior to untangle and properly assess the consumption and the investment components. The fact that the return to high school and to higher education has been about as large as the return to conventional forms of capital when all of the costs of such education including income foregone by students are allocated to the investment component, creates a strong presumption that there has been underinvestment since, surely, much education is cultural and in that sense it is consumption. It is no wonder, in view of these circumstances, that there should be substantial underinvestment in human beings, even though we take pride, and properly so, in the support that we have given to education and to other activities that contribute to such investments.

8. Should the returns from public investment in human capital accrue to the individuals in whom it is made? The policy issues implicit in this question run deep and they are full of perplexities pertaining both to resource allocation and to welfare. Physical capital that is formed by public investment is not transferred

as a rule to particular individuals as a gift. It would greatly simplify the allocative process if public investment in human capital were placed on the same footing. What then is the logical basis for treating public investment in human capital differently? Presumably it turns on ideas about welfare. A strong welfare goal of our community is to reduce the unequal distribution of personal income among individuals and families. Our community has relied heavily on progressive income and inheritance taxation. Given public revenue from these sources, it may well be true that public investment in human capital, notably that entering into general education, is an effective and efficient set of expenditures for attaining this goal. Let me stress, however, that the state of knowledge about these issues is woefully meager.

9. My last policy comment is on assistance to underdeveloped countries. Here, even more than in domestic affairs, investment in human beings is likely to be underrated and neglected. It is inherent in the intellectual climate in which leaders and spokesmen of many of these countries find themselves. Our export of growth doctrines has contributed. These typically assign the stellar role to the formation of nonhuman capital, and take as an obvious fact the superabundance of human resources. Steel mills are the real symbol of industrialization. After all, the early industrialization of England did not depend on investments in the labor force. New funds and agencies are being authorized to transfer capital for physical goods to these countries. The World Bank and our Export-Import Bank have already had much experience. Then, too, measures have been taken to pave the way for the investment of more private (nonhuman) capital abroad. This one-sided effort is under way in spite of the fact that the knowledge and skills required to take on and use efficiently the superior techniques of production, the most valuable resource that we could make available to them, is in very short supply in these underdeveloped countries. Some growth of course can be had from the increase in more conventional capital even though the labor that is available is lacking both in skill and knowledge. But the rate of growth will be seriously limited. It simply is not possible to have the fruits of a modern agriculture and the abundance of modern industry without making large investments in human beings.

Truly, the most distinctive feature of our economic system is the growth in human capital. Without it there would be only hard, manual work and poverty except for those who have income from property. There is an early morning scene in Faulkner's *Intruder in the Dust,* of a poor, solitary cultivator at work in a field. Let me paraphrase that line, "The man without skills and knowledge leaning terrifically against nothing."

33

Economic Growth as an Objective of Government Policy

Should the nation have an "economic growth" goal, along with its other big economic objectives? Professor Tobin says yes, and supports his answer with several arguments. Dr. Stein has serious doubts, and sharpens some of the issues we face on this score.

James Tobin is Sterling Professor of Economics at Yale University. Herbert Stein is Director of Research for the Committee for Economic Development, an organization of leading businessmen.

JAMES TOBIN, WITH COMMENT BY HERBERT STEIN

In recent years economic growth has come to occupy an exalted position in the hierarchy of goals of government policy, both in the United States and abroad, both in advanced and in less developed countries, both in centrally controlled and decentralized economies. National governments proclaim target growth rates for such diverse economies as the Soviet Union, Yugoslavia, India, Sweden, France, Japan—and even for the United Kingdom and the United States, where the targets indicate dissatisfaction with past performance. Growth is an international goal, too. The Organization for Economic Cooperation and Development aims at a 50 per cent increase in the collective gross output of the Atlantic Community over the current decade.

Growth has become a good word. And the better a word becomes, the more it is invoked to bless a variety of causes and the more it loses specific meaning. At least in professional economic discussion, we need to give a definite and distinctive meaning to growth as a policy objective. Let it be neither a new synonym for good things in general nor a fashionable way to describe other economic objectives. Let growth be something it is possible to oppose as well as to favor, depending on judgments of social priorities and opportunities.

Excerpted from "Economic Growth as an Objective of Government Policy," by James Tobin and "Comment," by Herbert Stein, *American Economic Review*, May, 1964, pp. 4–8, 10–15. Reprinted by permission.

I

In essence the question of growth is nothing new, but a new disguise for an age-old issue, one which has always intrigued and preoccupied economists: the present versus the future. How should society divide its resources between current needs and pleasures and those of next year, next decade, next generation?

The choice can be formalized in a way that makes clear what is essentially at stake. A consumption path or program for an economy describes its rate of consumption at every time point beginning now and extending indefinitely into the future. Not all imaginable consumption paths are feasible. At any moment future possibilities are limited by our inherited stocks of productive resources and technological knowledge and by our prospects for autonomous future increase in these stocks. Of feasible paths, some dominate others; i.e., path A dominates B if consumption along path A exceeds consumption along path B at every point of time. I hope I will incur no one's wrath by asserting that in almost everyone's value scheme more is better than less (or certainly not worse), at least if we are careful to specify more or less of what. If this assertion is accepted, the interesting

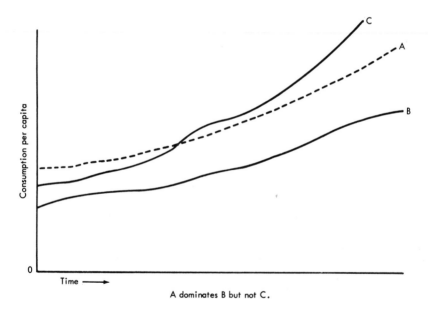

A dominates B but not C.

Fig. 1.   Alternative Consumption Paths.

choices are between undominated or efficient feasible paths; e.g., between a pair A and C where A promises more consumption at some points in time but less at others. See Figure 1. In particular, I take growthmanship to be advocacy of paths that promise more consumption later in return for less earlier.

*   *   *

1. Growth Versus Full Employment

To accelerate growth is not the same thing as to increase the utilization of existing resources, manpower, and capital capacity. In the formulation sketched above, a consumption path with underutilization is dominated or inefficient. By putting the idle resources to work, consumption can be increased both now and in the future. The same is true of other measures to improve the efficiency of allocation of resources. We can all agree, I presume, on the desirability of growth measures free of any cost. If that is the meaning of growth policy, there is no issue.

For short periods of time, stepping up the utilization of capacity can increase the recorded rate of growth of output and consumption. But over the decades fluctuations in the utilization of capacity will have a minor influence compared to the growth of capacity itself. To express the same point somewhat differently, the subject of economic growth refers mainly to supply, or capacity to produce, rather than to demand. In the short run, accelerating the growth of demand for goods and services can, by increasing the rate of utilization of capacity, speed the growth of output. But in the long run, output and real demand cannot grow faster than capacity. If monetary demand is made to set a faster pace, it will be frustrated by a rate of inflation that cuts real demand down to size.

Public policy affecting aggregate demand should be aimed at maintaining a desired rate of utilization of capacity. Economists and other citizens will differ on how high this rate should be, because they differ in the weights they attach to additional employment and output, on the one hand, and to the risks of faster price inflation, on the other. But however this balance is struck, monetary and fiscal policies can in principle hit the target utilization rate just as well whether the economy's capacity is growing at five per cent or three per cent or zero per cent.

Full employment is, therefore, not a reason for faster economic growth; each is an objective in its own right. In an economy suffering from low rates of utilization of manpower and capital resources, accelerating the growth of aggregate demand may well be the need of the hour. But this ought not be considered growth policy in the more fundamental sense. Tax reduction today has sufficient justification as a means of expanding demand and raising the rate of utilization. It is probably an unfortunate confusion to bill it as a growth measure, too.

I do not mean, of course, that the rate of growth of the economy's capacity is in practice wholly independent of its rate of utilization. In principle they may be independent. Demand can be expanded in ways that do not accelerate, indeed may even retard, the growth in capacity itself. But as a rule some of the output resulting from an increase in utilization will be used in ways that expand future capacity. Thus the Great Depression deprived the nation and the world of investment as well as consumption; we, as well as our fathers, bear the cost. The proposed tax reduction, even though its major impact is to stimulate consumption, will nonetheless increase the share of national capacity devoted to capital accumulation. It is in this sense that it can be called a growth measure. But there may be ways to expand demand and utilization to the same degree while at the same time providing both more stimulus for and more economic room for capacity-building uses of resources now idle.

2. Noneconomic Reasons for Growth

Economic growth may be a national objective for noneconomic reasons, for national prestige or national strength or national purpose.

No doubt much of the recent dissatisfaction with U.S. growth is motivated by unfavorable comparisons with other countries, especially the Soviet Union. If current rates are mechanically extrapolated, it is easy to calculate that the U.S. will not be first in the international statistical comparisons in our great-grandchildren's textbooks. Presumably the American nation could somehow stand and even rationalize this blow to our national pride, even as we survive quadrennial defeats by Russian hordes in the Olympics. At any rate, it is not for professional economists to advise the country to act differently just to win a race in statistical yearbooks. The cold war will not be so easily won, or lost, or ended.

International competition in growth may, however, be of importance in the battle for prestige and allegiance among the "uncommitted" and less developed countries. These nations place a high premium on rapid economic progress. They will not—so the argument runs—choose the democratic way in preference to communism, or market economies in preference to centrally directed economies, unless our institutions show by example that they can outperform rival systems. A political psychologist rather than an economist should evaluate this claim. But it has several apparent weaknesses: (a) Rate of growth is not the only dimension of economic performance by which our society will be judged by outside observers. Equality of opportunity and of condition, humanity, understanding, and generosity in relation to less privileged people in our own society and abroad—these are perhaps more important dimensions. (b) The U.S. is not the only noncommunist economy. The examples of Western Europe (in particular the contrast of Western to Eastern Germany) and Japan are more relevant to the rest of the world, and they give convincing evidence of the economic vitality of free societies. (c) What is much more important is a demonstration that an underdeveloped country can progress rapidly under democratic auspices. Without this kind of demonstration, faster growth of affluence in already affluent societies may cause more disaffection than admiration.

On the score of national strength, there is a case for growth. But it is more subtle than the facile association of military power with generalized civilian economic capacity. Nuclear technology has made this connection looser than ever. A country is not necessarily stronger than another just because it has a higher GNP. Great productive capacity may have been the decisive reserve of military strength in the last two World Wars, but nowadays it is useless if it remains unmobilized until the cataclysmic buttons are pushed. A country with smaller GNP can be as strong or even stronger if it persistently allocates enough of its GNP to military purposes. And in the age of overkill, apparently there can be a point of saturation.

Should we grow faster to be better prepared to meet possible future needs for output for military purposes—or for other uses connected with national foreign policy? If we do not, we will have to meet such needs when they arise by depriving other claimants on national production, principally consumption, at the time. But in order to grow faster, we have to deprive these claimants now. Hence the national power argument seems to boil down to the economist's calculation after all; i.e., to the terms of trade between current and future consumption.

But there is an important exception. Some hazards are great enough to bias our choice to favor the future over the present, to accept less favorable payoffs than we otherwise would. We might conceivably be challenged one day to a duel of overriding priority, involving all-out commitment of resources to military uses, foreign aid, space adventures, or all of these together. A high GNP might be the difference between victory and defeat rather than the difference between more or less consumption. In other words, this contingency is one that could be met only by sacrifices of consumption in advance, not by sacrifices at the time.

As for national purpose, it is surely conceivable that a growth target could inspire, galvanize, and unite the nation. But it is not the only objective that could serve this purpose, nor is it necessarily the best candidate.

3. Growth in What?

The formulation of the growth issue sketched above presents it as a choice among available consumption paths. The concentration on consumption deserves some elaboration and explanation—especially because growth performance and aspiration are popularly expressed in terms of gross or net national product.

Some of the noneconomic reasons for favoring faster growth also suggest that GNP is the relevant measure, especially if it is the most usual and visible measure. But as economists we would make welfare or utility depend on consumption. We would require the investment part of GNP to derive its value from the future consumption it supports. After all, a future in which the rate of growth of GNP reaches fantastic heights has no appeal if the fruits of the achievement are never consumed. We must heed the "golden rule" of capital accumulation: there is a saving ratio and a corresponding capital intensity that maximize consumption. Persistent saving in excess of the rule makes GNP higher but consumption lower.

Neither GNP nor consumption, as ordinarily measured, counts leisure. Yet I do not understand advocates of faster growth to be taking a stand in favor of goods and services priced in the market and against leisure. Should the trend toward shorter hours, longer vacations, and earlier retirements accelerate, the rate of growth of consumption as measured in the national accounts might decline. But a decline for this reason should not bother a growth-oriented economist. The *Affluent Society* to the contrary notwithstanding, the conventional wisdom of economics was long since liberated from the fallacy that only produced goods and services yield utility and welfare. Economists do have prejudices against biasing the price system in favor of leisure and against forcing the leisure of involuntary unemployment on anyone. But those are other matters. The consumption whose growth path concerns us should include leisure valued at the real wage. Needless to say, it should also allow for consumption goods and services provided by government.

Finally, is the relevant measure aggregate consumption or consumption per capita? Later in the lecture I shall be concerned with social indifference curves between consumption at one date and at a later date. . . . What measure of consumption should the axes of such a diagram represent? The answer depends on questions like the following: Do we discharge our obligation to the next generation if we enable them to enjoy the same aggregate consumption even though there will be more of them to share it? Should we, on the other hand, sacrifice today in order to raise per capita consumption half a century from now just because there will then be more consumers? Or should generations count in some sense equally regardless of size?

These are not easy questions for the social philosopher, but revealed social preferences lean towards per capita consumption. Presumably we do not value increase in population for its own sake. We might if sheer numbers were important for national power. But in general we are content to leave population trends to free choice; indeed, we seek to enlarge parents' ability to limit births at their discretion. Neither immigration nor subsidies for child-bearing are advanced as growth proposals. In the world at large, certainly, the commonly accepted aim is to retard the growth of population, not to accelerate it.

*   *   *

III

In this section I propose to argue: (1) that government might legitimately have a growth policy, and indeed could scarcely avoid having one, even if private capital markets were perfect; (2) that capital markets are far from perfect and that private saving decisions are therefore based on an overconservative estimate of the social return to saving; and (3) that the terms on which even so advanced an economy as our own can trade present for future consumption seem to be very attractive.

1. Government Neutrality in Intertemporal Choice

Many economists and many other citizens will argue that the government should be neutral as between present and future. In their view the capital markets produce an optimal result, balancing the time preferences of individuals, freely expressed through their consumption and saving behavior, against the technological opportunities for substituting consumption tomorrow for consumption today. Let us assume for the moment that government can be neutral in some meaningful sense and that the capital markets perform their assigned function. Even so, I believe government should have a growth policy, and only by accident a neutral one.

I fail to see why economists should advise the public that it is wrong for them collectively to supplement (or diminish) the provisions for the future they are making individually. I agree to the desirability of satisfying human preferences— that is what our kind of society and economy is all about. But I have never been able to understand why the preferences of individuals are worthy of respect only when they are expressed in the market, why the preferences of the very same individuals expressed politically should be regarded as distortions. Sometimes economists come close to rationalizing all market results and private institutions by the argument that they would not occur and survive if they were not optimally satisfying individuals' preferences. But political results and public institutions are not granted the benefit of presumptive justification-through-existence.

In both arenas preferences certainly need to be guided by full and accurate information. In the arena of government policy, it is the business of economists to help the society know what it is doing, to understand the choices, benefits, costs, and risks it confronts, not simply to repeat *ad nauseam* that the best thing to do is nothing.

The case for explicit government policy in intertemporal social choice is especially strong. More than any other social institution, government represents the permanence and continuity of the society. And in a democracy one way in which each generation uses government is to protect the interests of unborn generations against its own shortsighted and selfish instincts.

We cannot be sure that lineal family ties will give individuals sufficient motivation to provide for society's future. Suppose the individuals of a whole generation, deciding that their children and grandchildren might better start from scratch, were to proceed to consume their capital. Good capital markets might reflect this epidemic of acute time preference in a perfectly Pareto-optimal way. But would we as a nation feel that we were collectively discharging our obligations to our successors?

Through many activities of government, including conservation and public education, we have recognized a generalized obligation to equip the next generation—an obligation wholly distinct from our individual provisions for our own children. This generalized obligation acquires special force if we take seriously our ideals of equality of opportunity. We like to think that our society gives the members of each generation an equal chance in the race, or at least that their chances are not pre-determined by family backgrounds. Besides requiring investment in human beings on a basis other than ability to pay, this ideal suggests redistributive taxation of estates. And if estate taxation dulls incentives to save for specific heirs, the government needs to replenish saving collectively.

But what is growth-neutral government finance anyway? I have already dismissed as farfetched one answer; namely, that any government finance is growth neutral when it is fully and accurately foreseen, and accordingly offset, by taxpayers and by the beneficiaries of government services. Often a balanced budget is considered a growth-neutral fiscal policy. The budget in this rule is not, of course, the conventional U.S. administrative budget. Rather the rule suggests that (a) net government investment should be covered by borrowing, with the Treasury competing in the capital markets with private investors for private saving, and that (b) other government expenditure, including allowance for consumption of public capital, should be covered by current taxes or fees.

The rule is clear cut and has intuitive appeal. But it seems to bias social choice against the future when there is simply a shift in public preference from private consumption, present and future, to collective consumption, present and future. The rule would levy only enough new taxes to cover the additional collective consumption. But the evidence is that taxpayers would pay some of these new taxes from saving (especially if the collective consumption the taxes finance were of regrettable necessities like national defense rather than of services that clearly yield utility now and in the future). Interest rates would rise and investment would be curtailed, even though no shift in social time preference has occurred. Clearly the 10 per cent of GNP which the cold war has forced us to devote persistently to national defense has not come wholly from private or public consumption. True neutrality evidently would require a tighter fiscal policy the bigger the government's budget for current consumption.

But in any case, the quest for neutrality is probably a search for a will-of-the-wisp. For it is not only the overall budget position of government but also the specifics of taxation and expenditure which affect intertemporal choices. We have not yet learned how to implement the welfare economist's lump-sum taxes. I have already given one example of a tax which is desirable in view of other social objectives but is bound to affect incentives for private accumulation of wealth. It will suffice to remind you also that our methods of taxation necessarily favor one kind of current consumption, leisure, both as against other current consumption and as against future consumption of products and leisure.

The major policy proposals of growthmen boil down to the suggestion that government should save—or save more—by making investments on its own account, subsidizing the investments of others, or by channeling tax money through the capital markets into private investment. This last item is the major purpose of the full employment budget surplus for which Councils of Economic Advisers longed under both Presidents Eisenhower and Kennedy.

It is now widely recognized that in principle the government can match aggregate demand to the economy's capacity in a variety of ways. Its various instruments for regulating or stabilizing demand affect consumption and investment differently. A strong pro-growth policy would restrict consumption by taxation or by economy in government's current expenditure while stepping up public investment and encouraging private investment through tax incentives or low interest rates and high liquidity. The government cannot avoid choosing some combination of its demand-regulating instruments. Therefore government is bound to affect the composition of current output and society's provision for the future. Let us debate this choice of policy mixtures on its merits, weighing growth against its costs and against other objectives of policy, without encumbering the debate with a search for that combination which meets some elusive criterion of neutrality.

2. Imperfections in Private Capital Markets

I turn now to the second subject: the efficiency of the capital markets. Do private saving decisions reflect the real payoffs which nature and technology offer the economy? There are several reasons to believe that the answer is negative.

Monopoly and Restrictions of Entry. The evidence is that the rates of return required of real investment projects by U.S. business corporations are very high —typically more than 10 per cent after allowance for depreciation, obsolescence, and taxes. Rates of this magnitude are not only required *ex ante* but realized *ex post.* Why do these rates so greatly exceed the cost of borrowed funds, the earnings-to-price ratio of equity issues, and in general the rates of return available to savers?

One reason clearly is that the relevant markets are not purely competitive. A monopolistic or oligopolistic firm limits its expansion in product markets, its purchases in factor markets, and its calls on capital markets, because the firm takes into account that prices and rates in these markets will turn against it. The managers seek to maintain a market valuation of the firm in excess of the replacement cost of its assets, the difference representing the capitalized value of its monopoly power, often euphemistically called good will. Restrictions and costs of entry prevent other firms from competing this difference away. Foresighted and lucky investors receive the increases in the firm's market value in the form of capital gains. But the willingness of savers to value the assets of the firm above their cost, i.e., to supply capital at a lower rate of return than the firm earns internally, is not translated into investment either by this firm or by others. One effect is to depress rates of return in more competitive sectors of the economy. But another result is to restrict total saving and investment.

Risks, Private and Social. Risks provide a second reason for the observed divergence between the rates of return satisfactory to savers and those typically required of real investment projects. Some of these are risks to the economy as well as to the owners of the business: technological hazards, uncertainties about consumer acceptance of new products, or uncertainties about the future availability and social opportunity cost of needed factors of production. Even though these are social as well as private risks, it is not clear that society should take a risk-averse position towards them and charge a risk premium against those projects entailing more uncertainties than others. Presumably society can pool such risks and realize with a very small margin of uncertainty the actuarial return on investments.

Moreover, some of the private risks are not social risks at all. Consider, for example, uncertainties about competition and market shares; if several rivals are introducing a new process or new product, the main uncertainties in the investment calculation of each are the future actions of the others. Consider, further, the high and sometimes prohibitive cost which many firms impute to external funds—apparently as insurance against loss of control to new shareowners, or, with extremely bad luck, to bondholders. If savers were offered the rates of return asked of and earned by business investments, in the form of assets that impose no more risk on the holder than is commensurate to the social risks involved, presumably they would choose to save more.

It is true, on the other hand, that some net saving is now motivated by personal contingencies that are likewise social risks of a much smaller order. But our society has created insuring institutions, both private and public, to reduce the need for oversaving to meet such contingencies. Except in the field of residential construction, it has created few similar institutions to prevent private risk-aversion from leading to under-investment.

External Returns to Investment. Some investments yield benefits which cannot be captured by the individual or firm making the initial outlay. Research and development expenditures and outlays for training of personnel are obvious cases in point. Government policy has already recognized this fact both in tax law and in government expenditures, and it is difficult to judge whether this recognition is sufficient. Kenneth Arrow has pointed out that not only R and D but all forms of investment activity share in some degree the property that B may learn from A's doing. The support which this observation gives to a general policy of encouraging investment is somewhat tempered by reflecting that the same social process of "learning by doing" can occur in production of goods and services for current consumption. However, experience is most important as a teacher in new situations, and innovations are likely to require investment.

In regard to investment in human capacities and talents, it is by no means clear that public outlays are yet sufficient to reap the external benefits involved, or even that the relevant capital markets are sufficiently developed to permit individuals to earn the private benefits. I recognize that calculations of the rate of return to educational outlays depend critically on how much of these outlays are charged to current consumption. As an educator and ex-student I am inclined to rate high the immediate utility-producing powers of education.

3. The Payoff to Social Saving

The burden of my remarks so far is that we cannot escape considering growth or, more precisely, intertemporal choice as an issue of public economic policy. We cannot assume, either, that the market settles the issue optimally or that government can be guided by some simple rules of neutrality. We—and there I mean the economics profession and the country and not the three of us speaking tonight—must confront head-on the question whether the social payoff of faster growth in higher future consumption validates its cost in consumption foregone today. The issue that needs to be joined is typified by the contrast between Denison, who estimates a very high investment requirement for a one point increase in the medium-term growth rate (a ten point increase in the ratio of current gross investment to GNP) and Solow, who calculates a marginal investment requirement only about one-fifth as high.

Fortunately the profession has now begun the task of computing rates of return on various kinds of investment, tangible and intangible. Thanks to theoretical advances in growth models and in handling the knotty problems of technological progress, vintage capital, and obsolescence, we have a better conceptual foundation for these tasks than we did only a few years ago. Phelps, using the same conceptual approach as Solow, has estimated the overall rate of return on tangible investment in the U.S. to be about 14 per cent in 1954. And even this figure seems conservative in relation to some target rates of return of large industrial corporations reported by Lanzillotti.

*   *   *

"COMMENT"—by Herbert Stein

First, we are not impartial between generations. The next generation is our children and we are a child-oriented society. There is an old story about the immigrant who never in his life got to eat the white meat of chicken. When he was a child in the old country the parents got the white meat and when he became a parent in America the children got the white meat. We may all value white meat tomorrow less than white meat today, but some of us value white meat for our children more than white meat for ourselves.

Second, I suspect, though I have taken no census, that people in general tend to underestimate the rate at which incomes will rise through time and therefore overestimate the need for saving.

Third, people save for protection against private risks which would not require saving by the society as a whole.

Fourth, apparently a large sector of the population is driven by what a colleague of Professor Tobin has called "the Puritan ethic," which embodies a strong compulsion to save.

However, let us assume that we have discovered that we are saving too little. Let us assume further that we have persuaded everyone to accept the moral imperative: take what thou hast and give to the rich, that is to the future, so that they may be richer still. I shall not stop to ask what arguments could be used to persuade someone who did not find this idea spontaneously appealing. I would like to ask how the government gets into this picture, since Professor Tobin's paper is about growth as an objective of government policy.

Why should individuals require the help of government in order to carry out temporally impartial savings decisions if that is what individuals want to do? Ample savings media exist without further action by government. The effectiveness of one individual's saving does not depend on whether other people are also saving. There is no critical mass that the savings must reach. It is not necessary that everyone should save in some particular way, which has to be specified by a central authority.

I suppose that government enters the picture if an effective majority of the population desires to save at the socially appropriate rate but some significant minority does not. Then government becomes the instrument by which the majority forces the minority to save more than it wishes. I do not think we can brand this as illegitimate a priori. Government is an instrument of force, and we use it properly for many important purposes. But the use of force deprives some people of some part of their freedom. This is a cost and it should be minimized, or not incurred except for highly important gains. If we take the position that every departure from any optimum calls for government action, that not a sparrow falleth without becoming a concern of government, I fear we shall have more government than we can manage and less freedom than we would like.

In a special way, Professor Tobin's paper recognizes this. I refer to his few comments on population policy. If we are concerned, as Professor Tobin suggests we should be, with the growth of per capita incomes, it would seem natural that we should be concerned with the growth of population. But he accepts the fact that we do not have, and should not have, a government population policy. I think this is because he recognizes that the private freedom involved here is too important to be impaired for the sake of optimizing the rate of growth of per capita consumption.

Does not the same kind of question arise, even though on a different emotional scale, with respect to individuals' freedom to use their own incomes? Don't we have to ask not only whether saving and investment are below the social optimum but also whether the deficiency is so great and the consequence so serious as to justify government action?

This leads me to Professor Tobin's discussion of government neutrality towards growth. He demonstrates convincingly that government cannot be neutral with respect to growth, but inevitably affects growth in a variety of ways. If I have used the word "neutral" in this connection in the past, I recant. I would offer as a substitute for the word "neutral" the word "indifferent." Surely the government can be indifferent about economic growth. We would not expect the government to have a policy about every consequence of its actions. The pattern of government expenditures affects the distribution of the population among states and localities. But this does not require the government to have a policy about the regional distribution of the population, and we do not, except in extreme cases where there is distress. Something does not become an objective of government policy simply by being a consequence of government policy.

I do not want to run the notion of indifference into the ground. I only offer it as a feasible alternative to growth policy—more feasible than neutrality. There may be cases in which government action impairs growth and serves no other useful purpose. Such cases would call for correction. But we would expect these cases to be few and quantitatively unimportant. The big government actions that affect growth also have other objectives and effects. The import of a policy of indifference is that these actions should be determined by consideration of objectives other than speeding up growth—primarily and in general.

In the end, as Professor Tobin said at the beginning, the question is whether more growth is worth its cost. He has computed the cost in terms of present consumption foregone, compared it with the discounted value of the future consumption gained, and concluded that there would be a net gain. Whether such a computation can be done with any objectivity, especially in view of the difference in income levels between present and future generations is doubtful. Whether, however it is done, the result would come out in the direction indicated, is at least uncertain. But if I remain skeptical, it is not primarily for these reasons. It is primarily because of the costs not included in this calculation. These are the costs of the measures that government may have to take in order to make us save substantially more. Among these possible costs are reduction in our freedom to dispose of our own incomes, growth in the role of government as investor, impairment of the equity of the tax system, reduction of important government expenditures that do not qualify as investment, and diversion of the limited problem-solving capacities of government from other critical issues. These are the risks that make me hesitate to raise the further enrichment of our grandchildren into the top ranks of government policy objectives.

If any grandchildren of mine should ever read these words, I hope they will not think that I disregard their interests. I expect that they will be richer than we are, and hope that they will be even richer than I expect them to be. But to make them richer still is not, in my opinion, among the most valuable things we can do for them. It is much more important to pass on to them a world of reasonable security, in which they have substantial freedom to manage their own affairs and dispose of their own incomes, in which the relatively poor among them are relatively less poor, and in which the Indians and Guatemalans and Ghanaians are much less poor relative to the Americans. If we can do this, our grandchildren will have no cause to think bad of us. Perhaps we can achieve this and still accelerate future growth. But our energies and intelligence, our capacities for leadership and followership, our ability to govern ourselves, our stock of objectivity and altruism are all limited—more limited than our national income. I fear that if we set ourselves too many high-priority goals we shall achieve none of them. The best is the enemy of the good. May we not have to forego the effort to achieve the best of all possible worlds in order to increase the chance of achieving the merely good?

This presentation of monetary and fiscal
policies that could be used to promote
faster growth, without regard to political
feasibility or the impact of these policies
on other aspects of the economy, should
help you evaluate the wide range of growth
policy alternatives in terms of your own
objectives.

*Paul A. Samuelson is Professor of
Economics at Massachusetts Institute of
Technology.*

34

Fiscal and Financial
Policies for Growth

PAUL A. SAMUELSON

*   *   *

Before presenting the following list, I want to make clear its essential
nature. It is a list of programs that can have important bearings on economic growth. It is a fairly comprehensive list. But it most definitely is
not the list of measures that I personally would favor for the United States.
It is not even a list of measures that I personally would favor if there were
no political feasibility constraints upon American policy.

An example may make this clear. In the following list, I mention the
possibility of replacing graduated income taxes by indirect taxes, such as
federal excises or value-added taxes. This is not politically feasible, in my
amateur's view. But even if it were politically feasible, I personally would
be opposed to such a move: it would offend against my sense of "equity";
its desired effects could be achieved by other programs that are less ob-
jectionable and even if this were not so, I might as a personal value
judgment feel that this deliberate fostering of inequality represented
too stiff a price to pay for some extra growth. Nevertheless, I have put
this item on the agenda for discussion because it is a policy with a bearing on growth. Similarly, I mention in the list the problem of a changed
external value of the dollar. I do not do this because I favor such a move
or consider it at all politically feasible; I include this subject on the agenda
because it is a topic that some economists think is relevant to the problem
of growth.

From the *Proceedings of a Symposium on Economic Growth* sponsored by the
American Bankers Association, February 25, 1963, pp. 89–100. Reprinted by permission.

I do not know how to make clear enough that this is in the real sense of the term an "academic" roundup of all the topics related to our subject here today.

GOVERNMENT EXPENDITURE POLICY FOR GROWTH

1. Expenditure on useful public assets that are *durable* is more conducive to growth than expenditure on current public items.

2. Government expenditure, directly or by subsidy, to basic and applied *science* and to *research and development* is an important growth policy. (Why shouldn't private enterprise carry this ball? It does in part; but since no private firm can hope to keep to itself the social fruits of its innovational work, there is a prima-facie case for public expenditure and subsidy. While improvements in knowledge are an unmixed blessing, the effect of rapid innovation *can* be to lower profits and to intensify the problem of sluggish investment; or it *can* stimulate profits and investment, depending upon its qualitative character.)

3. Public expenditure on *education* and *training* programs can contribute much to growth. Human capital has a profit yield like that of material capital, but our market system does not carry human investment to an optimal point. (I personally believe that much of education ought to be defended on other grounds than growth, and suspect that many current economists have gone overboard in reckoning the social yield on educational investment in humans. But, like all professors, I am for more and better education on its own current merits.)

4. Public expenditure on *health research and care*, by the Federal Government or by its subsidies to states and localities, can contribute to growth. (I personally think this effect may be overrated and that these should stand and fall largely on their great human welfare merits in the here and now.)

5. Public expenditure on various forms of *social overhead capital*, including conservation and perhaps some cautious experiments with "indicative planning" of the French type, are policies conducive to growth.

6. Public expenditure to *reduce risk of private investments*, by insurance, subsidy or bail-out devices, or by joint participation or direct Government ownership and operation represents contributions to growth that are not quite the same thing as the ordinary notion of Government capital formation. Provided the good effects are not offset by harmful effects (psychological and/or real), these could be further devices for accelerating growth. Also, many public expenditure programs have directly favorable effects on private production and should be expanded in a balanced program for growth.

All the above public expenditure programs were designed to increase the rate at which America's full-employment potential national product can be made to grow. The next point has relevance to the problem of helping achieve growth by contriving to reduce underemployment and cut into the gap between actual and potential production.

7. *Any public expenditure on goods and services,* if not offset by more-than-equivalent new taxes and if it impinges on an underemployed economy which, for balance-of-payments or other reasons, cannot be brought to full employment by expansionary monetary policy, will cause real GNP to grow; aside from the first-round creation of useful public product, there will be the induced further rounds of private product (consumption and investment). In all candor, if one takes very seriously the international constraint and the ideological constraint

against large deficits, then the Administration's avoidance of expanding civilian Government expenditures cannot be defended as economically mandatory.

8. Expansion of *welfare transfer expenditure,* not offset by taxation, would also have the above effects. But there is no presumption that this can be done with less need to create a sizable deficit.

TAX POLICIES FOR GROWTH

9. Obviously, tax policies designed to spur *research* are desirable. We have already legislated loopholes in our tax law to encourage patents, and the 1963 tax bill will further liberalize the right to expand research expenditures. There is really not much more that taxation can do in this important field.

10. Allowing *faster depreciation* for tax purposes can stimulate capital formation and growth. The 1954 legislative change and the 1963 guidelines are important here. Policies, like those in Germany, Sweden and other nations, in which a large fraction of the value of an asset can be written off in the first and second year, *cannot* be justified as a return to fair recognition of true economic depreciation (inclusive of obsolescence) needed to measure true *money income;* let us face it, they are deliberate bribes to coax out faster growth. (Note that faster depreciation of an item merely puts off the day of taxes: it is an interest-free, equity type loan from government to business, and if business is already liquid, its effect can be weak.)

11. *The tax investment credit,* proposed by Kennedy and Dillon and so spurned by business, is a genuine give-away designed to coax out investment. The ante on this could be raised.

12. *Permitting assets to be depreciated on a base that is inflated along with the price level* would represent a change from the present system that taxes money income toward a new system that taxes *real* income. This ought to shift the balance away from hoarding money toward investing in things—just as our present LIFO methods for treatment of inventory represent a give-away from the standpoint of correct taxation of *money* income.

13. *Lenient treatment and definition of what is called "capital gain"* rather than ordinary income ought to encourage "venturesome" investment. Indeed, raising ordinary tax rates and lowering "capital-gains rates" should be very stimulating to investment and capital formation as well as to wheeler-dealer speculation. Loopholes can be bribes to coax out investment, albeit they can also distort resource use.

14. Improving devices for *"tax averaging,"* through generous carrybacks and carryforwards and other income-spreading devices, should remove the most important penalties against risk taking in our tax system. This gets the least attention in popular discussions of the present day, but it is economically about the most important policy for growth and equity. If the 1963 Kennedy-Dillon spreading reforms are enacted, our tax structure will be fairly optimal in this vital respect.

15. Changing from a graduated system of income taxation to a *graduated system of consumption and wealth taxation,* if it were politically and administratively feasible, would perhaps be the single most important policy to achieve growth without sacrifice of "equity." The penalty on investing for the future would then be removed, and the fruits of windfall gains would get taxed when spent or held.

16. It is popularly believed that our *high marginal rates of taxation on upper incomes* are the most important obstacle to dynamic investment and growth and reducing them is crucial. Careful study of the effects upon personal effort and on risk taking show this popular notion to be much exaggerated, and even to be possibly the reverse of the truth. The present system practically drives a rich man into venturesome investment, so as to convert ordinary income into what are treated as capital gains. I favor the Kennedy-Dillon 1963 tax package in which high marginal rates are brought down from a 91 to a 65 per cent top. But I do so primarily because the present system, in which people are subject to high rates which they can avoid by taking advantage of loopholes, is both unaesthetic and distorting. It is not because I expect it immediately to give our system a strong fillip toward growth and capital formation.

17. *A reduction in the corporate tax rate* might be stimulating to investment and growth.[1] Corporations early in 1963 look to be rather unusually liquid, so the actual increase in the funds left with them perhaps cannot be expected to be as stimulating to investment as in more normal times. There are some economists who think that excess capacity implies a marginal profitability to further investment of practically zero, so that it would be much more potent to engineer an increase in output toward capacity than to try to induce an increase in the ratio of capital to existing output. I am not of this school, but I must admit that events of the last few years have not strengthened my case. This group believes that stimulating current investment, so that you engineer a spurt like that of 1956–57, will merely mean excess capacity in subsequent years and you will pay in sluggishness then for anything you contrive now. (A shrewd Wall Street analyst told me he disliked the fast depreciation of the 1954 tax code because he thought it had led to the 1956–57 overinvestment which was eroding profits; he favored a cut in corporate taxes instead, precisely because he thought it would accrue to the stockholders and not be used to stimulate capital formation and undermine profits.)

Whether a cut in the corporate tax rate will stimulate investment much depends on the perplexing problem of the incidence of that tax. Gaylord Freeman, Vice-Chairman of The First National Bank of Chicago, told a recent *Life* forum on tax cutting that such a tax may well get passed on to consumers; so removing it would not swell profits and thereby coax out investment. Professor Richard Musgrave, at the same conference, reported on a statistical investigation in which he found that the corporate tax was shifted on to consumers. Even if it were true that the tax was shifted completely on to consumers but that the mechanism by which this came about was through the creation of less capital formation, this Musgrave-Freeman point would not invalidate the hope that cutting rates from 52 per cent to 47 per cent or lower would stimulate investment and growth. (This has been pointed out by the C.E.D. report, "Reducing Tax Rates for Production and Growth," December 1962, pp. 15–26.) Musgrave, however, suspects that the incidence takes place primarily through the fact that businessmen will administer their prices at lower levels if they have to pay less corporate tax: I must confess that this notion that businessmen are successful in pricing to a certain after-tax profit and no more seems unlikely to me. And I must report that Professor Arnold

[1] Wiping out the corporate layer of taxation is an extreme case of this. Back in 1945 when many economists favored such a move, I regarded the corporate tax as a lesser evil than any feasible alternatives, precisely because corporations are good poolers of risks.

Harberger of Chicago has done research that casts doubt on the shifting of the corporate tax away from capital.

It would seem plausible that certain modernization and other investment projects that yield only a 16 per cent before-tax profit and a bare 8 per cent after-tax profit might be refused by business this year; however, a sizable reduction in the corporate or individual tax rate could convert the after-tax yield into a return high enough to motivate this investment. To be sure, lowering the cost of debt and equity capital by massive Federal Reserve expansionary credit policies could achieve this same result and more; but a country—like Canada—with an over-valued currency might not be able to afford such policies, whereas the tax-cut route could extend to domestic investors, a privilege not bestowed on investment abroad. If this be discrimination, lay the blame on the overvaluation of the currency.

Fifteen years ago Musgrave, together with Professor Evsey Domar (now of M.I.T.), made an important point that is overlooked in most modern discussions. When the Government taxes so as to become your senior partner, it shares in your losses as well as gains; so *reducing* the tax rate does to some degree have the offsetting result of *increasing* the riskiness of private investment. It is not necessary that businessmen master this argument for it to be valid; it is enough that their profits be subject to the effect, and that habits and decisions adjust to the facts of the situation. This is not the place for me to become technical; but you can see that depressing points like this are what undermine to some extent the rosy hopes for strong results from business tax reduction. Later a similar point will come out.

18. *Shifting from a system that depends heavily on graduated income taxes to one that depends on ungraduated consumption taxation would be conducive to thriftiness out of a full-employment income.* If such thriftiness tended to become abortive and led to unemployment, growth would be hurt not helped. The result could be a mix of demand at full employment more conducive to capital formation rather than current consumption. Historically, capitalism has, teleologically speaking, used income inequality as a source of growth. If profits are the reward to people with a knack for picking good investment and if such people are thrifty, then leaving profits in their hands ought to lead to a good qualitative mix of venturesome investment as well as to a good overall total of investment. Whether modern democracies wish to purchase growth of this type at this cost is not a matter that I pronounce on here.

It is important to note that the mere fact that a man is in a high tax bracket does not discourage his investment. If I can expense my investment by ultrafast depreciation or by any means, or if my 90 per cent tax is one based upon my consumption, then wiping out all taxation would seem to convert a project with a before-tax return of 20 per cent and an after-tax return of 2 per cent into a project with after- and before-tax return of 20 per cent. What could be more stimulating to investment than that after-tax rise from 2 to 20 per cent, a tenfold change? Alas, the calculation is wrong and misleading. While subject to a 90 per cent tax, a dollar of investment does not cost me $1 but rather only 10¢ since the Government pays the other 90 per cent. If I relate my 2¢ gain to *my* 10¢ investment, I come out with the same 20 per cent after-tax return that 20¢ on a dollar gives me when there is no tax at all.[2] New businesses, it is true, do not have this advantage.

---

[2] The day after writing these lines I met the head of a large corporation who mentioned that they were test marketing a profitable new product "half at government expense."

While countries like Germany and Sweden and Britain tax relatively more than we do, they get a smaller fraction of their revenues from graduated income taxes. In the case of Sweden and Britain, this is not because our marginal rates are so much higher than theirs: at comparable levels of income they are not even so high. But it is because we are more prosperous, so that many more of our people are in high enough income brackets to pay appreciable direct taxes. Fostering inequality to stimulate capital formation, as we have seen, does have cause-and-effect validity. There is an alternative way of producing the same increase in capital formation but leaving its fruits more evenly divided among the populace; but this will appear later in the "expansionary credit policy *cum* fiscal austerity package" discussion.

If I were hired as an economist for the whole group of people who have incomes above $15,000 per year and asked to develop a program best designed in terms of their self-interest, I could not come up with any proposal better than that our present reliance on graduated income taxes be altered by drastically reducing the degree of graduation, exchanging for much of the revenue lost a sales or value-added tax at the Federal level. Professional ethics would require me to state to my clients that the evidence does not suggest to me that, in the present decade, such a change would contribute much to economic growth or to overall efficiency; but it would have significant effects (what we economists call "income" rather than "substitution" effects) in moving us back toward the greater inequality of incomes that prevailed in 1929. If hired by the rest of the community, it would of course be my duty to make this last point clear to the public.

19. *Using ad hoc tax baits to promote worthy causes could be part of a growth program.* I may illustrate this point by quoting a German economist who appeared as a guest at a C.E.D. meeting:

> I realize that the American and German practices are quite different. We in Germany are supposed to be a free enterprise economy, but we freely use the tax system to accomplish what we think needs to be accomplished. Thus, if we want more construction, Dr. Erhard shapes tax programs that subsidize building. If we wish to push exports, we use the tax system to do so. Then, when times change and we don't want these activities emphasized, we remove the tax bait and push something else. On the other hand, you economists in America seem to try to set up fairly what is to be defined as true income and then you try to tax the different kinds of incomes at uniform rates: while there is much to be said for this as a matter of equity, it ties your hand as far as achieving special purposes.

I think this quotation speaks for itself and needs no comment from me.

MONETARY POLICY AND FISCAL POLICY

Here at the end I come to the most important part of my subject. While it is right that fiscal policy should receive much emphasis these days, it is in the realm of monetary policy that a mixed enterprise system like ours can do the most to slow down or step up its rate of growth. Classical economists have always emphasized that channeling resources away from current consumption and toward capital formation is an important way of increasing the ability of an economic system to produce more in the future. Indeed the classical economists were hipped on this subject and tended to place all their emphasis on capital formation as the sole source of progress. Today we have redressed the balance: we also emphasize the crucial role of the technical innovations that can take place even when a nation is doing no net saving according to the usual way of measuring saving and capital formation. Perhaps we have gone too far in redressing the balance: numerous studies by Solow, Fabricant, Kendrick, and others abroad have led to the tentative conclusion that the largest fraction of progress comes from changes in the production function rather than from increases in the stock of capital. Nonetheless, for each extra dollar of resources that the nation can channel into capital formation, there is made possible more than a dollar of additional future consumption: depending upon whether you believe the estimates of Denison or other writers, you will find that society earns 10 to 20 per cent per annum on its effective investments. These rates are not riskless, to be sure; but they are far greater than the four per cent gilt-edge rates which prevail for long-term bonds of the highest quality.

20. *Central bank credit policies that reduce the cost of borrowing and increase the availability of credit to formers of real capital are the single most important programs for causing the "deepening of capital" which steps up the growth potential of a nation.* It is odd that the expressions "easy money" or "cheap money" have such a risqué connotation to them: actually they are the puritanical way of shifting a well-run nation away from consumption and toward more rapid growth. If Max Weber, Tawney, and Sombart wanted to preach the Protestant Ethic for a Twentieth Century economy, their emphasis would have to shift away from the Calvinist emphasis upon nonconsumption toward programs which ensure the channeling of resources into capital formation. For me to give up wanting to buy today's bread is not enough to guarantee that bridges and plants will get built: only if the interest rate and capital market mechanisms which create an effective demand for capital are brought into play does my Calvinistic abstention result in anything but unemployment and unused capacity. How wrong, therefore, on cause-and-effect grounds are arguments like the following, which I collect in my files from utterances by distinguished men of affairs: "Higher interest rates will encourage more saving and less consumption; since we need more investment, the best thing the Federal Reserve can do to promote capital formation is make money tight enough to cause interest rates to firm up." Economists regard this as a fine example of incorrect reasoning; and if this day's sun sets after having had someone here make sense of it, I shall consider today's visit the most valuable one of the year, for it will have taught me something very important.

I realize, of course, that our present international balance of payments makes it difficult to use this most important growth policy and will comment on that matter in a moment. I realize, too, that when easy money brings a nation too much demand-pull, this can contribute to inflation and have bad social effects and bad repercussions for growth; my next point will deal with that matter. But right here I ought to comment on whether an easy money policy which is good for the country is also good for the banking industry and for property owners generally. On the whole, since there is considerable evidence that the relative shares of property and of labor do not change much, one would expect that the owners of property as a whole are benefited by an easy money growth policy. I do not see that banks are any exception to this rule, and indeed policies which expand their reserves and earning assets might be expected to help them even when other property owners are being hurt by a decline in yields. The whole point of such a growth policy is to cause investment to take place that will bring down yields; so particular *rentiers,* particularly retired persons, might find themselves worse off even when the total return to property has gone up. And I must admit that there is the possibility that inducing a "deepening" of capital could cause its yield to decline at such a rate as to reduce the total return to property. Even a euthanasia of the *rentier* class is an eventual possibility, though unlikely: this points up the fact that there need not always be a harmony of interest between the part and the whole; what is good for the United States need not be good for some special part of it.

A number of recent econometric studies suggest that lower interest rates do have a stimulating effect on capital formation spending, which is in contrast to the more pessimistic findings of economists one or two decades ago. I do not wish to make too much of such fragmentary studies. And one has to admit that much of capital formation is financed by large corporations out of internal funds generated from undistributed profits and from depreciation accruals. Short-run variations in Federal Reserve policy are not likely to affect much the decision of the Aluminum Company or of du Pont to build a factory that is clearly needed. Yet even their decisions can, in the longer run, be influenced by the general environment of credit tightness or ease. This general environment can influence stock prices and corporate payout ratios. It can encourage or discourage firms from using their internal funds to buy up other firms or to go into new lines. While internal funds can be thought of as a separate pool from external funds, these two are loosely interconnected. Just as the Pacific and Atlantic oceans do not have the same level, as the locks in the Panama Canal show, so the effective yields externally may differ from those internally. But there is enough indirect connection between the two oceans to keep their levels from deviating by too much; and in the same way, lowering the levels of yields in the external market can help bring down gradually the yields within even the largest firms.

21. *A strong growth-inducing policy of monetary ease, if it succeeds in producing overall employment, can be combined with an austere fiscal policy, in which tax rates are kept high enough and/or expenditure rates low enough, so as to remove inflationary pressures of the demand-pull type and succeed in increasing the net capital formation share of our full-employment income at the expense of the current consumption share.* Such a package has been advocated for many years by such liberal economists as James Tobin, E. C. Brown, R. A. Musgrave, and me; and it has been greeted with some skepticism by the labor movement and by such economists as Alvin Hansen, Gerhard Colm, Robert Eisner, and Leon Keyserling. The Kennedy Administration, because of the international deficit problem, has not been able to make progress with such a program. So long as monetary policy is limited by international constraints, this "new look" program cannot get off the ground. If such a program cannot be tried, or if it actually lacks technical potency because of the impossibility of engineering an increase in the capital-output ratio by increasing the availability of capital, then a nontotalitarian economy like ours cannot do a great deal to speed up its growth.

22. *To the extent that a currency is temporarily or permanently overvalued, the case is strengthened for various unorthodox monetary policies designed to reduce long-term interest rates and increase the availability of risk-capital to domestic users, while not at the same time letting short-term interest rates fall to levels that will cause cool money to migrate to foreign markets and thereby worsen our international balance of payments.* Thus, the costs in terms of growth of an adherence to a "bills only" (or "—preferably") doctrine would be intensified in an era of international deficits. Conventional monetary policy has not usually been interpreted

to include policies designed to bring the rates of risky investment down toward the gilt-edge rates; if such measures could be devised, they would do much to energize private capital and promote growth.

The wage inflation that is now going on in Europe is doing as much to correct our international balance of payments as anything we have yet contrived. Still there are some academic economists who claim that this is too slow a process and that the American dollar may be overvalued. If that should some day prove to be so, some of them would favor direct import and capital controls. Some would favor suspending gold payments and letting the dollar be a floating currency. To the criticism that other countries can be expected to devalue as much as the United States, this reply is given: "If other countries are willing to hold our obligations at the same value in terms of their own currencies, well and good; the important thing is not to hamstring employment and growth domestically." Because some members of the press construed my remarks as favoring or contemplating a change in the external value of the dollar, I want to repeat that the above remarks report on academic attitudes and refer to vague future contingencies rather than to present actualities. What I do personally want to stress is this: When a currency is overvalued, adjusting to that situation by running a sluggish slow-growth economy is a remedy worse than the disease. The correct things should be done, and if that should reveal the untenability of existing parities, it will have been time to learn about the hard facts of life.

One final apology: I wish I could have come here and promised that balancing the budget, preserving monetary discipline, reducing Government expenditures, and busting the monopoly powers of labor unions would usher in an era of prosperity and growth without inflation or tears. It was not my heart that kept me from doing so; it was my head, and my fear of being in violation of the laws of fraud, that compelled me to say less agreeable words.

35
Why
Are We Blessed?

In the eyes of many of the world's poorer peoples America is rich beyond comprehension. Two reporters who have seen much of the world's misery ponder America's abundance and ask what can be done, beyond cold-war measures, to help the poor nations.

Peggy and Pierre Streit are writers on economic affairs.

PEGGY AND PIERRE STREIT

Shiraz, Iran

"Eighty-eight per cent of the people in America own television sets." There it is, the shortest of items in today's local English-language newspaper—there, amid the news about Iran, the cold war, and world crisis. "Eighty-eight per cent of the people in America own television sets"—the mere tick of a statistic, addressed, as it were, to whom it may concern. And our thoughts turn back to seven years of travel in the Middle East and Asia.

We think of India and the daily drive we made to New Delhi from our home on the outskirts of the city. On the way there was a small refugee village and in it a dump heap. Each day, as we passed, we watched the village dogs and the village women, side by side, clawing through the refuse with unnerving intensity for scraps of food.

And we remember Kabul, Afghanistan, its newly paved streets dusted with a thin coat of sand blown in from the plains. Roaming those streets was a band of dirty, barefoot scavenger boys—all seven or eight years old, each with a square metal can strapped to his back. They followed the carriages, searching for horse droppings, and when they found some they scooped up the manure with their small hands and, with a deft practiced motion, tossed it over their shoulders into the cans, to be sold later to Afghan farmers.

We remember, a few winters ago, a little girl on the sleet-covered streets of South Teheran. Her head was bent into a wind that blew her cotton dress against her legs. She was barefoot. As she walked the flesh of her heels, cracked by the cold, left little arcs of blood in the snow.

And so, this morning, as we read that 88 per cent of all Americans own television sets, we ask ourselves, as we have so often before, what we and what our countrymen have done to merit the bounty and the comfort with which we live, and what so much of the world has done to warrant its destitution.

Why is it that we can look forward this evening to the quiet comfort of an ample meal while, not two miles away, thousands of drought-driven Iranian nomads are on their weary way south in search of food for themselves and their gaunt animals? Why is it that we can buy clothes—clothes we don't really need—while in Calcutta thousands of men, women, and children who sleep under bridges and in doorways lack even a piece of cloth to put between themselves and the pavement?

Why are we permitted to look to tomorrow without fear of want, when for so many in this world, tomorrow may well bring flood, famine, or disease to destroy all that they cherish? Why are we permitted to enjoy the blessings of freedom and security, knowing that well-established democratic institutions in the United States have peacefully elected a new President, while in most of the underdeveloped world there is no freedom, there are no democratic institutions— or even much understanding of them or hope that they may soon provide the blessings enjoyed in the West?

Why have we been so fortunate? It would be pleasant to believe we have earned our good fortune because we have worked harder than the millions of people we see toiling on barren land. But we know better.

We have seen too many Indian farmers trudging behind primitive, wooden plows under a searing sun; we have seen too many Nepalese women bent double in their rice fields, their legs covered with leeches; we have seen too many Iranian children hunched over their ill-lit carpet looms, to have any such illusions. We know that never in our lives have we worked, one day, as hard as most of the people in the world work each day. We cannot lay claim to our comfortable lives because of diligence.

Perhaps we have been luckier than most because we are wiser, and wisdom brings its just rewards. But we are mindful of the many thoughtful, stimulating evenings spent under thatched roofs discussing the problems of the world with illiterate Indian or Afghan or Iranian farmers. It has been made abundantly clear to us that a man may be uneducated, but he may also be wise; he may be poor, but he may also have dignity; he may be hard-pressed, but he may also maintain his pride. Thus, we cannot believe that we or our countrymen are more fortunate than others because we have a monopoly on intelligence.

Perhaps we are blessed above others because we are more generous, more honest, or more dedicated. But this is not a point we would care to have to defend against the hungry peasants who have insisted on sharing their meals with us; against impoverished farmers who have gone to great lengths to return to us things we left in their villages; against the hundreds of young people we have met whose work for their young, struggling countries demands a kind of personal sacrifice we have never known.

We ask ourselves, then, if perhaps our good fortune is not due to our system of government, to our freedom and democracy, and if these are not our just inheritance from the men who won them in the United States—from George Washington, Thomas Jefferson, and Abraham Lincoln. But this, too, we must reject.

For, we ask, what have *we personally* ever done, more than most of the other people of the world, to earn or merit these blessings?

We can find no satisfactory reason, in short, to explain why, in a world that now has the capability of caring for *all* its people, there are so many poor and so few rich. And we feel very strongly that in this fact—in the very magnitude of the disparity of living standards, in the very number of people involved, in the very enormity of the injustice—a self-evident truth emerges: that apart from preserving the peace, the first, overriding, frighteningly pressing task of this year and this century is to feed, clothe, and unleash from fear the millions who, through no fault of their own, live in such desolation.

This is a massive and urgent undertaking. It is no longer one for a few missionaries or teachers but one requiring the marshaling of the intellectual, material, and spiritual resources of nations—nations rich enough to provide 88 per cent of their people with television sets. Whatever contributes to this mobilization, whatever speeds this process must be welcomed.

What *could* speed this process? To date, the greatest—one might almost say the only—impetus to this mobilization has been the cold war.

In the past fifteen years the tremendous job of bridging the gap between the affluence of the West and the poverty of the East has begun. In the seven years we have been travelling in this part of the world we have seen enormous accomplishment. Much of it has been due to Western aid. But a big part has also been played by the Russians.

Honesty compels us to admit, however, that the principal reason the United States has undertaken to help raise the world's standard of living is not that there are poor people who rightfully should be sharing more equally the good things of the earth, but that Americans are afraid that if they do not do something about their misery, the miserable will turn to the Communists in desperation. And undoubtedly the forces that motivate the Communists are very similar. The Soviets have undertaken a share of the burden, not because the welfare of the people is a primary concern, but because they want their ideology to prevail and aid is one means to that end.

It would be pleasant to believe that were East and West not embroiled in a cold war both the United States and the Soviet Union would continue their help to the underdeveloped world. But, regretfully, we haven't that much faith. If the cold war ended tomorrow, so, we fear, would the bulk of the efforts being made to help the earth's unfortunates.

We wonder, actually, whether when the history of these days is written a century from now, the cold war may not emerge as one of the greatest boons that mankind has ever known. Certainly, it seems to have been the one force powerful enough to marshal the intellectual and material resources of the United States on a national scale in behalf of the underprivileged, and to cause other countries to follow the American lead with aid programs of their own.

But we wonder if the cold war may not also emerge as a boon to the overprivileged—the 88 per centers. One can hope that it may prove to be a force that, carrying Americans to the far corners of the earth and opening their front pages, their eyes, and their hearts to the needs around them, will finally transform a response based on fear and self-preservation into a true concern for justice and the welfare of all men.

Using a broad brush, Professor Rostow
generalizes from historical experience, and
identifies five big stages of economic
growth from economic backwardness to a
mature, high-consumption society. He
discusses the implications of his conclusions
for the problems of underdeveloped
areas, and examines the role of
American government and business in
aiding the growth process.

*W. W. Rostow has served as an official
in the United States Department of State,
on leave from his position as Professor
of Economic History at Massachusetts
Institute of Technology.*

36
Economics for
the Nuclear Age

W. W. ROSTOW

There are two important problems that must be solved before our nation can, in peace, fully enjoy the products and services which the continued growth of the American economy and the world's technology offer
us and our children. One of these two problems, the arms race with Russia,
is so immediately pressing, so serious in its implications, that we are
tempted to ignore the other problem. The second issue is how to help
underdeveloped nations maintain their independence and progress democratically from their present relative stagnation toward sustained growth
and technological maturity. This second issue is no less important to the
future security and prosperity of the United States than the first.

Even if we find the way to call a halt to the arms race with Russia, what
happens if nations like India, Egypt, Argentina, Brazil, Venezuela, and the
emergent states of Africa adopt forms of government that are inimical to
democracy? Our problem with Communist China is a clear warning. How
can we assist these nations to grow along lines that make it likely they
will choose democratic rather than totalitarian forms of government? How
can we reduce the temptations to military adventures of the type that so
many of the now mature nations succumbed to during our century?
In the end, how can both the United States *and* Russia make sure that
any such temptations that do arise do not include those of nuclear warfare?

From *Harvard Business Review,* January–February, 1960, p. 41 ff. Reprinted by
permission.

STAGES OF GROWTH

These two great issues of the second half of the century are illuminated by an understanding of how the process of growth has unfolded in the past. Certainly, the future will be full of surprises, of events and situations that no one can predict; but some of our problems and choices can be clarified by looking back as well as forward, and trying to generalize what we can learn of the past.

As a social scientist I have gradually come to the view that it is possible and useful to identify all societies as lying within one of five categories:

1. The traditional society.
2. The transitional society.
3. The society in the crucial process of take-off.
4. The society in the drive to technological maturity.
5. The society which has reached the age of mass consumption.

Based on a dynamic theory of production, the theory of these five stages of growth contains one key position: *at any period of time the momentum of an economy is maintained by the rapid rate of growth in a relatively few key, leading sectors.* Cotton textiles, for example, has been in some periods of growth a leading sector, as have railways, chemicals, electricity, and the automobile in others. As a consequence of their rapid expansion, the society experiences a direct demand for new inputs of capital to consolidate the new growth and to establish new growth industries. Some of the developments in this snowballing of the economy are indirect. For example, Sweden, because of a lack of coal, plunged into the electrification of its railways, and thus laid the basis indirectly for a first-class electrical engineering industry.

Each set of leading sectors slows down, as time passes; but, in successful societies, each is superseded by a new set, which carries the process of growth forward. An understanding of this principle may help to explain phenomena like the unique depression of the 1930's:

> This economic reversal, with its resultant unemployment, was due, not to long-run diminishing returns, but to (1) Western Europe's failure to create a setting for a prompt move into high mass consumption, and (2) America's failure to create, through public policy, a renewed setting for full employment permitting the new leading sectors—suburban housing, automobiles, durable consumer goods and services—to roll forward and beyond 1929.

> Today, however, modern democratic nations recognize the sensitivity of the political process even to small pockets of unemployment, and, to boom a flagging economy, would quickly institute policies to encourage new leading sectors.

More than the history of technology is involved, however. As growth proceeds, each stage of development is marked by certain characteristic ranges of per capita income. These, in turn, influence the kinds and amounts of goods consumers demand, and have important characteristic playback effects on production. To understand the stage of a society, we must look at both its technology and how it spends its income—at demand as well as at supply.

But a detailed discussion of all this would go beyond the intent of the present article. Those who are interested in a more technical discussion of these points may refer to my article in *The Economic History Review,*[1] and readers who seek

---

[1] "The Stages of Economic Growth," August 1959, p. 1.

a more popular version may turn to the presentation prepared by the editors of of *The Economist*.[2] Here I shall summarize only briefly the stages of growth, and then consider some issues of possible special interest to the readers of this magazine.

Traditional Society

First comes the traditional society—one whose structure is developed within limited production functions, based on pre-Newtonian science and technology. Because this society is basically agrarian, with few technological innovations occurring in its limited industry, its productivity fluctuates with harvests, wars, plagues, discoveries of new crops, and so on. But the central fact about the traditional society is that a ceiling exists on the level of attainable output per head. This ceiling stems from the fact that the potentialities which flow from modern science and technology either are not available or are not applied in a regular flow.

In terms of history, then, the phrase "traditional society" groups the whole pre-Newtonian world: the dynasties in China, the civilizations of the Middle East and the Mediterranean, the world of medieval Europe. To these we must add the post-Newtonian societies which, for a time, remained untouched or unmoved by man's new capability for regularly manipulating his environment to his economic advantage. Few of these still remain, except for certain regions in Africa.

Transitional Society

During the period when the preconditions for take-off are developed, a society may be said to be in transition. Usually in modern history this period has been initiated as a result of aggression by more advanced societies, an intrusion which mortally wounds the traditional society, although its death is a lingering one and it is superseded slowly and painfully. Gradually, there emerges a new consensus: that economic progress not only is possible but is, in fact, a necessary condition for some other good purpose—national dignity, private profit, general welfare, or a better life for the children.

Technically speaking, there are in the preconditions period three leading sectors whose transformation is a necessary condition for sustained industrial growth:

> 1. *Agriculture*—A productivity revolution in agriculture is required to feed the expanding population, especially the population of the cities which are likely to be growing at higher rates than the overall national average.
> 2. *The export sector*—The earliest stages of industrialization are likely to create an expanded bill for imports, which can only be met by quickly applying modern techniques to the extraction and processing of natural resources.
> 3. *Social overhead capital*—When growth becomes relatively automatic, large outlays on transport, education, sources of power, and the like, are required.

Once the transition has begun, new types of enterprising men come forward who, in both private and governmental finance, show a willingness to mobilize savings and take risks in pursuit of profit or modernization. As banks appear and investment increases, the scope of commerce broadens. Here and there, modern manufacturing enterprises spring up to utilize the new methods of production. But all this activity proceeds at a limited pace within an economy and a society

[2] "Rostow on Growth," August 15, 1959, p. 409, and August 22, 1959, p. 524, summarizing a set of lectures delivered at Cambridge University and shortly to be published by Cambridge University Press as a book, *The Stages of Economic Growth: A Non-Communist Manifesto*. At some points in this article, I have made use of *The Economist's* paraphrasing.

still mainly characterized by traditional low-productivity methods, by the old social structure and values, and by the regionally based political institutions that developed in conjunction with them. One central task of the preconditions is to develop an effective, centralized national state, in opposition to the traditional landed interests of the regions or the colonial power, or both. The take-off can only begin, in most cases, when there exists an effective central government that means business as far as growth is concerned.

The Take-Off

During the interval when the old blocks and resistances to steady growth are finally overcome, the crucial process of take-off begins. The forces pressing for economic progress come to dominate the society; growth becomes its normal condition. Compound interest becomes built, as it were, into its structure.

In Great Britain, and the well-endowed parts of the world populated substantially from Great Britain (the United States and Canada), the proximate stimulus for take-off was mainly—but not wholly—technological. The original sector of primary growth in Great Britain was cotton textiles, but this is hardly a representative case. The substitution of a modern cotton textile industry for imports has more typically marked the pretake-off period. The most powerful single initiator of take-offs has been, as one would suspect, the introduction of railways.

During the take-off, some of the following conditions manifest themselves. The rate of effective investment and savings may rise from, say, five per cent of the national income to 10 per cent or more. New industries expand rapidly, yielding profits which are largely reinvested in new plants. As a result, a demand for industrial labor results, new urban areas develop around the factories, service industries and businesses spring up, and a new class of entrepreneurs is born to direct the enlarging flow of investment in the private sector.

To compensate for the diversion of manpower into industries (and to feed the cities), new methods of agriculture and of extracting natural resources must be developed. It is, therefore, one of the technical preconditions for take-off in the transitional areas that governments come to power which are prepared to channel a high proportion of their people's energies, talents, and resources into the tasks of economic growth as opposed to other possible objectives. One can approximate the take-off of Great Britain to the two decades after 1783; France and the United States to the several decades preceding 1860; Germany, the third quarter of the nineteenth century; Japan, the fourth quarter of the nineteenth century; Russia and Canada, the quarter century or so preceding 1914. Over the past five years India and China have, in quite different ways, launched their respective take-offs.

Technological Maturity

Some 60 years after a society begins take-off (or approximately 40 years after the end of the take-off), technological maturity is generally attained. On the road to this maturity, however, the make-up of the economy changes unceasingly as technology improves. New industries accelerate, older industries level off. The economy finds its place in the world of international trade. Goods formerly imported are produced at home; as a result, new import requirements develop, with new export commodities to match.

Once maturity has been reached, the economy has extended its range into more refined and often more complex technological processes. There may be, for example, a shift in focus from the coal, iron, and heavy engineering industries of the railway phase to machine tools, chemicals, and electrical equipment. This was the transition through which Germany, Great Britain, France, and the United States had passed by the end of the nineteenth century, or shortly thereafter.

Thus, we can formally define maturity as the stage in which an economy demonstrates its capacity to move beyond the original industries which powered its take-off and to absorb and apply efficiently, over virtually the whole range of its resources, the most advanced fruits of (then) modern technology. This is the stage in which an economy demonstrates that it has the technological and entre-preneurial skills to produce, perhaps not everything, but anything it chooses to produce.

Mass Consumption

We come now to a period in the growth of a nation in which mass consumption of durable consumers' goods and services becomes the central dynamic force in economic (and social) life. This is a phase from which Americans are beginning to emerge, whose not unequivocal joys Western Europe and Japan are beginning energetically to probe, and with which the Soviet regime uneasily flirts.

As societies achieved maturity in the twentieth century, two things happened:

> 1. Real income per person rose to a point where a large number of people gained a command over consumption transcending basic food, shelter, and clothing.
> 2. The structure of the working force changed in ways which increased not only the proportion of urban to total population, but also the proportion of the population in white- and blue-collar jobs, aware of and anxious to acquire the consumption fruits of a mature economy.

It is at this stage that, through the political process, Western societies have chosen to allocate increased resources to social welfare and security. The emergence of the welfare state is one manifestation of a society's moving beyond technological maturity. But it is also at this stage that resources tend increasingly to be directed to the production of consumers' durables and to the diffusion of services on a mass basis, if consumers' sovereignty reigns. The sewing machine, the bicycle, and then the various electric-powered household gadgets were gradually diffused. Historically, however, the decisive element, or leading sector, has been the cheap mass automobile with its quite revolutionary effects, social as well as economic, on the life and expectations of society.

For the United States, the turning point, perhaps, was Henry Ford's moving assembly line of 1913–1914. But it was in the 1920's, and again in the postwar decade of 1946–1956, that this stage of growth was pressed virtually to its logical conclusion. During the 1950's, Western Europe and Japan appear to have fully entered this phase, accounting substantially for a momentum in their economies quite unexpected in the immediate postwar years. The Soviet Union is technically ready for this stage and, by every sign, its citizens hunger for it. But communist leaders face some difficult political and social problems of adjustment if this stage is wholeheartedly launched. At the moment, they draw back from the mass-produced automobile and the single-family suburban house.

Future Development

Beyond this fifth stage of growth, it is impossible to predict, except, perhaps, to observe that Americans at least have behaved in the past decade as if diminishing relative marginal utility sets in, after a point, for durable consumers' goods; and they have chosen, at the margin, larger families. That is, Americans have behaved as if, having been born into a system that provided economic security and high mass consumption, they placed a lower valuation on acquiring additional increments of real income in the conventional form as opposed to the advantages and values of an enlarged family.

*   *   *

UNDERDEVELOPED AREAS

We come now to the problem of the underdeveloped areas. What light do the stages of growth analysis throw on their problems? What can and ought we as Americans do about them?

The first thing to be said about the underdeveloped areas is that, of course, they stand at various stages of the growth process. The phrase "underdeveloped" is inexact. Some of them are actually in the take-off: e.g., Mexico, Argentina, Brazil, Venezuela, and, above all, China and India. These societies face many vicissitudes; but I believe the bases have been laid for sustained growth.

Elsewhere there are societies in the late stages of the preconditions period: Iran, Iraq, Egypt, Morocco, for example, and several of the Latin American states. Indonesia, Pakistan, and Burma are only a little behind, if at all. I do not believe the beginnings of their take-offs are likely to be delayed more than a decade. But south of the Sahara in Africa there are societies close to the traditional stage which may have to pass through longer preconditioning processes before sustained growth can be undertaken.

The question now arises whether it is scientifically correct to use my concept of the stages of growth, derived from a generalization of the historical past, to analyze the contemporary problems of the underdeveloped areas.

In part, there is much that is familiar to the historian in the current scene. The technical problems of the preconditions still center about the three leading sectors of that stage—social overhead capital, the generation of increased exports, and a technological revolution in agriculture.

The social and psychological transformations that must occur are, again, broadly familiar from the past; they are the problem of siphoning off land rents into the modern sector, the changing of peasant attitudes, and the training of a new leadership—public, private, or both in various combinations—capable of bringing modern techniques to bear in the various sectors of the economy. And, above all, we can again see, as in the past, that a reactive nationalism, tempted to move in directions other than economic growth, lies close to the heart of the political process in many of these regions.

Two-Way Difference

There is a major technical difference, however. The pool of technology available to these underdeveloped nations is greater than ever before. Other latecomers have enjoyed this advantage to a degree—e.g., Germany, Russia, and Japan in the half century before World War I, coming a bit later than Great Britain and the United States. But in degree we must admit that there is a substantial difference between the present and the past, stemming from the size of the pool of unapplied technology.

This difference, however, cuts both ways: it not only offers the possibility of accelerating growth but complicates the problem of growth. The complication arises because the availability of modern techniques of medicine and public health leads to a radical fall in death rates, which yields much higher rates of population increase than those in most transitional societies in the past. Except for the United States and Russia, the population increase ratios in the precondition and take-off stages have been under 1.5 per cent—generally about 1 per cent. (The United States and Russia had reserves of good land that permitted high rates of population increase to be sustained—reserves which are not now available to the underdeveloped areas in most parts of the world.)

But these newer nations are trying to move forward with population increase rates of 2 per cent and more. This means, in general, that higher rates of investment must be generated to achieve sustained growth; and, even more precisely, it means that the revolution in agricultural technique must be pressed forward with great vigor if the whole development process is not to be throttled for lack of food.

In these circumstances, how can the United States help? By taking all three of these steps, each one essential:

> 1. Offering the underdeveloped areas ample supplies of capital, to ease the general problem of capital formation under regimes of high rates of population increase.
> 2. Providing these nations special assistance which helps them achieve prompt and radical increases in agricultural output, including supplies of chemical fertilizers and aid in building irrigation facilities.
> 3. Developing policies which encourage the local politicians to concentrate their hopes and their energies on the task of economic development, and avoiding policies which tend to divert them from these objectives.

The Price

This is going to cost us money. Loans or grants in themselves cannot do the job. But there is a minimum price tag which the United States and the Free World generally must accept if we are to make a serious contribution to the problem of the underdeveloped areas.

How much? Estimates made independently by many different groups come out at about the same point: something like an extra $3 billion a year, for all the underdeveloped areas of Asia, the Middle East, Africa, and Latin America. Of this sum, half perhaps ought to be provided by the United States, half by Western Europe, Canada, and Japan. Arithmetic of this kind lay behind the proposal of the Senate Foreign Relations Committee to expand the Development Loan Fund to make $1.5 billion available from the United States for each of the next five years. This compares with an American GNP approaching $500 billion and with American military expenditures of over $40 billion annually.

Never, even under the Marshall Plan, have such large stakes hinged on so modest a sum.

Dramatic Question

The urgency and drama of the problem are illustrated by the question of India's Third Five Year Plan. Here is a nation of some 400 million people, representing about 40 per cent of the population of the underdeveloped countries. It is committed in the next five years to attempt the take-off; that is, to move out of its present relative stagnation into sustained economic growth. It has accumulated considerable assets for this decisive effort: a government seeking to organize its resources and talents around the tasks of modernization, a competent civil service, and an expanding corps of private businessmen of competence, willing to accept new methods and to plough profits back into new capacity. Moreover, important capacity in steel and electric power has been developed in the past decade. The tasks of producing a sufficient increase in food to feed the expanding population and of getting enough foreign exchange in this decisive period to import what is needed are the two great remaining problems.

Of the total increase in loans I suggested as necessary, India needs about 40 per cent or $1.2 billion for each year in the Third Plan. The food problems India must basically solve for itself, although our technical assistance and some food surpluses could be helpful.

If India demonstrates that a take-off under democratic auspices is possible with American and Western European help, then other nations of Asia, the Middle East, and Africa will take heart; and the most powerful single argument for communism will be weakened. If in India the present government fails, the break-down of confidence in democracy and in association with the West may spread across the whole southern half of the globe, to our enormous cost.

This is a test which will now take place, whether we like it or not. Success or failure of India in the next five years will have immense consequences for ourselves and our children. Our choice is to ignore it, observe it, or participate in it with the vigor we once threw into the Marshall Plan.

What is true of India is only in degree less true and urgent in the other under-developed areas. Can noncommunist governments, in association with the West, create the preconditions for take-off and guide their societies through the precarious crucial take-off process? This is the question and the challenge.

THE BUSINESSMAN'S ROLE

What special bearing, if any, does this argument have on the life and profession of the American businessman?

Perhaps its greatest technical importance is to provide some insight into the peculiar problems of the underdeveloped areas with which the American business-man increasingly must deal. Some such analysis as this, properly developed, should permit us roughly to establish where, in the stages of growth, a particular region stands. Is it close to the traditional society, like many parts of Africa? Close to the take-off, like Egypt and Pakistan? Attempting the take-off, like India? Or in the early stages of the drive to technological maturity, like Mexico?

In this perspective, businessmen can have some notion of what the problems of doing business are likely to be and what to expect and what not to expect of a given society over a reasonable business-planning period. For example, businessmen should come to regard as normal a phase of nationalism focused against foreign business interests at times during the preconditioning process, for a reactive nationalism is typically the engine which uproots the traditional society and prepares it for modernization and growth.

Furthermore, businessmen should expect governments to play an important role in the economic process in the preconditioning and the take-off, when the build-up of social overhead capital constitutes so high a proportion of investment and the supply of energetic local businessmen is somewhat thin. On the other hand, this historical perspective might lead the American businessman to expect that, as the take-off proceeds and the new nation gains confidence and momentum, attitudes toward foreign business will become more temperate and sensible. Moreover, if communism does not seize these areas, we can expect the private business sector to grow and the role of government in economic affairs to diminish somewhat.

In a quite different dimension, the stages-of-growth analysis helps explain the nature of the boom in Western Europe and Japan, for those regions have entered the stage of high mass consumption, and are going through changes in their structure and momentum similar to those in the United States during the 1920's.

But ultimately, the relevance of this argument to the American businessman is its pertinence to him as an American citizen. It may be one way of helping us all to understand the inner meaning of this precarious stage of history which Mr. Khrushchev calls competitive coexistence. Whether the outcome of this stage is, as Mr. Khrushchev hopes, the isolation and defeat of the United States as a world power, as Asia, the Middle East, and Africa go communist—or whether it ends in earnest settlement, in which the Russians become convinced that their best option is to make a serious armaments control agreement and settle down within their present borders to enjoy the age of high mass consumption—either outcome depends on what we Americans do, both individually as citizens and nationally as leaders of the Free World alliance.

What we Americans do, finally, depends on the willingness of our citizens to lift their eyes from their own narrow concerns and to make their contribution in talent and in taxes to every dimension of this competition—from the deterrence of war to the provision of adequate assistance to the underdeveloped areas. In helping this country to accept Mr. Khrushchev's challenge, and in creating, over the next decade, a situation where peace—rather than world dominance—is the only realistic option available to Moscow, the American businessman has a decisive role to play, both as a citizen and as a community leader.

37
Development
Program
in Afghanistan

The very modest beginnings of a program
designed to raise living standards in
rural areas are described in this U.N.
report. It shows how hard it is to introduce
even the simplest changes in a backward
society.

UNITED NATIONS REVIEW

In Afghanistan, where 85 per cent of an estimated population of 13.8
million live in small villages, the first five-year community development
program, aimed at raising the living standards in rural areas, has just been
completed.

With the help of United Nations technical assistance advisers, eight
comprehensive community development projects, covering almost all facets
of rural life, were in operation by the end of 1961. Working cooperatively
with the government's Rural Development Department, specialists from
the United Nations and its specialized agencies are assisting some 420,000
people in more than 900 villages in such fields as education, agriculture,
health and sanitation, industrial cooperatives, training, leather tanning
and cottage industries, women's welfare, and planning and administration.

On duty in Afghanistan, as the community development program con-
tinues to expand, are technical advisers from the United Nations, the
Food and Agriculture Organization, the World Health Organization, the
United Nations Educational, Scientific, and Cultural Organization
(UNESCO), the International Labor Organization, and the United Nations
Children's Fund.

Now, according to Ch'un Wu, a Chinese community development adviser, a second five-year plan is under way and will be responsible for
setting up 17 additional community development projects, each of which
will affect some 50,000 rural inhabitants.

Mr. Wu, who recently returned to United Nations Headquarters after
five years in Afghanistan, has described the program as "highly successful"

From *United Nations Review,* May, 1962, p. 29.

and one in which the top government officials are "keenly interested because they now realize that it is most important to raise the living standards of the population living in rural areas."

"The essence of the program," he declared, "is to help the people help themselves."

By 1967, Mr. Wu estimates, the rural development program is likely to reach approximately one and a quarter million people, or one out of ten persons in the country. Within the next 15–20 years, if present plans materialize, the entire nation would be covered by about 250 projects.

The program is financed under the national budget, assisted by external aid and the contributions of the people themselves. Among the factors contributing to the rapid enlargement of the program is the administrative organization set up by the government under the Rural Development Department, which acts as the central executing agency functions under the direction and supervision of the Office of the Prime Minister and the cooperation of the rural people themselves.

The basic operating unit of the program is the individual "project" which roughly would cover a 450 square mile area with a population of about 50,000. For each project there is a project officer in charge, under whom work a group of "subject-matter" specialists and village workers, an assistant project officer, and administrative staff.

The village workers are "multi-purpose" in the sense that they have been trained to work with the villagers in a variety of fields corresponding to the special subjects recommended by the "subject-matter" specialists. Each village worker covers one or several villages with a population ranging from 50–6,000. There are 101 village workers for the 913 villages included in the eight projects operating at present. Thus, each village worker is responsible for about nine villages.

Much of the success of the community development program in this rugged hill country is due to the importance attached to the training of project personnel. Among those trained under the existing programs were 45 "subject-matter" specialists; 10 project officers and supervisory staff; 177 village workers; 120 village leaders; and 209 fundamental education organizers, 11 of whom were trained in industrial cooperatives and 33 in carpentry.

In the field of *agriculture* there are now 40 demonstration farms in the program area, 20 of which were established in the past two years. As against 8,600 animals treated and vaccinated in 1956–57, almost 83,000 animals received such care in 1960–61.

As regards *education*, there was only one village boys' school in the program area in 1957. There are now 64 such schools; similarly the number of girls' schools has risen from one to 48 during the same period.

Health services are organized primarily through rural health units in each project area. Their major activities consist of surveying existing health needs and control of communicable diseases; maternal and child health; vital statistics; school health services; treatment and environmental sanitation. There are now in operation eight main health centers and 17 sub-centers which, together, have treated some 500,000 persons. More than 18,000 persons have been vaccinated against small-pox; and 42,000 have received inoculations against cholera, typhoid, and paratyphoid.

The sanitation aspect of the program has made considerable headway.

In the field of *small-scale industries,* a fertilizer demonstration project has been set up to train local personnel in the use of locally-available waste material as a substitute for imported fertilizer. Larger units, operated on a commercial basis are to be installed shortly. A model tannery, utilizing modern machinery and equipment, has been established to train local tanners in finishing hides and skins.

Social Welfare: One center and two sub-centers have been established for training women in home economics and handicrafts; there are 59 village development councils and five youth centers.

"The figures," said Mr. Wu, "speak for themselves." But much remains to be done, particularly in the construction of village roads. Roads, important in any country, are of special importance in a land-locked country such as Afghanistan where, Mr. Wu explained, there are no railroads or waterways of any kind. Thus, adequate village roads would not only promote solidarity within the community, Mr. Wu declared, they would also facilitate participation of villagers in community affairs and develop local leadership. A doctor can be brought to a village to visit a sick child; agricultural produce can be brought to market; and commercial activities introduced into the village.

38
Economic Development: Rival Systems and Comparative Advantage

The undeveloped countries face a choice
between Western democratic methods and
the Marxist political and economic
design. Dr. Galbraith compares the two
approaches, and argues that a critical
advantage of the Western model is its
emphasis on liberty and constitutional
process.

JOHN KENNETH GALBRAITH

*John Kenneth Galbraith is Professor of
Economics at Harvard University.*

One of the well-observed features of economic development in the 20th
century is the need to choose between two broad political and economic
designs. This choice, one from which developing nations of the 18th and
19th centuries were conveniently exempt, is between Western constitutional organization on the one hand and Marxian and neo-Marxian polity
and economic organization on the other.

These are not, as everyone knows, homogeneous alternatives. Wide
differences separate a state such as Poland, where the agriculture, and
hence close to half the economy, remains in private hands and subject
to market influences, from the far more completely socialized economy
of the Chinese mainland. There are similar distinctions between the non-
Marxian economies, which, in this case, are enlarged by terminological
preference and political semantics. In Scandinavia, the United Kingdom, and modern India the word "socialism" is politically evocative. As a
result politicians try to find as much of it as possible. In the United
States, steps that would elsewhere be identified with socialist enlightenment—social security, agricultural price guarantees, even the public development of public power sites—are firmly for the purpose of making
private enterprise function better.

Also one must be cautious in speaking of a "choice" between the two
designs. Geography and the proximity of military power have had much
to do with the decision. Had Poland, to select a country not unaccustomed
to movement, been radically relocated after World War II to approxi-

Address before the Commonwealth Club, San Francisco, California, on June 4,
1962, published in the *Department of State Bulletin*, July 2, 1962, pp. 13–17.

mately the position of Paraguay, her subsequent economic and political history would have been rather different. Individuals do commit themselves as a matter of free choice to a Marxian political and economic design. But nations have rarely done so in the normal course of unmanaged elections—a relucance, incidentally, which was foreseen by both Marx and Lenin.

Nevertheless these broad alternatives exist. My purpose is to weigh their advantages and disadvantages from the standpoint of the developing country. I am aware that an American ambassador will not be considered by everyone a wholly impartial judge. And even in this liberal and sophisticated gathering there would doubtless be eyebrow-lifting if my evidence were to lead me to the wrong conclusion.

But the choice merits serious assessment. Much of the present literature consists of declarations of superiority by one side or the other. We share with the Communists a strong faith in the value of robust assertion. Were the advantage all on our side, we would have little reason to worry. But we do worry, and it might be well, accordingly, for us to have a moderately unemotional appraisal of what we have to offer the developing nations as compared with the Communists.

THE GOAL OF DEVELOPING COUNTRIES

The goal of the developing country can be quickly stated: It is to bring itself as rapidly as possible into the 20th century and with the apparatus of individual and group well-being—food, clothing, education, health services, housing, entertainment, and automobiles—which is associated in every mind, urban and rural, bourgeois and Bolshevist, with 20th-century existence. Here and there are some that demur. But in my observation the most monastic Christian, the most contemplative Buddhist, and the most devout Gandhian cannot be considered completely secure against the charms of the bicycle, motor scooter, or transistor radio.

The things associated with modern civilization are now denied by backwardness and poverty. The task of the two systems is to overcome this poverty. The causes of poverty, in turn, are not simple—although the problem has suffered prodigiously from oversimplification. One cause, clearly, is an oppressive social structure which channels return from the many to the few and which denies the individual the natural reward of his efforts at self-improvement. Another is a feeble, nonexistent, or corrupt apparatus of public administration which denies to the country the things—law and order, education, investment in roads, power, manufacturing—which are possible only where there is effective public authority. Or poverty may be itself a cause of poverty; it denies the country capital for investment, revenues for education, or purchasing power for consumer products which, in turn, are an incentive to effort. Thus poverty perpetuates itself. Such are the fundamentals that both systems must attack. It is unlikely that the same causes operate in the same form and with the same intensity in any two cases. An effective attack, therefore, requires not only efficient remedies but effective diagnosis of the condition to be cured.

Both systems agree on a number of important points. It is common ground that a shortage of capital is a likely cause of stagnation. Both agree on the need for a massive volume of investment to initiate and stimulate not only economic but social advance. There is agreement also that this investment should be in accordance with a carefully conceived plan. (Here we have paid the Soviets the compliment of appropriating an important idea.) There is increasing agreement that a principal object of this investment must be in the educational and cultural improvement of people themselves. The visitor to the more remote parts of Soviet Asia is immediately impressed by the volume of resources going into schools, colleges, adult education programs, and other forms of cultural extension as part of the attack on the traditional backwardness of these areas. If, in the years following World War II, we thought too much of investment in terms of physical capital and too little of the importance of a literate and educated populace, this is an error we are now correcting.

There are, however—and this will doubtless come as a relief—important differences between the two approaches, and these are vital. The first lies in the diagnosis of the causes of poverty and the related remedy. The second difference is in the way development is organized. The third is in the political and constitutional environment of development. Let me take up each of these differences in turn.

DIAGNOSING THE CAUSES OF POVERTY

In the Marxian view poverty is principally caused by institutions which chain the country to its past—which hold it in colonial subjection, which exploit and subjugate the masses and deny them the reward of their labor, which make government not the efficient servant of the many but the corrupt handmaiden of the few.

In the predominant Western view the poor are the victims of their poverty. All societies have capacity for growth; the poor society lacks the resources to invest in growth. Having less than enough for its current needs for food, clothing, and shelter, it has nothing for investment in education, improved agriculture, transportation, public utilities, or industrial enterprise.

Each of these views leads naturally to a prescription. If institutions hold a country to its past, the answer is the elimination of these institutions. If the problem is the self-perpetuating character of privation, the answer is to provide the catalyzing resources—specifically, economic aid and assistance in its use—which the country cannot supply to itself.

This is the first difference. The Marxian emphasis is on the institutions that inhibit progress and the need to eliminate them. Our emphasis is on the self-perpetuating character of poverty and the catalyzing role of aid. It will be noted that each system has a cause and remedy that is not without convenience to itself. The Soviets, at least until recently, were short of capital. They had a revolution which could be exported at moderate expense. Accordingly it was convenient to associate backwardness with colonialism, feudalism, and repressive capitalism, all of which could be eliminated by revolution. By contrast, we had capital. This we could export with greater ease than comprehensive social change.

The second difference is in the way development is organized. Although there is room for some national preference, and heresy cannot be entirely eliminated, the Marxian commitment is still to state ownership of the means of production—of land, capital plant, and natural resources. Private ownership of productive resources and their use for private gain is one of the retarding institutions. Its elimination leaves the state in possession and this continues. Incentives to individual and group effort are strongly supported. But incentives which use the device of property ownership to combine reward for individual effort with reward for management of property are excluded in principle and in large measure in practice.

The non-Marxian design for organizing development is not so easily characterized. In the past many countries—Japan, Germany, Canada, and to a remarkable degree also the United States—have made state ownership of canals, turn-pikes, railroads, electric power and other utilities, and even steel mills the fulcrum of development policy. India, Egypt, and some South American countries are taking the same course today. However, the main and indeed overwhelming reliance in non-Marxian development, both in agriculture and industry, is on private ownership of productive plant. This is true of countries, such as India, which choose to describe themselves as socialist.

WESTERN ADVANTAGE IN PROVIDING CAPITAL

The foregoing differences are sufficiently sharp so that we can relate them to results. And in Eastern Europe and China, not to mention the much older case of the Soviet Union, there is now an ample experience of Marxian development on which to draw.

Two major advantages lie with the Western or non-Marxian alternatives. There is, we have anciently been advised, a certain physical difficulty in extracting blood from a stone. This, however, is comparatively easy as compared with getting savings out of a poor society. When people do not have enough to eat, they are loathe to forego any part of their meal in order to eat better in the future. Pleas on behalf of children and grandchildren leave the man of simple, uncomplicated intelligence unmoved; he reflects that starvation will prevent his having children and, *pro tanto*, grandchildren as well. But Marxian no less than non-Marxian societies must have savings; without them there can be no growth. Accordingly, the Western pattern of development, with its prospect of assistance from outside the country, eases one of the most painful problems of development. This is why economic aid has become such an important feature of Western foreign policy. It is the process by which savings are transferred from countries where saving is comparatively unpainful to those where it is very painful. It exploits one of the major advantages of our system.

The Communist countries are not without resources in this respect. The Soviet Union, though its capacity has been far less than ours, has spared some savings for other countries. Communist economic and political organization deals more effectively—or ruthlessly—with unproductive and excessively luxurious consumption, of which there is always some and may be much in the poor country. And Communist organization can, within limits, squeeze blood from its turnip. The penalty is the pain, and this cannot be avoided. The rioting in Poland in 1956 which brought Mr. Gomulka to power was occasioned in large measure by the enforcement of a rate of saving that was too grim for the people to bear. These last years on the Chinese mainland have evidently been ones of serious trouble and tension. Part of the problem is inherent in socialist organization of agriculture to which I will advert in a moment. But some has certainly been the consequence of squeezing a large volume of savings out of a very poor population.

The larger consequence is that Marxian development risks the alienation of the people as non-Marxian development does not. It seems doubtful if a majority of the Chinese people are very pleased with their government and would vote for it in an uninhibited poll. By contrast, in India, after a decade of development, there has been an overwhelming vote for the government that led the task. If the Indian Government had to subtract the $7.3 billions it has received from the West in overseas loans and grants since independence from the meager incomes—an average of about $70 per year—of its own people, its popularity might well have suffered. We see in India, in remarkably clear relief, the advantages of the Western design in providing capital.

WESTERN ADVANTAGE IN AGRICULTURE

The second and equally substantial advantage of Western development is in the matter of agriculture. Industry, on the record at least, is fairly tolerant as to forms of organization. American industry works well under private ownership. Even the most reluctant among us must agree that the Soviets have made considerable progress with socialism. So no decisive contrast can be registered here. But the underdeveloped country is, by definition, a pastoral or agrarian community. The agricultural policy is, accordingly, vital. And it is far from clear, as a practical matter, whether it is possible to socialize a small-scale, densely populated, peasant agriculture. Even in the Soviet Union the agricultural problem has not been wholly solved. And here, at least, there is no serious talk of catching up. Each year we insouciantly extend our advantage in manhour productivity without effort and somewhat to our regret. Outside the Soviet Union, agriculture has been even more of a problem. Poland and Yugoslavia have had to revert to private ownership. In China, by all external evidence, the effort to socialize agriculture has brought a serious crisis. Certainly it has forced her to turn to the West for the largest food imports in history.

There are good reasons for this failure. Farmers, when they are small and numerous, cannot be brought unwillingly into a state-run system of agriculture for they can defeat any system that is available for their control. The employees of a factory, like the men of an army, are subject to external discipline. Failure in performance can be detected, judged, and penalized. (The same rule holds for certain types of plantation agriculture.) A scattered peasantry, carrying on the diverse tasks of crop and especially of livestock husbandry cannot be so regimented. As a consequence, productivity falls off. Working for others, the farmer works at the minimum rather than the maximum, and the difference between the two is enormous. He can be made to work at the maximum by giving him land to work and rewarding him with the fruits of his labor or some substantial share to consume or exchange as he wishes. But this is to restore individual proprietorship—private capitalism—which its doctrine excludes.

One day the Marxian economies may succeed in socializing agriculture—no effort is being spared. And the ability of the small man in agriculture to sabotage a system he dislikes or which treats him badly is not confined to communism. It is the reason for the low productivity and backwardness of the latifundia of Latin America and the feudal domains of the Middle East. But the fact that it accepts independent agricultural proprietorship is the second clear advantage of Western development.

ELIMINATING RETARDING INSTITUTIONS

I come now to a disadvantage of Western development. The Marxian alternative, I have noted, emphasizes the destruction of the bonds that tie the economy to the past. Our emphasis is on capital, education, technical assistance, and the other instruments that allow change. Until recently, at least, we have been tempted to suppose that any society is a platform on which, given these missing elements, development can be built.

In fact, institutions do chain economies to the past, and the breaking of these chains is essential for progress. The promise that this will be done is a valid and an appealing part of the Marxian case. There is no chance of agricultural development in the underdeveloped and hence agricultural country under systems of absentee landlordism, with the workers or sharecroppers confined by law and tradition to a minor share of a meager product. And feudal systems of farming extend their corrupting influence to government, to the provision of public sinecures to those who lack a claim on the land, to the milking of middle-class and industrial enterprise, and to the destruction of incentives and the morale of the society itself. "In our country," a South American guide once told me, "those who do the least get the most. I hear that in the United States it is the other way around. It's a better system." Progress does require the radical elimination of retarding institutions. If elimination can be had from no other source, the Marxian alternative will sooner or later be tried. The revolution they offer here, we should remind ourselves, is less the Russian Revolution than the French Revolution.

POLITICAL ENVIRONMENT

I come now to the final point of comparison—one, unfortunately, which has been much damaged by bad rhetoric. From the earliest days of their development, personal liberty, equal justice under law, and constitutional government have been important to Englishmen and to Americans. They haven't been the concern of everyone, but we have never supposed they were the fad of the esoteric and privileged minority.

And so it is in the undeveloped country today. The Andean Indian and the landless worker in the Indian village do have a preoccupying concern with keeping themselves fed. But the general yearning for the dignity of democratic and constitutional government is very great. No people who live under a dictatorship ever feel themselves to be first-class citizens.

There can be little question that most people believe that liberty and constitutional process are safer with the Western than with the Marxian alternative. We haven't, in my view, made as much of this advantage as we might. But the Communists are under the considerable handicap that their alternative involves a step into the dark. And while the details are obscure, most people know that it does not involve free selection of rulers by the governed, *habeas corpus,* equal justice under law, and a voluntary return to other economic arrangements should the experiment prove unpalatable.

MAKING USE OF THE ADVANTAGES

On first assessment, then, the advantage of the non-Marxian alternative for the developing country is considerable. It promises at least a partial avoidance of the pain that for the poor country is inherent in finding savings for investment and growth. It promises an acceptable and viable system of agriculture rather than a certain unpalatable and possibly unworkable one. And it offers personal liberty and constitutional process. Against this the Marxian alternative promises a more rigorous attack on the institutions—the unproductive claims on revenue and especially the feudal control of land—which exclude change.

But this is not a game where one can count the cards and decide the winner.

Some cards count for more than others, and there is the unfortunate possibility that some good cards will not get played.

The Marxian promise can be decisive. That is because the things we offer are only effective and attractive after the retarding institutions are eliminated. In a country where land and other resources are held by and operated for the benefit of a slight minority and where the apparatus of government serves principally to reinforce such privilege, aid is not of much use. It will also benefit not the many but the few. Our promise of independent proprietorship is obviously nullified so long as land remains in the hands of the few. And personal liberty and constitutional government have little meaning in countries where government is of the privileged for the rich.

We must, in short, meet the Marxian promise of reform of retarding institutions. We cannot organize revolution. We can place our influence solidly on the side of reform. Having done this, our cards give us a clear advantage. To be sure, we must play them. We must make good with aid on our promise of a less painful savings and investment process. We must give firm support to the small farmer. We must be clear in our commitment to constitutional process and personal liberty. We cannot suppose that these are wanted only by people of Anglo-Saxon origin of good income. And we must not excuse dictatorship on grounds of anti-communism or convenience in the absence of visible alternatives. The price of doing so, as we have so painfully learned, is disaster magnified by postponement.

These are highly practical matters. If there are no advantages in our alternative, it won't be chosen. The first resort to the Marxian alternative in this hemisphere was in a country where the concentration of wealth and land ownership was extreme, where these had extended a corrupting influence to other economic life and to government, and where dictatorship had been endemic. This being the experience with the Western alternative, it was not remarkable that so many were so little perturbed by the alternative. India, in face of formidable difficulties, is firmly committed to development on the Western model. That is because already in British India and over the whole country at the time of independence there was a strong attack on retarding institutions—especially on the feudal claims of princes, zamindars and great landlords, and government which was an extension of this landed power; because a substantial measure of peasant ownership had replaced the old system; because aid from outside eased the problem of supply capital; and because people felt secure in the protection of constitutional guarantees and representative government.

The lesson is clear. The advantages are with us. We must, however, have confidence in them and exploit them to the full.

39

Foreign Aid? Yes, But With a New Approach

Our foreign aid has not often won the lasting gratitude of the recipients. Senator Fulbright asserts that U.S. economic development aid cannot be successful on a bilateral basis, and makes the radical proposal that all development loan funds should be channeled through an international agency.

Senator J. W. Fulbright (Dem., Arkansas) is Chairman of the Senate Foreign Relations Committee.

SENATOR J. W. FULBRIGHT

Washington.

Difficult as the effort might be, it would be salutary for Americans to try to imagine exactly how they might feel as recipients of economic aid—and all that goes with it—from foreign countries.

How, for example, would the management and employes of the bankrupt New Haven Railroad feel if they were placed under the tutelage of a mission of, say, German transportation experts—who, for all they might do to show us how to run a railroad, would also be living purveyors of the message that "we Germans know how to do something you Americans don't know how to do"?

Or consider how a Texas rancher might feel as the pupil of a group of agronomists from Colombia assigned to teach him how to grow coffee. Would he be humbly and touchingly grateful? Or would his gratitude be tinged with a touch of rancor toward his benefactors because his pride was injured by the feeling of being a suppliant and a recipient?

Imagine, to take another example, how the recent flood victims of Oregon and California might have felt, having lost their homes and possessions and perhaps members of their families, if they were then asked to participate in little picture-taking ceremonies with beaming foreign ambassadors dispensing food and blankets labeled "Gift of the French People" or "Gift of the Russian People." If we can imagine ourselves in this position, I think we might agree that it is not an altogether heartwarming experience to be confronted with a gift of food whose label seems to convey the message that "the soup which you are about to consume is a charity from the great and generous and affluent people of someplace or other."

Several years ago, during a visit to a country which was then receiving American aid, I attended an informal supper with some local officials and American diplomats. One of the Americans favored us with an explanation of the costs and logistics of an impending disaster-relief mission in which American supplies were involved. As he warmed to his subject, I noticed our hosts becoming increasingly preoccupied with their soup. The American official was clearly well-informed on all the details of our mission of mercy, but the local officials did not seem to appreciate it.

I do not think they were ungrateful for our relief supplies. I think what they failed to appreciate was the strong and clear suggestion that they were our wards and we their patrons, that they were benighted and we were blessed, that they were incompetent and needy while we were rich and happy and very tenderhearted besides.

They did not seem to appreciate this at all, and I did not appreciate it either. In the course of a recent trip to Yugoslavia, I had the honor to decline to participate in an airport ceremony at Zagreb, where American planes were arriving with bedding supplies for victims of a major flood.

These are extreme examples of what might be called extreme bilateralism in relations between a rich country and a poor country. They are by no means representative of how most of our aid is extended and received, but they do, I think, illustrate the psychological problem that is inherent in every manifestation of *direct* American assistance to underdeveloped countries.

It is a problem of pride and self-respect, which has everything to do with a country's will and capacity to foster its own development. There is an inescapable element of charity in bilateral aid, and charity, over a long period of time, has a debilitating effect on both the recipient and the donor. It fosters attitudes of cranky dependency or simple anger on the part of the recipient and of self-righteous frustration on the part of the donor—attitudes which, once formed, feed destructively upon each other.

*   *   *

Of all the changes that are needed in our foreign aid, the most important is a change in our own attitude. In the long run, no policy can be sustained by the sole force of cold-blooded self-interest. We do not provide social security to the unemployed simply because it helps to quiet them and makes the possessing classes more secure in their affluence, although social security undoubtedly does contribute to that end. We do it because it seems decent and proper, because we feel some sense of responsibility. If we are at all sincere in our aspiration to achieve a world community of nations, we must bring something of the same spirit to our modest efforts to assist the poor nations in their struggle for a decent life. We must recognize that aid is a humane as well as a practical program, that, as Woodrow Wilson said of the League of Nations, there is a "pulse of sympathy in it" and "a compulsion of conscience throughout it."

The difficulties with foreign aid which we are now experiencing are attributable to the fact that the authorization of American aid has become deeply involved in Congressional politics and controversy, while the disbursement of our aid has involved the United States too deeply in the politics of too many countries. A new approach is needed. To this end, I propose the three following fundamental changes in our foreign aid program.

I—PUT ECONOMIC AID ON A LONG-TERM BASIS

Congress should cease its annual reviews of foreign aid and place the program under long-term authorizations. The case for doing so is both familiar and persuasive, and just about everybody involved with foreign aid agrees to it—except Congress.

A long-term authorization would not, of course, remove the foreign-aid program from direct Congressional authority; the funds authorized would still have to be appropriated annually. It might be possible, however, by putting the authorizing legislation, which sets maximum amounts and is intended to govern policy, on a three-year or four-year basis, to insulate the program from transitory waves of emotion.

A long-term authorization might have the effect of reversing the pernicious tendency to write binding restrictions into law in response to some transitory irritation, such as an insult from Nasser or Sukarno or a vote in the United Nations that displeases us. Such annoyances are genuine enough but they are often forgotten very quickly as events move on, while the legislative proscriptions to which they gave rise remain to govern—or to frustrate—policy.

Economic development is a long-term process which does not lend itself to the one-year legislative cycle of the American Congress. The conventional short-term approach greatly impedes planning by the aid recipient while the donor is denied the opportunity to offer incentives to recipients to make necessary internal economic reforms. There has been a tendency in the experience of AID and its predecessor agencies to hasten to commit funds as the end of a fiscal year approaches with the result that recipients may be pushed into premature commitments.

The Foreign Assistance Act of 1961, which in my opinion was the best aid bill we have ever enacted, provided long-term authorizations both for the Alliance for Progress and for development lending to Asian and African countries. The Congress, most unwisely, has been tampering with these legislative provisions ever since, so that we are in effect back on a year-to-year basis.

The very nature of the economic development process requires the casting of foreign aid in a new time perspective. The Congress of the United States could make an important contribution to this end by adopting foreign-aid authorization bills of four or three or, at least, two years.

II—DON'T CONFUSE ECONOMIC AND MILITARY AID

My second proposal is the separation of the economic and military components of foreign aid—or, more exactly, of those forms of aid which pertain to the economic development of underdeveloped countries from those which pertain to the maintenance of armed forces, supporting assistance for security purposes, and political loans which are really designed to influence a country's posture in the cold war or the outcome of its next election.

The distinction, in any case, is not merely a legislative one; it is an operative distinction of great importance, pertaining to functions which are quite distinct and not always even compatible.

The fundamental distinction between economic and military-political assistance —and it could hardly be more fundamental—is that one is designed to alter a status quo and the other is usually designed to preserve it. The relationship between the two is that politico-military assistance is intended, or should be intended, to buy time for the more fundamental purpose of developing the nation.

Military assistance is administered by the Department of Defense with the Secretary of State and the administrator of AID acting as policy coordinators. Military and economic assistance are thus overlapping in operation and merged in legislative authorization, giving rise to the constant possibility that recipients will suspect—perhaps rightly—that conditions attached to one form of aid are in reality intended to advance the purpose of the other. I believe that the two functions should be separated to the greatest possible extent, because of the vital importance, *for purposes of economic growth*, of maintaining the economic integrity of economic programs—both in the mind of the recipient and in the policy of the donor.

The same considerations apply with even greater force to those forms of aid which are designed to have nothing more than short-term political effects. I have no firm opinion, frankly, as to whether the United States has any business—or can be expected to gain in the long run—in trying to buy a vote in the United Nations or influence the election of a government. But even if we grant that political bribery is a necessary part of foreign policy, it is perfectly clear that it has nothing to do with economic development, that it is much more nearly a proper function for the C.I.A. than for AID.

As a Democrat, I do not make a habit of supporting my positions on issues with Republican campaign materials. In this case, however, I find myself impressed with a cogent case made in a 1964 publication of the Republican Critical Issues Council for separating economic-development aid from aid for short-term political purposes. The latter, says the Republican task force on foreign aid, should be provided from a special emergency fund at the disposal of the President: "It should not be confused with economic and technical assistance directed toward what we believe is foreign aid's appropriate role in achieving constructive longer-range purposes."

A corollary to the need for separating development assistance from military and short-term political assistance is the need for even greater selectivity—although this principle has in fact been accepted and to a great extent implemented by Presidents Kennedy and Johnson.

The United States nonetheless maintains aid programs in about 90 countries. Few of these contribute appreciably to economic development or to our security. Many are token programs designed to maintain an American "presence," which I take to be a euphemism for the exertion of one form or another of political leverage.

It is an open question whether an American aid "presence" gains any more leverage than it gives. Recent events in Egypt and Indonesia, where we have carefully cultivated our "presence," suggest that when a nationalist leader is feeling angry toward the United States he is unlikely to be deterred by a token or even a substantial American aid program and, further, that a threat to cut off our aid is far less likely to restrain a proud nationalist like Nasser than to goad him into further statements or actions hostile to the United States.

I was recently visited by the American Ambassador to an African country who expressed the view that the best way we can maintain friendly relations with the smaller African countries is by maintaining no "presence" whatever in them except normal diplomatic representation.

There is often far more to be gained by a conspicuous American "absence" from a country than by an American "presence." It is just about inevitable that any small and weak but proud country will view any great power that snuggles too close as a threat to its dignity and independence. I think we would be wise indeed to respect that feeling by vacating those many American "aid" missions whose function is not aid at all, and certainly not development aid, but merely the maintenance of an irritating and unnecessary American "presence."

I think that the President—the President, not the Congress—would be well-advised to terminate aid programs, such as that in Indonesia, which contribute nothing to economic development and exert far more leverage in arousing the ill temper of Congress than in influencing the political behavior of the recipient. If we take these steps, we may find that we have saved some libraries, some embassy windows, a small amount of money, and a large amount of good will.

III—MAKE ECONOMIC AID AN INTERNATIONAL AFFAIR

My third and, I believe, most important proposal for a new approach to foreign aid is that we cease to administer our economic development assistance on a bilateral basis. Let us instead place most, or all, of the funds made available for this purpose at the disposal of the international lending agencies, notably the World Bank and its affiliate, the International Development Association.

The fundamental difference between bilateralism and multilateralism in foreign aid is psychological. The one carries a connotation of charity, of patron and ward, of arrogance and humiliation; the other has the more dignified connotation of a community organized to meet its common and rightful responsibilities toward its less fortunate members. The one is appropriate to a world of nation states with unlimited sovereignty, the other to a world that is at least groping toward a broader community.

Unlike any single nation, an international agency like the World Bank is capable of entering into an *institutional* relationship with the recipient of its aid. It is true, of course, that the international agencies draw most of their resources from the same countries that provide bilateral aid, but, as the former president of the World Bank, Eugene Black, has pointed out, "the act of generosity is one stage removed, and this is quite enough to draw its sting."

Greatly as they want our aid, the poor nations of the world want our respect no less. Above all, they need the self-respect that will enable them to go forward confidently in building their own societies. I believe we can help to make this possible by multilateralizing our aid. And in so doing, we will also be advancing our own security by the cultivation of stable and mutually respectful relations.

By the reckoning of the Johnson Administration, 85 per cent of United States development loans in Asia and Africa will be committed under international arrangements in the next fiscal year, and, it is pointed out, most United States aid to Latin America is provided through the international channels of the Alliance for Progress. This is fine as far as it goes, but that is not really very far toward true multilateralism. The arrangements referred to consist largely of procedures of consulation and coordination, while final decisions about kinds and amounts of aid and the execution of programs remain bilateral.

The kind of multilateralism which is needed is one which will vest in an international agency such as the World Bank full authority to determine, *according to objective economic criteria,* who will receive aid and the amounts, kinds and conditions of aid. The United States and other donors would, of course, reserve to themselves final decisions as to the amounts of money they were prepared to contribute to the international agency, although it would be useful and proper for the international organ to suggest equitable contributions by the participating countries.

Specifically, I suggest that all development loan funds now administered by our Agency for International Development be turned over to the World Bank's International Development Association (I.D.A.) to be used for long-term low-interest development lending for programs that cannot be financed by conventional loans. This is precisely the purpose for which our development loans are intended and precisely the purpose for which the I.D.A. was set up.

I think that the assignment of these funds to the I.D.A. should be accompanied by an effort to persuade other countries to do the same thing, or at least to increase their contributions to I.D.A. I would not, however, make this a condition of our own contributions, because I believe it is in our interests to channel our development lending through an international agency whether others do so or not.

It should be understood that while the Bank and the I.D.A. are independent international agencies, the influence of the United States on their policies is considerable because decisions on loans are made by votes weighted according to contributions. As the largest single contributor, the United States has the greatest voting power. In channeling its development loans through the I.D.A., therefore, the United States would be renouncing exclusive control, with its attendant disadvantages, while retaining great influence on the disposition of its contributions.

The fundamental and, I think, inescapable limit on bilateral aid programs is that, however well and honestly they are administered, they cannot escape political pressure—or, what is just as bad, the suspicion of political pressure.

PART THREE

Markets, The Price System, and the Allocation of Resources

In 1776 Adam Smith described an economic world in which individual self-interest, balanced by the competitive self-interest of others, brought order out of economic chaos, and directed the society as if by an "invisible hand." Adam Smith's ideas have influenced economists and statesmen for almost two centuries, and still have tremendous appeal.

Robert L. Heilbroner is a member of the faculty at the New School for Social Research and a well-known free lance writer.

40

The Wonderful World of Adam Smith

ROBERT L. HEILBRONER

A visitor to England in the 1760's would quite probably have learned of a certain Dr. Smith of the University of Glasgow. Dr. Smith was a well-known, if not a famous, man; Voltaire had heard of him, David Hume was his intimate, students had traveled all the way from Russia to hear his labored but enthusiastic discourse. In addition to his scholastic accomplishments, Dr. Smith was known as a rather remarkable personality. He was, for example, notoriously absent-minded: once he had fallen into a tanning pit walking along in earnest disquisition with a friend, and it was said that he had brewed himself a beverage of bread and butter and pronounced it the worst cup of tea he had ever tasted. But his personal quirks, which were many, did not interfere with his intellectual abilities. Dr. Smith was among the foremost philosophers of his age.

At Glasgow Dr. Smith lectured on problems of Moral Philosophy, a discipline a great deal more broadly conceived in that day than in ours. Moral Philosophy covered Natural Theology, Ethics, Jurisprudence, and Political Economy: it thus ranged all the way from man's sublimest impulses toward order and harmony to his somewhat less orderly and harmonious activities in the grimmer business of gouging out a living for himself.

Natural theology—the search for design in the confusion of the cosmos—has been an object of the human rationalizing impulse from earliest times; our traveler would have felt quite at ease as Dr. Smith expounded the natural laws that underlay the seeming chaos of the universe. But when it came to the other end of the spectrum—the search for a grand architecture beneath the hurly-burly of daily life—our traveler might have felt that Dr. Smith was really stretching philosophy beyond its proper limits.

For if the English social scene of the late eighteenth century suggested anything, it was most emphatically not rational order nor moral purpose. As soon as one looked away from the elegant lives of the leisure classes, society presented itself as a brute struggle for existence in its meanest form. Outside the drawing rooms of London or the pleasant rich estates of the counties, all that one saw was rapacity, cruelty, and degradation mingled with the most irrational and bewildering customs and traditions of some still earlier and already anachronistic day. Rather than a carefully engineered machine where each part could be seen to contribute to the whole, the body social resembled one of James Watt's strange steam machines: black, noisy, inefficient, dangerous. How curious that Dr. Smith should have professed to see order, design, and purpose in all of this.

Suppose, for example, our visitor had gone to see the tin mines of Cornwall. There he would have watched miners lower themselves down the black shafts, and on reaching bottom draw a candle from their belts and stretch out for a sleep until the candle guttered. Then for two or three hours they would work the ore until the next traditional break, this time for as long as it took to smoke a pipe. A full half day was spent in lounging, half in picking at the seams. But had our visitor traveled up north and nerved himself against a descent into the pits of Durham or Northumberland, he would have seen something quite different. Here men and women worked together, stripped to the waist, and sometimes reduced from pure fatigue to a whimpering half-human state. The wildest and most brutish customs were practiced; sexual appetites aroused at a glance were gratified down some deserted shaftway; children of seven or ten who never saw daylight during the winter months were used and abused and paid a pittance by the miners to help drag away their tubs of coal; pregnant women drew coal cars like horses and even gave birth in the dark black caverns.

But it was not just in the mines that life appeared colorful, traditional, or ferocious. On the land, too, an observant traveler would have seen sights hardly more suggestive of order, harmony, and design. In many parts of the country bands of agricultural poor roamed in search of work. From the Welsh highlands, Companies of Ancient Britons (as they styled themselves) would come trooping down at harvest time; sometimes they had one horse, unsaddled and unbridled, for the entire company; sometimes they all simply walked. Not infrequently there would be only one of the lot who spoke English and so could serve as intermediary between the band and the gentlemen-farmers whose lands they asked permission to aid in harvesting. It is not surprising that wages were as low as sixpence a day.

And finally, had our visitor stopped at a manufacturing town, he would have seen still other remarkable sights—but again, not such as to betoken order to the uneducated eye. He might have marveled at the factory built by the brothers Lombe in 1742. It was a huge building (for those days), five hundred feet long and six stories high, and inside were machines described by Daniel Defoe as consisting of "26,586 Wheels and 97,746 Movements, which work 73,726 Yards of Silk-Thread every time the Water-Wheel goes round, which is three times in one minute." Equally worthy of note were the children who tended the machines round the clock for twelve or fourteen hours at a turn, cooked their meals on the grimly black boilers, and were boarded in shifts in barracks where, it was said, the beds were always warm.

A strange, cruel, haphazard world this must have appeared to eighteenth-century as well as to our modern eyes.

All the more remarkable, then, to find that it could be reconciled with a scheme of Moral Philosophy envisioned by Dr. Smith, and that that learned man actually claimed to fathom within it the clear-cut outlines of great purposeful laws fitting an overarching and meaningful whole.

What sort of man was this urbane philosopher?

"I am a beau in nothing but my books," was the way Adam Smith once described himself, proudly showing off his treasured library to a friend. He was certainly not a handsome man. A medallion profile shows us a protruding lower lip thrust up to meet a large aquiline nose and heavy bulging eyes looking out from heavy lids. All his life Smith was troubled with a nervous affliction; his head shook, and he had an odd and stumbling manner of speech.

In addition, there was his notorious absent-mindedness. In the 1780's when Smith was in his late fifties, the inhabitants of Edinburgh were regularly treated to the amusing spectacle of their most illustrious citizen, attired in a light-colored coat, knee breeches, white silk stockings, buckle shoes, flat broad-brimmed beaver hat, and cane, walking down the cobbled streets with his eyes fixed on infinity and his lips moving in silent discourse. Every pace or two he would hesitate as if to change his direction or even reverse it; his gait was described by a friend as "vermicular."

Accounts of his absence of mind were common. On one occasion, he descended into his garden clad only in a dressing gown and, falling into a reverie, walked fifteen miles before coming to. Another time while walking with an eminent friend in Edinburgh, a guard presented his pike in salute. Smith, who had been thus honored on countless occasions, was suddenly hypnotized by the saluting soldier. He returned the honor with his cane and then further astonished his guest by following exactly in the guard's footsteps, duplicating with his cane every motion of the pike. When the spell was broken, Smith was standing at the head of a long flight of steps, cane held at the ready. Having no idea that he had done anything out of the ordinary, he grounded his stick and took up his conversation where he had left off.

This absent-minded professor was born in 1723 in the town of Kirkcaldy, County Fife, Scotland. Kirkcaldy boasted a population of fifteen hundred; at the time of Smith's birth, nails were still used as money by some of the local townspeople. When he was four years old, a most curious incident took place. Smith was kidnaped by a band of passing gypsies. Through the efforts of his uncle (his father had died before his birth), the gypsies were traced and pursued, and in their flight they abandoned young Adam by the roadside. "He would have made, I fear, a poor gypsy," says one of his biographers.

From his earliest days, Smith was an apt pupil, although even as a child given to fits of abstraction. He was obviously destined for teaching and so at seventeen he went to Oxford on a scholarship—making the journey on horseback—and there he remained for six years. But Oxford was not then the citadel of learning which it later became. Most of the public professors had long ago given up even a pretense of teaching. A foreign traveler recounts his astonishment over a public debate there in 1788. All four participants passed the allotted time in profound silence, each absorbed in reading a popular novel of the day. Since instruction was the exception rather than the rule, Smith spent the years largely untutored and untaught, reading as he saw fit. In fact he was once nearly expelled from the university because a copy of David Hume's *A Treatise of Human Nature* was found in his rooms—Hume was no fit reading matter, even for a would-be philosopher.

In 1751—he was then twenty-eight—Smith was offered the Chair of Logic at the University of Glasgow, and shortly thereafter he was given the Chair of Moral Philosophy. Unlike Oxford, Glasgow was a serious center of study, and boasted a galaxy of talent. But it still differed considerably from the modern conception of a university. The prim professional group did not entirely appreciate a certain levity and enthusiasm in Smith's manner. He was accused of sometimes smiling during religious services (no doubt during a reverie), of being a firm friend of that outrageous Hume, of not holding Sunday classes on Christian Evidences, of petitioning the Senatus Academicus for permission to dispense with prayers on the opening of class, and of delivering prayers that smacked of a certain "natural religion." Perhaps this all fits into better perspective if we remember that Smith's own teacher, Hutcheson, broke new ground at Glasgow by refusing to lecture to his students in Latin!

But for all the inevitable academic rivalry, Smith was happy at Glasgow. In the evenings he played whist—his absent-mindedness made him a somewhat undependable player—attended learned societies, and lived a quiet and sheltered life. He was beloved of his students, noted as a lecturer—even Boswell came to hear him—and his odd gait and manner of speech gained the homage of imitation. Little busts of himself even appeared in booksellers' windows.

It was not merely his eccentric personality that gave him prestige. In 1759 he published a book which made an immediate sensation. It was entitled *The Theory of Moral Sentiments,* and it catapulted Smith immediately into the forefront of English philosophers. The *Theory* was an inquiry into the origin of moral approbation and disapproval. How does it happen that man, who is a creature of self-interest, can form moral judgments in which self-interest seems to be held in abeyance or transmuted to a higher plane? Smith held that the answer lay in our ability to put ourselves in the position of a third person, an impartial observer, and in this way to form a sympathetic notion of the moral (as opposed to the selfish) merits of a case.

The book and its problems attracted immediate interest. In Germany *das Adam Smith Problem* became a favorite subject for debate. More importantly, from our point of view, the treatise met with the favor of a brillant and intriguing man named Charles Townshend.

Townshend is one of those wonderful figures with which the eighteenth century seems to abound. A witty and even learned man, Townshend was, in the words of Horace Walpole, "a man endowed with every great talent, who must have been the greatest man of his age, if only he had common sincerity, common steadiness, and common sense." Townshend's fickleness was notorious; a quip of the times put it that Mr. Townshend was ill of a pain in his side, but declined to specify which side. As evidence of his lack of common sense, it was Townshend, as Chancellor of the Exchequer, who helped precipitate the American Revolution, first by refusing the colonists the right to elect their own judges and then by imposing a heavy duty on American tea.

But his political shortsightedness notwithstanding, Townshend was a sincere student of philosophy and politics, and as such a devotee of Adam Smith. What is more important, he was in a position to make him an unusual offer. In 1754

Townshend had made a brilliant and lucrative marriage to the Countess of Dalkeith, the widow of the Duke of Buccleuch, and he now found himself casting about for a tutor for his wife's son. Education for a young man of the upper classes consisted largely of the Grand Tour, a stay in Europe where one might acquire that polished finish so highly praised by Lord Chesterfield. Dr. Adam Smith would be an ideal companion for the young duke, thought Townshend, and accordingly he offered him three hundred pounds a year plus expenses and a pension of three hundred pounds a year for life. It was too good an offer to be declined. At best Smith never realized more than one hundred seventy pounds from the fees which, in those days, professors collected directly from their students. It is pleasant to note that his pupils refused to accept a refund from Dr. Smith when he left, saying that they had already been more than recompensed.

The tutor and His young Grace left for France in 1764. For eighteen months they stayed in Toulouse where a combination of abominably boring company and Smith's execrable French made his sedate life at Glasgow look like dissipation. Then they moved on to the south of France (where he met and worshiped Voltaire and repulsed the attentions of an amorous marquise), thence to Geneva, and finally to Paris. To relieve the tedium of the provinces, Smith began work on a treatise of political economy, a subject on which he had lectured at Glasgow, debated many evenings at the Select Society in Edinburgh, and discussed at length with his beloved friend David Hume. The book was to be the *Wealth of Nations*, but it would be twelve years before it was finished.

Paris was better going. By this time Smith's French, although dreadful, was good enough to enable him to talk at length with the foremost economic thinker in France. This was a M. Quesnay, a physician in the court of Louis XV and personal doctor to Mme. Pompadour. Quesnay had propounded a school of economics known as Physiocracy and devised a chart of the economy called a *tableau économique*. The *tableau* was truly a physician's insight: in contradistinction to the ideas of the day which still held that wealth was the solid stuff of gold and silver, Quesnay insisted that wealth sprang from production and that it flowed through the nation, from hand to hand, replenishing the body social like the circulation of blood. The *tableau* made a vast impression—Mirabeau the elder characterized it as an invention deserving of equal rank with writing and money. But the trouble with Physiocracy was that it insisted that only the agricultural classes produced true "wealth" and that the manufacturing and commercial classes merely manipulated it in a sterile way. Hence Quesnay's system had but limited usefulness for practical policy. True, it advocated a policy of *laissez faire*—a radical departure for the times. But in denigrating the industrial side of life it flew against the sense of history, for the whole development of capitalism unmistakably pointed to the emergence of the industrial classes to a position of superiority over the landed classes.

This was not a congenial philosophy to Adam Smith. The notion of the circulation of wealth he gladly accepted and acknowledged, but the idea that industry was somehow sterile and barren struck him as a peculiar construction of the world. After all, had he not grown up in Kirkcaldy and Glasgow where one could see wealth being created at every hand in the workshops and factories of craftsmen? But despite his rejection of the agricultural orientation of the Physiocrat cult (M. Quesnay's followers, like Mirabeau, were nothing if not adulatory), Smith had a profound personal admiration for the French doctor. Had it not been for Quesnay's death, the *Wealth of Nations* would have been dedicated to him.

In 1766 the tour was brought to an abrupt halt when the duke's younger brother, who had joined them, was murdered in the streets of Paris. His Grace returned to his estates at Dalkeith, and Smith went first to London, and then to Kirkcaldy. Despite Hume's entreaties, there he stayed, for the better part of the next ten years, while the great treatise took shape. Most of it he dictated, standing against his fireplace and nervously rubbing his head against the wall until his pomade had made a dark streak on the paneling. Occasionally he would visit his former charge on his estates at Dalkeith, and once in a while he would go to London to discuss his ideas with the literati of the day. One of them was Dr. Samuel Johnson, to whose select club Smith belonged, although he and the venerable lexicographer had hardly met under the most amiable of circumstances. Sir Walter Scott tells us that Johnson, on first seeing Smith, attacked him for some statement he had made. Smith vindicated the truth of his contention. "What did Johnson say?" was the universal inquiry. "Why, he said," said Smith, with the deepest impression of resentment, "he said, 'You lie!'" "And what did you reply?" "I said, 'You are a son of a —!'" On such terms, says Scott, did these two great moralists first meet and part, and such was the classical dialogue between two great teachers of philosophy.

Smith met as well a charming and intelligent American, one Benjamin Franklin, who provided him with a wealth of facts about the American colonies and a deep appreciation of the role which they might someday play. It is undoubtedly due to Franklin's influence that Smith subsequently wrote of the colonies that they constituted a nation "which, indeed, seems very likely to become one of the greatest and most formidable that ever was in the world."

In 1776, *Wealth of Nations* was published. Two years later Smith was appointed Commissioner of Customs for Edinburgh, a sinecure worth six hundred pounds a year. With his mother, who lived until she was ninety, Smith lived out his bachelor's life in peace and quiet; serene, content, and absent-minded to the end.

And the book?

It has been called "the outpouring not only of a great mind, but of a whole epoch." Yet it is not, in the strict sense of the word, an "original" book. There is a long line of observers before Smith who have approached his understanding of the world: Locke, Stewart, Law, Mandeville, Petty, Cantillon, not to mention Quesnay and Hume again. Smith took from all of them: there are over a hundred authors mentioned by name in his treatise. But where others had fished here and there, Smith spread his net wide; where others had clarified this and that issue, Smith illuminated the entire landscape. The *Wealth of Nations* may not be an original book, but it is unquestionably a masterpiece.

It is, first of all, a huge panorama. It opens with a famous passage describing the minute specialization of labor in the manufacture of pins, and covers, before it is done, such a variety of subjects as "the late disturbances in the American colonies" (evidently Smith thought the Revolutionary War would be over by the time his book reached the press), the wastefulness of the student's life at Oxford, and the statistics on the herring catch since 1771.

A glance at the index compiled for a later edition by Cannan shows the range of Smith's references and thoughts. Here are a dozen entries from the letter A:

> Abassides, opulence of Saracen empire under
> Abraham, weighed shekels

Abyssinia, salt money
Actors, public, paid for the contempt attending their profession
Africa, powerful king much worse off than European peasant
Alehouses, the number of, not the efficient cause of drunkenness
Ambassadors, the first motive of their appointment
America [a solid page of references follows]
Apprenticeship, the nature . . . of this bond servitude explained
Arabs, their manner of supporting war
Army, . . . no security to the sovereign against a disaffected clergy

In fine print the index goes on for sixty-three pages: before it ends it has touched on everything: "Riches, the chief enjoyment of, consists in the parade of; Poverty, sometimes urges nation to inhuman customs; Stomach, desire for food bounded by narrow capacity of the; Butcher, brutal and odious business." When we have finished the nine hundred pages of the book we have a living picture of England in the 1770's, of apprentices and journeymen and rising capitalists, of landlords and clergymen and kings, of factories and farms and foreign trade.

The book is heavy going. It moves with all the deliberation of an encyclopedic mind, but not with the precision of an orderly one. This was an age when authors did not stop to qualify their ideas with ifs, ands, and buts, and it was an era when it was quite possible for a man of Smith's intellectual stature virtually to embrace the great body of knowledge of his times. Hence the book ducks nothing, minimizes nothing, fears nothing. What an exasperating book! Again and again it refuses to wrap up in a concise sentence a conclusion it has laboriously arrived at over fifty pages. The argument is so full of detail and observation that one constantly has to chip away the ornamentation to find the steel structure which holds it together underneath. Coming to silver, Smith detours for seventy-five pages to write a "diversion" of it; coming to religion, he wanders off in a chapter on the sociology of morality. But for all its weightiness, the text is shot through with insights, observation, and well-turned phrases that imbue this great lecture with life. It was Smith who first called England "a nation of shopkeepers"; it was Smith who wrote, "By nature a philosopher is not in genius and disposition half so different from a street porter, as a mastiff is from a greyhound." And of the East India Company, which was then ravaging the East, he wrote: "It is a very singular government in which every member of the administration wishes to get out of the country . . . as soon as he can, and to whose interest, the day after he has left it and carried his whole fortune with him, it is perfectly indifferent though the whole country was swallowed up by an earthquake."

The *Wealth of Nations* is in no sense a textbook. Adam Smith is writing to his age, not to his classroom; he is expounding a doctrine which is meant to be of importance in running an empire, not an abstract treatise for scholastic distribution. The dragons which he slays (such as the Mercantile System, which takes over two hundred pages to die) were alive and panting, if a little tired, in his day.

And finally, the book is a revolutionary one. To be sure, Smith would hardly have countenanced an upheaval which disordered the gentlemanly classes and enthroned the common poor. But the import of the *Wealth of Nations* is revolutionary, nonetheless. Smith is not, as is commonly supposed, an apologist for the up-and-coming bourgeois; as we shall see, he is an admirer of their work but suspicious of their motives, and mindful of the needs of the great laboring mass.

But it is not his aim to espouse the interests of any class. He is concerned with promoting the wealth of the entire nation. And wealth, to Adam Smith, consists of the goods which *all* the people of society consume; note *all*—this is a democratic, and hence radical, philosophy of wealth. Gone is the notion of gold, treasures, kingly hoards; gone the prerogatives of merchants or farmers or working guilds. We are in the modern world where the flow of goods and services consumed by everyone constitutes the ultimate aim and end of economic life.

And now, what of the lessons of the text?

Two great problems absorb Adam Smith's attention. First, he is interested in laying bare the mechanism by which society hangs together. How is it possible for a community in which everyone is busily following his self-interest not to fly apart from sheer centrifugal force? What is it which guides each individual's private business so that it conforms to the needs of the group? With no central planning authority and no steadying influence of age-old tradition, how does society manage to get those tasks done which are necessary for survival?

These questions lead Smith to a formulation of the laws of the market. What he sought was "the invisible hand," as he called it, whereby "the private interests and passions of men" are led in the direction "which is most agreeable to the interest of the whole society."

But the laws of the market will be only a part of Smith's inquiry. There is another question which interests him: whither society? The laws of the market are like the laws which explain how a spinning top stays upright; but there is also the question of whether the top, by virtue of its spinning, will be moved along the table.

To Smith and the great economists who followed him, society is not conceived as a static achievement of mankind which will go on reproducing itself, unchanged and unchanging, from one generation to the next. On the contrary, society is seen as an organism which has its own life history. To discover the shape of things to come, to isolate the forces which impel society along its path—this is the grand objective of economic science.

But until we have followed Smith's unraveling of the laws of the market, we cannot rush to this larger and more fascinating problem. For the laws of the market themselves will be an integral part of the larger laws which cause society to prosper or decay. The mechanism by which the heedless individual is kept in line with everybody else will affect the mechanism by which society itself changes over the years.

Hence we begin with a look at the market mechanism. It is not the stuff that excites the imagination or stirs the pulse. Yet, for all its dryness, it has an immediacy which should lead us to consider it with a respectful eye. Not only are the laws of the market essential to an understanding of the world of Adam Smith, but these same laws will underlie the very different world of Karl Marx, and the still different world in which we live today. Since we are all, knowingly or otherwise, under their sovereignty, it behooves us to scrutinize them rather carefully.

Adam Smith's laws of the market are basically simple. They tell us that the outcome of a certain kind of behavior in a certain social framework will bring about perfectly definite and foreseeable results. Specifically they show us how the drive of individual self-interest in an environment of similarly motivated individuals will result in competition; and they further demonstrate how competition will result in the provision of those goods that society wants, in the quantities that society desires, and at the prices society is prepared to pay. Let us see how this comes about.

It comes about in the first place because self-interest acts as a driving power to guide men to whatever work society is willing to pay for. "It is not from the benevolence of the butcher, the brewer, or the baker that we expect our dinner," says Smith, "but from their regard to their self-interest. We address ourselves, not to their humanity, but to their self-love, and never talk to them of our necessities, but of their advantages."

But self-interest is only half the picture. It drives men to action. Something else must prevent the pushing of profit-hungry individuals from holding society up to exorbitant ransom: a community activated only by self-interest would be a community of ruthless profiteers. This regulator is competition, the socially beneficial consequence of the conflicting self-interests of all the members of society. For each man, out to do his best for himself with no thought of social cost, is faced with a flock of similarly motivated individuals who are in exactly the same boat. Each is only too eager to take advantage of his neighbor's greed if it urges him to exceed a common denominator of acceptable behavior. A man who permits his self-interest to run away with him will find that competitors have slipped in to take his trade away; if he charges too much for his wares or if he refuses to pay as much as everybody else for his workers, he will find himself without buyers in the one case and without employees in the other. Thus very much as in the *Theory of Moral Sentiments*, the selfish motives of men are transmuted by interaction to yield the most unexpected of results: social harmony.

Consider, for example, the problem of high prices. Suppose we have one hundred manufacturers of gloves. The self-interest of each one will cause him to wish to raise his price above his cost of production and thereby to realize an extra profit. But he cannot. If he raises his price, his competitors will step in and take his market away from him by underselling him. Only if all glove manufacturers combine and agree to maintain a solid front will an unduly high price be charged. And in this case, the collusive coalition could be broken by an enterprising manufacturer from another field—say, shoemaking—who decided to move his capital into glove manufacture where he could steal away the market by shading his prices.

But the laws of the market not only impose a competitive price on products. They also see to it that the producers of society heed society's demands for the *quantities* of goods it wants. Let us suppose that consumers decide they want more gloves than are being turned out, and fewer shoes. Accordingly the public will scramble for the stock of gloves on the market, and the shoe business will be dull. As a result glove prices will tend to rise as consumers try to buy more of them than there are ready at hand, and shoe prices will tend to fall as the public passes the shoe stores by. But as glove prices rise, profits in the glove industry will rise, too; and as shoe prices fall, profits in shoe manufacturing will slump. Again self-interest will step in to right the balance. Workers will be released from the shoe business as shoe factories contract their output; they will move to the glove business where business is booming. The result is quite obvious: glove production will rise and shoe production fall.

And this is exactly what society wanted in the first place. As more gloves come on the market to meet demand, glove prices will fall back into line. As fewer shoes are produced, the surplus of shoes will soon disappear and shoe prices will again rise up to normal. Through the mechanism of the market, society will have changed the allocation of its elements of production to fit its new desires. Yet no one has issued a dictum, and no planning authority has established schedules of output. Self-interest and competition, acting one against the other, have accomplished the transition.

And one final accomplishment. Just as the market regulates both prices and quantities of *goods* according to the final arbiter of public demand, so it also regulates the *incomes* of those who cooperate to produce those goods. If profits in one line of business are unduly large, there will be a rush of other businessmen into that field until competition has lowered surpluses. If wages are out of line in one kind of work, there will be a rush of men into the favored occupation until it pays no more than comparable jobs of that degree of skill and training. Conversely, if profits or wages are too low in one trade area, there will be an exodus of capital and labor until the supply is better adjusted to the demand.

All this may seem somewhat elementary. But consider what Adam Smith has done, with his impetus of self-interest and his regulator of competition. First, he has explained how prices are kept from ranging arbitrarily away from the actual cost of producing a good. Second, he has explained how society can induce its producers of commodities to provide it with what it wants. Third, he has pointed out why high prices are a self-curing disease, for they cause production in those lines to increase. And finally, he has accounted for a basic similarity of incomes at each level of the great producing strata of the nation. In a word, he has found in the mechanism of the market a self-regulating system for society's orderly provisioning.

Note "self-regulating." The beautiful consequence of the market is that it is its own guardian. If output or prices or certain kinds of remuneration stray away from their socially ordained levels, forces are set into motion to bring them back to the fold. It is a curious paradox which thus ensues: the market, which is the acme of individual economic freedom, is the strictest taskmaster of all. One may appeal the ruling of a planning board or win the dispensation of a minister; but there is no appeal, no dispensation, from the anonymous pressures of the market mechanism. Economic freedom is thus more illusory than at first appears. One can do as one pleases in the market. But if one pleases to do what the market disapproves, the price of individual freedom is economic ruination.

Does the world really work this way? To a very real degree it did in the days of Adam Smith. Even in his time, of course, there were already factors which acted as restraints against the free operation of the market system. There were combinations of manufacturers who rigged prices artificially high and associations of journeymen who resisted the pressures of competition when it acted to lower their wages. And already there were more disquieting signs to be read. The Lombe brothers' factory was more than a mere marvel of engineering and a source of wonderment to the visitor: it betokened the coming of large-scale industry and the emergence of employers who were immensely powerful individual actors in the market. The children in the cotton mills could surely not be considered market factors of equal power with the employers who bedded, boarded, and exploited them. But for all its ominous portents, eighteenth-century England approached, even if it did not wholly conform to, the model which Adam Smith had in mind. Business *was* competitive, the average factory *was* small, prices *did* rise and fall as demand ebbed and rose, and prices *did* invoke changes in output and occupation. The world of Adam Smith has been called a world of atomistic competition; a world in which no part of the productive mechanism, laborer or capitalist, was large enough to interfere with or to resist the pressures of competition. It was a world in which each agent was forced to scurry after his self-interest in a vast social free-for-all.

And today? Does the competitive market mechanism still operate?

This is not a question to which it is possible to give a simple answer. The nature of the market has changed vastly since the eighteenth century. We no longer live in a world of atomistic competition in which no man can afford to swim against the current. Today's market mechanism is characterized by the huge size of its participants: giant corporations and equally giant labor unions obviously do not behave as if they were individual proprietors and workers. Their very bulk enables them to stand out against the pressures of competition, to disregard price signals, and to consider what their self-interest shall be in the long run rather than in the immediate press of each day's buying and selling.

Then, in addition, the growth of government intervention has altered the scope of the market mechanism. Like a medieval lord, the government does not recognize its master in the market; more often than not it *sets* the market rather than abiding by it. That all these factors have weakened the primary guiding function of the market is apparent: later we will be concerned with what contemporary economists have to say about this problem. But it would seem, nonetheless, that for all the new quality of twentieth-century industrial society, the great principles of self-interest and competition, however watered down or hedged about, still provide basic rules of behavior which no economic participant can afford to disregard entirely. It is not the neat world of Adam Smith in which we live, but the laws of the market can still be discerned in it if we look beneath the surface.

But the laws of the market are only a description of the behavior which gives society its cohesiveness. Something else must make it go. Ninety years after the *Wealth of Nations*, Karl Marx was to make the portentous announcement that he had unearthed "laws of motion" which described how capitalism proceeded slowly, unwillingly, but ineluctably to its doom. But the *Wealth of Nations* already had its own laws of motion. However, quite unlike the Marxist prognosis, Adam Smith's world went slowly, quite willingly, and more or less inevitably to Valhalla.

Valhalla would have been the last destination that most observers would have predicted. Sir John Byng, touring the North Country in 1792, looked from his coach window and wrote: "Why, here now, is a great flaring mill . . . all the Vale is disturb'd. . . . Sir Richard Arkwright may have introduced Much Wealth into his Family and into his Country, but, as a Tourist, I execrate his Schemes, which having crept into every Pastoral Vale, have destroyed the course, and the Beauty of Nature." "Oh! What a dog's hole is Manchester," said Sir John on arriving there.

In truth, much of England was a dog's hole. The three centuries of turmoil which had prodded land, labor, and capital into existence seemed to have been only a preparation for still further upheaval, for the recently freed agents of production began to be combined in a new and ugly form: the factory. And with the factory came new problems. Twenty years before Sir John's tour, Richard Arkwright, who had gotten together a little capital peddling women's hair to make wigs, invented (or stole) the spinning throstle. But having constructed his machine, he found it was not so easy to staff it. Local labor could not keep up with the "regular celerity" of the process—wagework was still generally despised, and many a capitalist found his new-built factory burned to the ground out of sheer blind malice. Arkwright was forced to turn to children—"their small fingers being active." Furthermore, since they were unused to the independent life of farming or crafts, children adapted themselves more readily to the discipline of factory life. The move was hailed as a philanthropic gesture—would not the employment of children help to alleviate the condition of the "unprofitable poor"?

For it any problem absorbed the public mind, besides its mixed admiration of and horror at the factory, it was this omnipresent problem of the unprofitable poor. In 1720 England was crowded with a million and a half of them—a staggering figure when we realize that her total population was only twelve or thirteen million. Hence the air was full of schemes for their disposition. Despairing schemes, mostly. For the common complaint was the ineradicable sloth of the pauper, and this was mixed with consternation at the way in which the lower orders aped their betters. Workpeople were actually drinking tea! The common folk seemed to prefer wheaten bread to their traditional loaf of rye or barley! Where would all this lead to, asked the thinkers of the day; were not the wants of the poor ("which it would be prudence to relieve, but folly to cure," as a contemporary pamphlet expressed it) essential for the welfare of the state? What would happen to society if the indispensable gradations of society were allowed to disappear?

But if consternation described the prevalent attitude of the day toward the great amorphous mass of working England, it certainly did not describe Adam Smith's philosophy. "No society can surely be flourishing and happy, of which by far the greater part of the numbers are poor and miserable," he said. And not only did he have the temerity to make so radical a statement, but he proceeded to demonstrate that society was in fact constantly improving; that it was being propelled, willy-nilly, toward a positive goal. It was not moving because anyone willed it to, or because Parliament might pass laws, or England win a battle. It moved because there was a concealed dynamic beneath the surface of things which powered the social whole like an enormous engine.

For one salient fact struck Adam Smith as he looked at the English scene. This was the tremendous gain in productivity which sprang from the minute division and specialization of labor. Going into a pin factory, this is what Smith saw:

> One man draws out the wire, another straights it, a third cuts it, a fourth points it, a fifth grinds it at the top for receiving the head; to make the head requires two or three distinct operations; to put it on is a peculiar business; to whiten it is another; it is even a trade by itself to put them into paper. . . . I have seen a small manufactory of this kind where ten men only were employed and where some of them consequently performed two or three distinct operations. But though they were very poor, and therefore but indifferently accommodated with the necessary machinery, they could, when they exerted themselves, make among them about twelve pounds of pins in a day. There are in a pound upwards of four thousand pins of a middling size. Those ten persons, therefore, could make among them upwards of forty-eight thousand pins in a day. . . . But if they had all wrought separately and independently . . . they certainly could not each of them make twenty, perhaps not one pin in a day. . . .

There is hardly any need to point out how infinitely more complex present-day production methods are from those of the eighteenth century. Smith, for all his disclaimers, was sufficiently impressed with a small factory of ten people to comment on it; what would he have thought of one employing ten thousand! But the great gift of the division of labor is not its complexity—indeed it simplifies most toil. Its advantage lies in its capacity to increase what Smith calls "that universal opulence which extends itself to the lowest ranks of the people." That universal opulence of the eighteenth century looks like a grim existence from our modern vantage point. But if we view the matter in its historical perspective, if we compare the lot of the workingman in eighteenth-century England to his predecessor a century or two before, it is clear that mean as his existence was, it constituted a considerable advance. Smith makes the point vividly:

> Observe the accommodation of the most common artificer or day labourer in a civilized and thriving country, and you will perceive that the number of people of whose industry a part, though but a small part, has been employed in procuring him this accommodation, exceeds all computation. The woolen coat, for example, which covers the day-labourer, as coarse and rough as it may seem, is the produce of the joint labour of a great multitude of workmen. The shepherd, the sorter of the wool, the wool-comber or carder, the dyer, the scribbler, the spinner, the weaver, the fuller, the dresser, with many others, must all join their different arts in order to complete even this homely production. How many merchants and carriers, besides, must have been employed . . . how much commerce and navigation . . . how many ship-builders, sailors, sail-makers, rope makers. . . .
>
> Were we to examine, in the same manner, all the different parts of his dress and household furniture, the coarse linen shirt which he wears next to his skin, the shoes which cover his feet, the bed which he lies on . . . the kitchen-grate at which he prepares his victuals, the coals which he makes use of for that purpose, dug from the bowels of the earth, and brought to him perhaps by a long sea and a long land carriage, all the other utensils of his kitchen, all the furniture of his table, the knives and forks, the earthen or pewter plates upon which he serves up and divides his victuals, the different hands employed in preparing his bread and his beer, the glass window which lets in the heat and the light, and keeps out the wind and the rain, with all the knowledge and art requisite for preparing that beautiful and happy invention . . . ; if we examine, I say, all those things . . . we shall be sensible that without the assistance and cooperation of many thousands, the very meanest person in a civilized country could not be provided, even according to what we very falsely imagine, the easy and simple manner in which he is commonly accommodated. Compared indeed with the more extravagant luxury of the great, his accommodation must no doubt appear extremely simple and easy; and yet it may be true, perhaps, that the accommodation of a European prince does not always so much exceed that of an industrious and frugal peasant, as the accommodation of the latter exceeds that of many an African king, the absolute master of the lives and liberties of ten thousand naked savages.

What is it that drives society to this wonderful multiplication of wealth and riches? Partly it is the market mechanism itself, for the market harnesses man's creative powers in a milieu which encourages him, even forces him, to invent, innovate, expand, take risks. But there are more fundamental pressures behind the restless activity of the market. In fact, Smith sees deep-seated laws of evolution which propel the market system in an ascending spiral of productivity.

The first of these is the Law of Accumulation.

Let us remember that Adam Smith lived at a time when the rising industrial capitalist could and did realize a fortune from his investments. Richard Arkwright, apprenticed to a barber as a young man, died in 1792 leaving an estate of £500,000. Samuel Walker, who started a forge going in an old nailshop in Rotherham, left a steel foundry on that site worth £200,000. Josiah Wedgwood, who stumped about his pottery factory on a wooden leg scrawling, "This won't do for Jos.

Wedgwood" wherever he saw evidence of careless work, left an estate of
£240,000 and much landed property. The Industrial Revolution in its early
stages provided a veritable grab bag of riches for whoever was quick enough,
shrewd enough, industrious enough to ride with its current.

And the object of the great majority of the rising capitalists was first, last, and
always, to accumulate their savings. At the beginning of the nineteenth century,
£2,500 was collected in Manchester for the foundation of Sunday schools. The
sum total contributed to this worthy cause by the single largest employers in the
district, the cotton spinners, was £90. The young industrial aristocracy had better
things to do with its money than contribute to unproductive charities—it had to
accumulate, and Adam Smith approved wholeheartedly. Woe to him who did not
accumulate. And as for one who encroached on his capital—"like him who perverts
the revenues of some pious foundation to profane purposes, he pays the wages
of idleness with those funds which the frugality of his forefathers had, as it were,
consecrated to the maintenance of industry."

But Adam Smith did not approve of accumulation for accumulation's sake.
He was, after all, a philosopher, with a philosopher's disdain for the vanity of
riches. Rather, in the accumulation of capital Smith saw a vast benefit to society.
For capital—if put to use in machinery—provided just that wonderful division of
labor which multiplies man's productive energy. Hence accumulation becomes
another of Smith's two-edged swords: the avarice of private greed again redounding
to the welfare of the community. Smith is not worried over the problem which
will face twentieth-century economists: will private accumulations actually find
their way back into more employment? For him the world is capable of indefinite
improvement and the size of the market is limited only by its geographical extent.
Accumulate and the world will benefit, says Smith. And certainly in the lusty
atmosphere of his time there was no evidence of any unwillingness to accumulate
on the part of those who were in a position to do so.

But—and here is a difficulty—accumulation would soon lead to a situation where
further accumulation would be impossible. For accumulation meant more
machinery, and more machinery meant more demand for workmen. And this in
turn would sooner or later lead to higher and higher wages, until profits—the
source of accumulation—were eaten away. How is this hurdle surmounted?

It is surmounted by the second great law of the system: the Law of Population.

To Adam Smith, laborers, like any other commodity, could be produced according to the demand. If wages were high, the number of workpeople would
multiply; if wages fell, the numbers of the working class would decrease.

Nor is this quite so naïve a conception as it appears at first blush. In Smith's
day infant mortality among the lower classes was shockingly high. "It is not uncommon," says Smith, ". . . in the Highlands of Scotland for a mother who has
borne twenty children not to have two alive." In many places in England, half the
children died before they were four, and almost everywhere half the children only
lived to the age of nine or ten. Malnutrition, evil living conditions, cold, and
disease took a horrendous toll among the poorer element. Hence although higher
wages may have affected the birth rate only slightly, it could be expected to have
a considerable influence on the number of children who would grow to working
age.

Hence if the first effect of accumulation would be to raise the wages of the
working class, this in turn would bring about an increase in the number of
workers. And now the market mechanism takes over. Just as higher prices on the

market will bring about a larger production of gloves and the larger number of gloves in turn press down the higher prices of gloves, so higher wages will bring about a larger number of workers, and the increase in their numbers will set up a reverse pressure on the level of their wages. Population, like glove production, is a self-curing disease—as far as wages are concerned.

And this meant that accumulation might go safely on. The rise in wages which it caused and which threatened to make further accumulation unprofitable is tempered by the rise in population. Accumulation leads to its own undoing, and then is rescued in the nick of time. The obstacle of higher wages is undone by the growth in population which those very higher wages made feasible. There is something fascinating in this automatic process of aggravation and cure, stimulus and response, in which the very factor which seems to be leading the system to its doom is also slyly bringing about the conditions necessary for its further health.

And now observe that Smith has constructed for society a giant endless chain. As regularly and as inevitably as a series of interlocked mathematical propositions, society is started on an upward march. From any starting point the probing mechanism of the market first equalizes the returns to labor and capital in all its different uses, sees to it that those commodities demanded are produced in the right quantities, and further ensures that prices for commodities are constantly competed down to their costs of production. But further than this, society is dynamic. From its starting point accumulation of wealth will take place, and this accumulation will result in increased facilities for production and in a greater division of labor. So far, all to the good. But accumulation will also raise wages as capitalists bid for workers to man the new factories. As wages rise further accumulation begins to look unprofitable. The system threatens to level off. But meanwhile workmen will have used their higher wages to rear their children with fewer mortalities. Hence the supply of workmen will increase. As population swells, the competition between workmen will press down on wages again. And so accumulation will continue, and another spiral in the ascent of society will begin.

This is no business cycle which Smith describes. It is a long-term process, a secular evolution. And it is wonderfully certain. Provided only that the market mechanism is not tampered with, everything is inexorably determined by the preceding link. A vast reciprocating machinery is set up with all of society inside it: only the tastes of the public—to guide producers—and the actual physical geography of the nation are outside the chain of cause and effect.

And observe, furthermore, that what is foreseen is a constantly improving state of affairs. True, the rise in the working population will always force wages back toward a subsistence level. But *toward* is not *to*; as long as the accumulation process continues—and Smith sees no reason why it should cease—there is a virtually endless opportunity for society to improve its lot. Smith did not imply that this was the best of all possible worlds: he had read Voltaire's *Candide* and was no Dr. Pangloss himself. But there was no reason why the world should not *move* in the direction of improvement and progress. Indeed, if one left the market mechanism alone and allowed it and the great social laws to work themselves out, it was inevitable that progress would result.

In the very long run, well beyond the horizon, one could just discern the final destination for society. By then the "natural" level of wages would have risen considerably (for Smith assumed that basic subsistence wages were a sociological phenomenon rather than a brute animal fact). The landlord would also have fared well, for population would be large and pressing on what was, after all, a God-given and fixed supply of land. The capitalist alone would have suffered a difficult fate; since riches would have multiplied almost beyond calculation, the capitalist would realize the wages of management, but precious little profit beyond that: he would be a hard-working, well-remunerated, but certainly not luxuriously rich person. A strange paradise of hard work, much real wealth, and little leisure this would be.

But the road to society's eventual resting place was long and there was too much to be done between the world of Adam Smith and that final campground to warrant spending much time on its detail. The *Wealth of Nations* is a program for action, not a blueprint for Utopia.

Oddly enough, the book did not immediately take hold. It was actually ridiculed by Charles James Fox, the most powerful man in Parliament, and it was to be eight years until the book was quoted in Commons. Then when recognition came —as it did—it was from an unexpected ally. The rising capitalists—and let us remember that this sturdy, upstart class of parvenus was not bothered with twentieth-century ideas about equality or economic justice—found in Smith's treatise the perfect theoretical justification for their own opposition to factory legislation. The fact that Smith had written of "the mean rapacity, the monopolizing spirit of the merchants and manufacturers" and that he had said they "neither are, nor ought to be, the rulers of mankind"—all this was ignored in favor of the great point which Smith drew from his inquiry: *let the market alone.*

What Smith had meant by this was one thing; what his proponents made him out to mean was another. Smith, as we have said, was not the proponent of any one class. He was a slave to his system. His whole economic philosophy stemmed from his unquestioning faith in the ability of the market to guide the system to its point of highest return. The market—that wonderful social machine—would take care of society's needs *if it was left alone,* so that the laws of evolution might take over to lift society toward its promised reward. Smith was neither antilabor nor anticapital; if he had any bias it was in favor of the consumer. "Consumption is the sole end and purpose of all production," he wrote, and then proceeded to castigate those systems which placed the interest of the producer over that of the consuming public.

But in Smith's panegyric of a free and unfettered market the rising industrialists found the theoretical justification they needed to block the first government attempts to remedy the scandalous conditions of the times. For Smith's theory does unquestionably lead to a doctrine of *laissez faire.* To Adam Smith the least government is certainly the best: governments are spendthrift, irresponsible, and unproductive. And yet Adam Smith is not necessarily opposed—as his posthumous admirers made him out to be—to *all* government action which has as its end the promotion of the general welfare. He warns, for example, of the stultifying effect of mass production, which robs men of their creative natural powers, and prophesies a decline in the manly virtues of the laborer, "unless the government takes some pains to prevent it." Similarly he is in favor of public education to raise the citizenry above the level of mere uncomprehending cogs in a vast machine.

What Smith *is* against is the meddling of the government with the market mechanism. He is against restraints on imports and bounties on exports, against government laws which shelter industry from competition, and against government spending for unproductive ends. Notice that these activities of the government largely have the interest of the *merchant* class at heart. Smith never faced the problem—which was to cause such intellectual agony for later generations—of whether the government is weakening or strengthening the market mechanism when it steps in with welfare legislation. Aside from poor relief, there was virtually no welfare legislation in Smith's day—the government was the unabashed ally of the governing classes, and the great tussle within the government was whether it should be the landowning or the industrial classes who should most benefit. The question of whether the working class should have a voice in the direction of economic affairs simply did not enter any respectable person's mind.

The great enemy to Adam Smith's system is not so much government per se as monopoly—in any form. "People of the same trade seldom meet together," says Adam Smith, "but the conversation ends in a conspiracy against the public, or in some diversion to raise prices." And the trouble with such goings on is not so much that they are morally reprehensible in themselves—they are, after all, only the inevitable consequence of man's self-interest—as that they impede the fluid working of the market. And of course Smith is right. If the working of the market is trusted to produce the greatest number of goods at the lowest possible prices, anything that interferes with the market necessarily lowers social welfare. If, as in Smith's time, no master hatter anywhere in England could employ more than two apprentices or no master cutler in Sheffield more than one, the market system cannot possibly yield its full benefits. If, as in Smith's time, paupers are tied to their local parishes and prevented from seeking work where work might be found, the market cannot attract labor where labor is wanted. If, as in Smith's time, great companies are given monopolies of foreign trade, the public cannot realize the full benefits of cheaper foreign produce.

Hence, says Smith, all these impediments must go. The market must be left free to find its own natural levels of prices and wages and profits and production; whatever interferes with the market does so only at the expense of the true wealth of the nation. But because any act of the government—even such laws as those requiring the whitewashing of factories or preventing the shackling of children to machines—could be interpreted as hampering the free operation of the market, the *Wealth of Nations* was liberally quoted to oppose the first humanitarian legislation. Thus by a strange injustice the man who warned that the grasping eighteenth-century industrialists "generally have an interest to deceive and even to oppress the public" came to be regarded as their economic patron saint. Even today—in blithe disregard of his actual philosophy—Smith is generally regarded as a *conservative* economist, whereas in fact, he was more avowedly hostile to the *motives* of businessmen than most New Deal economists.

In a sense the whole wonderful world of Adam Smith is a testimony to the eighteenth-century belief in the inevitable triumph of rationality and order over arbitrariness and chaos. Don't try to do good, says Smith. Let good emerge as the by-product of selfishness. How like the philosopher to place such faith in a vast social machinery and to rationalize selfish instincts into social virtues! There is nothing halfhearted about Smith's abiding trust in the consequences of his philosophical beliefs. He urges that judges should be paid by the litigants rather than by the state, since in that way their self-interest will lead them to expedite the cases brought before them. He sees little future for the newly emerging business organizations called corporations since it seems highly improbable that such impersonal bodies could muster the necessary self-interest to pursue complex and arduous undertakings. Even the greatest humanitarian movements, such as the abolition of slavery, are defended in his own terms; best abolish slavery, says Adam Smith, since to do so will probably be cheaper in the end.

The whole complex irrational world is reduced to a kind of rational scheme where human particles are nicely magnetized in a simple polarity toward profit and away from loss. The great system works, not because man directs it, but because self-interest and competition line up the filings in the proper way; the most that man can do is to help this natural social magnetism along, to remove whatever barriers stand before the free working out of this social physics, and to cease his misguided efforts to escape from its thralldom.

And yet for all its eighteenth-century flavor, its belief in rationality, natural law, and the mechanized chain of human action and reaction, the world of Adam Smith is not without its warmer values. Do not forget that the great beneficiary of the system was the consumer—not the producer. For the first time in the philosophy of everyday life, the consumer is king.

Of the whole, what has survived?

Not the great scheme of evolution. We shall see that profoundly altered by the great economists to follow. But let us not regard the world of Adam Smith as merely a primitive attempt to arrive at formulations which were beyond his grasp. Smith was the economist of preindustrial capitalism; he did not live to see the market system threatened by enormous enterprises or his laws of accumulation and population upset by sociological developments fifty years off. When Smith lived and wrote there had not yet been a recognizable phenomenon which might be called a "business cycle." The world he wrote about actually existed, and his systematization of it, mechanical though it was, provides as good an explanation as any.

Yet something must have been missing from Smith's conception. For although he saw an evolution for society, he did not see a revolution—the Industrial Revolution. Smith did not see in the ugly factory system, in the newly tried corporate form of business organization, or in the weak attempts of journeymen to form protective organizations, the first appearance of new and disruptively powerful social forces. In a sense his system presupposes that eighteenth-century England will remain unchanged forever. Only in quantity will it grow: more people, more goods, more wealth; its quality will remain unchanged. His are the dynamics of a static community; it grows but it never matures.

But although the system of evolution has been discarded, the great panorama of the market remains as a major achievement. To be sure, Smith did not "discover" the market; others had preceded him in pointing out how the interaction of self-interest and competition brought about the provision of society. But Smith was the first to understand the full philosophy of action which such a conception demanded, the first to formulate the entire scheme in a wide and systematic fashion. He was the man who made England, and then the whole Western World, understand just how the market kept society together and the first to build an edifice of social order on the understanding he achieved. Later economists will embroider Smith's description of the market and will inquire anxiously into the defects which subsequently appeared in it. None will improve on the richness and life with which Smith imbued this aspect of the world.

For Smith's encyclopedic scope and knowledge there can be only admiration. It was only in the eighteenth century that so huge, all-embracing, secure, caustic, and profound a book could have been written. Smith anticipated Veblen by a hundred and fifty years when he wrote: "With the greater part of rich people, the chief enjoyment of riches consists in the parade of riches, which in their eye is never so complete as when they appear to possess those decisive marks of opulence which nobody can possess but themselves." He was a statesman ahead of his time when he wrote: "If any of the provinces of the British Empire cannot be made to contribute towards the support of the whole empire, it is surely time that Great Britain should free herself from the expense of defending those provinces in time of war, and of supporting any part of their civil or military establishments in time of peace, and endeavour to accommodate her future views and designs to the real mediocrity of her circumstances."

And perhaps no economist will ever again so utterly encompass his age as Adam Smith. Certainly none was ever so serene, so devoid of contumacy, so penetratingly critical without rancor, and so optimistic without being utopian. To be sure, he shared the beliefs of his day, in fact he helped to forge them. It was an age of humanism and reason, and while both could be perverted for the cruelest and most violent purposes, Smith was never chauvinist, apologist, or compromiser. "For to what purpose," he wrote in the *Theory of Moral Sentiments*, "is all the toil and bustle of this world? What is the end of avarice and ambition, of the pursuit of wealth, of power, and pre-eminence?" The *Wealth of Nations* provides his answer: all the grubby scrabbling for wealth and glory has its ultimate justification in the welfare of the common man.

At the end of his life, Smith was ripe with honors and respect. Burke traveled to Edinburgh to see him; he was elected Lord Rector at his old University of Glasgow; he saw the *Wealth of Nations* translated into Danish, French, German, Italian, Spanish. Only Oxford ignored him; it never deigned to give him an honorary degree. At one time Pitt The Younger, then Prime Minister, was meeting with Addington, Wilberforce, and Grenville, and Adam Smith had been invited to attend. As the old philosopher walked into the room, everyone rose. "Be seated, gentlemen," he said. "No," replied Pitt, "we will stand until you are first seated, for we are all your scholars."

In 1790 Smith died; he was sixty-seven. Curiously, his passing attracted relatively little notice; perhaps people were too busy worrying about the French Revolution and the repercussions it might have on the English countryside. He was buried in the Canongate churchyard with an unpretentious tombstone; it states that Adam Smith, author of *Wealth of Nations*, lies here. It would be hard to conceive of a more durable monument.

41

Who Gives
Free Enterprise
Its Sense
of Direction?

Who gives direction to the marvelously
intricate and efficient economic machine
that is the American free enterprise system?
Mr. Randall argues cogently that
businessmen, motivated by financial gain,
but tempered with a high sense of social
responsibility, perform this function,
and perform it well.

*Clarence B. Randall is a former President
of Inland Steel Company. He has also
held several high government posts.*

CLARENCE B. RANDALL

American businessmen are being driven these days to take a hard second look at the philosophy and the practices of free enterprise.

This system of accumulating private capital under single control—and
risking it for gain simply because of individual initiative—has come to
businesmen as instinctively as the act of breathing. In fact, until recently,
some of them lacked even a rudimentary awareness that there *are* in the
world other systems for the production and distribution of goods.

All this is changing, thanks to the Russians. Instead of concealing their
strength until they could choose their time to strike, they rather naively
rang the alarm bell by rocketing Sputnik into orbit, and by putting the first
man into space. Now the American businessman knows that the way
of life to which his entire effort is dedicated is under severe challenge nearly
everywhere in the world, and that he must either justify it by his conduct, or face the grim prospect that his grandchildren may lose it. He is
staggered by the sudden realization that free enterprise does not automatically export itself, and that new nations, when given an opportunity
for a free choice, are apt to reject it, and to accept the Communist program. Vigorous person that he is, he resents this incredible phenomenon,
and a highly creditable determination to do something about it is seizing
him.

When he takes this hard second look at himself and his way of life,
what does he find? What are the "truths" which he holds to be "self-
evident"?

His first truth is that the principle of freedom, upon which our form of democracy must irrevocably be based, is indivisible. There are no separate freedoms that may be specifically allocated to particular groups or institutions. The right to make private decisions with respect to the production of goods is precisely the same right exercised by the professor at the university who insists upon teaching whatever economic doctrine he believes to be true. Each must fight to the death to protect the right of the other, or all will be betrayed together. Whatever restricts one restricts both, and all who believe in freedom must jointly resist limitation wherever it appears, without immediate thought of self. We need all hands on deck all of the time if "life, liberty, and the pursuit of happiness," the national goals proclaims in our Declaration of Independence, are to be preserved.

Filled with Freedom

It is this freedom, applied in industry to the point of saturation, which has given the American economy its enormous vitality and resiliency, and which the businessman is determined to see preserved at all cost.

This is so because no other system of production has yet been conceived which so effectively releases the full creative effort of each individual involved. Our industrial way of life dignifies the worth of the individual, first, by preserving for him full choice as to what calling he will embark upon, and, second, by rewarding him in direct ratio to the contribution he makes to society.

We believe that the incentives created by monetary compensation are both effective and moral. We have proved by our long history that the sum total of all effort when given freely, and with enthusiasm, in our form of society, is greater than the resultant of total effort that is brought forth by compulsion under collectivism. And we see not the slightest wrong in doing well by those who try, and not so well by those who do not. We believe that in granting rewards that are proportionate to effort we are merely giving recognition to the fact that in a free society the goals of the individual and those of society are not in conflict, but parallel.

In support of these truths, powerful testimony is now coming from behind the Iron Curtain. Of all people, the Communists are the most thorough-going of pragmatists. A thing has to work or it will be discarded. They boastfully began the reorientation of their industry on the starry-eyed theory that society would take from every man according to his ability, and grant him his share of the total production in strict accordance to his need, regardless of his effort. Now they know better. Quietly, they have dropped that theory, and now employ a wide range of group bonuses, and of individual incentives accomplished through both salary and emoluments. In a land that has few automobiles, a limousine and chauffeur can create powerful motivation. Add a *dacha* on the Black Sea, and the upward surge of production can be pronounced. In fact, incredible as it seems, the spread between the compensation of the manager of a steel plant in Russia, and that of the lowest paid worker is unquestionably greater than the comparable difference in the United States.

We apply this principle of freedom that saturates not only to the production of goods, but to their sale and distribution as well. We have no lonely commissar pontificating by himself as to what quantities and qualities of merchandise we should turn out. We vote all day every day as to what they should be. Every time a housewife goes into a supermarket and buys a package, she casts a ballot, as does her husband when he makes the down payment on an automobile. By totaling the resultant from an infinite number of such free choices, we arrive at consensus as to our goals.

In fact, the basic concept that underlies everything we do is the idea that the wisdom of the many is at all times more to be trusted than the wisdom of the few. There is always the chance under communism that a commissar may display great genius, but there is a still greater chance that he may display colossal ignorance and stupidity, and only fools would knowingly take such risks.

We employ the same principle of freedom that saturates in the formulation and gathering of the capital required in building and equipping our industrial plan, and in financing our operations. We rely on no other force than the incentive of intelligent self-interest for providing our funds. No individual is required to save. He may eat today and starve tomorrow, if he so elects. No part of that share of the product of his toil which has been allocated to him will ever be taken from him against his will in order that capital may be accumulated. But as a rational being, he soon senses that there is a future, and that for him and his family it will be a better future if he withdraws a part of his earnings from immediate consumption, and risks it for further gain by buying common stock of his company, or of another if he prefers.

This broad diffusion of ownership does two things. First, it keeps management on its toes; unless industry fully measures up and gives full value in terms of return on investment, the flow of capital will stop; people will spend and not save. And, second, those who own want to understand, and a means of communication is established by which people everywhere acquire insight into the problems of the national economy.

The powerful magnetic force which keeps the compass of industry pointing true north, to the welfare of society as a whole, is competition. The rule of survival of the fittest, the counterpart of freedom of enterprise, sternly demands that each separate unit of production put forth its utmost effort at all times, and that is social gain of a high order. We speak of ours as a profit system, but actually it is a profit and loss system, and the two forces of hope and fear operate in parallel to eliminate those whom in America we call the "free riders."

Danger Signs

When one businessman enters into a secret agreement with another businessman to restrict competition, he is either guilty of moral turpitude or ignorant of the enterprise system. The pegging of prices, the arbitrary dividing of territories, the withholding for a fixed period of advances in technology, and all similar devices which evil minds can think up to fatten profits at the expense of the consumer are a denial of our heritage. And they will destroy the enterprise system if they are allowed to persist. Such power over society cannot be lodged in private hands, and an angry public, when fully roused, will punish us all by withdrawing the privileges which it has bestowed in the field of private endeavor.

This, of course, raises the whole question of the importance of moral attitudes in the preservation of the enterprise system. It is actually more important that we be right than that we be effective. The very highest standards of ethics must henceforth govern the conduct of industrial leaders if society is not to turn against us; and we in the United States now comprehend this clearly.

We still have areas of weakness, however. Take executive salaries, for example. It is urgent and right that men who bear great responsibility should be generously compensated, but when moderation yields to avarice, hostile social forces are swiftly set in motion.

Here are some of the danger signs. When the top man has the highest salary in his industry, he may be justified, for someone has to be the high man, but he should be put upon great caution to be sure he is right. And when the top man submits his proposed compensation to no one but an "inside board," namely a group of directors who work for him, he is clearly vulnerable.

We have erred, too, with respect to expense accounts. Under our law, legitimate entertaining may be deducted as a cost for purposes of computing the corporate income tax. But when the company president gives a champagne party at a night club, or uses the company airplane to take his friends on a duck-hunting trip, he steps far over the line of propriety. His conduct poses a threat to the survival of the entire private enterprise regime. His subversion and the Communist's differ only in degree.

On the other hand, there have been great advances in general probity during the years of the present generation. In my day, for example, I have seen commercial bribery all but completely eliminated. Time was that one company would place an industrial spy in the research department of a competitor, or when a supplier would buy the favor of a purchasing agent, but those moral lapses have been cleaned up—and cleaned up by industry itself, without the necessity for new laws.

In fact, the outstanding characteristic of the entire business community in the United States today, and the one which holds the greatest promise for the future, is its high sense of social responsibility. We now see clearly that the welfare of a particular enterprise and of the area in which it is located are inseparably linked, and we see further that the welfare of industry as a whole and of our country are likewise indivisible. It has taken a long time for this full sense of social mission to become the dominant philosophy of our industrial leadership, but such is now the unquestionable fact.

New Role for Businessmen

And it is right that this should be so. It is merely the logical extrapolation of a principle which, once accepted, could lead to only one conclusion: for every privilege bestowed upon individuals in a democratic society there is a corresponding obligation. Such is the essence of freedom. In the past, we have heard too much about our rights, not enough about our responsibilities. All this is now undergoing revolutionary change, and the businessman is assuming an important role in this significant transformation as he takes his hard second look at the enterprise system.

Nearly all leading American firms, for example, now set aside a part of their profits for philanthropy. Most of them do this by establishing a charitable foundation, which is administered by a special staff, and not by the board of directors. Through this medium they give support to hospitals, homes for the aged, child welfare institutions, health programs, and a wide variety of social agencies. This is only the beginning, however, and in large corporations literally hundreds of worthy causes will be assisted. Education stands high on the list, and liberal arts colleges are supported in parity with those which turn out technically trained graduates. Above all, the motive behind the allocation of such funds is not to help the company, but solely to serve the community and the nation. That is industrial statesmanship of the highest sort. We had a little trouble with the lawyers on this at the start, but it is now entirely clear that under our law a corporation may use its funds for the common good, as, of course, it should.

Moreover, businessmen in the United States now give themselves in addition to their money. You will find them lending their management skills to community institutions by taking unpaid executive posts, or by serving on boards of trustees, and you will find them employing their promotional gifts in leading fund-raising campaigns for charitable purposes. They are establishing by their conduct the proposition that free enterprise not only receives from society, but gives full value in return.

You will find businessmen in our government these days, too, at every level, carrying heavy responsibility at substantial financial sacrifice, and doing so with distinction. When, unexpectedly, a corporation officer is asked to close his desk for a term of years and go to Washington, or to his state capital, he does so in a high spirit of dedication. He knows that in this world of crises the demand for talent in government has greatly exceeded the supply, and he answers the call in the spirit of his new philosophy of social mission. Actually, the combination of the mature executive from business, paired with a career officer, makes a strong team. The professional provides the indispensable familiarity with the subject matter and the knowledge of how government operates; the amateur brings awareness of the state of public opinion and the courage to take a fresh approach, inasmuch as his own future is never at stake in anything he does. His greatest desire is to get the job done worthily, and go home.

Leaders in American industry are thus in many ways rising magnificently to the challenge of a world in torment and distress. They believe fervently that the forces of private initiative as released into the field of production in a free and democratic society bring greater good to more human beings than is possible under communism. But they also know that freedom brings responsibility, and that production as such is not a goal in itself. They are fully aware of their social obligations, and are determined to fulfill them abundantly.

42

On the Principle of Consumers' Sovereignty

In a competitive world, the economy's production is guided by the "dollar votes" of consumers. Professor Scitovsky argues that in our modern economic society, consumer choices are so complex and influenced so much by advertising, that the simple "consumers' sovereignty" principle needs drastic modification.

Tibor Scitovsky is Professor of Economics at the University of California, Berkeley.

TIBOR SCITOVSKY

Many attacks from many quarters have been launched in recent years on the principle of consumers' sovereignty. They have questioned the economist's wisdom in putting too great and exclusive a trust in the consumer's wisdom; and it is regrettable that these attacks have shaken the public's faith in the economist but have not shaken the economist out of his established modes of thought. Indeed, American economists have largely ignored these attacks, following an old American tradition of keeping hands off welfare economics—applying its results but refusing to cast a critical look at the derivation of these results. I have been fighting this tradition for some time, because I believe that much of the criticism is valid and economists should take it to heart. I have much more to say on the subject than time to say it in, and have said much of it already, so I shall confine myself here to two issues: the choice between market and collective goods, and the problem of whether the market can cater to consumers' tastes truly and well.

The first issue stems from the realization that the sovereignty of the consumer is not at all the same thing as the sovereignty of the individual or citizen. The consumer is just one facet of the individual—the one that has to do with the consumption of goods sold through the market. The consumer's welfare therefore is only a part of man's welfare and only a part even of his economic welfare. Choosing between market and collective goods, deciding whether a given service is better provided through the market or by public spending, determining the best allocation of public

From *The American Economic Review*, May, 1962, pp. 262–268. Reprinted by permission.

funds among their various uses—all these are economic choices no different and no less important than the consumer's choice between two market goods; and yet, our society has failed to develop adequate machinery through which the public could express its preferences on these issues. For, as Galbraith pointed out, advertising, the American tradition of self-reliance, belief in the advantages of private enterprise, and the economist's excessive preoccupation with consumer's choice in the market, not only have biased the American public against collective goods but even prevent its forming and expressing rational preferences on the economic aspects of any choice involving them, so much are these issues befogged by ideological considerations. The more's the pity, because a variety of recent changes and developments are rendering these choices ever more important.

Historically, there is plenty of excuse for such bias. For many centuries, food, clothing, and shelter symbolized market goods, while cathedrals, palaces, and armies were the symbols of collective spending; and most of us would favor absolute priority of the first over the second group. The tendency to think in these terms persists today, although in most developed countries the choice has long ceased to be so simple. On the margin, which is where choices are made, most expenditures in a developed economy have to do with leisure; and today, society's marginal choice between market and collective expenditures is no longer a choice between more bread and more palaces but more nearly that between TV sets and other gadgets and appliances on the market side and public services and recreational and educational facilities on the collective side. This is the kind of choice that the Planning Commission of France must have had in mind when they recommended a faster expansion of collective services than of the consumption sector and warned against the social malaise that might result from catering to the consumer's every whim.

Another explanation of our undue emphasis on the consumption of market goods may be the fact that our economic thinking was formulated at a time when many collective goods were free but which today are no longer free. The increase in population density and man's tendency to fill the countryside with factories, automobiles, and empty beer cans have created a world in which fresh air, clean water, and the enjoyment of nature are no longer free goods. Smog control and the decontamination of polluted rivers are expensive operations, and so is the creation and maintenance of "nature areas" in a world whose wide open spaces are rapidly being subdivided into quarter-acre lots. The external diseconomies of the production and consumption of market goods render such collective goods increasingly scarce and expensive; but economic theory, social accounting, and most public policy still proceed on the fiction that external diseconomies are small enough to be neglected.

Besides the rise in living standards and the crowding of space, increased life expectancy, secular inflation, and uneven progress and the resulting change in relative prices are all among the factors that call either for more provision of collective goods and services or at least for a reconsideration of the question which goods and services should be provided collectively and which through the market. Increased life expectancy demands of the individual more and more careful long-run budgeting at the very time when secular inflation and the uncertainty it creates are diminishing the market's ability to handle long-run budgeting. This, together with the changing nature of the family, which no longer provides a place for the aged, explains the rising demand and rising recognition of demand for the collective provision of social security. Increased life expectancy is also bringing about a situation in which the leisure classes are no longer the rich but the aged, who however are at the same time also the poor modern society. This too is causing many people to wish to do some reallocating of spending from market goods to collective services.

Changing relative prices are another factor relevant here, because they can change people's ideas on which services should be distributed free and paid out of public funds, which should be subsidized, and which sold at full cost through the market. This is so, because given the distribution of income and wealth, the inequality with which a particular good is distributed depends on its price in relation to other prices. The higher its relative price, the more unequally the market distributes it. It can happen, therefore, that the rise in the price of a good should increase the inequality of its distribution beyond the point tolerated by public opinion, which will then demand either its subsidization and sale below cost or its free provision out of public funds. In this age of fast and uneven technical progress there are many instances of this happening. An illustration is the increasing public demand in developed countries for national health insurance or free medical care.

In discussing some of the factors that in today's more complex world call for greater reliance on collective goods and services, I am not forgetting the arguments against the element of compulsion and the lesser safeguards against inefficiency and waste in the public sector. In the past, we have fought these troubles the easy way by trying to minimize the public sector itself. Its growth and the increasing need for it may compel us to fight the hard way for its more satisfactory performance.

We can now proceed to our other subject: the criticism of consumers' sovereignty in the narrow sense. The two main objections here are, first, that in this age, when man's control over his fellowmen's beliefs is almost as great as his control over nature, the economist should still continue to regard consumers' preferences as a datum and the standard by which to judge the performance of the economy; and, second, that even by the questionable standard of consumers' preferences, the market economy performs badly, and for reasons not even considered in traditional economic analysis.

In the days of the handicraft economy, every piece of clothing, every piece of furniture was made to the specifications of the person who bought it; but from this position of 100 per cent consumer sovereignty we have retreated long ago. Consumers yielded their dominance first to merchants, who had the initiative in placing orders and specifying the nature and design of products for a long period, and later to manufacturers, who now decide themselves what to produce. The consumer's loss of initiative involves no great loss of sovereignty as long as he is given an adequate range of alternatives to choose from and is able to distinguish the good from the bad and to recognize solid construction, good design, and practical and imaginative ideas. These conditions, however, are the less fulfilled, the more the economy and technology progress.

Economies of scale not only cheapen large-scale production but by raising wages they also raise the cost and diminish the profitability of small-scale production. This in turn raises the minimum volume of sales necessary to render production profitable and thus leads to an ever increasing narrowing of the range of variants of products offered and neglect of minority needs and tastes in the nature and design of goods produced and marketed.

The increasing neglect of minority preferences is a bad thing, because it is illiberal, makes for uniformity, and destroys to some degree the principal merit of the market economy: its ability to cater separately and simultaneously to different people's differing needs and tastes. Also, the more the market loses this ability, the greater the extent to which majority preferences are imposed upon minorities and the more do the nature and formation of these majority preferences become matters of public concern.

Now the very failure of the market to cater to minority preferences may have undesirable effects upon the development of majority preferences as well. Even the most ardent believers in consumer sovereignty must realize that most tastes are acquired, that bad tastes are as easy to acquire as good ones, and that the best one can hope for is that by example and imitation the good will prevail over the bad if given an even chance. An additional advantage, therefore, of a market that caters to diffeernt people's differing tastes is that it gives those with informed tastes a chance to set an example to the rest of the community. Informed people, however, are always a minority; and when they are too small a minority—or economies of scale are too great—for producers to cater to their demand, then they are unable to set an example and fulfill their educative function.

Informed people are partly the experts who either as professionals or as amateurs have an intimate knowledge of a particular type of consumers' good—and it goes without saying that the expert public for music is generally a different group of people from the expert buyers of automobiles. A second part of the informed public is composed of generally educated people, who either are informed or if not know how to inform themselves.

I should like to see the tastes of experts catered to, because they know something about technical excellence. I should like to have the preferences of the generally educated public respected, because they have a wider perspective, apply a variety of criteria, and pay attention to the relation and connection between different criteria.

I admit, of course, that the preference for an educated taste is simply the subjective preference of educated people; but they, or most of them, have the tremendous advantage of having, at an earlier stage, been uneducated and uninformed themselves. In the early work on the theory of consumer satisfaction, the Greeks could never resolve the problem whether men or women enjoyed more the pleasures of love, because they could not draw on the experience of people who had tasted these pleasures in both capacities. In approaching our problem we have no such handicap. I cannot claim that an informed person's tastes are better by any test than an uninformed person's, or that they are more conducive to happiness or more appropriate to the atomic age; but I can claim that they are based on knowledge of a wider range of alternatives, which includes the alternatives available to the uninformed person.

Let me also recall that the issue is not whether uninformed tastes should or should not be suppressed and displaced by informed ones. I am merely deploring and criticizing the tendency of scale economies to keep the market more and more from catering to informed, or, if you wish, highbrow, tastes and thus to keep these tastes from competing on an equal basis with uninformed and lowbrow tastes in molding the preferences of the public at large.

Who then influences the majority's preferences and how? I can think of several channels through which is imposed what David Riesman called "other directedness," not so much the taste of the representative consumer as what public-opinion experts believe to be his taste. As already mentioned, the increasing importance of scale economies has greatly raised the penalty producers have to pay for making the wrong guesses about consumers' tastes and putting unpopular products on the market. Hence the tendency of producers in an increasing number of fields to play safe and not to risk imaginative innovations in the new products, services, and publications they put on the market but to rely instead on market research into the consumer's unfulfilled desires. At its best, this can slow down genuine progress and innovation in the design of products; at its worst, it can lead to a serious misreading of the public taste and the imposition of a mythical majority taste that in fact few people share. The automobile industry, with its hand on the consumer's pulse, has for many years diagnosed a chronic yearning for longer and wider and more powerful cars; and had it not been for foreign competition, we— and they—might never have found out how wrong they were. Similarly, Hollywood used to proclaim twelve as the median age of the American movie audiences; and if it had not been for the success of foreign films, we would still live under the shadow of this depressing thought.

One trouble with such misreadings of the majority's mind is the difficulty of finding out how wrong they are. Competition seems no adequate safeguard. The consumer is all too often in the position of the voter who has but one candidate to vote for or several candidates who all stand for the same thing. And to complete the simile, the consumer too is subjected to a barrage of advertising to persuade him that he really wants the product which is the designer's realization of what the market researcher believes to be the average consumer's wishdream.

Another factor responsible for the other-directedness of the consumer's taste has to do with the increasing importance of durable goods in the consumer's budget. The most important of these, cars and houses, are bought not only for consumption but also as an investment for their resale value; and buying for high resale value means buying not what one wants but what one believes other people want. The consumer buys extra trim on his car, not necessarily because he wants it, but because the salesman assures him that it will raise the blue-book value of his car in the secondhand market. He is forced to avoid all but the most conventional design and construction in his house, because to get a good mortgage, the house must conform to what the appraiser believes, perhaps wrongly, the majority taste to be. Accordingly, house construction is governed to quite an extent not by what the consumer wants but what an unimaginative and not very expert middleman expects other consumers to want.

Luckily for the consumer, his writ still runs in many areas; but it is none too soon to start thinking about how to remedy the situation. Also, the above points were merely a sample of the things that are wrong with consumer's sovereignty but a sufficiently representative sample to raise the question of remedies and policies. Most economists seem reluctant to face up to these questions, presumably because they visualize the dictatorship of an economic planner as the only alternative to the present situation. Such an attitude, however, shows a misunderstanding of the issues involved. Most critics object not to the consumer's sovereignty but to the ignorance and restrictions to which his reign is subject and to the influence businessmen have over it. We cannot and do not want to turn the clock back and return to a handicraft economy; and some shortcomings we may choose to put up with. However, some of those discussed in this paper can be remedied; and we may be able to establish safeguards to assure the satisfaction of a wider range of consumers and to guard against the undue and undesirable influencing of consumer's tastes. The choice is not whether consumers or a central planner should exercise sovereignty but whether and how the producer's power to ignore some consumers and influence the preferences of others should be curbed and modified.

This is not the place to discuss in detail the nature of a constructive answer to any of these questions; but a few precedents may be mentioned. Public carriers are required to offer service in off-peak hours and on little-traveled routes; the Pure Food and Drug Administration does impose curbs on a highly competitive industry; and Britain's Independent Television Authority is an excellent and successful example of how the influencing of consumers' tastes by market-research and public-opinion experts can be curbed, modified, and supplemented by the influence of Distinguished Citizens. In a slightly different area, the survival of opera and serious drama and the publication of scholarly books are assured by subsidies—from the state in Western Europe, from other sources here.

All these, of course, are examples of exceptional cases justified by special circumstances. To extend them into a general rule would be much harder and more momentous than their admission as exceptions. Also, the further such policies are extended and the more the unfettered operation of the market is encroached upon, the more value judgments are involved. And here I should like to end on a note I started out with: the economist could wash his hands of value judgments only if the public's preferences were really given and he could accept them as such. As soon as this ceases to be true and the public's preferences are influenced by economic agents and the economic environment, value judgments on whether this influence is good or bad, in need of restraint or reform, cannot be avoided. If the economist feels incompetent to make such judgments himself, he should at least admit their legitimacy and provide the analytical framework to help others to make these judgments.

Different firms set prices in different
ways. Three economists describe in detail
how the prices of steel and consumer
appliances were established by some
leading firms.

A. D. H. Kaplan is a senior staff member
of The Brookings Institution, and
Research Professor of Economics, George
Washington University; Joel B. Dirlam
is Professor of Economics at Connecticut
College; and Robert F. Lanzilotti is
Professor and Head of Economics
Department, Michigan State University.

43

Pricing in Steel and Consumer Appliances

A. D. H. KAPLAN, JOEL B. DIRLAM, ROBERT F. LANZILOTTI

STEEL

The pricing process in steel reflects the industry's history of price leadership and the influence of vertical integration. Earlier studies of steel pricing
have concentrated on such factors as the forward integration of the major
steel producers, the method of price quotation, the heavy investment and
overhead costs, and the peculiarities of demand.[1] In the present context,
however, interest is focused on the determinants of policy as they appear
to a leading firm. Hence, little purpose would be served by attempting a
detailed summary of factors that may affect steel pricing. Nevertheless,
certain aspects of the price history of steel that are directly relevant to an
interpretation of the views of management require consideration.

The quoted base price for basic steel and steel products tends to be
uniform among firms following the lead of United States Steel. Finished
steel is sold mostly by specification—this being true not only of highly
fabricated pieces like structural steel, but also of the general run of sheets,
plates, bars, rods, etc. Extra charges, which are imposed for variations in
alloy and other specifications, are important in the final delivered price.
Up to the Second World War, the industry apparently agreed on uniform
extras to tie in differences in specifications with a uniform base price;

From *Pricing in Big Business* by A. D. H. Kaplan, Joel B. Dirlam, and Robert F.
Lanzilotto (The Brookings Institution, 1958), pp. 13–23, 55–65. Reprinted by permission.

[1] E.g. Carroll R. Daugherty, Melvin G. deChazeau, and Samuel S. Stratton, *The
Economics of the Iron and Steel Industry* (1937).

but in recent years, this practice seems to have become less prevalent.[2] Room is left for differentials among companies in the final price, despite the fact that most standard products are quoted at base prices plus extras showing no appreciable spread from the quotations of U.S. Steel. There still remains the freight advantage or disadvantage of location in relation to particular market outlets.

Mechanics of Pricing

United States Steel states that it employs a "stable margin" price policy, that is, in general it aims at maintaining margins despite variations in sales volume. In so doing it uses standard costs,[3] computed on the basis of 80 per cent of capacity as normal, and including an assignment of overhead burden to every product. Although the company continuously watches actual costs, it follows standard cost logic for pricing purposes. Standard costs are revised annually to account for such factors as increased labor costs, rising markets, new machines, new processes, new kinds of coal used, and similar factors affecting actual costs.[4]

Standard costs are determined for each mill, but these individual standards are used primarily for gauging efficiency and for stimulating incentive at the local level. For pricing purposes, the standard cost used is an average, weighted by the volumes at respective mills. This means that in addition to changes in the factors mentioned above, as occasioning revisions in standard cost, allowance is also made for higher capital costs of new facilities. Thus, high capital costs exert an upward push on company-wide weighted standard costs and prices.

The company stresses the distinction it makes between what it calls "price structure" and "price level." Price structure involves "a hard-boiled application of standard costs in pricing individual products"; price level is concerned with the general or average level of prices for the corporation, which in the final determination of prices involves much more than standard costs. The distinction can be seen more clearly by a discussion of the use of standard costs in connection with the

[2] Special prices are made for large contracts, and there is evidence that charges for extras are less uniform than they once were. In this connection, there is strong opinion among producers that discrimination and secret price cuts are not characteristic in the industry. The reason offered by one steel executive is that virtually everyone knows everyone else's costs; in effect, that the industry operates in a gold fish bowl. Also "the price cuts of the thirties taught everyone a lesson."

[3] Standard cost may be defined as "predetermined cost for each operation, or each unit of finished product . . . intended to represent the value of direct material, direct labor, and manufacturing burden normally required under efficient conditions at normal capacity to process a unit of prdouct." E. A. Green, National Association of Cost Accountants Bulletin, Vol. 16, cited in *Accountants' Handbook* (1944), p. 225.

One of the main purposes of employing standard costs is to avoid the presumption of significant changes in profits or efficiency when these may be due in a particular instance to a temporary change in the cost or market situation respecting a specific item. To provide for these shifting situations, cost standards are used to make the stated costs of parts, assemblies, and finished products accord more closely with planned objectives. A common objective to which standard costs are frequently geared is a break-even point regarded as normal or optimum —*e.g.*, 70 or 80 per cent of capacity. Another purpose of standard costs is to control plant operations by developing and analyzing variances or differences between standard and actual costs; or by developing cost ratios or trends which use the standard costs as measuring rods.

[4] The market against which U.S. Steel measures adequacy of its capacity and its hoped-for share of sales is the projected total national market (including imports), broken down by individual product groups, by regions and mills. On the basis of these figures and the amount of various products the company feels it can and wishes to sell, the company's "operating plan" for the year is determined.

mechanics of an actual price change, such as occurred following the wage settlement of 1956.

General Price Revision, August 1956

The average increase of $8.50 per ton in steel prices on August 7, 1956 was determined essentially as follows: With the wage negotiations as a backdrop, the Executive Vice-President, Commercial, directed his Price Division to recommend price schedules on the basis of hypothetical wage settlements.[5] According to a tradition in the steel industry, each cent-per-hour increase in direct labor costs adds another cent to steelmakers' non-wage costs per ton of steel. This working figure has been derived from experience in earlier wage settlements. With this labor-to-total cost ratio, the anticipated wage settlement is roughly doubled and multiplied by a traditional figure of twenty man-hours (more recently a figure of fifteen has been used to reflect higher efficiency) to yield the expected cost of a new wage package per ton of steel. Since the new contract (July 1956) was estimated to add 24 cents to the company's hourly labor cost per ton, an increase of $9.60 per ton was indicated.[6]

The Price Division bases its recommendations on more than this rule of thumb. It also makes a product-by-product analysis in which it considers proposals of the various product departments regarding changes in individual products. Whenever a product section of the company feels a change in base price is needed, it makes such recommendations in writing to the Commercial Department. The form used for this purpose calls for a detailed justification of the recommendation in terms of the pricing history and competitive information on the product and the expected impact of the proposed revision on specific company accounts or industries. The recommendation is accompanied by financial information prepared by the comptroller showing on a per-ton basis the present and proposed cost, together with the present and expected profit or loss.

These recommendations and attached supporting information are presented to the director of the Price Division for his evaluation and in turn are submitted to the Vice-President, Commercial, for final action. It is important to note the kinds of information before the price makers at this level of management (which actually evaluates proposed price changes and determines the changes to be made, when, and by how much). The changes are considered in terms of profit return on *sales*, not investment. This illustrates, as in the case of other companies in the sample, the way in which pricing officials view their product pricing problems, in contrast to the top level management, which views price policy primarily in terms of return on investment, but which does not actually determine prices.

Although the 1956 general price revision increased the composite average 6.25 per cent ($8.50 per ton), the prices of different products were not raised uniformly. Many products were raised more than 6.25 per cent, some less. The items tabulated . . . taken from U.S. Steel quotations announced immediately after the wage settlement illustrate the variations in the price increases.

---

[5] The Price Division consists of four or five price analysts charged with the responsibility of continuing examination of the price problem from many different angles (demand, costs, competition, market strategy, etc.).

[6] The custom of using this crude method of estimating price increases largely explains the expectation of the "trade" generally that prices would go up by at least $9.60 per ton. Some estimates ran as high as $12 per ton on the average, since in 1955 the industry used a 2.5 to 1 basis of estimating the total cost impact of the wage settlement. *Business Week*, Aug. 11, 1956, p. 25.

These differences show, among other considerations, such factors as: holding back on changes during the year, the post-wage settlement being regarded as the most propitious time for a complete revision of prices; the labor cost factor in the

	Aug. 7, 1956 Price (Per ton)	Previous Price (Per ton)	Per Cent Increase
Alloy steel			
Billets, blooms, slabs	$107	$ 96	11.5
Hot rolled strip and sheet	155	144	7.6
Wire—Premier spring, high carbon	168	152	10.5
Wire products			
Nails	167	152	9.9
Barbed wire	187	175	6.9
Carbon steel			
Cold finished bars	137	125	9.6
Light rails	120	113	6.2
Plates, high strength (Man-Ten S)	127	120	5.8

given product; the company's leadership position in the product; expectations of the trade (and the potential pressure from congressional committees and the public). With the 1956 three-year contract, management expected to make more selective price changes as it deemed appropriate, rather than follow its earlier practice of general annual changes.[7]

Cost-Price Relationships

That standard-cost doctrine has not been rigidly followed by the company in pricing is suggested by price changes that do not seem to conform to the usual varieties of standard-cost plus target-return pricing. Standard-cost pricing is designed to avoid the necessity for making short-run changes in burden that would result if adjustments were continuously made for temporary changes in volume. Actually, U.S. Steel has not been able to ignore short-term shrinkage of demand. Moreover, it has not been able to carry its "fair return" logic to the point of forcing price increases in depressions to offset higher unit costs at low volume, because its competitors would not follow. Nor has it cut prices in boom periods, which would be the corollary of price increases in depressions.

Differences in margins among products were not demonstrated by the corporation in terms of cost and price data on given product lines, but were assumed to be generally recognized in the industry. Mill prices cannot be directly related to costs for U.S. Steel or its competitors, whose prices, with certain exceptions noted below, are generally designed to meet the corporation's prices. United States Steel has the same prices at Pittsburgh and in Ohio, Illinois, Indiana, and Alabama, and apparently averages mill costs to get such equalization.[8]

The Competitive Impact on Pricing

The intensity of competition from other steel companies varies with the effectiveness of U.S. Steel's price leadership. With swings in the business cycle, there

[7] This selective policy apparently was not followed in the general price increase of $6 per ton announced by U.S. Steel on July 1, 1957.

[8] According to one pricing official, "standard costs on most products are much closer among mills than is commonly supposed: the variations run about five per cent." The Fairless Works is evidently an exception.

has been some modification of the "full-cost stable-margin" pricing philosophy of U.S. Steel and its leading competitors. Competitors of the corporation are more likely to take premiums in periods of prosperity, while U.S. Steel appears to demand no more than its published prices. In recession, however, the company has followed the trend toward concessions initiated by competitors. United States Steel has tended to be the laggard in recognizing the price cuts of its rivals. The ostensible regularity and comparative rigidity in steel prices have been appreciably modified by the policies of steel companies other than U.S. Steel. From 1946 to 1950 the prices of many steel producers were substantially higher than those of U.S. Steel.

When pricing through the basing point system was in effect, there were apparently fewer exceptions to the leader-follower pattern. Yet, even in 1936 U.S. Steel had to cut its base prices to reflect levels prevailing generally in the industry but not yet "official." With all mills on an f.o.b. basis, when demand is heavy, there is perhaps less of a disposition on the part of competitors to follow U.S. Steel. The corporation's public announcement of October 1953, reiterated in its *Annual Report* for 1953—that when necessary to get the business, it would meet the lower delivered price of a competitor—suggests that when rivals expect operation will be less than capacity, they are more disposed to undercut U.S. Steel.[9] There is no indication that the October 1953 policy resulted in U.S. Steel's having to match price reductions that yielded its competitors a lower base price than U.S. Steel had set.

Opportunities to differentiate prices to take advantage of locations within a given natural market may vary with the particular products and sections of the country that are involved. In the East, for example, where Bethlehem Steel has four mills, the mill prices for semifinished steel plates, bars, and sheets are the same at all its mills and identical with Pittsburgh prices. Structural prices are slightly higher than Pittsburgh, but are the same at all its mills, even Johnstown, which is near Pittsburgh. Yet, Sparrows Point prices are higher than Pittsburgh on wire rods, wire, and tin mill products. Some of these are made at the Johnstown mill, but for these products Pittsburgh prices are applied. Similarly, U.S. Steel's Fairless Works enjoys a $3.00 per ton price differential over other mills on standard bars, small shapes, and special quality and concrete reinforcing bars, and a $1.00 differential on hot- and cold-rolled sheets. Farther west, National Steel's Great Lakes plant near Detroit has enjoyed a differential over Pittsburgh of $2.00 (formerly $4.00) per ton on sheets. It is a moot question whether such differentials could be maintained in conditions of slack demand and underutilization of plant capacity by other steel producers, such as prevailed in 1953–54.

It also seems clear that firms will quote outside their natural territory and absorb freight. United States Steel management indicated in interviews that the 1953 announcement regarding its intention to meet the delivered prices of com-

---

[9] "Under the revised policy, U.S. Steel will continue to quote prices f.o.b. its mills, or, if the customer so desires, it will quote delivered prices which reflect full transportation charges from shipping mill to destination. The revised policy, however, permits the meeting of a lower delivered price of a competitor when necessary and commercially desirable in order to participate in the business of an individual customer. This change in policy is consistent with the stand long taken by U.S. Steel—that it has the right to compete in good faith in any market for the business of any consumer. This provision for meeting the lower delivered price of a competitor does not constitute a return to the so-called multiple basing point pricing method which was abandoned by the steel industry in 1948." U.S. Steel Corporation, *Annual Report, 1953*, p. 12.

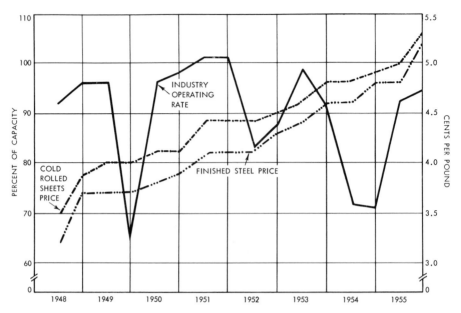

Average Prices of Steel Products and Average Capacity Operated, 1948–1955

petitors should not be taken to mean that it will shade its base prices to meet individual situations. An officer explained that the company "is committed to a one-price policy; if it is deemed desirable to change price, it will be an across-the-board change." The management stated that it will do no more than equalize the freight disadvantage, even in those instances when U.S. Steel's base price is higher than a competitor's.[10] The company's determination to implement this policy strictly has been spelled out in a memorandum to all sales offices, with specific instructions respecting the conditions under which freight absorption cases would be considered by the Commercial Department.

Competitors, meanwhile, complain that prices on many steel products, even after the broad price readjustments carried through in 1956, have not been high enough to stimulate the desirable level of new investment in the industry. Generally, the assertion takes the form of the specific accusation that U.S. Steel is pricing as though new capacity cost $100 instead of the current $300 a ton. United States Steel has joined in complaints of an insufficient return, yet apparently does not intend to relieve the pressure on its competitors.[11] A campaign by steel

[10] This would appear to be somewhat inconsistent with the earlier announcement about "meeting the delivered prices of competitors." Also, it is difficult to understand how customers could be gained or held (except in periods of steel shortage) if it meant that U.S. Steel's delivered price (with freight equalized) would still be higher than that of a rival steelmaker. It would appear that U.S. Steel will not *initiate any price shading,* but if threatened with loss of customers will retaliate as necessary to keep them—*e.g.,* by freight absorption.

[11] Since 1940, according to a statement made by Mr. Fairless in 1953, U.S. Steel had not, in ten out of twelve years, recouped "a dime of added profit on the millions of extra tons of steel that [it] produced for the people of this nation," nor earned "one cent of increased return on the billion and a half of additional capital that has been poured into [its] business." *New York Times,* Apr. 26, 1953, p. 5.

men to boost prices was dampened when U.S. Steel would not go along with a general price increase in the fall of 1955.

Although steel producers have complained, it is evident that the "art of follower-ship" is still deeply embedded in the philosophy of pricing in the steel industry. National Steel has been a price follower in every line in which it engages, in two of which (tin plate and light sheet steel) it has been an important producer. Despite former President Weir's adoption of the position that steel prices should be based on full cost of the most efficient firm, the company nevertheless has rested profitably under the umbrella of U.S. Steel prices during a large part of its history.[12] National's price has generally followed the Pittsburgh price, with freight allowed when necessary. While the company unhesitatingly meets price cuts—and does so by reducing the base price rather than the extras—it makes no effort to lead in price reductions.

Thus, U.S. Steel's competitors, except to the extent that they produce specialities or otherwise tailor their services, feel forced to go along with the U.S. Steel base price plus transportation cost in "normal" times when demand is heavy. By con-centrating in those areas of steel making, particularly tin plate, where it can operate at low cost and raise technical standards, National appears to have been a successful operator. Indeed, one officer of U.S. Steel who has been with the cor-poration for many years has expressed the opinion that companies like National and Bethlehem, with more centrally located facilities, have been able to improve those facilities at the same location. United States Steel, by contrast, was disinclined to abandon its original locations and less adaptable steel capacity "because of long-continued obligations to community and to staff." Hence, it has had greater over-head burdens and lower margins in comparison with other steel companies. These disadvantages have been offset in part by the advantages accruing from "a very broad product line and also complete geographic coverage."

Patently U.S. Steel's policies pervade the pricing structure and price levels for all steel products. Even with products numbered in the thousands, and customers exceeding 100,000, the company has sought to apply a uniform, universally ap-plicable pricing policy. Its price policy was characterized by one of the senior officials interviewed as follows: "U.S. Steel has never tried to price to maximum profit not only in the short run but even in the long run." It appears that U.S. Steel holds the philosophy of cost-plus pricing. Nonetheless, even such a company has difficulty in following a formula in pricing steel products—partly because of the differences in costs among plants and the heavy overhead factor, and partly from the desire to hold customers.

The corporation has given evidence of limiting profits and refraining from exploitation of shortages, which can be viewed as manifestations of awareness of its responsibilities and vulnerability as the largest and dominant firm in the industry. In the past, according to U.S. Steel, it has refrained from cutting off its semi-integrated customer-competitors in periods of shortage when it could make higher profits by sharply raising prices or by finishing the steel products itself—a problem that is not so important today with increased integration of smaller mills. President Fairless testified that the company has checked with its customers before raising prices and has held off in reducing published prices, in

[12] Recently the pinch of higher costs has led to industry criticism of prices under U.S. Steel's leadership as being inadequate to provide for depreciation and new capacity. National Steel Corporation, *Annual Report, 1955,* p. 6, and *1956,* p. 5.

the interest of customers with heavy inventories. Moreover, on occasion it has accepted orders for certain items at a loss to keep its regular customers. Competitors, on the other hand, even when they believe that U.S. Steel's prices are not high enough, will not ordinarily go above them. The period following the Second World War was an exception. When U.S. Steel has suffered a decline in volume, as in 1954, its pricing philosophy has predisposed it to resist significant cuts. The relative regularity of steel prices through marked changes in operating levels occurring since 1947 seems to bear out the traditional tendency to resist price revisions in steel until action is unavoidable.

*   *   *

CONSUMER APPLIANCES

There are several stages in the pricing process of a major consumer appliance. During the early period of development of the new piece of equipment—automatic washing machine, refrigerator, TV set—prices differ widely as experience accumulates to determine the most wanted type. After the experimental years, when the consumer has come to know the general character of the product, the result of continuing surveys of dealers' experiences and consumers' reactions is to produce a consensus on what constitutes the "right" price for retail distribution. In the case of 1954 models of automatic washers, there was apparently a general understanding that $300 was the "right" figure to aim at in producing the standard model, for among twenty-four leading manufacturers' brands of automatic washing machines two out of three were priced at $299.95, or within a dollar of that figure. The list price being accepted as the starting point, the problem shifts to a consideration of what the manufacturer can profitably put into the product.

The information on consumer appliances (as with other electrical equipment) has for the most part been supplied by General Electric, the only electrical equipment company in the sample; but in the case of the automatic dishwasher, the cost and price breakdown given below was provided by a large appliance manufacturer not interviewed for this study. It will serve, nevertheless, to illuminate several aspects of pricing policy enunciated by General Electric representatives in respect to consumer appliances.

Starting from the retail list price of $299.95, the manufacturer deducts 40 per cent for the retailer's margin and about 7½ per cent for the wholesale distributors' margin, leaving roughly $156 out of which the manufacturer must get his cost plus profit. With all manufacturers having a similar target to work on, the competition appears to turn mainly on whether one manufacturer can put into the $156 more appeal value than another.

The competition can be shifted to greater emphasis on price by carrying in addition to the standard "de luxe" models more or less stripped models, which eliminate certain automatic controls or trims featured in the former. At this lower level ($239.95 was a common figure), the manufacturers' standard brands encountered the private label brands of the mail order houses and the brands of various manufacturers catering to price-conscious buyers.

General Electric does not follow cost-plus pricing in the sense that it would determine the selling price from a calculation of its own costs. It prices for the market, actual or estimated. In pricing a new item, it prefers to go directly by market surveys to the consumer buyer where a controlled pricing experiment offers the same product with different prices in different areas and also, where feasible, through different channels of distribution.

In the opinion of a General Electric executive, the firm's experience shows that neither distributors and dealers nor the company's salesmen and executives are fully dependable in their guesses of what the consumer will pay for a product. Direct access to the consumers, confronting them with a real choice in a realistic selling environment, is the way to get answers to questions concerning the price-quantity relationship. Dealers can be more helpful in other aspects of marketing than pricing and determination of the features a product should have. This executive believes that in the future G.E. will pay more and more attention to the housewife in determining price and product features.

General Electric, like the other leading manufacturers, carried a $299.95 model among its 1954 automatic washers. But, unlike its competitors, G.E. featured its $349.95 model and treated its $299.95 as a partially stripped version of its standard model.

General Electric's approach to pricing a new consumer product can be illustrated directly by its development for the market in 1949 of a portable dishwasher. The dishwasher was tested in three markets, and the following three prices were set: $149.50; $169.50; $189.50. Each of these prices represented a different method of distribution, ranging from home demonstration at the top price to orthodox department store distribution without demonstration. (Several hundred dishwashers were made by essentially hand processes for this test.) The company thus learned about the relative effectiveness of various distribution methods and what needed to be improved in the product, particularly in styling, to make it more salable. General Electric price policy does not stress, indeed G.E. does not consider desirable, the use of low price in the early stages of development of a product as the means of tapping new markets and expanding uses. For example, when the new dishwasher was sold at $200 instead of $250, no more than 5 per cent of additional sales was believed to result. This was because the "service" idea of an automatic electric dishwasher was not yet so fully accepted as to make a price concession expand sales significantly. When the service idea caught on so that the sales reached about 15 per cent of the market potential, demand became very responsive to price. Similarly, in this early stage the stripped models of dishwashers were not particularly effective. The new portable dishwasher, for example, "looked too cheap." Another $5.00 spent on streamlining and in embellishment made it look like another $30 to the customer.

In its present policy on appliances, G.E. apparently exercises a degree of independence associated with maintenance of quality prestige for its products. Thus G.E. itself adheres to quoted prices. At the end of a year, when a new model is coming out, G.E. gives notices to distributors and dealers and expects them to work off their inventory before the new model comes along.[13]

At the level of distributors, and more importantly at the level of dealers, it is recognized that quoted prices are as a rule not strictly adhered to. General Electric

[13] This was contrasted with the practice of some rivals of making early price cuts on the old model. One manufacturer has been known to make large additional quantities at the end of the model year and to dump the old model at low prices, while simultaneously selling the new. The general impression is given that large companies typically adhere to quoted prices of major appliances and that small companies with less well-established brands are less punctilious on this score; but this was not explicitly stated to the interviewer.

does not fair trade its major appliance lines. Executives explain that the techniques of indirect price concession on "big ticket" items have been so finely developed "that it would take a large staff of lawyers to police fair trading in 40 states." Evasions through trade-ins and wiring charges are hard to detect and harder to prevent. These General Electric products, however, have been fair traded in a few states where distributors make the decision. While G.E. has no right to tell distributors to whom to sell, and at what price, it does believe in maintenance of the margins considered necessary to perform adequate service. It is interested in seeing that service does not deteriorate.

Whether to advertise prices of major appliances nationally has been a moot question at G.E. During the immediate postwar inflation, the policy of advertising prices nationally was abandoned because of unsettled conditions, in which production of the advertising frequently lagged behind the rising cost level.[14]

The experience with television sets, which in 1948 and 1949 were selling at about a 20 per cent mark-up in New York City rather than the larger margin allowed for in the suggested list price, illustrated the difficulty of preventing price shading at the dealer level. The irregularities were related to the mortality rates of independent dealers in different areas. From the standpoint of General Electric, a fair estimate is that a dealer who carries major appliances and electronic items needs about 2,000 wired homes. This is probably a factor in its selection of dealers. The company likes to see dealers big enough to have at least two outside salesmen.

Although G.E. does not regard itself as operating on a cost-plus basis in the field of consumer appliances, its realizations nevertheless do not change drastically over time, partly due to the tendency noted above for manufacturers to settle through experience on a customary price and then adjust cost to price with a "normal" profit margin in mind. What changes there are would not be mainly attributable to departure of actual prices from quoted prices but rather to variations in the proportions of long and short margin products. This type of variation is not regarded as very important. However, there is a broad secular downward change in percentage of net profit to sales as well as cyclical fluctuation.

Small portable appliances, which are sold by G.E. to a great variety of dealers, were generally fair traded in the interest of maintaining profitable margins for the dealers. The small appliance fair trading unit of General Electric has pointed out that the number of small appliances it is possible to dispose of is largely dependent on ability to attract dealers. Up to a point, sales volume may be determined by consumer elasticity of demand, but as soon as the retail price is reduced to the point at which the dealer's profit margin begins to be undermined, there is a progressive decline in the number of dealers willing to carry the article and in the extent to which they will push its sale. The problem of the manufacturer, therefore, is to set the "optimum" price, which is the one that combines attractiveness to the consumer with a profit margin satisfactory to the dealer, and ensure it through fair trading. Since many of these items are supplied as gifts, their biggest sales occurring before Christmas and on other gift-giving occasions, the company may concentrate on building consumer prestige through attractiveness rather than on an effort to be the lowest priced producer in the line.

General Electric has supplied the following case history of a small specialty

---

[14] However, on small appliances under $25, which were fair-traded until 1958, prices have been nationally advertised.

item that is not fair traded, as an example of the tests applied to determine the "right price" to be suggested to retailers.

Adjustable Night Light

The market for night lights has been well established in the American retail economy. Introduced more than twenty years ago, these small lights have increased in sales until today the annual sales volume is several million units. General Electric played a dominant role in introducing the original night lights and has enjoyed a satisfactory market position ever since. Several retail channels handle the sale of these lights. Variety chains were among the first actively to promote the item, but hardware stores, drug stores, and more recently food stores have all successfully merchandised night lights.

Recently General Electric looked for product innovations which would help:

1. Expand the market.
2. Add features to better suit the customer needs.
3. Secure larger share of available market.
4. Improve G.E.'s profit position.
5. Enhance the value of the entire G.E. Wiring Device Consumer Line.

General Electric recognized that if they were to find such a product it would be necessary to employ the "double profit" system, a profit for the manufacturer and a larger profit or benefit for the customer. The question arose as to what additional features, performance, or attractiveness could be added to the present product to increase the appeal to the customer. Actually, performance and attractiveness of the present night lights left little to be desired so it appeared that the solution must involve the matter of product features.

The Marketing Section had long realized that customers' comments concerning the present night lights were centered on two general areas:

1. *Quality of Light*—Some customers complained that there was too much light —others too little. There was no control of the intensity of the light in the present products. Light intensity control was particularly desirable in a sickroom.

2. *Position*—Two forms of night light were available. In one form the light was essentially parallel to the wall where it was out of the way and could not easily be disturbed in passing. However, since some outlets are mounted vertically and the remainder horizontally, some customers would find the night light in a vertical position and others in a horizontal position. Customers generally preferred the light to be vertical. In the second type, the light protruded straight out from the wall. This light was adjustable so that light always shone down but had the disadvantage that it was easily disturbed by persons passing by.

Product Planning Specifications. The Marketing Section decided that if they could have a "de luxe" item with the above two features at the "right price," they would have a product that would satisfy the requirements. But what was the "right price"? The earlier night lights had a retail price of about 59 cents. How much would the customers pay for the additional features? The Marketing Section concluded that since this was largely an impulse item, a top price of 98 cents was desirable. Further, since more and more retail outlets were going to self-service, the package became more important since it must do the selling job to a large extent.

A preliminary investigation indicated that an attractive number of customers were willing to pay this premium for the "de luxe" item. A Product Planning specification was prepared describing the desired features, performance and attractiveness of the product. It was recognized that color was important since the item must attract attention on the counter. Conventional night light colors are brown, ivory, pink, and blue. Ivory was rejected because it was too translucent to achieve desired lighting effect (see below); brown was rejected because it was relatively unattractive; pink and blue were selected for thir attractiveness on the counter as well as their nursery appeal. G.E. felt that the higher-priced item would be more attractive as a gift than the conventional 59 cent item. Further, it was hoped that the new item would not only appeal to the new customers but would also be sufficiently attractive to cause persons who had previously purchased night lights to purchase the new, more desirable one.

Engineering Problem. The major engineering problem consisted in finding a suitable means of dimming the light that would not be too costly. Conventional methods of dimming by the use of variable resistors or variable auto transformers were rejected because of cost and size. Finally, an ingenious means of dimming the light by a mechanical shutter was devised and this was designed into a light using the "Moon and Stars" as the motif. For full brightness the shutter was adiusted mechanically to "Full Moon" effect. For lowest brightness the shutter could be adjusted so that only the "Stars" gave off light. This design was found to be patentable.

The cost estimates, based upon this design, were somewhat disappointing. Since a lower than normal return would be realized at the previously considered retail price of 98 cents, the entire price question was re-opened.

Setting Selling Price. In the final determination of price it was necessary to review the objective of the development.

1. The new light was not intended to replace existing lights but rather to upgrade a portion of the market. Even though the total annual volume of night lights was several million units, the sale of anything over 100,000 units would be considered satisfactory for the new product. Costs were essentially constant after this volume was achieved.

2. This new light was originally conceived as a 98 cent item because this is the generally considered top price for "impulse" items. However, with price inflation, customers were conditioned to seeing items of this type move up beyond the dollar figure. Also, because this was conceived as being a gift item, the higher retail price might attract more customers. Since there was no competitive product, the customer had no direct method of establishing value and could only compare it to the then available but less desirable products selling at 59 cents. However, one difficulty with even the 98 cent price was that this item was designed to be sold on the electrical counter of the retail outlets previously mentioned. Since most items on this counter sold for a much lower price, there was the question of customer resistance to a product of this price being sold on this counter.

[It was noted that from the standpoint of the retailer the item must produce a profit compatible with the counter space required to display it. A higher priced item might produce for him more dollars of profit than one selling at a lower price with higher volume. Consequently a lower sales volume (with a higher price) could justify the necessary counter space as against a drive for volume through low margin pricing.]

3. A study was made of volume-selling price relationship required to achieve the same dollar profit to the Department. These data were calculated at 99 cents, $1.09, $1.19, and $1.29 selling prices. The study disclosed that it was necessary to sell

twice as many at 99 cents as was necessary at $1.09 to achieve the same dollars of profit for the manufacturer. It was necessary to sell twice as many at $1.09 as at $1.29 to achieve the same dollar profit. Four times the volume was required at 99 cents as was required at $1.29 to produce the same dollar profit. Furthermore, since costs were estimated to vary only slightly with volume above 100,000, the higher selling price provided a better return on investment.

4. Items of this type often require special pricing for special promotions. The selling price was established high enough to allow for this type of promotion on a profitable basis.

5. The final question was the effect of pricing on volume in actual test situations. If the higher price reduced sales much below 100,000, it would not be considered despite the reasons cited above. Tests were conducted in various retail outlets in selected cities to test the effect of price on sales. These tests indicated that price was not a particular factor up to and including $1.29 but that sales fell off above this figure. Consequently, the item was introduced with a suggested retail of $1.29. However, since none of our wiring devices is fair traded and no effort is made to control or establish retail prices, we have no assurance that the price was followed in all instances.

44

The Price
of Gasoline

In most places the retail price of gasoline
is about the same at all service stations.
Does this demonstrate that the retail
gasoline business is highly competitive,
or does it suggest collusion? This article
gives the industry's point of view on how
prices are set.

HIGHWAY HIGHLIGHTS

*   *   *

The charge that retail gasoline prices are identical within a community
has led some consumers and legislators to conclude that gasoline suppliers
must get together to fix prices. Otherwise, the reasoning goes, some service
stations would be selling at much lower prices than others.

However, a careful investigation would probably show a significant
variation in gasoline prices within a community of any size. Price similarities within a community may occur around what might be called clusters
of competition. Service stations engaged in direct competition with each
other generally charge identical or nearly identical prices for gasoline, except for such differences as may result from off-brand gasoline being sold
at a lower price than well known brands.

COMPETITIVE MARKET

The fact is that similar or identical gasoline prices in an area actually reflect intense competition, rather than the opposite. When a product like
gasoline is sold in a truly competitive market, no one can charge significantly higher prices than his competitors and keep his customers.
Gasoline consumers are on wheels. They can look around and compare
posted service station prices.

On the other hand, if one dealer charges prices substantially lower
than the others in an area, business will gravitate to him. His competitors

From *Highway Highlights*, April, 1962, pp. 8 ff. Published by the National Highway Users Conference. Reprinted by permission.

will either have to cut their prices to meet his or watch their volume decline to ruinously low levels.

Thus, competition in gasoline marketing acts as a brake on higher prices. Even in the more thinly-populated states many supplying companies compete for the market in addition to the private brands marketed by local suppliers. With the number of aggressive competitors in the field, it is impossible for any one company or group of companies to determine or control the price level. With a wide choice of competing brands the motorist is not at the seller's mercy. On the contrary, each seller must keep up with competition to survive. The oil business has become one of the most fiercely competitive in the country.

Gasoline prices—like the prices of other things—are not the same everywhere. But there is really no mystery about wide variations in prices—be they gasoline prices or prices of any other commodities. A number of economic factors have an important influence in determining the various price levels. Among these are transportation costs, which vary not only according to the distances involved but also according to the means of transportation available; storage expenses, wages and salaries, land values, taxes, local laws regulating the transportation or storage of gasoline, market conditions, and the intensity of competition. Further, in some areas of the country, climate and geography play an important role because gasoline consumption drops in the winter when climatic conditions discourage all but essential driving.

In sparsely-populated states the unit cost of transporting and marketing gasoline tends to be quite high.

DEALER'S PROBLEMS

At the retail level the gasoline dealer has somewhat the same problem as the refiner. The dealer also has fixed costs to contend with—rent or property taxes, wages for his employees, the cost of his equipment and inventory. As in the case of the refiner, the dealer's unit costs go down as his sales volume rises, because his overhead costs remain more or less constant whether he is pumping 10,000 gallons of gasoline a month or 50,000.

But some dealers are situated in places where their gasoline sales volume is restricted by circumstances over which they have no control. That explains why, for example, a service station on a back road, serving neighborhood needs, often tends to charge somewhat more for gasoline than a service station on a heavily traveled main road—where competition is much more intense and the unit cost of selling gasoline is lessened by a big volume of sales.

The rural gasoline dealer in a state with low population and sharp seasonal changes is at a real disadvantage. He must provide the same services and maintain the same basic equipment as a dealer serving a busy main highway, but his sales volume is necessarily much lower and subject to a sharp decline when adverse weather sets in to discourage driving.

In New Hampshire, for instance, highway consumption of gasoline is 62 per cent lower during the month of February than in August. In Wisconsin, motor vehicles consume 71 per cent less gasoline in February than in June. In Montana, there is a 53 per cent decline in January over August. These seasonal setbacks for the gasoline dealer hurt because most of his fixed costs continue, and in the winter, when gasoline sales are slack, his overhead costs mount with the added cost of heating his service station.

Thus, dealers located off the beaten track must seek a bigger gross margin per sale than urban competitors.

PRICE WARS

Why do companies seem to raise and lower their prices simultaneously?

The key is in the two words "seem to." Neither wholesale nor retail prices of different companies change "simultaneously"; they only *seem* to.

It has already been noted that gasoline prices tend to be similar within a given market area. Gasoline prices do change, however, and when they do it means that someone has taken the initiative. When a single seller lowers his price, he does so with the intention of gaining greater volume to make up the reduction in profit he suffers on each gallon he sells. Greater volume, however, can only come at the expense of the dealer's competitors. And these competitors must cut their prices or risk losing a large part of their sales to the lower priced station.

Price increases are even more hazardous. Unless based on a sound appraisal of the market in terms of supply, demand, and cost, the results of a price increase can be disastrous for the company which initiates it. If the market analysis is incorrect, and conditions do not convince other companies to follow, a severe drop in sales would be the immediate result for the initiating company. This company may thus be forced to revert to the price level of its competitors.

Sometimes the marketer who takes the initiative in a price adjustment is the one with the greatest share of the market; sometimes it is another company. Often in today's market place the leader in a price move is an independent marketer.

DETROIT EXAMPLE

In 1961 there was a widespread and long drawn-out price war in Detroit. When it finally ended and a uniform price prevailed, there were demands for investigation of "big," "simultaneous" price increases. However, *The Detroit News-Times*, after an investigation of its own, told its readers:

> The gasoline industry is highly competitive, at both retail and producer level. It was bristling competition which brought prices steadily down (with no political yelps about "collusion") to the level from which they have not rebounded so sharply. It is that same competition which will prevent the current price from sticking if it is in fact too high.

In the final analysis under the competitive enterprise system, each competitor faces the challenge of making a profit, and if he fails to meet that challenge, his business will fail. In order to make a profit he must give the public what it wants at prices the public is willing to pay. The desires of the consuming public shape and give direction to all business activity.

As an exceptionally competitive industry, petroleum is particularly sensitive, and therefore responsive, to the public's preferences in product quality, service, and price. Every company in every branch of the oil business must keep up with the pace of competition in order to hold its place in the market against the rival firms that are constantly pressing to capture some of its business.

45

The Revenue Maximization Hypothesis

Economists traditionally explain that businessmen try to maximize profits. Professor Baumol believes that although profits are important, most businesses are more concerned with expanding their total sales.

William J. Baumol is Professor of Economics at Princeton University.

WILLIAM BAUMOL

Before turning to the substantive material of this brief chapter, it is necessary to explain the limitations of the evidence on which its allegations, and some of those which occur later, . . . are based. Essentially, the assertions are no more than impressions gathered through casual observation of the operation of a number of business firms. In my work I have had occasion to examine in detail some of their decisions and the data on which they were based. Perhaps equally illuminating have been management's reactions to our own recommendations. These reactions certainly seemed indicative of the nature of management's objectives and, in particular, its attitude toward profit maximization. As we shall see, this will play an important part in the sequel.

It must be emphasized, then, that the empirical observations which are reported here were highly unsystematic and represent a sample which, as statistical studies go, must be considered extremely small. Their only and peculiar virtue is that they can lay claim to having come, as it were, from the inside.

Let us turn now to the real matter of this chapter. I shall take the position that, *in day-to-day decision-making*, oligopolistic interdependence plays only a small role. Of course, plans for the launching of a really major advertising campaign, or for the introduction of a radically new line of products does usually involve some discussion of the probable competitive response. But often, even in fairly crucial decisions, and almost always in routine policy-making, only the most cursory attention is paid to competitive reactions. This apparently dangerous attitude does not usually lead the business-man into serious difficulty because, I believe, his more ordinary decisions are rarely met by prompt aggressive countermoves of the sort envisaged in many of our models. There are several reasons why this should be so.

1. Complexity of Internal Organization

The modern industrial giant is a mammoth organization which is almost always engaged in many activities—some of them highly diverse in character. Its great size and complexity have been accompanied by a correspondingly large and involved managerial organization. Proposals are characteristically inaugurated at points in the organization far removed from the makers of the final decisions. Moreover, because of the multiplicity of departments usually involved, and the uneasy truce between highly centralized control and departmental autonomy, responsibility is frequently divided and is rarely well defined. As a result decision-making is often a lengthy process whose outcome is fairly unpredictable.

This decision-making apparatus is too clumsy and slow-moving for effective interplay of strategy and counterstrategy among competing firms. A move by one of them, *provided it is not too radical,* may just be ignored by the others, simply because divided responsibility invites each decision-maker to shift the responsibility on to others. Even if some countermove is proposed, the suggestion is likely to be watered down as it passes through various echelons and committee meetings. And what finally does come through is very likely to come only after a very consider-able lapse of time.

2. The Use of Rules of Thumb

Top executives are usually too busy, and their computational skills are sometimes too limited for them to be able to probe very deeply into every business problem. Management's difficulty is that it must retain some measure of control over the operations of the firm without, at the same time, tying itself up in operational detail. This problem is solved by the frequent use of rules of thumb—prices are set by applying a standard markup to costs; advertising expenditures are deter-mined by setting aside a fixed percentage of total revenues; and inventories are required to meet a preset turnover norm.

These rules of thumb do not work out too badly. They translate hopelessly involved problems into simple, orderly routines. They save executive time and permit a degree of centralized control over the firm's farflung operations. By and large, they probably contribute considerably to overall operating efficiency. Most executives appear to recognize these rules for what they are—imperfect expedients designed to cope, in a rough and ready manner, with a difficult control and decision problem. This is one reason frequently given for asking the advice of operations researchers.

But rules of thumb tend to reduce competitive give and take among oligopolistic enterprises. Because they must be relatively simple in order to be useful, these rules do not make provision for a variety of contingencies. For example, an aver-age cost pricing rule takes no explicit account of recent trends in the decision patterns of other firms in the industry. It provides no elaborate directions for adaptation to each of the many possible moves of competitors.

In one rather typical case, the manufacturer of a fuel kept his price just slightly above that of the nearest competing fuel because his large overheads made his average cost rather high. When it was pointed out to him that a lower price could reduce his average costs substantially through an increase in his sales volume, he accepted the suggestion with apparently little concern for the possibility that his rival would retaliate by also cutting his price. Moreover, his confidence seems to have been justified by the results. It should be added that in this industry firms in many other cities seem to have had the same experience. Very likely, the manufacturers of the competing fuels failed to meet these price cuts because they too were using average cost pricing procedures.

3. Desire for the Quiet Life

In recent years the managers of large firms have displayed signs of a desire for respectability and security. To avoid difficulties with public regulatory authorities as well as with their own stockholders, managements have veered away from the rough and tumble. But firms who wish to live and let live are not likely to be anxious to make life unpredictable for one another. And it is my impression that business organizations have, to some extent, come to depend on each other to be well-behaved. In fact, they frequently seem to expect others to go along with their decisions and, if anything, to adjust their policies in a cooperative spirit. In some cases I have even seen the possibility of competitive countermoves considered as a sort of breach of etiquette—as a slightly shocking possibility.

4. Reservations

In making a case of this sort it is quite easy to exaggerate, and doubtlessly, I have somewhat overstated the point. It is not true that a reign of perfect and universal mutual inattention has descended upon our oligopolies. Among many firms there are unsettled border disputes which lead to occasional forays. For example, in one industry where pricing seems otherwise to be conducted on a gentlemanly basis, there is mutual suspicion of the discounts that are offered (for advertising purposes) for the use of their products by nonprofit organizations! One firm undertook a sort of cloak-and-dagger investigation to find out what rebates were really being offered, and indicated that it was prepared to do whatever was necessary to get its products displayed through this channel.

Moreover, it must be recognized that while it does not usually consist of a series of strategic moves and quick responses, vigorous competitive activity does take place. The oligopolist has a fiercely tender regard for his share of the market and, if ever he finds himself losing out, energetic steps may be expected. I will discuss some implications of this attitude later in the book. But for the moment it suffices to recognize its existence, and for me to reassert my belief that in its day-to-day pricing and output decisions, the oligopolistic firm takes only the most cursory glance at the probable reactions of its competitors in the confident expectation that their unresponsiveness (so long as there is no large change in market share) will continue very similar to its own.

It must be emphasized that there still remains a very important role to be played by the theory of oligopolistic interdependence and its analysis with the aid of tools like those provided by game theory. For decisions relating to radical changes in policy these are usually as relevant as our theory has always supposed. However, the ordinary problems of value theory, the routine pricing, and advertising decisions are generally not beset by these complications. This has been the burden of the argument of this chapter. Since the remainder of Part I of this book is concerned with just such problems of value theory no more will be said about questions of interdependence until Part II.

If interdependence is demoted from its central role in the theory of oligopoly, some alternative must be chosen to replace it. The obvious alternative is to assume that each firm tries to maximize its profits as though it were in isolation.

However, the consequences of such an assumption are not particularly satisfying. As I shall point out later, it leaves unexplained some frequently noted features of oligopolistic behavior. Moreover, my experience, and apparently that of some others who have worked with business firms, is that profits do not constitute the prime objective of the large modern business enterprise. It must be made clear that I am not trying to reopen the tired and tiresome argument against the economic man. Doubtlessly, he never existed and does not now, but he is still a very useful approximation. On the contrary, I believe the businessman can usefully be viewed as a calculating individual, but one whose calculations take account of profits in a manner which differs somewhat from the standard view.

I shall maintain that the size of the firm's operations shares with profits the role of prime objective. For the moment I shall say no more about this hypothesis. . . . But first, to lay the ground for some of my later discussion, and to help supply plausibility to my hypothesis, I shall argue in the next chapter that even to the profit maximizing firm the scale of its operation can become an important proximate objective.

THE REVENUE MAXIMIZATION HYPOTHESIS

Though businessmen are interested in the scale of their operations partly because they see some connection between scale and profits, I think management's concern with the level of sales goes considerably further. In my dealings with them I have been struck with the importance which the oligopolistic enterprises attach to the value of their sales. A small reversal in an upward sales trend which can quite reasonably be dismissed as a random movement sometimes leads to a major review of the concern's selling and production methods, its product lines, and even its internal organizational structure.

Before going on I must make an important terminological point. In ordinary business parlance the term "sales" refers not to the number of physical units of one of its products which has been sold but, rather, to the *total revenue* obtained by the firm from the purchases of its customers. In the near universal multiproduct firm any measure of overall physical volume must involve index number problems, and the adoption of a value measure is doubtless to be expected. In any event, in the sequel I shall adhere to the businessman's practice and use the terms "sales" and "total revenue" as synonyms. As a reminder, however, I will frequently employ "dollar sales" or "sales revenue" or some other such expressions.

1. Disadvantages of Declining Sales

There are many reasons why the businessman should show such concern about the magnitude of his sales. Declining sales can bring with them all sorts of disadvantages: there is reason to fear that consumers will shun a product if they feel it is declining in popularity, though their information on these matters is doubtless often spotty. Banks and the money market will tend to be less receptive to the desires of a firm whose absolute or relative sales volume is declining. Perhaps even more important in this connection is the very real danger that firms whose sales are declining will lose distributors—a major marketing setback. Management also is not unmoved by the fact that in a declining firm personnel relations are made much more difficult when firing rather than hiring is the order of the day. The firm which declines (or which remains small when others expand) can lose monopoly power and the power to adopt an effective competitive counterstrategy when it is called for. And it may become more vulnerable to a general deterioration in business conditions. For all these reasons the executive may reasonably conclude that maintenance of as large a sales volume as possible is the only way to succeed in business.

Even if size did not promote profits, personal self-interest could well induce the managers of a firm to seek to maximize sales. Executive salaries appear to be far more closely correlated with the scale of operations of the firm than with its profitability. And in the modern corporation, which is characterized so often by separation of ownership from management, many executives find it politic to avoid an absolute or relative decline in their operations. Here, management's concern with the volume of sales is compounded of its very conscientious concern with the responsibilities of its trusteeship and a desire to play good stockholder politics. In any event the effects are the same—the volume of sales achieves the status of a prime business objective.

2. Sales as an Ultimate Objective

Up to this point, I have, in essence, been arguing that the firm may be expected to promote sales as a means to further its other objectives—operational efficiency and, ultimately, profits. So far, there is no necessary clash with orthodox analysis.

But now I propose to take the next step and suggest that the businessman has gone still further in his regard for sales volume. I believe that to him sales have become an end in and of themselves.

It must be made clear to begin with, that this hypothesis in no way conflicts with an assumption of rationality. People's objectives are whatever they are. Irrationality surely must be defined to consist in decision patterns which make it more difficult to attain one's own ends, and not in choosing ends that are, for some reason, considered to be wrong. Unless we are prepared to determine other people's values, or unless they pursue incompatible objectives, we must class behavior as rational if it efficiently pursues whatever goals happen to have been chosen.

The evidence for my hypothesis that sales volume ranks ahead of profits as the main object of the oligopolist's concern, is again highly impressionistic; but I believe it is quite strong. Surely it is common experience that, when one asks an executive, "How's business?," he will answer that his *sales* have been increasing (or decreasing), and talk about his profit only as an afterthought, if at all. And I am told the requirements for acceptance to membership in the Young Presidents Organization (an honorific society) are that the applicant be under 40 years of age and president of a company whose annual volume is over a million dollars. Presumably it makes no difference if this firm is in imminent danger of bankruptcy.

Nor is this failure to emphasize profits a pure rationalization or a mere matter of careless phrasing. Almost every time I have come across a case of conflict between profits and sales the businessmen with whom I worked left little doubt as to where their hearts lay. It is not unusual to find a profitable firm, in which some segment of its sales can be shown to be highly unprofitable. For example, I have encountered several firms who were losing money on their sales in markets quite distant from the plant where local competition forced the product price down to a level which did not cover transportation costs. Another case was that of a watch distributor whose sales to small retailers in sparsely settled districts were so few and far between that the salesmen's wages were not made up by the total revenues which they brought in. When such a case is pointed out to management, it is usually quite reluctant to abandon its unprofitable markets. Businessmen may consider seriously proposals which promise to put these sales on a profitable basis. There may be some hope for the adoption of a suggestion that a new plant be built nearer the market to which current transportation costs are too high, or that watch salesmen be transferred to markets with greater sales potential and a mail order selling system be substituted for direct selling in little populated regions. But a program which explictly proposes any cut in sales volume, whatever the profit considerations, is likely to meet a cold reception. In many cases firms do finally perform the radical surgery involved in cutting out an unprofitable line or territory, but this usually occurs after much heart-searching and delay.

3. The Role of Profits

It is tempting to object that along this road lies bankruptcy; and so it would if management were prepared not only to subordinate profit considerations to sales, but to disregard profits altogether. After all, maximum sales might require prices so low that the costs would nowhere be covered. It is quite true that there is some conflict between the firm's sales goal and its profit objectives, and, as is to be expected, the matter is settled by compromise. The compromise is, of course, usually tacit, its terms ill-defined, and doubtless, it varies from case to case. But I think it is, nevertheless, possible to set up a formal relationship which is analytically useful and, at the same time, provides us with a reasonably close approximation to the facts.

The nature of this approximation is again best suggested by an illustrative experience. A manufacturer of a new synthetic yarn indicated that he was reluctant to promote sales by introducing his product at a price which would not cover the cost of his small initial outputs. The firm's usual rate of return on investment played an explicit and very fundamental role in these deliberations. It was made clear that management was not concerned to obtain profits higher than this. Once this minimum profit level was achieved, sales revenues rather than profits became the overriding goal.

I suspect that the much publicized practice of average-cost pricing is a crude attempt to achieve just this sort of goal. Prices are set at a fixed markup above average costs, not only because this is a convenient rule of thumb, but also because the practice appears to set a floor under the rate of return. Of course, it does not always work out in that way because volume can be miscalculated and cost estimates may therefore turn out to be incorrect. But the objective of the procedure seems clear nevertheless.

I am prepared to generalize from these observations and assert that the typical oligopolist's objectives can usefully be characterized, approximately, as sales maximization subject to a minimum profit constraint. Doubtless this premise over-specifies a rather vague set of attitudes, but I believe it is not too far from the truth. So long as profits are high enough to keep stockholders satisfied and contribute adequately to the financing of company growth, management will bend its efforts to the augmentation of sales revenues rather than to further increases in profits.

*   *   *

46

Another View of Corporate Capitalism

Does market power make any difference in the operation of a private enterprise system? Professor Kaysen argues that in many cases competition does not provide a tight constraint on management behavior, and that management often has a considerable range of freedom in decision making which is not accurately represented by profit-maximizing models.

CARL KAYSEN

Carl Kaysen is Professor of Economics at Harvard University.

The vigor of Professor Peterson's attack on the heralds of a new "corporate capitalism," differing fundamentally from the competitive private enterprise system which it is supplanting, is perhaps proportional to the breadth and vagueness of the propositions that some of them have advanced. To just this extent, he evokes a sympathetic response, even in a writer who is among his targets. But arguments that are loosely stated, or strongly overstated, are not necessarily wrong, and I believe that Peterson's defense of the old time religion errs in the same ways, but in the opposite direction.

As I read it, his paper advances three major propositions:

1. In the representative firm, even the representative large managerial firm, margins between revenues and costs are too narrow, and both minuend and subtrahend too fluctuating, to permit management any significant departure from the goal of profit maximization. If departures exist, they are transitory or trivial, not appropriate material for theory building.

2. Any departures from the traditional mechanism of close market constraint over business decisions are the consequence of market power, not of change in the internal structure of the corporate enterprise that has brought new relations between owners and managers not contemplated in the classical model.

3. No more than price, output, and investment decisions, are decisions on the distribution of corporate income the product of unrestrained managerial discretion. Rather, the close constraints imposed by the workings

Reprinted by permission of publisher from the *Quarterly Journal of Economics*, February, 1965, pp. 41–46, Cambridge, Mass., Harvard University Press, Copyright, 1965, by the President and Fellows of Harvard College.

of the capital markets, reinforced by the legal rights of stockholders and the legal duties of managements to manage in their interests, leads to just those rewards to scarce capital which classical theory predicts.

Together, these three propositions lead to the conclusion that the changes which the new views purport to expound and interpret are superficial, not essential, and new corporate capitalism is just old private enterprise described in the language of public relations.

I wish to argue that the first and third of these propositions are wrong in essential respects, while the second, by adding a false dichotomy to a correct statement, leads the argument just as far astray. Further, there are aspects of the problem omitted from Peterson's discussion which are as deserving of attention as those he has singled out for comment. Thus neither his central propositions, nor argument and evidence more broadly viewed, support his conclusion.

How narrow must a profit margin be, how uncontrollable the cost and revenue components which determine it, before we can dismiss the discretion which corporate managers exercise as marginal or uninteresting? Peterson notes the exceptional case of the pharmaceutical industry in a footnote. How about the exceptional case of General Motors, whose profit on capital after taxes in 1963 was over 22 per cent?[1] Or the exceptional case of the steel industry, which was able at the end of the fifties to raise its prices and profits in the face of a declining level of capacity utilization, and unfilled orders which were falling in relation to sales?[2] Or the other cases of the concentrated industries with high entry barriers, whose generally high profits Bain has examined?[3]

Nor can the proposition be discussed merely in terms of profit margins for industries or particular firms. Reported figures show only realized profits, not the potential scope of discretion of managements in pushing costs down or prices up. Glimpses into the internal workings of large firms with significant market power, fragmentary as they are, frequently reveal practices which depart widely from cost minimization, or full exploitation of potential monopoly gains. The typical large firm sells many products in many markets; its reported profit rate is an average over a variety of operations. To what extent average profits in the aggregate conceal wide variations among departments is only rarely discoverable; yet knowledge in this point is highly revelant to a judgment of how wide or narrow the decision margin open to management. One piece of indirect evidence on this point worth considering is the infrequency with which large firms divest themselves of old operations, old divisions, even old products, in relation to the generally high rate of return criteria they employ for new investments. Rational profit maximizers, whether so by necessity or desire, would use the same rate of return criteria, applied to the anticipated sales value of subsidiaries, divisions, etc., to decide whether to keep rather than sell them as they do to evaluate prospective new investments. Yet how often do we read of DuPont selling a rayon plant, or U.S. Steel a cement plant, because the rate of return on the anticipated sales

[1] *The Fortune Directory*, 500 Largest U.S. Industrial Corporations, August 1964, p. 2.

[2] Otto Eckstein and Gary Fromm, *Steel and the Postwar Inflation*, Study Paper No. 2, Study of Employment Growth and Price Levels, Joint Economic Committee, 86th Congress, 1st Session, 1959.

[3] J. S. Bain, *Barriers to New Competition* (Cambridge: Harvard University Press, 1956), pp. 190–201.

value is not up to the firm's target investment criterion? But if we admit the relevance of other goals, especially internal organizational ones, and the discretion to pursue them to some extent, the absence of such action is less surprising.

There is, however, another level on which we can examine the first proposition, which brings out some deeper problems. In the context of competitive product and factor markets, profit maximization has a well-defined meaning. Further, the constraints of the market are such that the firm has no choice but to strive to maximize profits: the alternative is failure to survive.[4] But for a firm which operates in product and factor markets which depart substantially from competitive conditions, these statements are no longer true. In many such markets firms are characteristically large, and long-lived, they look forward far into the future, and often make expenditures whose benefits extend over fairly long periods. Risk, uncertainty, the evaluation of future streams of income necessarily enter into the calculations of firms so situated. At the minimum, the one-dimensional profit variable turns into a distribution of possible profit streams, and profit-maximization must become the maximization of some function of that distribution. Need every firm seek to maximize the same function? Need the function a particular firm seeks to maximize be invariant over time? If the answers to these questions are in the negative, as I think they clearly are, the definiteness of our behavioral rule begins to fade. And it fades even more, when we consider the many decisions which such firms face where the alternatives cannot readily be translated into changes in the probability distribution of streams of profit. Could it be wise, for example, for a firm to decide to fight its union over a work-rules issue as a "matter of principle" even though the immediately calculable costs involved in the rule change are not large compared to the wage elements in the proposed settlement? To assert that a decision on a question of this sort must indicate a calculation on the long-run cost advantages of the two courses—even if it is an implicit or unconscious calculation—is to empty the notion of profit maximization of its content. It is one thing to say that, other things being equal, all firms, large or small, competitive or less competitive, prefer a larger to a smaller profit prospect; it is quite another to assert that there are in general neither significant other things to consider nor ambiguities about which is the larger and which the smaller prospective profit stream.

At this point, our discussion has carried us to the second summary proposition. Market power of particular firms—the absence of competition as a close constraint on them—is just what we have been examining, and thus we are in accord with the first half of the proposition. The last half, however, is a *non sequitur*, and a puzzling one. If we could assert, with Peterson, that stockholder interests in maximum income, whether exercised directly through stockholder influence on the board, or indirectly through the mechanism of the capital market, rule

---

[4] We could elaborate on this proposition to discuss entrepreneurs accepting lower than market wages in order to remain self-employed, or other owners of rent-yielding factors in intra-marginal firms extracting less than the maximum rent, etc., but the principle is clear. Even where assumptions about foresight and knowledge are made more general than in the usual perfect competitive model, the investment decision is like a lottery ticket purchase; it is either right, and earns just normal returns, or it is wrong, and the entrepreneur must take a loss on it. In such a more general model, entrepreneurs need not be identical, and there would be intra-marginal lucky entrepreneurs who made less than the proportion of bad guesses that marginal entrepreneurs made, and accordingly received larger profits. But this would simply change the distribution of rewards in the lottery.

management choices, then the existence of market power in any particular case would mean only that maximum income is larger than it would otherwise be. But the larger income would be translated into whatever combination of larger dividends and larger investment maximized the stockholders' returns. Both the behavioral consequences for the firm and the distributive consequences of market power would be clear. But this is not the case, and it is precisely the interaction between the existence of market power in product markets and labor markets, and the degree of choice that managements have in their relations with owners that raises the more interesting questions about the nature and consequences of "corporate capitalism." To put it another way, if appreciable departures from competition occurred only in product markets, and both labor and capital markets were competitive, the existence of noncompetitive product markets would result in extra earnings to the owners of the monopoly firms. If these are publicly-owned corporations, the extra earnings would be capitalized in their share prices, which would then sell in the markets at competitive prices in relation to earnings. In fact, however, the typical large firm operating in one or more product markets in which it exercises significant power is also faced with an imperfect labor market, and an imperfect capital market. Thus the question of to what degree and with what results managements use the area of discretion the combination of imperfect markets provides becomes a richer and more interesting one. Wage earners, as well as stockholders and managements themselves, become potential claimants to some of the gains. Wage determination in a number of key industries characterized by large firms, concentrated markets, and strong unions cannot be explained without reference to market behavior in those industries, and the interaction of price and wage determination is only poorly represented in terms of neo-Marshallian profit-maximizing decisions.[5]

All this may be true, but is it quantitatively important? Peterson, without quite saying it in so many words, conveys the thought that the existence of significant market power—to the extent that it raises questions worth notice at all—is an aberrational phenomenon, not a characteristic of important sectors of the economy. Is he correct? This is not a question which is easy to answer, or on which there is a wide professional consensus on one answer. I have myself made one of the few attempts at a comprehensive answer, and though it is now six years old, I am aware of no more recent one on a similarly comprehensive basis.[6] The conclusion of that study was that in manufacturing and mining, industries with oligopolistic structures accounted for a major share of both the number and the gross output of all industries in these sectors, and that they were particularly conspicuous in the strategic investment-goods and consumer-durables industries. Not all industries which have oligopolistic structures depart significantly from competitive behavior; but in the absence of detailed study of particular markets, the existence of oligopoly structures at least raises the question. Besides the oligopolistic markets in mining and manufacturing, we should take into account transportation and public utilities. These are regulated industries, but the regulatory constraints are often loose, or even perverse; typical firms are large, and the "natural" market structures in them are oligopolistic or monopolistic. Together, these sectors and the oligopolistic sectors in mining and manufacturing produce at least 20 per cent, and probably

---

[5] See O. Eckstein and T. A. Wilson "The Determination of Money Wages in American Industry," *Quarterly Journal of Economics*, LXXVI (August 1962).

[6] C. Kaysen and D. F. Turner, *Antitrust Policy, An Economic and Legal Analysis* (Cambridge: Harvard University Press, 1959), Chap. II and Appendixes.

more like 25 per cent of the national income.[7] Again, we cannot translate this measure into a distribution of output within these sectors by a measure of market power; but we can certainly say that the broad picture is not that of an episodic or negligible phenomenon.

* * *

---

[7] *Ibid.*

47

The Electric
Conspiracy Case

Agreements among producers to fix prices
and market shares are illegal and
inconsistent with the principles of a
competitive society. This article discusses
the development of an industrial
conspiracy in the electrical equipment
industry, and provides some insight into
the problems and attitudes of the
executives who were involved.

WALL STREET JOURNAL

THE PROBLEMS OF PRICE FIXING

For a number of years various electrical companies and individuals successfully evaded the antitrust laws. They periodically met to fix prices,
divide up markets, and otherwise cartellize their industry.

But examination of court records of the cases indicates the conspiracy
was not a very successful one. Prices were not fixed except temporarily—
some one of the conspirators was forever evading the intent of conspiracy.

Markets were divided somewhat more successfully, but here again the
planners of the market were always running afoul of new circumstances
which did not fit into the master plan. Certainly the attempt to evade the
give and take of the market place meant for the people and companies
involved a good deal of unforeseen trouble—the law aside. Red tape
flourished; bureaucracy, unofficial and perhaps illegal though it may have
have been, grew apace. The need for conspiratorial gatherings mounted,
all as man-made rules were substituted for competition.

For example, the circuit breaker conspiracy involving General Electric,
Westinghouse, Allis-Chalmers, and Federal Pacific ran into this problem
in 1958—what to do about the entrance onto the scene of a new company? While a new competitor is never an easy matter for an individual
company, it was also quite complex for the conspirators.

What happened was that I-T-E Circuit Breaker Co., a factor in other
aspects of the electrical equipment business, in 1958 bought out a small
company and wanted to enter the circuit breaker field where prices were
being fixed and markets allotted on a percentage basis.

From *The Wall Street Journal*, January 10, 12, 1962. Reprinted by permission.

"Now, room had to be made for I-T-E," Antitrust Chief Bicks noted in remarks at the arraignment of the defendants. "So a series of meetings began in January of 1958, at which I-T-E indicated its desire for some business. I-T-E had bought a company; it wanted to get into the business.

"The knowledge by I-T-E that it was entering into a pre-existing conspiracy is clear beyond doubt from the pattern of events in early 1958. I-T-E began meeting with the four conspirators that had been going, going more or less smoothly, it's true, with greater or less success, with greater or less mutual confidence that each of the conspirators was living up to his part of the deal, but, nonetheless, one constant conspiracy I-T-E sought to get in."

Overall Policy

"In early 1958 I-T-E secured an agreement as to the overall pricing policy leaving the allocation aside.

"The nature of that agreement arrived at in early 1958 at a series of meetings was roughly this, that general pricing would be tied to G.E.'s book price, that I-T-E in the southern part of California would be allowed 15 per cent off, that I-T-E nationally would be allowed 5 per cent off. . . . Remaining to be finalized was I-T-E's allocation share of the sealed bid business. This was discussed . . . I-T-E was cut in for a share of 4 per cent following a series of conferences, and so from 1958 on everybody cut back a bit except Federal Pacific. . . .

"The three big companies, G.E., Westinghouse, Allis-Chalmers . . . cut down their percentage. Federal Pacific came up from 10 to 15. I-T-E was cut in for 4. That was roughly the pattern of the conspiracy that kept on until the date of the indictment."

I-T-E, seeking to plead no contest in this case, said among other things that it was charged with being only a small factor in the industry for a short period of time. It has told its men to stay away from competitors, that if they're caught in such activities again they'll be fired.

It was one thing, as in the circuit breaker case, to agree that a certain company would get a specific piece of sealed-bid business. It was something else again to see that the designated company actually got the job. Here, again according to Mr. Bicks' statement to the court, is how that worked, amid burgeoning red tape.

"At a working level meeting where a particular big job was up for discussion the percentages initially would be reviewed in light of what was known as the ledger list, which had on it recent sealed-bid jobs given to the other defendants. In light of that ledger list it was decided which of the companies, to keep the percentages constant, would get the job. Now if that company was prepared to say the price at which it was going to bid, then the other companies could discuss among themselves what they would bid, add on for accessories, to make sure to give . . . the company . . . whose turn it was to get the job, the best shot at it.

Numbers Code

"If the company, whose job the particular rigged job was supposed to be did not know the price, there would be later communication, either by phone to homes with just the first names used, or by letter to homes with just first names of senders, with no return address, and this wonderful code . . . The numbers were 1, General Electric; 2, Westinghouse; 3, Allis-Chalmers; and 7, Federal Pacific. What happened to 4 or 5 and 6 until I-T-E, came in remains a mystery."

One of the great ironies of the conspiracies was that no matter how hard the participants schemed, no matter how friendly their meetings and communications might be, there was an innate tendency to compete. Someone was always violating the agreements to get more business, and this continually called for new illegal plans. For example, price-cutting in sales of power switching equipment to government agencies was getting out of hand in late 1958. This led to the "quadrant" system of dividing markets.

"So," declared Baddia Rashid, chief of the trial section of the antitrust division, "at a meeting in November of 1958 at Philadelphia . . . they decided that the best way to handle the sealed-bid market was to allocate the business; however, since there were sixteen companies involved in this particular conspiracy it would have been difficult to try to allocate the business as in other cases on a percentage basis, and therefore it was decided that it would be best to divide the country into four separate geographical areas which were called quadrants—the northwest quadrant, the southwest quadrant, the southeast quadrant, and the northeast quadrant.

"Four companies were assigned to participate in each quadrant, and one of the company representatives in that quadrant was designated as a secretary for the purpose of handling the allocation within the particular quadrant." For example, ". . . in the northeast quadrant . . . meetings were held, and it was decided that the business within that quadrant would be allocated in an alphabetical rotation . . ."

This plan did not work to everyone's satisfaction, but rather than fall back on the give and take of the market place, which the law requires, the conspirators formulated another plan.

"In September of 1959, however, there were some complaints that had arisen because some companies felt they were not getting a sufficient share of the business . . . it appeared that certain of the quadrants were obtaining more sealed-bid business than other quadrants. Therefore, they held a meeting in Pittsburgh . . . in September, 1959 . . . and they discussed this situation. . . . After some discussion it was finally decided that perhaps the best way to do it would be to go back to a national allocation scheme at which each company would be allotted a certain percentage of the business. They all agreed to that plan, and each company was then asked to indicate what percentage of the sealed-bid market it felt it should obtain. . . . An individual from one of the . . . companies was designated to act as secretary. . . ."

But the basic problem, in this industry where price fluctuations were sometimes drastic, was "stabilizing" prices, and efforts to bring this about spawned many a difficulty.

Reviewing the Books

In one case one conspirator sneaked in a bid on a product below the price level which had been agreed upon, the government said. Discussions among the conspirators followed, and the offending company was asked to bring in its books so they could be checked. The representatives of the other companies reviewed them and decided "that this company had deviated from the established prices. So the representative from this company indicated that henceforward he would try to control it a little better." Such meetings to keep the co-price-fixers in line were frequent in other cases.

In a case involving industrial controls these meetings became quite numerous. The government characterizes this case as perhaps the most serious price-fixing case encountered in the "past five or ten years." It counted 31 separate meetings from 1955 until the date of the indictment by the defendants, General Electric, Westinghouse, Square D Co., Cutler-Hammer Co., Clark Controller Co., and Allen-Bradley Co. Mr. Rashid spelled out some of the details for the court.

"The first [meeting] occurred in August of 1955, in Maine. At this meeting all of the defendants except a representative of General Electric were present . . . the individuals present agreed to increase the prices of industrial control equipment by 10 per cent and to put this price increase into effect the following September. They mutually agreed that Cutler-Hammer would be the first to announce the price change and that the rest would follow thereafter.

"There was another meeting in November of 1955 at Atlantic City, New Jersey, in which again all the defendants except General Electric met to discuss the effect this recent price increase was having on the market.

"This was followed by a meeting in April of 1956 at Cleveland, Ohio. Between the November, 1955 meeting and the April, 1956 meeting, General Electric had unilaterally put into effect a price increase. The rest of the companies therefore met in April of 1956 to decide what they would do. . . . They had a discussion and decided that with respect to some products they would all follow G.E.'s prices; with respect to other products they would not follow it.

"When this was agreed upon General Electric thereafter retracted its price increase with respect to those products that the other companies did not agree to.

Mutual Complaints

"There was another meeting in May of 1956 at Hot Springs, Virginia, which was a so-called price-cutting-discussion meeting at which the companies got together to complain against each other when they were cutting prices from those that had been agreed upon."

In a framework of fixing prices, there arose also the problem of how to price a new product. In some cases the pricing problem evidently stymied introduction of the product.

At a meeting in May of 1957 at Hot Springs, Mr. Rashid declared, there was discussion of the Double O starter that Cutler-Hammer wanted to market. After general discussion there was a "consensus" reached "that it should sell for about two-thirds of the price of the starter then in existence. They tentatively agreed that this new product should be put on the market . . . on or about January 1, 1960."

The following November some of the conspirators met in the suite of Allen-Bradley at the Traymore Hotel in Atlantic City, the government alleged.

"Cutler-Hammer at this meeting wanted to put on the market a low-quality starter; the other defendants (G.E. was not present) were complaining to Cutler-Hammer that that was a bad practice, that what Cutler-Hammer should do should be to put on the market a high-quality standard and that the price of that product should be comparable to the price of existing starters, so that as Cutler-Hammer was contemplating reducing the price of this new starter by about 20 per cent or 25 per cent, that would have cut into the market of the starter that was then being marketed."

Then at a meeting on January 9, 1958, the government said, ". . . they resumed a discussion of the Double O starter, and they again criticized Cutler-Hammer for wanting a low-quality starter, and in the end the other companies won, and it was agreed that Cutler-Hammer would put out a high-quality starter."

At the same meeting, "Square D Co. was criticized for having put out a new oil-type pushbutton enclosure. . . . The reason they were criticized . . . was the price . . . was lower than the prices of comparable products then in existence."

These then are some of the unexpected tangles that developed from the electrical equipment conspiracies. No matter how diligently plans and schemes were laid, they somehow could not defeat the basic economic factors, which insisted on responding to the inherent forces of the free market.

*   *   *

Potentials for Trouble

Certainly the climate in which the individuals and companies in the heavy electrical equipment industry operated was loaded with potentials for trouble, and these may well have been the genesis of the legal difficulties which came to afflict a large segment.

The industry is a relatively compact one. Its members range from very large enterprises to relatively small ones. For example, among those indicted in the case were General Electric with $4 billion annual sales and Joslyn Manufacturing and Supply Co. of Chicago with annual sales of less than $2 million and only 45 production employees.

The industry is tightly-knit with many friendships among executives of competing firms; indeed, officials of smaller firms sometimes are former General Electric or Westinghouse Electric executives. The men involved oftentimes had similar educational backgrounds also—college graduates in engineering with a rise through technical ranks into the world of sales. There sometimes existed on the part of the men with the bigger companies an almost protective, big brother attitude toward the smaller companies; this was reciprocated.

And the friendships were not only professional but often quite personal. Trade association meetings fostered these. It was perhaps easy in the camaraderie of these meetings at upper-bracket hotels, amid speeches typical of any association lauding the industry's members and "mission," to draw even closer than business and background indicated. It was perhaps easy, with wives and children present, and acquainted from past conventions, to drift into the belief that nothing could be very wrong in such an atmosphere.

Darkening Grays

Indeed, many of the meetings took place at the conventions of the National Electrical Manufacturers Association and other trade groups. Rather typically, after a conventional and perfectly lawful meeting of some kind, certain members would adjourn for a rump session and a few drinks in someone's suite. It seemed natural enough that mutual business problems would be discussed—specifications, for example—and like as not prices would come up. In time it was easy enough to drift from general talk about prices into what should be done about them—and finally into separate meetings to fix them for everyone's mutual benefit.

Thus purely legal gatherings might have drifted into ones with increasingly dark shades of gray and finally into ones that were pretty black; more than one moralist has noted that it isn't the blacks and whites of situations that get initially law-abiding citizens into trouble; rather it is a progressive inability to distinguish between shades of gray.

It was especially easy in this industry to get into price discussions.

The economic position of the various companies has often been one of feast or famine—large orders or none at all for the gigantic pieces of equipment manufactured. Widespread overcapacity after World War II brought intermittent price warring. In 1955, for example, there occurred a price war, known throughout the industry as the "white sale," which saw some prices cut as much as 50 per cent. Profit losses resulted and in some cases red ink. Again in 1957 there was a lesser wave of competitive cutting. At least during the "white sale" General Electric and Westinghouse wound up with most of the business. By reports then current some smaller companies were seeking government intervention under the Sherman Act's anti-monopoly provisions.

The case has a number of ironic aspects, but one of the great ones is that men in the large companies believed they had to protect the position of the smaller companies or run the risk of antitrust prosecution. Another is that much of the overcapacity underlying the "need" to fix prices was government spurred. Fast tax write-offs, growing out of two wars in two decades, brought the greater capacity for defense that the government wanted, but they also left the manufacturers with an embarrassing amount of plant.

As a result of this industry makeup, the friendships, and the price-capacity situation, there evidently developed in wide segments the philosophy that collusive activity was ethical, illegal though it might be.

Perhaps an extreme exponent of this view, though expressing a widespread one, is F. F. Loock, president, general manager, and sales manager of Allen-Bradley Co. of Milwaukee, who has pleaded guilty.

Looking back on what happened, he says: "No one attending the gatherings [in the electrical controls industry] was so stupid he didn't know [the meetings] were in violation of the law. But it is the only way a business can be run. It is free enterprise."

Price fixing is not usually associated with the idea of free enterprise, with the idea that the market mechanism is to be the ultimate controlling factor, and that this mechanism must remain unimpaired either by individuals or governments. But there is a rationale for the cartel system which permits the general type of collusive activity the electrical men were engaged in. According to it, markets are divided and prices fixed so everyone involved can "get along." Even the consumer is supposed to benefit because stable markets aid stable production and supposedly costs can thus be stabilized.

"Protection Against Buyers"

Price competition is anathema to such a setup. Mr. Loock says one reason for the gatherings in his industry was "we also need protection against buyers" and the "illegal meetings gave us such protection."

Elaborating on the need for "protection," Mr. Loock cites one instance in which the purchasing agent of a major Detroit manufacturer told the electrical manufacturer another one had offered a lower price. "By discussing the matter, which was not true, among ourselves, we were able to iron out the problem." He concludes: "I believe that in an industry where money is necessary to continue research and development of products, we should have some protection against the crookedness of some buyers."

There was also a feeling in the industry that the antitrust laws were unjust. With a rationale developed of friendly live and let live among competitors, laws designed to force competition seemed "government interference." The question was also asked in the industry: If such getting together was all right under the old N.R.A., why isn't it all right now? Of course the N.R.A. of the 1930's was declared unconstitutional by the Supreme Court, but some say the industry's philosophy of "getting together" has roots in that era.

But if illegal "stabilization" was an industry way of life, it should not be assumed that relations were continually rosy among competitors, or that all authority in the industry was bent on collusive activity.

Getting together to fix prices did not alter the basically competitive situation prevailing in the industry's markets. Indeed, it often seems some attendance at the collusive meetings was with tongue in cheek as to stabilizing prices, with a real reason of finding out what the rest of the industry was up to in order to get the jump in the next price cutting wave. Too, some of the conspirators pretty much inherited their roles from predecessors, older men who may have felt more of a tug from the industry's "way of life" than they did. In fact there was personal dislike among some of the individual conspirators; perhaps an individual who did not like himself for conspiring had little respect for others also so engaged.

*   *   *

This paper, written when Justice Fortas was in private legal practice, presents a practical analysis of the current state of antitrust policy, with emphasis on mergers as the current major issue facing policy makers. He analyzes policy formation as a combination of decisions by the F.T.C., the Department of Justice, and the Supreme Court.

Abe Fortas is a prominent attorney and public servant who was appointed to the Supreme Court by President Johnson in 1965.

48

Portents of New Antitrust Policy

ABE FORTAS

*   *   *

In the beginning, antitrust was considered principally a specific to purge the body politic of trusts. It's not much used for that any more. Maybe that's because the form of monopoly has changed; maybe it's because we've grown fond of them and don't want them purged. Maybe it's because, like many strains of virus, they've developed an immunity to antitrust antibiotics.—I don't know.—All I can say is that if you're the Number One company; if you're dominant and don't have any skeletons of previous acquisitions in your closet; if you can control prices, and supply, and the rate of technical innovation without agreement with others, you need not be too fearful of antitrust. Just don't be too greedy. You need not fear the mighty purgative of the anti-monopoly ingredient of Section 2 of the Sherman Act. As I sniff the witches' cauldron, I detect no signs of renewed agitation of this dormant ingredient.

Later, as you know, antitrust had its principal role as a purgative of various types of collusive and predatory practices—product allocation, territorial division, price fixing, boycotts, and so on. The purge was administered with a certain gaiety and abandon during the tenure of my partner, Thurman Arnold, as chief physician. He became so enchanted by its results that he even tried it on labor unions, but with negative results. He still thinks he was right.

Antitrust continues to be an important and effective medicine for collusive and restrictive arrangements. I think most businessmen now accept

From *Proceedings of the Third Annual Corporate Counsel Institute* held at Northwestern School of Law on October 15 and 16, 1964. Reprinted by permission.

the diagnosis that they're sick, and that antitrust may be applied without offense to holy scripture if they engage in collusive price-fixing, division of territories, boycotts, and similar practices. There are still a few whose attitude is like that of the fellow who came to his lawyer during the days of OPA and asked him for advice as to how he could violate OPA legally. There are even—I regret to say— a few who don't care, and, who will run for luck in a collusive arrangement, hoping they won't get caught. There are, however, still many gray areas and gray situations where it is difficult to say whether the arrangement is in fact and in law an agreement in unlawful restraint of trade, and whether antitrust does apply. And there is the never-ending controversy about the desirability of resale price maintenance laws—retail price fixing of branded merchandise by manufacturers.

Except for the latter—resale price maintenance—I see no prospect or possibility of change. I think we are fairly united that collusive price-fixing, collusive allowances and discounts, agreements to boycott, collusive division of territories, etc.— all of the *per se* practices—are undesirable and should be outlawed. As to resale price maintenance, I am constantly surprised at the widespread support which it has. Even my friend, Hubert Humphrey, seems more impressed by his recollections of the hardships of being a retail druggist than he is by what seems to me the obvious undesirability to American business and our economy of resale price maintenance.

Currently, the great antitrust issue relates to mergers and acquisitions—to the application of Section 7 of the Clayton Act. I think that it is important to try to evaluate this problem in some depth.

In 1963, there were about 1,300 corporate acquisitions in commerce. Only 17 of them were the subject of legal proceedings brought by the Department of Justice and the Federal Trade Commission. These figures, however, do not begin to indicate the effect of antitrust enforcement on corporate merger activity. Its real effect is subterranean—the effect of enforcement attitudes in discouraging mergers before they have taken off from the table of corporate officers or their counsel. If this figure could be ascertained, it would doubtless show that the number of mergers averted because of antitrust is extremely large.

These aborted mergers—mergers which were considered and discarded because of antitrust phobia—are probably important far beyond their number. They probably concern primarily relatively large companies in areas of our economy where there is a good deal of concentration. This is so because these are the companies that are likely to be sensitive to antitrust danger and to weigh seriously and fearfully the possibilities of attack.

Similarly, many of the 1,300 mergers which took place without attack are relatively small and unimportant in a national sense.

Now I suppose it is possible to argue—and some people believe this—that there is no such thing as a good merger—that an acquisition of control of one company by another is contrary to the national interest—regardless of effect or lack of effect on competition: In other words, that it is cannibalism; and everybody knows that people shouldn't eat people.

Of course, that's not what Section 7 says. Section 7 prohibits an acquisition only if it may reasonably be anticipated that the effect upon competition will be adverse and substantial. The battleground is precisely here: Between those on the one hand who believe that this mandate should be applied broadly, with almost complete reliance merely upon share of market figures and with nothing more than a tipping of the hat to the specific competitive consequences, and on the other hand, those who insist upon a specific demonstration of tangible anti-competitive consequences before Section 7 is applied to forbid the combination of business enterprises.

Let me say at the outset that, as I read the decisions, the Supreme Court has not to this date applied Section 7 except when its analysis—rightly or wrongly—led it to conclude that specific, defined anti-competitive results could be antici-pated from the combination of the acquired and acquiring companies.

In other words, despite global language which appears here and there in the opinions, the Supreme Court's decisions have not yet gone to the point of holding that there can be inferred from *mere aggregation,* in the absence of the specific elimination of direct competition, the actual or potential injury to competition required by the statute.

In short, the Court has to date set aside only acquisitions where it found, rightly or wrongly, existing, planned, or reasonably anticipatable *direct competi-tion* between the acquired and the acquiring company, or a direct *vertical* relation-ship between the two.

This observation, however, is of limited utility. In the first place, on the horizon are cases, heading for the Court, like *Clorox*—involving "conglomerate" acquisitions—a fancy term for acquisitions *not* characterized by direct, specific competition or a vertical relationship between the acquired and the acquiring company. In the second place, there are the cases, such as *Consolidated Foods,* involving the intricate question of reciprocity. In addition, there remains con-stantly the vexatious, subtle, and difficult question of whether *any* direct, present, or prospective competition or vertical relationship, however slight, suffices to bring the case within the prohibition of Section 7—or whether some quantum—some significant kind or degree or quality of threat to competition—is necessary.

This is the battleground, I think, of the next few years. This, I think, together with the perennial issue of resale price maintenance, will be the antitrust ground that is fought over in the courts, the agencies, the forum of public opinion, and in the halls of the Congress.

I believe that we can confidently predict that the Supreme Court will be in-clined to validate agency action—whether it is an FTC decision or a decision by the Department of Justice to attack an acquisition—that the Supreme Court will validate the agency action if, on the record, it can discover *any* basis, even though it be slight, for finding a present or prospective threat to competition. In short, we can predict the Supreme Court will be resourceful in finding that the facts show that competition *may* be affected by the acquisition within the broad lan-guage of Section 7—and that the Court will not weigh whether the net effect upon competition is good or bad. That is the portent I derive from examining, in soothsayer's fashion, the entrails of recent opinions and the exhalations of the Justices of the Court.

I hasten to say that this does not mean that the Court will agree with the ex-treme position that any acquisition is *per se* unlawful. I think it will continue to insist upon the necessity of demonstrating that some present or prospective injury to competition can be distilled from the facts—however low the proof.

Now, this means, in my view, that the FTC and the Department of Justice have a profound obligation carefully to determine when and whether the public interest will be served by attacking an acquisition. I submit that it is their duty to acknowledge that their policy—their decisions—as to the types of acquisitions which they will challenge—whether by the jawbone method of investigations and threats of prosecution or by the actual institution of proceedings—it is their duty to acknowledge that their policy is *not* just law enforcement—but that it is economic regulation.

In short, the broadly tolerant view which the Supreme Court is likely to take of agency decisions to prosecute acquisitions makes it imperative, in my view, that the agencies candidly and thoughtfully face the full implications of their roles.—Antitrust is not just law enforcement. It is not a branch of whodunit law enforcement. Antitrust is economic regulation, cast in the form of individual, adversary proceedings.—Those in charge of it cannot take refuge in saying, like the cop on the old television series, that all we want are the facts, ma'am. They must justify their actions and their policy not only in terms of whether they win the case in the courts (they usually *will*), but in terms of economic effect.

Now this is a simple problem for those who believe that *all* acquisitions are bad; and it's equally simple for those who believe that the law should not prohibit *any* acquisition, however monopolistic the result.

But for us unfortunate people in the middle, the problem of determining which types of acquisitions should be permitted and which should be attacked is difficult and vexatious. Most of us, I think, believe that there are many situations in which mergers and acquisitions may be beneficial, and not harmful, to the economy. For example, this *may* be the case when a merger results in creating a new enterprise which can challenge a dominant company possessed of monopoly power without increasing the competitive disadvantages of other companies in the industry; or when the acquired and the acquiring company are in different trading areas, are not directly competitive, and when their amalgamation will result in financial or economic benefits through diversification, shared research expenditures, or otherwise—without substantial threat to competitors.

Basically, I think, there is substance to the view that our relatively free-wheeling economic system requires—among many other things—tolerance for mobility; a presumption, if you will, that no avenue of growth or even of change—whether by acquisitions or otherwise—should be arbitrarily foreclosed except on the basis of a serious, sober showing of overriding public necessity in the particular case or type of case.

*　　*　　*

49

The Guidepost Approach to Price Stability

In recent years the government has aimed many of its anti-inflation policies at key private decision makers in labor and business. In addition to promoting price competition, the federal government has described guides for noninflationary wage and price behavior. The government's suggested "guideposts" for wages and price behavior are restated in the *1964 Report* of the Council of Economic Advisers, and the recent effects of this "jawbone" policy are evaluated in an excerpt from the *1965 Report*.

COUNCIL OF ECONOMIC ADVISERS

ANTI-INFLATIONARY POLICIES FOR HIGH EMPLOYMENT

It is the business of responsible government to try to achieve the best possible balance among such major economic objectives as full employment, economic growth, reasonable price stability, and the promotion of economic freedom and opportunity. The importance of price stability as compared with the other goals is sometimes minimized. But there are compelling reasons why we can ill afford to neglect prices.

The Need for Stability

First, inflation redistributes real incomes and wealth arbitrarily. When prices rise, those groups that are able to expand profits and wages most rapidly improve their situation at the expense of those whose incomes respond slowly. Inflation erodes the real value of public assistance and makes it difficult for local governments to maintain adequate standards of education and other essential services. It also reduces the purchasing power of retirement pensions and other fixed incomes—in effect, subjecting them to a discriminatory tax. Fixed-income assets lose value, while the prices of equity securities and other properties rise.

A second cost of inflation that we cannot afford is its adverse impact on our balance of trade and on our balance of payments. During most of the 1950's the pricing of American industrial products caused some loss of competitive ground to the products of other industrial countries. From

From *Economic Report of the President, January, 1964*, pp. 116–120 and *Economic Report of the President, January 1965*, pp. 57–59.

1953 to 1958, the overall wholesale price index rose only moderately more than the comparable indexes in most Western European countries and Japan. But the prices of certain goods important among U.S. exports rose substantially faster in the United States than in most of the countries with which we compete. Table 22

Table 22

Changes in Wholesale Prices in Selected Industrialized Countries, 1953 to 1958

	Percentage Change in Wholesale Prices		
	Total	*Steel*	*Machinery and Equipment* [1]
United States	8.3	24.0	20.2
France [2]	9.8	5.2	5.1
Italy	.9	[3]	2.6
Japan [4]	−1.3	16.5 [5]	6.8 [6]
United Kingdom	11.4	1.8	18.2
West Germany	3.0	9.1	6.0

[1] Implicit deflator for machinery and equipment component of gross national product used for all countries except Japan.

[2] Adjusted for change in exchange rate in 1958.

[3] Not available.

[4] Change from 1954 to 1958.

[5] Iron and steel.

[6] Machinery.

Sources: Organization for Economic Cooperation and Development, Japanese Economic Planning Agency, and Council of Economic Advisers.

indicates the deterioration of our relative price position particularly in the crucial areas of steel and machinery and equipment during the period 1953 to 1958.

Since 1958 the relative movement of overall prices has begun to be reversed, partly because our unit labor costs have declined in comparison with those in most European countries. . . . The competitive price position of American producers has improved both in their home markets and overseas. It would be foolishly complacent, however, to believe that these recent gains can be extended, or even retained, without special effort. The European countries have been striving to establish rigorous "income policies" to restrain wages and prices. Despite recent setbacks, they will continue to press these efforts. In doing so, some European nations are willing to accept substantial interventions into private decision making. The United States is not. If we would compete with them successfully over the long pull, we shall need to achieve a high degree of price stability by means that are consistent with our traditions and values.

A third cost of inflation that we can ill afford is the compromise it could impose on our pursuit of full production and full employment. If cost and price pressures should arise through the exercise of market power while the economy is still climbing toward high output and employment levels, we would be forced once more into the dreary calculus of the appropriate trade-off between "acceptable" additional unemployment and "acceptable" inflation. This could result in a serious setback to attainment of our national goals.

The choice for key private decision makers is clear. It is a particularly critical choice as the economy, after six years of excessive slack and unemployment, progresses toward full employment after enactment of the tax cut. For several years now many observers, including many leaders of the business and labor communities, have been saying that we have solved the cost-push inflation problem that appeared in the mid-fifties to have become endemic. This hopeful appraisal could not be demonstrated conclusively in a period when unemployment averaged six per cent. But, given a combination of private and public efforts, we will have the opportunity to prove it in 1964 and later years.

Government Actions

For its part, the government will be striving energetically to reinforce one of the most significant comparative advantages that the American economy has over nearly all other industrialized nations—namely, a tradition and an institutional structure that nurture vigorous internal competition.

In the period ahead the Administration plans actively to enforce the Nation's antitrust laws, in part choosing its cases and concentrating its enforcement energies so as to curb price-fixing and those proposed mergers and other business practices and structures that tend to make for anticompetitive enhancement of prices. Likewise, it will resist proposals—such as the revival of resale price maintenance now before the Congress in the so-called Quality Stabilization Bill—that would inhibit price competition and reduce the competitive vitality of our marketing system. In its efforts to promote freer international trade the government typically is not unmindful of the effects that import competition has on domestic American pricing practices. And it will continue to promote and encourage vigorous price competition by United States exporters.

At the same time, existing, expanding, and new labor market programs, already enacted by the Congress or proposed by the Administration, will help firms meet their labor needs without raising costs and prices. These programs will increase labor mobility, provide opportunities for training and retraining, and improve education at all levels.

The government also will be making a determined and continuing effort, . . . to promote what are by all odds the best anti-inflationary measures of all—large and sustainable productivity improvements, which allow both wages and profits to increase with stable prices. The pending tax bill will have a major effect of this kind through its lasting stimulus to investment.

Finally, as the economy's single largest buyer of goods and services, the Federal Government will redouble its efforts in 1964 to get full value for each dollar it spends.

Private Decisions and the Price-Wage Guideposts

Government policies can only provide an environment conducive to responsible private price and wage decision making. By choice, our government can advise, inform, and bring to bear the pressure of public opinion—but it cannot direct.

With so much at stake, however, the government's opportunity to advise and inform the public is one it must seize. In the Kennedy Administration, general advice as to the pattern of private price-wage decision making that would take account of the public's interest in avoiding market-power inflation was first formally set forth in the Economic Report of January 1962. The "guideposts" therein described—and repeated in the 1963 Report—offered standards by which union and business leaders themselves—along with the general public—could appraise particular wage and price decisions. They are restated here.

The guideposts contain two key propositions. The first—the general guidepost for wages—says that, in a particular firm or industry, the appropriate noninflationary standard for annual percentage increases in total employee compensation per man-hour (not just in straight-time hourly rates) is the annual increase in *national trend* output per man-hour. The standard is not the productivity trend in the particular firm or industry in question. Nor is it the particular year's productivity change, which can be influenced by short-run transitory factors.

The general guidepost for prices specifies that when an industry's trend productivity is growing less rapidly than the national trend, prices can appropriately rise enough to accommodate the labor cost increases indicated by the general wage guidepost. Similarly, in an industry whose trend productivity is growing more rapidly than the national average, product prices should be lowered enough to distribute to the industry's customers the labor-cost savings it would make under the general wage guidepost.

It should be emphasized that the general price guidepost does not counsel against price changes per se in a particular firm or industry. On the contrary, it contemplates changes in specific prices—downward in industries with high rates of productivity gain, as well as upward in industries with lower-than-average productivity gains.

Adherence to these general guideposts not only would make for overall price stability but would be generally consistent with the tendencies of competitive labor and product markets. The principles established by the guideposts do not imply that the entire gains from productivity improvement should go either to labor or to capital. Rather, they suggest a proportionate sharing of average national productivity gains among labor, capital, and the other related factors of production throughout the economy.

The general guideposts can cover the vast majority of wage and price decisions, but cannot provide for all of the adjustments the economy requires, especially over an extended period. Hence, the guideposts, as originally expounded in 1962, appropriately included a set of exceptions that reflected certain considerations of equity and resource allocation.

On the wage side, it was suggested that exceptions might be made to adjust for labor supply conditions and for wages that are exceptionally high or low compared with the average for comparable work. Price exceptions took into consideration capital requirements, nonlabor costs, and profits based on excessive market power.

The original formulation of the guideposts in the January 1962 Report of the Council of Economic Advisers also noted that ". . . Although output per man-hour rises mainly in response to improvements in the quantity and quality of capital goods with which employees are equipped, employees are often able to improve their performance by means within their own control. It is obviously in the public interest that incentives be preserved which would reward employees for such efforts."

These modifications of the general guideposts still apply, but it must be emphasized that they are intended to apply to only a relatively few cases. Particularly at a time when our national capabilities for responsible price and wage making may undergo a more serious test than in recent years, the most constructive private policy in the great majority of situations would be to arrive at price decisions and wage bargains consistent with the general guideposts.

Two other comments on the guideposts seem appropriate this year. First, it is not the purpose of these advisory policies permanently to freeze the labor and nonlabor shares of total industrial income, as would a rigorous, unrelieved application of the general guideposts. The 1962 Report noted that: "The proportions in which labor and nonlabor income shares the product of industry have not been immutable throughout history. . . ." It went on to point out that bargaining over the shares is consistent with the guideposts if it is conducted "within the bounds of noninflationary price behavior." Specifically, this means that it is consistent with the guideposts for wage and profit shares to be bid up or down in a particular industry *so long as price behavior in that industry remains consistent with the general price guidepost indicated above.*

Second, it is appropriate to focus special attention this year on *price reductions.* The guideposts call for reductions in those industries whose trend productivity gains exceed the national trend. It is fair to say that large industrial enterprises thus far have not widely heeded this advice. And yet, as noted earlier, there will be ample room for such price reductions in 1964. If they are not forthcoming, overall price stability will be rendered more difficult, since price increases are likely in industries that are progressing at a less-than-average rate. Moreover, in industries whose trend of productivity rises faster than the national average, if wages conform more nearly to national than to industry productivity trends (as the guideposts would have them do), failure to follow the general price guide will cause profits to pile up. Such profits become highly visible to the public and constitute a lure for strongly intensified wage demands.

Such circumstances pose a most unattractive dilemma from the viewpoint of the public interest. On the one hand, extra increases in wages or fringe benefits might tend to spread to other industries, creating a general cost-push from the wage side. On the other hand, there is no justification, on either economic or equity grounds, for distributing above-average gains in productivity exclusively through the profits channel. The real way out of this dilemma is for the firms involved to remove its cause by reducing prices.

*   *   *

Prices by Industries

Overall price movements are the result of a continuous stream of price changes in individual industries—upward and downward. In industries where productivity rises slowly, unit labor costs tend to rise, while in industries where productivity rises more rapidly, unit labor costs tend to fall. During periods of expansion, industries with rising unit labor costs can easily pass them along in higher prices. But achievement of overall price stability requires that savings resulting from faster than average increases in productivity be passed along in lower prices. Chart 8, which compares price and productivity trends for 19 manufacturing industries for which satisfactory physical output data are available, suggests that both developments have generally occurred during the current expansion.

However, in some instances, industries with large productivity gains made only token reductions in prices, or even raised them. Except where these movements reflect divergent movements in nonlabor costs, such cases give an upward bias to the overall price level. Moreover, they tend to produce unusually high profits (as in the automobile industry) which serve as inviting targets for wage increases that exceed the general, economy-wide trend of productivity gains. If such wage increases were generalized, overall price stability would be threatened.

Despite occasional exceptions—as in automobiles and construction—the general pattern of recent wage and price changes has closely approximated the government's wage-price guideposts.

To be sure, the guideposts have not been completely effective either in stimulating all warranted price reductions, or in preventing some individual wage and price increases that are not in accord with their criteria. Nevertheless, the very fact that representatives of both labor and management have often explicitly indicated their compliance with, or tried to justify any deviations from, the guidepost standards suggests that these standards have had a useful influence.

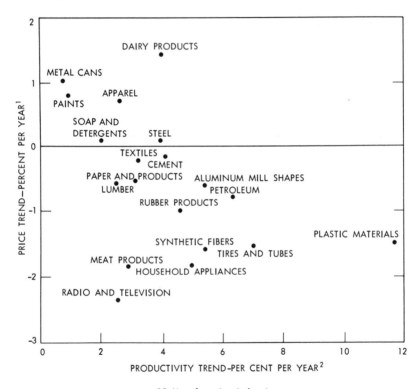

19 Manufacturing Industries

Chart 8. Price and Productivity Trends

[1] Average annual percentage change in Wholesale Price Index, 1959–64.
[2] Average annual percentage change in output per employee man-hour, 1959–64.
Source: Council of Economic Advisers (based on data from Department of Labor and Board of Governors of the Federal Reserve System).

In addition to any direct influence that they may have had on the wage and price policies of unions and managements, the guideposts have helped to create a new climate of opinion. Many groups in our society now have a better understanding of the relationships between costs and prices. There is increasing realization that it is appropriate—indeed necessary—to consider whether a proposed course of action, if followed by others in similar circumstances, would be consistent with overall stability. Decision makers in unions and managements are increasingly aware both of the fact that their decisions affect the public interest and of the fact that the public is interested in their decisions.

The government's wage-price guideposts have been subject to strong criticism by labor, management, and academic economists. Professor Burns, Chairman of President Eisenhower's Council of Economic Advisers, argues that they are largely unworkable, will interfere with the operation of our market economy, will throttle competition, and will involve excessive government controls.

Arthur F. Burns is John Bates Clark, Professor of Economics at Columbia University and President of the National Bureau of Economic Research. He served as Chairman of President Eisenhower's Council of Economic Advisers from 1953 through 1956.

50

Wages and Prices by Formula

ARTHUR F. BURNS

ADVENT OF GUIDEPOSTS

Exhortation with regard to prices or wages is by no means a novel practice of government. In its days of secular authority, the Church spoke firmly on the need for just pricing. In later times governments often blamed profiteers for increases in food prices. In the postwar period it has become customary for governments to stress the importance of stability in the *general level* of prices rather than the rectitude of individual prices. As of old, however, the authorities seek to limit private power in the marketplace by moral suasion. In today's world, as everyone knows, some trade unions can raise wages beyond the level that would prevail in a competitive labor market, just as some corporations have the power to push prices above competitive levels.

It is understandable enough, therefore, why our successive Presidents in the postwar period have seen fit to lecture the private community on the need for noninflationary conduct. General Eisenhower, for example, warned during his presidency that "businesses must recognize the broad public interest in the prices set on their products and services" and that "greater stability of the general level of prices" is "unlikely unless the national average of increases in wage and salary rates and related labor benefits remains within the limits of national productivity gains."

In the last few years governmental pronouncements of this sort have become more frequent and louder. In fact, the urging of moderation on

From the *Harvard Business Review,* March–April, 1965, pp. 57–64. Reprinted by permission.

private parties has reached a scale that marks something of a break from the earlier policy of dealing with inflation. Thus:

> On the one hand, the classical weapons of monetary and fiscal restraint, which in the past were relied on as the main defense against inflation, are now frowned on.
>
> On the other hand, general appeals to public responsibility are being implemented by wage and price guideposts. Trade unions and business firms, in other words, are no longer merely asked or admonished to moderate their private power in the public interest; they are advised with a show of specificity *how this can best be done.*

Once exhortation has been fortified by formula, it can no longer be dismissed as sheer rhetoric. It then takes on new authority over the minds of men, and its capacity for good or ill becomes much greater.

Intended Nature

The guideposts have been a major part of the Administration's economic policy since early 1962, when they were first set forth by the Council of Economic Advisers. What are these guideposts or guidelines?

> 1. *Wages*—This guideline specifies that the annual rate of increase in wage rates, including fringe benefits, should be equal in a particular firm or industry to the annual trend increase in national productivity, that is, to the average annual percentage rate of growth over a term of years in the output per man-hour of the economy at large.
>
> 2. *Prices*—This guideline specifies that when the trend of an industry's productivity rises less than the national trend of productivity, its prices "can appropriately rise enough" to accommodate the rise in labor costs per unit of output that is indicated by the wage guideline; and that when an industry's productivity rises more rapidly than the national average, its prices "should be lowered" in keeping with the decline in unit labor costs.

The Council originally characterized its pronouncement on the guidelines as a contribution to public discussion of how the national interest may be judged in the case of private wage and price decisions. The guidelines were certainly not intended to be interpreted as directives to industry or labor. In fact, they were described by the Council as "general guideposts" which still had to be reconciled in individual situations with "objectives of equity and efficiency." In other words, "specific modifications" were required to adapt the guidelines "to the circumstances of particular industries."

The more important types of modification that would be likely to arise in practice were actually listed by the Council. For example, the suggestion was advanced that wage increases should exceed the "general guide rate" if the bargaining position of workers in a particular industry or locality had previously been weak or if an industry was unable to attract sufficient labor.

Actual Effect

As was bound to happen, however, it was the crisp formula of the "general guideposts," not the qualifications or disclaimers, that mainly caught the public eye. And, with the passage of time, the Administration has itself become bolder. Thus:

> The January 1964 Report of the Council no longer speaks of the guidelines as a contribution to public discussion of how the national interest may be judged;

instead, it describes them as a "standard" for private wage and price decisions.

The Report of 1962 had avoided specifying the annual trend increase of national productivity on the ground that this was "a large and complex subject and there is much still to be learned." The Report of 1964, on the other hand, is free from all methodological doubts and presents without qualification a figure of 3.2 per cent as the annual trend increase of productivity in the private economy that is currently applicable.

The Report of 1962 had indicated that the "general guideposts" were "only first approximations" that would need to be adapted extensively "to the circumstances of particular industries." The Report of 1964, on the other hand, states flatly that the guideposts "can cover the vast majority of wage and price decisions" and, while the modifications that had been suggested earlier "still apply, . . . it must be emphasized that they are intended to apply to only a relatively few cases."

Thus, the official position, as now developed or clarified, is that the national interest can be best served by setting wages and prices in accordance with the formula of the general guidelines—not, to be sure, in every instance, but almost that.

TROUBLESOME CONSEQUENCES

As every economist knows, there are only two ways of raising the real earnings of labor. They can be raised by (1) increasing output per man-hour of work or (2) enlarging the share of total income that accrues to wage and salary workers.

Of these two sources, the first is basic, and it has always been vastly more important in our country than the second. The guidelines have the great merit of calling attention to this fact. Taking the economy as a whole, it is the cost of labor that dominates production costs. If the cost of labor per unit of output rises, business firms will ordinarily seek to protect their profit margins by raising prices. But a rise in wage rates, using this term broadly so as to include fringe benefits, need not involve a rise in production costs. It will do that only if the rise in the hourly wage rate is proportionately greater than the increase in output per man-hour. Therefore, if the average percentage increase in wage rates across the nation merely equals the average percentage increase in output per man-hour, the general level of prices could remain stable without reducing the fraction of the nation's output accruing to stockholders and other income claimants.

By expressing this basic truth, the guideposts have helped to direct the attention of thoughtful citizens to ways of raising output per man-hour—ways such as investing in more and better tools of production, improving the education and skills of workers, improving the quality of management, and eliminating featherbedding and restrictive trading practices.

Public enlightenment, however, has been an incidental aspect of the guideposts. Being a tool of policy, they point to a course of action. Their essential purpose is to curb inflation—or, more precisely, to permit monetary and fiscal policies to stimulate production and employment without stirring up inflationary pressures from trade unions or corporations. And if the guidelines for prices and wages were generally observed, it is indeed true that the existing links between the flow of money to markets, on the one hand, and the flow of goods and services to purchasers, on the other, would be broken. In such a world the levels of wages and prices would be governed by formula, and they would no longer reflect the changing forces of market demand and market supply—as they now do.

If the policy of the guideposts became fully effective, it would therefore change drastically the workings of our commodity and labor markets, and thereby modify —for better or worse—the character of our economic system.

Practical Effects

Let us try to visualize a little more definitely how the guideposts, if they were generally and fully respected, would work out in practice.

Statistical records stretching back into the nineteenth century demonstrate that, although the overall productivity of our economy occasionally declines, its trend has been steadily upward. If this continues to be true, as we may reasonably suppose, general observance of the guidelines will result in higher wages every year, regardless of the stage of the business cycle or the level of unemployment or the state of the balance of payments. The rise of wages will be the same, on the average, in years of recession as in years of prosperity; but in any given recession the rise of wages could easily be larger than in the preceding years of prosperity. Furthermore, the average wage will tend to rise in any given year by the same percentage in every firm, regardless of its profitability or the state of the market for different kinds of labor.

However, general observance of the guidepost for prices will not freeze individual prices or the relations among them. What it would tend to freeze is (1) the general level of prices and (2) the ratio of individual prices to unit labor costs of production. The tendency of the price-cost ratio to remain constant will be stronger in some industries than in others. Strictly speaking, the guidepost for prices specifies merely that the ratio of price to unit labor cost of production should not rise; it does not argue against a decline of the price-cost ratio. Hence, firms or industries experiencing a weak demand for their products or keen foreign competition may need to be content with prices that decline relative to their unit labor costs. On the other hand, firms or industries that are favored in the marketplace would be unable to raise prices relative to their unit labor costs even if their incoming orders were many times as large as their production. Nor would they be able to raise prices to compensate for increases in costs of production other than those of labor.

The broad effect of these tendencies would be to keep more or less constant the percentage share of the national income—or of national output—going to labor. Changes in the use of capital relative to the use of labor, whether upward or downward, could still have a large influence on the size of the national income but not on the proportion of income accruing to labor. Unless major shifts occurred in the occupational or industrial distribution of employment, any fluctuation in labor's percentage share of the national income would be due primarily to the discrepancy between the movement of overall productivity in a particular year and the corresponding trend increase. Nonlabor income, in the aggregate, would also tend to be a constant percentage of the national income.

It is well to bear in mind, however, that since profits are only a fraction of nonlabor income, the share of profits in the total national income could either rise or decline. In the postwar period, the amount paid by corporations on account of excises, customs duties, property taxes, licensing fees, and other indirect taxes has risen more rapidly than their net output. If this trend continues, the income share of investors in the corporate sector will tend to undergo a persistent decline, while that of labor will tend to remain constant.

Throttling of Competition

In the hypothetical economy that I have sketched, monopolies—whether of business or labor—would no longer have the power to push up the price level. Put more precisely, if trade unions and business firms complied voluntarily with the guidelines, they would relinquish any market power that they have not yet used or that they might gain in the future. This is worth noting, but it is not the main point.

The *fundamental* point of the preceding analysis is that general observance of the guideposts would throttle the forces of competition no less effectively than those of monopoly. The point is important because, unlike much of the rest of the world, the rivalry among U.S. business firms is very keen. Even in industries where a few corporations dominate the market—as in the case of automobiles, steel, and aluminum—each corporation competes actively against the others in its industry, against rival products of other industries, and against foreign suppliers. Competition in labor markets is also stronger than casual references to labor monopoly may suggest. After all, only a little over a fourth of the population working for wages or salaries is unionized, and many of the trade unions are weak. By and large, it is competition—not monopoly—that has vast sweep and power in our everyday life. Since free competitive markets would virtually cease to exist in an economy that observed the guidelines, this transformation of the economy merits serious reflection.

To be sure, compliance with the guidelines would be voluntary in the economy we are considering. That, however, may not mean much. For when economic freedom is not exercised, it is no longer a part of life. As far as I can see, an economy in which wages and prices are set voluntarily according to a formula suggested by the government would be almost indistinguishable from an economy in which wages and prices are directly fixed by governmental authorities. In either case—

> . . . the movement of resources toward uses that are favored by the buying public would be impeded;
> . . . the tendency to economize on the use of what happens to be especially scarce, whether it be materials or labor or equipment, would be weakened;
> . . . since prices will no longer tend to equate demand and supply in individual markets, some form of rationing would need to be practiced.

In all likelihood, therefore, a shift from our present market economy to one of voluntary compliance with the guidelines would adversely affect efficiency. It would also adversely affect the rate of economic growth and the rate of improvement of the general standard of living.

It is true, of course, that controlled economies can and do escape complete rigidity. The exigencies of life do not permit their authorities to be blind to considerations of efficiency or social harmony, so that price and wage edicts have to be modified here and there. Black markets tend to develop, and—despite their unsavory character—they often perform a useful function in facilitating production. Moreover, managers gradually become skillful in "gray practices," such as reclassifying labor in order to escape the wage restraints or modifying products in order to escape the price restraints. Our hypothetical economy of voluntary compliance would also have its safety valve; that is to say, the guidelines would be modified in "a relatively few cases" in the interest of equity or efficiency. However, gray or black markets, which impart some fluidity and resilience to authoritarian economies, could not exist in the economy of voluntary compliance that we have been considering here.

ARE THE GUIDES WORKABLE?

This theoretical sketch of how our economy would work if the guidelines were generally and fully observed has blinked institutional factors—such as the adjustments caused by the disappearance of auction markets, the new role of trade unions, and so on. Moreover, our theoretical sketch has tacitly assumed that voluntary compliance with the guidelines is merely a matter of will. Life is not that simple. Even if everyone responded to the government's plea for "cooperation" and sought faithfully to act in accordance with the guidelines, it would frequently be difficult or actually impossible to do so.

There is, first of all, a vast gap in our statistical arsenal. To comply with the guideline for *wages,* businessmen would need to know the trend increase of the overall output of the nation per man-hour. Once this highly complex magnitude had been estimated by the government, it would presumably be subjected to outside review, revised if need be, and accompanied by a specification of the boundaries of the year (if a year be the interval) to which it would apply. All firms dealing with labor, except those newly established, would then know what wage adjustment was expected of them.

Compliance with the *price* guideline would be infinitely harder. For this purpose, every company would need to know the trend increase in the productivity of its own industry and how this increase compares with the trend increase of overall productivity of the economy. Such information is not generally available, nor is it readily usable.

Applying the Indexes

The productivity indexes now being published, besides being often out of date, lump together a great variety of products. In time, more detailed and more current indexes of productivity will doubtless be constructed, but there are limits to what is statistically feasible. Even if measures of this type become available for each of a thousand or ten thousand industries, much confusion or perplexity will still remain:

- Should a manufacturer of bricks, for example, be guided in his pricing by an index of productivity for the stone, clay, and glass group or by an index confined to brick manufacture?
- If the latter, is the pertinent index a nationwide measure, one confined to his region, or perhaps to his locality or plant?
- How should a manufacturing firm proceed when its output is not standardized or when it makes a hundred different items, instead of just one product?
- If the appropriate index is not available, as may long remain the case for many firms, especially in the service trades, what is the best "proxy" for it?
- Will the judgment of a company's management on such issues, even if made entirely in good faith, be acceptable to others—such as its trade union, the Council of Economic Advisers, or the general public—who also seek only what is right?

Better statistics on productivity will reduce these difficulties; however, they cannot possibly remove them.

Changes in Work Force

Another puzzling problem would be posed by changes in the composition of labor that is used in industry. Consider, for example, the case of a company that has recently decided to employ more skilled workers of different sorts and less unskilled labor:

> Since skilled labor is compensated at a higher rate, the average wage per hour that is paid by the company to its workers will go up, quite apart from any wage increase that may be needed for the individual grades of labor. Let us now suppose that the wage guidepost calls for an increase of, say, 3 per cent. Then the company's employees will naturally expect an increase of this size in their individual rates of pay.
>
> But may not the company's personnel executive, who has become steeped in the mathematics of the guidelines, properly insist that the average wage has already gone up this much or more on account of the more intensive use of skilled labor and that no increase of wage rates is therefore warranted by the government's guideline? Will the trade union's representative grasp this statistical subtlety? Will he not argue that the guideline requires an increase of 3 per cent, that other organizations are putting through such increases, and that simple justice requires that the same be done by this company?
>
> Suppose that the personnel executive perseveres and finally convinces the union's representative. Will the latter, in turn, be able to persuade the company's employees? Can we even be sure that the company's board of directors will be convinced by the argument of its personnel officer?

In view of modern trends that emphasize the use of higher skills, this sort of difficulty would be bound to occur frequently in an economy of voluntary compliance.

Other Pitfalls and Puzzles

A related puzzle with which businessmen would need to grapple arises from changes in the composition of output. Suppose that a firm has two plants, that each of them makes a unique product, that the output per man-hour is constant in each plant, but that the two plants differ in efficiency. If the wage guidepost calls for a 3 per cent increase in wages, it might appear, since no improvement of productivity has occurred in either plant, that a corresponding increase in the price of each of the two products is justified by the guideline for prices. But are price advances really proper if the firm has shifted some workers from the less efficient to the more efficient of its two plants and thereby raised the output per man-hour of the entire firm as much as or more than the trend increase of national productivity? In that event, does the guidepost for prices require that the productivity of each plant be taken separately or that the two be taken in combination?

Another problem that businessmen and trade-union leaders would need to face is whether the modifications of the guideposts that the Council of Economic Advisers has officially sanctioned apply in a particular case. In assuming, as I have, a general willingness to comply with the guidelines, I have not meant to abstract from human nature entirely. Since the modifications suggested by the Council are phrased in very general terms, men acting in good faith may feel that their situation is precisely the kind of rare case that permits some departure from the guidelines. But will business managers and labor leaders always or even frequently agree in their interpretation of what modifications are permissible? In any event, is it not likely that the modifications will turn out to be numerous, rather than, as now intended by the Administration, relatively few?

In view of these and many other problems that are bound to arise in practice, the guidelines would prove unworkable over a very large segment of industry, even if everyone sought conscientiously to observe them. To deal with this critical difficulty, a new governmental apparatus might need to be established; its function would be to spell out detailed rules and to interpret them in individual cases. Although there is no way of telling just how such an agency would work, it seems reasonable to expect that not a few of its clarifying rules and interpretations would be arbitrary, that its advisory rulings would at times involve considerable delay and thereby cause some economic trouble, and that the rulings themselves would have at least some inflationary bias. These factors inevitably cast a cloud over the preceding analysis of how an economy of voluntary compliance would function, but they hardly make the prospect more inviting.

SPECTER OF CONTROLS

I have as yet said nothing about the aspect of guidepost policy that has aroused the most skepticism—namely, the likelihood of general observance on a voluntary basis. In recent years unemployment has been fairly large, and many industries have had sufficient capacity to increase output readily. Under such conditions, upward pressure on prices cannot be great. Even so, the guidelines have been sharply criticized or defied by powerful segments of the business and labor community. The critical test of the inhibiting power of the guidelines will come, of course, when both labor and commodity markets become appreciably tighter— and this test may come soon. If the recent wage settlement in the automobile industry is at all indicative, expectations of a high degree of compliance with the guidelines are hardly warranted. Similar experiments in other countries also suggest that general price stability will not long be maintained through voluntary restraint.

But once the government in power has committed itself to a policy, it may become difficult to move off in a new direction. A strong commitment to the policy of the guidelines inevitably means that any extensive private defiance would, besides frustrating the government's anti-inflation policy, injure its prestige. There is always a possibility, therefore, that failure to comply voluntarily with the guidelines will be followed by some coercive measure. This might initially take the form, as has frequently been proposed, of a review by a governmental board of the facts surrounding the price or wage changes that are being contemplated. The thought behind proposals of this nature is that once the facts are clearly developed, the force of public opinion will ordinarily suffice to ensure "responsible" action by corporations and trade unions.

No one can be sure whether this expectation will be fulfilled. But if it is, the governmental review board will have virtually become an agency for fixing prices and wages. If, on the other hand, the board's reports were flouted with any frequency, the next step might well be outright price and wage fixing by the government. It would seem, therefore, that from whatever angle we examine the guidelines, direct controls pop up dangerously around the corner.

Incipient Realities

This danger must not be dismissed as an illusion. Although the guidelines are still in their infancy, they have already hardened, as I previously indicated. Nor has the evolution of the Administration's thinking concerning the guidelines been confined to a literary plane. In April 1962, only three months after the announcement of the guidelines, the Administration moved sternly to force the leading steel companies to cancel the price increases that they had just posted. This interference with the workings of a private market had no clear sanction in law, and it caused consternation in business circles. Fortunately, a crisis was avoided by a prompt and concerted effort of the Administration, in which President Kennedy himself took the leading part, to restore business confidence.

Since then, the government has been more cautious. But it has continued to espouse the need for moderation in the matter of wages and prices, and now and then has even gently rattled its sword. Early in 1964 President Johnson requested the Council to reaffirm the guideposts. He emphasized his commitment to this policy by adding that he would "keep a close watch on price and wage developments, with the aid of an early warning system which is being set up." Last summer, when intimations of a rise in the price of steel appeared in the press, the President lost no time in declaring that such action would "strongly conflict with our national interest in price stability."

TOWARD SOUNDER POLICIES

As this account of recent history suggests, the guidepost policy may, under the pressure of events, move our nation's economy in an authoritarian direction. The danger may not yet be large, in view of prevailing political attitudes, but it could become serious in a time of trouble or emergency. And this is not the only risk, as I shall presently note. However, the fact that many citizens both within and outside government favor the guidelines must also be considered, for it means that they see smaller risks or larger advantages in this policy than I do.

It may readily be granted that the guidepost policy has the meritorious objective of blunting the power of monopolists to push up the price level. This is the feature of the policy that its proponents often stress. Indeed, they are apt to argue that it matters little in practice whether or not the bulk of the economic community pays any attention to the guidelines—as long as the major corporations and trade unions do so.

But if the guidelines are circumscribed in this fashion, they are still subject to the criticism of interfering with the competitive forces of the markets in which many major corporations actually operate. Moreover, the absence of a precise indication of what firms, industries, or trade unions are covered by the guidelines can create a mood of uncertainty that will militate against compliance. Not least important, the effectiveness of the guidelines in curbing inflation becomes doubtful when their application is restricted. For the very limitation on wage and price increases in the guideline sector of the economy would facilitate increases in the uncovered sector whenever an expansive economic policy generated a monetary demand that grew faster than the supply of goods and services.

Another argument frequently advanced in favor of the guideposts is that if they were in fact respected on a sufficient scale, then profit margins would tend to be maintained and the chances of prolonging the current business expansion would therefore be improved. This consideration is bound to count in men's thinking at a time when our nation is striving to reduce unemployment and to spread prosperity.

We must not, however, become so absorbed in today's problems that we overlook those that will haunt us in a later day. If the guidelines may stretch out the expansion now by helping to maintain the relatively high profit margins of prosperity, may they not at some later time stretch out contraction by serving to maintain the low profit margins of recession?

Let me add, also, that I recognize that the guideline policy was adopted by the Administration only after it had given serious consideration to alternatives. The thought of its economists apparently is that, in general:

- Monetary and fiscal tools must be used to promote expansion as long as the economy is not operating at full employment.
- Other devices must therefore be employed (in the absence of full employment) to prevent inflation.
- Policies aiming to increase competition or to improve productivity cannot accomplish much in the short run or cannot be pushed hard for political reasons.
- Direct controls of wages and prices cannot and should not be seriously considered under peacetime conditions.
- Consequently, there is only one major way left for curbing immediate inflation—namely, through devices of exhortation.
- And the guidelines for wages and prices are merely a promising specific application of the technique of exhortation.

Locus of Responsibility

Space will not permit me to unravel this complicated argument, but I at least want to suggest why I think it may be faulty. Once the government looks to trade unions and business firms to stave off inflation, there is a danger that it will not discharge adequately its own traditional responsibility of controlling the money supply and of maintaining an environment of competition. In the past our own and other governments have often found it convenient to blame profiteers, corporations, or trade unions for a rising price level. Only rarely have they pointed the finger of blame at their own policies—such as flooding the economy with newly created currency or bank deposits.

To the extent that the government relies on private compliance with its guidelines for prices and wages, it may more easily be tempted to push an expansive monetary and fiscal policy beyond prudent limits. Besides, it may fail to resist strongly enough the political pressure for higher minimum wages, larger trade union immunities, higher farm price supports, higher import duties, more import quotas, larger stockpiling programs, and other protective measures that serve either to raise prices or to prevent them from falling.

One of the major needs of our times is to give less heed to special interest groups and to reassert the paramount interest of consumers in vigorous competition. The political obstacles to reducing artificial props for prices are undoubtedly formidable. However, reforms of this type—supplemented by more stringent antitrust laws, effective enforcement of these laws, and reasonable steps to curb featherbedding— are likely to contribute more to the maintenance of reasonable stability in the general price level than will the guidelines for wages and prices on which we have recently come to rely.

This article argues that the wage-price guideposts provide a reasonable basis for a working consensus among labor, management, and government in a democratic society, and that so used the guideposts can play a useful, though limited, role in helping to achieve high employment without inflation.

G. L. Bach is Maurice Falk Professor of Economics at Carnegie Institute of Technology.

51

Inflation—

Danger Ahead?

G. L. BACH

G. L. Bach is Maurice Falk Professor of Economics at Carnegie Institute of Technology.

NEED FOR AGREEMENT

In the United States, as elsewhere, the backbone of a high-employment-without-inflation policy must be a stable growth in aggregate demand, with total spending growing roughly in step with the growth in capacity of the fully employed economy at stable prices. But for even the most effectively managed aggregate demand policy to succeed we must have strong public consensus on what wage and price policies are acceptable in the public interest. This consensus must be reflected in Congressional attitudes and in the behavior of the Administration and Federal Reserve officials, and thus be increasingly accepted as reasonable and forceful by business and labor leaders.

Even a "perfect" aggregate demand policy (as defined above) will fail if important labor and business units insist on trying to increase wages and profits faster than is consistent with increasing productivity on the average. For then the "perfect" aggregate demand will mean unemployment and slack in the economy, since aggregate demand will not rise fast enough to buy the high-employment output at the new higher costs and prices.

If every market in the economy were perfectly competitive, stable aggregate demand alone could do the job, for then no units would be powerful enough to push up wages or prices beyond the levels set by competition in the market. Temporary waves of consumer buying or employer optimism and demand for labor might bid up prices and wages

From the *Harvard Business Review*, July–August, 1964, pp. 49–61. Reprinted by permission.

in particular industries, but these could hardly force us into a major-jobs-versus-inflation dilemma.

But many markets are *not* perfectly competitive; big unions and big business are real, and they do have considerable power to push up wages and prices, at least temporarily, beyond purely competitive levels. Given this concentration of market power, at least in key industries which are important pattern setters, some pressure to assure reasonable wage and price behavior becomes essential if we are to avoid both inflation, on the one hand, and, on the other, unemployment induced by excessive wage and price demands when aggregate spending is held down by monetary-fiscal policy.

Put bluntly, labor cannot expect wages, on the average, to rise much faster than the growth in productivity per man-hour unless it is to generate inflation, or unless it is to generate unemployment in case monetary-fiscal policy holds the aggregate demand to noninflationary levels. Similarly, business cannot expect profits to soar rapidly over the long pull without facing the same results. Equally, business cannot expect organized labor to moderate its wage demands if profits soar rapidly, nor can labor expect businessmen to accept wage demands which persistently squeeze profits. What I argue is that *unless business and labor do accept wages and prices set within this general framework, given prevailing governmental and public attitudes toward avoiding inflation, they are more likely to cut their own throats through inducing unemployment and lower profits than to achieve the higher real wages and profits they seek.*

But to expect them voluntarily to accept such a constraint is asking a great deal in a highly competitive American world. What can hold wage and price increases in line? Monetary-fiscal restraint can do it alone, but at a probable cost of wasteful unemployment and slack. Monetary-fiscal restraint can do the job right if it has the aid of strong public pressure (exerted directly on unions and business firms, and through Congress and government officials) to keep key wages and prices within the bounds consistent with high employment and no inflation. Broad public consensus on controversial issues is hard to achieve, but without that consensus (including important members of Congress, the Administration, and the Federal Reserve) the horns of our dilemma look painfully sharp.

What could be the basis for such a working consensus? Has such an approach any practical chance of working in a free society like ours? Let us see.

Basis for Consensus

Economists have long agreed on the broad outlines of a wage and price policy which should prevail if we are to have a high-employment-without-inflation economy—this long before the "guideposts" suggested by the Kennedy Administration in 1962. These are roughly the wage and price developments that would occur from the force of the market if highly competitive labor and product markets prevailed everywhere.

For the economy as a whole, assuming any given rate of productivity increase (increase in output per man-hour or per man-year), the pattern should be this. Wage payments (including fringes and the like) *on the average for the whole economy* can increase at about the same rate as output per man without leading business firms to increase prices, while also permitting profits to increase at roughly the same rate. (If the society is dissatisfied with the existing division of the total national income between profits and wages, wages may increase faster or more slowly than the rate of productivity advance to produce a corresponding redistribution with a stable price level.)

Individual wages and prices should be set, as far as possible, by the force of competition in individual markets. But where purely competitive forces do *not* prevail, the guidelines for individual wage and price changes are these:

1. Unless there is a special reason to the contrary, wages in particular industries should rise by *about the same rate as average productivity increases for the economy as a whole.* (This is roughly what would occur in highly competitive markets with high labor mobility.) Wages in particular industries *should not* be directly related to productivity changes in that industry. Thus, if productivity in the automobile industry increases 5 per cent per year, but only 3 per cent for the economy as a whole, this does not justify a 5 per cent wage increase in the auto industry, but rather, as indicated below, a decline in the average price of automobiles.

2. Prices should remain approximately stable in industries which have an average rate of productivity increase, if wages conform to the guideline above. Where productivity increases faster than the national average (that is, where costs fall faster than the average), selling prices should decline roughly in proportion to the faster rate of increase in productivity. Where productivity increases more slowly than the average (that is, where average costs rise), prices should be expected to rise. (Again, this is roughly what would happen in highly competitive markets.)

3. Wages should rise less than the national average in industries where labor is plentiful and unemployment persists, to discourage additional workers from entering the industry and to encourage employers to use more labor in that industry. Wages should be expected to rise faster than the average for the economy in industries where labor is scarce, in order to induce more workers to come into the industry and to encourage employers to economize on labor. (Again, these are the results to be expected from highly competitive markets.)

4. If obvious inequities exist at the outset, individual wages should move faster or slower than the average to adjust these inequities.

5. Economy-wide productivity changes over one year, or even several years, may be distorted by cyclical or other forces. Thus, the average productivity increase over several years (say, five) provides a more reliable guide than does the very recent past. But to use too long a past trend might unacceptably speed or slow wage changes if productivity does speed up or slow down rapidly. A compromise like five years would provide considerable stability in the rate of wage advances, minimizing the impact of jerky annual and cyclical changes. It would permit labor to reap the benefits of productivity speedups without unrealistically long delays for union leaders. Finally, it would still leave on profits much of their present residual burden of decline in cycle downswings and rapid climbs in upswings.

But, most important, the critical point is that *the great bulk of wage bargains* would probably fall close to the economy-wide average increase in productivity, and *the great bulk of individual prices* should not have to be raised or lowered *because of the wage bargains reached* (although, of course, they might rise or fall reflecting varying rates of productivity increases or demand changes in different industries).

These guides, if they were widely accepted for wage bargaining and price behavior, would create a general *presumption;* they would not prescribe individual prices or wage rates. The framework emphasizes that, on the average and for the economy as a whole, these results need roughly to prevail. But it reaffirms that individual wage bargains should be determined by collective bargaining and that individual prices should be set by business firms in the industries concerned.

The establishment of presumptions is the essence of democratic, managerial, and legal control in our society, in every phase of our day-to-day lives. We should not be surprised to think of doing so here. Every manager presumes that his employees will arrive at work on time, and most employees share his expectation.

This presumption generally works without compulsion, because it is agreed upon. Many of our presumptions are established by law or by special agreements such as collective bargaining contracts. Many others are unwritten, yet have very strong force. An example is our widespread presumption of "first-come, first-served" in queuing up in cafeteria lines and ticket offices. The force of widely held presumptions should never be underrated in a society that is democratically oriented.

THE "GUIDEPOSTS"

In 1962, President Kennedy's Council of Economic Advisers took a first tentative step toward suggesting this widely accepted economic analysis as a set of "guideposts," or presumptions, for wage and price setting. Seldom has the wrath of virtually everyone been so centered on one pronouncement by a group of economists. In particular:

—Businessmen were horrified because, they alleged, the suggested guideposts would mean governmental intervention in price setting; and, as a practical matter, the suggested national average productivity increase for wages would serve merely as a floor for union demands.

—Union leaders were equally horrified because the guideposts might lead to governmental restrictions on wage increases, and, they alleged, because the suggested productivity-wage increases would serve as a ceiling for the increases they might extract from employers.

—Collective bargaining experts were horrified because the guideposts would interfere with "free collective bargaining," yet the *process* of "free" collective bargaining itself is the important virtue in our society, not the quality of the outcome of the bargaining.

—Some traditional economists were horrified because, they alleged, markets should be left completely free to set individual wages and prices within only the constraint of a properly determined level of aggregate demand.

In retrospect, I suspect that all these groups were too ready to jump on the guideposts of 1962 (which have been repeated in the Council's Reports for 1963 and 1964). Why do I believe this? First, because the guideposts make sense as national policy (albeit as only one modest part of an overall approach to obtaining high-level employment without inflation); and, second, because both business and labor stand to gain, rather than to lose, from widespread public acceptance of the kind of framework proposed by the guideposts.

The degree of misunderstanding and pure misinformation about the Council's proposal was incredible. It was clear from their statements that many who cried the loudest alarms had not even bothered to read the Council report. The general business belief that the guideposts would hold profits stable while giving all the benefits of productivity increases to wages merely reflected misunderstanding, or failure to read the proposal, or it could simply have been a mistake in arithmetic.

The flatly contradictory fears of business and labor that the economy-wide productivity increase would serve as, respectively, a floor or a ceiling for wage demands suggests that the guideposts were treading heavily on self-interests, and that they may have been about right for sound public policy.

The widespread fear that the guideposts might become an entering wedge for more direct intervention in wage and price setting was a far more valid concern. Such a result would indeed be unfortunate. Most Americans are firmly against this approach—I among them. A return to NRA-type tripartite government-business-labor "planning" or direct government control over individual wages and prices would be a colossal blunder indeed.

Government Bugaboo

The case for the guideposts is that they promise to *reduce* the likelihood of direct government intervention, not to increase it. The guideposts as a nationally accepted presumption would lessen the necessity for individual direct governmental intervention, because they would induce more responsible collective bargaining and business price policies that would be consistent with national goals.

There is always the danger that governmental authorities may become too worried about deviations from their policies and too enthusiastic about calling such deviations to the public's attention, thus edging over the line into direct intervention in wage bargaining or price setting. But the chance of minimizing such governmental intervention is greater if we have some reasonably well-defined guides to acceptable behavior than if we refuse to face the fundamental issues and wait for *ad hoc* crises to arise. For when such a crisis arises (say, because an excessive wage bargain clearly threatens to trigger an outburst of inflation), public pressures for governmental intervention are likely to be very strong indeed. And *ad hoc* intervention, without guideposts, has a very poor record indeed.

The other major attack on the guideposts has been the argument that they will not work if they are merely exhortation. Thus if we rule out direct government control over individual wages and prices, they will be merely pious pronouncements. It is both stylish and correct to say that mere Presidential exhortation to labor and business to behave has seldom made much difference. But the sophisticated case for a consensus based on the guideposts is, I think, quite different from merely saying that we should exhort businesses and labor unions to behave.

This more sensible argument holds that in a democracy the only reliable basis for preservation of individual freedoms within the market is a widespread voluntary consensus as to what is reasonable and how the market shall work. To say, as Adam Smith economics does, that individual price and wage setting should be left completely to the play of the free market is unacceptable where concentrated power exists in important markets, where there is little likelihood of diffusion of that power, and where, as a consequence, the level of aggregate demand itself is not independent of the actions of important wage and price setters.

In fact, public consensus does play an important role in determining the framework for most of our economic activity—for example, in determining the meaning of acceptable competitive behavior in the markets and the limits to monopoly. Public consensus to establish loose limits on reasonable wage and price behavior is in keeping with the same practical approach to the functioning of a market economy.

Reasonable Restraint

Public consensus can and does exert great power, for good or for ill. Such consensus is communicated to and often shared by influential legislators in Congress and by members of the Administration in power. To some extent it may bear directly on union leaders and businessmen responsible for key wage bargains and price policies, as in the late 1950's. Perhaps more important, public attitudes do influence Congressmen and government officials, including Federal Reserve officials. The Congress not only makes fiscal policy but also communicates its attitudes strongly to labor and business participants in the economic process. Administration leaders and officials of the Federal Reserve have strong direct powers to change aggregate demand levels if they do wish, as they must in many cases, to use this power.

During the late 1950's, for example, a consensus developed (among the public, many Congressmen, many officials of the Administration and the Federal Reserve, and, indeed, many union members) that wages were rising too fast, that profits were being squeezed unreasonably, and that price inflation could be pinned in considerable part on excessive wage demands. This widespread agreement led to strong public pressures for wage and price restraint, to stiffened business resistance to rising wages, to moderating unions' push for larger increases, and, perhaps most important, to strong governmental pressures to limit such wage and price excesses. Neither unions nor businesses are insensitive to public or to Congressional attitudes. In particular, monetary policy after 1957 was much tighter than before. It held aggregate demand down and should probably have a substantial share of the credit (or blame) for bringing the wage inflation to a gradual halt, leading to the recent extended period of substantially stable unit labor costs in the American economy.

But to see only the restrictive effect of monetary policy after 1957 is to miss an important part of the total operation of our modern American economy. Public attitudes are formed slowly and haltingly on most big issues such as inflationary wage demands and price policies. Their impact is thus often halting and gradual. There is no simple way to measure what part of the policy positions developed in Washington come from public attitudes and what part independently from the views of the officials concerned. There is no direct way of measuring how much of the wage moderation after 1957 was attributable to hard-boiled business resistance because of the profit squeeze and how much to changing public and governmental attitudes and policies. But to cast aside the force of public consensus because it is not readily measurable by economists and statisticians is to make a serious mistake indeed.

The greatest potential of the guideposts is to help crystallize a latent, widely shared feeling that "reasonable" wage-price behavior is needed to help us achieve continuing prosperity without inflation—when there is a reasonably strong readiness for consensus. If major economic groups perceive their own interests as drastically conflicting, there is probably little hope that something like the guideposts can help much. In such a climate, government advocacy might do more harm than good, since obvious failure could seriously impair future chances of achieving acceptance. However, I believe there is much latent support today for "reasonable" wage-price restraint. The guideposts can help to give content to this desire.

CONCLUSION

The central case for the guideposts, properly understood, is that with a working consensus based on them we can free the monetary and fiscal authorities to follow effective policies to produce high-level employment without inflation. Without some such working consensus, the Federal Reserve and the Congress will be intermittently, or persistently, up against the dilemma of validating inflationary wage and price increases or holding the price line at the cost of accepting low employment and slack.

A stable value of the monetary unit is a proper central objective of any responsible government. But to ask responsible officials, either elected or appointed, to enforce stable prices at the cost of persistent unemployment is neither realistic nor desirable. To break up all business and labor groups into smaller, more highly competitive units could obviate the need for anything like the guideposts in markets where now big labor meets big business. But there is no evidence that this will soon occur.

If this argument is correct, both business and labor, as well as the public at large, stand to gain from development of a working consensus on something like the guideposts. But wages and prices are set by individual unions and individual firms in individual industries. Is it reasonable to expect, or hope, that in the press of individual collective bargaining the guideposts can play an important role without the strong threat of direct governmental intervention or punishment for deviation?

In small individual bargains, such as many between the building trades and the construction industry, probably the answer is no. But in the big pattern-setting bargains, such as steel, autos, electrical equipment, and the like, consensus on the guideposts *can* exert a real pressure on the bargaining parties.

There is, indeed, some inequity in any policy that operates primarily through its impact on particular groups in society. But, in fact, most of our written and unwritten regulations operate to some extent in this way, for a very practical reason. Here big bargains are the important ones, and they are the only ones that loom large enough in the national picture for strong public consensus to come to bear on them. Temporary deviations by small units in the economy may provide special, and inequitable, advantages to them temporarily. If, however, the big bargains are consistent with the guideposts, and if monetary-fiscal policy stands its ground against inflationary pressures on the average, the resulting inequities are unlikely to be large. Little unions and little businesses are unlikely to be able to move far out of line with major markets for long. Unfortunately, even small-market deviations from presumptive policies may be disruptive because they make it harder for big unions and big business to live by the guideposts. But the price of direct government intervention to police little bargains below the level of public attention and consensus would far exceed any possible advantages.

The establishment of widespread democratic consensus on big issues is at best low and uncertain. It is not surprising that the guideposts raised a storm of protest in 1962. That they are, in fact, more widely accepted now is encouraging. (Note the pressure Walter Reuther obviously feels to claim that his wage demands are in keeping with guideposts.) Restrictions on individual behavior in our economy run against strong negative presumptions, for we instinctively distrust suggestions that the government ought to have anything to say about how we set our wages and our prices. But the only lasting foundation for effective operation of a basically free economy is a working consensus on the rules of the game that the major participants play.

Achievement of high employment without inflation is a very important part of our total economic game, and it is increasingly clear that we must rethink our attitudes and policies if a free market economy is to generate the result that virtually everyone wants. Important as they are, the best aggregate demand policies will fail unless over the years we come to insist that business and labor live within a framework consistent with our basic national goals.

Part of the thorny farm problem lies in the very efficiency of American agriculture. We can produce more than the nation will buy at currently supported prices. To alleviate these problems, the Committee for Economic Development proposes a long-range program to move resources—people and land—out of agriculture, while cushioning the short-run impact of the changes on farm families.

The Committee for Economic Development is a group of approximately 200 leading businessmen who are presidents and board chairmen of large corporations.

52

A Program for Agricultural Adjustment

COMMITTEE FOR ECONOMIC DEVELOPMENT

A PROGRAM FOR AGRICULTURAL ADJUSTMENT
calls (a) for policies and programs to attract excess resources from use in farm production, and (b) for measures to cushion the effects of the adjustment on property and people.

First and fundamentally, we propose a set of measures assigned to bring about a condition in which:

1. A much smaller total quantity of resources will be used in agricultural production;
2. This smaller total of resources at use in farm production will be composed of a much smaller amount of labor, and, possibly, somewhat less capital;
3. Production per unit of resources used in agriculture will be higher;
4. Earnings per unit of resources used in agriculture will be higher, on the average, and these earnings will be obtained through sale of farm products without government subsidy or support.

Adjustment of farming to this condition is basic to solution of the farm problem.

Second, we propose a set of temporary, transitional measures designed to:

1. Prevent a sharp decline in farm incomes, and
2. Avoid further additions to stocks of farm goods, while the basic adjustment to the condition sketched above is being brought about.

From *An Adaptive Program for Agriculture* (New York: Committee for Economic Development, 1962), pp. 31–51. Reprinted by permission.

It is an essential characteristic of these transitional programs that they should cushion the adjustment, but should do so in ways that do not prevent or retard the adjustment.

ATTRACTING EXCESS RESOURCES FROM USE IN FARM PRODUCTION

This is the heart of the matter in agricultural adjustment. Excess resources in use in the production of farm goods *is* the farm problem. Everything else suggested here is for the purpose of facilitating the fundamental transaction—withdrawal of excess resources from agricultural production—or serves to hold things steady while the basic transition is taking place.

AN IMPROVED LABOR MARKET

Some of the measures we are suggesting here are broader than the program traditionally associated with agricultural policy, or lie outside what has been the usual farm policy scope. The fact is that the well-being of agriculture cannot be assured by programs having to do only with the production and marketing of farm goods: healthy agriculture requires a healthy economy as a whole and healthy relations between the farm and nonfarm sectors. It is obvious, therefore, that the Department of Agriculture would not be called upon to administer all the programs suggested here, but that, regardless of the fact that they are suggested in connection with solving the farm problem, they should be administered by agencies best able to do so.

1. High Employment

The maintenance of employment opportunities in nonagricultural industry and services is an essential condition for the most satisfactory agricultural adjustment.

In our diagnosis, the problem of getting excess resources out of agriculture is a nonfarm employment problem: resources, particularly labor, are engaged in farming when they could produce more, and earn more, outside agriculture. This implies that opportunities for their employment exist or can be created outside of agriculture. If this were not true, the problem of agriculture would be basically different.

We believe, of course, that high and growing employment can be maintained in the nonfarm economy. We have discussed the steps necessary to achieve this result in a recent statement that emphasized:

> (a) The potential contribution of monetary and fiscal policy to a steady rate of growth in total expenditures for goods and services, and
> (b) Moderation of the rate of increase of wages and other labor costs, so that the rise of total expenditures is not absorbed by higher prices, but takes effect in raising production and employment.

The importance of high employment for a resolution of the farm problem must be emphasized. The movement of labor from agriculture has shown itself to be responsive to the state of the nonagricultural labor market. A sustained period of high employment would itself make a major contribution to agricultural adjustment, and would contribute to the success of any other measures that may be undertaken.

While emphasizing the importance of high employment in the nonagricultural economy for the speed with which agricultural adjustment can be effected, we do not mean to suggest that the other parts of the program recommended here must await the achievement of high employment or should be suspended in the event of future departures from high employment. There has been significant movement of people from agriculture even in recent years when unemployment was unsatisfactorily high, and even in such circumstances measures to facilitate the outmovement will have constructive results.

2. Education

. . . 44 per cent of the farm population is presently below the age of 20.

Here, in our opinion, is a main key to agricultural adjustment: we have an opportunity to secure long-lasting relief from the overburden of people pressing upon farm income by getting a large number of people out of agriculture before they are committed to it as a career.

It is obvious that the extent to which we may be successful in using this key will depend upon the impression the farm youth gets when he looks at the nonfarm economy with an eye to uprooting himself permanently from farming. If employment prospects off the farm are high and growing, the attraction to farm youths of training for nonfarm careers will be strong; if the current prospects for employment off the farm are not attractive, young people deciding whether to commit themselves to a career on the farm or in the nonfarm economy can be expected to decide in large numbers that the long term prospects are best in farming. This tends to perpetuate the farm problem.

Recent studies have brought out that fewer farm youths than others (a) graduate from high school, (b) enter college, and (c) graduate from college.

Attendance of boys at school falls off sharply in countryside school districts, by comparison with the nation as a whole and with urban schools, beginning with the 16–17 year old age brackets (final years of high school).

Per Cent of Males Enrolled in School *

| | | Place of Residence October, 1960 | | | |
Age Groups	Total	Urban	Rural Nonfarm	Farm	Usual School Grade
5 years	64.1	74.1	58.0	33.7	Kindergarten
6 years	97.8	98.8	98.0	92.7	First
7 to 9 years	99.6	99.6	99.7	99.7	2–3–4
10 to 13 years	99.4	99.5	99.5	98.6	5–6–7–8
14 & 15 years	97.9	98.0	98.3	96.3	Fr & S, H.S.
16 & 17 years	84.5	85.1	85.4	79.7	Jr. & Sr, H.S.
18 & 19 years	47.8	51.4	46.8	33.5	Fr & S, Col.
20 & 21 years	27.1	31.1	20.8	18.8	Jr. & Sr, Col.

* Bureau of the Census, Current Population Report (school grades supplied).

. . . the United States as a whole derives 4.3 per cent of its personal income from farming, and no state derives more than 26.1 per cent; yet the nation devotes 44.5 per cent of its vocational education funds, exclusive of funds for home economics training, to training for agriculture. In the 20 states getting the highest percentage of personal income from farming (North Dakota, 26.1 per cent to Texas, 6.5 per cent), all but two—Arizona and Vermont—spend over half of their vocational education funds, excepting home economics, for training in the skills of farming.

This means that in many states where farming is strongest vocational education tends to perpetuate the farm problem of too many people in agriculture by holding out extraordinary opportunities to train for farming as a vocation.

America's Resources of Specialized Talent,[1] a study published in 1954, gave the following summary of the relationship between the father's occupation and higher education:

The tendency for farm youths to have fewer years of schooling, and the emphasis on vocational education for farming, together with the above figures show-

Father's Occupation	Percentage of High School Graduates Entering College	Percentage of High School Graduates Graduating from College
Professional and semiprofessional	67%	40%
Managerial	50	28
White collar (clerical, sales, service)	48	27
Factory, craftsman, unskilled, etc.	26	15
Farmer	24	11

ing the relatively low proportion of farm youths in colleges, indicate that it is necessary to give attention to the amount and the kind of education farm youths get below the college level.

We have three recommendations on this vital aspect of the farm problem.

(a) *This Committee has recommended a program for Federal aid to public education below the college level in the low income states.* If this program were put into effect, its preponderant effects in the improvement of educational attainments would be felt in lower income farm states. *We once again urge adoption of this program, and rejection of proposals for aid to all states.*

(b) *Vocational education should be revamped to place its emphasis upon training in skills needed by expanding industries.* This means that vocational education in farming areas should be mainly for industrial, not agricultural, skills. There is need, as this Committee has pointed out elsewhere, for an expanded Federal effort to provide research and information to help guide state education departments and local school boards in what skills are in demand or coming into demand.

(c) *Public and private policy should take dual account of the national needs (i) to reduce the number of people committed for their livelihood to farming, and (ii) to raise the national educational attainment, by measures to bring the participation of farm youths in higher education up to the national standard.* Our recommendation (a) above tends in this direction, by increasing opportunities for youths in lower income farm states to qualify for college. There should also be a general increase in the availability on the basis of need and merit of loans and scholarship grants for college education. State and private funds for this purpose have been increasing and should continue to do so. Federal loan and scholarship funds for needy farm youths qualified for college study should be

[1] Report of the Commission on Human Resources and Advanced Training (Harper & Row, Publishers, New York), Dael Wolfle, Director.

provided during the transition period in which a rapid migration from agriculture is needed. Here also, as in (a) above, major effects would be felt in lower income farm states.

It should be recognized by all agencies, public and private, that on the average the farm youth, more often than the nonfarm youth, will have to live away from home while he is at college, and that a college education therefore tends to be more "expensive" for farm youths than for others. This should be taken into account in judging need for financial help.

3. Mobility

Early in 1962, a Federal *Manpower Development and Training Act* was enacted. The objectives of the Act are to "appraise the manpower requirements and resources of the nation, and to develop and apply the information and methods needed to deal with the problems of unemployment resulting from automation and technological changes and other types of persistent unemployment."

In farming the counterpart of unemployment resulting from automation and technological changes is underemployment, or, as we have discussed it here, excess use of resources.

We are glad to see the problem of the excess use of resources *in farming,* particularly excess commitment of people, integrated with the *general* problem of the nation's manpower requirements, and the national, general need for policies to help the nation adapt to the ever changing skill requirements of the economy.

This coincides with our view, basic to the adaptive approach we are recommending for solution of the farm problem, that the farm problem is not unique, but is, rather, the leading case of a large class of problems where an industry is using too many resources, and, that solution of the farm problem lies in policies tending to improve, generally and overall, the efficient use of our resources, rather than in protectionist, specialized "farm policy."

The provisions of the new Manpower Act can be an important step in guiding and easing the movement out of farming of a large number of people in a short time, if the Act's purposes are interpreted as applying fully and specifically to the farm problem, and if they are vigorously pursued in that light. This includes:

Job Information

The Act requires the Secretary of Labor to promote, encourage or directly engage in programs of information and communication concerning manpower requirements and improvement in the mobility of workers. We recommend additionally that:

> *The Federal-State Employment Service be expanded to rural areas,* and its coverage made national and regional, rather than local only, and that:
> *The present farm labor service should expand its responsibility to include placement in off-farm work,* instead of limiting its referrals to farm employment.

Careful attention should be given to the impact of the foreign worker program upon the wages of domestic migrant farm workers.

Retraining and Movement

The new Act establishes procedures for selecting and training workers for occupations requiring new skills. It specifies that workers in farm families with annual net income under $1,200 are eligible for retraining assistance under the Act. The Act provides allowances for training, subsistence, and transportation, and for Federal assistance for state and private occupational training schools.

The adjustments required in agriculture will call for the movement of many people who would not be eligible for retraining under the provisions of the Act. It confines retraining allowances and other assistance to workers in farm families with net annual income below $1,200. Basically our objective should be to provide assistance for retraining where the individual will not get it without assistance and where the retraining will substantially increase his ability to produce and earn income. Some arbitrary definition of eligibility may be necessary for administration of the Act, but *we believe that the present definition is too restrictive so far as agriculture is concerned.*

The retraining of farm workers leaving farming should be considered one of the principal objectives of the new Act. Those responsible for the administration of the Act should have it clearly in mind that farming is the leading case of misuse of resources in the American economy, that overcommitment of people to farming for their livelihood is the special form of the use of excess resources in agriculture, and that the Manpower and Training Act should consequently be applied with all vigor to solution of the farm problem.

The provisions in the Act limiting and qualifying direct help programs to avoid abuse should be fully and carefully observed.

We recommend that retrained farm workers leaving farming should be assisted in moving to nonfarm work sites, by a program of loans to cover the cost of moving themselves and their families. Such assistance should be given once only for the purpose of leaving farming. It should be given only for movement from areas where there is excess labor supply and only for movements in excess of, say, 50 miles.

It should be emphasized that all such direct help programs should apply to farm tenants, hired hands and domestic migrant workers, as well as to farm proprietors and their families.

We regard direct help to farm people in finding better opportunities in the nonfarm labor force as necessary and desirable, because we believe that a small fraction of the funds now spent on agricultural subsidies would, if spent in ways that tended positively to induce the needed movement of human resources out of farming, result in higher national income and lower national outlays on subsidies.

ADJUSTMENT OF AGRICULTURAL PRICES

The basic adjustment required to solve the farm problem, adjustment of the resources used to produce farm goods, cannot be expected to take place unless the price system is permitted to signal to farmers how much is wanted, of what.[2]

Therefore, it is recommended that a Price Adjustment Program be instituted.

[2] The importance of the correct price signals for farm products was highlighted by recent developments in the dairy industry. During 1960, production and consumption of dairy products were about in balance, and the government had to purchase only small amounts of surpluses. Then, in late 1960 and early 1961, the support price for dairy products was increased. This higher support price, together with lower feed grain prices, induced a sharp increase in the production of dairy products at a time when the demand for dairy products was not expanding. The result has been more resources in dairying, more output, and sharply increased expenditures for acquisition of surpluses to support prices of dairy products.

In order that the prices of our major farm products should give the correct signals for investment and production, *the prices of cotton, wheat, rice, and feed grains and related products now supported should be allowed to reflect the estimated long-run "adjustment price" of these products.*

The adjustment price would simultaneously satisfy two conditions. *First,* it is a price at which the total output of the commodity can be sold to domestic consumers or in commercial export markets without government subsidy. *Second,* it is a price at which resources efficiently employed in agriculture, after a period of maximum freedom to move out, could earn incomes equivalent to those earned in the nonfarm economy.

For most of these commodities the adjustment price is below the present support price and is likely to remain so even after a period of stimulated out-movement. This means that at prices below the present support prices sufficient resources would prefer to remain in agriculture, rather than move out under favorable conditions, to produce as large a volume of these commodities as would be bought by consumers, at home and abroad, at these lower prices. The willingness of labor to remain in agriculture after a period of maximum opportunity to move out, with the incomes they can earn at these lower prices, will be objective evidence that these incomes are "satisfactory." It will be possible for labor to earn satisfactory incomes at lower commodity prices because output per worker will be increased by two developments: (a) the number of workers will be substantially reduced, which will increase the capital each worker has to work with, and (b) restrictions on output per worker will be removed.

While the adjustment price for most of the major commodities is below the present support level, it is above the price that would result if the total output that the resources now in agriculture would produce were sold in an unsupported market. Such a purely free market price would be lower than the adjustment price we have in mind because it would result from marketing crops without previous adjustment of the resources used in their production. We propose below two measures, an expanded Soil Bank and a Cropland Adjustment Program, to keep production from exceeding demand at the adjustment prices during the transition period while the basic out-movement of resources is taking place.

The purpose of setting the adjustment price is to give farmers the best possible indication of the prices they may expect to receive during and at the end of the transition period, so that those farmers who do not think they can earn incomes they regard as satisfactory at those prices can take advantage of the transition period to move out. It is not proposed that the government should support prices at the adjusment price levels after the transition period. Neither should it be expected that market prices will remain permanently at the adjustment price levels after the transition period. The long-run course of agricultural prices will depend mainly upon the rate of growth of agricultural productivity and the rate of movement of resources into and out of agriculture.

We do not favor a gradual lowering of farm prices to the adjustment level, although we took a position in our statement on farm policy in 1956 favoring gradualism. Gradual price reductions in recent years have not affected the resources used in farming fast enough and have not allowed total production to flow into use. Therefore,

it is recommended that the price supports for wheat, cotton, rice, feed grains and related crops now under price supports be reduced immediately to the prices that could be expected to balance output and use, after the transition period, without new additions to government stocks.

The undesirable effects on farm incomes during the transition period should be handled separately and simultaneously as suggested later.

The importance of such price adjustments should not be underestimated. The lower price levels would discourage further commitment of new productive resources to those crops unless it appeared profitable at the lower prices. Also, the lower prices would induce some increased sales of these products both at home and abroad. Some of these crops are heavily dependent upon export markets. Finally, these price adjustments would put the United States into position to begin disentangling itself from export subsidies, import quotas, and other inconsistent policies which now surround our foreign trade in these farm products.

Specific adjustment prices to satisfy these principles will have to be estimated when the program is initiated, in terms of the facts and outlook at that time. It appears that at the present time (mid-1962) the adjustment price would be, for cotton about 22 cents a pound, for rice about $3 a hundredweight, for wheat about $1.35 a bushel, and for feed grains the equivalent of about $1 a bushel for corn.

These prices for wheat, rice, and cotton are believed to approximate the prices at which these crops would be sold in the market without further accumulation of surpluses. The suggested price for feed grains is about the level that had been maintained for feed grains for two years prior to 1961.

To keep feed grain production from outrunning usage at the suggested adjustment price, we recommend below a Temporary Soil Bank, designed to hold output of feed grains below 155 million tons a year.

Consequently, although government supports of the crops designated above would continue at the adjustment price levels during the five-year adjustment period, *it is not expected that the government would acquire surpluses except under exceptional and temporary circumstances.*

The effects of the adjustment prices would reach beyond our borders. The adjustment price suggested for cotton would permit our domestic cotton mills to compete on a more even basis with foreign mills, in our markets and in foreign markets. At present, foreign mills can buy United States cotton more cheaply than can our domestic cotton producers. The same would be true of our domestic flour millers and rice exporters.

An estimate of the market adjustment price for farm products will be partly a matter of judgment as long as markets are not free and earnings in farming are too low. However, this judgment must be made, and the preferable direction of error, if any, is clear in our present situation.

For several reasons it is important that price supports be moved to levels that, if wrong, will be low rather than high.

First, price supports on the low side will test the market demand for farm products. If this demand turns out to be higher than output at the support level we can meet the needs from our huge stocks.

Second, new resources (especially people) should be discouraged from entering agriculture, at least during the adjustment period, and the rate of entry in the longer run should not be excessive. Price supports set too high will tend to continue the errors of recent years.

Therefore, the costs of errors of setting supports too low initially are virtually zero as long as the income of farm people does not suffer as a result, whereas the errors of too high a level can only be corrected at considerable expense either to farmers or the public, or both.

If it is demonstrated over a period of time that the adjustment prices originally determined are too high or too low, the adjustment price should be corrected accordingly.

Where support prices are reduced to an adjustment level, production restrictions should be abolished.

In explanation:

Given two cushioning programs discussed later—a Cropland Adjustment Program and a Temporary Soil Bank—the output of the products for which we are suggesting reduction of supports to an adjustment price should be approximately in balance with domestic and export use at the recommended prices. Where it is exceptionally advantageous to produce these crops, producers would find it profitable to expand output at the adjustment price. Such would be the case for cotton in California and wheat in certain areas of the Plains.

On the other hand, in other areas farmers would find alternatives more attractive than continued production of the crops for which supports had been lowered. In some cases the alternative would be nonfarm employment. In other cases, the alternative would be the production of farm goods for which demand is rising fast (meat, for instance, as contrasted with wheat).

CUSHIONING THE PROCESS OF ADJUSTING THE RESOURCES USED IN FARM PRODUCTION—A CROPLAND ADJUSTMENT PROGRAM

What we are recommending with respect to land use is a program designed to turn land being misused in agriculture to better agricultural use. It is not a program to take land out of farming where there is no nonagricultural alternative use, since that would be wasteful. Our suggestions concern mainly the Western Plains and Mountain area. They are designed to convert land being used for the production of crops back to grassland. It is anticipated that if wheat is priced lower, farmers in this area will have better income raising livestock on this land, once it is returned to grass, than they have as arid country wheat farmers. The object of the program we are suggesting is to assist them in converting their farms from plowland to livestock grasslands.

It is recommended that a Cropland Adjustment Program be instituted, to induce the reconversion of at least 20 million acres of Western Plains, and Mountain Region land from crop use to grass, as rapidly as possible.

To induce a farmer to convert from wheat production to grassland, the government would:

> 1. Pay an amount equal to the expected income from producing a crop, so that these conversion payments, together with the income protection payments mentioned later, would provide, over the adjustment period, an income equivalent to what the farmer would get if he produced a crop.
> 2. Make available technical assistance and planning in the conversion of cropland to grass, and share the costs of conservation practices, where applicable.
> 3. Require agreements on the part of the owner that, once converted, the land would not be returned to the production of wheat for some specified period.

This program is an extension and enlargement of the Great Plains Conservation Program started in 1956 and continued until the present time. What is proposed is an expansion and extension of its scope to induce greater participation.

The extraordinary demands of World War II and the immediate post-war period brought favorable wheat prices. These prices induced a substantial expansion in wheat acreage in the United States, from a low of 57 million acres in the early war period to over 77 million acres in the late 1940's. The increase in production was intensified by good weather. This expansion included a marked increase in the total acreage in the low rainfall areas of the Western Great Plains.

When wheat surpluses appeared, acreage allotments were inaugurated and land was forced out of wheat. However, in this western region grain sorghums have been developed that are an alternative dry country crop to wheat—*as long as wheat and feed grain prices are maintained high enough to keep sorghum prices high.* In the Plains and Mountain region harvested wheat acreage declined by 9 million acres from 1952–53 (the last years before allotments) to 1957–58. Feed grain acreage meanwhile increased by over 12 million acres. This additional 12 million acres in feed grains can produce just about the amount of *surplus* feed grain produced annually in recent years before 1961. Moreover, total wheat production in this region still substantially exceeds prewar production despite the acreage allotments.

These basic facts point directly at what should be done:

    1. Acreage converted to cropland in the dry areas must be returned to grass.

    2. Wheat and feed grain prices should be allowed to tell farmers how much of each is wanted. That is, the price signals should be allowed to work.

As long as five years may be required to return this plowed land to grass. During this period farm operators would have to forego all or a major portion of their cash income and at the same time incur some out-of-pocket expenses. Even though the long run income prospects in the dry area would be higher from a grassland-livestock program than from wheat, if wheat were priced correctly, few farmers can afford to forego current income to make the change.

This is why we recommend a Cropland Adjustment Program. Payments under the plan should reflect the length of time required to establish grass. This will differ in various areas. Payments should end at the end of that time.

Payments under the Cropland Adjustment Program would be on a declining schedule, to mesh with the growth of new income from different use of the land.

A TEMPORARY INCOME PROTECTION PROGRAM

If price supports for wheat, rice, and cotton were reduced immediately to the level at which adjustment of resources would begin to take place, the income of the producers of these crops would decline sharply in the absence of any compensatory public policy. While such a quick and sharp decline in income might conceivably increase the rate at which needed adjustments took place, it would exact a high cost in terms of suffering of the farm people displaced.

Therefore:

We suggest that a *Temporary Income Protection Program be inaugurated,* to prevent the major impact of the required price adjustments from bearing excessively upon the farm community.

We recommend Temporary Income Protection payments only for wheat, rice, and cotton because the price drop in other crops would be much less than for these three.

The Temporary Income Protection Program would have five controlling features:

> 1. Payments should be made only to farmers who now have acreage allotments for wheat, rice, and cotton. The adjustment payments should be based upon a quantity of the product determined by the present acreage allotment and the normal yield of the farm for the previous two years prior to the beginning of the program.
> 2. The program would continue only five years.
> 3. Payments would be a declining percentage of the excess of the 1960 support prices over the adjustment price.
> 4. Payments would be independent of further production of these crops.
> 5. Payments would decline to zero within five years.

To illustrate the workings of the program in the case of wheat farming:

The farmer has a base period quantity of wheat, computed as above in Point 1. Let us assume that this quantity, for a particular farmer, is 1,000 bushels. The support price for wheat in 1960 was $1.78 a bushel. If the adjustment price, as described earlier, is $1.35 a bushel, this leaves a difference of 43 cents a bushel. In the first year of the program, the farmer would receive 1,000 times 43 cents, or $430. In the second year he would get 80 per cent of that amount, or $344. In the third year he would get 60 per cent of $430, or $258, and so on. In the sixth and succeeding years, there would be no income protection payments.

The farmer would get the income protection payments, based upon his former marketing quota, no matter how much wheat he grew, and even if he grew no wheat or grew something else. This provision is essential. The farmer should decide how much wheat to produce, if any, on the basis of what is profitable for him to do at $1.35 a bushel. It is essential that receipt of the supplemental payment should not be dependent upon the production of wheat. Otherwise the supplemental payment would simply be an additional price for wheat and an additional inducement to produce wheat, beyond what would be induced by the adjustment price.

The foregoing example has assumed that the adjustment price is constant during the five-year period, but, as noted earlier, the adjustment price might be changed if circumstances indicated that it was too high or too low.

To put the above into the form of rules for the program, the income protection payments should:

> 1. be based upon (a) the acreage allotment held by the farmer and a marketing quota, converted to an income protection base derived from it, and (a) the difference between supports in 1960, and the new adjustment price;
> 2. decline to zero by the end of five years;
> 3. be made whether or not a crop was produced.

A TEMPORARY SOIL BANK

The third measure for cushioning adjustment should be a Temporary Soil Bank, to prevent feed grain production from exceeding demand in the next few years.

It is recommended that a Temporary Soil Bank should be established, to last not more than five years, and to hold feed grain output, during that time, to not over 150–155 million tons a year. The Temporary Soil Bank would extend, under conditions set forth below, the existing Soil Bank.

If feed utilization per animal continued at the rate of recent years, it appears that by 1965 the domestic demand for livestock products will require the use of about 165 million tons of feed grains annually, at about 1960–61 prices. This would mean that feed grain and livestock prices should stabilize at about 1960–61 levels without the accumulation of feed grain stocks. Until such time as this balance is achieved, a Soil Bank program should be utilized in order to prevent low livestock prices or continued accumulation of feed grains.

The Temporary Soil Bank should be on a whole farm basis. First, the retirement of whole farms is less expensive in terms of the inducement needed to obtain the necessary land. *Second,* the whole farm retirement also retires both labor and capital from farming, thereby shrinking the total resource base in agriculture.

There has been much objection to the whole farm Soil Bank Program from the nonfarm people in rural communities. They have objected to the loss of sales and to the competition from farm people in the local labor market. However, the impact of the Soil Bank on adjacent communities will depend very much on the state of economic activity in the economy generally. Moreover, the program should be operated so that its impact will be minimized on individual communities or areas.

53
Statement in
Reply to the CED

Secretary of Agriculture Freeman argues
that the CED proposals (see the previous
article) would hurt farmers and would
seriously disrupt the rest of the economy.
The proposals would also, he argues,
threaten the family farm.

ORVILLE L. FREEMAN

THE SECRETARY OF AGRICULTURE COMMENTS ON THE CED PROPOSALS

"The whole premise of the CED five-year plan is based on the stated
goal of doubling the expected exodus from farming, pushing it up to a
level of two million farm workers in the next five years, by means of an
administered decline in farm income. This artificially accelerated dislocation of two million farmers seeking nonfarm jobs, together with the disruption of their families, plus the effects on the businessmen on Main Street
and on those in rural towns and villages who provide professional and
public services, all add up to a serious burden of adjustment and critically
handicap the rest of the economy. A rate of economic growth sufficient to
achieve satisfactory employment levels under normal conditions could be
thrown out of balance by this additional load.

"Second, the CED five-year plan to end farm programs threatens to
alter the basic character of American agriculture. If government made
good on its determination to stay out of the picture after five years, farmers
would be faced with low and fluctuating farm prices. They would be left
to deal with business firms in other sectors of the economy having monopolistic control over their markets. The result would be a disorganized
agriculture where farmers were exploited by the large firms with whom
they dealt in selling their products and buying farm supplies. Even the
most efficient family farm would find it difficult to survive this type of
economic pressure, and the control of agricultural resources would be-

Statement of Secretary of Agriculture Orville L. Freeman, July 18, 1962, as reported in *Current*, September, 1962. Reprinted by permission.

come increasingly concentrated into the hands of firms outside agriculture—firms which could and would begin to join together to raise prices to increase profits. . . .

"The real threat to the independent family is not, in most cases, the giant factory-scale corporation-owned farm employing labor in large crews. Rather, it is through the imposition of a pattern of controls by centralized private authority over the existing family-farming pattern." In the broiler industry, for example, which is dominated by large producers who process and market their own produce, "the independent farmer cannot compete with the integrated industry because he cannot gain access to improved breeds and strains of poultry stock, he cannot secure financing on equal terms, he cannot keep up with the rate of technological and managerial advance where research information is available only through private channels controlled by the integrators, or where access to markets is controlled by the integrators. . . .

"Moreover, the CED has apparently not been concerned with the class of farmers from which this out-migration would principally occur. If, for example, we were to move out of agriculture and into improved nonfarm job opportunities the least productive 44 per cent—grossing less than $2,500 a year—we would go a long way toward solving the problem of rural poverty for this group. But we would reduce total farm marketings by only five per cent, and the remaining 56 per cent of the farmers would have to face the disastrously low level of unsupported prices on high unrestrained production levels.

"If two million farmers were moved out of commercial agriculture (grossing over $2,500 per year), the decline in production would indeed be drastic, at least until science, technology, and machinery could catch up.

"Probably there would be some out-migration from all income classes of farmers. If trends of the past few years were to continue most of it would come from the $2,500 to $5,000 gross income class. It is our best judgment that this out-migration could be forced and accelerated somewhat—although not to the extent of two million in five years—if we wish to pay the price in increased competition for nonfarm employment, increased social and economic problems in urban areas, and the drastic decline in business on Main Street in small towns of rural America.

"It is also our best judgment that, even if we were to pay this price, the out-migration would not be sufficient to leave adequate incomes, under 'free market' prices, to those who do remain."

Finally, the ultimate aim of the CED program—the abandonment of all farm programs—would "alter the nature of the nation's agriculture and seriously threaten the family farm system that has created the world's most successful agricultural productivity. The national economy and general welfare would suffer from the absence, in the CED program, of some of the major constructive aspects of the Administration's food and agriculture program, such as rural area development and the wise use of land resources to meet growing needs for conservation, wildlife, and outdoor recreation."

PART FOUR

The Distribution of Income

54

Geographic
Mobility of ········
American Workers

American workers are constantly on the
move in the process of adjusting to change
in the economy. This analysis of the
geographic labor mobility demonstrates
how private labor markets function, and
provides a basis for evaluating their
effectiveness.

MANPOWER REPORT OF THE PRESIDENT

Because of the dynamic nature of the American economy, changes in
the numbers and types of workers needed by employers take place continually throughout the country. The result is frequent local imbalances
between labor demand and labor supply, which are always in the process
of correction as workers move to jobs and jobs to workers.

One of the great historic movements of workers—the migration from
the South—exemplifies the combinations of factors which can contribute
to worker mobility. High birth rates and the discrimination against Negro
workers in the South, together with rising farm productivity and underemployment of farm workers, have tended to push workers out, while
the rapid growth of industry in the North and later the West have pulled
them in these directions. The resulting migration has reduced, though by
no means eliminated, underemployment and poverty among Southern
farm workers.

The persistent labor surpluses which have developed in all too many
local areas, as a result usually of declining or departed industries, have
been another source of economic pressure for migration. This has been
true, for example, in the coal mining areas of Appalachia and the former
textile towns of New England. Many workers have left such areas. Yet
many are still there who have little or no work and live in poverty but
lack the means or motivation to look for and find employment elsewhere.

In some areas, jobs have disappeared almost overnight. Plant shutdowns

From *Manpower Report of the President* and *A Report on Manpower Requirements, Resources, Utilization, and Training* by the United States Department of
Labor, March 1965, pp. 145–151, 153, 154.

or severe employment cutbacks, stemming sometimes from technological change-overs or other company actions and sometimes from the ending of work on government contracts, can eliminate in a very short time many of the jobs on which a community has depended. The result can be a community-wide disaster unless advance plans have been made by the company, in cooperation with community and government agencies, to aid the affected workers in qualifying for and obtaining new jobs—preferably within, but if necessary outside, the area.

In sharp contrast are the labor shortages and consequent need for in-migration of workers which have been created in some areas by the building of defense installations or other new plants. In general, professional and skilled workers have been in great demand in these places and many have been recruited from other localities.

HIGHLIGHTS OF THE FINDINGS AND NEEDED DIRECTIONS OF ACTION

There is evidence that migration of workers has eased but by no means eliminated local imbalances in labor demand and supply and the corollary problems of joblessness or, in some cases, labor scarcity. Before the effectiveness of migration in matching men and jobs can be properly evaluated, a number of important questions must be answered. How likely are workers to move in response to the lack of employment opportunities in depressed areas or the attraction of better opportunities elsewhere? How many of those who migrate thereby succeed in improving their employment situation? And how many make uninformed and ill-advised moves and thus merely add to the pool of jobless workers in the community to which they go? What steps need to be taken to increase the gains and diminish the costs of worker migration, from the viewpoint both of the individuals and of the communities involved?

These are some of the questions to which this chapter is addressed.[1]

In evaluating the contributions worker migration makes to the matching of men and jobs, there is much one sees that is encouraging. In general, workers have gravitated in recent years toward areas of better employment opportunity. Men leaving depressed areas have usually fared better than those remaining there, and men entering prosperous areas have frequently shared in the favorable opportunities they offer. Areas of high employment have provided jobs for many low-skilled as well as higher-skilled migrants, and for Negroes as well as whites. Even workers who had been unemployed for long periods have often improved their job situations by migrating. Also, workers previously employed as laborers have sometimes succeeded in getting higher-level jobs.

Nevertheless, some workers are no better off—or even worse off—after migrating than they were before. Although people tend to migrate to areas with good opportunities, a considerable number—including many Negroes—mistakenly go to areas where there is little chance of employment, particularly if one is unskilled. Many areas which formerly offered opportunities for large numbers of unskilled workers no longer do so. And in some areas, the job market situation can change sharply within a short period of time. Therefore, migrants who do not have recent,

[1] The analysis in this chapter is based primarily on data from (a) U.S. Department of Commerce, Bureau of the Census, *U.S. Census of Population: 1960,* and (b) U.S. Department of Labor, Bureau of Labor Statistics, *Geographic Mobility and Employment Status,* Special Labor Force Report 44 (1964).

accurate information on opportunities in other areas or jobs lined up in advance run a great risk of unemployment after reaching their destinations.

Older workers, the unskilled, and the uneducated are those least likely to move and those who fare worst when they do. They are the ones with least resources for moving and least access to information on employment opportunities elsewhere. They are also much less likely than more skilled workers to have firm offers of jobs in other areas. When they do move—possibly as a last resort after a long and fruitless search for work locally—they may go to communities where there is no more demand for their services than there was in their home community. As a result, unskilled workers who migrate are subject to recurring unemployment and tend to make repeated moves. Many return to their home communities to resume the hunt for employment.

In contrast, the better educated young people, who are those most likely to migrate, generally have good opportunities for employment after moving. Their exodus from depressed areas—and, in the case of Negroes, from the South generally—is usually to their personal benefit. This outflow has serious consequences, however, for the areas they leave. In losing many of their most promising young men and women, these areas lose a resource of critical importance to their economic and social development.

These findings indicate a need for action, far beyond that already underway, in five general directions:

First, *more and better information on employment opportunities in job market areas throughout the country* should be widely available to guide potential migrants, especially those planning moves to distant communities. Special efforts are needed to tell workers that such information can be obtained from public employment offices. At the same time, the interarea information and placement services provided by the employment service system should be strengthened. These measures should help to reduce the large amount of misdirected mobility, and thus prevent needless hardship to individuals and burdens on the community.

Second, *financial and other aids to migration* should be provided for workers who would improve their job situation by moving but cannot do so for lack of funds or knowledge of how and where to look for jobs. Unemployed workers caught in depressed areas, even some with relatively little skill, could often find employment by moving to more prosperous communities. Improved interarea informational and job finding services would help such workers. But many also need financial aids, such as will be provided to a few by the new pilot program of relocation allowances set up under the Manpower Development and Training Act.

Third, migrants need much *more help in finding jobs* in the communities to which they move. Many go through a prolonged period of joblessness after reaching their destinations. Here again, what is needed is wider public knowledge of the placement and other services available through the public employment offices and a strengthening of these services.

Fourth, unskilled workers need *greater opportunities for training and retraining*, including more basic education if necessary, to qualify them for jobs either in or outside their home communities. Many unemployed workers at the lowest levels of skill are unable to move. Some would be no better off if they did. For such workers and for those with obsolete skills, training for currently available employment is necessary whether they move or not.

Fifth, expanded efforts are needed to speed the *economic development of depressed areas,* thus bringing jobs to workers. The continual outflow of the younger, better-educated workers is draining the economic potential of many areas—leaving unskilled and older workers stranded. These findings underline the importance of continued and expanded area redevelopment programs and of the broad regional development programs recently recommended by the President.

MIGRATION AND THE SEARCH FOR WORK

About one out of 15 persons migrates each year—that is, moves from one county to another. About half of them move to another state. Many of the migrants are young people whose mobility is associated with an attempt to find a job, a discharge from military service, completion of education, and personal considerations such as marriage.

Most men are employed when they migrate, and many move to take other— presumably better—jobs. About two-thirds of all men 18 to 64 years old who moved between March 1962 and March 1963 were employed at the beginning of the period. Nevertheless, the rate of migration was about twice as high among unemployed as employed workers—11 compared with 6 per cent. Clearly, unemployment and the search for work are very important motivations for migration.

In general, migrants have an above-average level of education. Of the 25- to 29-year-old men who migrated between 1955 and 1960, for example, 25 per cent were college graduates, as compared with 9 per cent of the nonmigrants. And a lower proportion of the migrants than of the nonmigrants in this age group had completed only eight years or less of school (14 and 23 per cent, respectively). To look at the figures a different way, 55 per cent of all male college graduates 25 to 29 years old lived in a different county in 1960 than in 1955, compared with only 29 per cent of the men who had completed but not gone beyond high school. It is apparent that geographic mobility drops off sharply with decreasing education.

Similarly, professional workers have much greater geographic mobility than any other occupational group. About half the men 25 to 29 years of age in professional, technical, and kindred occupations migrated between 1955 and 1960, as compared with less than a third of the clerical workers and even smaller proportions of the blue-collar workers. . . .

Migration rates for the white population are much higher than for the nonwhite. This is true for both employed and unemployed workers. The low migration rate of nonwhite workers is probably associated with the fact that relatively few of them have had a chance to qualify for the higher skilled occupations. Also, nonwhites less often receive offers of employment in other areas. Altogether, only one out of every five nonwhite men migrants reported that he moved to "take a job" or "because of a transfer" between March 1962 and March 1963—just about half the corresponding figure for white men. (See Chart 27.)

Reasons for Migration

Reasons related to employment explain at least half of the moves made by workers. Twelve per cent of the men who migrated between March 1962 and March 1963 reported that they moved "to look for work" and 38 per cent to "take a job" or because of "job transfer." Employment prospects were certainly important considerations also in the moves made by workers who said they migrated primarily for personal or family reasons. . . .

Some of the men who reported that they moved to "take a job" had undoubtedly searched for this job before moving. This was easiest for persons who moved only

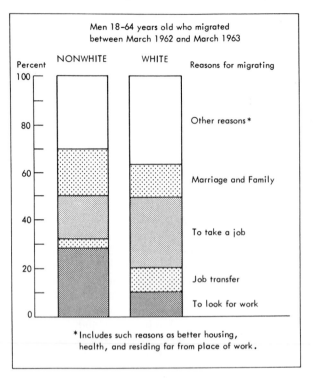

Chart 27.   Relatively More Nonwhite Than White Migrants Move to Look for Work—Relatively Fewer Have Jobs Arranged in Advance.

Source: U.S. Department of Labor.

short distances and could explore job possibilities before shifting their residence. Those who moved over long distances had had much less chance to do this and more often had periods of unemployment after they moved.[2]

These long-distance migrants are particularly in need of assistance in job seeking after they reach their destinations. In many cases, the trip back would be prohibitively expensive, and relatives and friends who might provide financial aid or help in finding a job are no longer nearby.

The particularly high rate of geographic movement among professional, technical, and kindred workers referred to earlier is explained, in part, by the geographic concentrations of jobs in certain professions. An extreme example is the localization of employment opportunities for specialists in atomic energy in a few scattered areas. On the other hand, in some other professions where employment is widespread (for example, teaching and social work), the demand for qualified personnel is so great that many opportunities arise to fill jobs elsewhere, and an

---

[2] Data for a period shortly after World War II show that the proportion of male migrants who moved to look for work was twice as high among interstate migrants as among migrants who moved within a state. See U.S. Department of Commerce, Bureau of the Census, *Current Population Reports*, Series P–20, No. 4 (Washington: U.S. Government Printing Office, 1947).

individual's rate of advancement may depend to a considerable extent on his willingness to move to a new area. The professions are also relatively well-paid occupations, where financial resources for moving are usually available, sources of information on job opportunities throughout the country are better than average, and motivation to advance is generally keen.

Among unskilled and semiskilled workers the situation is reversed. These workers have much lower rates of migration because they usually lack information about job opportunities, seldom have the resources for moving, and have limited employment opportunities in other areas, as well as locally. The barriers to migration of unskilled workers make it very difficult for them to move even from the worst depressed areas, where their competitive difficulties in finding jobs are compounded by the presence of jobless workers with higher qualifications. However, unskilled workers who do migrate may significantly increase their opportunities for higher-level jobs. Almost 30 per cent of the migrants who had been nonfarm laborers in March 1962 had jobs as operatives in March 1963.

Employment Effects of Migration

Jobless workers who move to other areas are often able to improve their employment situation in the process. Among men 25 to 44 years old who were unemployed in March 1962, about four-fifths of those who migrated in the following year were employed in March 1963, compared with only three-fifths of those who did not migrate. (See Chart 28. . . .) Even among workers who were job-

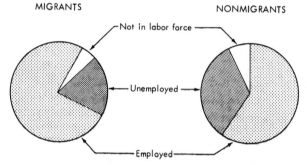

MIGRANTS   NONMIGRANTS

Not in labor force

Unemployed

Employed

Civilian labor force status in March 1963 of men 25–44 years old who were unemployed in March 1962

Chart 28. Unemployed Workers Who Migrate Are More Likely to Find Jobs Than Nonmigrants.

Source: U.S. Department of Labor.

less both in March 1962 and just before they moved, most found jobs after moving.

Nevertheless, migration, unless well planned and well informed, is no sure road to immediate improvement in a worker's employment situation. Workers who recently migrated have higher unemployment rates than nonmigrants. This is true in all age groups over 35, with the greatest differences occurring at the oldest ages. . . . Even migrants who move to take jobs already arranged for are sometimes unable to meet the demands of the new job or are laid off because of changing employment requirements.

Migrants 45 years old and over have a more severe unemployment problem after they move than men 25 to 44 years old. They have less education and face age discrimination. And since community and family ties are stronger among older persons, migration is probably a last resort for this greatly disadvantaged group.

The difficulties in finding jobs encountered by some migrants diminish with the passage of time, however. Thus, the 1960 unemployment rate for men who had migrated sometime during the preceding five years was only half the unemployment rate for those who had migrated within the preceding year. Even migrants over 45 had a much lower unemployment rate several years after migrating than during the first year after arrival in a new community.

On the other hand, many migrants tend to be repeat movers, and many actually return to their homes. As a result, they have to make the adjustments accompanying migration more than once. This is particularly true of unskilled workers.

There is other evidence that moves made by the lower skilled workers are less certain to result in improvement in their job situation than those made by the more skilled. Of the nonfarm laborers who migrated between March 1962 and March 1963, 26 out of 100 moved to look for work, compared with only 2 out of 100 professional and technical workers, most of whom have jobs arranged in advance. Clearly, the lack of advance contacts with employers, as well as of good information on the geographic availability of jobs, is greatest among low-skilled workers—those most subject to unemployment and most likely to have difficulty in locating jobs.

*   *   *

Character of Areas with Migration Gains and Losses

In the country generally, migration losses have been greatest in the sections which are most rural. This is shown by an analysis of net migration losses and gains between 1950 and 1960 for counties classified according to the urban-rural distribution of their population in 1950.

All groups of counties where more than half of the population was rural had migration losses. And the higher the proportion of the county population in rural areas, the higher the rate of migration loss—still another reflection of the shrinking employment opportunities in agriculture.

The groups of counties that were predominantly urban gained population. However, the gains were sharpest not within big cities but in less urbanized counties, including rapidly growing suburbs and middle-sized cities.

Just as people migrate from rural to urban areas, they move from areas of low income to areas of high income. Counties with low average family incomes lost people through migration between 1950 and 1960, with the heaviest losses in the lowest income counties. (See Chart 29.) Gains through migration occurred only in the group of counties with median family incomes of $6,000 and over. The counties where the median family income was $3,000 or less lost half of their young adults, probably their most valuable resource.

*   *   *

Migration Into and Out of Areas of High and Low Unemployment

Since the net migration changes we have so far observed are only the differences between in-migration and out-migration, they often mask important information about these component elements. For this reason, it is necessary to examine the "gross" figures on in-migrants and out-migrants separately. The findings of such

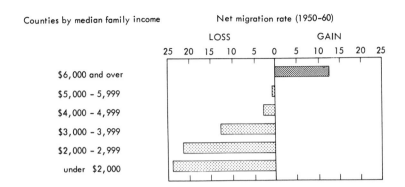

Counties by median family income   Net migration rate (1950–60)

Chart 29. High Income Counties Attract Population While the Lowest Show the Largest Losses.

Source: U.S. Department of Labor, based on data from U.S. Department of Agriculture.

an examination are here presented for persons entering and leaving 20 Standard Metropolitan Statistical Areas between 1955 and 1960. . . . In order to study the relationship between the character of these migrants and the employment situation in the areas they entered or left, 10 areas with very high unemployment and 10 with relatively low unemployment were selected.

One major finding, which suggests how deceptive net migration figures can be is that although the high unemployment areas lost population on balance and the low unemployment areas had gains, the gross flow of out-migrants was relatively less from the areas of high unemployment (10 per cent versus 14 per cent). The explanation of this seeming contradiction lies in the smaller proportion of persons entering the areas which had high unemployment (7 per cent versus 17 per cent). The net result of these separate movements was a migration loss of 3 per cent from the ten depressed areas—whereas the more prosperous areas had a migration gain of 3 per cent.

It is significant also that relatively few of the unskilled or semiskilled workers in high unemployment areas left and few entered. The workers leaving these areas, like migrants generally, were younger and had more education to equip them for job opportunities elsewhere than those who did not leave. . . . The median age of the out-migrants was only 26½ years, or about eight years less than the average age of the residents (age data are for males five years old and over). And the proportion of men in professional and technical occupations was nearly twice as high for the out-migrants as for residents. Furthermore, the unemployment rate of the men who had left these high unemployment areas was slightly lower in 1960 than that of the men still residing there, despite the difficult period of adjustment experienced by many migrants.

In contrast, men who had left the more prosperous areas of good employment opportunities had higher rates of unemployment than those who remained there. Their unemployment rates were also higher than those for men who had entered these areas. Moreover, judging from information on the 1959 family income of migrants and nonmigrants, men who left the low unemployment areas fared worse financially than those who remained in or entered these areas and were able to benefit from the good economic conditions there. Median family incomes of these groups were $6,200 for migrants who left these areas, compared with about $7,000 for persons who remained and $6,700 for those who entered.

Job opportunities in the prosperous areas attracted considerable numbers of blue-collar as well as white-collar workers. Thus, the increase in nonfarm laborers resulting from net in-migration between 1955 and 1960 accounted for 7 per cent of all laborers in these areas in 1960.

The population increase resulting from net in-migration in areas of low unemployment was somewhat sharper among Negro than white men. Relatively fewer Negroes than whites entered such areas, but so few Negroes left that, on balance, there was a greater gain in the Negro than in the white population. It is noteworthy also that, in these areas, the net gains in the number of Negro workers brought about by migration extended to all major occupational groups (exclusive of farm workers).

In the high unemployment areas, Negroes had a lower rate of net out-migration than whites. This difference resulted mainly from the smaller proportion of Negroes than of whites leaving these depressed areas, rather than from white-nonwhite differences in rates of entry.

It was, of course, greatly to the Negroes' disadvantage that they did not leave the high unemployment areas at as great a rate as whites. It is also most unfortunate that they entered areas of low unemployment at a lower rate than whites but moved into high unemployment areas at almost as rapid a rate as white workers. Because of the stiff competition for jobs in these latter areas and the discrimination which all too often confronts Negro workers, a very high proportion of the Negro men who moved into these areas were jobless in 1960. Their rate of unemployment was 22 per cent, as compared with 7 per cent for all men in-migrants.

These figures stand in sharp contrast to the rates for the men who made better advised moves to areas of low unemployment. There, only 8.5 per cent of the non-white men and 3.7 per cent of all men in-migrants were unemployed.

To summarize briefly:

> High unemployment areas lost population through migration between 1955 and 1960, while low unemployment areas gained population. The gross number of out-migrants from high unemployment areas was not large, but relatively fewer persons entered these areas than moved to areas of better economic opportunity.
>
> On balance, workers tended to move toward areas with low unemployment, which offered job opportunities in a wide range of occupations for both white and Negro workers.
>
> Men entering low unemployment areas—including Negroes—were able to share in the better opportunities in these areas while those entering areas with poor economic conditions fared badly.
>
> Men who left high unemployment areas tended to be younger, better educated, and more highly skilled and to have less unemployment than those who remained. Also, Negro men less often left these areas than white men. It thus appears that the groups with the greatest competitive disadvantages in the job market were the ones most likely to remain in depressed areas.
>
> Though Negroes entered areas with low unemployment at a much lower rate than white men, they moved to areas with substantial unemployment at almost as high a rate as whites. Yet the choice between moving to a good or to a poor economic area is especially critical for Negroes, because of their particularly high rates of unemployment in depressed areas and their low rates of out-migration from such areas.

55

Why Workers Hate to Change Jobs

The effectiveness of a free labor market depends on labor mobility. This article shows how fringe benefits (for example, pension plans) and the age composition of the labor force have contributed to a decline in labor mobility, but predicts better results in the long run.

BUSINESS WEEK

Sarah Williams is a laid-off auto worker with 13 years' seniority. If the auto industry prospers, she may be called back to her $2.40-an-hour job of running a sewing machine in the upholstery department at the Dodge plant in Detroit.

While she's waiting to be called back, she isn't trying to get a permanent job elsewhere. And temporary work is almost nonexistent. So she remains unemployed.

Sarah Williams is a living example of the immobility that seniority rights are building into the labor force. If it were not for the equity she has built up in 13 years at the Dodge plant, she could get a full-time job tomorrow in the garment industry, where skilled operators are at a premium.

As it is, she doesn't want to lose her pension rights and other benefits, particularly not for lower pay than she was getting—and even if she did, employers in the garment trade would think twice about hiring a woman who would quit as soon as Dodge recalled her.

Vested Interest

There are many workers who have the same problem as Sarah Williams.

"Employees try to ride out layoffs and come back," says an executive of an auto company. "There's less tendency to have a 'float' in the labor market after employees have built up equity in various benefit plans."

Seniority itself is not one of these benefits, but it is closely related to the

Reprinted from the June 6, 1959 issue of *Business Week* by special permission; copyright 1959 by the McGraw-Hill Book Company, Inc.

package of rights that make up the employee's equity: supplementary unemployment benefits, pensions, holidays, paid vacations, health plans. The more seniority a worker has, the greater this equity and the greater his reluctance to change jobs. And this reluctance extends to workers who are nearing the point of gaining greater equity in these benefits.

This tends to leave only the youngest workers with any great freedom to change jobs without sacrifice of equity under seniority rights. And there are fewer of the youngest generation of workers, because of the low birth rate of the Depression years.

I. EMPLOYER'S ATTITUDE

The big factor is pension rights; most other benefits are so widespread that they have little effect on a worker's willingness to move from one job to another. They work two ways. They govern an employer's hiring policies about as much as they tend to freeze workers on their high-seniority jobs.

This shows up particularly in a key management decision: Do we hire more people or do we pay overtime to the present work force? The costs of "fringe" benefits are no longer marginal costs, from the employer's viewpoint, and management often decides it's cheaper to pay overtime at premium rates than to hire additional workers for what may be a short time.

Not Marginal Costs

According to the U.S. Chamber of Commerce, the costs of labor benefits, having doubled in 12 years, now average 22 per cent of payroll.

A national food concern estimates its overall costs for the so-called fringe benefits at 78¢ an hour for each employee. It figures retirement plans, social security, unemployment benefits, and workmen's compensation at 23.6¢ an hour; military leave, holidays, vacations, premiums, lunch and rest periods, and shift differentials at 54.4¢ an hour.

A farm equipment manufacturer estimates employee benefits at slightly more than 50¢ an hour. The American Iron & Steel Institute cites 70¢ an hour for such benefits in the steel industry, and the auto industry calculates 62¢ an hour. These costs depend more on the number of men at work than on the number of payroll hours. So up to a point it may cost no more to pay premium rates for overtime work than to add new people with a corresponding increase in fringe costs.

In weighing overtime against new hirings, management must also consider other costs that are hard to pin down, such as retraining of new people and the cost of additional foremen for the new work crews.

A Black Eye

For two other reasons, too, employers often elect to work people overtime, regardless of out-of-pocket costs, rather than hire new workers who may have to be laid off in a few months.

One reason is the touchy question of public relations. Layoffs give an employer a black eye among the company's total work force, in the plant's community, even in the financial world. "The bad publicity just isn't worth it," an auto executive says.

The other reason is the measurable effect on the company's rates for unemployment benefits. To hire a man and then lay him off after six months will hurt the employer's rated experience, which determines the premiums or taxes for these benefits. A bad employment experience rating in Michigan, for example, can cost the employer up to 4.5 per cent of taxable payroll, or up to 12¢ an hour.

II. HOLDDOWN ON MOBILITY

The ability and inclination of workers to move from job to job has been one of the great strengths of the American economy. Generations of historians have cited this factor as a major force in keeping the economy flexible and dynamic, nourishing the development of new frontier regions and new industries. That's why so many economists today are worrying about evidence that workers are less willing to move.

Most observers agree that the decline in mobility of labor is real and serious. They point to figures that the Bureau of Labor Statistics keeps on the number of "quits" in industry. Allowing for business ups and downs, this quit rate shows an apparent long-term tapering. In a report to the Fund for the Republic entitled *Pension Funds and Economic Freedom*, Robert Tilove says: "The conclusion seems inescapable that most private pension plans . . . exercise a restraining influence on labor mobility."

The Restless Young

Part of the change, however, must be attributed not to pensions but to a shrinkage in the number of the younger workers—the most mobile group, still searching for a permanent niche and not yet tied economically to any employer.

As early as 1913–14, a study showed that 81.3 per cent of all workers "separated" had been on the payroll less than a year. Arthur M. Ross, a University of California economist, mentions a 1949 study of manual workers in New Haven, mostly nonunion labor. This survey found that 71 per cent of the voluntary changers of jobs had less than three years' service, 80 per cent less than five years, 94 per cent less than 10 years.

It's an assumption among most experts that the lowest seniority is among the younger workers. That group is shrinking as a proportion of the total labor force. In 1940, the civilian labor force had 14.5 per cent in the 20–24 age group; in 1956, only 8.8 per cent. In 1940, the group between 45 and 64 years old made up 27.2 per cent of the total; in 1956, a full 33 per cent.

Problems in Manufacturing

The percentage shift has probably been even higher in manufacturing, which has more problems than employers as a whole must face. The actual number of production workers in manufacturing has not increased since 1951, while employment has boomed in wholesale and retail trades, finance, insurance, and government.

For one thing, manufacturing seems less attractive to the young, although its wage rates are high enough to hold onto the older workers. Mechanization has eliminated many jobs where a beginner might have gotten his start a generation ago.

Thus, manufacturing is more and more isolated from the rest of the labor market, in contrast to its former role as a vast pool with workers coming in and going out. With today's specialized technology, it is harder, for example, for a farm boy to become a machine operator, than to move out into retailing or banking.

III. MORE MOBILITY AHEAD?

At any time, in any economy, some people should be shifting from job to job. If manpower should become inflexible and immobile, the U.S. would be confronted with a serious economic problem.

Some people think this problem is developing right now, but others see signs of a change. The current trend toward immobility contains the seeds of its own counter-trend, some experts say.

Pension Influence

For example, pension plans now act as a drag on job-changing, but they may prove eventually to have an equal and opposite effect.

Gerry E. Morse, industrial relations vice-president of Minneapolis-Honeywell Regulator Co., notes that a 10-year minimum for pension eligibility allows companies to hire overage men (retired policemen as guards, for instance) without adding to pension costs.

Moreover, says Robert Tilove, "if a worker knows that pension plans—from the new job and perhaps from the old one as well—will still give him security in his years of retirement, he can feel a little freer to apply his personal savings to the risks of changing jobs."

"Money in the bank is an element of freedom," says Tilove. "And the ultimate right to a pension may offer some of the liberating influence of liquid assets."

Tilove adds that the vesting of pension rights (giving the worker an equity that he can take with him upon leaving a company) will also enlarge mobility, though fully vested plans will doubtless remain a rarity as far as blue-collar workers are concerned.

Early Retirement

More important to the mobility of the labor force, says Tilove, is the prospect that pensions can free workers from physically demanding jobs at an age early enough to let people take lighter jobs afterward.

Tilove cites the pension plan of United Parcel Service of New York, Inc., which has enabled some men in the 55 to 64 age bracket to retire. A high proportion of these men have gone into less demanding jobs, such as clerk, time-keeper, school bus driver, bank guard, messenger, dispatcher, and butter and eggs salesman.

This sort of development, Tilove points out, "may in time make a major contribution to labor mobility, to an extension of the working life, and therefore to national production."

Mobility within a given industry is already being aided by negotiation of industrywide pensions and by reciprocity between pension funds. A New York truck driver, for example, can switch to coverage in a New Jersey pension fund without sacrificing any retirement benefits, and a ship's officer can move from an East Coast to a West Coast company under similar terms.

IV. TURNING POINT

In any case, the economists' worries about labor mobility will almost certainly end in the next half-dozen years.

The U.S. has reached a turning point in the composition of its labor force. The proportion of young people has in all probability hit bottom. The "hollow generation" born in the Depression years is already at work, and the input of young workers will increase rapidly as the wartime children come of age.

Entrance of large numbers of young people into the labor market is bound to boost the quit rate. Young people jump from job to job, exploring the possibilities open to them, with little regard for the fringe benefits they aren't yet entitled to. And their search for the "right" job can be expected to restore normal mobility to the labor force as a whole.

56

Sit-Down
at General Motors

It is easy to forget the frequently violent
and emotional background of industrial
unionism. This vignette of labor history
describes the period when management
had not yet recognized the right of
employees to bargain through unions of
their own choice. Unions defied companies,
the courts, and police in their struggle
for recognition.

HERBERT HARRIS

*   *   *

The "sit-down" which between September 1, 1936, and June 1, 1937,
involved 484,711 American workers not only in motors but in rubber,
steel, textiles, shipbuilding, subways, oil-refining, shoes, newspaper pub-
lishing, baking, aircraft, and countless other manufacturing service and
retailing spheres, is a strike of a very special kind. Whereas in the everyday
variety employees leave mill or mine or store or factory to picket outside
their place of business, in the sit-down they remain inside at or near their
usual posts but do no work. They just sit or stretch out on the floor or
benches or loll around on their feet. And if a sit-down lasts long enough—
dozens of them in mass-production plants last only a few minutes or a few
hours—it becomes a stay-in, properly speaking, though the term sit-down is
already a colloquialism used to describe this technique, per se, whatever
its duration.

Its advantages are obvious. Police and militia can more easily disperse
a picket line in the open than an "occupied" plant where windows may
be barricaded and gates barred. "You can't ride a horse through a brick
wall," remarked a grizzled old unionist in Detroit during the General
Motors stay-ins. "With the sit-down today the boys don't have to put up
with that, anyway."

*   *   *

From *American Labor,* by Herbert Harris (New Haven: Yale University Press,
1938), pp. 288, 296–304. Reprinted by permission.

From the mists and fogs of emotion-charged words marking the discussion of the sit-down one clear question emerges: Is purely legal title to a producing property the only right that should be recognized in the American democracy? The answer of the United Automobile Workers was put by its "in-and-out" vice-president, Wyndham Mortimer, when he inquired:

> Is it wrong for a worker to stay at his job? The laws of state and nation, in a hundred ways, recognize that the worker has a definite claim upon his job; more fundamentally . . . every workman has a moral right to continue on his job unless some definite misconduct justifies his discharge. These sit-down strikers [i.e., in Flint and elsewhere] are staying at their work-places; no one has a better right to be there than these men themselves. . . . The sit-down strikers have performed valuable services in those factories; General Motors and the public alike have profited. . . . To call them trespassers now, and to deny their right as human beings to remain with their jobs . . . is manifestly unjust.

In Flint, Michigan, the power of General Motors was arrayed against the implications of this view in a community where, out of 165,000 inhabitants, 50,000 depended directly upon the company for livelihoods gained from Buick, Chevrolet, and Fisher Body Plants. Anti-sit-down sentiment, after the first days of the strike, was crystallized by an organization called the Flint Alliance. It was in theory composed of "loyal employees" most of whom somehow contrived to resemble barflies and poolroom toughs from nearby Detroit. The Alliance also contained a sprinkling of General Motors executives and subadministrators and people from its technical and commercial divisions, some local businessmen, and almost all the vigilante-minded personalities in the vicinity, the kind of men, and there are many of them, who in their perpetual adolescence come fully alive only when they can have "adventure" by doing physical injury to others. The Alliance's propaganda was fabricated by the high-pressure, high-priced Floyd E. Williamson who, himself an "outsider" imported from Manhattan for his special purpose, amusingly enough based a large part of his anti-union blasts upon the "un-American activities" of "outside" organizers. The chairman of the Alliance was George E. Boysen, former paymaster in a Buick factory, and latterly himself the owner of a spark-plug concern. As the sit-down progressed, Alliance spokesmen grew daily more vociferous in their demands for violence, some of them promising that soon law and order committees of indignant citizenry would forcibly evict the sit-downers who by the thousand had "dug-in" for a long siege.

To oust the strikers, General Motors had secured from Judge Edward Black an injunction which commanded them to vacate company property and also forbade picketing. Although he owned nearly $200,000 worth of General Motors stock, Judge Black considered himself sufficiently impartial to issue his edict, a belief not entirely in accord with the more commendable traditions of the American bench. When Sheriff Wolcott delivered the Black document to the sit-downers he was jeered and good-naturedly told to go home. Meantime, company officials, both local and national, and U.A.W. and C.I.O. leaders were busy fencing, mustering all their skill for parry and riposte, all of them with an eye on the public gallery.

On January 12, the company shut off the heat in Fisher Body Plant No. 2 and its own gray-uniformed police, reinforced by regulars from the local Flint force, were instructed to prevent the shipment of food into the building. It was hoped that this "diet of cold and hunger" would break the morale of the sit-downers.

Inside the plant, the men missed their lunch, shivered, and grew restive at the prospect of being also deprived of their dinner. Shortly before seven o'clock that evening, a United Automobile Workers sound truck rolled up before the great rectangle of Fisher No. 2, with Victor Reuther, a top-notch organizer for the union, at the microphone. At first he politely asked the police, both public and private, for permission to have food sent in to the sit-downers from the union's kitchen. The metallic lungs of the amplifier lifted his voice high above the sounds of the street until everyone within a half-mile radius could hear his plea. The officers, both the gray and the blue, were mute. Reuther tried another tack. He appealed to them as workers, urging the necessity for cooperation among all kinds and degrees of labor. There was no response, save the cheers of the sit-downers. He then became more aggressive, assuring the officers that strikers outside the plant would get food to the sitters. Some fifteen minutes later a group of pickets carrying pails of coffee and cartons of buns, like an oversized backfield, starting on an end run, bowled over the police guarding the door to the plant and brought food to their famished friends.

At 8:45 some sixty policemen set upon pickets stationed at plant entrances, clubbed them with night-sticks, and drove them inside the building. A sergeant smashed a glass pane in one of the doors and thrust the nozzle of a tear-gas gun through the jagged space, pumping shells into the vast interior. Other officers fired buckshot into pickets and men clustered near the door, wounding fourteen who were later removed to the hospital.

The sit-downers replied to this attack with literally everything they had: coffee-mugs, pop-bottles, and steel automobile hinges weighing two pounds each. At the beginning of the battle, a clarion voice from the sound truck cried: "We wanted peace. General Motors chose war. Give it to 'em!" In the road strikers formed a phalanx around the sound truck, repelled all efforts of police to dismantle it, and overturned three police cars and another belonging to the sheriff.

At midnight the policemen closed in their ranks and, with guns cracking, tried to rush the main entrance, only to be met by a devastating stream of water from a big fire hose which, along with the steel-hinge missiles, compelled them to retreat and finally to abandon their assault. This affair was promptly named "The Battle of the Running Bulls."

The bloodshed of that night, and the fears of more violence to come, resulted in the appearance of 1,500 of Michigan's National Guardsmen in Flint. Acting under instructions from the cool-headed, humanitarian Governor Murphy, who was valiantly seeking to settle the strike by pacific means, they managed on the whole to preserve order almost impartially, though various commanders chafed at the restraints placed on them and would have preferred to try out their new machine guns, howitzers, and knowledge of the "how to quell" riots sections of military manuals on the sit-downers, in response to the beseechings of the Flint Alliance that the requirements of patriotism be fulfilled.[1]

Meantime—after the strikers by a ruse had captured the crucial Chevrolet motor assembly plant No. 4, and John L. Lewis had called on President Roosevelt to intercede for them against the "economic royalists represented by General Motors and the Du Ponts," who had opposed his reelection with the same fervor that the auto workers had supported it; and also after Washington conferences between Secretary of Labor Frances Perkins and Alfred P. Sloan, president, and

---

[1] One major in particular confessed his bitter disappointment that he was unable to test the value of his pet idea, shooting vomiting gas into the sit-downers via the plants' ventilating systems.

William S. Knudsen, vice-president of the company, had produced mutual re-criminations—General Motors obtained from Circuit Judge Paul V. Gadola a significant and sweeping court order. It directed the sit-downers to evacuate company-owned plants under penalty of imprisonment for contempt of court and a fine of $15,000,000, the estimated value of the invested properties. Again Sheriff Wolcott served to mocking and derisive groups of determined men the order that set 3 P.M. on February 3 as the deadline for leaving the struck plants.

In reply the sit-downers sent telegrams to Governor Murphy, who was still exerting almost superhuman patience and persuasion to bring both sides into agreement. The message from Fisher Body Plant No. 1 read in part:

> We the workers . . . have carried on a stay-in strike over a month in order to make General Motors Corporation obey the law [2] and engage in collective bargaining. . . . Unarmed as we are, the introduction of the militia, sheriffs, or police with murderous weapons will mean a blood-bath of unarmed workers. . . . We have decided to stay. . . . We have no illusions about the sacrifices which this decision will entail. We fully expect that if a violent effort to oust us is made many of us will be killed, and we take this means of making it known to our wives, our children, to the people of the state of Michigan, and the country that if this result follows from the attempt to eject us, you are the one who must be held responsible for our deaths.

The night before the "zero hour" day of February 3, the sit-downers, pallid under blazing arc-lights, listened grimly to their radios, or played cards or parcheesi or checkers or dominoes, or tried to lose themselves in newspapers or magazines, or talked in subdued tones. Many were convinced that the morrow meant massacre. For defense against expected machine guns, inadequate clubs dangled from their belts. An air of almost Oriental passivity, as of men who wait in resignation for the beat of destiny's drum, hung over them. Their faces were stern and thoughtful, and few slept.

In the morning roads leading into Flint were filled with cars and trucks carrying union sympathizers from Akron, Lansing, Detroit, and Toledo, who by the thousand swarmed over the town and had to take over the direction of traffic themselves, for no policemen were in sight. The visitors moved toward the various sit-down plants, and only the women's emergency brigades, with their red and green berets, brought color to a somber procession that for weapons held pokers, broom handles, and pieces of pipe.

While Flint's clocks ticked on toward the showdown hour of three in the afternoon, Governor Murphy in Detroit finally succeeded in arranging a conference between William S. Knudsen for the company and John L. Lewis for the United Automobile Workers. To Sheriff Wolcott, who had the duty of enforcing the Gadola eviction order, Governor Murphy wired that everything should be held in abeyance during the Knudsen-Lewis conversations; and the Sheriff, more than pleased to oblige, suddenly discovered that he lacked proper legal sanction, anyway, along with a sufficient force to carry out the Gadola edict, although the Flint Alliance and the company's legal staff in Flint assured him that they could together remedy both deficiencies.

When this turn of events was made known, sit-downers, pickets, and unionists from other cities made high holiday. Their violins, saxophones, banjos, cornets

[2] The National Labor Relations Act.

struck up hill-billy airs and square-dance tunes, and men and women swung partners joyously over the frozen lawns surrounding the various plants.

Next day the company complied with President Roosevelt's request that in the public interest its representatives should again meet with spokesmen of the strikers. A wearing week of conferences ensued between William S. Knudsen, G. Donaldson Brown, and John Thomas Smith for General Motors, and John L. Lewis, Lee Pressman (general counsel for the C.I.O.), Homer Martin, and Wyndham Mortimer for the strikers. Time after time only the moral strength and suasions of Governor Murphy, who presided over the negotiations, prevented their collapse, and cigarette and cigar ashes spilled over trays amid the temper-fraying clashes of strong wills and stronger wants.

Eight days later, the Governor, his face haggard with strain and lack of sleep, had the great personal triumph of seeing at long last a meeting of minds out of which came the agreement terminating one of the most important capital-labor disputes in recent times.

The contract signed by General Motors and the United Automobile Workers was a great step forward for unionism in motors and contained seven basic provisions: (1) recognition was to be granted to the U.A.W. for its members only, and not as sole collective bargaining agent; (2) straight seniority rules were to prevail after six months of service; (3) shop committees were to be set up to smooth out grievances on the job; (4) a survey of speed-up evils was to be made; (5) the forty-hour week was to continue in force; (6) time and a half for overtime was to prevail; (7) no discrimination was to be exercised against unionists, who could wear their union buttons and talk about their organization during lunch hours.

The union requests for a uniform minimum wage, affecting plants in all parts of the country, and for the thirty-hour week were both denied.

Primarily as the result of its sit-downers' forty-four-day defiance of General Motors, the United Automobile Workers (late in 1938) has some 370,000 dues-paying members out of an industry-wide maximum potential of 450,000. It is thus the third largest among the C.I.O. unions. It has collective bargaining agreements with all of the independents and with two of the Big Three, General Motors and Chrysler. Currently it is trying to unionize Ford against an opposition as stubborn as a peasant's prejudice and as strong as a billion dollars.

The U.A.W. is doubly young—both in its short time of existence as a union and in its membership, since the industry still places a premium upon speed and endurance in its workers, attributes most generally found in men and women under forty, even under thirty-five. The union's maverick sit-downs, condemned by motor magnates and (some of them) by Martin himself, have derived from a new sense of liberation from oppression; from flawed methods of adjusting "line" and departmental grievances; from foremen-worker antagonisms that had been piling up for years and were often aggravated by both the self-assertion of the new unionists and the desire of the straw boss to show them that he was still top-dog. Many of the pettier officials, indeed, still believe it their purpose in life to bring obloquy upon the union whenever possible; [3] and neither side has as yet been "educated up" to the patience and will to good will necessary for a harmonious management-union relationship.

---

[3] General Motors has discharged a superintendent who by "riding" unionists tried to provoke them into sit-down action.

57

The Influence
of Unions
on Relative Earning

What appears to be obvious is not always
true. Professor Rees asks how much unions
have actually affected wages, and
concludes that the answer varies from
very little to moderately in different
markets.

ALBERT REES

*Albert Rees is Professor of Economics
at the University of Chicago.*

*   *   *

Research on the impact of the union on wages has proceeded along two
lines. One group of studies has examined a large number of industries
simultaneously, classifying them according to the degree of unionization.[1]
A second group of studies is based on the intensive examination of the
effects of unions on earnings in a single industry.[2] Most of the cross-
section studies fall in this group.

Reprinted from *The Economics of Trade Unions*, by Albert Rees, by permission
of The University of Chicago Press. © by the Univ. of Chicago, pp. 75–80, 94–99.

[1] See Arthur M. Ross, "The Influence of Unionism upon Earnings," *Quarterly
Journal of Economics*, February, 1948; Arthur M. Ross and William Goldner,
"Factors Affecting the Interindustry Wage Structure," *Quarterly Journal of Economics*, May, 1950; and Harold M. Levinson, *Unionism, Wage Trends, and Income
Distribution* (Ann Arbor: University of Michigan Press, 1951). A new study of this
general type is now being conducted by Professor H. Gregg Lewis. His preliminary
results were reported in a paper entitled "The Effects of Unions on Industrial Wage
Differentials" presented at Princeton, New Jersey, April, 1960, to a conference on
labor economics held by the National Bureau of Economic Research.

[2] See Stephen P. Sobotka, "Union Influence on Wages: The Construction In-
dustry," *Journal of Political Economy*, April, 1953; Joseph Scherer, "The Union
Impact on Wages: The Case of the Year-Round Hotel Industry," *Industrial and
Labor Relations Review*, January, 1956; Elton Rayack, "The Impact of Unionism on
Wages in the Men's Clothing Industry, 1911–1956," *Labor Law Journal*, September, 1958; Melvin Lurie, "The Effect of Unionization on Wages in the Transit Industry," *Journal of Political Economy*, June, 1961; and Rush V. Greenslade, "The
Economic Effects of Collective Bargaining in Bituminous Coal Mining" (unpub-
lished Ph.D. dissertation, University of Chicago, 1952).

Because I shall rely rather heavily in what follows on the estimates made in some of these studies, it is desirable to give some explanation of the estimating techniques that have been used. To use the time-series technique, one must construct a historical wage series for the unionized group going back far enough to include a period in which it was not unionized. It is also necessary to have a comparison or "base" series, often much broader in scope, showing the movement of wages or earnings for a group of workers who remain unorganized throughout the period of the study, or whose extent of unionization is appreciably less. If the workers of the base group are unorganized throughout, the analysis might proceed as follows: Suppose that in the period before the formation of the union under study, the average ratio of wages in the study group to wages in the base group in years of reasonably full employment was 1.20 to 1 and that in the period after the unionization of the study group this average ratio was 1.40 to 1 in comparable years. The estimate of the relative effect of unions on wages would then be approximately 17 per cent.[3] Before the estimate could be accepted, it would have to be determined whether factors other than unionization might account for changes in the ratio. It might also be possible to attach significance to changes in the ratio during the period of unionization.

The cross-section technique refers to a particular year. It can most easily be described for the case in which it is applied to separate local labor markets, in each of which the group under study can be described as entirely unionized or entirely nonunionized. For each market the wages of workers in the study group are divided by the wages of workers in some common base group in which workers are nowhere extensively unionized, such as retail trade, or in which there is little variation in the extent of unionization from place to place. If the base group is nowhere unionized, the estimate is made as follows: Suppose that the average ratio of wages in the study group to those in the base group is 1.40 to 1 in the unionized cities and 1.20 to 1 in the nonunion cities. Then the estimate of the relative wage effect of the union in the year studied is again 17 per cent. The purpose of the use of the base group is to eliminate or reduce the effect of differences in wage levels among places that are not the result of unionization.[4]

Having sketched briefly the nature of the research techniques that have been used, I shall now attempt to summarize the findings of this body of research and to make some educated guesses to fill in the gaps. The summary will attempt to indicate both the possible average effect of unions on relative wages, and the range of variation among unions in these effects, though the estimates of the latter kind will be subject to large errors. Initially, the effects will be stated in terms of the percentage by which unions raise relative earnings in periods of reasonably full employment and reasonably stable prices.

Strong American unions seem to be able to raise the relative earnings of their members by 15 to 25 per cent. Sobotka's study of the skilled building trades

[3] This figure is obtained by dividing 1.40 by 1.20 and subtracting 1.00. The result is then expressed as a percentage by multiplying it by 100.

[4] If the industry or occupation in question is one in which the extent of unionization varies continuously from one market to another, the cross-section technique can still be used. It will then involve estimating a regression equation in which the dependent variable is the ratio of wages in the study group to wages in the base group, and the independent variable is the percentage of workers in the study group who are organized. Ideally, the measure of union effect as we have defined it is the difference in the level of the regression line at zero and 100 per cent unionization, though this measure is subject to error if, for example, either extreme lies outside the actual range of observations. Readers with no background in statistics may safely ignore this footnote and rely on the text.

unions, as reinterpreted by H. G. Lewis, suggests a figure toward the high end of this range. It seems probable that craft unions in the printing, railroad, and entertainment industries have at times had effects of this general magnitude, though in recent years declines in demand and technological change may be eroding the power of some of them. Some industrial unions also seem to have effects of this order. Greenslade's study indicates that the United Mine Workers had an effect of at least 20 per cent on relative earnings in 1950–51, and Rayack has estimated that the effect of unionization in men's clothing was about 20 per cent in the early 1920's. Although no study of this type has been made of the teamsters' union, its rapid growth and generally aggressive attitude might lead one to classify it among the strong unions, at least for a large portion of its jurisdiction.

Little research has been done on the effects on earnings of industrial unions in the mass-production manufacturing industries during periods of reasonably stable prices. In the light of what we know about other unions, an effect of 10 to 15 per cent for the strong unions in this group, such as the steelworkers, does not seem unreasonable.

Some recent studies have found periods of stable prices and high employment in which the unions studied had no measurable influence on earnings. The unions for which this was found are of two general types. First, there are those which bargain with firms selling in national product markets and which have failed to organize a substantial majority of the firms in their industry. At the present time, the unions in the textile industry are the best example of this situation. Wage increases in the unionized sector that exceed those in the nonunion sector give the nonunion firms a competitive advantage in the product market and therefore have large effects on employment in union firms. The union lacks power because the products of nonunion labor are an almost perfect substitute for the products of union labor.

There are other cases in which unions have little or no measurable effect on earnings even though they have organized almost all of the firms in their jurisdictions. Two such cases that have been studied are those of the Amalgamated Clothing Workers and the Amalgamated Association of Street Railway and Motor Coach Operators in the period since World War II. Both of these unions had had substantial effects on the earnings of their members in earlier periods. The relevant common factor is that both unions operate in industries where the demand for the final product has been declining in recent years. The resulting declines in employment and the precarious financial position of many employers have apparently made the unions unwilling to risk further losses in employment by an aggressive wage policy. This attitude is reinforced by the effect of declining employment in raising the average age of union members. Older workers are less mobile and have poorer alternatives in the labor market and will therefore be more concerned with saving their jobs than with higher wage rates.

My own best guess of the average effects of all American unions on the wages of their members in recent years would lie somewhere between 10 and 15 per cent. This is within the range of the estimates being made by H. G. Lewis in his current work covering the whole economy, though his results would not rule out an average effect somewhat higher than this.

The preceding discussion has taken conditions of relatively stable prices and relatively full employment as a norm for measuring union effects on relative wages. We must now ask what deviations from these effects occur under other conditions.

In periods of rapid and unexpected inflation, such as occurred from 1941 to 1948, even the strongest unions seem to have no effect on relative earnings, or to lose most of any effect they previously had. During rapid inflations, demand forces pull up product prices and wage rates in nonunion markets. Agreements fixing wages for a period of time, or even long-term agreements providing for periodic wage increases according to some preagreed formula or schedule can leave unions at a relative disadvantage. The presence of a union, with its power to resist wage cuts at a later date, can also dissuade employers from using wage increases to deal with temporary labor shortages.

The sluggishness in wage adjustment created by collective bargaining, which acts to a union's disadvantage in periods of very rapid price and wage increases, becomes an advantage in periods of recession or in the early stages of a depression. Here union wages may remain fixed while other wages decline, increasing the union's normal effect on relative wages. Such an effect operated in the building and printing industries from 1929 to 1931, as may be seen by comparing their wage movements with those of other industries in which there are a large number of small employers. Because the recessions of the past fifteen years have been comparatively mild, effects of this sort have not been of appreciable importance since 1945. When a depression becomes prolonged and severe, as in 1931–33, the union effect on relative earnings again tends to disappear. Some unions lose their bargaining rights over much of their jurisdictions, some accept wage cuts that wipe out their relative advantages, and still others preserve the union scale, but permit such substantial amounts of work to be done at wages below the scale that the scale becomes largely a fiction. Fortunately, we have had no opportunity to observe how the stronger unionism of today would adjust to severe depression.

*   *   *

§7. THE UNION INFLUENCE ON LABOR'S SHARE

Many people view trade unions as a device for increasing the worker's share in the distribution of income at the expense of capital; that is, at the expense of the receivers of rent, interest, and profits. Attempts to test this view, which is often expressed by the unions themselves, have led to a number of studies of the effect of unions on labor's share. The studies to date must be regarded as highly inconclusive; no union effect on labor's share can be discovered with any consistency. The ratio of wages and salaries to national income has been rising steadily for a long time. This rise, however, largely reflects the shift of labor from unincorporated business, especially farms (where the labor of the owners or operators is compensated by what appears in the national accounts as profits), to corporate enterprise where all labor is paid by wages and salaries. The statistical adjustments needed to convert the original figures into estimates of the total labor share, including the share of owner labor, are difficult and the results of different procedures do not usually agree. However, all have the effect of reducing the rise in labor's share and leaving a remainder that shows no particular relation to union power.[5]

It may seem very strange that statistical studies can find a considerable effect

[5] See D. Gale Johnson, "The Functional Distribution of Income in the United States, 1850–1952," *Review of Economics and Statistics,* May, 1954. Johnson finds an increase in labor's functional share of national income from about 68 per cent in 1890 to about 75 per cent in 1952 but notes that almost half of the increase was achieved before 1929, while unions were still weak. See also Irving Kravis, "Relative Income Shares in Fact and Theory," *American Economic Review,* December, 1959.

of unions on wages and none on labor's share. On further consideration, however, this result is quite reasonable. First, the global studies of labor's share cover all the workers in the economy, including the self-employed. Only about one-fourth of this total labor force consists of union members, and some of these are in unions too weak to raise the relative earnings of their members. Even if effective unions raise labor's share in their own industries, the effect would be highly diluted and thus difficult to observe when spread over the whole economy. Second, just as we assume that changes in wages can affect capital's share, so we must recognize that disturbances in the rewards to capital will affect labor's share. An obvious example of this is the rise of labor's share during depressions as a direct result of the fall in profits. These independent changes in the reward to capital again tend to obscure any effects of unions on labor's share. By far the most fundamental point, however, is that a successful union will not necessarily raise labor's share even in its own industry. The wage bill will rise following a wage increase if the demand for labor is inelastic (that is, if the percentage reduction in employment is smaller than the percentage increase in wages), and this will raise labor's share in the short run. But as time passes the employer will tend to substitute capital for labor, as we have seen in the case of the coal industry. The price of capital to a particular industry will not usually decline as more of it is used, so that the total payments to capital may rise by more than the rise in the wage bill. In extreme cases, total wage payments may fall as employment contracts so that they are smaller than they were before the wage increase. (In other words, the long-run demand for wage-earner labor may be elastic in certain industries.) It is thus entirely possible for a union simultaneously to raise the relative wages of its members and to reduce their aggregate share of income arising in their industry.

If we have no evidence that the union's gains have generally been made at the expense of capital, we may ask from whom they have been made. One answer has been suggested in the preceding section; they may be made in large part at the expense of nonunion labor. That is, the likeliest effect of unions on the distribution of income is to redistribute it among workers. In real terms, this redistribution can be thought of as arising in either or both of two ways: first, the money wages of nonunion workers may be held down by the reallocation of labor produced by unionism; second, the nonunion workers may have to pay more for the products produced by union labor. The union reply to this position is that nonunion workers should organize. But even if all workers were organized into unions, it does not follow that union gains would all be at the expense of capital. It would still be possible for strong unions to make gains at the expense of weak ones, and under a decentralized system of collective bargaining, they undoubtedly would.

§8. THE UNION INFLUENCE ON THE SIZE DISTRIBUTION OF INCOME

People are interested in the functional distribution of income (its division between capital and labor) in part because they believe it to be related to the size distribution, the share of income going to people at different income levels. Most people would like to see this size distribution become more equal, at least to the extent of improving the lot of those at the very bottom. The simplest view of the relation between the two distributions is that workers are poor and the receivers of property income are rich. A union that can raise labor's share can then be viewed as a latter-day version of Robin Hood's merry men, with their headquarters removed from Sherwood Forest to a storefront opposite the mill.

Of course, this view of income distribution is much too simple. In fact, there are relatively few employed manual workers at the bottom of the income distribution. Of the 8.7 million families with 1957 incomes under $2,500, only 1.5 million were headed by employed craftsmen, operatives, or nonfarm laborers—that is by people in the major occupation groups strongly organized by unions. Perhaps in the absence of unions this number would be somewhat larger, but it seems clear that low wages are no longer a principal cause of poverty, if they ever were. Almost half of these low income families had heads who were not employed in 1957, and many of these had aged heads, presumably retired. Because large numbers of retired people depend on rents, interests, and dividends for much of their income, it seems probable that income from capital is more important at the very bottom of the income distribution than anywhere else except at the very top.

The union influence on relative earnings implies an influence on the size distribution of income even if there is none on the functional distribution, provided only that the members of effective unions are not equally distributed throughout the size distribution. But this proviso is clearly met, for manual workers are highly concentrated in the middle ranges of the income distribution. To get some idea of the probable union effect on the size distribution, we must look in some detail at the income position of the occupations represented by effective unions.

For 1949, the median wage and salary incomes for 118 rather detailed male occupations have been arranged by Miller in deciles based on the number of workers in each occupation. Occupations in which most workers are union members appear throughout the distribution. However, the top deciles of the distribution contain a large number of skilled craft occupations of the kind for which both theory and empirical research suggest that unions have the greatest influence on earnings. The top decile contains railroad conductors, compositors, locomotive engineers, and printing craftsmen other than compositors. The other occupations in this decile are all managerial, professional, or supervisory. The second highest decile contains brakemen, structural metal workers, plumbers, locomotive firemen, electricians, boilermakers, telegraph operators, and (rather surprisingly) baggagemen, express messengers, and railway mail clerks. The highest ranking occupation organized by an industrial union appears in the third decile from the top: operatives, motor vehicle. In all these occupations, the median income from wages and salaries alone is far above the median income from all sources of all males with income in 1949; it is also above the median income from all sources of all white, nonfarm males with income, in most cases substantially so. It is true, however, that within these high-income manual occupations the dispersion of income is rather small, so that few manual workers get into the highest income brackets. For example, only 0.2 per cent of locomotive engineers had wage and salary income in 1949 of $10,000 and over, as compared with 17.9 per cent of managers and officials, manufacturing.

Perhaps the best summary statement that can be made from the available evidence about the effect of unions on the size distribution of income is that unions have probably raised many higher income workers from an initial position somewhat above the middle of the income distribution to a present position closer to the top. They have narrowed the gap between the best paid manual workers and the very rich, and widened the gap between these workers and the very poor. This effect cannot be completely described by calling it either an increase or a decrease in the equality of income distribution, though it seems closer to the latter than to the former.

In most cases, union government does
not conform to the traditional two-party
system of our democracy. Clark Kerr
examines some of the pressures which help
enforce leadership responsiveness to
membership interests. He asserts that it
is essential for this purpose that union
constitutions guarantee effective
competition for elective offices.

*Clark Kerr is President of the University
of California, and formerly Professor of
Economics at that University.*

58

Union Democracy

CLARK KERR

THE CENTRAL ISSUE—UNION IMPACT ON WORKER FREEDOM

Of the several issues involving labor today three are inherently simple
issues. They are confined to specific segments of the labor movement but
at the same time run into American life generally. These three issues are
corruption, collusion, and violence.

Corruption exists and it is bad: but right and wrong are evident and
hardly open to debate. Few unions are involved and other institutions in
society have known and do know it also. Some remedies, including proper
accounting procedures, are relatively easy to identify, although not always so easy to apply effectively.

Collusion also exists and it also is bad; but again the nature of virtue is
not hard to define, although the line where it ends may be hard to draw
in particular cases. (Virtue and the drawing of proper lines have met
before on other stages.) Relatively few unions are affected and then nearly
always jointly with their employers; and collusion, too, accompanies
human nature almost throughout the span of social relationships.

Violence also is to be condemned. It has decreased greatly as a union
tactic, however, and is subject to control by the many devices civilized man
has created to insure law and order.

These are issues—they probably will be for a long time, and they deserve
attention. But they are peripheral to the main controversy today.

Excerpted from *Unions and Union Leaders of Their Own Choosing,* by Clark
Kerr (New York: Center for the Study of Democratic Institutions, December, 1957),
pp. 6–19. Reprinted by permission.

The great current issue is the impact of the union on the freedom of the worker. This issue is not simple; it is most complex. It is one that runs through all or nearly all of the union movement and is central to its very existence. While not unknown as an issue in the spheres of government and the corporation, it is less intensely manifested there at the present time. Our nation has had a long, successful experience in creating a democratic framework for our government and protecting the liberties of individual citizens. Our corporations are not expected to be run on a democratic basis. They are founded on the model of the individual entrepreneur making his own decisions; and corporations seldom have either a captive labor force or captive consumers (when they do have captive consumers they are usually subject to state control).

The unions are different. They have not had, like our government, a long and successful experience in developing a system of checks and balances, in limiting their sphere of endeavor, in defining and protecting the internal rights of their members. Unlike the corporation, they are founded on the assumption of internal democracy. They are associations of individuals, not collections of capital funds. Moreover, increasingly they have a captive membership. It is usually not possible for a union member just to withdraw in protest, without penalty, if he does not like the organization, its leaders, or its policy. We have here, most frequently, a more or less compulsory organization with substantial impact on the lives of its members.

American unions do make a major overall contribution to a democratic industrial society—this is the first and most important observation to be made about their impact on worker freedom. They usually create a two-party legislative system governing the life of the work-place. In their absence, the rules would be set exclusively by the employer. Through the unions, the workers can have a direct influence on the nature of the rules under which they work. (Without a union they can also have an impact, by their choice of employers, but this is much less direct.) Also, unions usually insist on a grievance mechanism, and this brings a judicial process into industrial life which is more impartial than when the employer sits as both prosecutor and judge. Beyond that, unions create a new power center which can, if it wishes, stand against the power centers of the state and the corporation, and these latter power centers have gained greatly in recent years in their absolute strength. A rough balance among private and public power centers is the essence of a pluralistic society, and a pluralistic society is the only firm foundation for democracy in an economy based on industrial production.

Thus the unions have generally brought a better legislative and judicial process into industrial life and a better balance among the power groups of society. They have done this without the consequences that were so feared in times just past. It was believed that industrial conflict would tear society apart; the fact is that industrial peace is now the commonplace, and, except for the few unions still under Communist domination, American unions most certainly contribute to the social stability and security of our whole system. It was feared that unions would hamper productive efficiency and stifle progress; undoubtedly many union rules do retard production but there is no evidence that the overall effect has been anything but relatively minor, and some new methods have been better received because of union consultation than they otherwise would have been in the light of the inherent conservatism of the work-place. It was feared that unions might distort inter-industry wage structures and that their actions would assure wild inflation; in fact, it is one of the wonders of the economic world that unions have had so little effect on wage structures; and their impact on price levels, while open to dispute, has certainly been no more than moderate. The fears of costly social conflict, of strangled production, of rampant inflation because of unions have proved largely without substance.

But a fear does remain that unions may take too much freedom from the worker, and this fear may not prove so groundless. If they do, they will not be the only institutions in our mass society which have conduced toward conformity. Big unions, big corporations, big government, and small individuals seem to be the order of the day.

If freedom is defined as the absence of external restraint, then unions reduce freedom, for they restrain the worker in many ways. They help to establish formal wage structures, seniority rosters, work schedules, pace of output, and the pattern of occupational opportunities, all of which limit his freedom of choice. They decide when he shall strike and not strike. They are—and this is one of the essentials to an understanding of unionism—disciplinary agents within society. They add to the total network of discipline already surrounding the workers through the practices and rules of the employer. They too insist upon order and obedience. It is inherent in their very existence. Two bosses now grow where only one grew before.[1]

Some loss of freedom, however, is inevitable in an effective industrial system. It will occur, more or less, whether the system is run by the employers alone, by the state alone, or even by the unions alone. Industrial society requires many rules and reasonable conformity to these rules. There must be a wage structure, a work schedule, and so forth, no matter who operates the system. This loss of freedom is one of the prices paid by man for the many benefits in income and leisure that can flow from industrial society. The challenge is that this price not be any higher than necessary. The issue lies in the "more or less." The loss of freedom of the industrial worker will be substantial, as compared with the self-employed farmer or craftsman, but it may be less rather than more; and unions can make it either less or more.

UNION DEMOCRACY—DIFFICULTIES, DETRIMENTS, VIRTUES

Before we can determine how the reduction of freedom may be less rather than more, three introductory observations should be made:

(1) Democracy in unions is inherently difficult to achieve. A union is variously expected to be at one and the same time—as Muste pointed out long ago—an army, a business, and a town meeting. Unions have usually ended up by being a business, serving the members but sometimes with those members having little more influence over the conduct of the business than stockholders have over a corporation. Unions have sometimes ended up as an army and have justified it, as Lloyd Fisher once remarked, in the terms the Communists have used to justify their "people's democracy," by reference to "capitalist encirclement." Unions have almost never ended up as a town meeting.

(2) A good deal more democracy exists in unions than these comments and most outside observation would indicate. The national unions are the most visible

---

[1] This is not to suggest that it is not often and perhaps almost always better to have two bosses rather than one, for the union boss may help liberate the worker from the unilateral rule of the employer boss; but the worker is still subject to a web of rules, and this web tends to be more thickly woven as a result of the presence of the union.

entities, and they are usually the least subject to democratic pressures. But at the local level, in many unions, there are contested elections, substantial turnover of officers, and face-to-face relations between members and leaders—here is the least entrenched bureaucracy. Particularly at the shop level, the relationship between shop stewards and workers is a responsive one. This local level is usually the most important to the workers. This is where he lives and where his grievances are handled.

(3) It is sometimes argued that unions need not or even should not be democratic. Different reasons are given for this conclusion. One line of argument is that unions have become largely functionless organizations and nobody really cares whether they are democratic or not. The state guarantees full employment and social security, and the employer has been seduced by human relations. Consequently, the worker has a job—often paid above the contract rate—a pension, and a friend, perhaps even a psychiatrist; and there is nothing for the union to do. Or, it is sometimes said, unions have become quasi-governmental bureaus. They help set minimum wages and schedules of hours, and they process grievances, as government bureaus sometimes do both here and abroad. Their work is largely routine and best handled in bureaucratic fashion; and so, again, why worry about democracy? Occasionally it is also said, unions function best if they are removed from the pressures of democratic life. They must respond to many pressures, not those of the membership alone but also the needs of the industry, the welfare of society, the concerns of other unions. They should take a longer view of events than the current membership is likely to take, for they are organizations with a continuing life. They will be more widely responsible to society and more business-like in their operations if they are not subject to the demands and uncertainties of active democratic participation. The conclusion to this argument is that democracy causes internal and external strife and irresponsibility.

Each of these reasons has some point to it. Unions perform less of a function than they did two decades ago; their work has become more routine as pattern-following and grievance precedents have become established; and internal democracy can cause external trouble, particularly for employers.

But the case for democracy can still be persuasive. If democracy is a superior form of government, as most of us would insist, it should be preferred in practice wherever it is possible.

Second, the workers can have a more effective voice in industry if they have an effective voice in their unions; and they are more likely to be satisfied with society if they have a sense of participation.

Third, if the unions lose their responsiveness to the interests of the workers, an opportunity is created for other organized elements, more politically motivated, to move in to represent these interests, as has happened in certain European countries.

ONE-PARTY GOVERNMENT—THE UNION CASE

The overwhelming majority of all the organizations of man throughout history have been ruled by one-party governments. Most of the time in most parts of the world all organizations have been under one-party rule. In certain parts of the world at certain times in history there have been a few two-party (or multi-party) organizations; but one-party rule is the standard and well-nigh universal case. The trade union is no exception. The International Typographical Union is the single deviant specimen on a national level in the United States.

Even in the democratic United States, the corporation, the political party, the fraternal order, the religious denomination, the farm organization, the welfare group, the student government are all one-party organizations. Only in the public area, where it is by all odds the most essential, do we have two-party government.

The neglect of the one-party model of government, in view of its significance, is astounding. The rare instances of two-party and multi-party government have attracted most of the study. Certainly two-party government, as Lipset has persuasively argued, has much to recommend it. It provides criticism of the existing government, it makes ready an alternative government if the members want it, it reduces apathy, and does much else of value. But most men all of the time, and all men some of the time, function in one-party social organizations; and so do union members.

Why are unions one-party governments? There are several reasons. Partly, it is the requirement of unity in the face of external conflict. Partly, it is the control exercised by the leaders over the mechanism of the organization. But the answer lies much deeper than the fear of the enemy and the desires of the leaders. It is that there are no continuing conflicts except over ideology, and ideological conflicts tend to split unions rather than to create two-party systems within them. Witness the separate unions in several European countries and the split-off of Communist unions in the United States. Issues over wage increases, the handling of grievances, and so forth may lead to factions and leadership rivalry but not to two-party systems on a continuing basis.

Does one-party government mean that unions are inevitably "undemocratic"? If only two-party systems are really democratic, then the answer is obviously in the affirmative. But if organizations where the supreme power is retained by the members and which are reasonably responsive to membership desires may be called "democratic," even in the absence of a two-party system, then unions may be and many are "democratic."

There are dangers in any one-party government, but the system may serve its members well. It is most likely to do so, however, in the long run, if it is under the proper pressures. Traditionally, this pressure on trade-union government in the United States has come from four sources, all of them, unfortunately, now largely of historical importance only. In the passing of these four sources of pressure lies much of our current problem.

(1) When union membership was more voluntary, leaders had to be responsive to the workers to get and retain members, and this was an effective check on authority. As noted earlier, union membership is now, one way or another, often compulsory, the law notwithstanding; and it is likely to become more so. Union security, with all its other advantages, and leadership responsiveness tend to move in somewhat opposite directions; the voluntary sale and the forced sale lead to different behavior in any walk of life. This is not to support voluntary membership through the compulsion of the state for it seems neither possible in many situations nor, on balance, wise.

(2) When dual unionism, now largely a relic, was an active force, it had somewhat the same impact as voluntary membership. Not individuals but groups could and did shift allegiance, and this acted as a check and balance. The idea of one union in one jurisdiction, however, is so firmly embedded in American union philosophy that dual unionism can exist only sporadically and temporarily.

(3) The more or less permanent faction, stopping short of a second party but hovering in the wings ready to rush out on any inappropriate occasion, was a check on the leadership in many unions. The old-line Socialists served this func-

tion for many years, but the New Deal and time brought their demise. The Catholic faction continues in a few unions, but usually only in those under left-wing control; otherwise there is little basis for a Catholic faction. There are few permanent factions today and fewer still in prospect.

(4) The employer, particularly the recalcitrant employer, has historically been a check and balance on the union leadership. If the two organizations—the company and the union—appealing to the same constituency are in conflict, each will criticize the other and may even stand ready to try to destroy the other. But the day of fighting the unions is largely past, at least under conditions of full employment. The separation of interests between the leaders of the two organizations is decaying because industrial peace pays. Consequently, company pressure on most unions has been greatly reduced and in some instances has entirely disappeared.

UNION DEMOCRACY—THE POSSIBILITIES

With union membership increasingly compulsory, dual unionism declining, the permanent faction disappearing, and company opposition more rare, is there any hope for "democracy" or leadership responsiveness to membership interests in trade unions? There still is, for there are substitutes for these historical pressures. Six such possibilities will be suggested, with particular emphasis on the sixth.

1 *Membership interest.* Union memberships are traditionally apathetic except in some crisis, and very little can be done about it. Compulsory strike votes proved a farce in World War II, and most bargaining issues cannot properly be put to membership vote. But some experiments might be undertaken with the polling of membership opinion, with advisory referenda, and even with the use of television as a way for leaders to reach members, who will seldom come to meetings.

2 *"Professional" leaders.* Much is written about management as a profession. Perhaps union leaders might also become professional in the sense that they might be specifically trained for their jobs and might develop an "ethic" to guide their conduct—an ethic which sets boundaries to their behavior. They might, like city managers, be specifically trained for their jobs and responsible to an elected governing board.

3 *A new faith for the union movement.* Certain leaders today, in unions where the last vestiges of active democracy disappeared long ago, still serve their members well because of their adherence to the "old faith" of the union movement. But the "old faith" attracts few new followers. It was a fighting faith that grew out of evil conditions for the workers and union-busting by the employers. The conditions which gave rise to it no longer exist in the United States, although they continue to a degree in England and Germany, where the "old faith" still sets standards for union leaders. The social reformer holds himself—and is held by his environment—to a higher code of conduct than the business leader of the business union who quickly takes on the coloration of the industry with which he deals. If its ethics are high, his will be also; if they are low, so are his. The business union is a segment of the business.

What might this new faith be? It cannot be either "more, more, more, and now." It cannot be a vision of class conflict. It might lie, as suggested later, in the development of unions as a liberating force in industrial society; and this might carry the union leader more into the intellectual and less into the business community.

4 *Local autonomy.*   Local unions, by their inherent nature, clearly can provide more opportunities for democratic participation by the members than can national unions. Consequently, the more autonomy there is at the local level, the greater the democratic life of the union movement is likely to be. The big drop in democratic participation comes in the move from the one-plant to the multi-plant local or the district union. In the one-plant local, rival leaders can get known and be effective, issues can be discussed on a face-to-face basis, and democracy can be effective. In several European countries, for example, it is the local Works Council, with substantial powers, which arouses worker interest and participation. The multi-plant unit serves the interests of the entrenched leadership in a most emphatic way. The one-plant local with real authority is the most democratic entity in the trade-union movement. Considerable constitutional reform in most unions would be prerequisite to effective single-plant locals. Among other things, the institution of the "receivership" by regional and national officials would need to be curtailed.

5 *Union decertification.*   It is certainly desirable to continue some mechanism through which members can exercise an option in favor of another union, or of no union at all. Such an option will rarely be employed but it should be available. If it is available and is used occasionally, it can act as a minor check and balance on union leadership.

6 *Discharge through rebellion.*   The two-party system within unions, as we have seen, is an historical oddity. The regularly contested election is a rarity. Yet union officials do get changed other than as a result of death or retirement. Union officials are, in effect, "hired" by the membership for the duration of their good behavior, as tested imprecisely by the membership. The trouble comes when they need to be "fired." The mechanism then is a contested election in which the old leader is voted out of office. For such a contested election to take place two prerequisites are necessary: (1) It must be possible for a faction to form and for its members to be reasonably free from retaliation through the operation of an impartial judicial process; and (2) there must be secret elections at appropriate intervals. Other actors must be allowed to stand in the wings and be permitted to move on stage when the audience calls them. The dissatisfied individual and the antagonistic faction must be given an opportunity.

The term "competitive discharge" might be used in the sense that the leader is subject to constant evaluation by the members and is also subject to discharge through the process of electing a competitor who is free to appear when the conditions warrant. In the two-party system, the question is as to the better person; in the "competitive discharge" case, it is whether the incumbent should be fired or not. Deposed union leaders usually feel—and they are right—that they have been fired, not that they have been defeated. Among other things, they almost never seek election again once they have been discharged. They are like the old bull in the buffalo herd brought to his knees by the young challenger.

If trade-union democracy is defined as a system of government where the supreme power is largely retained by the members and can be exercised by them in an emergency at any and all levels, then the effective right of competitive discharge, by itself, is a sufficient basis for trade-union democracy. The essential feature of a trade-union constitution is whether it guarantees this right of competitive discharge. This is the most we can reasonably expect, and it is also probably enough.

*   *   *

59

Good Profits
Promote Progress

What role do profits really play in our economy? Mr. Kappel argues that realized profits, not just the profit motive, are essential, and that profits are essential for efficient management.

Frederick R. Kappel is Chairman of the Board of The American Telephone and Telegraph Company.

FREDERICK R. KAPPEL

A few years ago, a group of Bell System managers made an intensive study of the relationship between profits and performance in American industry. They started with two questions: "Does profit do anything? Is it only a result or does it also cause things to happen that affect our economy?"

Their broad conclusion was that good profit, good business performance, and healthy economic progress all go together. But the men who made the study went further. Good profit, they suggested, does much more than parallel good performance. It is one of the essential factors in bringing good performance about. (The other essentials named were good management and a good product.) In other words, good profit is by no means merely a result; it is also causative, dynamic, and energizing.

These conclusions were based on the group's study of the actual case histories of companies in several industries. The weight of the evidence was that where profits have been relatively good, performance has also been relatively good, measured by several important criteria. Of the businesses analyzed, those that earned well had better growth records—with all that connotes of value delivered to consumers—than those that earned poorly. The more profitable companies put more investment (including more retained earnings) into new and improved equipment; they did more research and more innovating; they offered better job opportunities; and they contributed more to community well-being.

Thus, the study group suggested that good profit should be regarded as

From *Business Horizons,* Winter, 1961, pp. 21–28. Reprinted by permission of the author, *Business Horizons,* and the University of Indiana.

a prime *cause* of economic and social progress. Profit, they felt is not merely an end result of the business process, but a lively functional element that does indeed "cause things to happen."

The idea has had a mixed reception. Many people have said to me that they think it makes excellent sense; others have been critical. They have argued that, while good performance may indeed produce good profit, it is not demonstrable that good profit will generate good performance. Our study group, they contend, must have been putting its carts before its horses.

This critical reaction is not surprising. It is, after all, a new thought that profit can be causative in the sense suggested. For generations, profit has been regarded mainly as a result, a residue, a remainder, and this is still the popular notion. It is a notion derived, perhaps, from nothing more complicated than the classroom illustration that if a man grows an apple for eight cents and sells it for 10, he is left with two cents profit. Or it may be that the classical economists of the last century are partly responsible. As they saw the matter, according to the *Encyclopaedia of the Social Sciences:*

> There was first a separation between rent and a kind of gross income of the capitalist, as the businessman was then more or less correctly called; subsequently the latter fund was divided between the capitalist and the laboring classes. Wages were supposed to be determined independently, the final share of the capitalist being left as a residuum.

Residuum—there is something lifeless and inert about the very word. It gives linguistic support to the view that the figures on the bottom line belong also at the bottom of our scale of values; and perhaps the typical form of income statement, showing profit at the bottom, further encourages this view. This is too bad, for as I see it, the fact that profit is something left over does not in any sense define its character. Its appearance as a remainder merely reflects its place in time, which is necessarily after the transactions that produced it. But this is no clue to its nature or potential.

Thinking about this, I was interested when someone the other day called to my attention the views of Francis Amasa Walker, as discussed by John Chamberlain in his book *The Roots of Capitalism*. According to Chamberlain, Walker, a Civil War general, teacher at Yale, and later president of M.I.T., "isolated profit as the driving force of industrial progress." While Walker too saw profit as a result, he saw it also as something more. Profit, said Walker, is the special creation of the gifted enterpriser. He produces it "by his comprehension of the demands of the market; . . . by his organizing force and administrative ability; by his energy, economy, and prudence." Thus, profit is more than a result; it is the instrument of dynamic change.

The classical concept of profit as mere residue suggests that when profit has been gained, its vitality ends. It is not useful to society; rather, it is likely to serve only the convenience and comfort of those who have possession of it. All this fits in with many people's feeling that while a little bit of profit may do no harm, profits for the most part are bad. To what degree public distrust of business profits may be derived from the concept of profit as a residue or any other economic theory, I am not able to say. More important is the fact that there is at present little or no theory of the kind that might dispel distrust. So far as I can see, profits are distrusted largely because the public sees them as a manifestation of economic power; because there is evidence every now and then that certain profits have not been honestly earned; and because of the belief that profit is often a reflection of the ability of some people to gain at others' expense. But these are political, ethical, and emotional considerations. They have nothing to do with any principle of business profit as such. It will be a pity, therefore, if we cannot gain acceptance for some view of profit other than one that, implicitly at any rate, deprecates its social usefulness. From the concept of profit as mere residue it is only a step to the moral contention that paucity of profit is a demonstration of virtue, and only one more step to the proposition that if scant profit is a mark of high integrity, then no profit at all must be a mark of the highest.

The danger is that noneconomic considerations may in the end determine what is to be done about profit. We need, on the one hand, a clear understanding that aberrations in business practice, unwarranted exercise of power, and the like are in no sense indicators of the function of profit. On the other hand, we need a concept of profit so satisfying that it will be impossible to identify ethical failure with failure of the profit principle.

Let us go back a moment now to Walker, who found in profit the driving force of industrial progress. Today one hears countless voices that seem to be saying much the same thing. I have in mind all the economists and journalists who echo and re-echo the refrain that "the profit motive" is the dynamo of enterprise. But for some reason, at least in this country, it seems to me there is much more applause for the profit motive than there is for profits. It is almost as though there were two kinds of thought: One has something in common with Walker's views, except that the modern stress, as I have said, is on the motive alone, whereas Walker did not stop there; the other, which is strengthened by the residue theory, if not derived from it, appraises profit with a wary eye, as something acceptable only when it is scant.

THE PROFIT DILEMMA

In short, we are seriously at odds with ourselves about profits. Our attitude is: Hurrah for the profit motive and down with profits. Or as a Latin might put it, "Motive *si,* profit *no.*" We want people to work for profits, but we are not at all sure that we want them to be earned. This is economic schizophrenia. It is absurd to hold that profit is a desirable incentive but a poor achievement. Men cannot work on the basis that it is right and necessary for them to pursue a goal that, when they reach it, will prove a sterile thing at best, and at worst a harmful one.

The Russians, I may remark, are in no such dilemma. They want profits, the genuine article, and not just "the profit motive." Witness this statement from the draft program of the Soviet Communist party as translated by Tass and printed in *The New York Times* on August 1, 1961: "It is necessary to promote profitable operation of enterprises, to work for lower production costs and higher profitability."

Wouldn't it be interesting some day to see a platform of the Republican or Democratic party calling for higher profitability? I am sure we can count on both parties to continue advocating prosperity, but it would be a great thing for the country if we might also find included—say in 1964—a recommendation in favor of higher profitability, the necessary ingredient of that prosperity.

THE BENEFITS OF PROFIT

I have a good many reasons for believing that a plus in business profits fairly earned is a plus for everybody. *The profitable business has freedom to do what is right.* I did not say has freedom to throw money around. The business that is profitable can operate much more economically than the one that is not, for the profitable operation does not have to defer current expenditures that will improve long-run performance. The company that puts off doing what it ought to do, because it cannot afford it at the time, inevitably sacrifices long-run economies.

I could sum up much of what is in my mind by saying that good profits facilitate good management judgment, but since this statement needs particularizing, I shall try to illustrate.

Training

Let us look first at the training of people. This is essential to the vitality of any business enterprise and its ability to contribute to economic progress. The selection of able people is a crucial task requiring thought, time, and money, and it is but the start of a long-range development process that calls for more of all three. I am not thinking of formal training procedures alone, but of the whole complex of effort needed to bring about conditions that encourage personal growth, inspire quality performance, and enable the individual to realize deep satisfaction in his work. The business that has adequate means available is far more likely, I think, to make the conscious and continuous effort needed than the business that is hard up.

There is growing conviction that the best way to test managerial talent is to give young people from the start assignments that truly challenge their capacity —in preference to training routines that impose a minimum of responsibility, fail to offer the trainee any sense of having a real job, bore him unutterably, and give him sore feet from standing around. One of the good arguments in favor of testing men early in their careers is that they will learn from their mistakes. In saying this, I am not advocating mistakes at any time; we have, however, to be realistic. If we are going to give people responsibility in this way, there are bound to be some errors, and they are bound to cost money (albeit less than the cost of bigger errors the same people might make in later years if they did not have the judgment gained from making little ones). But if we cannot stand the cost of the small errors, we are not going to assign the responsibility. In other words, we are not going to do what we know we ought to do to build the future.

It may be said that these examples hardly provide all the evidence needed to support the case for healthy profit. I agree. Before offering more illustrations, however, let me remind the reader that these I have mentioned lie in an area of special importance for the future. With the advance of technology, there is an ever-growing need for the training and retraining of men and women in almost every phase of industry. People must learn to use new arts effectively, find new markets for new products and services, and function to best advantage in new forms of organization. In short, industry in the years ahead faces a tremendous task in education, and if industry cannot earn the means, the task is simply not going to be done well. To put it another way, the country is well aware that the schools face a problem of unprecedented scope. But as we all know, education is not completed at school; it only begins there. This is the recurrent theme of every college commencement, and with good reason. Starting where the schools leave off, industry must shoulder a considerable part of the total responsibility for future education—quite apart from its financial contributions to the schools.

Physical Plant and Engineering

Another aspect of what I choose to call the vital or causative function of profit lies in the area of engineering and building plant facilities. Let us look at an example drawn from the telephone business, which must make heavy investment in physical plant in order to serve its customers.

A telephone engineer is called on to decide what size of telephone cable should be installed to serve a growing neighborhood. He knows it must serve perhaps 200 homes immediately. He is also reasonably confident that, in another couple of years, possibly 200 more homes will want service. Putting in a cable today that is big enough to serve all 400 homes will obviously cost more now than putting in one that will serve only 200. The carrying charges will be higher, too, of course. But if the engineer puts in the cable today that will serve only 200 homes, and another of equal size is needed two years later, the total cost and carrying charges will be considerably more in the long run.

So what will the engineer do?

If the company he is working for is hard up, he will have to put in the smaller cable because that is cheaper *now*, even though it is obvious that this course will be more expensive in the end. If, however, the company is in good financial shape, if it can readily get the capital needed for investment in the larger cable, and if the general level of earnings permits absorbing the higher carrying cost of the bigger cable until its full capacity is utilized, then the engineer will be encouraged to install the bigger cable. Again I point out that good profit favors doing what ought to be done.

It is a commonplace that profit or the prospect of profit is necessary to attract capital. Less emphasized, but no less important, is the fact that healthy profit in countless instances promotes capital's effective and efficient application. The example I have cited is not an isolated instance; telephone people, and no doubt others in many different lines of business, have to make thousands of decisions like the one mentioned above. In the making of all such decisions, reasonable present prosperity helps to promote long-run economy and progress.

In the last year or so, much public attention has centered on the fact that a large proportion of America's industrial plant is growing old. Surveys that have been made indicate that about a third of it is now so old and inefficient that it ought to be scrapped. The Secretary of the Treasury has said that the average age of the nation's plant is twenty-four years, and the President has observed that some two-thirds of our machine tools are more than ten years old.

Aging plant is progressively more inefficient. We need to modernize our productive facilities to compete more effectively in world markets, help balance our international payments, and create job opportunities for our growing work force. Why then does industry retain so much old and inefficient plant? One important reason is that our tax laws do not allow industry enough depreciation expense, either in total or year by year. The result is understatement of true costs, corresponding overstatement of income, and, in consequence, a tax on capital. (Any levy on a proper expense that the law requires to be mislabeled as income must be a levy on capital; it cannot be anything else.) In any event, adequate depreciation plus adequate real profit has been made impossible.

I have been arguing my conviction that good profit works in favor of productive efficiency. It seems to me that the apprehensions about inadequate depreciation and the movement to find some remedy support this argument. In essence, what we have here is a growing concern that capable and effective businesses should be able to earn the real profits they need in order to become more productive. Maybe some people in government have not thought the matter through in this way; if they have not, I wish they would. Knowing the problem for what it really is might lead also to better understanding of the function of profit in other respects.

Lean Leavings Not Enough

The main effort in this article has been to suggest the meaning of a concept that says that profit is not something merely residual, but is causative and energizing. At this point, however, someone may well say, "Look here, this is all very well, but are you really talking about profit per se and how much of it there ought to be? It seems to me you are talking rather about some of the things a well-managed business needs to do *before* it makes a profit—before it is able to deposit that residue. There are other accomplishments that are also important: good wages and working conditions, for instance, safe working practices, research and development, the introduction of new products and services, alertness to consumer needs, and so on. So long as you accomplish these and still have something left over, this is what really counts, isn't it? And where is your proof that the residue, the profit, needs to be more than minimal?"

I can only answer that last question from actual experience as a manager, and this experience has convinced me that the quality of management performance is influenced in every aspect by the prospect of good earnings on the one hand, or of lean leavings on the other. For evidence, I have to turn again to events in the Bell System. This is not intended as special pleading, and I hope it will not be so interpreted. The fact is simply that to speak from experience, it is necessary to refer to it.

Our overall earnings situation in the years soon after the war was poor. In the early 1950's, there was a slight improvement, and in the last few years there has been further improvement. What one may trace rather easily, as earnings have risen, is an acceleration of projects that markedly increase the quality, dependability, and convenience of the service rendered.

For example, we measure the quality of telephone transmission in terms of how people might hear each other if they were conversing in a quiet open field. In 1950, transmission on the average long distance call was as though the talkers were standing 15 feet apart. In the ten years following, this distance was reduced some 20 per cent—to about 12 feet. But with a better profit margin at hand, we are now working on a program to cut the distance down to less than 5 feet by 1970. This will make an enormous difference in the ease of conversation.

Perhaps it has been noticed also that as Bell System earnings improved in the later 1950's, there came a succession of new telephone instruments and systems for homes and offices. Direct distance dialing spread rapidly so that today about three-quarters of all our customers can dial their own calls to all parts of the nation. Ocean telephone cables to Europe, Alaska, and Hawaii have resulted in a great improvement in overseas services.

Today a program is under way to sharply reduce the occasions when people wanting to telephone in the busier periods of the day will find no circuits available. Another important project is construction of a bomb-resistant underground communications system across the continent. Our direct distance dialing program is proceeding on a schedule that will make such calling available to nearly every Bell System customer in the next four years. Means for automatically identifying the calling number are being installed under an accelerated program. Data-Phone services, which enable machines to communicate with other machines through the regular nation-wide telephone network, are being rapidly extended. Millions of dollars are being spent for the development of communications satellites that may permit global communications, including television and data as well as voice transmission, on a scale hitherto impossible.

Were the profits of the Bell System today no better than they were in the 1940's and well into the 1950's, it would be impossible for us to push ahead with anything like the same vigor. And if we could not maintain good earnings, we would necessarily have to put a checkrein on forward undertakings. Prudence would demand this.

Not that profit can or ever should be assured. It must be worked for and earned in every sense of the word. But if the ultimate end in sight is meager, few managers will bend extra effort to develop and proceed with new and useful long-range projects that increase current costs, or build additional excellence into their product, or take special pains with their maintenance, or spend either a million dollars or a hundred to make their plant and facilities more efficient. More likely, they will feel pressed to move in the reverse direction. They may compromise on quality; they may skimp on maintenance, or even do none for as long as possible. They may rely protractedly on the outmoded and outworn. Against his better judgment, against all his instincts to do the job well, the manager is pushed into ill-advised corner-cutting, into expedients and substitutes, into deletions and omissions that may not show immediately but will ultimately sap the long-run vigor and strength of the enterprise. In short, if he has no hope of prosperity by the means that will most benefit his customers and his company, which is to give real value and earn an equivalent reward, he is forced into the situation of trying to keep integrity in his financial statements by taking it away from his business.

THE BROADER VIEW

Earlier in this article I put some stress on the difficulties we get into if we admire profit as a goal but deplore it as an achievement. We cannot be half for profit and half against it. I wonder if the reason some of the critics of profit get into this situation may not be that they see business managers as dedicated *solely* to profit. Perhaps some managers are so dedicated. However, my observation is that most of them have a broader view. In a business like the one I am in, the question is ever present, "Which comes first, service or profits?" Our license, of course, is only to serve, nothing else. But to answer the question by separating the one from the other is difficult indeed. Years ago, the answer was given in these words, and I find it hard to improve them: "We must serve well to prosper. We must prosper to serve well."

I have omitted from this discussion such an obvious point as the fact that prosperity pays taxes. All it appears necessary to say is that if the government wants revenues, the government will do more than give lip service to the profit goal—it will really encourage the making of real profits, and rejoice in the result.

No discussion of business profits can be conclusive. But to refer again to the study mentioned at the start, where there is overwhelming evidence that profit, performance, and progress are intimately linked, may there not be wisdom in accepting the likelihood that profit is in fact an essential contributing factor? I realize that economics is not an exact science. By the same token, however, it seems necessary to say that no theory that denies a causative, creative role to business profits can be taken as definitive. From experience and observation, I am persuaded that good profits not only accompany and make manifest sound progress, but do in fact make important contributions to it, and must be regarded as essential to promote economic growth and the achievement of desirable economic goals. Only an economy in which industry and government see eye to eye on this, and work in harmony to nourish business profit, will realize its full potential in creating productive efficiency, in delivering the greatest value to the consuming public, and in raising living standards.

Everyone is against poverty, but Dr. Reid argues that the problem has been exaggerated. She criticizes the poverty yardstick used by the Council of Economic Advisers, and argues that the Administration's antipoverty program will have little effect on the great bulk of the really poor.

Dr. Margaret G. Reid is Professor of Economics at the University of Chicago.

60

Poverty—Defining the Problem

MARGARET G. REID

* * *

This bill has something to say about poverty, and a great deal of the discussion of it, both inside and outside the government, has dealt with poverty.

As I read the discussion, I find an enormous amount of confusion; in fact, I would say that the discussion is full of confusion. Some speakers and writers seem to say that the great upsurge of productivity that has come in the past few decades has bypassed many people. Undoubtedly, all groups in the population have not shared equally in the increases.

In our dynamic society, sharing tends to change as the technology and choices of consumers change the demand for various skills. In spite of all this, workers on farms and in cities, white and Negro workers, young and elderly workers have shared importantly in the secular rise in national income.

These are matters on which there are no questions.

For the population in general, there has been a decline in the frequency of inadequate diets, of housing without plumbing facilities, and of children who have had to drop out of school because of low income of parents. All of these trends have been very carefully measured and are generally accepted.

In addition, new products such as television sets have come quickly into

Statement by Dr. Margaret G. Reid, *Hearings* before the Subcommittee on the War on Poverty, U.S. House of Representatives, 88th Congress, April 23–28, 1964, pp. 1427–1438.

universal use, testifying to the equality of sharing of consumption experiences. These and other trends indicate an ever-widening diffusion of welfare levels.

With the rise in income and its diffusion throughout the population, a marked decline has occurred in poverty, if one measures poverty in terms of consumer products and services. This decline has been documented in a recent report of the U.S. Bureau of the Census, and in some of my writings.

Poverty, in the basic sense of how well people live, has declined markedly in the United States. It will decline further as productivity rises. Why then, all this hullaballoo about poverty?

The overtones of much of the discussion and its sudden eruption create the impression that we are in the throes of another emotional jag. Not long ago there was an outpouring of books and articles in magazines and newspapers on affluence. We were pictured as satiated, but not very wise, consumers: Every household with an electric refrigerator stocked with soft drinks and every household with one or more TV sets to provide entertainment with a generous supplement of comics to further relieve the tedium of life.

I am sure many of you have had this brought to your attention. A dearth of consumption for our public needs, such as roads and schools, was stressed. Affluence is now being overshadowed. We are portrayed as a poverty-ridden society and urged to undertake a large-scale program for increasing economic opportunity.

Extravagant estimates of poverty have appeared, some indicating as much as two-fifths of the population poverty stricken.

The Council of Economic Advisers to the President has used $3,000 as the poverty point. There are many other estimates. We are, in fact, witnessing a veritable battle of the poverty yardsticks.

Who is going to win out and say what is poverty? And this battle is likely to continue because there is no definite way of resolving the arguments.

There is no scientific method for determining the income necessary to prevent poverty. The policymaker who needs a measure of poverty can choose one suitable for his purpose. Once he has chosen it, he is likely to say, along with Humpty Dumpty, that "when I use the word, it means what I choose it to mean, neither more or less."

A poverty yardstick suitable for his purpose would show the amount of poverty that serves the purpose of the policy. The claims must not appear absurd, but they must be impressive. The Council of Economic Advisers reached the conclusion that 33 to 35 million American people were living at or below the boundary of poverty in 1962, nearly one-fifth of the population. Such a judgment will of course be impressive to those people who are unaware of how it was reached.

There is no scientific method of defining poverty. Even so, something definite can be said about the meaning of any yardstick used.

For example, if a yardstick calls for money income of $3,000, then this test will overstate the number of people whose consumption is below $3,000. Current income of some families with incomes under $3,000 is less than usual, and their consumption is likely to be higher than their income. They are drawing on past assets, accumulated earlier, or they are borrowing on the basis of expected future income. Examples are easily found.

The ups and downs of annual incomes are experienced by many families and these changes get represented in the income data because the income data describe the situation for only a given year. Their presence cannot be readily seen except in consumption surveys.

These surveys more fully than income surveys indicate the conditions associated with incomes in any one year.

I would like to point out that all the estimates we have floating around in regard to poverty have used income distribution data, they have not used consumption data, and very few people are acquainted with the consumption studies in the policy field. I find this over and over again in my experience even with students who come to me on research problems. They do not know how to use the consumption data, and the volume is much smaller than the income data, so lots and lots of judgments based on the income data are quite unrealistic. So families reporting low income have consumption expenditures much in excess of income.

In order to give some examples of this, I pulled down some reports that are just now reaching my desk from the U.S. Bureau of Labor statistics. They made a large-scale consumption survey for the year 1960, and the reports are just coming out.

For example, a consumption survey of 1960 reported for Washington only two families with incomes under $1,000. Their average expenditure, including their income tax payments and personal instance, was $5,404. In other words, their outlays were more than five times their income. In fact, it was more than that. Their average income was about $600. They were almost 10 times above their income.

It seems highly unlikely that either of these families should be classed as important. These are not isolated examples.

For the large cities of the United States, in 1960 consumers with incomes under $1,000 were spending $224 for every $100 of income received, and those with incomes from $2,000 to $3,000 were spending $116. Many low current incomes reported in surveys understate ability to pay. This understatement that I have given these examples for come from the fact that in any one year you go to make a survey, you catch in it low-income group people who are below their normal income position, and in addition, it has been fully documented in the studies of income that a large number of the low-income people do not report their income. They are much more likely to underreport their income than to underreport their consumption expenditures. They are rather practiced in underreporting incomes in the way means tests are used for those seeking help.

However, there are other things that make the use of a $3,000 income meaningless in terms of what its relationship to welfare and consumption is. Money income also understates the consumption of families because they have income in kind apart from the money income. Farm families provide a notable example. Much of their food and housing is in addition to money income. This is recognized clearly in consumption studies, but often overlooked by those who attempt to relate the distribution of money income to welfare.

Poverty, judged in terms of money income, greatly exaggerates the proportion of the poor that live on farms.

That is only looking within the entire structure of the group that someone decides to call poor because they have decided to use a certain money income as the test. In that particular kind of testing, you get an exaggerated notion of the poverty of the farm people.

Extravagant claims as to the number of poor may influence the reception accorded this bill. The measures proposed, however, have very little to do with the families whose normal incomes, that is income year after year, including their income in kind, is less than $3,000.

The provisions of the bill deal, however, with enlarging the economic opportunity of some persons through education and training and thus enhancing their ability to earn and work. The great bulk of the really poor are going to be untouched by these programs.

The programs proposed would undoubtedly result in some persons having higher incomes than they would otherwise achieve. That the programs would add to general productivity and welfare is by no means so clear. It is in such terms that the merits of the bill should be appraised. There are many questions to debate—how many people would benefit by the programs?

To what extent might they be served by existing programs?

To what extent are the programs proposed geared to modern technology?

To what extent was the development of the program influenced by the experience of the great depression?

Surely we have come a long way since then in terms of the type of training needed and the initiation of workers to jobs appropriate to 1933. There is also the matter of how the costs of the program bear on other uses of resources, including a reduction of the income tax imposed on them who are reported to be poverty ridden.

If you look at the consumption data, which includes the full outlay of consumers, you can see where the income tax falls where you have a judgment such as has been rendered.

The bill only marginally relates to poverty. To sell it as a poverty bill is misleading advertising. Alas, sellers of the bill are not subject to our truth-in-advertising laws, legislation that I am currently discussing in my class.

This critic of President Johnson's antipoverty program regards it as too little and poorly constructed. It is described as a "war on the poor" that has little chance of substantial success. The author believes that an "effective" attack on poverty would require a major change in our political climate.

61
Johnson
vs. Poverty

Christopher Jencks is a Fellow for the Institute for Policy Studies, and formerly served as a member of the Board of Editors of The New Republic.

CHRISTOPHER JENCKS

*   *   *

IS IT EFFECTIVE?

Does all this add up to an effective attack on poverty? To answer that question one must consider some of the possible alternatives.

A more obvious approach was initiated during the New Deal: direct welfare payments to those whose standard of living falls below subsistence level. The difficulty is that legislators regard such payments as a "give away." Neither Congress nor any state legislature has shown any inclination to set either social security or welfare payments high enough to support a decent life. Benefits are so low that the recipient cannot afford a balanced diet, regular medical and dental care, warm clothes, adequate housing, or the "incidental" expenses of educating his children. Payments would have to quadruple to assure every American family $60 a week and every individual $30.

A second approach to the poor, also initiated during the New Deal, is to subsidize the goods and services they need. This would mean additional low-cost housing, expanding the food stamp plan which subsidizes the grocery purchases of welfare recipients, expanding the Kerr-Mills bill which pays some of the hospital costs of the medically indigent, providing hospital insurance for the aged, and so on. The Johnson Administration has backed such measures, but Congress has been conspicuously hostile. There

From *The New Republic*, March 28, 1964, pp. 17–18. © 1964, Harrison-Blaine of New Jersey, Inc. Reprinted by permission.

is little in the mood of the country at present to suggest that this hostility to "socialism" will diminish in the next few years.

Since the architects of the poverty program could not realistically hope to subsidize those with low earnings, their only alternative was to help them earn more. There is a widespread tendency, in the Administration and elsewhere, to assume this means putting the unemployed back to work. Actually, poverty and unemployment are only loosely connected. Most of the unemployed have enough savings, unemployment compensation, or other workers in their families, to keep them above the poverty line. Conversely, most poor families must blame their troubles on something other than unemployment. The fact is that only six per cent of all poor families are headed by a man or woman who is seeking work and unable to find it. By comparison, half are headed by a man or woman with a job that pays less than $3,000 a year. Another 44 per cent are headed by a man or woman too old, too sick, too busy with children, or too apathetic to hold a regular job.

The situation is dramatized by a statistic: there are about four million unemployed in America, but there are about seven million men and 13 million women who are earning less than $3,000 a year. Of course not all these low-paid jobs must be upgraded in order to eliminate poverty. Many are held by men or women who have no dependents, and others are held by members of families with several workers, who pool their incomes and so escape poverty. Nevertheless, it is clear that the elimination of poverty depends far more on changing the overall wage structure than on eliminating unemployment.

To win the war on poverty in a decade would require a rate of sustained growth achieved only once in recent American history. During the years 1939–44 the quantity of goods and services produced in America rose by 11 per cent annually. Unemployment sank to one per cent. During the years 1941–45, the purchasing power of the poorest fifth of all Americans rose by a third—equal to their gain since 1945. These gains were, however, achieved only by Draconian methods. Government deficits were higher than ever before or since. Price controls were necessary to restrain inflation, and even so prices rose seven per cent annually. (The economic gains cited above take this into account, however.) Government intervened in every phase of the private economy. Shortages of men, materials, and consumer goods were chronic.

The poor did well during World War II because there was an acute labor shortage and employers had no alternative to hiring every applicant. Employers did not welcome the necessity then, and they would not welcome it now. The poor are for the most part uneducated and unskilled. They are sick more often than other workers, have more accidents, make more mistakes, require more supervision, skip work more often, quarrel more with other workers. Before hiring such men and women most employers will do their utmost to find better qualified applicants. Their utmost usually includes offering higher wages than other employers, starting an inflationary spiral. Only when this tactic fails will employers accept the poorer workers.

Since the Johnson Administration has largely accepted the American taboo against inflationary policies, it inevitably rejected efforts to help the poor by stimulating extremely rapid economic growth. It did, of course, back the tax cut. This will take up some of the economic slack, but it will hardly begin to generate the kind of expansion needed to improve the wages of the poor substantially. That would take not only a tax cut but a rapid expansion of public investment and public expenditures. Congress has repeatedly refused to tolerate such expansion. State and local governments have done better, but not enough better. The private sector has done nothing at all. (The President's 1964 Manpower Report shows that expansion of private demand since 1957 has not created a single new job. Increases in productivity have abolished jobs, especially farm jobs, as fast as rising demand created them. *All* new jobs since 1957 have resulted from expanded employment by government and nonprofit organizations, and increased government demand for private goods and services, like missiles and highways.)

Mr. Johnson proposes to allocate only $75 million of his $962 million poverty package to increasing the number of good permanent jobs open to the poor. Of this $75 million, $25 million would go to the Area Redevelopment Administration to encourage new enterprises which would hire the long-term unemployed, and $50 million to the Agriculture Department's "land reform" program.

CONSERVATIVE APPROACH

Mr. Johnson's approach is, then, fundamentally conservative. It assumes that the poor are poor not because the economy is mismanaged but because the poor themselves have something wrong with them. They live in the wrong place and won't move. They have the wrong skills—or no skills at all—and won't enroll in training programs. They have too little education and won't go back to school. They have the wrong personality traits or bad health. They are too profligate to save when their earning power is high, and so have nothing left to supplement their inadequate relief or Social Security benefits. They are too short-sighted to use contraceptives, and wind up with unwanted children.

What has been launched is therefore not just a war on poverty but a war on the poor, aiming to change them beyond all recognition. The aim is not just to provide them with a lower-middle class standard of living, but also with the lower-middle class virtues, such as they are. Out of $962 million, $887 million is to be spent on education, training and character building.

Can such a plan succeed? Not this year or next, certainly. Nor, probably, in a decade or a generation. President Johnson has asserted that for the first time America has the means to abolish poverty. If poverty is understood in the narrow economic sense, this is true. But have we the means to abolish the attributes of the poor? Ignorance? Incompetence? Short-sightedness? Apathy? Despair? Illness? Not for $1 billion a year, and probably not for $10 billion either.

And what if the "causes" of poverty were eliminated? Suppose that every American family were headed by a healthy white male college graduate between 25 and 55, living in a large metropolitan area outside the South. In today's economy, some would still be unemployed—presumably those who had the poorest college records. Many would have to choose between poor jobs and no jobs. Those with the lowest IQs would tend to lose their jobs through automation. Many employers would still prefer to hire one bright PhD at $20,000 a year rather than two not-so-bright BA's at $10,000 each. Viewed in this light, the problem is not just to raise the competence of the poor, but to narrow the gap between the most desirable employees and the least desirable. If this gap cannot be narrowed, the bottom fifth of the nation will remain economically expendable, as it is today. If it is expendable—if it cannot contribute significantly to the output of goods and services—then it will not be allowed much of a share in consumption.

Despite Mr. Johnson's efforts, a substantial fraction of the American people will remain unproductive. The only way to help them is to give them money or free goods and services. To do this would require a major change in the American political climate.

The poor have only two political weapons: votes and the threat of violence. Judging by recent Negro experience, the latter is more effective than the former. Congress likes to pretend that threats only stiffen its back. But recent history suggests otherwise. It is true that Negro militancy has produced the beginnings of a white counter-reformation. But without Negro militancy Congress would not have come as close as it has to action on civil rights. Nor, I suspect, would the poverty program have as good a chance as it now has. A really massive attack on poverty must, however, await similar pressures from other poor groups.

62
Approaches
to the Reduction
of Poverty

Professor Lampman played a key role in mapping out the "war on poverty" when he was a member of the staff of the President's Council of Economic Advisers. This analysis of the problem should help you make an objective evaluation of the major policy alternatives.

ROBERT L. LAMPMAN

Robert J. Lampman is Professor of Economics at the University of Wisconsin.

The greatest accomplishment of modern economies has been the raising of living standards of the common man and the reduction of the share of the population in poverty. Contrary to the gloomy predictions of Malthus, production has increased faster than population, and, unlike the expectations of Marx, inequality of income has not steadily increased. The growth in value of product per person is generally understood to arise out of more capital, economies of scale and specialization, better management and organization, innovation with regard both to end products and techniques of production, greater mobility of factors, and improved quality of labor. All of these in turn yield additional income which, in a benign spiral, makes possible more and higher quality inputs for further growth.

The process of growth has not meant simply higher property incomes. As a matter of fact, income from property has fallen as a share of national income. Neither has growth meant a widening of differential for skill in labor incomes. Rates of pay for the most menial of tasks have tended to rise with average productivity. Social policies in fields such as labor and education aimed at assuring opportunities for all have narrowed initial advantages of the more fortunate. Such policies, along with taxation, social insurance, and public assistance measures which redistribute income toward the poor have tended to stabilize if not reduce the degree of income inequality.

A growth in productivity of 2 per cent per person per year and a relatively fixed pattern of income inequality probably have combined to yield

From the *American Economic Review*, May, 1965, pp. 521–529. Reprinted by permission.

a net reduction in poverty in most decades of American history. However, the rate of reduction has undoubtedly varied with changes in the growth rate, shifts from prosperity to depression, changes in immigration, in age composition, and in differential family size by income level.

THE POVERTY RATE AND THE POVERTY INCOME GAP

Using a present-day standard for poverty and even without recognizing the relativity of poverty over long periods, we would estimate that poverty had become a condition that afflicted only a minority of Americans by the second decade of this century. This situation was upset by the Great Depression of the 1930's but later restored by the booming economy of World War II. The postwar period has yielded a somewhat above average rate of growth in productivity and a reduction in poverty which probably is at least average for recent decades. The number of families in poverty (as marked off from nonpoverty by a $3,000 income at 1962 prices) fell from 12 million in 1947 to 9 million in 1963. This was a drop from 32 per cent to 19 per cent of families.

The rate of reduction one records or predicts will vary somewhat with the definition of poverty which he adopts. The Council of Economic Advisers adopted an income cut-off of $3,000 of total money income for families and $1,500 for unrelated individuals. It is not inconsistent with those guidelines to make further modification for family size, using $3,000 as the mark for an urban family of four persons with variations of $500 per person and to set a lower mark for rural families. Such a procedure yields a slightly lower rate of reduction in the percentage of all persons in poverty than is suggested by the 32 to 19 drop shown above. This discrepancy is due to a shift in family size and the rural to urban migration during the postwar years.

It is possible that consideration of personal income as opposed to total money income, of average rather than one year's income, of assets and extraordinary needs as well as income, and of related matters would alter our understanding of how poverty has been reduced. It is clear that some of these considerations affect the number and the composition of the population counted as poor; and it is obvious that the rate of reduction would vary if we varied the poverty line over time.

These matters of definition are important to a refinement of the generalized goal of elimination of poverty to which President Johnson has called us. Economists can assist in reaching a national consensus on the specific nature of the goal, of ways to measure the distance from and rate of movement toward the goal. Currently we are in the stage of goal-setting with poverty that occurred in 1946 with unemployment and that we have experienced with respect to other national goals such as price stability and economic growth. Hopefully, out of current controversy there will emerge a refined and only infrequently changed measurement of poverty reduction which will take its place along with the unemployment rate and the growth rate and the consumer price index as guides to appraisal of the performance of the economy. In the meantime, we can carry on our discussion of ways and means to achieve the general goal with the rough and ready measures that are at hand.

At this point in time, poverty is clearly a condition which afflicts only a minority—a dwindling minority—of Americans. The recent average rate of change, namely, a fall in the percentage of families in poverty by one percentage point per year, suggests that the poverty problem is about twenty years from solution. This rate of reduction may be difficult to maintain as we get down to a hard core of poverty and a situation in which further growth will not contribute to the reduction of the poverty rate. My own view is that this rate is still highly responsive to changes in the growth rate and that it will continue to be so for some time ahead. The relationship between the two rates is a complex one and is influenced by such things as demographic change, changes in labor force participation, occupational shifts in demands for labor, and derived changes in property incomes and social security benefits. Some groups—notably the aged, the disabled, and the broken families—have poverty rates that appear to be relatively immune to growth in average income. One powerful drag on the responsiveness of the poverty rate to growth, which has now about run its course and will shortly reverse, is the aging and reduction in labor force participation of family heads.

While the size of the poverty population is dwindling, the size of what can be called the "poverty income gap" is diminishing. This gap—the aggregate amount by which the present poor population's income falls short of $3,000 per family or $1,500 per unrelated individual—is now about $12 billion, or 2 per cent of GNP. As time goes on, this gap will assuredly be less, both because of economic growth and because of scheduled increases in social insurance benefits. (Transfers now make up about $10 billion of the $25 billion income of the poor.) Projecting recent rates of change suggests that by 1975 the poor will be no more than 12 per cent of the population and the poverty income gap will be as little as 1 per cent of that year's GNP.

As I see it, the goal of eliminating poverty needs to have a time dimension and intermediate targets. I assume we want a rate of progress at least as fast as that of recent years. Further, it helps to think of the goal in two parts: the reduction of the poverty rate and the reduction of the poverty income gap. This means we want to work from the top down and from the bottom up, so to speak. The aim of policy should be to do each type of reduction without slowing the other and to do both with the least possible sacrifice of and the greatest possible contribution to other important goals.

WHY POVERTY PERSISTS

As background to such strategic decisions, it is useful to categorize the causes of poverty in today's economy. But perhaps it is necessary first to brush aside the idea that there has to be some given amount of poverty. Most economists have long since given up the idea that a progressive society needs the threat of poverty to induce work and sobriety in the lower classes. Similarly, one can consign to folklore the ideas that some are rich only because others are poor and exploited, that if none were poor, then necessary but unpleasant jobs would go undone, that the middle class has a psychological need to exclude a minority from above-poverty living standards, and that poverty is a necessary concomitant of the unemployment, which necessarily accompanies economic growth.

Why, then, is it that there remains a minority of persons who are involuntarily poor in this affluent society? How does our system select the particular members for this minority? To the latter question we offer a three-part answer: (1) Events external to individuals select a number to be poor. (2) Social barriers of caste, class, and custom denominate persons with certain characteristics to run a high risk of being poor. (3) The market assigns a high risk of being poor to those with limited ability or motivations.

One cannot look at the data on who are the poor without sensing that many are poor because of events beyond their control. Over a third of the 35 million poor are children whose misfortune arises out of the chance assignment to poor parents. In some cases this poverty comes out of being members of unusually large families. Among the poor adults, about a third have either suffered a disability, premature death of the family breadwinner, or family dissolution. A considerable number have confronted a declining demand for services in their chosen occupation, industry, or place of residence. Some have outlived their savings or have lost them due to inflation or bank failure. For many persons who are otherwise "normal" poverty may be said to arise out of one or a combination of such happenings.

A second factor that operates in the selection of persons to be poor is the maintenance of social barriers in the form of caste, class, and custom. The clearest example of this, of course, is racial discrimination with regard to opportunities to qualify for and to obtain work. (It is perhaps worth emphasizing here that only a fifth of the present poor are nonwhite, and that only a minority of the nonwhites are presently poor.) Similar types of arbitrary barriers or market imperfections are observable in the case of sex, age, residence, religion, education, and seniority. They are formalized in employer hiring procedures, in the rules of unions and professional and trade associations, in governmental regulations concerning housing and welfare and other programs, and are informally expressed in customer preferences. Barriers, once established, tend to be reinforced from the poverty side by the alienated themselves. The poor tend to be cut off from not only opportunity but even from information about opportunity. A poverty subculture develops which sustains attitudes and values that are hostile to escape from poverty. These barriers combine to make events nonrandom; e.g., unemployment is slanted away from those inside the feudalistic walls of collective bargaining, disability more commonly occurs in jobs reserved for those outside the barriers, the subculture of poverty invites or is prone to self-realizing forecasts of disaster.

The third factor involved in selecting persons out of the affluent society to be poor is limited ability or motivation of persons to earn and to protect themselves against events and to fight their way over the barriers. To the extent that the market is perfect one can rationalize the selection for poverty (insofar as earnings alone are considered) on the basis of the abilities and skills needed by the market and the distribution of those abilities and skills in the population. But we note that ability is to some extent acquired or environmentally determined and that poverty tends to create personalities who will be de-selected by the market as inadequate on the basis of ability or motivation.

COUNTERING "EVENTS"

Approaches to the reduction of poverty can be seen as parallel to the causes or bases for selection recounted above. The first approach, then, is to prevent or counter the events or happenings which select some persons for poverty status. The poverty rate could be lessened by any reduction in early death, disability, family desertion, what Galbraith referred to as excessive procreation by the poor, or by containment of inflation and other hazards to financial security. Among the important events in this context the one most relevant to public policy consideration at this time is excessive unemployment. It would appear that if the recent level of over 5 per cent unemployment could be reduced to 4 per cent, the poverty rate would drop by about one percentage point.[1] Further fall in the poverty rate would follow if—by retraining and relocation of some workers—long-term unemployment could be cut or if unemployment could be more widely shared with the nonpoor.

To the extent that events are beyond prevention, some, for example, disability, can be countered by remedial measures. Where neither the preventive nor the remedial approach is suitable, only the alleviative measures of social insurance and public assistance remain. And the sufficiency of these measures will help determine the poverty rate and the size of the poverty income gap. It is interesting to note that our system of public income maintenance, which now pays out $35 billion in benefits per year, is aimed more at the problem of income insecurity of the middle class and at blocking returns to poverty than in facilitating exits from poverty for those who have never been out of poverty. The nonpoor have the major claim to social insurance benefits, the levels of which in most cases are not adequate in themselves to keep a family out of poverty. Assistance payments of $4 billion now go to 8 million persons, all of whom are in the ranks of the poor, but about half of the 35 million poor receive neither assistance nor social insurance payments. One important step in the campaign against poverty would be to reexamine our insurance and assistance programs to discover ways in which they could be more effective in helping people to get out of poverty. Among the ideas to be considered along this line are easier eligibility for benefits, higher minimum benefits, incentives to earn while receiving benefits, ways to combine work-relief, retraining, rehabilitation, and relocation with receipt of benefits.

Among the several events that select people for poverty, the ones about which we have done the least by social policy are family break-up by other than death and the event of being born poor. Both of these could be alleviated by a family allowance system, which the U.S., almost alone among Western nations, lacks. We do, of course, have arrangements in the federal individual income tax for personal deductions and exemptions whereby families of different size and composition are ranked for the imposition of progressive rates. However, it is a major irony of this system that it does not extend the full force of its allowances for children to the really poor. In order to do so, the tax system could be converted to have negative as well as positive rates, paying out grants as well as forgiving taxes on the basis of already adopted exemptions and rates. At present there are almost $20 billion of unused exemptions and deductions, most of which relate to families with children. Restricting the plan to such families and applying a negative tax rate of, say, 20 per cent, to this amount would "yield" an allowance total of almost $4 billion. This would not in itself take many people out of poverty, but it would go a considerable distance toward closing the poverty income gap, which now aggregates about $12 billion.

[1] Unemployment is not strikingly different among the poor than the nonpoor. Nonparticipation in the labor force is more markedly associated with poverty than is unemployment. However, it seems that about one million poor family heads experience unemployment during the year. (*Census Population Reports,* P-60, No. 39, Feb. 28, 1963, Tables 15 and 16.) If half of this group were moved out of poverty by more nearly full employment, then the poverty rate would be one percentage point lower. Another way to estimate this is as follows. The national income would be $30 billion higher than it is if we had full employment. And a $30 billion increase in recent years has generally meant a full percentage point drop in the per cent of families in poverty.

It would, of course, be possible to go considerably further by this device without significantly impairing incentive to work and save. First, however, let me reject as unworkable any simple plan to assure a minimum income of $3,000. To make such an assurance would induce many now earning less than and even some earning slightly more than $3,000 to forego earnings opportunities and to accept the grant. Hence the poverty income gap of $12 billion would far understate the cost of such a minimum income plan. However, it would be practicable to enact a system of progressive rates articulated with the present income tax schedule. The present rates fall from 70 per cent at the top to 14 per cent at income just above $3,700 for a family of five, to zero per cent for income below $3,700. The average negative tax rates could move, then, from zero per cent to minus 14 per cent for, say, the unused exemptions that total $500, to 20 per cent for those that total $1,000 and 40 per cent for those that total $3,700. This would amount to a minimum income of $1,480 for a family of five; it would retain positive incentives through a set of grants that would gradually diminish as earned income rose.

The total amount to be paid out (interestingly, this would be shown in the federal budget as a net reduction in tax collections) under such a program would obviously depend upon the particular rates selected, the definition of income used, the types of income-receiving units declared eligible, and the offsets made in public assistance payments. But it clearly could be more than the $4 billion mentioned in connection with the more limited plan of a standard 20 per cent negative tax rate. At the outset it might involve half the poverty income gap and total about $6 billion. This amount is approximately equal to the total federal, state, and local taxes now paid by the poor. Hence it would amount to a remission of taxes paid. As the number in poverty fell, the amount paid out under this plan would in turn diminish.

BREAKING DOWN BARRIERS

The approaches discussed thus far are consistent with the view that poverty is the result of events which happen to people. But there are other approaches, including those aimed at removing barriers which keep people in poverty. Legislation and private, volunteer efforts to assure equal educational and employment opportunities can make a contribution in this direction. Efforts to randomize unemployment by area redevelopment and relocation can in some cases work to break down "islands of poverty." Public policy can prevent or modify the forming of a poverty subculture by city zoning laws, by public housing and by regulations of private housing, by school redistricting, by recreational, cultural, and public health programs. It is curious that medieval cities built walls to keep poverty outside. Present arrangements often work to bottle it up inside cities or parts of cities and thereby encourage poverty to function as its own cause.

IMPROVING ABILITIES AND MOTIVATIONS

The third broad approach to accelerated reduction of poverty relates to the basis for selection referred to above as limited ability or motivation. The process of economic growth works the poverty line progressively deeper into the ranks of people who are below average in ability or motivation, but meantime it should be possible to raise the ability and motivation levels of the lowest. It is interesting that few children, even those of below average ability, who are not born and raised in poverty, actually end up in poverty as adults. This suggests that poverty is to some extent an inherited disease. But it also suggests that if poor children had the same opportunities, including preschool training and remedial health care, as the nonpoor (even assuming no great break-throughs of scientific understanding), the rate of escape from poverty would be higher. Even more fundamentally, we know that mental retardation as well as infant mortality and morbidity have an important causal connection with inadequate prenatal care, which in turn relates to low income of parents.

A belief in the economic responsiveness of poor youngsters to improved educational opportunities underlies policies advocated by many educational theorists from Bentham to Conant. And this widely shared belief no doubt explains the emphasis which the Economic Opportunity Act places upon education and training. The appropriation under that Act, while it seems small relative to the poverty income gap, is large relative to present outlays for education of the poor. I would estimate that the half-billion dollars or so thereby added increases the national expenditure for this purpose by about one-seventh. To raise the level of educational expenditure for poor children—who are one-fifth of the nation's children but who consume about a tenth of educational outlay—to equal that of the average would cost in the neighborhood of $3 billion. Such an emphasis upon education and training is justified by the fact that families headed by young adults will tend, in a few years, to be the most rapidly increasing group of poor families.

SUMMARY

Past experience provides a basis for the belief that poverty can be eliminated in the U.S. in this generation. The poverty rate has been reduced at the rate of one percentage point a year; the poverty income gap is now down to 2 per cent of GNP.

Preventing and countering the "events" which select people for poverty can help to maintain or accelerate the rate at which we have been making progress against poverty. For example, by returning to the 4 per cent "full employment" rate of unemployment, we would instantaneously reduce the poverty rate by one percentage point. For another example, we could make a great stride toward early closing of the poverty income gap by modifying the income tax to pay out family allowances.

Another broad approach to the elimination of poverty is to break down the social barriers which restrict opportunities for the poor. Examples of this are legislating against practices of discrimination and making plans to bring the poor into the mainstream of community life.

The third approach is to make progressively greater investment in improving the abilities and motivations of the poor. Substantial increase in outlays for education and training is a promising example of this approach.

Reduction of poverty hinges on the attainment of other goals such as economic growth, full employment, income security, and equal opportunity. But it also turns upon the reduction of poverty itself since poverty to an important degree causes itself. Hence, any favorable break in the circle makes the next step easier. More nearly full employment makes barriers less meaningful; lower barriers shrink differences in motivation. Similarly, higher incomes for the poor work to reduce both acquired and at-birth limitations of ability.

But any one of the approaches will involve costs, and it would be valuable to know their comparative cost-benefit ratios. It is on this that, by theoretical and empirical research, including intercountry study, social scientists can make a distinctive contribution to the long-dreamed-of, but now explicitly stated, goal of eliminating poverty.

63
The Making
of a
Negro
Middle Class

It is not a simple matter to stimulate small business enterprise in the Negro community. This author argues, however, that the success of programs may play an important role in the future social and political stability of our society.

Hannah Lees is a Philadelphia free-lance writer.

HANNAH LEES

Philadelphia

A Negro who wants to get ahead is less apt to think of starting his own business than of making the bigger and more demanding jump into law, medicine, or another profession. Matriarchal dreams of my-son-the-doctor-lawyer-professor are partly responsible, but a more obvious factor has been the almost total roadblock when it came to borrowing money. It has been easier for an ambitious young Negro to borrow money to go to college and on to professional school than to borrow a much smaller sum to start a business. Similarly, it has been easier for a Negro to get scholarships for his children than to borrow the money necessary to expand his business so that he could send them to college himself. Since the prosperous small businessman is an important stabilizing factor in any neighborhood, providing leadership and continuity, his absence in the Negro communities in our big cities has left a vacuum. He is not there to be consulted; his voice is not there representing his neighborhood in the chamber of commerce and other civic organizations. Most Negroes in business just scrape along, and a man just scraping along has neither the time, energy, nor prestige to be a civic or even a neighborhood leader.

The recent explosion of rioting and looting in Philadelphia is a painful and instructive example of what happens inside this vacuum. Columbia Avenue, where most of the violence occurred, is the chief shopping street for thousands of low-income Negroes who live in North Philadel-

Excerpted from "The Making of a Negro Middle Class," *The Reporter,* October 8, 1964, pp. 41–44. Reprinted by permission.

phia. Its shops are at least ninety per cent white-owned, and white shopkeepers, together with white landlords, have become an increasing and often legitimate symbol of exploitation. It is reasonable to wonder if the looting would have occurred if the shops had been Negro-owned. After the carnage was over, scattered small shops with crudely lettered "Negro Owned" signs stood unscathed among the rubble. But the most these owners could do was save themselves. There were none with voices loud or impressive enough to join the Negro ministers who drove around with the police broadcasting appeals for a return to sanity. If there had been, the original riot might never have spread at all.

LEARNING TO THINK SMALL

The Small Business Administration (SBA), a Federal agency now eleven years old, did nothing at all to help this situation in the first ten years of its existence. Discrimination was not a factor; SBA was simply not thinking small enough. Its ceiling for loans was $350,000, and though its theoretical floor was $200, it seldom dealt with such small figures. During 1963, for example, the branch that serves all of Pennsylvania, New Jersey, and Delaware granted only 206 loans, dispersing in the process almost $15 million, which made the average loan over $72,000. Only six of the loans were under $6,000. And during its first decade it made only seven loans to Negro businessmen.

Last year, however, a nonprofit group called the Small Business Opportunities Corporation (SBOC) was formed in Philadelphia under a three-year, $330,000 grant from the Area Redevelopment Administration, which has broad powers and millions of dollars at its disposal to stimulate enterprise and employment in depressed areas. The sole function of the SBOC was to help the SBA meet the needs of the very small businessman and to teach the businessman at the same time how to use SBA loans as stepping-stones to expansion and profit.

*   *   *

The new loan opportunities, immediately nicknamed "6-by-6," were announced to the public last January 28 with considerable radio and TV coverage, and immediately there were swarms of applicants. SBOC, expecting to start slowly and make perhaps fifty loans the first year, had set up temporary quarters in a conference room in the Fellowship Commission. It was swamped. SBA had sent four credit men to do the initial interviewing, but an SOS had to be sent out to the banks, which sent more trained interviewers. The first quarterly report of SBOC listed 1,380 applicants, of whom about a third (430) had been sufficiently qualified to send on to SBA. By August 1, SBOC had heard from 2,315 applicants, of whom 988 seemed qualified, and the Small Business Administration had made 152 loans in the 6-by-6 program with another 155 approved and nearly ready for disbursement. Forty per cent of these loans had been to Negroes. So far there have been no defaults.

Loans are obtained for a variety of purposes. Mrs. Gwynn Williams has a loan of $2,500 to enlarge her employment and job-training center, and to move it to a better location. William McElhney has a loan of $3,000 to buy trucks and equipment for an exterminating service. Leon Cornwall got $6,000 to stock an electrical appliance and service shop. Two young housewives borrowed $200 to start a children's day-care center. But these and all the other successful loan applicants are not enough to satisfy Dr. Thomas Roberts, who left the chair of economics at Villanova University to become executive director of the Small Business Opportunities Corporation. They are just beginning, he said, to realize the dimensions of the job—and of the problem.

EXPANDING THE BENEFITS

The small businessman has for some time been a victim of the cult of big bigness, but many social scientists feel that his day is coming back, that people are tired of being chain-served. The Urban League estimates that there may be seven thousand small Negro businesses in Philadelphia, including the very smallest. Most of them are one-man operations, but if they had loans many of them could expand, and, like Eason Peel, increase employment. Since the first big wave, however, they have not come in as fast as SBOC would like.

Many who came in have not been eligible and have gone out feeling and saying that SBOC is a fake. Of those approved and given papers to fill out, half never return. The basic problem is that most men with marginal businesses, and particularly Negroes with their background of limited opportunity, simply lack the schooling to cope with the forms and requirements SBA finds necessary. Obtaining letters from two banks that have refused them loans and a signed report from an accountant on their financial position simply throws them into a panic. They also feel the loan program is not as represented. And there has been a good deal of resistance from accountants, who have been telling applicants that if they are eligible for a SBA loan they can get the money more easily from a bank. This is totally untrue of the 6-by-6 program, but the accountants have tended to exaggerate the cost of preparing a presentation and the difficulty of having a loan approved.

The Small Business Opportunities Corporation is aware of these problems and is working on them. It hopes to explain its program to every small businessman in Philadelphia before very long. It has already persuaded SBA to reduce a five-page form to two sides of a single sheet and is hoping for still more simplification. It is trying to make accountants realize that their negative attitude is losing them money. One accountant who was initially very skeptical has since brought in six applicants for 6-by-6 loans and gotten them all accepted. He now thinks the program is great. The credit man for a big dairy, curious about 6-by-6, came in with one of his firm's retailers who wanted a loan and went away promising to urge the dairy's distributors to spread the word.

More important than a loan to many small businessmen is better understanding of sound business methods and careful discussion of the project they are undertaking. They are sometimes advised not to take a loan. A young clerk in a chain food store who had a wife and two small children wanted to open his own shop. Roberts said to him: "Are you prepared to work six and a half days a week and every evening? Are you prepared for the constant worry of whether you've bought the right stock or are being undersold? Are you, in fact, willing to put your store ahead of your family or any life of your own for years?" The clerk decided he was not.

Business-management courses are offered to any who want to take them, with evening sessions in business law, in keeping proper records, in how to hire, how to get new business, stockkeeping, and buying. Of the two hundred men and women who have already taken these courses about sixty per cent are Negroes.

Half of them, surprisingly, were not even applying for loans. What they wanted most was knowhow.

The program is still not quite the stimulus to Negro private enterprise that it was designed to be. Philadelphia's Negro leaders have given it little more than lip service. This is not surprising, since the Negro leadership in Philadelphia comes mainly from ministers and lawyers. Thus far, they have been too busy affirming rights, enforcing laws, and demanding equal job opportunities to see that crass, materialistic profits, if they are Negro profits, may do more for their cause than militancy. For every Negro businessman who prospers starts a chain reaction. He achieves status; he brings leadership to his neighborhood; he reduces unemployment and raises the living standard of every extra man and woman he hires; they have more to spend, which helps other Negro businesses; and so on. Perhaps there will have to be more businessmen among the Negro leaders before they add equal business opportunity to their crusades.

The regional approach to economic problems has been symbolized by the special program put together to aid "Appalachia." This author complains that the Administration's Appalachia Program does not meet the real needs of the region and provides aid mainly for those who need it least.

Harry M. Caudill, author of Night Comes to the Cumberlands, *his biography of a depressed area, is a Kentucky lawyer and former state legislator.*

64
Misdeal
in Appalachia

HARRY M. CAUDILL

Appalachia is a region as large as all Great Britain and the home of fifteen million Americans. Once, long ago, it was green and rich. For years it has been sick and now it is dying, a charity patient of affluent America.

Conscience-ridden by Appalachia's old and numerous social and economic ills, the federal government has enacted into law the Appalachian Regional Development Act, a program two years in the drafting and hailed by its sponsors as the cure for Appalachia. The act is a grim hoax. It won't restore Appalachia and its millions of poor to health and hope; more likely it will speed their descent into the depths of despondency.

President Kennedy was deeply distressed by the destitution and demoralization he encountered in West Virginia during the preferential primary in 1960. He created the President's Appalachian Regional Commission (PARC), to consult with the governors of the eleven states having counties in the Appalachian Mountains and to formulate a regional program calculated to bring prosperity to the jaded highland communities.

There is every reason to believe that President Kennedy sincerely desired to aid the area and that President Johnson has come to share his concern. But both President Johnson and the Congress appear to have assumed that the commission's recommendations as embodied in the act constitute a comprehensive redevelopment program. The assumption is unfounded, and both the President and the Congress have been sold a bill of shoddy goods.

The President's Appalachian Regional Commission was headed by Franklin D. Roosevelt, Jr., Undersecretary of Commerce. It held extensive hearings and made every effort to devise a program acceptable to the states involved. Unfortunately, the commission seems to have decided at an early date that gaining acceptance of the program by the governors was more important than finding effective solutions. To placate the governors, some of whom showed little initial enthusiasm for the project, the commission revived the hoary theory of nullification. Each state was authorized to veto any proposal which it deemed unsatisfactory, whether advanced by Washington or by another state. This new partnership arrangement, by which the federal government provides the lion's share (80 per cent) of the money and the state governments (whose historic dereliction brought about most of the trouble) get the lion's share of the resulting political credit, was hailed by PARC and Appalachian congressmen as a significant advance in state-federal relationships.

The state-veto provision is of doubtful constitutionality. It is unlikely, however, that the veto will have to be invoked, because there is little in the planned program that could arouse the ire of a governor, let alone kindle hope in the thousands of impoverished mountaineers.

The redevelopment scheme produced by PARC is not only bland; it borders on the insignificant. Appalachia is a mammoth island of backwardness, and millions of its people are paupers. Impressive as it may appear to those who have to pay it in taxes, the $1 billion to be spent for the region's supposed rehabilitation is little more than a drop of aid in a bucket of need.

Roving reporters and probing television cameras have brought the face of Appalachian misery into every American living room. The bleak hillsides, the gray mining camps, the littered roadsides, the rickety houses, and the tattered, dispirited people have haunted millions. Shocked Americans everywhere have demanded that Appalachia be rescued by the government that found it possible to rescue Europe with the Marshall Plan and to nourish the once desolate Tennessee Valley through the TVA.

What most people may not suspect is that Appalachia has two faces. They have seen the face of Appalachian poverty. The face of Appalachian affluence has remained discreetly out of view. Absenteeism and anonymity curtain the vast domain of giant corporations which own the region's wealth.

The nation's great steel and manufacturing corporations—including United States Steel, Inland Steel, Bethlehem Steel, Republic Steel, Jones & Laughlin, and International Harvester—own immense boundaries of coal, oil, gas, limestone, and other minerals, which were bought cheaply from their original owners nearly three quarters of a century ago and have been held ever since at little more than nominal taxation.

State and local taxing officials have bowed to the ancient argument that to impose fair levies on the extractive industries "will kill the goose that lays the golden egg." For example, eight years ago Pittsburgh-Consolidation Coal Corporation sold a part of its eastern Kentucky holdings to a subsidiary of Bethlehem Steel. The purchase price was nearly $16 million, but the assessed valuation of the same property was less than $4 million. These corporations and their allies, the electric utilities, the railroads, the huge real estate corporations, and the coal-mining companies, have a gigantic stake in the status quo.

Not all state and local officials are uncaring about Appalachia's ills, but in sum the state and local governments are little more than fronts for the absentee corporations which control the economic destinies of the region. The wealth—and it is almost immeasurable—is in "foreign" ownership as surely as are most of the riches of Central America.

The power of the region's economic overlords was demonstrated in the West Virginia legislature in 1953. Governor William Casey Marland struggled unsuccessfully to persuade the assembly to levy a general fund tax on the privilege of severing coal and other nonrenewable resources from the state. Today an indigent coal miner must pay a tax for the privilege of removing a loaf of bread from a grocer's shelf, but the world's largest steel corporation can remove trainloads of coal daily from the Appalachian hills without paying a tax for the right to do so.

Economically, Appalachia is little more than an internal colonial appendage of the industrial North and Midwest. Its plight is worse than that of a banana republic receiving U.S. foreign aid. Its exploitative economy generates much wealth and much poverty. The wealth flows to distant cities; the poverty accumulates at home. Like Latin America, Appalachia can find no relief for its dilemma until there is far-reaching tax reform and an overhaul of the antiquated political structure. But here the parallel ends. In the Alliance for Progress program, Washington insists on Latin American reform as the price of aid. For Appalachia, Washington has devised a plan of relief that will leave the old pattern unchanged. While the politicians can speak piously of Appalachian rejuvenation, they lack the guts to break the iron vise that grips the territory and its inhabitants. Any basic change in the situation would send wrathful reverberations through the boardrooms of dozens of huge firms.

PARC in its joint labors with the state governments discovered that whatever aimed at effective reorganization of the decrepit economy ran afoul of the entrenched absentee-owned interests and the political power structure which they dominate. So the search turned toward palliatives rather than remedies. The commission decided to spend $840 million in five years on new highways and access roads. The construction of roads will make it even easier for the nonresident owners to market their minerals and timber. Roads are popular with the mountaineers, too, so more than 80 per cent of the money could go for this one item with seemingly happy results.

The remaining funds are allocated at the rate of $41,000,000 for hospital construction, $28,000,000 for hospital maintenance, $16,000,000 for the building of vocational schools, $5,000,000 for development of timber stands, $6,000,000 for sewage-treatment systems, $36,500,000 for reclamation of strip-mined lands, and $2,400,000 for administration. None of these measures strikes at the real roots of Appalachia's troubles. They will not restore health, because the malaise is too critical.

The redevelopment program is noteworthy because of its glaring omissions. Appalachia is a beautiful country whose major resource is bituminous coal. Its wooded hills are stuffed with the fuel, and mining has shaped its tragic history. Any effort to revitalize this region without giving serious attention to the chaotic coal industry is nonsensical.

Until about 1948 coal was an immense industry, the counterpart of steel. As a mass employer, it was beset by oil and gas and advancing mining technology, and collapsed abruptly. Scores of coal companies were forced out of business in the 1950s, and those remaining in operation were compelled to mechanize to an astonishing degree. Thus hordes of industrial workmen were left stranded in the mining communities. They were men who had been educated for the mines;

their communities were poorly built and were without decent schools, hospitals, or roads. In the last decade the jerry-built communities have turned into peoplesties. The land is scarred with crumbling shacks, tipples, commissaries, and culm heaps. The demoralized people, long dependent on public assistance for their bread, have littered the roadsides and streams with countless automobile hulks and trash dumps. The creeks and rivers are reeking sewers.

Many miners earn a subsistence living digging coal with hand tools from thin seams. These "dog-hole" operations lack the protection of the federal mine safety code and are in a hopeless competition with strip mines and the large mechanized pits. The land is being ripped apart by surface miners. Simply put, the region's main source of income, its coal industry, borders on anarchy. PARC, however, blandly ignored this salient fact.

The commission might have recommended a giant cleanup campaign for Appalachia; without this, it is impossible to see how the morale of the people can be restored. Children growing up in the incredible squalor of the typical mining community fall naturally into the ruinous, sometimes rapacious habits of their elders. Yet the possibility of clearing away the befouled landscape was not even considered.

The rest of the nation has cause for alarm in the pollution constantly emanating from this tortured region. Some five hundred gigantic culm heaps—man-made mountains of mining wastes and low-grade coal—containing millions of tons of fuel, are forever burning. Their acrid fumes cloak countless valleys. Simultaneously, billions of gallons of sulfuric acid water drain daily from unsealed mines and open coal auger holes. These nauseous contaminants must be restrained if Appalachia is to shed its grim reputation. A feeble start toward this goal is authorized by the legislation, but the task will be hard, and its ultimate cost will be high indeed.

The zooming American population gives Appalachia a genuine potential as a recreation area, but this potential is being aborted by the ravages of strip mining. New machines, including the giant rubber-tire high lifts now coming on the market, make it certain that surface mines will multiply and that their onslaught upon the land will quicken. A feeble gesture at alleviating this murder of the land is proposed in the legislation, but an amendment to the bill limits reclamation to publicly owned land. Since nearly all the torn earth is privately owned, the section dealing with strip mining is without practical meaning. According to the testimony of Pennsylvania Governor William Scranton, a quarter of a million acres of land in his state have already been ruined. Unless strip mining is prohibited in the near future, the coalfields will be churned into total wreckage.

The coal industry urgently needs a stable year-round market. Such a market is available, but PARC and Congress are ignoring it. The Edison Electric Institute has estimated that $175 billion will have to be invested in new electricity-generating facilities within twenty years if a power shortage is to be averted. The trend in the electric-power industry is toward large mine-mouth generators, the power going to market by extra-high-voltage transmission lines. Such plants could be constructed in Appalachia with their power output carried cheaply and efficiently into all the great cities east of the Mississippi. The American Public Power Association, the National Rural Electric Cooperative Association, and a research group sponsored by Lockheed Space and Missile Company have concluded that these plants are feasible and that their product could be profitably marketed. And a small developmental royalty of perhaps one half mill per kilowatt hour produced would plow hundreds of millions of dollars back into regional facilities and services within a decade or two. Thus Appalachia could in large measure finance its own rehabilitation.

Such plants would make cheap power available everywhere in the Appalachian range. The lakes created to provide cooling water for the huge coal-burning generators would curtail the ravages of floods, simultaneously supplying water for new industries which the low-cost electricity would attract to the area. As in the Tennessee Valley, the lakes would bring fishermen, sportsmen, and vacationers. The modern trinity—electricity, water, and fertilizer—which has wrought such miracles for the TVA, is sorely needed in the valleys of Appalachia, but PARC and the Congress refused to learn from the nation's first great and successful attempt to rejuvenate a dying segment of the country.

To its credit, PARC considered electric-power development as a means of aiding the region's economy and requested congressional authorization for a full-scale power study. The Congress, goaded by lobbyists for the private power interests, moved with alacrity in the opposite direction and expressly prohibited the use of Appalachian Redevelopment Funds for the generation, transmission, or sale of electricity. Thus Appalachia, a land of heavy rainfall and vast coal reserves, is denied the blessings of cheap power—blessings bestowed by federal action on the Tennessee Valley and most of the West.

The great need of the Appalachian people is education. The schools everywhere are poor, often abominable. Most of America's one-room schools are in highland counties, 40 per cent of them in eastern Kentucky alone. The adult illiteracy rate is appallingly high. Teachers' salaries average about $1,000 per year under national averages. The best teachers moved away years ago. The states refuse to levy severance taxes on minerals for the support of the schools. New generations are born into the old relentless cycle of poor people, poor schools, poor job preparation, poor pay, more poor people. Yet except for a modest appropriation for vocational education, PARC made no recommendations for improvement of the public schools. As matters now stand, the Administration's pending aid-to-education bill offers more long-range hope to the mountaineers than do PARC's remedial measures.

Another notion that a serious program would have embraced is the concept of new towns. At least two thirds of the existing housing is dilapidated. Much of the populace is spread out in string towns that stretch up the winding creek valleys. Other tens of thousands are clustered in crumbling coal camps. All these communities lack adequate water supplies, and the available water is generally polluted. In fact, public health officials in one typical eastern Kentucky county recently estimated that 76 per cent of the drinking water is "grossly contaminated." It is practically impossible to service the communities with adequate public facilities. Student transportation alone is a back-breaking burden on the meager school systems. The roads are for the most part ribbons of mud, and if new ones are built, maintenance costs will be extremely high. The people spread out in this fashion years ago when "new ground" farming was their principal livelihood. Now farming is passé. Even the family vegetable garden is disappearing. No valid justification for living on rough and isolated creeks exists at the present time.

By every reasonable standard the people would be far better off living in towns, where the amenities of life could be supplied at bearable costs. A few well-planned, solidly built, and strongly organized new municipalities would absorb much of the present dwindling population and would bring new talent into the region. Both the Atomic Energy Commission and the Tennessee Valley Authority have had experience in building new cities. Their experience could have been invaluable in any undertaking to organize, house, and service the Appalachian population properly. The "new town" concept was urged upon PARC as an obvious and much-needed remedial measure, but those bold planners wasted no thought upon it.

The provision for building and financing hospitals is a patent absurdity. New hospitals can be built, and under some circumstances funds can be made available for their operation, but existing hospitals cannot be aided. Ten hospitals owned by Appalachian Regional Hospitals, Incorporated, were bought from the United Mine Workers of America's Health and Welfare Fund with federal money advanced by the Area Redevelopment Administration. This nonprofit corporation has done an excellent job of administering the hospital chain, maintaining superb standards and paying union wages to its employees. It has begun to operate in the black despite a fantastically high charity load. Yet these institutions—the best public facilities in Appalachia—are threatened with extinction for lack of operating capital. The administrators of the Appalachian Regional Development Act will be powerless to aid them. They may be compelled to watch these immensely beneficial hospitals close for lack of funds while simultaneously financing the construction of others.

An effort to obtain an amendment beneficial to satisfactory existing hospitals brought stern admonitions from PARC and congressional sponsors of the act that no changes could be tolerated, not even so much as "a single comma." However, when it came to another matter, Senator Robert Kennedy of New York was not deterred by such notions. His amendment to add thirteen relatively prosperous New York counties to Appalachia was promptly approved, and by legislative fiat the prosperous inhabitants of comparatively scrubbed upstate New York cities and towns became fellow sufferers with the miserable people of the Cumberland Plateau.

Paradoxically, not all of Appalachia is poor. There are "growth centers" within the region which are prosperous by national norms. In these areas—for example, Kingsport, Tennessee—industry has begun to diversify. Bank deposits are high. Schools, hospitals, libraries, and other public facilities and services are good by Appalachian standards. These islands of affluence in a sea of poverty grow as much by attracting people from other parts of America as by drawing highlanders out of the surrounding countryside. A cruel provision in the legislation requires all the development funds to be spent in such a manner as to expedite the expansion of these fortunate centers of prosperity and growth. The fact that only a relative handful of mountaineers live there did not deter PARC's planners. The growth of a few small cities will not affect the tens of thousands of people stranded in such abysmal backwaters as Hellier, Kentucky, and Stonega, Virginia.

Sorely needed is a plan of development based on the total environment of Appalachia, a plan that indexes and utilizes all its resources of people, soil, water, timber, and minerals to build a viable economy and a healthy social order for the entire territory. The accentuation of a spotty prosperity will make the rich wealthier still without alleviating the misery of the poor. This is a reversal of American policy in the development of the Tennessee Valley and of our great Western territories. Here is a new national policy which declares that when an American region falls into misfortune, only a few of the people and only a part of the land will be rescued, with the aid going to those who need it least.

What, then, will be the consequence of this loudly trumpeted legislation for putting more than $1 billion of taxpayers' money into Appalachia? If we ask, in a paraphrase of John Kennedy, not what it will do for us but for our country, the answer has to be a dismal one. The future of Appalachia is bleak indeed. The absentee landlords are pillaging the countryside of its coal, oil, gas, and timber. With the exception of a few counties in Pennsylvania, Tennessee, and North Carolina, little of value is being manufactured anywhere in the huge territory. PARC's scheme will accelerate the bleeding of resources without relieving the region's most pressing ills. The hopes of the people have been stirred. Disillusionment is sure to follow. The old people are dying. The young are leaving. The middle-aged subsist on the dole. In the estimation of the corporations that control the resources, most of the inhabitants are simply superfluous. Their lands are worn out. They possess no skills that the nation needs. Perhaps if they are retrained, they, too, will go away and stop bothering the public conscience. Appalachia is becoming a dark island near the heart of America, peopled in large measure by benumbed human relics and totally despoiled of its natural resources.

Perhaps the superhighways the governors, PARC, and Congress have prescribed will bring some tourists to shake their heads sadly over this end result of man's greed and folly. It has been said that Appalachia, like Rip Van Winkle, slept through an entire age. Its backwoods people went to sleep in the agricultural age and were little disturbed until the dawn of the age of cybernetics.

Perhaps so. In any event, those who had hoped for a meaningful Appalachian development program as far-reaching and revolutionary as was TVA thirty years ago have been bitterly disappointed. Unless Congress takes a new look at its number one trouble spot and unless the American public is aroused as the people of England were aroused over the fate of Wales forty years ago, Appalachia can go back to sleep—the sodden sleep of the impoverished, the embittered, and the hopeless.

65

No More Pork Barrel: The Appalachia Approach

This article presents a friendlier view of the Appalachia Program. Some of its virtues are reviewed, including the innovation of delegating a major share of decision making to the participating states. The author argues that the program is a pragmatic response to political and economic realities.

Jerald Ter Horst is chief of the Washington bureau of the Detroit News.

JERALD TER HORST

If imitation is the sincerest form of flattery, then the Appalachia redevelopment program may indeed be the forerunner of a new era in Federal public-works spending. Similar programs are already being proposed for the Ozarks, the New England States, and the Upper Great Lakes area, each fashioned in the belief that the gateway to the Great Society is through regional concentration of Federal money instead of scattershot spending in the fifty states.

In its purest form, the 1965 Appalachia proposal would mean that the states and counties actually could tell Washington where and how to spend Federal tax dollars to achieve the economic and social uplift of a particular region. Ordinarily this alone would engender stiff opposition in Congress. But the eleven-state Appalachia concept dares to go several steps further. Federal money would go primarily to a region, not directly to impoverished people. It would not necessarily go to the neediest towns and counties, either, but to those with the greatest potential for economic growth. And the benefits, assuming that the program is successful, would not be immediately translatable into votes.

THE GOVERNORS' IDEA

This tradition-shattering concept did not originate in Washington. It was the collective idea of a group of governors who began meeting periodically in the late 1950's in an effort to seek solutions to the common economic blight affecting many areas of their states. By May 20, 1960, the con-

From *The Reporter,* March 11, 1965, pp. 27–29. Reprinted by permission.

sultations had reached the point where the group, meeting in Annapolis, Maryland, formally created the Conference of Appalachian Governors. The following October, meeting in Lexington, Kentucky, the conference gave birth to "a special regional program of development" that envisaged a combined attack on their problems through the resources of the local, state, and Federal governments, and the assistance of private industry, civic groups, and philanthropic foundations. At the meeting were the governors of Alabama, Georgia, Kentucky, Maryland, North Carolina, Pennsylvania, Tennessee, Virginia, and West Virginia. Joined later by Ohio and South Carolina, the group represents that portion of the Appalachian Mountains ranging from northern Pennsylvania into southern Alabama, an area largely bypassed by the tremendous economic changes at work in the rest of the country since the Second World War.

In 1963, the Appalachia governors prevailed on President Kennedy to create the Appalachian Regional Commission to analyze the needs of the region and develop a co-ordinated plan for attempting some permanent cures of their chronic problems. Represented on the commission were the states and all the Federal agencies involved in such aid programs as highways, hospitals, public health, education, timber, crops, livestock, manpower retraining, mining, flood control and stream pollution, wildlife, and recreation. Under its chairman, Under Secretary of Commerce Franklin D. Roosevelt, Jr., the commission toured Appalachia twice and discussed the region's needs with public and private experts in the various states. Its report last spring to President Johnson set the stage for an unusual concerted program of economic-resource development by the cities, counties, and states and the Federal government.

The various subregions of Appalachia, the commission said, share this unhappy distinction: "Rural Appalachia lags behind rural America, urban Appalachia lags behind urban America, and metropolitan Appalachia lags behind metropolitan America." It found, for example, that one-third of Appalachia's families earn less than $3,000 annually; two-thirds of its people do not finish school; unemployment is half again the national average, and out-migration is at the high rate of 200,000 persons a year. "The most serious problems which beset Appalachia are low income, high unemployment, lack of urbanization, low educational achievement, and a comparatively low standard of living."

BREAKING NEW GROUND

At first glance, the 1965 Appalachia program appears to be the usual grab bag of projects—new roads, soil improvement and erosion control, timber development, hospitals and treatment centers, vocational-education, sewage-treatment works, strip-mine reclamation, fish and wildlife projects—all intended to help Appalachia catch up with the rest of the nation.

But closer examination discloses that the Appalachia planners have broken new ground in the formulation and management of public-works spending. For the first time, the Federal government would delegate a major share of the decision-making to the participating states. The master plan for economic rehabilitation would be devised by the states or groups of counties in a multistate area with contiguous land and common problems.

While the actual operation of aid projects would be under the appropriate Federal agencies, the supervision and co-ordination of the whole Appalachia program would be vested in the Appalachian Regional Commission, to consist of the governor of each participating state, or his designee, and one Federal representative named by the President. Decisions would be made by a majority vote of the state members, plus the affirmative vote of the Federal representative, who would, in effect, have a veto over proposals by the state members of the commission. But the veto could be substantially limited, since a majority of state members could counter any move toward Federal "dictation" by withholding their votes.

This check-and-balance formula represents a major shift in bureaucratic thinking in Washington. It has inspired heated debate inside the administration and in Congress. Veteran agency heads still question the wisdom of letting states have such a large share of the decision-making process when most of the money comes from Federal revenue.

Congress has also been historically reluctant to appropriate money without a certain supervision over the decision-makers. This it can do most easily when funds are expended by Federal agencies—even to the extent of cranking into a program a few pet projects of a committee chairman and influential lawmakers. It is a precept of pork-barrel doctrine that a congressman and his constituents have a right to expect certain Federal benefits for their district to flow from his membership on key committees. Thus it comes as a minor miracle to find that both Federal bureaucrats and members of Congress seem willing to relinquish some of their authority in order to give the Appalachia program a trial.

One of the surprise converts is the Bureau of the Budget, known best as the "No" agency of government. "To be honest, this is a new venture," conceded Charles L. Schultze, until recently an assistant Budget Bureau director. "We are doing something different. While not saying it is experimental, we think it is an exceedingly interesting approach. We are going to have to work our way through this."

In his testimony before the House Public Works Committee, Schultze described the proposed Appalachia concept of multistate planning under Federal supervision as "a nice balance" of authority. Still to be tested, however, is just how the states will exercise their new license to tell Washington where to send Federal dollars. What's likely to happen, according to Senator Jennings Randolph, the West Virginia Democrat who steered the bill through the Senate, is that most of the hard bargaining will be done outside the commission's chambers. An Appalachia planner agreed. "We'll work it out informally before we take something in for a vote—just like they do in Congress."

The basis for this hope lies in the considerable give-and-take among the Appalachia governors and the Federal representatives in working out the terms of the legislation. For example, Georgia, North Carolina, and Maryland, because their needs are not so great, have consented to a smaller allocation of primary highway corridor mileage than is intended for West Virginia and Pennsylvania. Similarly, the governors of South Carolina and Alabama have agreed to take a smaller share of development highway money because their Appalachia counties will be adequately served by the Federal interstate highway program.

The spirit of compromise was equally apparent in Congress. The administration and Capitol Hill Democrats consented to a proposal by Senator Jacob K. Javits (R., New York) that no program for Appalachia should be implemented until the Appalachia commission had consulted with appropriate state officials and received their recommendations. The acid test, however, will come when individual lawmakers make their customary demands on Federal agencies for inclusion of projects dear to their constituents.

LEADING FROM STRENGTH

Another radical departure from tradition is the Appalachia concept of skipping the customary "means test" to determine which areas will be helped. The Area Redevelopment program, for example, uses specific criteria for establishing eligibility for Federal aid. A county must have a certain rate of unemployment in order to qualify for job-creating projects. But the Appalachia approach relies on "regional growth potential," a theory that economic uplift should be concentrated on certain cities or counties that have prospered in spite of Appalachia's general distress.

There is a hint of economic predestination here; the belief that many economically weak towns and counties do not have the potential to become thriving, prosperous centers of population. Instead, Appalachia planners believe that the economically strong places should be strengthened to support the weaker surrounding areas. One example is Huntsville, Alabama, with its space-industry complex and college environment in the midst of a depressed area. "Instead of trying to build up the area to compete with Huntsville, we should try to find ways of helping the rest of the region become auxiliary to Huntsville," one planner explained. "This could be done by improving the road network, providing sewer and water facilities for residential expansion, perhaps improving farm production and recreational opportunities in some sectors of the region."

Wilkes-Barre, Pennsylvania, is considered another center for regional growth potential that could attract more industries and commerce and provide new job opportunities through co-ordinated planning designed to increase the "social overhead capital" needed for area self-sufficiency. In all, there are probably fifty such core cities or counties in the 360 counties included in the Appalachia region.

One of the continuing controversies in the Appalachia program is its heavy emphasis on roadbuilding. About one thousand miles will be "local access" roads, intended primarily to link Appalachia's almost inaccessible valleys with nearby cities and towns. Another 2,350 miles would be designated as "development highways," linking core cities with each other and with areas outside Appalachia.

"There's been a sort of liberal versus pragmatist debate on this thing," said John L. Sweeney, the able young administrator the President chose as chairman of the Federal Development Planning Committee for Appalachia. "Most programs of economic help in the past have been based on the theory that a man has a right to a job where he lives and that government should help bring him that job. The Appalachia approach is that a man has a right to a job, but it is reasonable to expect him to be willing to commute to it or move to it if necessary."

Using a mile-a-minute yardstick, Appalachia planners think it logical to expect people to travel forty minutes to reach their places of employment, a vocational school, or even a hospital. Thus a core-city plan will encompass an area extending as far as forty miles from the center, crossing county and state boundaries when necessary.

ROADS OR EDUCATION?

Not all economic and social planners agree, however, with the priority on roads. Doubts about its importance were heard at the American Institute of Planners conference in Newark, New Jersey, last year. One said he wished he could be "czar" of the Appalachia program just long enough to scrap the highway priority. Others said education should get first priority. An earlier Ford Foundation study concluded that the unemployed and unskilled coal and steel workers in Appalachia "must be written off so far as any major economic contribution is concerned." It advocated massive Federal aid to education, increased out-migration, and birth control.

The Appalachia rebuttal is both intriguing and indignant. "If we are going to be politically realistic about the Appalachia program, it is necessary to design a program that mirrors the political realities of the states involved," said Stuart F. Feldman, top staff aide for the Appalachia Development Committee. And the political realities are that the governors, senators, and representatives of the Appalachia states wanted a priority on roads—and so did the planning experts for the committee.

"From the point of view of public policy," Feldman told the planners' conference, "it is evident that Appalachia is an ongoing region whose 167,000 square miles, numerous metropolitan areas, and population of of over sixteen million people represent a resource and an investment this nation cannot abandon through policies that encourage an outmigration of the able."

There is both historic and contemporary justification for the road priority. Appalachia once had been opened by the railroads, which came to fetch the coal for the steel mills and electric-power generation. But automation has hit each of the region's big three—coal, steel, and the railroads—throwing thousands upon thousands of men and their sons out of manual-labor jobs. Oil and natural gas became victorious competitors of coal for the fuel market; even the coal-burning locomotives gave way to diesels. In the old days, rail spurs ran back into almost every Appalachia hollow to reach the mines; because they were not built for private gain, roads seldom followed. There are still hamlets whose only connection with the outside world is over the abandoned rail roadbeds.

The Federal interstate highway system has helped to open Appalachia. But states and communities with a low tax base haven't been able to raise extra funds for the auxiliary highways and local access roads. In mountainous areas of West Virginia, for example, Appalachia planners note that it costs $2 million a mile to construct a two-lane paved highway. Moreover, Appalachia needs road money not so much to accommodate existing traffic as to stimulate new traffic.

Surprisingly, the press has been rather uncritical in reporting that seventy-six per cent, or $840 million, of the Appalachia program's $1.1-billion price tag is for roadbuilding. The road money actually is a five-year authorization; the rest of the money for other Appalachian needs covers the first two years only. Seen in perspective, then, the road ratio is not so lopsided as it appears.

The debate will be more intense over another aspect of the Appalachia program —namely, its assumption that there should be preferential treatment for an eleven-state area, as well as internal discrimination inherent in selecting one town as a growth center while bypassing another. One of Appalachia's problems is the inability of counties and cities to raise the usual local share necessary to obtain Federal matching funds for such things as airports, hospitals, vocational education facilities, libraries, and flood control. The Appalachia bill will make it possible for the Federal government to pay up to eighty per cent of the total cost in such instances, even if other regions of the country would get only fifty per cent Federal aid. Additionally, there are special supplemental funds to cover actual operating costs of hospitals for up to two years, plus a $36.5-million fund to alleviate land damage wrought by collapsed coal mines, underground fires, and acid seepage into streams. And Republicans charge gross discrimination in that the road program "is almost as large as the annual program for construction of Federal-aid primary and secondary highways" for the entire country.

There has been, inevitably, some compromise. The bill's current dollar total is about one-third of the $3 billion in Federal money originally sought. A proposed public development corporation, to be financed by bond sales and Federal funds, had to be scrapped when it appeared to be just another back-door raid on the Treasury. Western cattle interests knocked out a $17-million program for pastureland improvement. And administration lobbyists have had to tell envious lawmakers from other areas that if they will go along with the Appalachia plan, the White House will entertain similar regional development programs for other parts of the country.

Behind it all lies a growing conviction in Congress and in the councils of a Democratic administration that pork-barreling, accelerated public-works spending, and such things as the Area Redevelopment program—generally classed as economic pump priming—have missed the mark. The past, however, has not been a complete loss, at least not in the view of the President's Council of Economic Advisers. The council has analyzed the weaknesses of these earlier programs, and all of its conclusions point toward more Appalachia-type solutions. Add a pinch of Johnsonian consensus, and the rationale is simply that states and local communities cannot do the job alone—and that the Federal government should not.

One often forgets that social problems
involve people, not just statistics.
Mr. Harrington provides a graphic portrait
of the eroding impact of dependence
on the aged poor, and illustrates some
problems faced in relief administration.

*Michael Harrington was formerly
editor of* New America *and is the author
of* Accidental Century, *Macmillan, 1965.*

MICHAEL HARRINGTON

The aging woman in New York called her social worker on the telephone. She was in tears. Her check had not come from Welfare on the
expected day, and she was terrified that she had been cut off, that now she
would literally face starvation. Her life, like those of many in her situation,
was suspended by a thread from the city's welfare system. The social
worker was her symbol of hope.

The social worker: It is inevitable that this figure should emerge in a
book on poverty. In every part of the other America there are social
workers. Among the gangs of the city slums, it is even considered a mark
of honor to have a full-time worker assigned to a particular group. It shows
that the authorities are taking them seriously. In the Negro ghetto, once
the social worker becomes known, he or she is the one person from the
outside who can move with a certain ease down the streets.

But it is particularly fitting that the social worker appear in a chapter on
the misery of age in contemporary America. For the millions of aging poor,
and particularly for those who live alone, one of the main facts about life
is that it becomes totally dependent. At best, they must count on the
charity and love of a family; at worst, their fate belongs to the stranger
from Welfare.

Much has been written against the social worker in the United States.
The argument usually runs that callousness and cynicism are the inherent
products of public charity. Unquestionably, social work has created some
bureaucratic, unfeeling personalities, individuals who see only statistics

and the mass, who never really look into the human face of poverty. There is a sort of welfare-state Lady Bountiful who subsists on a patronizing, routinized *noblesse oblige.* As time has gone on, the "clients" of these social workers have become wise. They adopt the jargon; they give the right answers; they become bureaucratically adept.

But this acid portrait is only part of the picture. To a considerable extent social workers are as they are because the funds with which they work are completely inadequate to solve the problems that confront Welfare. The case load is usually overwhelming. Often, good, warm, and sincere people who genuinely want to help human beings are simply submerged in a routine that is not of their own making. (An irony: some years ago, a union of social workers in New York struck against the authorities by staying late on their own time and writing all of the money authorizations that were legally possible.) I remember a teacher in St. Louis who moved into the slum neighborhood of her school in order to be with the people all of the time. She is a symbol of the best in the social-work impulse.

If it is tragic that a bureaucratic impersonality is imposed on many social workers throughout the other America, that fact becomes most intolerable in relation to the aged poor. These are people whose plight is expressed in a torment of loneliness and isolation. They require, above all, individual and particular care. And no matter how passionately committed to humanity a social worker is, this requires a certain amount of money. America has not provided it.

In the fifties, a young woman social worker for the aged at the Montgomery County Relief Area settled in Dayton, Ohio. What follows in the next few pages is a summation of her impressions of the reality of social work in that place.

In Ohio, relief programs are on the basis of county administration (or were in the mid-fifties, the period from which this description is taken). Standards were set for minimal payments required to give the people the basis of a subsistence existence. Then, as so often happens in the other America, each county would decide what percentage of the minimum it would provide. (Relief and welfare programs throughout the United States are completely uneven; it is much better to be poor in New York City than in Montgomery County, and better to be poor in almost any place than in Mississippi.) In Montgomery County the percentage of the minimum was 90 per cent—fairly high for the state.

The first thing that an older person would encounter when coming to the relief area was the necessity of documenting eligibility. In some cases proof of age was required, and there could be a long postponement, or even a rejection, if the proper papers were not produced. Some of the programs had a residency requirement that the individual had lived in the state for five out of the last nine years.

In this particular office, the young woman relates, the screening was carried on by people who were hostile to the applicants. They regarded most of those who came to them as "dead-beats" and "bums," and they were determined to keep freeloaders off the public rolls. As a result, they have achieved a rejection rate of 55 per cent, and they were quite proud of it and determined to keep it there.

To a person from the middle class, the fact that documents are required by a public agency seems to be obvious and rational. Yet this judgment misses a basic fact about the poor generally, and the aged poor in particular: that they are precisely the ones least equipped to deal with the bureaucracy of the welfare state. Some of the American poor have difficulty with the English language, and almost all of them are undereducated. There are those who develop their relations with welfare into a fine art, but there are many more who are literally terrified by the forms and the apparatus of a relief office.

This is doubly true for the aged. They are in failing health, and are completely and totally dependent upon the authorities. A trip to the relief office is a matter of life and death for them. And they tend to be bewildered by the routines of a world in which they did not grow up. The people described by the young social worker in Montgomery County were consciously hostile to those who came to them for help. But even those who are solicitous are forced to act in somewhat the same way. Money is limited, and in order to see that everyone gets something it is necessary to be brutal and probing.

In Montgomery County there were some who tried to steer the aged poor away from clinics. They felt that if a person went to a clinic where all kinds of complaints were treated, there would be a tendency to invent illness so as to get more out of the state. So they preferred to send them to individual doctors, and to certify treatment for a single ailment.

But within the present setup the single-doctor approach is not a simple evil. One of the standard indignities in the clinic is that the doctor is likely to change with each visit. This means that the old person has to recite symptoms anew each time. Because of such repetition, it seemed to some of the people that they were beginning treatment over and over and that nothing was really being done for them. (In New York, for instance, one old man I know goes to a clinic and an individual doctor through the Welfare Department. He feels that the doctor is really helping him, but the routine of the clinic has convinced him that nothing is being done for his condition.)

But again, all this is part of the poverty of public facilities in the affluent society. In Montgomery County, for example, there was a woman who would be confined to her bed unless she had a wheel chair. A relatively small expenditure of money would have made her life infinitely more decent and dignified. When the social worker proposed that this be done, her superiors told her that there were hundreds of others who needed wheel chairs (to translate: hundreds of others who, by receiving a simple device, could have the horizons of their life broadened). The authorities granted that this particular case was a worthy one and that the benefits would be immediate and obvious, but they were afraid that it would start a run on wheel chairs. The woman stayed in bed.

In the incident of the wheel chair, the lack of public funds prolonged and made more miserable an already existing illness. In other cases, sickness and suffering are created by the squalor of the welfare services. Mrs. H_____ was seventy-five. Her husband had suffered a stroke and a bad fall, and had lost control of his bowel and bladder functions. She tried to care for him, lift him, wash his sheets and underwear, and so on. There was enough government money to "live" on, but her life was near collapse, and she had already been stricken by one siege of pneumonia.

Mrs. H_____ was not an isolated individual. This is how the young social worker described the living conditions of her "clients": "They live in furnished rooms, as boarders with a family, in small furnished and unfurnished apartments, in homes of their own, in trailers and rest homes. Those in the furnished rooms are probably on the whole the most pitiable. Generally they are alone—single, widowed or widower, divorced—they live in complete seclusion, terribly lonely, yet deliberately cutting themselves off from their neighbors whose gossip they fear. They do not want it known that they are "on relief."

"If they are fortunate, they can find one neighbor whom they can learn to trust. That neighbor will function as a companion and, equally important, as a responsible protector who will call the doctor or get the client into the hospital, or who will call the case worker if the client is too sick to do so. If this neighbor moves away they may never find another to rely on."

Another hard fact of this life comes from the bureaucratic demand that there be some *quid pro quo* for relief payments. In many areas, going on relief requires the signing of a lien on all property so that Welfare has the first claim against the estate. Usually, this is a technicality, since these people have no money and no assets in any case. But for those who have saved and skimped and bought a home during their middle years, this provision is a trauma, a sort of ultimate deprivation that puts an official stamp on society's rejection of them. And for almost all, whether there are assets or not, it is an emotional experience in which life itself is being signed away in a legal document. The individual is being made the property of the state in return for three inadequate meals a day, rent money, and some medical care.

There is a woman in New York who had been a vaudeville head-liner in the old days. When she was making money, she spent it foolishly, signing away rights and a fortune. Now she is on relief, and Welfare has demanded that she sign over her estate. There is a possibility that a movie may be made about her life. In her old age she has finally become crafty. Because she signed too much away when she was young, she is balking now. And perhaps she won't get care as a result.

At the end of the road, there is the county home. The staff people around Dayton are quite proud of this institution, the young woman relates. They regard it as adequate to the needs of the people who are sent to them. But many of the aged themselves are terrified by the idea of the county home. In the popular feeling of America, there is something utterly degrading in the very name. (The popular feeling is partly right; the utter inadequacy of a good many of these places will be described shortly.)

How representative are these details of welfare administration in Ohio? As noted before, there is great variation in these programs from state to state, from city to city. But there are also the inescapable mathematics of the inadequacy of social security and other Federal programs and of the various local systems. As it is, the aged poor in America are condemned to deal with a bureaucratic, impersonal, frustrated setup.

The payroll tax rate now required to
finance social security benefits, including
Medicare, may have reached a practical
maximum. But any move to finance
improved social security benefits from
general tax sources conflicts with the
historical basis of our social security system
as an "insurance" program. The author
argues that we must face this dilemma
soon.

67

What Future
for Social Security

*Merton C. Bernstein is an attorney,
a labor arbitrator, and a lecturer at Yale
Law School. He is the author of* The
Future of Private Pensions (*The Free
Press*).

MERTON C. BERNSTEIN

Hard and crucial decisions about Social Security confront us. At least
we should confront *them.* Since its inception in 1935, Old Age, Survivors',
and Disability Insurance has been financed wholly by payroll taxes, paid
in equal parts by employer and employees. Unless augmented by funds
drawn from general federal revenues—an innovation as unpalatable to
many of its staunchest supporters as to its most carping critics—benefits will
remain woefully inadequate to the needs of the elderly, who already comprise about 10 per cent of our population. If this transformation is not
accomplished, or is done only timidly, private pensions must provide substantial supplements to most of our future retirees—a task for which private
pensions now are ill-fitted.

The great likelihood is that, unless basic improvements are made in *both*
public and private systems, an appallingly large majority of the elderly
will continue to drag out their last years in poverty. Enactment of the
Medicare program will not solve the problem—indeed, it will crystallize
and accelerate the predicament which is imposed by the limits that are
inherent in the OASDI program as presently constructed. If the public
desires improvements in coverage and benefits, they must learn more about
both the public and private systems, and grapple with the dilemmas
posed.

*　　*　　*

In the view of many, most notably Senator Ribicoff, former Secretary
of Health, Education, and Welfare, the *rate* of tax is approaching the

From *The New Republic,* January 9, 1965, pp. 9–11. © 1965, Harrison-Blaine
of New Jersey, Inc. Reprinted by permission.

maximum that is feasible. Payroll tax increases required by the enactment of Medicare, and the small money benefit improvements of the bill passed by the Senate last fall, would bring the combined employee-employer rate to what is regarded as the limit—10 per cent; in addition, a boost of taxable payroll to $5,600 a year would be necessary. As the rate of tax is uniform for all, and as it is really inconceivable that low-paid workers can or should be taxed at any higher rate, how are we to finance further OASDI benefit improvements which are urgently, often desperately, needed?

*   *   *

. . . Quite clearly, higher payroll taxes are out of the question, for, with enactment of Medicare, the uniform, hence regressive tax, will go as high as low wage earners can bear. If we are to remain within the "principle" that OASDI payroll tax revenues must pay completely for benefits, future increases must come from raising the amount of wages and salaries that are taxable. How much of a boost would depend upon the benefit increase that is sought. An aggregate benefit boost of 50 per cent—which in terms of need is modest—simply could not be paid for in this manner, even if there is *no* limit on the amount of earnings subject to this tax. If the limited hospitalization program of the 1964 bill that the Senate passed were enacted (with its benefits extended to retirees 62 and over, and to the disabled), money-benefit improvements of 14 per cent would use up all of the funds available from a combined 10 per cent payroll tax applied to *all* wages and salaries without upper limit.

The dilemma then becomes either to enact whatever modest improvements can be paid for by payroll taxes, or to modify the principle that such taxes can be the sole source of revenue for this program. Such a change cannot be made lightly, because the OASDI payroll-tax pattern has been a key factor in the relative ease with which repeated liberalizations of OASDI have been legislated since 1950. While there was opposition to just about every improvement, it was slight compared to the phalanxes that would have done battle were the financing derived from general revenues themselves, derived in the main from corporate taxes and the more or less progressive individual income tax. Then such improvements would have constituted just another "spending program," in competition for insufficient funds from a usually tight-fisted Congress.

Another alternative, chilling to the liberal heart, is to seek medical care for the aged outside the Social Security system. Such a separate program would be meaningless unless much of its funds came from general revenues, but *without* a means test. The United States has yet to adopt a social-welfare program paid for by general revenues which does not include the odious needs test. Furthermore, benefits under these programs have been anything but generous.

If the elderly are to participate in the Great Society, something has to give—specifically, the Social Security "principle" of beneficiaries paying the whole freight under a tax scheme that is doubly regressive (uniform rates applicable only to the low end of wages and salaries); or else we must turn, in part, to general revenues derived under moderately progressive rates, without attaching a needs test. Many European countries—notably Sweden and Britain—pay for the bulk of their social insurance from general tax sources.

There is real question that we are ready for such a move, although last fall the Senate, without a murmur, included some three million non-OASDI participants in the Medicare program, with their benefits to be paid from general revenues without a means test. But that provision would be temporary because, before long, practically all those turning 65 will qualify for OASDI.

It remains to be seen whether the staunchest advocates of OASDI improvements are willing to risk the future of the program by abandoning the conservative funding "principle" that has eased their task during the last decade and a half, and probably was crucial in the adoption of the disability program. (The argument that retirees "pay" for their benefits, and so cannot be deprived of them by Congress, has suffered a major rebuff in the Supreme Court; hence that reason for resistance seems unrealistic.) Perhaps those most devoted to Social Security will see that the program has little future, at least slight prospect of substantial improvement, unless they move to higher ideological ground. A society such as ours is disgraced by the plight of our elderly, and the resources of the entire nation should be mobilized to help provide a decent standard of living upon retirement. Indeed many European retirement programs, both private and public, provide benefit increases reflecting wage improvements occurring *after* retirement, on the theory that former workers helped build the economic system and are entitled to share equally in its progress. We subsidize less laudable activities, which supposedly redound to the general public interest, although quite exclusive groups are the direct beneficiaries of the public largesse.

Even with Democratic majorities of two-to-one in both houses of Congress, I wonder whether we are ready for the bold departures described. If an advance is not made quickly and decisively, another opportunity will be long in coming. If a basic and ambitious reconstruction of OASDI and proposed medical care for the aged programs are not accomplished, we had better become reconciled to the long-term limits of Social Security, and recognize the broad role that must be performed by private pension plans. Then we must turn to the urgent business of rendering them fit to assure broad and meaningful coverage and adequate benefits. As we most often do things by halves—at best—probably both courses must be pursued.

PART FIVE

The Public Sector

Writing as the Senator from
Massachusetts, President Kennedy
describes the variety of pressures under
which decisions are made by the Congress,
and discusses the nature of the
Congressman's responsibility to his
constituents. This perceptive analysis of
legislative behavior is a useful supplement
to economic analysis in the examination
of public policy issues.

*The late President John F. Kennedy
was United States Senator from
Massachusetts when he wrote* Profiles
in Courage.

68

Courage and Politics

JOHN F. KENNEDY

*   *   *

A nation which has forgotten the quality of courage which in the past has been brought to public life is not as likely to insist upon or reward that quality in its chosen leaders today—and in fact we have forgotten. We may remember how John Quincy Adams became President through the political schemes of Henry Clay, but we have forgotten how, as a young man, he gave up a promising Senatorial career to stand by the nation. We may remember Daniel Webster for his subservience to the National Bank throughout much of his career, but we have forgotten his sacrifice for the national good at the close of that career. We do not remember—and possibly we do not care.

"People don't give a damn," a syndicated columnist told millions of readers not so many years ago, "what the average Senator or Congressman says. The reason they don't care is that they know what you hear in Congress is 99 per cent tripe, ignorance, and demagoguery and not to be relied upon. . . ."

Earlier a member of the Cabinet had recorded in his diary:

> While I am reluctant to believe in the total depravity of the Senate, I place but little dependence on the honesty and truthfulness of a large portion of the Senators. A majority of them are small lights, mentally

weak, and wholly unfit to be Senators. Some are vulgar demagogues . . . some are men of wealth who have purchased their position . . . [some are] men of narrow intellect, limited comprehension, and low partisan prejudice. . . .

And still earlier a member of the Senate itself told his colleagues that "the confidence of the people is departing from us, owing to our unreasonable delays."

The Senate knows that many Americans today share these sentiments. Senators, we hear, must be politicians—and politicians must be concerned only with winning votes, not with statesmanship or courage. Mothers may still want their favorite sons to grow up to be President, but, according to a famous Gallop poll of some years ago, they do not want them to become politicians in the process.

Does this current rash of criticism and disrespect mean the quality of the Senate has declined? Certainly not. For of the three statements quoted above, the first was made in the twentieth century, the second in the nineteenth, and the third in the eighteenth (when the first Senate, barely underway, was debating where the Capitol should be located).

Does it mean, then, that the Senate can no longer boast of men of courage?

Walter Lippmann, after nearly half a century of careful observation, rendered in his recent book a harsh judgment both on the politician and the electorate:

> With exceptions so rare they are regarded as miracles of nature, successful democratic politicians are insecure and intimidated men. They advance politically only as they placate, appease, bribe, seduce, bamboozle, or otherwise manage to manipulate the demanding threatening elements in their constituencies. The decisive consideration is not whether the proposition is good but whether it is popular—not whether it will work well and prove itself, but whether the active-talking constituents like it immediately.

I am not so sure, after nearly ten years of living and working in the midst of "successful democratic politicians," that they are all "insecure and intimidated men." I am convinced that the complication of public business and the competition for the public's attention have obscured innumerable acts of political courage —large and small—performed almost daily in the Senate Chamber. I am convinced that the decline—if there has been a decline—has been less in the Senate than in the public's appreciation of the art of politics, of the nature and necessity for compromise and balance, and of the nature of the Senate as a legislative chamber. And, finally, I am convinced that we have criticized those who have followed the crowd—and at the same time criticized those who have defied it— because we have not fully understood the responsibility of a Senator to his constituents or recognized the difficulty facing a politician conscientiously desiring, in Webster's words, "to push [his] skiff from the shore alone" into a hostile and turbulent sea. Perhaps if the American people more fully comprehended the terrible pressures which discourage acts of political courage, which drive a Senator to abandon or subdue his conscience, then they might be less critical of those who take the easier road—and more appreciative of those still able to follow the path of courage.

The *first pressure* to be mentioned is a form of pressure rarely recognized by the general public. Americans want to be liked—and Senators are no exception. They are by nature—and of necessity—social animals. We enjoy the comradeship and approval of our friends and colleagues. We prefer praise to abuse, popularity to contempt. Realizing that the path of the conscientious insurgent must frequently be a lonely one, we are anxious to get along with our fellow legislators, our fellow members of the club, to abide by the clubhouse rules and patterns, not to pursue a unique and independent course which would embarrass or irritate the other members. We realize, moreover, that our influence in the club—and the extent to which we can accomplish our objectives and those of our constituents—are dependent in some measure on the esteem with which we are regarded by other Senators. "The way to get along," I was told when I entered Congress, "is to go along."

Going along means more than just good fellowship—it includes the use of compromise, the sense of things possible. We should not be too hasty in condemning all compromise as bad morals. For politics and legislation are not matters for inflexible principles or unattainable ideals. Politics, as John Morley has acutely observed, "is a field where action is one long second best, and where the choice constantly lies between two blunders"; and legislation, under the democratic way of life and the Federal system of Government, requires compromise between the desires of each individual and group and those around them. Henry Clay, who should have known, said compromise was the cement that held the Union together:

> All legislation . . . is founded upon the principle of mutual concession. . . . Let him who elevates himself above humanity, above its weaknesses, its infirmities, its wants, its necessities, say, if he pleases, "I never will compromise"; but let no one who is not above the frailties of our common nature disdain compromise.

It is compromise that prevents each set of reformers—the wets and the drys, the one-worlders and the isolationists, the vivisectionists and the anti-vivisectionists—from crushing the group on the extreme opposite end of the political spectrum. The fanatics and extremists and even those conscientiously devoted to hard and fast principles are always disappointed at the failure of their Government to rush to implement all of their principles and to denounce those of their opponents. But the legislator has some responsibility to conciliate those opposing forces within his state and party and to represent them in the larger clash of interests on the national level; and he alone knows that there are few if any issues where all the truth and all the right and all the angels are on one side.

Some of my colleagues who are criticized today for lack of forthright principles—or who are looked upon with scornful eyes as compromising "politicians"—are simply engaged in the fine art of conciliating, balancing, and interpreting the forces and factions of public opinion, an art essential to keeping our nation united and enabling our Government to function. Their consciences may direct them from time to time to take a more rigid stand for principle—but their intellects tell them that a fair or poor bill is better than no bill at all, and that only through the give-and-take of compromise will any bill receive the successive approval of the Senate, the House, the President, and the nation.

But the question is how we will compromise and with whom. For it is easy to seize upon unnecessary concessions, not as means of legitimately resolving conflicts but as methods of "going along."

There were further implications in the warning that I should "go along"—implications of the rewards that would follow fulfillment of my obligation to follow the party leadership whom I had helped select. All of us in the Congress are made fully aware of the importance of party unity (what sins have been committed in that name!) and the adverse effect upon our party's chances in the next election which any rebellious conduct might bring. Moreover, in these days of civil service, the loaves and fishes of patronage available to the legislator—for distribution to those earnest campaigners whose efforts were inspired by something more than mere conviction—are comparatively few; and he who breaks the party's ranks may find that there are suddenly none at all. Even the success of legislation in which he is interested depends in part on the extent to which his support of his party's programs has won him the assistance of his party's leaders. Finally, the Senator who follows the independent course of conscience is likely to discover that he has earned the disdain not only of his colleagues in the Senate and his associates in his party but also that of the all-important contributors to his campaign fund.

It is thinking of that next campaign—the desire to be re-elected—that provides the *second* pressure on the conscientious Senator. It should not automatically be assumed that this is a wholly selfish motive—although it is not unnatural that those who have chosen politics as their profession should seek to continue their careers—for Senators who go down to defeat in a vain defense of a single principle will not be on hand to fight for that or any other principle in the future.

Defeat, moreover, is not only a setback for the Senator himself—he is also obligated to consider the effect upon the party he supports, upon the friends and supporters who have "gone out on a limb" for him or invested their savings in his career, and even upon the wife and children whose happiness and security—often depending at least in part upon his success in office—may mean more to him than anything else.

Where else, in a nontotalitarian country, but in the political profession is the individual expected to sacrifice all—including his own career—for the national good? In private life, as in industry, we expect the individual to advance his own enlightened self-interest—within the limitations of the law—in order to achieve overall progress. But in public life we expect individuals to sacrifice their private interests to permit the national good to progress.

In no other occupation but politics is it expected that a man will sacrifice honors, prestige, and his chosen career on a single issue. Lawyers, businessmen, teachers, doctors, all face difficult personal decisions involving their integrity—but few, if any, face them in the glare of the spotlight as do those in public office. Few, if any, face the same dread finality of decision that confronts a Senator facing an important call of the roll. He may want more time for his decision—he may believe there is something to be said for both sides—he may feel that a slight amendment could remove all difficulties—but when that roll is called he cannot hide, he cannot equivocate, he cannot delay—and he senses that his constituency, like the Raven in Poe's poem, is perched there on his Senate desk, croaking "Nevermore" as he casts the vote that stakes his political future.

Few Senators "retire to Pocatello" by choice. The virus of Potomac Fever, which rages everywhere in Washington, breeds nowhere in more virulent form than on the Senate floor. The prospect of forced retirement from "the most exclusive club in the world," the possibilities of giving up the interesting work, the fascinating trappings and the impressive prerogatives of Congressional office, can cause even the most courageous politician serious loss of sleep. Thus, perhaps without realizing it, some Senators tend to take the easier, less troublesome path to harmonize or rationalize what at first appears to be a conflict between their conscience—or the result of their deliberations—and the majority opinion of their constituents. Such Senators are not political cowards—they have simply developed the habit of sincerely reaching conclusions inevitably in accordance with popular opinion.

Still other Senators have not developed that habit—they have neither conditioned nor subdued their consciences—but they feel, sincerely and without cynicism, that they must leave considerations of conscience aside if they are to be effective. The profession of politics, they would agree with political writer Frank Kent, is not immoral, simply nonmoral:

> Probably the most important single accomplishment for the politically ambitious is the fine art of seeming to say something without doing so. . . . The important thing is not to be on the right side of the current issue but on the popular side . . . regardless of your own convictions or of the facts. This business of getting the votes is a severely practical one into which matters of morality, of right and wrong, should not be allowed to intrude.

And Kent quotes the advice allegedly given during the 1920 campaign by former Senator Ashurst of Arizona to his colleague Mark Smith:

> Mark, the great trouble with you is that you refuse to be a demagogue. You will not submerge your principles in order to get yourself elected. *You must learn that there are times when a man in public life is compelled to rise above his principles.*

Not all Senators would agree—but few would deny that the desire to be re-elected exercises a strong brake on independent courage.

The *third* and most significant source of pressures which discourage political courage in the conscientious Senator or Congressman—and practically all of the problems described in this chapter apply equally to members of both Houses—is the pressure of his constituency, the interest groups, the organized letter writers, the economic blocs, and even the average voter. To cope with such pressures, to defy them or even to satisfy them, is a formidable task. All of us occasionally have the urge to follow the example of Congressman John Steven McGroarty of California, who wrote a constituent in 1934:

> One of the countless drawbacks of being in Congress is that I am compelled to receive impertinent letters from a jackass like you in which you say I promised to have the Sierra Madre mountains reforested and I have been in Congress two months and haven't done it. Will you please take two running jumps and go to hell.

Fortunately or unfortunately, few follow that urge—but the provocation is there —not only from unreasonable letters and impossible requests, but also from hopelessly inconsistent demands and endlessly unsatisfied grievances.

In my office today, for example, was a delegation representing New England textile mills, an industry essential to our prosperity. They want the tariff lowered on the imported wool they buy from Australia, and they want the tariff raised on the finished woolen goods imported from England with which they must compete. One of my Southern colleagues told me that a similar group visited him not long ago with the same requests—but further urging that he take steps to (1) end the low-wage competition from Japan, and (2) prevent the Congress from ending— through a higher minimum wage—the low-wage advantage they themselves enjoy to the dismay of my constituents. Only yesterday two groups called me off the Senate floor—the first was a group of businessmen seeking to have a local Government activity closed as unfair competition for private enterprise; and the other was a group representing the men who work in the Government installation and who are worried about their jobs.

All of us in the Senate meet endless examples of such conflicting pressures, which only reflect the inconsistencies inevitable in our complex economy. If we tell our constituents frankly that we can do nothing, they feel we are unsympathetic or inadequate. If we try and fail—usually meeting a counteraction from other Senators representing other interests—they say we are like all the rest of the politicians. All we can do is retreat into the Cloakroom and weep on the shoulder of a sympathetic colleague—or go home and snarl at our wives.

We may tell ourselves that these pressure groups and letter writers represent only a small percentage of the voters—and this is true. But they are the articulate few whose views cannot be ignored and who constitute the greater part of our contacts with the public at large, whose opinions we cannot know, whose vote we must obtain, and yet who in all probability have a limited idea of what we are trying to do. (One Senator, since retired, said that he voted with the special interests on every issue, hoping that by election time all of them added together would constitute nearly a majority that would remember him favorably, while the other members of the public would never know about—much less remember—his vote against their welfare. It is reassuring to know that this seemingly unbeatable formula did not work in his case.)

These, then, are some of the pressures which confront a man of conscience. He cannot ignore the pressure groups, his constituents, his party, the comradeship of his colleagues, the needs of his family, his own pride in office, the necessity for compromise, and the importance of remaining in office. He must judge for himself which path to chose, which step will most help or hinder the ideals to which he is committed. He realizes that once he begins to weigh each issue in terms of his chances for re-election, once he begins to compromise away his principles on one issue after another for fear that to do otherwise would halt his career and prevent future fights for principle, then he has lost the very freedom of conscience which justifies his continuance in office. But to decide at which point and on which issue he will risk his career is a difficult and soul-searching decision.

But this is no real problem, some will say. Always do what is right, regardless of whether it is popular. Ignore the pressures, the temptations, the false compromises.

That is an easy answer—but it is easy only for those who do not bear the responsibilities of elected office. For more is involved than pressure, politics, and personal ambitions. Are we rightfully entitled to ignore the demands of our constituents even if we are able and willing to do so? We have noted the pressures that make political courage a difficult course—let us turn now to those Constitutional and more theoretical obligations which cast doubt upon the propriety of such a course—obligations to our state and section, to our party, and above all, to our constituents.

The primary responsibility of a Senator, most people assume, is to represent the views of his state. Ours is a Federal system—a Union of relatively sovereign states whose needs differ greatly—and my Constitutional obligations as Senator would thus appear to require me to represent the interests of my state. Who will speak for Massachusetts if her own Senators do not? Her rights and even her identity become submerged. Her equal representation in Congress is lost. Her aspirations, however much they may from time to time be in the minority, are denied that equal opportunity to be heard to which all minority views are entitled.

Any Senator need not look very long to realize that his colleagues are representing *their* local interests. And if such interests are ever to be abandoned in favor of the national good, let the constituents—not the Senator—decide when and to what extent. For he is their agent in Washington, the protector of their rights, recognized by the Vice-President in the Senate Chamber as "the Senator from Massachusetts" or "the Senator from Texas."

But when all of this is said and admitted, we have not yet told the full story. For in Washington we are "United States Senators" and members of the Senate of the United States as well as Senators from Massachusetts and Texas. Our oath of office is administered by the Vice-President, not by the Governors of our respective states; and we come to Washington, to paraphrase Edmund Burke, not as hostile ambassadors or special pleaders for our state or section, in opposition to advocates and agents of other areas, but as members of the deliberative assembly of one nation with one interest. Of course, we should not ignore the needs of our area—nor could we easily as products of that area—but none could be found to look out for the national interest if local interests wholly dominated the role of each of us.

There are other obligations in addition to those of state and region—the obligations of the party whose pressures have already been described. Even if I can disregard those pressures, do I not have an obligation to go along with the party that placed me in office? We believe in this country in the principle of party responsibility, and we recognize the necessity of adhering to party platforms—if the party label is to mean anything to the voters. Only in this way can our basically two-party nation avoid the pitfalls of multiple splinter parties—whose purity and rigidity of principle, I might add—if I may suggest a sort of Gresham's Law of politics—increase inversely with the size of their membership.

And yet we cannot permit the pressures of party responsibility to submerge on every issue the call of personal responsibility. For the party which, in its drive for unity, discipline, and success, ever decides to exclude new ideas, independent conduct, or insurgent members, is in danger. In the words of Senator Albert Beveridge:

> A party can live only by growing, intolerance of ideas brings its death. . . . An organization that depends upon reproduction only for its vote, son taking the place of father, is not a political party, but a Chinese tong; not citizens brought together by thought and conscience, but an Indian tribe held together by blood and prejudice.

The two-party system remains not because both are rigid but because both are flexible. The Republican party when I entered Congress was big enough to hold, for example, both Robert Taft and Wayne Morse—and the Democratic side of the Senate in which I now serve can happily embrace, for example, both Harry Byrd and Wayne Morse.

Of course, both major parties today seek to serve the national interest. They would do so in order to obtain the broadest base of support, if for no nobler reason. But when party and officeholder differ as to how the national interest is to be served, we must place first the responsibility we owe not to our party or even to our constituents but to our individual consciences.

But it is a little easier to dismiss one's obligations to local interests and party ties than to face squarely the problem of one's responsibility to the will of his constituents. A Senator who avoids this responsibility would appear to be accountable to no one, and the basic safeguards of our democratic system would thus have vanished. He is no longer representative in the true sense, he has violated his public trust, he has betrayed the confidence demonstrated by those who voted for him to carry out their views. "Is the creature," as John Tyler asked the House of Representatives in his maiden speech, "to set himself in opposition to his Creator? Is the servant to disobey the wishes of his master?"

> How can he be regarded as representing the people when he speaks, not their language, but his own? He ceases to be their representative when he does so, and represents himself alone.

In short, according to this school of thought, if I am to be properly responsive to the will of my constituents, it is my duty to place their principles, not mine, above all else. This may not always be easy, but it nevertheless is the essence of democracy, faith in the wisdom of the people and their views. To be sure, the people will make mistakes—they will get no better government than they deserve —but that is far better than the representative of the people arrogating for himself the right to say he knows better than they what is good for them. Is he not chosen, the argument closes, to vote as they would vote were they in his place?

It is difficult to accept such a narrow view of the role of United States Senator —a view that assumes the people of Massachusetts sent me to Washington to serve merely as a seismograph to record shifts in popular opinion. I reject this view not because I lack faith in the "wisdom of the people," but because this concept of democracy actually puts too little faith in the people. Those who would deny the obligation of the representative to be bound by every impulse of the electorate— regardless of the conclusions his own deliberations direct—do trust in the wisdom of the people. They have faith in their ultimate sense of justice, faith in their ability to honor courage and respect judgment, and faith that in the long run they will act unselfishly for the good of the nation. It is that kind of faith on which democracy is based, not simply the often frustrated hope that public opinion will at all times under all circumstances promptly identify itself with the public interest.

The voters selected us, in short, because they had confidence in our judgment and our ability to exercise that judgment from a position where we could determine what were their own best interests, as a part of the nation's interests. This may mean that we must on occasion lead, inform, correct, and sometimes even ignore constituent opinion, if we are to exercise fully that judgment for which we were elected. But acting without selfish motive or private bias, those who follow the dictates of an intelligent conscience are not aristocrats, demagogues, eccentrics, or callous politicians insensitive to the feelings of the public. They expect—and not without considerable trepidation—their constituents to be the final judges of the wisdom of their course; but they have faith that those constituents—today, tomorrow, or even in another generation—will at least respect the principles that motivated their independent stand.

If their careers are temporarily or even permanently buried under an avalanche of abusive editorials, poison-pen letters, and opposition votes at the polls—as they sometimes are, for that is the risk they take—they await the future with hope and confidence, aware of the fact that the voting public frequently suffers from what ex-Congressman T. V. Smith called the lag "between our way of thought and our way of life." Smith compared it to the subject of the anonymous poem:

> There was a dachshund, once so long
> He hadn't any notion
> How long it took to notify
> His tail of his emotion;
> And so it happened, while his eyes
> Were filled with woe and sadness,
> His little tail went wagging on
> Because of previous gladness.

Moreover, I question whether any Senator, before we vote on a measure, can state with certainty exactly how the majority of his constituents feel on the issue as it is presented to the Senate. All of us in the Senate live in an iron lung—the iron lung of politics, and it is no easy task to emerge from that rarefied atmosphere in order to breathe the same fresh air our constituents breathe. It is difficult, too, to see in person an appreciable number of voters besides those professional hangers-on and vocal elements who gather about the politician on a trip home. In Washington I frequently find myself believing that forty or fifty letters, six visits from professional politicians and lobbyists, and three editorials in Massachusetts newspapers constitute public opinion on a given issue. Yet in truth I rarely know how the great majority of the voters feel, or even how much they know of the issues that seem so burning in Washington.

Today the challenge of political courage looms larger than ever before. For our everyday life is becoming so saturated with the tremendous power of mass communications that any unpopular or unorthodox course arouses a storm of protests such as John Quincy Adams—under attack in 1807—could never have envisioned. Our political life is becoming so expensive, so mechanized, and so dominated by professional politicians and public relations men that the idealist who dreams of independent statesmanship is rudely awakened by the necessities of election and accomplishment. And our public life is becoming so increasingly centered upon that seemingly unending war to which we have given the curious epithet "cold" that we tend to encourage rigid ideological unity and orthodox patterns of thought.

And thus, in the days ahead, only the very courageous will be able to take the hard and unpopular decisions necessary for our survival in the struggle with a powerful enemy—an enemy with leaders who need give little thought to the popularity of their course, who need pay little tribute to the public opinion they themselves manipulate, and who may force, without fear of retaliation at the polls, their citizens to sacrifice present laughter for future glory. And only the very courageous will be able to keep alive the spirit of individualism and dissent which gave birth to this nation, nourished it as an infant, and carried it through its severest tests upon the attainment of its maturity.

Of course, it would be much easier if we could all continue to think in traditional political patterns—of liberalism and conservatism, as Republicans and Democrats, from the viewpoint of North and South, management and labor, business and consumer, or some equally narrow framework. It would be more comfortable to continue to move and vote in platoons, joining whomever of our colleagues are equally enslaved by some current fashion, raging prejudice or popular movement. But today this nation cannot tolerate the luxury of such lazy political habits. Only the strength and progress and peaceful change that come from independent judgment and individual ideas—and even from the unorthodox and the eccentric—can enable us to surpass that foreign ideology that fears free thought more than it fears hydrogen bombs.

We shall need compromises in the days ahead, to be sure. But these will be, or should be, compromises of issues, not of principles. We can compromise our political positions, but not ourselves. We can resolve the clash of interests without conceding our ideals. And even the necessity for the right kind of compromise does not eliminate the need for those idealists and reformers who keep our compromises moving ahead, who prevent all political situations from meeting the description supplied by Shaw: "smirched with compromise, rotted with opportunism, mildewed by expedience, stretched out of shape with wirepulling, and putrefied with permeation." Compromise need not mean cowardice. Indeed it is frequently the compromisers and conciliators who are faced with the severest tests of political courage as they oppose the extremist views of their constituents. It was because Daniel Webster conscientiously favored compromise in 1850 that he earned a condemnation unsurpassed in the annals of political history.

His is a story worth remembering today. So, I believe, are the stories of other Senators of courage—men whose abiding loyalty to their nation triumphed over all personal and political considerations, men who showed the real meaning of courage and a real faith in democracy, men who made the Senate of the United States something more than a mere collection of robots dutifully recording the views of their constituents, or a gathering of time-servers skilled only in predicting and following the tides of public sentiment.

*   *   *

Our public economy allocates resources through taxation and government spending, following democratic election of representatives. J. S. Mill states the classic position that only those who pay the cost should have the voting franchise through which the expenditures and taxes are controlled.

John Stuart Mill was a prominent economist during the middle of the last century who also wrote influential pieces on politics and ethics.

69

Extension of Suffrage

JOHN STUART MILL

*   *   *

It is . . . important that the assembly which votes the taxes, either general or local, should be elected exclusively by those who pay something towards the taxes imposed. Those who pay no taxes, disposing by their votes of other people's money, have every motive to be lavish and none to economise. As far as money matters are concerned, any power of voting possessed by them is a violation of the fundamental principle of free government; a severance of the power of control from the interest in its beneficial exercise. It amounts to allowing them to put their hands into other people's pockets for any purpose which they think fit to call a public one; which in some of the great towns of the United States is known to have produced a scale of local taxation onerous beyond example, and wholly borne by the wealthier classes. That representation should be co-extensive with taxation, not stopping short of it, but also not going beyond it, is in accordance with the theory of British institutions. But to reconcile this, as a condition annexed to the representation, with universality, it is essential, as it is on many other accounts desirable, that taxation, in a visible shape, should descend to the poorest class. In this country, and in most others, there is probably no laboring family which does not contribute to the indirect taxes, by the purchase of tea, coffee, sugar, not to mention narcotics or stimulants. But this mode of defraying a share of the public expenses is hardly felt: the payer, unless a person of education and reflection, does not identify his interest with a low

Excerpted from John Stuart Mill's *Considerations on Representative Government;* first published in 1861.

scale of public expenditure as closely as when money for its support is demanded directly from himself; and even supposing him to do so, he would doubtless take care that, however lavish an expenditure he might, by his vote, assist in imposing upon the government, it should not be defrayed by any additional taxes on the articles which he himself consumes. It would be better that a direct tax in the simple form of a capitation, should be levied on every grown person in the community; or that every such person should be admitted an elector on allowing himself to be rated *extra ordinem* to the assessed taxes; or that a small annual payment, rising and falling with the gross expenditure of the country, should be required from every registered elector; that so every one might feel that the money which he assisted in voting was partly his own, and that he was interested in keeping down its amount.

However this may be, I regard it as required by first principles, that the receipt of parish relief should be a peremptory disqualification for the franchise. He who cannot by his labor suffice for his own support has no claim to the privilege of helping himself to the money of others. By becoming dependent on the remaining members of the community for actual subsistence, he abdicates his claim to equal rights with them in other respects. Those to whom he is indebted for the continuance of his very existence may justly claim the exclusive management of those common concerns, to which he now brings nothing, or less than he takes away. As a condition of the franchise, a term should be fixed, say five years previous to the registry, during which the applicant's name has not been on the parish books as a recipient of relief. To be an uncertified bankrupt, or to have taken the benefit of the Insolvent Act, should disqualify for the franchise until the person has paid his debts, or at least proved that he is not now, and has not for some long period been, dependent on eleemosynary support. Nonpayment of taxes, when so long persisted in that it cannot have arisen from inadvertence, should disqualify while it lasts. These exclusions are not in their nature permanent. They exact such conditions only as all are able, or ought to be able, to fulfil if they choose. They leave the suffrage accessible to all who are in the normal condition of a human being: and if any one has to forego it, he either does not care sufficiently for it to do for its sake what he is already bound to do, or he is in a general condition of depression and degradation in which this slight addition, necessary for the security of others, would be unfelt, and on emerging from which, this mark of inferiority would disappear with the rest.

*   *   *

70
The Theory
of Social Balance

Professor Galbraith argues that we allocate too many of our productive resources to unimportant private purposes and to creating artificial wants, too few to such social purposes as slum clearance, education, and cultural activities. The result is a social imbalance which he argues should be remedied.

JOHN KENNETH GALBRAITH

John Kenneth Galbraith is Professor of Economics at Harvard University.

> It is not till it is discovered that high individual incomes will not purchase the mass of mankind immunity from cholera, typhus, and ignorance, still less secure them the positive advantages of educational opportunity and economic security, that slowly and reluctantly, amid prophecies of moral degeneration and economic disaster, society begins to make collective provision for needs which no ordinary individual, even if he works overtime all his life, can provide himself.
>
> —R. H. TAWNEY [1]

The final problem of the productive society is what it produces. This manifests itself in an implacable tendency to provide an opulent supply of some things and a niggardly yield of others. This disparity carries to the point where it is a cause of social discomfort and social unhealth. The line which divides our area of wealth from our area of poverty is roughly that which divides privately produced and marketed goods and services from publicly rendered services. Our wealth in the first is not only in startling contrast with the meagerness of the latter, but our wealth in privately produced goods is, to a marked degree, the cause of crisis in the supply of public services. For we have failed to see the importance, indeed the urgent need, of maintaining a balance between the two.

This disparity between our flow of private and public goods and

This selection from John Kenneth Galbraith's *The Affluent Society,* 1958, pp. 251–269, is reprinted by permission of an arrangement with Houghton Mifflin Company, the authorized publishers.

[1] *Equality* (4th revised ed.), pp. 134–35.

services is no matter of subjective judgment. On the contrary, it is the source of the most extensive comment which only stops short of the direct contrast being made here. In the years following World War II, the papers of any major city—those of New York were an excellent example—told daily of the shortages and short-comings in the elementary municipal and metropolitan services. The schools were old and overcrowded. The police force was understrength and underpaid. The parks and playgrounds were insufficient. Streets and empty lots were filthy, and the sanitation staff was underequipped and in need of men. Access to the city by those who work there was uncertain and painful and becoming more so. In-ternal transportation was overcrowded, unhealthful, and dirty. So was the air. Parking on the streets had to be prohibited, and there was no space elsewhere. These deficiencies were not in new and novel services but in old and established ones. Cities have long swept their streets, helped their people move around, edu-cated them, kept order, and provided horse rails for vehicles which sought to pause. That their residents should have a nontoxic supply of air suggests no revo-lutionary dalliance with socialism.

The discussion of this public poverty competed, on the whole successfully, with the stories of ever-increasing opulence in privately produced goods. The Gross National Product was rising. So were retail sales. So was personal income. Labor productivity had also advanced. The automobiles that could not be parked were being produced at an expanded rate. The children, though without schools, sub-ject in the playgrounds to the affectionate interest of adults with odd tastes, and disposed to increasingly imaginative forms of delinquency, were admirably equipped with television sets. We had difficulty finding storage space for the great surpluses of food despite a national disposition to obesity. Food was grown and packaged under private auspices. The care and refreshment of the mind, in con-trast with the stomach, was principally in the public domain. Our colleges and uni-versities were severely overcrowded and underprovided, and the same was true of the mental hospitals.

The contrast was and remains evident not alone to those who read. The family which takes its mauve and cerise, air-conditioned, power-steered, and power-braked automobile out for a tour passes through cities that are badly paved, made hideous by litter, blighted buildings, billboards, and posts for wires that should long since have been put underground. They pass on into a countryside that has been rendered largely invisible by commercial art. (The goods which the latter advertise have an absolute priority in our value system. Such aesthetic considerations as a view of the countryside accordingly cóme second. On such matters we are con-sistent.) They picnic on exquisitely packaged food from a portable icebox by a polluted stream and go on to spend the night at a park which is a menace to public health and morals. Just before dozing off on an air mattress, beneath a nylon tent, amid the stench of decaying refuse, they may reflect vaguely on the curious unevenness of their blessings. Is this, indeed, the American genius?

II

In the production of goods within the private economy it has long been recognized that a tolerably close relationship must be maintained between the production of various kinds of products. The output of steel and oil and machine tools is re-lated to the production of automobiles. Investment in transportation must keep abreast of the output of goods to be transported. The supply of power must be abreast of the growth of industries requiring it. The existence of these relation-ships—coefficients to the economist—has made possible the construction of the input-output table which shows how changes in the production in one industry will increase or diminish the demands on other industries. To this table, and more especially to its ingenious author, Professor Wassily Leontief, the world is in-debted for one of its most important of modern insights into economic relation-ships. If expansion in one part of the economy were not matched by the requisite expansion in other parts—were the need for balance not respected—then bottle-necks and shortages, speculative hoarding of scarce supplies, and sharply increas-ing costs would ensue. Fortunately in peacetime the market system operates easily and effectively to maintain this balance, and this together with the existence of stocks and some flexibility in the coefficients as a result of substitution, insures that no serious difficulties will arise. We are reminded of the existence of the problem only by noticing how serious it is for those countries—Poland or, in a somewhat different form, India—which seek to solve the problem by planned measures and with a much smaller supply of resources.

Just as there must be balance in what a community produces, so there must also be balance in what the community consumes. An increase in the use of one product creates, ineluctably, a requirement for others. If we are to consume more automobiles, we must have more gasoline. There must be more insurance as well as more space on which to operate them. Beyond a certain point more and better food appears to mean increased need for medical services. This is the certain result of the increased consumption of tobacco and alcohol. More vacations require more hotels and more fishing rods. And so forth. With rare exceptions—shortages of doctors are an exception which suggests the rule—this balance is also maintained quite effortlessly so far as goods for private sale and consumption are concerned. The price system plus a rounded condition of opulence is again the agency.

However, the relationships we are here discussing are not confined to the private economy. They operate comprehensively over the whole span of private and public services. As surely as an increase in the output of automobiles puts new demands on the steel industry so, also, it places new demands on public services. Similarly, every increase in the consumption of private goods will normally mean some facili-tating or protective step by the state. In all cases if these services are not forth-coming, the consequences will be in some degree ill. It will be convenient to have a term which suggests a satisfactory relationship between the supply of privately produced goods and services and those of the state, and we may call it social balance.

The problem of social balance is ubiquitous, and frequently it is obtrusive. As noted, an increase in the consumption of automobiles requires a facilitating supply of streets, highways, traffic control, and parking space. The protective services of the police and the highway patrols must also be available, as must those of the hospitals. Although the need for balance here is extraordinarily clear, our use of privately produced vehicles has, on occasion, got far out of line with the supply of the related public services. The result has been hideous road congestion, an annual massacre of impressive proportions, and chronic colitis in the cities. As on the ground, so also in the air. Planes collide with disquieting consequences for those within when the public provision for air traffic control fails to keep pace with private use of the airways.

But the auto and the airplane, versus the space to use them, are merely an ex-ceptionally visible example of a requirement that is pervasive. The more goods people procure, the more packages they discard and the more trash that must be carried away. If the appropriate sanitation services are not provided, the counterpart of increasing opulence will be deepening filth. The greater the wealth the thicker will be the dirt. This indubitably describes a tendency of our time. As more goods are produced and owned, the greater are the opportunities for fraud and the more property that must be protected. If the provision of public law enforcement services does not keep pace, the counterpart of increased well-being will, we may be certain, be increased crime.

The city of Los Angeles, in modern times, is a near-classic study in the problem of social balance. Magnificently efficient factories and oil refineries, a lavish supply of automobiles, a vast consumption of handsomely packaged products, coupled with the absence of a municipal trash collection service which forced the use of home incinerators, made the air nearly unbreathable for an appreciable part of each year. Air pollution could be controlled only by a complex and highly developed set of public services—by better knowledge stemming from more research, better policing, a municipal trash collection service, and possibly the assertion of the priority of clean air over the production of goods. These were long in coming. The agony of a city without usable air was the result.

The issue of social balance can be identified in many other current problems. Thus an aspect of increasing private production is the appearance of an extraordinary number of things which lay claim to the interest of the young. Motion pictures, television, automobiles, and the vast opportunities which go with the mobility, together with such less enchanting merchandise as narcotics, comic books, and pornographia, are all included in an advancing gross national product. The child of a less opulent as well as a technologically more primitive age had far fewer such diversions. The red schoolhouse is remembered mainly because it had a paramount position in the lives of those who attended it that no modern school can hope to attain.

In a well-run and well-regulated community, with a sound school system, good recreational opportunities, and a good police force—in short a community where public services have kept pace with private production—the diversionary forces operating on the modern juvenile may do no great damage. Television and the violent mores of Hollywood and Madison Avenue must contend with the intellectual discipline of the school. The social, athletic, dramatic, and like attractions of the school also claim the attention of the child. These, together with the other recreational opportunities of the community, minimize the tendency to delinquency. Experiments with violence and immorality are checked by an effective law enforcement system before they become epidemic.

In a community where public services have failed to keep abreast of private consumption things are very different. Here, in an atmosphere of private opulence and public squalor, the private goods have full sway. Schools do not compete with television and the movies. The dubious heroes of the latter, not Miss Jones, become the idols of the young. The hot rod and the wild ride take the place of more sedentary sports for which there are inadequate facilities or provision. Comic books, alcohol, narcotics, and switchblade knives are, as noted, part of the increased flow of goods, and there is nothing to dispute their enjoyment. There is an ample supple of private wealth to be appropriated and not much to be feared from the police. An austere community is free from temptation. It can be austere in its public services. Not so a rich one.

Moreover, in a society which sets large store by production, and which has highly effective machinery for synthesizing private wants, there are strong pressures to have as many wage earners in the family as possible. As always all social behavior is part of a piece. If both parents are engaged in private production, the burden on the public services is further increased. Children, in effect, become the charge of the community for an appreciable part of the time. If the services of the community do not keep pace, this will be another source of disorder.

Residential housing also illustrates the problem of the social balance, although in a somewhat complex form. Few would wish to contend that, in the lower or even the middle-income brackets, Americans are munificently supplied with housing. A great many families would like better located or merely more houseroom, and no advertising is necessary to persuade them of their wish. And the provision of housing is in the private domain. At first glance at least, the line we draw between private and public seems not to be preventing a satisfactory allocation of resources to housing.

On closer examination, however, the problem turns out to be not greatly different from that of education. It is improbable that the housing industry is greatly more incompetent or inefficient in the United States than in those countries—Scandinavia, Holland, or (for the most part) England—where slums have been largely eliminated and where *minimum* standards of cleanliness and comfort are well above our own. As the experience of these countries shows, and as we have also been learning, the housing industry functions well only in combination with a large, complex, and costly array of public services. These include land purchase and clearance for redevelopment; good neighborhood and city planning, and effective and well-enforced zoning; a variety of financing and other aids to the housebuilder and owner; publicly supported research and architectural services for an industry which, by its nature, is equipped to do little on its own; and a considerable amount of direct or assisted public construction for families in the lowest income brackets. The quality of the housing depends not on the industry, which is given, but on what is invested in these supplements and supports.

III

The case for social balance has, so far, been put negatively. Failure to keep public services in minimal relation to private production and use of goods is a cause of social disorder or impairs economic performance. The matter may now be put affirmatively. By failing to exploit the opportunity to expand public production we are missing opportunities for enjoyment which otherwise we might have had. Presumably a community can be as well rewarded by buying better schools or better parks as by buying bigger automobiles. By concentrating on the latter rather than the former it is failing to maximize its satisfactions. As with schools in the community, so with public services over the country at large. It is scarcely sensible that we should satisfy our wants in private goods with reckless abundance, while in the case of public goods, on the evidence of the eye, we practice extreme self-denial. So, far from systematically exploiting the opportunities to derive use and pleasure from these services, we do not supply what would keep us out of trouble.

The conventional wisdom holds that the community, large or small, makes a decision as to how much it will devote to its public services. This decision is arrived at by democratic process. Subject to the imperfections and uncertainties of democracy, people decide how much of their private income and goods they will surrender in order to have public services of which they are in greater need. Thus there is a balance, however rough, in the enjoyments to be had from private goods and services and those rendered by public authority.

It will be obvious, however, that this view depends on the notion of independently determined consumer wants. In such a world one could with some reason defend the doctrine that the consumer, as a voter, makes an independent choice between public and private goods. But given the dependence effect—given that consumer wants are created by the process by which they are satisfied—the consumer makes no such choice. He is subject to the forces of advertising and emulation by which production creates its own demand. Advertising operates exclusively, and emulation mainly, on behalf of privately produced goods and services.[2] Since management and emulative effects operate on behalf of private production, public services will have an inherent tendency to lag behind. Automobile demand which is expensively synthesized will inevitably have a much larger claim on income than parks or public health or even roads where no such influence operates. The engines of mass communication, in their highest state of development, assail the eyes and ears of the community on behalf of more beer but not of more schools. Even in the conventional wisdom it will scarcely be contended that this leads to an equal choice between the two.

The competition is especially unequal for new products and services. Every corner of the public psyche is canvassed by some of the nation's most talented citizens to see if the desire for some merchantable product can be cultivated. No similar process operates on behalf of the nonmerchantable services of the state. Indeed, while we take the cultivation of new private wants for granted we would be measurably shocked to see it applied to public services. The scientist or engineer or advertising man who devotes himself to developing a new carburetor, cleanser, or depilatory for which the public recognizes no need and will feel none until an advertising campaign arouses it, is one of the valued members of our society. A politician or a public servant who dreams up a new public service is a wastrel. Few public offenses are more reprehensible.

So much for the influences which operate on the decision between public and private production. The calm decision between public and private consumption pictured by the conventional wisdom is, in fact, a remarkable example of the error which arises from viewing social behavior out of context. The inherent tendency will always be for public services to fall behind private production. We have here the first of the causes of social imbalance.

IV

Social balance is also the victim of two further features of our society—the truce on inequality and the tendency to inflation. Since these are now part of our context, their effect comes quickly into view.

With rare exceptions such as the post office, public services do not carry a price ticket to be paid for by the individual user. By their nature they must, ordinarily, be available to all. As a result, when they are improved or new services are initiated, there is the ancient and troublesome question of who is to pay. This, in turn, provokes to life the collateral but irrelevant debate over inequality. As

---

[2] Emulation does operate between communities. A new school or a new highway in one community does exert pressure on others to remain abreast. However, as compared with the pervasive effects of emulation in extending the demand for privately produced consumer's goods there will be agreement, I think, that this intercommunity effect is probably small.

with the use of taxation as an instrument of fiscal policy, the truce on inequality is broken. Liberals are obliged to argue that the services be paid for by progressive taxation which will reduce inequality. Committed as they are to the urgency of goods (and also, as we shall see in a later chapter, to a somewhat mechanical view of the way in which the level of output can be kept most secure) they must oppose sales and excise taxes. Conservatives rally to the defense of inequality—although without ever quite committing themselves in such uncouth terms—and oppose the use of income taxes. They, in effect, oppose the expenditure not on the merits of the service but on the demerits of the tax system. Since the debate over inequality cannot be resolved, the money is frequently not appropriated and the service not performed. It is a casualty of the economic goals of both liberals and conservatives for both of whom the questions of social balance are subordinate to those of production and, when it is evoked, of inequality.

In practice matters are better as well as worse than this statement of the basic forces suggests. Given the tax structure, the revenues of all levels of government grow with the growth of the economy. Services can be maintained and sometimes even improved out of this automatic accretion.

However, this effect is highly unequal. The revenues of the federal government, because of its heavy reliance on income taxes, increase more than proportionately with private economic growth. In addition, although the conventional wisdom greatly deplores the fact, federal appropriations have only an indirect bearing on taxation. Public services are considered and voted on in accordance with their seeming urgency. Initiation or improvement of a particular service is rarely, except for purposes of oratory, set against the specific effect on taxes. Tax policy, in turn, is decided on the basis of the level of economic activity, the resulting revenues, expediency, and other considerations. Among these the total of the thousands of individually considered appropriations is but one factor. In this process the ultimate tax consequence of any individual appropriation is *de minimus,* and the tendency to ignore it reflects the simple mathematics of the situation. Thus it is possible for the Congress to make decisions affecting the social balance without invoking the question of inequality.

Things are made worse, however, by the fact that a large proportion of the federal revenues are pre-empted by defense. The increase in defense costs has also tended to absorb a large share of the normal increase in tax revenues. The position of the federal government for improving the social balance has also been weakened since World War II by the strong, although receding, conviction that its taxes were at artificial wartime levels and that a tacit commitment exists to reduce taxes at the earliest opportunity.

In the states and localities the problem of social balance is much more severe. Here tax revenues—this is especially true of the general property tax—increase less than proportionately with increased private production. Budgeting too is far more closely circumscribed than in the case of the federal government—only the monetary authority enjoys the pleasant privilege of underwriting its own loans. Because of this, increased services for states and localities regularly pose the question of more revenues and more taxes. And here, with great regularity, the question of social balance is lost in the debate over equality and social equity.

Thus we currently find by far the most serious social imbalance in the services performed by local governments. The F.B.I. comes much more easily by funds than the city police force. The Department of Agriculture can more easily keep its pest control abreast of expanding agricultural output than the average city health service can keep up with the needs of an expanding industrial population. One consequence is that the federal government remains under constant pressure to use its superior revenue position to help redress the balance at the lower levels of government.

V

Finally, social imbalance is the natural offspring of persistent inflation. Inflation by its nature strikes different individuals and groups with highly discriminatory effect. The most nearly unrelieved victims, apart from those living on pensions or other fixed provision for personal security, are those who work for the state. In the private economy the firm which sells goods has, in general, an immediate accommodation to the inflationary movement. Its price increases are the inflation. The incomes of its owners and proprietors are automatically accommodated to the upward movement. To the extent that wage increases are part of the inflationary process, this is also true of organized industrial workers. Even unorganized white collar workers are in a milieu where prices and incomes are moving up. The adaption of their incomes, if less rapid than that of the industrial workers, is still reasonably prompt.

The position of the public employee is at the other extreme. His pay scales are highly formalized, and traditionally they have been subject to revision only at lengthy interval. In states and localities inflation does not automatically bring added revenues to pay higher salaries and incomes. Pay revision for all public workers is subject to the temptation to wait and see if the inflation isn't coming to an end. There will be some fear—this seems to have been more of a factor in England than in the United States—that advances in public wages will set a bad example for private employers and unions.

Inflation means that employment is pressing on the labor supply and that private wage and salary incomes are rising. Thus the opportunities for moving from public to private employment are especially favorable. Public employment, moreover, once had as a principal attraction a high measure of social security. Industrial workers were subject to the formidable threat of unemployment during depression. Public employees were comparatively secure, and this security was worth an adverse salary differential. But with improving economic security in general, this advantage has diminished. Private employment thus has come to provide better protection against inflation and little worse protection against other hazards. Though the dedicated may stay in public posts, the alert go.

The deterioration of the public services in the years of inflation has not gone unremarked. However, there has been a strong tendency to regard it as an adventitious misfortune—something which, like a nasty shower at a picnic, happened to blight a generally good time. Salaries were allowed to lag, which was a pity. This is a very inadequate view. Discrimination against the public services is an organic feature of inflation. Nothing so weakens government as persistent inflation. The public administration of France for many years, of Italy until recent times, and of other European and numerous South American countries have been deeply sapped and eroded by the effects of long-continued inflation. Social imbalance reflects itself in inability to enforce laws, including significantly those which protect and advance basic social justice, and in failure to maintain and improve essential services. One outgrowth of the resulting imbalance has been frustration and pervasive discontent. Over much of the world there is a rough and not entirely accidental correlation between the strength of indigenous communist parties or the frequency of revolutions and the persistence of inflation.

VI

A feature of the years immediately following World War II was a remarkable attack on the notion of expanding and improving public services. During the depression years such services had been elaborated and improved partly in order to fill some small part of the vacuum left by the shrinkage of private production. During the war years the role of government was vastly expanded. After that came the reaction. Much of it, unquestionably, was motivated by a desire to rehabilitate the prestige of private production and therewith of producers. No doubt some who joined the attack hoped, at least tacitly, that it might be possible to sidestep the truce on taxation vis-à-vis equality by having less taxation of all kinds. For a time the notion that our public services had somehow become inflated and excessive was all but axiomatic. Even liberal politicians did not seriously protest. They found it necessary to aver that they were in favor of public economy too.

In this discussion a certain mystique was attributed to the satisfaction of privately supplied wants. A community decision to have a new school means that the individual surrenders the necessary amount, willy-nilly, in his taxes. But if he is left with that income, he is a free man. He can decide between a better car or a television set. This was advanced with some solemnity as an argument for the TV set. The difficulty is that this argument leaves the community with no way of preferring the school. All private wants, where the individual can choose, are inherently superior to all public desires which must be paid for by taxation and with an inevitable component of compulsion.

The cost of public services was also held to be a desolating burden on private production, although this was at a time when the private production was burgeoning. Urgent warnings were issued of the unfavorable effects of taxation on investment—"I don't know of a surer way of killing off the incentive to invest than by imposing taxes which are regarded by people as punitive." [3] This was at a time when the inflationary effect of a very high level of investment was causing concern. The same individuals who were warning about the inimical effects of taxes were strongly advocating a monetary policy designed to reduce investment. However, an understanding of our economic discourse requires an appreciation of one of its basic rules: men of high position are allowed, by a special act of grace, to accommodate their reasoning to the answer they need. Logic is only required in those of lesser rank.

Finally it was argued, with no little vigor, that expanding government posed a grave threat to individual liberties. "Where distinction and rank is achieved almost exclusively by becoming a civil servant of the state . . . it is too much to expect that many will long prefer freedom to security." [4]

With time this attack on public services has somewhat subsided. The disorder associated with social imbalance has become visible even if the need for balance between private and public services is still imperfectly appreciated.

Freedom also seemed to be surviving. Perhaps it was realized that all organized activity requires concessions by the individual to the group. This is true of the

[3] Arthur F. Burns, Chairman of the President's Council of Economic Advisers, *U. S. News & World Report,* May 6, 1955.
[4] F. A. Hayek, *The Road to Serfdom* (London: Routledge & Kegan Paul, Ltd., 1944), p. 98.

policeman who joins the police force, the teacher who gets a job at the high school, and the executive who makes his way up the hierarchy of Du Pont. If there are differences between public and private organization, they are of kind rather than of degree. As this is written the pendulum has in fact swung back. Our liberties are now menaced by the conformity exacted by the large corporation and its impulse to create, for its own purposes, the organization man. This danger we may also survive.

Nonetheless, the postwar onslaught on the public services left a lasting imprint. To suggest that we canvass our public wants to see where happiness can be improved by more and better services has a sharply radical tone. Even public services to avoid disorder must be defended. By contrast the man who devises a nostrum for a nonexistent need and then successfully promotes both remains one of nature's noblemen.

71

Private and Public Expenditures: A Reappraisal

This vigorous attack on Galbraith's "Affluent Society" alleges that there is no real meaning to "social imbalance," and denies that the public sector should be expanded at the expense of the private sector.

Ernest van den Haag is Professor of Social Philosophy at New York University and a practicing psychoanalyst.

ERNEST VAN DEN HAAG

In *The Affluent Society,* John Kenneth Galbraith persuasively refurbishes the arguments in favor of widening the public and narrowing the private sector of our economy. Let me examine some of his major ideas.[1]

I

Galbraith argues foremost that there is an "imbalance" between the public and the private sector. Economists have overlooked that "imbalance" because their obsolete "conventional wisdom" leads them to focus on "scarcity," whereas we have "affluence."

Galbraith's argument here rests on his confusion or equivocation between the technical meaning of "scarcity"—*i.e.,* need for allocation—and the colloquial meaning—*i.e.,* insufficiency, or poverty. If the two meanings of scarcity are separated, his argument is seen to be without merit. Economists are aware that our affluence has increased (colloquial meaning): but affluence does not make rational allocation obsolete (technical meaning). Allocation, the subject matter of economics—the problem: how can we make the best use of our resources?—becomes "obsolete" only with the millennium. For, though we can and do produce a lot in temporal society, we cannot produce enough to satisfy all desires; thus it remains rational

From *Modern Age,* Spring, 1962, pp. 145–153. Reprinted by permission.

[1] Most of Galbraith's arguments, were they correct, would not be necessary, and altogether they are not sufficient, for the conclusions he draws. I have discussed *The Affluent Society* as a whole in *Commentary* (September, 1960, and January, 1961).

to allocate, *i.e.*, to choose between alternative satisfactions, and to economize, *i.e.*, to satisfy desires with the least expenditure of resources. Indeed, Galbraith himself advocates forcible reallocation of resources from the private to the public sector, thus implying that the scarcity, which makes allocation (choice) necessary, and which he is at pains to deny, is still with us. In his equivocation between the technical and colloquial meanings of scarcity, Galbraith is not altogether original. He follows the "conventional wisdom" of millenarians, Utopians, and Marxians. However, the chiliastic sects realized that there is scarcity in temporal society, and the Marxists realized that there is scarcity in noncommunist society. The discovery that scarcity is "obsolete" in *our* society is original with Galbraith but no improvement on "conventional wisdom." [2]

Galbraith's "imbalance" itself turns out to be a rhetorical device disguised as an argument. No indication is given—let alone substantiated—as to where a "balance" could be found, or by what means one might locate it. Hence the word "imbalance" does no more than denote Galbraith's dissatisfaction with the present allocation of resources between the public and the private sector; his conclusion merely restates that premise, and his reasoning but asseverates what it is supposed to prove, namely, that the public sector should be expanded. [3]

Economists took the idea of balance from mechanics to describe a state without endogenous tendency to change (equilibrium). Galbraith gives it a laudatory sense—balance becomes an unspecified but ideal distribution between public and private sector—and proceeds to use the descriptive term prescriptively. By this device, he retains the authority the term derived from its objective reference, though he has surreptitiously cut it adrift. This public relations stratagem has worked well; in defense of reason, I suggest that from now on, unless an author tells us how he determines "imbalance" in the economy, we ought to grant only that it exists in his mind.

Colin Clark has tried to prove that we suffer from the opposite imbalance, that the public sector is overexpanded whenever it uses (or, better, attempts to use) more than 25 per cent of the national income. When that happens, he thinks, the ostensive welfare goals are defeated, and the economy generally suffers. At least Clark tells us how to locate his imbalance and its effects. He tries to prove a meaningful proposition. I do not think he succeeds; but Galbraith does not even try—and for good reason: he does not have a genuine proposition to which evidence could be relevant.

In Galbraith's defense, one may argue that some public expenditures are directly complementary to private ones. Without roads, cars are of no use. But even here, "imbalance" is misleading. The proper quantitative relationship between road and car expenditures has not been worked out with any precision; and it may be impossible to do so in any way that would permit us to speak of a general "balance."

Here Galbraith follows convention, but would have done better to abandon it: we usually treat public expenditures as a dependent variable and the private

---

[2] The supposed disappearance of scarcity leads Galbraith to conclude that we need no longer emphasize productivity. A consistent conclusion, as dangerous as it is wrong.

[3] Galbraith suggests, often with striking illustrations, that specific public services are lagging. He takes it for granted that the lag is caused by insufficient financing. The term "imbalance" evades analysis of distribution and of effectiveness of money within the public sector, which are the actual problems causing most of the deficiencies Galbraith mentions. More money is not likely to improve matters and may make them worse. Reorganization is called for.

expeditures to be complemented by them as an independent one. Yet this is certainly wrong. Both must be treated as dependent variables. They are functionally interdependent. The problem is not how much road space is needed for automobile traffic growing at a given rate, but, how much automobile traffic should be supported, induced or balked, in view of public costs and various alternative expenditures and means of transportation. Roads invite automobile traffic as much as they accommodate it. (The underdeveloped countries illustrate very well that automobile traffic is as much a function of road building as *vice versa*.) Other factors—taxation, public transport, etc.—also influence automobile traffic.[4] When roads are built with public funds, surely we must base decisions on the comparative desirability of fostering and accommodating automobile traffic, and not exclusively on the desires of actual and prospective automobile users. (In the case of tollroads, this problem differs—although tollroads do cause costs in addition to those paid for by users.)

To treat public expenditures as a dependent variable complementing independent private expenditures is about as reasonable as it would be to say, "since many people want to drive at a speed of 100 m.p.h. injuring more pedestrians than we now can take care of, we must multiply hospitals and cemeteries." Shouldn't we instead, or as well, discourage speed, and other hazards, and perhaps traffic?

Whenever possible, the cost of the public complement to private expenditure should be defrayed by the most direct and main beneficiaries. A fuller application of this ancient rule of fiscal equity might, apart from its intrinsic merit, greatly reduce public expenditures: the private expenditures which are now subsidized by complementary public ones might be reduced if the complementary public costs were borne by the direct private beneficiaries through taxes.[5]

Though easily abused, the attempt to determine theoretically complementarities between specific public and private expenditures can be fruitful when the relationship between the interdependent variables is treated as independent, and *both* variables as dependent. I doubt, however, that the attempt to find a general balance between public and private expenditure is fruitful. I can conceive of situations where 70 per cent of the national income might well be spent publicly even in peacetime and of others where 10 per cent would be too much. So many variables are involved—*e.g.*, size and distribution of the national income, type of expenditure, tax structure—that I do not think a general rule can do justice to concrete situations unless it be interpreted as a warning to pay heed to the undesired and possibly self-defeating effects of very high general levels of taxation. Clark's attempt to weigh diminishing returns of taxation certainly has this merit.

II

Galbraith next offers a value judgment: consumers spend too much on trivialities. I share his judgment; but he misconceives the problem and proposes irrelevant and indefensible solutions likely to make matters worse.

Galbraith argues as though the problem simply that there are not so good

[4] Incidentally, I am convinced our cities will be choked by automobiles if the present favored tax treatment continues.

[5] The general sales tax proposed by Galbraith in place of the excise taxes here suggested would have the opposite effect.

(*i.e.*, private) and good (*i.e.*, public) expenditures; and he calls on all right-thinking citizens to make sure that the good guys (government) get more money and the bad guys (consumers) less. This will do for a Western; but is it economic analysis? It replaces the all too real problem: what values are we to live by, or how can people be free *and* wise?, with a pseudo-problem: how can we keep people right-thinking and buying?, and then offers a pseudo-solution: by letting the government spend more of their income for them.

Thoughtful men have always agreed that consumers prefer trivialities and vulgarities to the satisfaction of their real needs; but they have never agreed on the real needs that ought to be satisfied; or on how to make consumers do what is good for them. This is not a new problem arising from affluence and advertising, as Galbraith suggests. Nor is Galbraith's solution new. It ignores what makes the problem problematic: neither an objective nor an agreed upon standard by which purchases could be judged more or less trivial in general is available.[6] Since Plato, those who in the past proposed what Galbraith proposes—let the government decide (and spend) more, consumers less—were more consistent than he: they did not believe in individual freedom; and they felt that right values could be objectively ascertained and collectively imposed. If Galbraith held these views, his theory would be consistent, however unacceptable, to me. But though they are implied in much of *The Affluent Society*,[7] I think he would repudiate such views when stated explicitly.

Certainly trivialities and vulgarities are now a greater proportion of our total output than in the past, not because taste has deteriorated—it probably was always bad—but because it is satisfied more often. Affluence changes the ability to satisfy taste rather than the taste: whereas in the past only the rich had the privilege to indulge their taste, now the poor can too. I do not see why transferring expenditures to a government no wiser than the voters who elect it and less able to satisfy *individual* tastes would solve this problem. It would probably replace private folly with official silliness. *Si monumentum quaeris, circumspice.* And it would make harder satisfaction of the minority tastes, which are usually more interesting than those of the majority.

I see one advantage of democracy in making reasonably certain not that the government is better than the voters in general—but that it is not much worse; without democracy, this last happens quite easily. Still in a democracy, if the government is likely to be not worse than the average voter, it is also likely to be worse than some voters. Wherefore, the transfer of the power to decide from the individual to even a democratic government is justifiable only where the object is so indivisible, or indiscriminate, as to make collective decisions imperative.

The argument in favor of expansion of the public sector need not be based on the demerits of private expenditure alone. It can be based also on the merits of public expenditure. But these can never be general. Each expenditure must be considered on its own merits: will benefits exceed costs by more than the benefits of alternative expenditures, public or private, would? How are benefits and costs distributed? The admitted triviality of many private expenditures, as well as "imbalance"—whatever it means—are utterly irrelevant unless general

[6] I am making a factual statement: such a standard is not *available*. Nothing is implied about its existence; and should it exist, its nature, applicability or imposition.

[7] One of the major defects of that book is that it disguises inchoate and chaotic philosophical ideas as economic analysis.

superiority of public expenditures can be shown. By pointing to the triviality of private expenditures—which each consumer is likely to admit for all other consumers—Galbraith suggests that the government would restrain those other consumers; and that anyway it could not do worse. But it always can and usually does. (These two fallacies are perennial stand-bys of appeals for dictatorships: followers of would-be dictators usually think that matters can only improve; and that the dictator would frustrate the [trivial] wishes of others but not their own [untrivial] ones.)

III

Though lambasting consumers for their silliness, Galbraith does not hold them responsible for it: according to the principles of ritualistic liberalism, the people always have their heart (or is it their stomach?) in the right place; when they err, it is because they have misread their heart's prompting owing to some wicked seducer. This theory is popular all around: it enables people to eat their cake and profess that they didn't really want it; and it enables the theorists to have his cake (people are good) and eat it (people act bad). In the past, the seducers were devils, capitalists, or Jews. Madison Avenue is fast replacing them in the folklore of our society.[8]

Galbraith argues that consumers no longer satisfy endogenous desires, but exogenous ones "contrived" by advertising. Industry thus first produces the desires it then satisfies—whereas before *The Affluent Society*, the needs satisfied arose independently. Now, to the extent to which we grant the truth and undesirability of this "dependence effect," it might argue against advertising. Surprisingly, Galbraith seems to think of it as an argument for reducing the purchasing power of consumers and increasing that of the government by means of a general sales tax. His not entirely explicit train of thought seems to be: consumers' purchases are trivial; they satisfy a demand "contrived" by advertising; therefore, we should transfer purchasing power from consumers to the government; public expenditures will be less contrived and less trivial. There is no logical connection among the various parts of this argument. Why should the government not do worse than consumers? Why are public expenditures less (rather than differently) contrived than private ones? Is the political process that spontaneous? Why is "contrived," *i.e.*, influenced, demand better or worse (more or less trivial) than uncontrived, *i.e.*, uninfluenced (if that is conceivable), demand? Is the "contrived" demand for education, books, and soap worse than uncontrived spontaneous dirt and ignorance? One may spontaneously desire trivial things—as any child knows and does. Culture is contrivance, *i.e.*, social *"influence"*; and there is no society without it. There is no less contrivance in primitive, or for that matter, in Soviet, society than in ours. The problem is not that there is influence ("contrivance")

---

[8] Certainly recent myths are less convenient than the ancient ones. Jews and capitalists suffer from them—whereas in the past the devils were the main sufferers. Let me note that Galbraith's myth, though structurally analogous to those mentioned, if more urban, is functionally quite different: Galbraith does not urge liquidation of Jews, capitalists, or advertising men. His theoretical mountain gives birth to a quite modest, practical mouse: a general sales tax. But then mice can be quite voracious and they multiply fast. (The general sales tax may have technical merits as such. But Galbraith wants it because he believes it to be the best means to achieve his basic end of increasing the general level of taxation, of decreasing private and increasing public expenditure. I object to this end, rather than to a sales, as compared to an income tax.)

but the quality, source, and direction of such influence; above all, whether influence is monopolized or whether it comes from many competing sources. The high taxes Galbraith proposes obviously would not affect these problems except by reducing the power of individuals and adding to the power of the government.

Galbraith's argument is irrelevant then. Is it true? Are consumers hapless victims of Madison Avenue? One would expect that they bought Ford's Edsel car in droves and not small foreign cars; or that the political party that spends most on advertising always wins. Presidents Thomas Dewey and Richard Nixon, and the Republican Congressional majority would testify to these beliefs were they true. They aren't. But believers are unshaken by evidence.

Advertising is only one influence among others in political or purchasing decisions and is frequently offset by competing advertising. Yet, advertising men as well as their opponents (for different reasons) cherish the belief that advertising is always the decisive influence. Advertising agencies want to impress prospective clients with the importance of what they may do for them. The motivation of opponents is more complex though their faith is as strong. Some are looking for scapegoats; others are mildly paranoid; still others want to convince people that they lose nothing in getting government "protection" from their own use of freedom, since advertising mysteriously has deprived them of that freedom anyway.

Many consumers spend their money in ways many other consumers disapprove. The first group of consumers assumes that the second cannot possibly have freely decided to spend its money as it does. The disapproved expenditure pattern is taken for evidence of their lack of freedom—just as apologists for dictatorship have always presented election of a less than perfect democratic government or one they disapproved of, as evidence for lack of political freedom. If you don't "really" have it, what can you lose in giving it up? The moral connection between sumptuary and political freedom is anything but tenuous: if consumers are incapable of freely choosing among advertised products, why should they be deemed capable of freely choosing among propagandizing political parties? What is freedom if not the right to choose among competing influences? If these influences are considered coercion, or if people are deemed too incompetent to choose among them, freedom can never be more than sham, and we might just as well install a dictatorship.[9] But I like freedom because it allows me to make, and judge, my own choices, however foolish.

We might well oppose and seek to restrain seduction. But we cannot (unless it be practiced on the legally incompetent) treat it as though it were rape, precisely because it gives choice (and therewith part of the responsibility) to all parties concerned: it requires consent. Democracy does so not less than the "dependence effect": with freedom there always are competing influences. And advertisements for detergents no more hypnotize or coerce than advertisements for political candidates. If people are competent as citizens to choose among candidates, why should they not be competent as consumers to choose among goods? I find it hard to believe that those who confuse influence with coercion can be sincere, but I may overestimate both their intelligence and their malevolence.

Has the influence of advertising increased? The proportion of the population

[9] It would not follow that dictatorship will lead to better results; but there would be no reason to expect worse ones. We would give up something we never had, or were never able to use competently.

affected certainly has. Not, however, because Madison Avenue has discovered new tricks—there seems to have been little basic progress in propaganda techniques since Roman times—but because literacy and other communications media have spread; and because many people who did not in the past, do now have enough disposable income to follow fashions in purchasing. However, even the fixed purchasing patterns of the past were socially influenced. The peasant's dress, food, and housing were no more individual creations than the wigs of noblemen, or their extravagant garments. Nor were these things less trivial than the things advertised in *Vogue* today. Versailles, a medieval cathedral, or Vanderbilt's yacht were neither more of a necessity nor more spontaneous than our tailfinned cars, or a copy of *The Affluent Society*—though perhaps of more lasting value. The actual change that has occurred is not any new "dependence effect" but a general change from a pre-industrial, tradition-directed to industrial, consumer-directed society with its concomitant mass culture. Which means that social influences are more changeable, that they come more often from below—with people more attuned to them (more other-directed—rather than coming from nobility, king, and church; or, having been internalized, they come from a greater variety of sources; the advertising industry is among them, though it perhaps transmits more than it creates.

Characteristically, advertising agencies are not in the permanent service of a class, ideology, or church but of whoever hires them. Mostly private firms try to increase or maintain their profits by doing so. But firms are as interested in producing what people want as they are in making people want what they produce. The former is more profitable and more certain of success. In this sense, advertising probably is less engaged in "contriving" needs than the church was, or than Harvard University is when it raises funds. Indeed, the bad taste Mr. Galbraith deplores is indulged in largely because of the absence of the ancient contriving agencies—church and court. We are now catering to the taste of the masses, whereas before it could be ignored. There is no evidence to indicate that people would buy fewer or better things without advertising. They might buy slightly different things from slightly different people.

IV

The public expenditures Galbraith advocates to replace private expenditures—more public works, education, welfare services—are neither new nor supported by new arguments. This part of *The Affluent Society* amounts to tiresome exhortation. Yet a discussion of the specifics of public expenditures might have been fruitful. I am convinced that we do need public services not now undertaken; and that many public services presently offered at high cost to taxpayers are "contrived": they become necessary because the government prevents private industry from rendering them, or makes it excessively costly to do so, or, finally, because they offset noxious government activities elsewhere. What happens is classically illustrated in the case of farm subsidies.

The government raises farm prices, *i.e.*, the cost of living, mainly the price of food, but also of cotton, tobacco, etc., by means of price supports. The government spends more than $5 billion annually to give us the privilege of buying food at higher than free-market prices. This money is spent to buy supplies which would depress the market price, or to pay farmers for not producing them. No way to dispose of most of the supplies purchased has been found; they are stored at huge additional cost, until they spoil. Some are sold at a loss abroad or given away. The subsidy, of course, perpetuates the misallocation of resources between agriculture and the rest of the economy, which it is supposed to correct, and also within agriculture, so that more is produced of what is needed less, and less of what is needed more, *ad infinitum;* and subsidies are required *ad infinitum* to keep things that way.

There is no respectable argument known to economists for these subsidies. The argument usually heard is that without them the income of farmers would be lower than that of workers, or lower than it was in some past period. But most of the subsidy does not go to low-income farmers; their farms are so small and unproductive that higher prices, or payments for noncultivation of their property add little to their income. Most of the subsidy goes to big-scale producers of unneeded farm products. (50 per cent of our farmers produce less than 10 per cent of the agricultural output.)

If we wanted to help low income farmers, it would be simple to do so without raising food prices, without fostering misallocation, and without subsidizing farmers whose income far exceeds the income of the taxpayers who must pay the subsidy. Without changing the whole complex structure of present legislation—a task that should not be neglected, but that requires time—we could do so by simply purchasing only from farmers whose net income from all sources in any given year does not exceed, say, $7,000. (Surely farmers with higher incomes need no subsidies.) Any amount paid farmers whose income exceeds $7,000 must be returned—and the government can return what it purchased from them. In time, the government might limit itself to purchases from progressively older farmers. This ultimately would solve the problem; only those would remain or go into farming who can make an income that satisfies them by selling their crops at unsubsidized market prices. This, of course, would correct the allocation of resources and make further subsidies unnecessary.

I have briefly outlined elsewhere how this proposal could be carried out and what the effects would be. I have received heartening letters from economists. But nothing else. The mood of our times is such that if a problem can be perpetuated and made worse by high subsidies and brought nearer solution by low ones, we prefer high subsidies. I deliberately speak of the mood of the times. For in terms of their economic interests, the farmers who would not lose under the proposal—let alone consumers—constitute an overwhelming majority. But our general tendency is to make individual incomes less and less dependent on individual efforts, on the value placed by the market on one's product, and more and more on political considerations, on the political power exercised by a group, or the power that can be gained by catering to it. Above all, the nature of the subsidy is carefully hidden. We speak of price supports when we make relief payments to some farmers who need them (and who should be trained for a different occupation rather than kept farming to receive relief) and to many who do not. This careful disguise helps persuade taxpayers.

By now the farm program has become a classical case. Many newer, equally dubious, programs seem more complicated. Thus, the government feels it necessary to subsidize low and middle-rent appartment-house building in many cities. It is contended that low and middle-income families, although more affluent than ever before, cannot afford the rent for unsubsidized housing. But if their income is too small, we should subsidize them, not housing. Why a subsidy in kind, which deprives them of choice? Is it feared that they would make a choice that appears wrong to the government? What evidence is there to show that they are wrong and the government right? Does not our system rest on the premise that the individual knows best what he needs—not the government? Why then should he be incompetent to decide whether he should spend additional money best on housing, clothing, or, say, education? If, finally, it is believed not that people's income requires supplementing but that the cost of housing has risen disproportionately, we must ask (1) why people should not make a greater proportionate outlay for housing than they used to; or, (2) why the cost of housing has risen disproportionately. Certainly there are measures the government could take to reduce it without paying out subsidies. What about taxes, obsolete building codes, and local laws and required briberies which unnecessarily raise the cost of building? What about the steadily rising labor costs of building—disproportionately high wage rates, featherbedding, deliberate inefficiency—caused in no small measure by labor unions, whose power to raise costs is due in the main to the governmental protection they enjoy? Does not the government first raise the cost of housing, then point out that it is high and proceed to subsidize housing? One may find similar situations throughout our economy: *e.g.*, in urban transportation, railroads, the merchant marine. . . .

As soon as we turn from vacuous generalizations about the affluent private and the starved public sector of our economy to an actual scrutiny of public expenditures, we find that, though it is true that some needed services are not performed, or not performed well, it is also true that many unneeded services are performed at immense cost, and that they serve as pretexts to perform still other services, or to pay subsidies to offset the effect they have. Increasing public expenditure is unlikely to remedy this state of affairs—on the contrary, it will make it worse.

72

Can Benefits and Costs of Public Investments Be Measured?

This research report briefly summarizes a number of attempts to use benefit-cost analysis to appraise different public expenditures, and concludes that it provides a practical guide to public-expenditure decisions in only a limited number of areas.

BROOKINGS RESEARCH REPORT

Some economists [1] believe that the benefits of government projects can be appraised objectively and even quantitatively by applying benefit-cost analysis. They contend that analytical techniques similar to those used in evaluating investments in the private sector of the economy can be adapted to help guide public investment discussions.

Other economists are skeptical of the accuracy and the usefulness of benefit-cost analysis. They doubt whether the most important social effects of government investments can be appraised quantitatively by any formalized method. One skeptical view compares this problem of measurement to the appraisal of a horse-and-rabbit stew, the rabbit being cast as the consequences that can be measured and evaluated numerically, and the horse as the amalgam of external effects (social, emotional, and psychological) and historical and aesthetic considerations that can be adjudged only roughly and subjectively. Since the horse dominates the flavor of the stew, meticulous evaluation of the rabbit is hardly worthwhile.

The advocates of benefit-cost analysis agree that many important aspects of a public investment project are not amenable to quantitative appraisal. They recognize that benefit-cost analysis is largely an undeveloped art, and that even if one takes the most hopeful view of the future,

Brookings Research Report No. 32, Brookings Institution. Reprinted by permission. The Report presents some highlights of *Measuring Benefits of Government Investments*, edited by Robert Dorfman, copyright 1965 by the Brookings Institution.

[1] The findings and conclusions are those of the authors and do not purport to represent the views of the Brookings Institution, its trustees, officers, or other staff members.

some significant consequences of public undertakings must, it seems, always elude the craft of the quantifier. Nevertheless, in the field of water resources, public decisions have been made noticeably more rational and consistent by submitting project proposals to the discipline of comparing measurable costs with measurable benefits. At the very least, such a process, if applied to other investments, would focus attention on the question of whether the unmeasurable benefits are deemed impressive enough to justify sustaining the measurable costs that are not offset by measurable benefits.

The debate thus revolves around conjectures on whether the economist, the statistician, and the political scientist, working in cooperation, can devise means for quantifying a usefully large proportion of the consequences of public investment undertakings.

INCENTIVES FOR GOVERNMENT ENTERPRISE

In general, if a good or a service is desirable, its production will also be profitable; and if it is profitable, it will probably be provided by private enterprise. But where investments that businessmen would deem unprofitable are socially worthwhile, government must take the initiative.

The circumstances that favor government provision cluster around the concept of collectibility or, rather, uncollectibility. In the usual economic transaction, the user is charged for the good or service he consumes; the amount he is willing to pay measures the value of the commodity to him; and, since his use of the commodity precludes anyone else from benefiting from it, the value of the commodity to the user is also its value to society. This standard analysis of social value is not, however, strictly valid for all transactions; for a few types of transactions it is too wide of the mark to be acceptable. The most important of these latter types are (1) collective goods, and (2) goods that are characterized by external economics of consumption. In neither case is the provider of the good able to collect from beneficiaries a charge commensurate with the benefits conferred.

A collective good is a facility or service that is made freely available to all comers without charge. It is not feasible, for example, or desirable to levy a charge on every shipmaster who sees a lighthouse, or on every housewife when a health officer inspects a food market. Collective goods then, with rare exceptions, cannot be provided by private firms because they do not produce a flow of income to the provider. The responsibility for providing them, therefore, frequently falls to the government. Some important collective goods are national defense, civil and criminal justice, streets and most highways, and outdoor recreational facilities. The important factor is that, since collective goods are not sold, there are no market prices to assist in appraising their value.

Collective goods are allied to *external economies of consumption* but the latter come into being in a different way. When a man is treated for a communicable disease, the relief afforded him is only part of the social value; every resident of his community benefits from the reduced danger of infection. In other words, the consumer of a good or service is not the sole beneficiary, and the amount he is willing to pay does not measure the entire value of the good to society. The act of consumption, in effect, creates the collective good.

Another circumstance that calls for government initiative involves *economies of scale.* Some activities can be performed economically only at such a very large scale that for private enterprise to undertake them is neither feasible nor desirable.

For example, without invoking governmental power, it is not practicable to assemble the large areas of property required for highways, urban redevelopment, or hydroelectric projects. Whatever the condition of production, however, the government would not undertake a project unless important collective goods or external benefits were involved.

Applied research and development projects are sponsored by the government to secure a variety of benefits. Some, such as the bulk of the applied research supported by the department of Agriculture, are directed toward increasing productivity. Other projects, such as the work sponsored by the National Institutes of Health, seek to enhance the domestic welfare. Still other programs are concerned with reaping benefits in the sphere of international power politics and national prestige. The most obvious examples are the Defense Department's vast R&D effort, the military part of the R&D activities of the Atomic Energy Commission, and a substantial fraction of the rapidly growing programs of the National Aeronautics and Space Administration.

In the field of education there is serious national concern over the school "dropout." But is a dropout necessarily a "dropout problem"? In his paper, Weisbrod points out that a dropout becomes a problem when society feels that he or she is unable to adjust to the society and to the economy. If the problems of the dropout are handled directly by the individual, or within the family unit, "society" may be unconcerned. But the matter becomes a *social* problem when the consequences that are ignored by the individual begin to impinge seriously on others.

Sometimes government undertakings are stimulated by an incentive of quite a different sort: the desire to influence the distribution of income. The desire for a regional redistribution, for example, is one of the explicit motivations for the Appalachia program, and the desire for redistribution plays a large role in urban renewal programs.

As the above discussion of incentives suggests, the government tends to intervene in precisely those markets in which prices are either lacking or would seriously understate social values. It is inherent in government activities, therefore, that market prices cannot be used in appraising their social contributions. Still, some economic basis is needed for judging which potential government undertakings are worthwhile and which are not. Benefit-cost analysis attempts to provide such a basis.

BENEFIT-COST ANALYSIS

Benefit-cost analysis is closely analogous to the methods used by businessmen to appraise investment projects. The major difference is that estimates of social value are used in place of estimates of sales value when appropriate. A number of different formulas are used for comparing benefits and costs of government undertakings.

The starting point is a projection of the physical output of the undertaking, either in each year of its life or in some typical year of operation. If the undertaking is a highway, there would have to be estimates of the number of passenger-car miles, truck miles, and bus miles to be traveled on it in each year or in a typical year. Then estimates would be made of the social value of each unit of these physical outputs, be they passenger-car miles, kilowatt hours, or other. These two estimates can be used to estimate the gross social contribution of the enterprise in a single year.

At this point the different formulas begin to diverge. One approach is to perform the gross benefit calculation for a typical year and to make a parallel computation for social costs. The costs consist of two major components: *current costs* —the typical annual expenditures for operating and maintaining the facilities— and *capital costs*—a charge levied against a year's operations to amortize the initial expenses of construction and installation. The ratio of gross annual benefits to total annual costs is the benefit-cost ratio. This formula amounts to a businessman's calculation of the ratio of sales to cost of goods sold, or of a profit-sales ratio, except, of course, that the value of output used in a benefit-cost computation is the social rather than the market value.

An alternative formula subtracts current costs in each year from gross benefits to obtain an estimate of current net benefits. The current net benefits for each year are discounted back to the date of inception of the project and added up to obtain an estimate of the present value of discounted net benefits. The ratio of this figure to the estimated capital cost of the project is then the benefit-cost ratio. This formula is therefore analogous to a businessman's calculation of the rate of profit that can be earned by capital invested in the undertaking.

The precise formula used for consolidating and expressing the results of the benefit-cost analysis is not important: properly interpreted, all the formulas lead to the same conclusions. The heart of the matter lies in deciding what benefits should be included and how they should be valued. The debate about benefit-cost analysis centers on the question of whether the social value of benefits can be estimated reliably enough to justify the trouble and effort involved in a benefit-cost computation.

HIGHLIGHTS OF PROJECT EVALUATION

Although the subject matter of the papers ranges widely, a strong strain of similarity in treatment suggests that benefit-cost analysis may be the same wherever it is applied. Typically, the papers start out by listing the various social and economic groups likely to be affected by the particular problem or program under investigation.

The next step is usually an evaluation of the various impacts of the program on the groups which have been listed. Ruth Mack and Sumner Myers, for example, discuss the utilities of outdoor recreation in three different categories: immediate enjoyment, long-term benefits for the individual, and benefits to the nation as a whole.

Immediate enjoyment consists of the sense of pleasure experienced immediately before, during, and after participation in outdoor recreation. Long-term benefits, which are both physical and psychic, are more difficult to measure. Society places particular value on outdoor recreation because it builds strong bodies and because it does this in an environment that is credited with building healthy minds. Thirdly, outdoor recreation is important because it benefits the nation as a whole. It is an advantage to *all* people, and it encourages the conservation of natural wonders and beauties for the benefit of the pleasure to the inhabitants.

On the "dropout" problem, Burton Weisbrod discusses unemployment and its impact on the national scene. With respect to age and education, when unemployment is concentrated among young people, and particularly among the young dropouts, frustration and despair are likely consequences, from which individual delinquency, gang activity, and more serious crime are likely to spring. A broader distribution of unemployment by age, education, race, and geography results not only in savings in social costs to others, but also savings in transfer payments, as the extreme effects of long-term unemployment tend to be replaced by the less severe financial and psychological effects of more equally distributed unemployment. The need for welfare assistance, then, unemployment compensation, and other payments to the needy tend to decline.

The critical stage of the benefit-cost analysis follows when the authors of the papers attempt to place a unit value on each of the groups. They elaborate on the details here more than in any of the other sections. Weisbrod calculates that prevention of a white male student's dropout outside the South is "worth" $4,000 as of age 18, if a 5 per cent rate of discount is appropriate, or $1,740 if a 10 per cent rate is justified. It is striking to note that at the 5 per cent rate white dropouts of either sex are more costly in the South than in the North; the reason is that income differentials between the North and South narrow as the level of educational attainment rises. Hence, while Northern graduates and dropouts have larger incomes than their Southern counterparts, the expected monetary value of additional education is greater in the South.

In analyzing urban highway investments, Herbert Mohring assigns value to travel time because travel time turns out to be by far the most important cost of urban travel. He lists the average travel times and their costs per vehicle mile at various volume/capacity ratios and at alternative values of $1.55 and $2.80 per hour.

Herbert Klarman defines the economic benefits of a disease control program as the costs that are averted by the program. The costs attributable to the 119,600 cases of syphilis incurred in the United States in 1962 can be estimated, he explains, by taking into account medical care expenses, production loss from time spent in treatment, reduction of earnings resulting from the social "stigma" of having had syphilis, and the psychic loss to the sick individual resulting from his awareness of his affliction.

In estimating the benefits from the FAA aviation support system (largely airway and air-traffic operations and facilities), Fromm points out that the gains from these services reduce the elements of ineffectiveness in the system—the delays, diversions, cancellations, and accidents. Using data for 1960, he estimates the costs of such ineffectiveness—which are equal to the potential gains that might be realized if the aviation system were capable of operating without delays, diversions, cancellations, and accidents.

The final analysis of each paper deals with the adding of the measurable costs and benefits and a comparison of results, with due allowance for the unmeasurable components.

For example, the accompanying table from the paper by Rothenberg provides —for purposes of illustration only—numerical estimates of benefits and costs on three renewal projects in Chicago. In this particular case, the measured benefits are only a small proportion of the costs of each project. The "plus" marks indicate spillover benefits and benefits associated with decreasing cost of slums, which the author was not able to quantify in this paper. To determine the grand balance, the costs in the table would have to be compared with all the benefits; the

Summary Table of Benefit-Cost Analysis
of Three Urban Renewal Projects
(In thousands of dollars)

Project Costs and Benefits	Blue Island	Hyde Park "B"	Michael Reese
I. Resource Costs of Project			
1. Gross Project Costs	$396	$638	$6,235
2. Less Initial Value of Land	46	49	1,596
3. Equals Total Resource Costs	350	589	4,639
II. Benefits Produced by Project			
1. Increased Productivity of Site Land	$ 29	$ 30	$1,719
2. Increased Productivity of Neighboring Land and Improvements (Spillover)	+	+	+
3. Decreased Social Costs Associated with Slums	+	+	+
Total Costs not offset by Site Land Benefit (I-3 minus II-1)	$321	$559	$2,920

Note: "Plus" marks indicate nonmeasurable spillover benefits.

existence of significant nonmeasurable benefits is the source of much of the difficulty in practical policy-making.

The discussants' reactions to the papers were remarkably similar. Most of the debate revolved around the relative importance of the types of benefits which have been included in the value-totals as against the types that have been excluded. That something has been left out is agreed in every instance; and just as uniformly there is disagreement on whether enough has been included to make the exercise worth the effort.

CONCLUSION

The debate about benefit-cost analysis centers on the question of whether the social value of benefits can be estimated reliably enough to justify the trouble and effort involved in a benefit-cost computation. This issue cannot be resolved categorically. It is no accident that benefit-cost analysis had its origin and highest development in the field of water resources. That is the field in which government operations are most analogous to private business and in which the highest proportion of outputs—water and power—are salable commodities bearing relevant market prices. And nonpriceable, almost intangible consequences, though present, are less obtrusive than in other spheres of government activity.

The information presented by the seven authors on the selected government investment projects, and the evaluations of the advantages of the benefit-cost analysis method by both authors and discussants, will be useful as a guide for future work in this field. The difficulties encountered in these seven case studies are symptoms of the youngness of the field and of the opportunities still remaining for its development. The application of methods of benefit-cost analysis for use in decision-making by governmental bodies has only just begun.

Professor Wallich argues that our
present tax structure may inhibit economic
growth because we depend heavily on
high income taxes to finance public
expenditures. He discusses some of the
shortcomings of our present tax system and
suggests a federal sales tax as a possible
alternative.

*Henry C. Wallich is Professor of
Economics at Yale University.*

73

For Fastest Growth— What Kind of Tax?

HENRY C. WALLICH

More Americans pay a sales tax, and pay it more often, than any other kind of tax. Yet because so much of it is in pennies, the take from sales taxes is relatively modest. It does not begin to compare with the massive sums that some 40,000,000 income-tax payers annually turn over to the tax collector.

The present national argument about taxes—whether to cut them or to reform them, definitely not to abolish them—has brought out the interesting fact that Americans pay a higher proportion of their total taxes in the form of income taxes and other direct taxes than the citizens of almost any other industrial country. Conversely, they pay a lower proportion in the form of sales taxes and other indirect taxes.

The argument has also brought out that the industrial countries which have recently enjoyed the fastest economic growth are among those that rely much more on sales and similar taxes than on income taxes. This is strikingly true, for instance, as Prof. William J. Fellner of Yale has shown, of the European top-growth countries (France, Italy, and Germany) as well as of Japan. Other countries, relying more heavily on income taxes, have by and large grown less rapidly.

Findings like these do not prove anything conclusively, of course. The members of the "fast-growth club" may owe their success to some other factors, most likely to a variety of causes. And among the less developed countries of the world there are many that grow painfully slowly while relying exclusively on indirect taxes.

But in the cases of the successful countries of Europe, and of Japan, some logical connection between the tax system and growth does seem to emerge. No country can grow rapidly unless it plows back a high proportion of its output into productive investment. High income taxes probably tend to reduce the supply of savings that are needed, because they weigh most heavily on high-income earners who do the most saving. They may also undermine the incentive to invest, as well as the urge to work and make money.

The successful countries are all countries that save and invest a high proportion of their incomes. Recently, the rate of growth has slowed in some of them, for instance in Germany, though to a level still well above the growth of the United States. This has been accompanied by some slowing of investment. The Germans attribute this to overfull employment, shorter hours worked and a squeeze on profits through rising wages. The tax system, insofar as it has favored investment and growth in the past, still does so today.

The United States has been very successful throughout most of its history, but today it has become a low-investment country, and our growth has slowed. These are grounds for suspicion, at least, that our tax system may have been one of the culprits in a complicated case.

Tax comparisons among countries are the most odious of comparisons, because in no two countries are tax laws ever exactly comparable. The variety of taxes is a monument to the ingenuity of governments. The simple distinction of income and sales taxes does not begin to do it justice. Even the economists' distinction of direct and indirect taxes, which covers roughly the same ground, does not really bring order into this chaos.

In the United States, the Federal Government levies no sales taxes proper at all. It manages, however, to raise about 13 per cent of its budgetary revenues from excises on gasoline, liquor, and tobacco, on transportation, telephone calls, and entertainment, and on a number of other articles and activities as well as from customs duties.

These are sales taxes in economic effect, if not in legal terminology. All the rest comes from taxes on income in one form or another. State and local governments do get a much larger share of their considerably smaller income from sales-type and property taxes.

The net result is that we hand over 62 per cent of our taxes in the form of income taxes and 38 per cent as sales and similar taxes. Only Sweden levies a slightly higher proportion of direct taxes. Meanwhile, France obtains only 26 per cent from income taxes, the rest as sales and similar imposts; Italy 30 per cent, including in all cases state and local revenues, but excluding social-security taxes which do not seem to fit properly into either category. It is quite possible that these figures contain some of the European growth secret for which President Kennedy told his advisers to go looking.

How did the United States get so far out of line with the tax policies of the most successful countries? The United States had its first brush with the income tax during the Civil War. The tax was dropped thereafter, and did not rear its head again until 1913, following the passage of the Sixteenth Amendment. Introduced just in time to help finance World War I at rates up to 77 per cent, it was cut back to a top rate of 24 per cent during the Nineteen Twenties by Secretary of the Treasury Andrew W. Mellon. As a peace-time tax, it came to full flower (if that is the word) during the great depression. Its sponsors had in mind two principal purposes—to discourage people who want to save (their money is needed to finance growth), and to redistribute income. Politics aside, both purposes had their justification in the climate of the times.

Those were the days when it was believed, with some apparent basis in contemporary fact, that the United States economy had reached full maturity, that it offered few opportunities for new investment and could look forward to but little future growth. This meant that there was little need for new savings. Wealthy Mr. Smith, who saved a good part of his income, thereby merely cut down consumption and destroyed jobs. By taxing him and easing the tax burden on impecunious Mr. Jones, who spent most of what he earned, it was thought that a positive stimulus to the economy would be achieved. Redistribution of incomes, through taxes and public expenditures, seemed the only means of raising lower-bracket living standards in the absence of genuine growth.

Then came World War II, and with it tremendous financial needs and still higher taxes. In the different social climate of the post-World War II period, rates did not come down drastically as they did during the Twenties. Today, with a lowest bracket rate of 20 per cent and a top rate of 91 per cent, we are very close to all-time peak levels.

Income tax adherents rightly argue that the income tax is much more sophisticated than a tax on commodities. Taxes on the sale or transportation of commodities are easy to administer. Since the time immemorial, princes and potentates have levied them—at the city gate, at the harbor dock, at the places of primitive manufacture, or in the town market. The income tax is a tax on an abstract number which cannot be arrived at, for the larger taxpayers, without subtle accounting concepts like depreciation.

The income tax has been described as a fair tax because it demands more from the wealthy than from the poor. It also permits account to be taken of individual circumstances—such as the number of children, the age of the taxpayer, expense through illness, and the like—through appropriate exemptions and deductions. It is thought to encourage good citizenship because it is a clearly visible tax, allowing everyone to know exactly what the government costs him, in contrast to sales and excise taxes that can be concealed in the price.

Finally, the income tax seems attractive to many because it is flexible in recessions. When a taxpayer's income falls, the progressive feature of the tax, which makes the rate rise with the income bracket, goes into reverse. The taxpayer's liability falls faster than income and affords him relief.

But in the post-war years, the income tax has also revealed grave weaknesses. Tax rates designed to cope with supposedly permanent stagnation are out of place in an economy geared for growth. We can no longer afford to discourage saving—it is needed to finance growth. Even though, in the present state of the economy, there seem to be more savers than investors, that is largely a question of the business cycle and should not determine long-run tax policy.

We also have every reason not to discourage the willingness to work or invest. And we need no longer look to the redistribution of Smith's income to Jones as the principal means of raising Jones' living standards. Economic growth is a much more powerful lever than redistribution. If the two conflict, more is to be gained, for both Jones and Smith, if we go for growth than if we go for redistribution. All this suggests that a tax system relying less heavily on high income taxes may be more in tune with our times.

Practical experience with high tax rates has tarnished the glamour of the income tax in other ways. Tax avoidance and tax evasion have become familiar terms in the economic dictionary. Tax avoidance is the legitimate effort of the taxpayer to take advantage of all the facilities the law provides to hold his taxes down. A whole profession of tax specialists has been reared in the overheated tax climate of a 91 per cent top rate. In this strange world, a penny saved is ten pennies earned, and a penny of deductible expenditures is almost no cost at all. When a large part of a businessman's time is devoted to tax problems, and a large part of his decisions governed by their tax consequences, little good can be expected for the economy.

Tax evasion is the name of illegitimate efforts to minimize taxes—tax cheating, for short. The United States taxpayer is probably one of the world's most honest —many other countries do not trust their taxpayers to assess themselves, as we do, but prepare returns for them. Yet high taxes put a strain on the honesty and raise the possibility that tax morale may soften and be neglected.

The tremendous pressure of the top rates has knocked some highly inequitable breaches in the wall separating pre-tax from post-tax income. Groups with strong political backing have molded the law to fit their interests. It is possible today to write off the same building several times over, to deduct depletion on an oil well long after the investment has been repaid, to charge off business expenses that are pure fun, and to stash away income for the future with a minimum of present tax.

Whatever the logic behind these devices, they make a mockery of the rate structure, and they create invidious distinctions between those who have oil wells, expense accounts, or deductions and pension funds and those others with similar incomes who have not.

Even decisions regarding public expenditures are vitiated by high tax rates. When Mr. Jones, who has three children and pays a top rate of 20 per cent, looks at a proposal for Federal aid to higher education, he may feel that he would be sending his offspring to college rather cheaply at that price. Mr. Smith, who also has three children but pays a top rate of 70 per cent, figures that private education would cost him less.

Since in our taxable society there are more Joneses than Smiths, there is a chance that the Joneses may outvote the Smiths, and get the legislation passed. But the Smiths are apt to get more vocal about the matter, and perhaps they can pull the Congress their way. In any event, an arbitrary and irrational element is injected into national-expenditure decisions that distorts them one way or the other.

Even the ancient faith that income taxes cannot be shifted from seller to buyer has begun to wane. That many corporations can, in certain circumstances, pass along part or all of their income tax by raising prices has long been evident. Many corporate executives insist that this is precisely what they do. The personal income tax may be a little harder to shift. But the level of taxes certainly is a feature in wage negotiations. And would many corporate salaries be quite so high if executives could not point to the need to compensate for the tax bite?

The troubles of the income tax are beginning to make the sales tax intellectually respectable again. The new support comes from curiously ill-assorted elements. There are those who are concerned about economic growth and who believe that a little less income tax and a little more sales tax would be an improvement over the present mix. There are old-fashioned conservatives who are mainly concerned with getting their high rates down, and who see in a Federal sales tax a means of making that possible. And there are the liberals who want to raise public expenditures and who, feeling that the income tax has been milked almost dry, are trying to overcome their innate aversion to sales taxes.

For most liberals, to be sure, the sales tax still carries a stigma. But avant-garde thinkers like Harvard professors Alvin Hansen and John Kenneth Galbraith have given support to a Federal sales tax. Galbraith has argued, possibly to the chagrin of some of his disciples, that in an age of affluence a sales tax no longer means what a bread tax or a salt tax meant in ages gone by. Hansen has calculated that the income tax simply cannot yield the kind of money he believes the government should spend. Some former critics have sought to make their peace with the sales tax by suggesting that it be coupled with a special tax on luxuries. All in all, the sales tax seems to be coming up in the world. And there is work for it to do.

In trying to establish priorities among the various objectives of contemporary tax policy, the goal of faster growth strikes me as by far the most important. Faster growth will, in fact, give everybody pretty much what he wants. It will make the cost of big government easier to bear for the well-to-do. It will permit larger public expenditures to satisfy the proponents of social priorities. If we can speed up growth by cutting back the income tax and introducing a Federal sales tax, the effort would be worth while.

The evidence that the maneuver will succeed is not conclusive, to be sure. In any case, no very striking result could be expected from such a reform alone. But there probably is enough sensible economics behind the case to justify moving in that direction.

We would have to move cautiously, however, because pitfalls are sure to beset the unwary sales tax enthusiast. Sales taxes have been the province of state and local authorities. A Federal sales tax would have to be designed so as not to interfere with this traditional source of revenue.

The question of coverage needs to be faced. Should the tax cover only goods, or also services? Should food be excluded? Should the rate be the same for all items? If a great many things were excluded, to which purpose tremendous political pressures are sure to be mobilized, and if the rate were severely fragmented, we might end up with little more than what we have now—a set of arbitrary Federal excise taxes.

I do not believe that in the near future there is much hope of reaching a national consensus on any of these questions, or even on the basic principle of a Federal sales tax. The experience of this year's tax bill, on its tortuous way through Congress, has made clear how very difficult it is to reach agreement even on relatively minor tax reforms. As a practical matter, the most likely way in which we might some day get a Federal sales tax is through a national emergency calling for large extra revenues. A sales tax might then be introduced instead of or along with the traditional income tax hike. Obviously that is not a consummation to be wished.

*   *   *

74

The Effect
of High Tax Rates
on Executive Incentive

A leading businessman argues that our
high marginal income tax rates make it
difficult to induce men with ability to
enter the field of business, and that
capable individuals are discouraged from
exerting the effort necessary to make
their greatest contribution.

*Crawford H. Greenewalt is Chairman
of the Board of E. I. du Pont de Nemours
& Co.*

CRAWFORD H. GREENEWALT

*   *   *

. . . The views I shall express are those of an executive who must face
the very practical problems involved in the operation of a large corporation. These, of course, embrace the present, and the usual problems of
customer, employee, and stockholder relations. In a much more important
sense, however, they are problems of the future and comprise, insofar as
possible, the development of policies and practices which will insure continuing effective performance well beyond present horizons.

*   *   *

As our country has developed and matured, we have become increasingly dependent on an active and dynamic industry for our economic growth and prosperity. Without minimizing in the slightest the important contributions to our national economy made by the farmers, the
professions, the service trades, the fact is that our standard of living is
firmly anchored to our industrial development.

Since this is so, it follows that how business and industry fare must be
a matter of great importance to all Americans. Their standard of living,
their future well-being, are vitally dependent upon an American industry that continues to be dynamic, resourceful, and progressive. This
desirable state of affairs can continue only so long as industry can compete
successfully for the limited supply of talented people. For an industrial

Reprinted from *Federal Tax Policy for Economic Growth and Stability*. Papers
Submitted by Panelists Appearing before the Subcommittee on Tax Policy, Joint
Economic Committee on the Economic Report, November 9, 1955, pp. 185–188.

477

corporation is not a machine that can be run by automation. It is a team of human beings that must have first-class direction by intelligent and able management. And if we have learned one fundamental truth in industry, it is that first-class performance can never come from second-class performers.

*   *   *

The point I make is that industry, if it is to keep abreast of its responsibilities to the Nation, must have a great number of first-class minds at its disposal. It must compete for them with all other phases of our society, for there are never enough to go around. The fields of government, education, the military, the arts, the professions, all are seeking to persuade able young men to cast their lot with them. Each has its own type of incentive to offer, and the demand for talent always exceeds the supply.

THE ESSENTIAL QUESTION OF INCENTIVE

*   *   *

Adequate incentives, of course, differ with different people. Some are attracted most strongly by the promise of prestige. Some are more interested in leisure time, to follow scholarly pursuits or perhaps simply to meditate upon the ills of the world. To some people, public notice or outward signs of rank and importance are alluring goals. Some seek power. For most, however, the strongest and probably the most desirable incentive is financial reward. Furthermore, financial reward is not only an incentive in itself; it is the only fluid medium that can be used to balance the attractions of the more intangible compensations, such as prestige, power, or public notice.

There is another aspect of the monetary incentive that seems to me worthy of comment. It is the only reward that can be cut down on a basis of fixed percentages. We do not, for example, withhold 91 percent of an Oscar going to the best moving-picture actress of the year. The winner of a Nobel Prize does not have to give the Government a certain percentage of the prestige accruing to him. A brilliant violinist does not have to share his applause with the collector of internal revenue. These illustrations may seem facetious, yet they are based on a serious foundation, for we do in fact make the recipient of monetary rewards, and him alone, give up significant percentages in taxes. We are, that is, penalizing only one manifestation of success, and this seems to me, frankly, not only unfair but, for the future, a dangerous practice.

*   *   *

Business, for the most part, is in a poor position to compete in these intangible areas. With few exceptions executives of great ability remain relatively unknown. A player of even minor roles in the films, a leader of a jazz orchestra, or a writer of only average accomplishment may be far better known than many leaders of industry. For businessmen there are few medals, prizes, degrees, uniforms, patriotic citations, or grandiose honorifics. There are few featured players on the industrial stage.

There is, of course, the satisfaction that comes from work well done. But this is peculiar to no special section of our society; it is common to all. For the purposes of this discussion, it simply cancels out.

And so industry must rely most importantly on financial compensation. As it becomes increasingly less able to do so, it will lose its capacity to induce qualified people to make their careers in industry, or to seek to advance to their maximum capacity.

THE EROSION OF THE MONEY INCENTIVE

It is here, as I see it, that our danger lies. I am certain that the effectiveness of the money incentive is being eroded by the tax rates that prevail in the upper brackets today. While many companies are experimenting with nonmonetary incentives, basically industry must rely upon the coin of compensation most suitable to its character. I am afraid the raw truth is that, in the long run, we shall begin to lose out and our proportion of the available candidates will fall unless some relief can be obtained.

I am necessarily talking in the future tense, because it is quite clear that the point of concern is not the executive of today, or even of the immediate future. I think, if we are to focus the picture, we must rule out consideration of the present management group. I doubt that high personal taxation has had substantial effect upon the performance of present-day management people, even though they may not be happy over the realization that at top levels each additional dollar of gross income nets its earner about 9 cents. I confess to some pain in this respect myself, but I cannot say that I am inclined as a result to work less diligently or to take my responsibilities less seriously.

Today's executives are, I think, reasonably immune. By the time a man has reached a position of eminence within his organization, he is influenced importantly by his sense of loyalty, his sense of obligation, a preoccupying interest in the work, or, as has been unkindly suggested, by conditioned reflex.

The same applies, I would guess, to those who may be regarded as the immediate successors, for they too have reached a point where the challenge and associations of the work present an incentive that will probably override reduced financial motivations. . . .

There are two major areas of concern. There is, first, the effect of high income-tax rates on long-range monetary incentives, which promises to make it more difficult than heretofore to persuade young men with real ability to enter the rank of business. Let me make it clear that I am not asking for an improvement in industry's competitive position opposite the other fields of endeavor. I merely want to maintain it.

There is, second, increased difficulty, also tracing to high tax rates, in persuading men of ability who have risen to the point where they are in sight of reaching their top capacity to keep on going rather than to rest on their oars.

*   *   *

75

U. S. Exports Provide Jobs

The effects of international trade on domestic employment are not always easy to see. This article reports that in 1960, 3.1 million Americans had jobs which depended on our export trade.

THE NEW YORK TIMES

About 3,100,000 workers in the United States owed their jobs to the nation's export trade in 1960, the Labor Department reported today.

They were employed in that year to produce, transport, and market $20,700,000,000 worth of merchandise sold overseas, according to a study prepared by the Bureau of Labor Statistics.

The total of 3,100,000 jobs represents about one-seventeenth of the jobs in the private sector of the economy. The overall job total in the United States has been about 67,000,000 in recent months.

The study was released in conjunction with President Kennedy's message to Congress on foreign trade. Mr. Kennedy asked new authority to negotiate lower tariffs and to assist workers and industries affected by competing imports.

The bureau found that about 13 per cent of the total farm employment and 8 per cent of manufacturing employment was attributable to exports, with considerably higher percentages for such industries as chemicals and nonelectrical machinery.

POST-WAR TREND UNKNOWN

Jack Alterman, assistant chief of the bureau's division of productivity and technological developments, said there was no reliable figure on the post-war trend in export-generated employment. Exports have increased since 1945, but so has the amount produce by each worker.

"It is possible there has been relatively little change, or possibly a decline," he said.

Studies are under way dealing with the impact of imports on domestic job opportunities in 1960 and, for comparison purposes, on the export-import employment picture in 1953, Mr. Alterman said.

Of the 3,100,000 jobs created by exports in 1960, the report said, about 48 per cent were involved directly in the production, transportation, and marketing of exported goods. The remainder came in supporting industries, as in making the steel contained in exported machinery, for example, or fabricating the tires and upholstery on an exported auto.

About 2,100,000 of the export-created jobs were in nonfarm occupations. The individual manufacturing groups that were most affected were chemicals, primary metals, machinery, and automobiles and trucks.

INCLUDES FOREIGN AID

In 1960, the report said, the United States, including Alaska and Hawaii, exported merchandise valued at about $20,700,000,000, including military and economic aid. With transportation, insurance, and Federal export payments for farm and food products added, it said, the total industrial output attributable to exports was $22,055,300,000.

The leading industries helped by exports were nonelectrical machinery, with 15.5 per cent of its employment attributable to exports; primary metals, including steel, 14.4 per cent; chemicals and allied products, 14.4 per cent; tobacco products, 12.8 per cent; scientific and control instruments, 10.2 per cent; and transportation equipment, 7.8 per cent.

The trade and service industries were affected least, with only 2.1 per cent work forces affected by exports.

"It should be noted," the report stated, "that the share of the machinery and primary metals industries in total export employment would be even higher if it were possible to distribute by industry the indirect employment attributable to military goods production and employment attributable to replacement of plant and equipment."

"Petition from the Manufacturers of
Candles, Wax-lights, Lamps, Chandeliers,
Reflectors, Snuffers, Extinguishers; and
from the Producers of Tallow, Oil,
Resin, Alcohol, and Generally of Every
Thing Used for Lights."

Do we need a tariff to shut out the
sunlight so as to create jobs for candle-
makers? In a classic satire, Frederic
Bastiat exposes the fallacies underlying the
argument that we need tariffs to protect
workers against "unfair" foreign
competition.

*Frederic Bastiat was a noted French
economist of the nineteenth century.*

76
Petition from the Manufacturers of Candles

FREDERIC BASTIAT

To the Honorable Members of the Chamber of Deputies:

"GENTLEMEN,—You are in the right way: you reject abstract theories;
abundance, cheapness, concerns you little. You are entirely occupied with
the interest of the producer, whom you are anxious to free from foreign
competition. In a word, you wish to secure the *national market* to *national
labor.*

"We come now to offer you an admirable opportunity for the application
of your —— what shall we say? your theory? no, nothing is more deceiving
than theory;—your doctrine? your system? your principle? But you do not
like doctrines; you hold systems in horror; and, as for principles, you declare that there are no such things in political economy. We will say then,
your practice; your practice without theory, and without principle.

"We are subjected to the intolerable competition of a foreign rival, who
enjoys, it would seem, such superior facilities for the production of light,
that he is enabled to *inundate* our *national market* at so exceedingly reduced a price, that, the moment he makes his appearance, he draws off
all custom from us; and thus an important branch of French industry,
with all its innumerable ramifications, is suddenly reduced to a state of
complete stagnation. This rival, who is no other than the sun, carries on
so bitter a war against us, that we have every reason to believe that he has
been excited to this course by our perfidious neighbor England. (Good
diplomacy this, for the present time!) In this belief we are confirmed by
the fact that in all his transactions with this proud island, he is much
more moderate and careful than with us.

From *Sophisms of Protection* (New York: G. P. Putnam's Sons, 1874), pp. 73–80.

"Our petition is, that it would please your honorable body to pass a law whereby shall be directed the shutting up of all windows, dormers, sky-lights, shutters, curtains, vasistas, œil-de-bœufs, in a word, all openings, holes, chinks, and fissures through which the light of the sun is used to penetrate into our dwellings, to the prejudice of the profitable manufactures which we flatter ourselves we have been enabled to bestow upon the country; which country cannot, therefore, without ingratitude, leave us now to struggle unprotected through so unequal a contest.

"We pray your honorable body not to mistake our petition for a satire, nor to repulse us without at least hearing the reasons which we have to advance in its favor.

"And first, if, by shutting out as much as possible all access to natural light, you thus create the necessity for artificial light, is there in France an industrial pursuit which will not, through some connection with this important object, be benefited by it?

"If more tallow be consumed, there will arise a necessity for an increase of cattle and sheep. Thus artificial meadows must be in greater demand; and meat, wool, leather, and above all, manure, this basis of agricultural riches, must become more abundant.

"If more oil be consumed, it will cause an increase in the cultivation of the olive-tree. This plant, luxuriant and exhausting to the soil, will come in good time to profit by the increased fertility which the raising of cattle will have communicated to our fields.

"Our heaths will become covered with resinous trees. Numerous swarms of bees will gather upon our mountains the perfumed treasures, which are now cast upon the winds, useless as the blossoms from which they emanate. There is, in short, no branch of agriculture which would not be greatly developed by the granting of our petition.

"Navigation would equally profit. Thousands of vessels would soon be employed in the whale fisheries, and thence would arise a navy capable of sustaining the honor of France, and of responding to the patriotic sentiments of the undersigned petitioners, candle merchants, etc.

"But what words can express the magnificence which *Paris* will then exhibit! Cast an eye upon the future and behold the gildings, the bronzes, the magnificent crystal chandeliers, lamps, reflectors, and candelabras, which will glitter in the spacious stores, compared with which the splendor of the present day will appear trifling and insignificant.

"There is none, not even the poor manufacturer of resin in the midst of his pine forests, nor the miserable miner in his dark dwelling, but who would enjoy an increase of salary and of comforts.

"Gentlemen, if you will be pleased to reflect, you cannot fail to be convinced that there is perhaps not one Frenchman, from the opulent stock holder of Anzin down to the poorest vender of matches, who is not interested in the success of our petition.

"We foresee your objections, gentlemen; but there is not one that you can oppose to us which you will not be obliged to gather from the works of the partisans of free trade. We dare challenge you to pronounce one word against our petition, which is not equally opposed to your own practice and the principle which guides your policy.

"Do you tell us, that if we gain by this protection, France will not gain, the consumer must pay the price of it?

"We answer you:

"You have no longer any right to cite the interest of the consumer. For whenever this has been found to compete with that of the producer, you have invariably sacrificed the first. You have done this to *encourage labor, to increase the demand for labor.* The same reason should now induce you to act in the same manner.

"You have yourselves already answered the objection. When you were told: The consumer is interested in the free introduction of iron, coal, corn, wheat, cloths, etc., your answer was: Yes, but the producer is interested in their exclusion. Thus, also, if the consumer is interested in the admission of light, we, the producers, pray for its interdiction.

"You have also said, the producer and the consumer are one. If the manufacturer gains by protection, he will cause the agriculturist to gain also; if agriculture prospers, it opens a market for manufactured goods. Thus we, if you confer upon us the monopoly of furnishing light during the day, will as a first consequence buy large quantities of tallow, coals, oil, resin, wax, alcohol, silver, iron, bronze, crystal, for the supply of our business; and then we and our numerous contractors having become rich, our consumption will be great, and will become a means of contributing to the comfort and competency of the workers in every branch of national labor.

"Will you say that the light of the sun is a gratuitous gift, and that to repulse gratuitous gifts, is to repulse riches under pretence of encouraging the means of obtaining them?

"Take care,—you carry the deathblow to your own policy. Remember that hitherto you have always repulsed foreign produce, *because* it was an approach to a gratuitous gift, and *the more in proportion* as this approach was more close. You have, in obeying the wishes of other monopolists, acted only from a *half-motive;* to grant our petition there is a much *fuller inducement.* To repulse us, precisely for the reason that our case is a more complete one than any which have preceded it, would be to lay down the following equation: $+ \times + = -$; in other words, it would be to accumulate absurdity upon absurdity.

"Labor and Nature concur in different proportions, according to country and climate, in every article of production. The portion of Nature is always gratuitous; that of labor alone regulates the price.

"If a Lisbon orange can be sold at half the price of a Parisian one, it is because a natural and gratuitous heat does for the one, what the other only obtains from an artificial and consequently expensive one.

"When, therefore, we purchase a Portuguese orange, we may say that we obtain it half gratuitously and half by the right of labor; in other words, at *half price* compared to those of Paris.

"Now it is precisely on account of this *demi-gratuity* (excuse the word) that you argue in favor of exclusion. How, you say, could national labor sustain the competition of foreign labor, when the first has every thing to do, and the last is rid of half the trouble, the sun taking the rest of the business upon himself? If then the *demi-gratuity* can determine you to check competition, on what principle can the *entire gratuity* be alleged as a reason for admitting it? You are no logicians if, refusing the demi-gratuity as hurtful to human labor, you do not *à fortiori,* and with double zeal, reject the full gratuity.

"Again, when any article, as coal, iron, cheese, or cloth, comes to us from foreign countries with less labor than if we produced it ourselves, the difference in price is a *gratuitous gift* conferred upon us; and the gift is more or less considerable, according as the difference is greater or less. It is the quarter, the half, or the three-quarters of the value of the produce, in proportion as the foreign merchant requires the three-quarters, the half, or the quarter of the price. It is as complete as possible when the producer offers, as the sun does with light, the whole in free gift. The question is, and we put it formally, whether you wish for France the benefit of gratuitous consumption, or the supposed advantages of laborious production. Choose, but be consistent. And does it not argue the greatest inconsistency to check as you do the importation of coal, iron, cheese, and goods of foreign manufacture, merely because and even in proportion as their price approaches *zero,* while at the same time you freely admit, and without limitation, the light of the sun, whose price is during the whole day at *zero?"*

Here the head of a trade association
presents in vivid form the traditional
arguments of domestic industries for
protection against foreign competition that
promises to win away American markets
—in a statement intended to win
Congressional votes for continuation of
the tariff.

77

A Plea for Protection

B. C. Deuschle is President of the
Shears, Scissors, and Manicure Implement
Manufacturers Association.

B. C. DEUSCHLE

The association respectfully wishes to record with this committee its strong opposition to H.R. 9900 in its present form. This bill could destroy industries such as ours and add to the unemployment problem.

During the past 15 years representatives of our association have appeared before this committee and other congressional committees, the Committee for Reciprocity Information and the Tariff Commission, to present our views on the impact of imported scissors and shears on our domestic industry.

We have never requested or suggested that a complete embargo be placed on the import of scissors and shears. All that we have asked for and desire is a fair competitive opportunity, not an advantage.

To date we have not obtained relief in any form.

We believe that H.R. 9900 would make matters worse. H.R. 9900 provides for new Presidential authority to reduce or eliminate duties. We realize that Title III of H.R. 9900 provides for adjustment assistance, but the criteria are general and too much is left to the discretion of the President in granting assistance.

Injury or threat of injury as it is written into our present escape clause cannot be properly defined. When 42 manufacturers out of 50 cease manufacturing and go out of business within 12 years as a direct or indirect result of excessive imports, and the Tariff Commission as well as the President decide that there is no injury or threat of injury, something should be done.

From *Hearings Before the Committee on Ways and Means,* House of Representatives, 87th Congress, 2nd Session, on H.R. 9900, 1962, pp. 1656–59.

487

Imports of shears and scissors valued over $1.75 per dozen import value have reached the proportion that they represent 95 per cent of domestic production of scissors and shears in this category.

We realize that the domestic scissor and shear industry with its 1,000-plus employees accounts for only a fraction of 1 per cent of the gross national product, but we see this as no justification for letting the industry be completely destroyed by imports produced with low-cost labor.

The workers in the domestic scissor and shear industry do not want to become wards of the State; they want to use their skills, which have taken years to develop. These workers are not interested in retraining; over many years they have developed a skill they are proud of and want to continue the work they are happy doing.

If the scissors and shears imported during 1961 had been manufactured in the United States, it would have provided over two million man-hours of factory work, or full-time employment for over 1,000 American employees.

Domestic manufacturers of scissors and shears have modernized and automated their operations in an effort to meet foreign competition. But foreign manufacturers also have modern equipment and with their lower wage rates are underselling domestic firms in the U.S. market at today's rate of duty.

H.R. 9900 would give the President unrestricted authority to reduce duties and thereby further reduce the cost of imported scissors and shears in our market. Under the provisions of this bill, scissors and shears would be buried in a category with many other items and the duty cut 50 per cent.

This would mean a reduction of at least 20 cents per pair at the retail level for scissors and shears now being retailed at $1 to $1.29 per pair.

If this is permitted, we do not need a crystal ball to see the results. There are only eight domestic firms now remaining of the 50 operating in the United States prior to the 50 per cent reduction in import duty during 1950–51.

These few remaining manufacturers would be forced to close their doors and discharge their employees. The United States would then become wholly dependent on imported scissors and shears.

We cannot understand how it could be in the national interest to permit such a loss. We would lose the skills of the employees and management of the industry as well as the capital investment in production equipment. In the event of a national emergency and imports cutoff, the United States would be without a source of scissors and shears, basic tools for many industries and trades essential to our defense.

The scissor and shear industry is one of the oldest in the world. The skill was brought to the United States from Germany at a time when the United States needed new industry and a scissor and shear industry in particular.

Scissors and shears of all sizes and types are used in every school, retail establishment, office, factory, hospital, and home in the United States. Scissors cannot be classified as a luxury, gimmick, or novelty.

Scissors are used to separate us from our mothers at birth; to cut our toenails; to trim the leather in our shoes; to cut and trim the materials used in every piece of clothing that we wear.

They are used to cut our fingernails, to trim our mustaches, the hair in our ears and nose, and to cut the hair on our heads—even down to the end of the road when our best suit or dress is cut down the back so that the undertaker can dress us for the last ride. Scissors are truly used from birth to death. They are essential to our health, education, and general welfare.

I ask you, gentlemen, is this an industry that should be permitted to become extinct in this country?

78

Common Market—Lesson in Trade Expansion

The European Common Market is the biggest international economic development of our generation. Professor Kravis analyzes its success to date, and contrasts and compares it with American experience and trade policy.

Irving B. Kravis is Professor of Economics at the University of Pennsylvania.

IRVING B. KRAVIS

On November 28, 1961, the front page of the *New York Times* carried a remarkable statement by a high French official. He said that France had learned that she could do away with tariffs without harm to her industries. His statement—so remarkable because France had not long ago been one of the most protectionist countries in the Western world—was no idle boast.

In the previous three years, France had reduced tariffs by 30 per cent in her trade with the five other members of the European Economic Community—or the Common Market as it is more commonly referred to. The result? No important segment of the French economy appears to have suffered. Nor does there seem to be any fear or objection from any part of French industry about the prospect of the complete elimination of intra-community trade barriers within the next decade or so. The same statements can be made about the rest of "the Six"—Italy, West Germany, and the Benelux countries, Belgium, the Netherlands, and Luxembourg—who as members of the Common Market are, of course, making tariff reductions at the same pace as France, and none of their domestic industries appears to be endangered.

Is there a moral for United States tariff and trade policy to be drawn from this experience? Is trade expansion possible without injury to domestic industries? Or are there special circumstances that have made it possible for European countries to move safely toward freer trade, circumstances which do not apply to the United States?

From *Harvard Business Review,* March–April, 1962, pp. 6 ff. Reprinted by permission.

THE CONTRAST BETWEEN EUROPEAN AND U.S. TRADE POLICY

Merely raising these questions calls attention to the great difference between tariff and trade policy in Western Europe and in the U.S. And this difference has to be made clear before any answers can be found.

European Innovation

The Common Market's program for the elimination of trade barriers may be viewed as part of a more general movement toward freer trade in postwar Europe. The 18 members of OEEC, the Organization for European Economic Cooperation, succeeded during the late 1940's and in the 1950's in dismantling the great bulk of the quantitative restrictions on trade that had sprung up in depression and wartime. However, the OEEC was never successful in coping with tariff obstacles to trade, and these became more important as quotas were first expanded and then removed.

It was partly for this reason that the Six formed their Common Market. Earlier the Six had established free trade in coal and steel through the creation of the European Coal and Steel Community (ECSC). The countermovement, led by England and Sweden, of seven other countries into the European Free Trade Association (EFTA), while a less happy outcome than a Europe-wide agreement to reduce trade barriers, represented a further attack on tariff and other obstacles to trade. The EFTA countries are reducing tariffs among themselves at about the same rate as the Common Market countries.

It would be wrong to think that these organizations favoring trade-barrier reduction were created in a blaze of idealism over European unity that blinded men to their short-run self-interests. While the ideal of European integration was a powerful motive force, there was hard bargaining. Terms were hammered out that would reconcile and protect the interests and aspirations of each country.

This reconciliation was no easy task, particularly in the close association that was involved in the establishment of the Common Market. For instance:

> France wanted to be sure that her more generous scale for overtime pay and her more rigid adherence to the principle of equal pay for men and women would not handicap her industries in the free trade of the Common Market.
>
> Italy wanted to be certain that her efforts to industrialize would not be swamped by the superior industrial machines of Germany and the other member countries.
>
> West Germany had to be assured that her high-cost agriculture would not be inundated under a flood of low-cost Dutch and French products.
>
> The Benelux countries wanted to maintain their ability to purchase raw materials and semifinished goods for their processing industries at low world market prices.

Furthermore, no country was willing to sacrifice any major domestic industry, or even any well-established minor industry, on the altar of the pan-European ideal. Indeed, it is hardly an exaggeration to say that there has been an almost unspoken "no injury" rule in the framing and application of the new European trade arrangements.

The significant point, however, is that the avoidance of injury was not allowed to interfere with the reduction of trade barriers and the expansion of trade. This required great ingenuity. Some day historians may compare the boldness and imagination with which the potential trade and other conflicts were resolved in forming the new European institutions with the similar qualities that contributed to the drafting of the United States Constitution.

Before examining the reasons for European success in expanding trade without injury, let us refresh our memories about American tariff and trade policy over the past dozen years. In the councils of nations, under both the Democratic and Republican administrations, we have been vigorous advocates of freer trade. Unfortunately, our own actions at home have fallen short of the principles we espouse to a sufficient extent to arouse cynicism abroad and to weaken our leadership.

Our policies with respect to imports are governed largely by the Reciprocal Trade Agreements Act of 1934 as amended. This law gave the President powers to reduce tariffs below the levels set in the Tariff Act of 1930, but renewals have been necessary since the powers were limited in time and extent. There have been seven extensions since 1948, the last of which is due to expire in June 1962. Each renewal has been the occasion for a political donnybrook between the supporters of freer trade and the advocates of protection.

*   *   *

HOW EUROPE WAS ABLE TO EXPAND HER TRADE WITHOUT INJURY

How can we explain our preoccupation in post-war years with staving off the effects of foreign competition at a time when Europeans were reaching out for closer ties? In part, of course, the answer lies in the difference between the two situations. At the end of the war, Europe's trade barriers were higher and Europe's need to find ways to break out of these restrictions was greater and more urgent; i.e., the subdivision of the continent into small national units made "foreign" trade more essential.

Thus the Europeans were perhaps less fearful of foreign competition, or, since the gains of trade were more obvious and important to them, more willing to take risks. But, if this line of reasoning explains why Europe was willing to venture more, it does not explain why she succeeded in reducing barriers and expanding trade without injury to domestic industries. For there is little evidence that a decade of the OEEC program of trade liberalization and eight years of a common market in coal and steel have had seriously detrimental effects on any important industry in any country participating in either of these ventures.

While it is true that Belgian coal has been in trouble since 1958, its difficulties can hardly be ascribed to the functioning of the Common Market. In any case, safeguards were invoked and the operation of the Common Market was not allowed to worsen the position of Belgian coal. It is, of course, premature to evaluate the European Economic Community, but the record to date hardly seems inconsistent with a no-serious-injury rule.

Industries in the underdeveloped regions of Italy, agricultural processing industries in West Germany, and Benelux processing industries relying on low-cost imports from third countries have all been given special treatment to avoid injury.

Furthermore, not one of these forms of more or less intimate European cooperation shows substantial evidence of bringing about any significant shifts in the localization of European industry. Trade among the partners increased more than with third countries, but not as a result of the expansion of some industrial branches and the contraction of others in each of the countries. Nor does there appear to be an expectation in any responsible quarter that such shifts will occur in the future operation even of the Common Market, the closest of the forms of cooperation in Europe.

Favoring Circumstances

How did Europe manage to avoid economic injury and yet get trade expansion? The European leaders and technicians who formulated the new institutions are human enough to say, "We planned it that way," and realistic enough to add, "We were also lucky." They are right on both counts. Let us take a closer look at the factors—both planned and fortuitous—which played important roles in Europe's success:

1. *Economic expansion* Perhaps the most important circumstantial factor has been the rapid rate of economic growth which characterized the Six both before and after the establishment of the Common Market. From 1953 to 1960 their total gross product increased by 45 per cent (in constant prices) as compared to only 26 per cent for the rest of Europe and 15 per cent for the U.S. It is easy to make room for increased imports when domestic demand is booming. And in those sectors in which imports prove too competitive, it is not so difficult for businesses to find other lines which they can pursue with greater profit. Firm reciprocal demands for exports also help.

2. *Specialization in the fine* Economic expansion appears to have facilitated a form of specialization which differs from the usual textbook model. Most economics texts would lead us to believe that the expansion of trade is likely to involve the disappearance of some branches of industry in one country and their expansion in another. Instead, specialization tended to develop in terms of particular designs, qualities, or types of product. This tendency, observed first in the operation of the Benelux customs union, has been widely commented on, but has not been satisfactorily explained. It may be related to the movement toward larger plant size that is produced when market horizons are extended by a customs union or common market. There has also tended to be a reduction in the number of varieties of a product turned out in a plant of a given size.

3. *Business agreements* The development of product specialization and the avoidance of injury may be due also, to some degree, to agreements or combinations between producers in different countries. The European outlook on these matters is different from that of the United States. There is a closer working relationship in Europe between business and government, and the governments are more willing to rely on perhaps somewhat more highly organized trade and industrial associations to achieve governmentally desired ends. At the same time, business groups are more assured of a sympathetic and cooperative attitude on the part of the government in case difficulties are encountered, particularly if they arise from foreign competition.

Thus it is not surprising to find that European governments have sometimes called on business groups in the importing and exporting countries to negotiate solutions in cases where injury was caused or threatened. Perhaps the most extensive reliance on private business arrangements to cope with problems of international competition occurred in the Benelux customs union.

*   *   *

There is no denying that part of the success obtained by the Six in expanding trade without injury was due to a well-conceived strategy which had four essential points:

1. *Gradualism* Industry was placed on notice that free trade would be established, but in gradual stages. Gradualism meant time for adaptation. Provision was made for relief to adversely affected industries; however, it was limited in duration and intended only to aid the industries to adapt themselves to the new situation.

2. *Certainty* Thus it was made clear that the establishment of free trade could be expected with a high degree of certainty. As a result, the business community reached to the expectation of broadened markets and heightened competition by accelerating investment. High investment, in turn, played a significant part in creating and maintaining the prosperous conditions that made the adjustment to the Common Market easier. With less certainty—as there might have been if the escape clauses of the Treaty of Rome had not been so clearly phrased in terms of purely temporary exceptions—the possibility that trade barriers would not really come tumbling down or that they might be re-established might have encouraged businessmen to continue in their old paths rather than to seek new ones in preparation for increased foreign competition and opportunities.

3. *Readaptation* Provisions for readaptation, or adjustment assistance to use the American term, helped to disarm the fears and suspicions of labor. The economic purposes of the readaptation clauses—that is, actually easing the adjustments to changes in the location of industries—were probably more in the minds of the framers of the treaty establishing the coal and steel community than in the minds of the drafters of the Common Market treaty. The passing of six prosperous years had made readaptation seem less urgent and also had made it clearer that the national governments intended to discharge this task themselves. Conceivably, the readaptation provisions may still be called on to play a larger economic role, but thus far there has been little occasion to invoke them and their importance has been largely psychological and political.

4. *Joint responsibility* Again and again the provisions of the treaties establishing the new European organizations make it clear that there is a common concern for the difficulties that any one member country encounters. Indeed, one can almost say that the idea that the surplus country as well as the deficit country has a responsibility for finding solutions to imbalance (a concept well accepted for some years now in the field of international finance) is being extended to the field of international trade. In the trade area, the exporting and importing countries are concerned with the disruption of particular markets in the importing country rather than with balance-of-payments problems. The cooperation between the Dutch and Belgian governments to curb Dutch exports to Belgium, described above, is an illustration of an application of the principle of joint responsibility.

*   *   *

Relevant Implications

Even after admitting that [some] points favoring European trade expansion do not apply to the U.S., the fact remains that the bulk of what happened in Europe has direct lessons for us, and therefore is relevant.

Certainty

Making it absolutely certain that trade barriers are going to come down is the keystone of the whole approach. It is the business of businessmen to make adjustment to changing conditions, and this is, indeed, a main reason for the high rewards paid for successful business leadership. Once it is clear that trade barriers are really going to be eliminated, businessmen may be expected to meet this change as they do others—by making investment decisions that will minimize injury.

It cannot be presumed that American businessmen are less eager or less adept at survival than their European counterparts. Given the same certainty and the same degree of notice, there is every reason to believe that they will be just as successful in maintaining profitability by cutting costs or by developing new lines. Our past methods of advancing a half step toward freer trade and then taking a half step backward have created inducements for the avoidance of adjustment rather than for spontaneous adjustment.

Security

Businessmen in vulnerable industries must be given confidence that the government will not allow catastrophic disaster to befall them. The sudden disruption of markets for individual commodities should be avoided, if necessary by controls over the rate of increase in imports. Businessmen should also understand that the government will not be indifferent to their long-run difficulties when the trouble arises from increased imports.

Gradualism

Ample time must be given for adaptation to the freer entry of foreign competitors to the American market, and adjustment assistance should be promised. Some industries and firms will need more time than others. Where necessary, additional safeguards providing longer or even increased protection should be established, but only if linked to measures that will assure adaptation to the new conditions.

Adjustment Assistance

Provision should also be made to afford assistance to industries that have difficulty in adjusting to an upward trend of imports. Public funds should be available for resettlement and retraining of workers, for readaptation loans for affected enterprises, and perhaps also for new employment-creating investments in areas hit by import competition.

The purpose of this assistance should be to remove, as far as possible, the element of injury from the changes imposed by increased foreign competition. Of course, displacement itself—the need to shift out of old lines of work and away from the production of familiar products—is sometimes considered injurious in itself. However, if the adaptation to new lines and products can be brought about quickly or without loss of income either to capital or labor, real injury will be minimized.

Joint Responsibility

The exporting as well as the importing country should assume responsibility for avoiding the disruption of markets for individual commodities. In the past, controls over sudden and large increases in imports have largely been exercised unilaterally by the importing country. Recently, a new element has begun to be introduced: quotas governing the size of shipments have been determined by agreements between the exporting and importing countries. The arrangements between the United States and Japan with respect to cotton textiles represent the first extensive use of this technique by the U.S. Last July, an international textile conference in Geneva agreed on the broader use of this method. The exercise of joint responsibility should minimize the possibility of a spiral of retaliatory restrictions on trade that might develop if import controls were unilaterally established. It should also make possible gradual adjustment to trade patterns that conform to market forces.

Economic Expansion

In establishing the timing of trade barrier reductions, finally, we should bear in mind that adjustments to freer trade take place more easily during a period of rapid expansion. It would be unwise, however, to try to link the freeing of trade too closely to future cyclical conditions. The Common Market solution seems a good one here. A schedule could be established for the reduction of trade barriers which would include some flexibility for acceleration or retardation. Good economic conditions would then permit faster progress. If conditions were unfavorable, delays might be necessary.

A REVITALIZED TARIFF AND TRADE POLICY

These are the keys to Europe's success in expanding trade without injury. And they are available to us. We can, if we are determined and courageous enough, have free trade with no widespread injury to domestic industries. . . .

*   *   *

Mr. Hayes explains how the U. S. dollar
has become an international "key
currency" and the implications this
development has for our domestic and
international monetary policies. We are
now "banker to the world," with new
responsibilities and new problems,
including proper management of our gold
reserves.

Alfred Hayes is President of the
Federal Reserve Bank of New York.

79

International Financial
Problems and Policies

ALFRED HAYES

The present international financial system is, of course, the result
of gradual evolution over many years. The cornerstone of the whole
structure is the link between gold and the United States dollar, with the
dollar firmly anchored by its interconvertibility with gold at a fixed price
of $35 per fine ounce. Most other governments in the Western World
have established with the International Monetary Fund par values for
their currencies in terms of either gold or the dollar, and monetary authorities generally are committed to maintaining these par values by buying
or selling dollars in their exchange markets to maintain the rates for their
currencies within a relatively narrow range. This network of fixed exchange rates has greatly facilitated the growth of international trade and
capital movements, and has thereby contributed to the increasingly close
integration of world trade and payments.

In this international system the United States plays the dual role of the
most powerful trading nation and the foremost banker for the rest of the
world.

The role of the United States as the world's leading trader is based
upon many factors—the massive raw material requirements of our factories,
the high consumption demands of our people, the competitive strength of
many export industries, an abundant flow of private savings into investment abroad, and sizable governmental programs of foreign economic aid.
The growth of our foreign trade has been further strongly stimulated by

Excerpted from a statement by Alfred Hayes in *Hearings Before the Subcommittee
on International Exchange and Payments of the Joint Economic Committee,* Congress of the United States, June 2, 1961, pp. 83–92.

United States Government policy which has consistently sought to minimize artificial barriers to trade and payments between our domestic market and the rest of the world. Last year our total payments and receipts came to some $57 billion, with receipts falling short of the payments by $3.8 billion or, roughly, 13 per cent.

I am sure that many competent witnesses have already provided you with an exhaustive analysis of our balance-of-payments experience during recent years, and I shall try to highlight only a few points which, to me, seem particularly important.

As you know, the deficit position of 1960 was not something new. Indeed, such deficits have been a characteristic feature, except in 1957, of our balance of payments for more than a decade. Prior to 1958, however, these deficits generally ran in the magnitude of $1.0 to $2.0 billion and served the highly useful purpose of reconstituting foreign dollar balances and securing a more appropriate distribution of gold stocks. Such deficits, in fact, were instrumental in helping to bring about the rapid expansion of international trade and investment, the dismantling of discriminatory controls abroad, and the restoration of currency convertibility by the leading Western European countries at the end of 1958. While some might be tempted to criticize what seemed a delayed awakening by the United States to its growing balance-of-payments problem, full recognition must be given to the changing nature of the problem during these transitional years.

By late 1959 it was reasonably clear that convertibility was a solid success and that most of the leading trading nations had so reconstituted their international reserves that they had little need to build them up further. Moreover, there had been a very sizable increase in the dollar working balances in the hands of private foreign interests, and, with the restoration of confidence in European currencies, there was an increasing tendency for funds to flow to foreign financial centers where interest rates were most attractive. In this new context, and particularly with declining interest rates in the United States in 1960, the continuing balance-of-payments deficits of the United States took on a more ominous aspect. The storm signals had been raised.

I do not believe it is necessary to review with this group in any detail the various measures that were undertaken to defend the dollar. While I would reject the tying of United States foreign aid to the American market as a basic long-run principle of our aid program, I believe that the moves which have been taken in that direction since late 1959 are entirely appropriate under the circumstances. Subsequent measures and proposals designed to secure a more equitable sharing with our allies of economic and defense aid outlays, to stimulate exports, to economize on military expenditures abroad, to prohibit private United States ownership of gold abroad, and to reduce the duty-free allowances for returning tourists were all highly desirable. In addition, various official statements, especially President Kennedy's Message on Balance of Payments and Gold to the Congress in February of this year, had a highly beneficial effect, providing impressive reassurance to the world of our determination to defend the dollar. I have been particularly gratified that recourse to restrictive trade and other controls has had no part to play in this program. Continued efforts are still necessary to eliminate restrictions against United States exports and to encourage a number of countries to make their capital markets more freely accessible to foreign borrowers. We would only hurt ourselves by turning our backs on the principles of liberal trade and unrestricted international payments for which we have stood.

Much still needs to be done to create a sufficient awareness of the need to expand our exports. It is encouraging, however, that there are indications of a more vigorous pursuit of foreign markets. I have full confidence in the ability of American labor and management to rise to the challenge, with benefits to all concerned.

I should now like to turn to the role of the United States as banker for the rest of the Free World. As a central banker, I am of course particularly concerned with this banking function of the United States and with the role of the dollar as an international reserve currency. The Federal Reserve Bank of New York now maintains accounts for 97 central banks and monetary authorities throughout the world, and this brings us into close day-by-day contact with the many complex problems facing the dollar as a reserve currency.

As of the end of 1948, foreign official holdings of gold and dollar reserves amounted to $8.8 billion and $2.8 billion, respectively. Since then, there has been an impressive rise in both types of reserve assets, with foreign official holdings of gold amounting as of the end of March 1961 to nearly $21 billion, while official dollar reserves had risen to somewhat more than $11 billion as of the same date. We hold earmarked in our vaults in New York $9.5 billion, or nearly one half, of total foreign official gold holdings, and also hold for foreign official account roughly $6.5 billion of dollar balances and other liquid dollar assets. In addition to these official dollar holdings, foreign private and international holdings now amount to about $12 billion.

It is important to note that the $11 billion in official short-term balances is convertible into gold on demand. Balances held by foreign private interests, as well as those of domestic holders, acquire the convertibility privilege if they are shifted into foreign official accounts. Since the United States stands ready to convert, at a fixed price, foreign official dollar balances into gold on demand, these dollar balances are regarded by foreign countries as equivalent to gold itself and hence have been included in their official reserves. By thus serving as the banker for such a "gold exchange" or "dollar exchange" system, as it is sometimes called, the United States has made possible a massive reinforcement of international liquidity upon which the free flow of world trade so heavily depends.

There are many reasons why the dollar has acquired this status as a reserve or "key" currency and, of these, I would mention particularly its stability, its interconvertibility with gold, its widespread use in financing world trade, and the availability in New York of financial markets of unparalleled size and efficiency which permit dollar holdings to be readily put to work. These factors were instrumental in establishing the dollar equally with gold as the reference point for setting par values for other currencies with the International Monetary Fund. The emergence of the dollar as a "key" currency has been mainly a postwar phenomenon, although it had its beginnings in the prewar period when there was a massive inflow of capital from abroad in search of a safe haven.

It may be noted that the conditions which have made the dollar a reserve currency were not fostered solely, or even largely, for that purpose. Rather they are an integral part of our market economy and the result of our efforts to achieve much broader goals. The reserve currency status of the dollar thus ultimately flows from and depends upon the pre-eminent role of the United States in international trade and finance, a role which can be fulfilled only by continuing adherence to sound economic and financial policy. Any undermining of confidence in our ability to keep our financial house in order—any slackening of resolve in the pursuit of monetary stability or any weakening of fiscal responsibility—could result in a severe blow to the dollar as a reserve currency and, in fact, to the entire international financial system. This would be a development that would prejudice our economic well-being in the broadest sense by undermining the base on which so large a share of world trade and payments now depends. We, therefore, have a responsibility—and one not without advantages—which we have met, and should continue to meet, with a resolution equally as firm as that required for leadership in the security and economic progress of the Free World.

*   *   *

In conclusion, I should like to venture some comments on the question of the longer term problem of insuring an adequate growth of international liquidity over the years. It is sometimes contended that, if we succeed, as we must, in restoring balance-of-payments equilibrium, our very success will operate to the disadvantage of the rest of the world by limiting the amount of liquidity that will be added to the international financial system. I question seriously any such conclusion. Certainly there is at present a fully ample stock of world liquidity in the form of gold and foreign exchange balances and other forms of credit. While the rate of new gold production over the years may slip somewhat behind the growth of world trade, there is no particular reason to assume that world liquidity needs will rise automatically and proportionately with trade and investment. Just as we have developed within our economy increasingly efficient uses of money and credit, so also similar possibilities are available internationally through cooperative arrangements which will not impair the individual responsibilities of each country. Moreover, while the United States must keep its balance of payments under firm control, this does not preclude moderate flows of dollars abroad when such movements would serve a constructive purpose. Furthermore, to the extent that the United States may find it desirable to accumulate foreign exchange balances, new sources of liquidity would be opened up. In this connection, it is important to recognize that liquidity should not be defined narrowly with reference solely to existing stocks of gold and foreign exchange but should also be taken to include private and governmental credits, the intercentral bank credit facilities I have discussed, and the resources of the Monetary Fund.

If, therefore, domestic policies are appropriate and fashioned with due regard to international realities, and if means to deal with short-term capital flows are available and adequate, there is no reason, in my judgment, why the international financial system cannot work satisfactorily for at least the foreseeable future. I would thus conclude that there is no present need for far-reaching reforms which would basically alter the present financial structure, practices, and institutions of the world.

80

International Transmission of Business Cycles: Comment

In this article Professor Despres argues that business cycles are no longer likely to be transmitted directly from one country to another through international monetary channels. But widely varying rates of technological advance may nevertheless create difficult balance of payments problems, which may require new adjustment processes and new international monetary arrangements.

Emile Despres is Professor of Economics at Stanford University.

EMILE DESPRES

The papers of Mr. Gilbert and of Messrs. Polak and Rhomberg have provided further confirmation that short-term cyclical fluctuations—and their international propagation through the automatic operation of the foreign trade multiplier—are no longer problems of major importance for the industrially advanced countries. It is important to recognize, however, that we are by no means free of critical problems in this field.

The nature of the problem has changed. The chief present problem arises neither from short-term cyclical fluctuations nor from severe inflationary or deflationary developments in particular countries. It arises, rather, from rapid structural changes in the world economy within an international monetary and financial framework which is inadequate to accommodate the balance-of-payments consequences of these changes. This creates a serious danger of secular retardation of growth in countries suffering external deficits and its gradual propagation to other countries as well. Indeed, this process of secular retardation seems to have already begun.

The largest source of structural disturbance is the inevitable unevenness of improvements in productivity—unevenness from period to period, from industry to industry, and from country to country. Major structural changes are taking place today within a framework characterized by currency convertibility, relatively liberal commercial policies, and greatly constrained cyclical fluctuations. Within this framework, uneven rates of improvement in productivity tend to produce large shifts in trading patterns and large,

From a symposium in *The American Economic Review*, pp. 93–126, in which Professor Despres comments on various papers. Reprinted by permission.

prolonged swings in net current account balances which it would be undesirable to suppress. These swings are not short-term oscillations which cancel out in a few years; large imbalances in one direction or another should be expected to persist for a number of years. Although liberalized trading conditions widen the scope for eventual adaptation and adjustment of imbalances, this should not obscure the fact that, in the first instance, they allow such imbalances to become large and to persist for prolonged periods. Under the earlier regime of direct controls and inconvertibility, these imbalances could be quickly suppressed. Moreover, under our present system of quasi-fixed gold parities capital movements among the industrially advanced countries are more likely to reinforce than to neutralize the imbalances in current accounts.

Under today's conditions it is fatuous to expect balance-of-payments equilibrium, as conventionally defined, to be closely approximated from year to year or even over a period of several years. But the existing international monetary framework does not provide adequate facilities for financing the large and prolonged imbalances which, under liberalized trading conditions, are the reflection of a dynamic international economy.

Our international monetary institutions simply do not fit our newly liberalized trading and payments arrangements. This creates a striking lack of symmetry between the reaction of deficit countries and that of surplus countries. As their reserves become deficient, deficit countries find themselves under increasingly urgent pressure to correct their deficits; the pressure on surplus countries to halt the accumulation of redundant reserves, either by increasing their domestic effective demand or by providing the external finance which would permit continued surpluses in their international accounts, is not so urgently felt. This asymmetry introduces a pervasive deflationary bias into the world economy, which first impinges on the deficit countries and then is transmitted by them to the surplus countries both directly and through underdeveloped countries as intermediaries.

The most likely consequence, unless adequate financial mechanisms are created, is international propagation of secular retardation; i.e., sluggish growth. There is no likelihood today that any country would accept sharp, cumulative deflation, deep depression, and massive unemployment as a means of eliminating a deficit in its international accounts. On the other hand, monetary and fiscal policies in the United States, in Britain, and perhaps also in Japan are being based today on a delicate and uneasy compromise between domestic growth objectives and balance-of-payments considerations. The difference over five or ten years between a close approach to full employment and an average level of unemployment of 5 to 7 per cent is much greater than the simpler calculations on this subject reveal. The difference between full employment and moderate unemployment is not chiefly that output is raised by increasing labor input, nor is it primarily that aggregate investment is higher when employment is full. The chief difference is that the climate of buoyant demand and active use of productive resources which full employment entails is one in which innovations and improvements come forward rapidly and resources gain mobility, moving readily from obsolete fields into newer fields of growing competitive strength. This is the main difference between full employment and "high-level stagnation"—5 to 7 per cent unemployment. Fundamental correction of underlying deficits in external payments of structural origin requires an acceleration of innovations, more rapid improvements in technology, and the transfer of resources to new industrial fields. But as Britain's experience since World War I has demonstrated, these conditions could not be realized when aggregate demand was constrained by policies which almost continually reflected a preoccupation with the balance of payments. The uneasy compromise between domestic economic objectives and the so-called "discipline" of the balance of payments serves to hamper economic growth and needed structural change, and thus to perpetuate the imbalance in external payments. When the source of payments imbalances is structural, a substantial increase in deficits in the short and intermediate run is likely to be indispensable for constructive long-run adjustment. The Marshall Plan, even after allowance for the special circumstances, was a vividly dramatic illustration of this principle. Until conditions are gradually created under which international captial movements on private account can perform an equalizing role, payments imbalances among advanced countries will require official compensatory financing on a much larger scale and for longer periods than has hitherto been customary.

It is wrong to think that such financing merely postpones necessary adjustments. On the contrary, it makes possible the structural changes and adaptations in both deficit and surplus countries necessary for removing the causes of unbalanced international payments, without handicapping growth. It would be ironical indeed if the advanced industrial countries, having proclaimed through OECD ambitious growth targets for the sixties, did not adopt the basically simple international financial measures without which these growth targets will have little chance of being realized.

In this and the following selection, two
Yale professors differ sharply over the
risks for the United States in the present
international gold-and-dollar standard
system, under which foreign short-term
claims on U.S. gold have reached high
levels. Professor Triffin argues that the
parallel with the British situation in
1929–31 is a close one, and that the
danger of a major international financial
crisis is substantial.

Robert Triffin is Professor of Economics
at Yale University.

81
Will 1965
Repeat 1931?

ROBERT TRIFFIN

President Johnson, in his February 10 message to Congress on the
balance of payments and our gold position, agreed in effect with President
de Gaulle that the international monetary system of the 1920's "brought
us all to disaster in the early 1930's." The area of agreement unfortunately
stops there.

President de Gaulle is convinced that the system that failed us then
was a so-called "gold-exchange" or "key-currencies" standard, very similar
to the present one, except that the dollar has now replaced sterling in the
driver's seat of the old key-currency tandem. He fears that the new
system will lead us to a similar collapse, and wants it to undergo drastic
surgery before it is too late.

Mr. Johnson and the U.S. Treasury have no such fears. To them, what
failed in 1931 was not the gold-exchange standard but the gold standard,
which they think is precisely what de Gaulle wishes to restore. We should,
instead, said the President, "build on the system we now have, a system
which has served the world well during the past twenty years."

YES?

Much as I dislike to question the wisdom of our own Treasury, the facts
hardly bear out its interpretation of the 1931 monetary collapse. What collapsed then was not the pure *gold* standard of the pre-1914 era but the
gold exchange standard which de Gaulle feels is doomed to a similar fate
tomorrow. In the late 1920's, dollar and primarily sterling holdings made

From *The Reporter*, April 8, 1965, p. 27 ff. Reprinted by permission.

up more than a third of the total monetary reserves of countries other than Great Britain and the United States. It was the inability of Britain to convert into gold —or dollars—the large sterling balances accumulated by foreign central banks, particularly the Bank of France, that triggered the 1931 collapse of the world monetary system. Today, sterling and primarily dollar holdings account for more than two-fifths of other countries' monetary reserves, and for more than three-fourths of their increases over the last seven years. There can be no doubt that any massive demands for repayment of the huge dollar and sterling balances held today by central banks (about $23 billion) would put a dangerous strain on U.S. and British gold reserves (now about $17 billion). The British *net* reserves have long been in the red, while the U.S. *net* reserves have dropped precipitately from $16 billion at the end of 1957 to less than $300 million at the end of last year. If we also deducted—as the Department of Commerce does—our short-term liabilities to private dollar holders abroad, our liquid liabilities would exceed our liquid assets by more than $12 billion.

The parallelism between monetary and economic developments in Britain in the aftermath of the First World War and in the United States in the aftermath of the Second does not end there. It extends to the impact of capital flights from the Continent upon the pattern of exchange rates, and to the impact of the consequent underevaluation of European currencies upon economic activity. Booming conditions on the Continent in the late 1930's contrasted with unemployment and stagnation in Britain. When Continental currencies were finally stabilized, refugee capital moved back from London to the Continent, causing a heavy and persistent drain on Britain's slender monetary reserves.

The attempt to slow down the exodus of capital through high interest rates conflicted with the desire to revive economic activity through low interest rates. The Bank of England had to plead with the Continental central banks to refrain from converting into gold their increasing amounts of sterling reserves. The gold delegation of the League of Nations was still deadlocked in its marathon debate about the "gold shortage" when French demands for sterling repayment—inspired by political motives as well as by long-entrenched monetary traditions and conservation—finally unleashed a run on the Bank of England, the devaluation of sterling, and a world-wide collapse of the gold-exchange standard.

Substitute the United States for Britain, the "liquidity shortage" for the "gold shortage," and the "Group of Ten" for the "gold delegation" in the above account, and draw your own conclusions about what may happen tomorrow if the present deadlock between the French—and other Continentals—and the Anglo-Saxons continues much longer to frustrate agreement on international monetary reform.

NO?

There are, however, some major differences between the present situation and that of 1931. First of all, the world economy is in far better shape today than it was then, and the overall economic and financial position of the United States far stronger than that of Britain in 1931. Our current account surpluses, i.e., the excess of our exports over our imports of merchandise and services, reached a record high last year of $7 billion, and even more if we take into account the more than $1.5 billion of unrepatriated earnings on our foreign investments. Our losses of monetary reserves are entirely due to capital exports and are far more than balanced by growing and highly profitable long-term investments. Our net "foreign worth" even increased by more than $10 billion—from $42.2 billion to $52.3 billion—during the four years 1960–1963. We may become illiquid, but we are more and more solvent.

Second, and very important, world political and financial leaders are now keenly aware of the disaster that any repetition of 1931 could entail for the international monetary and economic order of the West. Since the Second World War they have developed deeply ingrained habits of co-operation and laid the foundations, at least, of the monetary institutions and policies that should enable them to organize a durable international monetary system adapted to the realities of the financial, economic, and political interdependence of their theoretically sovereign countries.

The negotiations of the Group of Ten have, moreover, already developed a large degree of consensus on the defects of the present system and on the alternative solutions available for its consolidation. The reports of both the Group of Ten (France, West Germany, Italy, Belgium, the Netherlands, Sweden, United Kingdom, Canada, Japan, and the U.S.) and the International Monetary Fund are unanimous in their rejection of flexible rates and of any change in the price of gold. They also recognize that neither gold production, future U.S. deficits, the multiplication of reserve currencies, the present IMF credit facilities, nor bilateral swap-standby agreements such as those negotiated by former Under Secretary of the Treasury Robert V. Roosa can be depended upon to meet all liquidity needs in the future. Steps are required, and have been taken already, to "provide a basis for multilateral surveillance of the various elements of liquidity creation"; and Pierre-Paul Schweitzer, managing director of IMF, affirmed in a recent speech the "emerging consensus among the international community that the creation of international liquidity, like the creation of domestic liquidity, should become a matter of deliberate decision."

Finally, a Study Group on the Creation of Reserve Assets has been established "to investigate the problems raised by the creation and use of . . . some additional kind of reserve asset, . . . the possible forms it might take, and the institutional aspects associated with it."

MAYBE

Nine-tenths of the road toward agreed international monetary reform has thus been covered already, but the Group of Ten has nevertheless been bogged down now for months in a deep conflict between the two key-currency countries, on the one hand—the United States and Britain—and the major reserve holders of the Continent—particularly the French—on the other.

The Anglo-Saxons see a potential shortage of liquidity as the main or only defect of the present system and argue for the creation of new reserve assets supplementary to rather than substituting for gold, dollars, and sterling.

The Continentals deny the existence of any proximate liquidity shortage and stress instead the haphazardness, inequity, and vulnerability of a system in which the bulk of world reserve increases—three-fourths or more in recent years—depends on the unpredictable size of U.S. payments deficits and on the precarious willingness of foreign central banks to finance them through the accumulation and retention of short-term dollar holdings as part and parcel of their international monetary reserves.

*   *   *

WHY GAMBLE?

If the present debate could be rescued from the political and emotional morass into which it is now sinking, the broad outline of a sensible solution would at once become apparent. Mr. Schweitzer has urged that "The creation of international liquidity should become a matter of deliberate decision," rather than be left to the hazards of gold production, Soviet gold sales, U.S. balance-of-payments deficits, and speculation about future changes in the gold price and dollar and sterling exchange rates. Thus, the French and other European dollar holders should agree to protect the present level of world liquidity against wanton and unfeasible conversions into gold metal of the huge *outstanding* dollar and sterling balances inherited from long years of past functioning of the gold-exchange standard. These balances should be transformed into IMF deposits or reserve certificates, carrying appropriate exchange-rate guarantees and remaining fully usable for the settlement of all international imbalances.

The Americans and the British, on the other hand, should recognize that they are facing the end of an era in which they alone could finance their deficits through the willing or reluctant accumulation of dollar and sterling holdings by foreign central banks. Their future deficits, like those of all other countries, should be paid in cash, i.e., through transfers of gold or IMF deposits to their creditors. Such deficits could also be paid in the new type of reserve assets proposed by the Group of Ten, which would be deliberately created for the specific purpose of adjusting the growth of world reserves to the legitimate, noninflationary requirements of an expanding world economy. Unlike the functioning of the two key currencies—the dollar and sterling—which rather haphazardly served this purpose in the past, both the creation of such reserve assets and the uses to which they are put should be the result of concerted decisions by the world community —through the IMF—or the major reserve holders.

Differences of views still exist concerning the appropriate forum for such decisions. Should the management of these funds be concentrated in the IMF, for instance, as generally favored by the Anglo-Saxons, or in the Group of Ten itself, as favored by the French and most Continental countries? I would favor a more decentralized approach as the most appropriate solution of what is essentially a conflict over relative voting rights and influence in these two organizations. Such conflicts could in large part be eliminated if due account were taken of the emergence of new regional economic and monetary unions—such as the European Economic Community—and if the creation and the management of the new reserve assets were divided between them and the IMF.

This problem, however, could be left to leisurely negotiations if the present level of world liquidity could be protected against sudden and massive contraction by an early agreement on the proposals outlined above with regard to outstanding dollar and sterling balances. The Ten have, indeed, unanimously agreed that the rapid increase of such balances over the last seven years has created ample levels of liquidity and made further increases unnecessary for some time.

ANSWERING THE TREASURY

The Treasury's main objection to this viewpoint is that it would deprive us of the facility with which we have financed our deficits through dollar accumulation by foreign central banks. We too might now have to pay gold for our future deficits. Morality and equity aside, there are three answers to this objection.

The first is that, in the absence of agreement, the United States is far more likely to be faced with further demands for gold conversion of dollar holdings accumulated abroad in the past than to benefit from continuing accumulation of dollar balances by foreign central banks.

The second is that our gold reserves—if protected against further conversion of outstanding dollar balances—are more than adequate to meet reasonable deficits, and could be supplemented, in case of need, by our drawing rights on the IMF, now amounting to nearly $5 billion and to be further increased by the forthcoming rise of IMF quotas, and by our probable participation in the use of the new reserve assets to be created in the future.

The third answer—and, I think, the most important—is that the agreement suggested above to provide protection against further raids on gold would eliminate the major cause of our deficits of recent years, i.e., the totally abnormal swing of short-term capital movements from net *inflows*—characteristic of a major world money center—of $50 million a year in the early 1950's and $1 billion a year in the late 1950's—to net *outflows* of $1.7 billion to more than $2 billion a year in 1960, 1961, 1962, and 1964. This swing began in 1960 with the sharp increase in gold prices in London and is undoubtedly due largely to rumors about the weakness of the dollar that have been engendered by our growing short-term indebtedness abroad.

Funds have been moved out of the dollar into foreign currencies, notably Deutschmarks, and also into gold and real assets abroad. Speculative positions in gold, however, would be highly vulnerable to any agreement which clearly removed any prospect of an official change in gold prices and which enabled central banks to regain full control of the market by using the proposed new type of reserve asset as a supplement- or even an alternative—to future gold accumulation.

We might then see a massive unloading of gold by speculators who have accumulated enormous hoards of the metal over many years past. The size of such gold sales might be expected to run into several billions of dollars, if we reflect that private gold purchases have risen since 1960 by $500 to $600 million each year over previous levels that already embodied large and sustained speculative purchases.

Substantial dollar inflows would then replace, once again, the abnormal outflows that are at the origin of most of our deficits and reserve losses of the last five years. Together with the other measures already taken to improve our balance of payments, this should suffice to bring us into equilibrium and possibly even into substantial surpluses in our international accounts. While removing the remaining tax provisions that discourage the repatriation of foreign earnings, we should then also be able to dispense with the recent capital controls proposed in the President's February 10 message, which if maintained for long would effectively kill the dollar as a key currency in world trade and finance.

Contrary to the judgment of many New York bankers, the survival of the dollar in this vital and fruitful role depends today on its elimination, rather than on its retention, as a reserve currency. In the latter role, the dollar will always be cashable into gold metal, either by cautious central bankers afraid of a gold revaluation or embargo, or by their political masters, eager to brandish the real or imaginary bargaining strength derived from their monetary *force de frappe*. Both may be wrong in their calculations, but the main threat to our international monetary order lies precisely in such miscalculations.

Professor Tobin argues that America
should put domestic prosperity and high
employment ahead of protection of the
U.S. gold stock as a goal of national
economic policy, and that excessive weight
is being given to the alleged current
threat to the soundness of the dollar and
to the stability of the U.S. economy.

*James Tobin is Sterling Professor
of Economics at Yale University.*

82

Europe and the Dollar

JAMES TOBIN

The dollar crisis will no doubt be surmounted. "The dollar" will be
saved. Its parity will be successfully maintained, and the world will be
spared that ultimate and unmentionable calamity whose consequences are
the more dreaded for never being described. The world monetary system
will stay afloat, and its captains on both sides of the Atlantic will congratu-
late themselves on their seamanship in weathering the storm.

But the storm is in good part their own making. And if the financial
ship has weathered it, it has done so only by jettisoning much of the
valuable cargo it was supposed to deliver. Currency parities have been
maintained, but full employment has not been. The economic growth
of half the advanced noncommunist world has been hobbled, to the detri-
ment of world trade in general and the exports of the developing countries
in particular. Currencies have become technically more convertible but
important and probably irreversible restrictions and discriminations on
trade and capital movements have been introduced. Some government
transactions of the highest priority for the foreign policy of the United
States and the West have been curtailed. Others have been "tied" to a
degree that impairs their efficiency and gives aid and comfort to the bizarre
principle that practices which are disreputably illiberal when applied to
private international transactions are acceptable when government money
is involved.

These are the costs. Were, and are, all these hardships necessary? To
what end have they been incurred?

Reprinted by permission of the publishers from *The Review of Economics and
Statistics*, May, 1964, pp. 123–126, Cambridge, Mass.; Harvard University Press,
Copyright 1964, by the President and Fellows of Harvard College.

They have been incurred in order to slow down and end the accumulations of dollar obligations in the hands of European central banks. It is fair to ask, therefore, whether these accumulations necessarily involved risks and costs serious enough for the countries concerned and for the world at large to justify the heavy costs of stopping them.

Which is easier? Which is less disruptive and less costly, now and in the long run? To stop the private or public transactions that lead one central bank to acquire another's currency? Or to compensate these transactions by official lending in the opposite direction? I do not suggest that the answer is always in favor of compensatory finance. But the issue always needs to be faced, and especially in the present case.

Several courses were open to European countries whose central banks had to purchase dollars in their exchange markets in recent years. (a) They could have built up their dollar holdings quietly and gladly, as they did before 1959. (b) By exercising their right to buy gold at the United States Treasury, they could have forced devaluation of the dollar or suspension of gold payments. (c) They could have taken various measures to correct and reverse chronic European payments surpluses. (d) By occasional withdrawals of gold and by constant complaints they could have brought tremendous pressure for "discipline" upon the United States without forcing a change in the dollar parity.

European central banks and governments chose the fourth course, with token admixtures of the third. They have made world opinion, and American opinion, believe there is no other choice. Almost everyone agrees that the pressure of the balance of payments deficit upon the United States is inescapable arithmetic rather than the deliberate policy of foreign governments. Yet for almost ten years previously, United States deficits were no problem. Clearly it is a change in human attitude and public policy, not inexorable circumstance, which has compelled us to take "corrective" actions.

It is true that the concern of financial officials about "the dollar" was only an echo—and a subdued echo at that—of the fears, hopes, anxieties, and speculations that arose in private financial circles in the late 1950's. But financial officials do not have to follow the private exchange markets; they can lead instead. By an equivocal attitude toward private suspicions of the dollar, European officials kept pressure on the United States. Never did they firmly say that they would not force devaluation or suspension of gold payments. Instead, they succeeded in making the maintenance of gold-dollar convertibility at $35 per ounce a unilateral commitment of the United States, under three successive Administrations. Once a banker has solemnly assured the world and his depositors that he will never fail, he is at the mercy of those depositors capable of making him fail.

Memories are short, and gratitude is not a consideration respected in international relations, especially when money is involved. But the United States had and has considerable moral claim on European governments and central banks.

The present excess supply of dollars is in many respects an unwinding of the dollar shortage of the immediate postwar period. Capital left Europe because the continent was vulnerable to military attack, its governments were unstable, its industries were prostrate and uncompetitive, and its currencies were inconvertible. Capital has returned to Europe when events have overcome the special advantages which North America seemed to have in these respects. It is therefore relevant to recall the behavior of the United States when the shoe was on the other foot.

During the dollar shortage the United States: gave Western European countries (other than Greece, Turkey, and Spain) $32 billions of military and economic aid; lent them $11 billions additional (in spite of the default of European governments of debts connected with World War I); acquiesced in substantial devaluations of European currencies, without which European exports would still not be competitive; and acquiesced in exchange controls, capital controls, quantitative restrictions on imports, and discriminations against the United States and other non-European countries—by no means all of which are liquidated even now. After enabling Europe to overcome the dollar shortage, the United States has been expected to adjust to its reversal *without* the tools that Europe used in its turn. Rightly so, because many of these tools were illiberal expedients—the more reason for replacing them now with compensatory intergovernmental finance.

The United States has undertaken, at considerable cost in real resources and foreign exchange, to defend Western Europe against the Soviet Union. This is in theory a joint effort, but European governments do not even yet fulfill their modest commitments to NATO. While European political leaders solicit constant reassurance that United States military power will remain visibly in Europe, their finance ministers and central bankers complain about the inflow of dollars.

The United States has not only tolerated but encouraged the development of a European customs union which attracts American capital and discriminates against American exports (especially the products of industries, notably agriculture, where North America has a clear comparative advantage).

The United States has borne a disproportionate share of the burden of assistance to uncommitted and underdeveloped nations, in which European countries have a common political and, one might hope, humanitarian interest.

The United States has provided a reserve currency. In the late forties no other international and intergovernmental money was available except gold; and the supply of gold was not keeping up with the demand. United States deficits filled the gap with dollars. It is true that this gave the United States a favored position among countries. Anyone who can print money can choose how new money will be first spent. The United States did not seek this privileged role; it arose by accidental evolution rather than conscious design. As it happens, the United States did not exploit it to live beyond our means, to make the American people more affluent. We used it rather for broad international purposes. No doubt in the long run the creation of new international money should be a privilege and responsibility more widely and symmetrically shared. But once the United States and the world are adjusted to the creation of international money via United States deficits, it is scarcely reasonable suddenly to ring a bell anouncing that the world's financial experts have now decided that these deficits—past, present, and future—are pernicious.

The United States has not pushed its moral case before world public opinion. This is because many Americans believe, or prefer to believe, that balance of payments deficits, like venereal diseases, betray and punish the sins of those whom they afflict. Others regard them as simply matters of arithmetic and circumstance. Still others are afraid that making a moral argument will indicate to our all-powerful European creditors insufficient resolution to overcome the difficulties. On their side, the Europeans have neatly segregated the contexts. Their financial officials wash their hands of tariff and trade policies, agricultural protection, defense and aid appropriations, and their governments' budgets. Any European failings on these counts are facts of life to which the United States must adjust, rather than reasons for more patience or more credit.

By the narrowest of bankers' criteria—all moral claims aside—the United States is a good credit risk. Its balance sheet vis-à-vis the rest of the world, not to mention its internal productive strength, indicates the capacity to service a considerably increased external public debt. The United States has been confined to the types of credit that can be given on the books of central banks. European Parliaments cannot be asked to vote long-term loans to Uncle Sam, although the American people voted through the Congress to tax themselves to finance the Marshall Plan when Europe's credit rating was nil.

Meanwhile, European central banks are uneasy holding short-term dollar assets. They prefer gold. Why? Because they might some day force us to give them a capital gain on gold holdings. We compensate them with interest on their dollar holdings when they forego this speculative possibility. But bygones are bygones; and past interest earnings are irrelevant when future capital gains beckon. On its side, the United States has had nothing to lose and much to gain in guaranteeing to maintain the value of official dollar holdings. After stubbornly resisting this suggestion on obscure grounds of principle, the United States Treasury now belatedly and selectively guarantees value in foreign currency.

The only remaining reason to refuse the United States credit is that the United States, like any other deficit country, must be "disciplined." Disciplined to do what?

To stop an orgy of inflation? The United States has the best price record of any country, except Canada, since 1958—before there was a Balance of Payments Problem. The rates of unemployment and excess capacity during the period scarcely suggest that the government has been recklessly overheating the economy with fiscal and monetary fuel.

Nevertheless, many Europeans say that when they buy dollars they are importing inflation. It is hard to take this claim seriously. First of all, if acquisitions of dollars are inflationary so are acquisitions of gold, and Europe shows no signs of saturation with gold. Second, the classic mechanism of international transmission of inflation is certainly not operating. We have not inflated ourselves into an import surplus adding to aggregate demand in Europe. To the contrary, we have maintained a large and secularly growing export surplus. Third, although central bank purchases of foreign exchange have the same expansionary monetary effects at home as other open market purchases, it is not beyond the wit or experience of man to neutralize these effects by open market sales or other monetary actions. Fourth, United States farmers and coal producers, and Japanese light manufacturers, among others, stand ready to help European governments reduce their living costs and their payment surpluses at the same time. The truth is that Europe does not really want a solution at the expense of its balance of trade.

Perhaps we are to be disciplined to cut foreign aid. European governments do not attach the same importance as we do to aid programs, especially in the Western Hemisphere. Clearly we need a better understanding on development assistance and "burden sharing" among the advanced countries.

Should the United States be disciplined in order to cut off private exports of capital, by controls or by tight monetary policy or both? This has been a major and successful focus of European pressure. The United States authorities have responded by pushing up United States interest rates, more than a full point at the short end, and by proposing the Interest Equalization Tax. European pressure is motivated in part by nationalistic and protectionist aims—keep the rich Americans from buying up or competing with local industry. This may or may not be a worthy objective, but its worth is the same whether international payments are in balance or not.

Two other issues are involved. The first concerns capital markets and controls. Should the United States move toward poorer and more autarkic capital markets, or should the Europeans move toward more efficient and freer capital markets? Much of United States long-term capital movement to Europe does not represent a transfer of real saving. Instead it is a link in a double trans-Atlantic chain connecting the European saver and the European investor. The saver wants a liquid, safe, short-term asset. The investor needs long-term finance or equity capital and seeks it in the United States. Unfortunately, another link in the same chain is official European holding of short-term dollar obligations. But the Europeans themselves could, through institutional reforms, do a great deal to connect their savers and investors more directly and to reduce the spread between their long and short interest rates.

The second issue is the appropriate international level of interest rates. Evidently national rates must be more closely aligned to each other as international money and capital markets improve. But surely the low-rate country should not always do the aligning. This would impart a deflationary bias to the system. In principle, easy fiscal policy could overcome this bias, but only at the expense of investment and growth. In the present situation European countries are fighting inflation by tightening their money markets rather than their budgets. They are forcing the United States to fight unemployment with a tight money-easy budget mixture. If interest rates are raised whenever a country faces either inflation or balance of payments difficulties, while expansionary fiscal policy is the only measure ever used to combat deflation, a number of swings in business activity and in payments will move the world to a mixture of policies quite unfavorable to long-run growth.

In summary, the adjustments forced on the United States to correct its payments deficit have not served the world economy well. Neither were they essential. European countries have had at their disposal several measures which are desirable in their own right, not just as correctives to the present temporary imbalance in payments. To the extent that they are unprepared to take these measures, they should willingly extend compensatory finance. International financial policy is too important to leave to financiers. There are more important accounts to balance than the records of international transactions, and more important markets to equilibrate than those in foreign exchange.

PART SEVEN

Perspectives on Economic Change

83

Some Myths
About Automation

This short statement illustrates the
extreme concern of those who fear that
our present institutions may not be able to
cope with the dramatic changes that
"automation" is expected to create.

JOHN I. SNYDER, JR.

*The late John I. Snyder, Jr. was chairman
and president of U.S. Industries, Inc.*

*   *   *

. . . My company designs and produces automation machinery; therefore, those of us in the management of the company feel a deep sense
of responsibility toward those people whom such machines are adversely
affecting. It is in the area of automation's effects on human beings that our
foundation is focusing its primary attention in the form of research and
study programs.

Our efforts are dramatically limited, however, when we view with care
the growing dimensions of our national manpower problem. Neither our
company nor the other automation machinery manufacturers possess the
kind of resources that enable us to bear the full burden, to assume the full
responsibility for all those people affected in one way or another by our
machines. This simply is not the kind of responsibility that can be delegated
to any one company or even group of companies. It is too large, too all-
encompassing, too serious a responsibility not to be everyone's.

Apart from the research and study efforts which I have mentioned,
our major task at the foundation is to tell the truth about automation—and
this is not an easy task. Too many people are willing to accept too many
myths about what is going on around us in our factories and offices. Too
few people accept the very few truthful facts which are being turned up
by real experience and intelligent study. Because I wholeheartedly believe
this to be the case, I have taken on the assignment of telling the truth—or

Statement of John I. Snyder, Jr. *Hearings before the Senate Subcommittee on
Employment and Manpower,* Eighty-Eighth Congress, First Session, October 3,
1963, Part 5, pp. 1649–1651.

at least what I consider the truth—about both the short- and long-range effects of automation and technological change.

Specifically, in regard to my own area of specialization, the manufacture and utilization of automated equipment, I can assure you that the problems are vast and complex in the area of conflict between the efficiencies of the machines and the nature of human needs. From a technological point of view automation is working; but the same thing cannot be said so confidently from the human point of view. The technologists have done and are doing their job. They have developed and are developing equipment that works miracles. But, as is too often the case in this age of the widening gap between scientific progress and man's ability to cope with it, we have failed to keep pace.

Much of this failure is due, I think, to the existence of a number of myths about automation, which, because they are so widely accepted, have had a deep tranquilizing effect on many of those who otherwise might make effective contributions toward solutions to the human problems created by automation. The most seductive of these myths is the claim that, for a number of reasons, automation is not going to eliminate many jobs. Last week, before a Senate Labor Subcommittee, a top productivity expert for the Bureau of Labor Statistics stated that the Department felt that rising productivity—another way of describing automation—would eliminate 200,000 jobs a year—or 4,000 jobs a week. Personally, I think this is a gross underestimate of the real situation and that automation is a major factor in eliminating jobs in the United States at the rate of more than 40,000 a week, as previous estimates have put it. We must also keep in mind that automation is not only displacing people directly, but also indirectly through what are called silent firings in reference to workers who would have been hired for jobs eliminated by automation.

A second myth is that automation will create jobs for workers not only in running the machines, but in maintaining and building them. The hard truth here is that modern automated equipment requires very little maintenance. If it did not, it would not pay to operate it; and if the equivalent number of workers replaced by automation were required to build the machines and systems, there would be no point in automating.

A third myth that needs to be laid to rest is the belief that those who lose their jobs to automation can be retrained and put into other jobs requiring higher skills and paying more money. As studies have shown, automation is more likely to reduce rather than increase the demands for skills and aptitudes and, besides, many workers are just not retrainable, due to their levels of intelligence, education, and age.

Still another myth is that workers replaced by automation in one part of the country can find jobs in other areas. The truth is that the workers thrown out of jobs are usually just those who are least able to move. They are the lower paid, the older, the unskilled. Either they cannot afford to move from an economic standpoint or they are psychologically incapable of beginning a new life in a strange area.

I have mentioned these myths or misconceptions because I feel strongly that they are unfortunately serving as easy palliatives for those who either cannot or will not come forward and grapple with the human problems caused by automation. It is much easier to look for proof that these problems do not exist than to admit their existence and move ahead toward a solution.

This general failure to face these problems, the attempt in many places to avoid them, to my way of thinking, represents a national moral weakness in itself; and I further believe that it can be an indication of a common failure to judge and understand the severe nature and extent of the thrust of this technological revolution. In the coming months and years, if we are to survive as a nation, we will need new sociological and economic ideas to solve the problems we face in this area. All of us, whether our desks are in the Congress, or in business offices, or at union headquarters, must work together as never before—to come up with such new ideas. We have a moral obligation to make a substantial contribution toward solving the problems that accompany rapid technological change. If we fail, we are handing our children an invitation to disaster—for failure to perceive the dimensions and the gravity of the human problems we are facing represents a moral breakdown of the gravest dimensions.

On the other hand, by meeting and overcoming the challenges that confront us—acting in the common good and by conquering ourselves as we have conquered the natural forces around us, we can gain the rich rewards of our scientific ingenuity for ourselves and for generations of Americans yet to come.

84
Technological Change and Aggregate Demand

Technological change is not a new phenomenon. In this analysis the Council of Economic Advisers attempts to place recent technological change in the perspective of time, and to assess its impact on the economy in the light of the available evidence.

ECONOMIC REPORT OF THE PRESIDENT

. . . In many applications, automated facilities—which control productive processes through servo-mechanical ("feed-back") devices—accomplish dramatic savings in direct labor. As with previous major technological changes, one can expect this innovation to be applied to an increasing number of activities. But merely because automation is technically feasible in many applications, it is not necessarily economically feasible, even though it may greatly reduce direct labor costs. Higher capital costs, lack of flexibility, and the necessity for large runs make automation noneconomic in thousands of applications where it is technically feasible. Moreover, even where it is economically advantageous eventually to substitute automated for nonautomated equipment, its introduction may well be delayed until the relative cost of operating the older equipment increases substantially. In a previous generation, electric power did not displace the steam engine overnight, nor did the steam engine in its time take over from the waterwheel overnight. Only a small fraction of the ultimate benefits of automation have yet been realized.

TECHNOLOGICAL CHANGE AND AGGREGATE DEMAND

Like all previous technological change, automation creates the necessity for many workers to change jobs during their lifetimes and for sons to find different work from that of their fathers. The problem created by these labor market adjustments is discussed in a later part of this chapter, together with the policies that can lubricate such adjustments and ease their human toll.

From *Economic Report of the President,* January, 1964, pp. 94–99.

The Expansion of Demand

Quite apart from these adjustment problems many are convinced that recent and current technological change is somehow different in its employment effects from all previous changes. This conviction rests upon one or both of the following propositions: (1) that our productive powers are now outstripping our wants and needs and ability to buy our own output, and thus our economy's ability to create new jobs; and (2) that technological change is now destroying jobs at a much faster rate than ever before.

If the Nation's ability and eagerness to buy output can and does keep pace with its ability to produce, a speeded-up pace of technological advance means that standards of living and economic security can rise more rapidly than ever. In this case, faster progress of productivity is to be sought and welcomed. Only if demand cannot keep pace (or if the required adjustments cannot readily be accommodated) is there a basis for fearing more rapid technological change.

Historically, there is surely no evidence of any inability of demand to rise along with productive capacity, or of any permanent inadequacy of total job opportunities. Rather, our technologically progressive economy has brought higher output and incomes, and more and better consumption and investment, along with the voluntary decision to take some of the fruits of progress in the form of leisure. Since 1929, for instance, output per worker has almost doubled. If total demand had not grown since 1929, and if we were still producing the 1929 level of output, using present methods of production and the present shorter workweek, it would take just 26 million workers to do it. This would leave two-thirds of our present labor force unemployed. Instead, the demand for output is almost three times as high, and employment is 50 per cent higher than in 1929. If total demand had grown since 1929 only as fast as population, 46 per cent of our labor force would now be unemployed as a result of the higher productivity.

Clearly, the increase in total demand for our potential output is the factor that has reconciled advancing technology with rising employment.

And it should continue to do so far into the future. Despite dramatic increases in average family income, American consumers have continued to spend a remarkably constant proportion of their disposable income on consumer goods and services. And a very large proportion of our families still earn very modest incomes. Millions of families live in actual poverty, as the preceding chapter has shown, and half of American families in 1963 had incomes below $6,200. If median family income increased at the same rate in the next 17 years as it has since 1947, half of American families in 1980 would still have incomes below $9,300 in today's prices. Today, even families at twice that level have no trouble finding ways to spend extra income. There is surely no reason to believe that any plausible rate of technical progress could lead to consumer satiation in the lifetimes of persons now on earth.

Technological change permits any given level of output to be produced with less labor and, in that sense, destroys jobs. But it also provides a significant spur to investment and consumption and thus creates jobs. Technological change makes existing capital equipment obsolete. New processes and products increase the profitability of investment and stimulate business demand for new machines, new equipment, and new buildings. Technological change both generates high levels of investment and gives consumers new purchasing incentives. Historically periods of rapid technological change have generally been periods of high and rising employment.

There is, of course, no automatic mechanism which guarantees that actual demand will grow each year at exactly the same rate as potential full-employment output. An economy characterized by technological change and growth always faces the challenge of maintaining a growth in demand sufficient for full employment, but not so high as to lead to inflation. Fortunately, growing sophistication in the uses of economic policy, particularly fiscal and monetary policy, make this goal more nearly attainable than ever before.

These tools of economic policy are capable of righting the balance whenever the job-destroying effects of technological progress outweigh its job-creating effects. They will succeed in this task, however, only if they are adjusted to take account of changes in the rate of productivity gains, whether from an altered pace of technological advance or from other sources.

The Trend of Labor Productivity

Some recent developments have been cited frequently to support the belief that technological change is accelerating. In certain instances, automation has greatly lifted output per man-hour and has revolutionized the productive process. These instances are highly dramatic, but they are insufficient for evaluating the overall impact of technological progress. Such an evaluation must be based on a study of the trend in overall productivity—output per man-hour—for the private economy.

The main difficulty in assessing the trend of productivity is that current output per man-hour is also affected by numerous transitory factors, most significantly by fluctuations in output and changes in the average age of the machinery in use. For example, during recessions employment falls proportionately less than output as a result of lags in employer reaction, uncertainty about the future, the need to retain the same supervisory and maintenance personnel over wide ranges of output, and hiring and firing costs. Employed manpower is not fully utilized, and the level of output per man-hour is depressed. This is usually followed by rapid rates of increase in labor productivity during the early phases of cyclical expansions. . . .

Moreover, our statistical measures of productivity are far from exact. Productivity is a ratio of recorded output to recorded labor input, and relatively small errors in measuring either the numerator or denominator can distort the pattern of change in productivity. Particularly in measuring productivity for *individual* sectors of the economy, there are statistical problems associated with the measurement of output change; and measures of labor input are also a source of difficulty. (Currently there are two separate official series on employment and man-hours—one based primarily on payroll data reported by business establishments and the other based on a monthly survey of households.) The Department of Commerce is now engaged in major revisions of output data, and the Bureau of Labor Statistics is planning to publish revised productivity indexes during 1964, based on the revised output data. Recorded changes in productivity for individual years and sectors must be viewed as a broad gauge—rather than a precise reading—of economic performance.

With these qualifications, productivity measurements for recent years are presented in Table 17, accompanied by some comparisons with longer-run trends. Labor input data are based on information collected primarily from establishments. The table shows that productivity gains have been healthy but not unprecedentedly large during the past three years. While improvement has varied among sectors, the average gain in each case has been greater during the past three years than in the preceding decade, but less than the average of 1947–50.

*   *   *

Table 17

*Changes in Output Per Man-hour
in the Private Economy, 1919–63*

| Period | Percentage change per year | | | | |
| | | | Nonagriculture | | |
	Total private	Agriculture	Total	Manufacturing *	Nonmanufacturing *
1919 to 1947	2.2	1.4	2.0	3.0 †	‡
1947 to 1963	3.2	6.1	2.6	2.7	2.5
1947 to 1950	4.5	8.8	3.7	4.3	3.4
1950 to 1960	2.7	5.4	2.1	2.0	2.2
1960 to 1963	3.5	5.5	3.2	3.7	2.9
1960 to 1961	3.3	5.9	2.9	2.6	3.1
1961 to 1962	3.9	3.4	3.8	5.4	2.9
1962 to 1963	3.5	7.4	3.0	3.1	2.8

* Department of Labor estimates for 1960–63 are in the course of revision and are not available. . . . Therefore estimates for all years beginning with 1947 have been made by the Council of Economic Advisers on a consistent basis using Department of Commerce net output estimates.
† Based on data from private sources.
‡ Not available.
Note: Man-hours are based primarily on establishment data.
Sources: Department of Commerce, Department of Labor, and Council of Economic Advisers.

Recent large gains could reflect no more than a possibly unusually cautious hiring policy on the part of business in the current expansion. Experience with the slack labor market of recent years may have deterred the anticipatory hiring of overhead and skilled personnel, which appears typically to take place during a business expansion as insurance against the possibility of future labor shortages. If so, the recent higher rates of productivity increase may prove to be transitory. Yet optimism may still be warranted. If objective analysis does not support a firm conclusion that the trend of productivity has accelerated, neither can that possibility be dismissed. Technological progress may indeed have accelerated, but its impact on productivity may be only gradually becoming visible because of the time that must elapse before innovations become embodied in new capital equipment and expressed in new organizational forms.

The Changing Distribution of Job Requirements

In the past decade, jobs have been destroyed and created at very unequal rates in various regions, occupations, and industries.

Changing *regional requirements* are illustrated by the fact that nonagricultural employment actually declined between 1953 and 1963 in Rhode Island, Pennsylvania, Michigan, and West Virginia, remained essentially unchanged in Maine and Ohio, and rose by 1.5 million (almost 40 per cent) in California, 65 per cent in Florida, 80 per cent in Arizona, and 97 per cent in Nevada. Even more striking disparities can be found among metropolitan areas.

Shifts in the *occupational distribution* of jobs have been equally dramatic. The number of farmers and farm workers declined by 2.8 million, or 40 per cent, between 1950 and 1960. In more narrowly defined occupations, there were employment declines of 25 per cent among locomotive engineers and firemen, 38 per cent among textile weavers and spinners, 42 per cent among telegraph operators, and 50 per cent among fishermen. During this same period, employment rose by 45 per cent among professional nurses, 49 per cent among teachers, and 60 per cent among engineers and draftsmen.

Changes in the *industrial composition* of jobs were highlighted by the continued decline in the importance of goods-producing industries as sources of employment. Total employment in manufacturing, mining, and construction declined by 2 per cent between 1953 and 1963. In contrast, employment increased by 65 per cent in state and local government, 41 per cent in services, 33 per cent in finance, and 16 per cent in trade.

Automation is often regarded as having a qualitatively different effect on worker displacement than did earlier forms of technological change. Specifically, it is suggested that automation requires a higher average level of education or skills than did earlier forms of technology, and that this complicates the adjustment process for displaced blue-collar workers whose old skills have been rendered obsolete while lack of adequate educational background disqualifies them from filling the new jobs created by automation.

However, the current changes in skill requirements appear to continue a long evolutionary process. Professional and technical workers and craftsmen, for instance, accounted for about 15 per cent of the work force in 1900, 23 per cent in 1950, and 26 per cent in 1960. In contrast, unskilled farm and nonfarm workers accounted for 30 per cent of the labor force in 1900, 11 per cent in 1950, and only 8 per cent in 1960. It is not clear whether automation has caused any acceleration in these trends. Further studies are needed, to which the proposed Commission on Automation should contribute.

*   *   *

Mr. Glazier points out that automation eliminates jobs and often diminishes skill requirements. Under these conditions, retraining cannot solve the unemployment problem, and the price of faster technological advance may be increased unemployment.

William Glazier is Assistant to the Director of the Salk Institute for Biological Studies, and for many years was associated with the International Longshoremen's and Warehousemen's Union.

85

Automation and Joblessness

WILLIAM GLAZIER

There are few important economic issues in our nation which are not in some way attributed to automation. Whether it be joblessness, apprehension over the increased power and market influence of dominant corporations, major collective-bargaining conflicts, or the indifferent prospects for capital investment and economic growth, automation seems to be lurking somewhere in the background.

Ironically enough, the same lack of balance which ascribes too much blame to automation is equally responsible for expecting too many blessings from this advanced technology. Although a great deal of today's unemployment is correctly attributed to the displacement of men by machines, these same machines are also confidently expected to create higher-skill job opportunities, which the unemployed can presumably fill after retraining.

The present Administration, beset with a nationwide joblessness which refused to melt away in the 1961 business revival, and armed with soothing projections demonstrating the higher-skill occupational requirements of an increasingly automated economy, has made a variety of proposals to facilitate the retraining of technologically displaced labor.

There is no denying the appeal of these proposals to retrain the unemployed. But, as so often is the case with complex economic problems, the simple solution is frequently either naïve or dangerously disingenuous.

Since World War II, unemployment in the troughs of each recession has averaged about 7.5 per cent of the labor force, but when the recovery peaks were reached, it was discovered that not all of those who lost their

From *The Atlantic Monthly*, Vol. 210, No. 2, August, 1962, pp. 43–47. Reprinted by permission of the author.

jobs during the recession had been re-employed. In the peak year 1953, 2.9 per cent of the labor force was jobless; in 1957 the proportion had climbed to 4.3 per cent; and in 1960, the most recent peak year, 5.6 per cent of the labor force was unable to find work.

Traditionally we have accepted the premise that the primary cause of jobless-ness is a temporary layoff during a business recession. With the help of unemploy-ment compensation, the worker is tided over until economic conditions improve and he is called back to work. But how can we explain an economic recovery which does not reabsorb the unemployed? And what can be done about it?

One of the more facile explanations of this disturbing phenomenon is that the hard core of the unemployed is composed of individuals who cannot find em-ployment primarily because they are not fitted for available job openings. They have either been technologically displaced or have reached working age without requisite industrial skills and training.

There is widespread agreement among congressmen of both parties that tech-nological change is primarily responsible for displacing unskilled and semiskilled workers and for making old skills obsolete; but simultaneously, so the theory goes, this same technological change is responsible for opening up new jobs, of a higher skill content. The conclusion is neat and plausible: train and retrain the jobless, and fit the unemployed worker to the unfilled job.

Not only are most senators and congressmen sold on retraining as the answer to current hard-core unemployment and the technological displacement of labor, but the general public seems to share the same illusion. According to the Gallup Poll, of all the proposals specified by the President in his second State of the Union message, the proposal to train the unemployed was cited by 67 per cent of those replying as one for which they were willing to make sacrifices. This was more than twice the support given any other recommendation.

The seriousness of the problem of persistent, hard-core unemployment cannot be exaggerated. When the National Planning Association studied the problem in early 1961, it found that the chronically unemployed had grown from fewer than 500,000 persons in late 1953 to about 1.5 million at the end of 1956 and to about 2 million at the beginning of 1960. The number has continued to grow since. Technological change, decline in some industries and growth in others, shifts in the geographical location of plants, and changes in consumer demand have caused these many millions of workers to be unemployed and have kept them that way. They are the victims of growth and progress in the American economy.

The consequential shifts in the structure of industry have left behind a grow-ing pool of unskilled and semiskilled workers handicapped by the limits of a grade school education, equipped with years of routine production-work experi-ence, and burdened with families to support. Many are members of minority groups. In addition, there are the young people under twenty-two years of age, who have the highest unemployment rate of any group in the nation today; half of them have still to get their first jobs. They are largely unskilled and untrained for employment.

Meanwhile, the paradox, as the advocates of training and retraining see it, is that all over the nation jobs go unfilled. In Detroit, with 12 to 14 per cent of the labor force unemployed, employers are unable to fill openings for electronics tech-nicians, computer operators, and bookkeeper system specialists. As the want ads demonstrate, there are nationwide shortages of draftsmen, technicians, and electronic, hydraulic, and pneumatic repairmen. There seems to be no lack of people on the one hand or unfilled jobs on the other; what appears to be lacking is people with sufficient training and the right skills. The jobless worker, in the wrong place with the wrong skills and aptitudes, has become the fall guy.

In most of the discussions about retraining, it is conveniently forgotten that the purpose of labor-saving technical improvements is to enable the same amount of product to be produced by fewer workers. Other things remaining equal, after a technological innovation has been applied in a factory or an office, some members of the work force will have lost their jobs. Moreover, technological progress as such is not going to reabsorb these workers. Only a sufficient increase in production, either in the plant or elsewhere, will provide alternative employment opportunities for the individuals whose labor and skills have been incorporated into a new piece of machinery. The nub of the problem is how to achieve this sufficiency of production.

Automation not only diminishes the number of workers employed in the factory, it also diminishes skill requirements. If this were not so, if the displacement of unskilled and semiskilled workers by machines necessitated the increased employment of higher-skilled, higher-paid workers, then obviously the whole evolution of production to a higher technological level would be economic foolishnesss.

Equally naïve is the expectation that as employment drops in the firms replacing men with machines, the displaced workers or their counterparts will find employment in building machines. If as many people were now employed in manufacturing the machines as had formerly been used in making the final product, there would be no point in substituting machines for people.

The immediate gains from rising productivity that result from the substitution of machines for men largely take the form of cost savings realized from the displacement of labor; this purpose would be frustrated if the labor savings at one point were contravened by increased labor costs elsewhere in the production cycle.

Of course, cases can be cited demonstrating that advanced technological innovations have come into a factory or office with few, if any, layoffs. For example, each of the dozen or so automation situations studied by the Bureau of Labor Statistics of the U.S. Department of Labor in 1960 and 1961 lends itself to the comforting conclusion that with proper preparation and planning, discharges can be virtually eliminated. But it would be unwise to generalize from these few instances in which technologically displaced workers were reabsorbed by their employers. The uniqueness of these particular experiences is demonstrated by the mounting number of technologically unemployed this same government agency reports each month.

Moreover, we cannot forget that the displacement of men by machines need not occur at the same time or even at the same place that the machine makes its appearance. When an auto manufacturer automates without layoffs, and in the process is able to manufacture a component formerly purchased from a supplier, the discharged employees of the supplier are as much the victims of automation as if they had been on the payroll of the automating firm. Or when workers who would have been hired by an automated firm no longer have job opportunities, they too are the victims of automation, of "silent firing."

In addition, the increase in the skill content of the work force in an automated factory is as elusive to pin down as the increase in new job opportunities.

As the studies made by Professor James Bright of the Harvard Business School a few years ago show, the effect of automation is more than likely to reduce—or, at least, not to increase—the demand for skills and abilities on the part of the direct production workers. The same tendency holds for the indirect production workers, the men who service and maintain the machines, in contrast to those who operate or supervise them. The complaints about shortages of skilled engineers, technicians, and craftsmen are more likely to be heard from the builders of automatic machinery than from the users, who are profitably replacing human labor and human skills with automatic machines and control devices.

Professor Bright could find "little justification for the popular belief that present labor is employable in automated plants only with extensive retraining, or that there is a major shortage of new skills in the automated factories." His observations are persuasive in the light of what we know about the diminution of labor and the transfer of skills from men to machines in the evolution of automation.

As a social objective, training or retraining employed and unemployed persons is much to be desired. It would improve the employability of workers, open up more attractive and higher-paid job opportunities, and raise the productive level of the entire nation. The debatable issue is the appropriateness of retraining as a remedy for the current chronic unemployment. In the enthusiastic endorsement of the retraining proposals embodied in the Manpower Development and Training Act of 1961, a rather important consideration became obscured: there must be job opportunities in prospect for the trainees, or all such programs become exercises in futility. Retraining a skilled, unemployed West Virginia coal miner as an auto mechanic does not accomplish much if he cannot find a job as an auto mechanic.

Retraining and relocating displaced and unemployed labor, useful and necessary when economic growth and progress are giving rise to many new jobs in new places, become of dubious value when the economy is producing job seekers faster than job opportunities.

In late 1960, after the Oklahoma City plant of Armour and Company had shut down, the tripartite Armour Automation Committee offered to help finance retraining for any of the 431 former production workers who showed promise of benefiting from some form of vocational training. Of the 170 who responded and were tested, 60 were found capable of retraining; the balance were told that the best chance for re-employment would be in manual labor. About one year later, according to the AFL-CIO, 13 had completed the retraining courses and 7 had found employment in their new skills. This experience convinced the union members of the committee that to retrain under these circumstances was simply to raise the educational level of the unemployed.

In 1959, unemployed workers in the state of California who had exhausted their unemployment benefits and were found eligible for extended benefits for an additional thirteen weeks were offered retraining to improve their chances of finding jobs. Some 50,000 unemployed were eligible to take these courses. In the entire state 38 applied for retraining; 26 were approved and took courses.

It is not surprising that unemployed workers are so markedly unenthusiastic about retraining when they have so few reasonable expectations for reemployment, despite the want ads.

The Administration proposal for retraining unemployed workers in vocational schools will cost the federal government approximately $83 million the first year and reach $238 million the fourth year. This compares with total expenditures on vocational school training in the United States of $238.7 million in 1960, which represented $111 million on the local level, $82.4 on the state level, and $45.3 on the federal level.

The contention of the vocational school administrators, who strongly endorsed the new legislation, that industrial skills are best learned in a vocational school is belied by the fact that three out of every five workers with special vocational skills have received their training on the job and through job progression. They worked up, step by step, to jobs of higher skills; training in most cases has been informal, and instruction and guidance have generally come from a foreman, supervisor, or more highly skilled fellow employee.

Training in new skills is much more practical and is likely to be more successful for both trainee and employer when the program is carried on within the plant and geared to specific job needs. An employer training or retraining his own employees knows whom he is retraining; he trains with specific job openings in view, and the program, no matter how informal, is tailored to the special needs of the plant or department.

On-the-job training is, of course, limited to workers already employed who have another job prospect at the same place. Unemployed persons, unless specifically hired for apprenticeship or training purposes, cannot be benefited. To recognize this is nevertheless no justification for arguing that vocational school training can be substituted with similar beneficial results for trainee and potential employer.

There is a good deal of confusion and exaggeration about just how much skill is included in a skilled or a semiskilled job, and just how much training is required before a worker acquires employable and useful skills. A recent New York state study covering manpower needs and technological change in some of the most diversified industrial, commercial, and business areas in the nation points out that the skills required for the bulk of industrial jobs are relatively simple ones. Most can be taught on a full-time basis in a few days, a few weeks, or a few months. Approximately two thirds of all jobs in New York state at the present time fall into this category. The specific skills required by these jobs are typically taught by employers, on the job. If the jobs are there, the job seekers will learn the skills quickly enough once they are employed.

On the other hand, only about one third of all jobs are accounted for by the skilled crafts, the professions, and technical and managerial occupations. These occupations require complex skills and a wide range of knowledge which can only be gained in a matter of years, not weeks or months. They are far beyond the competence of most of the hard-core unemployed.

The lack of enthusiasm which unemployed workers display toward retraining when there is no assurance of employment is matched by management under these same circumstances. Management has never had any hesitancy about conducting on-the-job training programs when unfilled jobs were holding up production plans. During and immediately after World War II, for example, when American industry was desperately short of labor, many firms enlarged the scope of on-the-job training, not only to upgrade their employees but to equip newly hired unskilled and semiskilled workers for the tasks at hand. However, when business and employment are not expanding, when new employees are not being added, any businessmen would be imprudent not to curtail such programs.

*   *   *

Mr. Fischer argues that technological change is eliminating many of the jobs our labor force is capable of performing, and that the I.Q. requirements for many of the new jobs are beyond the capacity of the available labor force. He urges that we must face the need to find useful jobs for workers with low intelligence levels.

John Fischer is Editor-in-Chief of Harper's Magazine.

86
The
Stupidity Problem

JOHN FISCHER

*   *   *

It is perfectly clear, to me at least, why Mr. Kennedy hasn't been able to find jobs for our three or four million unemployed. The human race—or anyhow that sample of it located in North America—no longer fits the kind of society it has to live in. Our society just doesn't have any jobs for certain types of people. If it continues to develop along its present course, the number of such unemployables seems likely to grow rather rapidly. Meanwhile, at the other end of the scale, an increasing number of important jobs will remain empty, because there aren't enough men and women able to fill them.

So the chief characteristic of The Overdeveloped Society (if that is the right label) will be a permanent surplus of some kinds of workers, together with a permanent shortage of others. For the assortment of jobs which need to be done is simply out of kilter with the natural distribution of brains.

A few figures show how this happened. According to the psychologists, intelligence seems to be parceled out among human beings in line with a fairly consistent pattern. If you should round up a hundred typical Americans off the street, getting a fair sample of our whole population, you would find that about 46 of them would have something close to "normal" intelligence—that is, Intelligence Quotients between 90 and 109. Another 29 would be quite bright, with IQs ranging from 110 to 139. And one or two would be really brilliant, with IQs of 140 or above.

On the other hand, 20 people in this group would have to be classed as fairly stupid, since their IQs would fall between 70 and 89. And two or three, with ratings below 70, would barely have enough sense to come in out of the rain.

From the beginning of history until fairly recently—say, a couple of generations ago—every society in the world had plenty of jobs for low IQ people. They could herd sheep, pick cotton, dig ditches (even the Erie Canal was made with spades), h'ist that bale and tote that load. Indeed, nearly all of the earth's work called for strong backs and weak minds—for drawers of water and hewers of wood. Jobs that demanded real intelligence, on the other hand, were strictly limited; most communities had room for only a few doctors, ministers, teachers, lawyers, and captains of industry. Scientists were practically unknown. (As Robert Oppenheimer once pointed out in these pages, quoting Professor Purcell of Harvard, 90 per cent of all the scientists that ever lived are living today.) Government administrators were almost as scarce; Alexander Hamilton could run the Treasury Department with five clerks. As a consequence, thousands of high IQ people lived in frustration, because they could find no work equal to their talents. In many parts of the world this is still true. Some of the brightest people I ever met—in Greece and Yugoslavia—are hauling nets, throwing the shuttle on hand looms, sweeping streets, and winnowing grain with a hand basket.

But in the industrialized countries, as we all know, human muscle has now become almost obsolete. Anything it can lift, a machine can lift better. Practically any task involving repetition of the same motions can be done faster and cheaper by a mechanical or electronic device. So the muscle-worker is out of luck. He can still find a few things to do—collecting garbage, for example, unloading trucks, replacing railway ties—but these are mostly in minor or backward industries which have not yet got around to complete mechanization. And the number of such low-IQ chores is dwindling every day.

Farming perhaps offers the most vivid illustration of what is happening. As recently as my grandfather's day, farming was a set of inherited motions, not very different from those used by the Babylonians. As a boy in Ohio, he sowed wheat by hand-broadcasting and harvested it with a scythe. Since neither of these operations strains the cerebral cortex, a youngster who was too dumb for anything else could always make a living on the farm; the demand for field hands was virtually unlimited.

Today, however, a successful farmer has to be a combination geneticist, mechanical engineer, chemist, cost accountant, agronomist, tax expert, and economist; in all likelihood he is a college graduate. While he may still hire some unskilled migrant labor for a few weeks a year to harvest certain fruit and vegetable crops, he can very frequently operate a big farm without any help outside the family. If he does take on a full-time hand, he looks for a smart one; no farmer wants to entrust $40,000 worth of complex agricultural machinery to a dope.

*   *   *

The youngsters who drop out of high school before graduation are a case in point. Most leave school, not because of economic problems, but because they can't keep up with the not-very-demanding work. The federal Bureau of Labor Statistics has reported that 80 per cent of the drop-outs are lagging by at least one grade; and Dr. Cronbach notes that "the very dull tend to drop out as soon as they reach age sixteen. . . . By the end of high school, almost no one with IQ below 85 is still in school." This is one reason why the unemployment rate for sixteen- to nineteen-year-olds is twice as high as for adults. A few get jobs as messengers, gas pump operators, or dishwashers. Many others drift straight from the classroom to the relief rolls, or to crime. For as our society is now organized, we can't find any use for most of these young dullards—a situation unjust and miserable to them, and to the rest of the community both costly and dangerous.

The counterpart of this situation is a severe and increasing shortage of people brainy enough to man the upper level jobs in our Overdeveloped Society. The design, supervision, and maintenance of automated equipment require a lot of smart, highly trained people—and even now industry can't find enough of them. Did you ever hear of a good computer-programmer who was out of work?

So too with the rest of our society. All the professions which demand better-than-average minds—medicine, law, journalism, teaching, the sciences, advertising, the military—are moaning about their difficulties in attracting enough competent recruits. And as the structure of society grows in both complexity and size, the need for able managers (in business and government alike) grows in almost geometric ratio. Our inability to locate enough first-rate managerial talent in many fields—from college presidents to corporate comptroller, from regional planner to operations analyst—may yet prove to be the breakdown point in our civilization.

For we have apparently built ourselves, unintentionally and without quite realizing it, a society which calls for a distribution of intelligence entirely different from that which God provided. It remains to be seen whether we can make it work.

*   *   *

We might also profit if we could change our national attitude toward certain kinds of employment.

From the earliest days of the Republic, most Americans have regarded personal service as somehow degrading. Hardly anybody wanted to be a housekeeper or cook, and those hapless widows who were forced into such work to avoid starvation usually did it bitterly and with little pride. Butlers and valets were legendary creatures who belonged in British country homes or Wodehouse novels, but had no place in democratic America. Waiting tables was, and is, so unpopular that many restaurants have to import their help from Europe or Puerto Rico.

These prejudices evidently are peculiar to America, not to democracies in general. In Switzerland, the oldest democracy in Europe, the profession of waiter is both honorable and much sought-after, while it is still possible to hire good-natured and efficient household help in Scandinavia, Ireland, and Greece. (In England, however, the Americanization of society has made the butler and the maid almost extinct; those few who still exist there are mostly imported from Sweden, Italy, and Eire.)

Whatever their origins, such attitudes are costly. Both the efficiency and the tone of American life would be vastly improved if personal service came to be regarded as an acceptable way to make a living. For we now have the curious spectacle of millions of people on relief, while at the same time millions of households are looking for desperately needed help—to care for elderly relatives, tend the children, and help with the heavier chores. If such help could be found, countless women—many of them highly educated—could be freed for teaching and other understaffed professions . . . innumerable old people would not have to be condemned to nursing homes . . . any number of businessmen could save the energy now dissipated in shoveling snow, putting up storm windows, and tinkering with balky plumbing. It might even become possible to get prompt and courteous service in the average hotel and restaurant—but no, that is carrying fantasy too far.

Such work demands no great intelligence and only a minimum of training. Yet it is scorned by nearly all the people on the unemployment rolls. That isn't our kind of work, they say—and relief officials ordinarily will not require their clients to accept any job opening outside their customary trade.

I have no idea how such ingrained attitudes might be changed. Perhaps it could be done by professionalizing service work, and thus removing the stigma of the servant. Already this is being attempted, with some success, by a few companies which send out crews of trained men and women to do spring housecleaning, household repair, and the like. Their workers wear snappy uniforms, they work for the company instead of the householder, and they put in a regular eight-hour day; as a consequence they seem to feel more independence and self-respect.

No doubt there are many other and better ways to find useful work for the low IQs, and to persuade them to do it. My main point is that nobody seems to be thinking about such things, because nobody is yet willing to admit publicly that the Stupidity Problem needs coping with. The steps taken by the Kennedy Administration to fight unemployment—new factories for distressed areas, retraining for technologically displaced workers, general stimulus of the economy—may be fine for their own purposes; but they ignore the special problem of the dullard. This is not only expensive, but dangerous. When you condemn people indefinitely to idleness and public charity, you condemn them also to frustration and bitterness —to the kind of discontent which may have a lot to do with the crime rate, drug addiction, and political unrest.

It ought not to be beyond human ingenuity to create worthwhile jobs for these people, if we only set our minds to it. If we tended our forests, for example, as carefully as the Germans do, we would need millions of man-hours of not-very-skilled work—and we would increase enormously the value of a precious national asset. We could use a lot of muscle power in deferred maintenance of our dilapidated railways. We might even set a few hundred thousand men to work cleaning the litter off our streets and the beer cans out of our trash-clogged parks and streams. And we might start now to devise an educational system which will candidly train every youngster for a level of work that fits his intelligence, instead of pretending that each of them is potential college material.

87

Unions and Automation:Truce on the West Coast

Can the problems of automation be handled by labor and management in the private sector without government help or interference? This article reports three important approaches which have been tried in recent years.

Bruce Bliven is a lecturer in journalism at Stanford University and was formerly editor of The New Republic.

BRUCE BLIVEN

Three union contracts on the West Coast seem to point a clear, broad road to voluntary peace between workers and employers on the greatest single issue now dividing them—automation. In each of these agreements, the union has abandoned all resistance to the introduction of laborsaving devices. In each, the employer is paying a stiff price for this concession, including a guarantee for a period of years that no worker will suffer hardships because machinery has eliminated his job. While prediction is always rash, strikes seem highly unlikely during any of these contracts. They have special significance at a time when Congress, struggling with the nationwide conflict between the railroads and their workers, has passed the first peacetime law in memory providing for compulsory arbitration.

The contracts in question are between the Southern Pacific railroad and its clerks, the shipowners and the longshoremen of the Pacific Coast and Hawaii, and the Kaiser Steel Corporation and its steelmakers.

Each of these agreements is the lengthened shadow of a man, and in each case he represents a different side of the triangular bargaining table that is becoming commonplace today. In the railroad dispute, the outstanding figure is Professor J. Keith Mann of the Stanford University Law School. The longshoremen's contract is chiefly the handiwork of the president of the union, Harry Bridges. The Kaiser settlement springs from the ideas of Edgar Kaiser, now the guiding spirit in the steel company and in most of the other enterprises founded by his father, Henry J. Kaiser.

These three agreements were hammered out within a few miles of each

From *The Reporter*, November 7, 1963, pp. 35 ff. Reprinted by permission.

other, the first two in San Francisco and the third at the Kaiser headquarters across the Bay in Oakland. This is only partly coincidence; the West seems somewhat freer from the rigidity of conservative tradition than the East, more willing to experiment boldly.

While these contracts have important elements in common, they also have sufficient differences to be discussed separately.

AUTOMATION AND ARBITRATION

Donald J. Russell, the hard-driving sixty-four-year-old president of the Southern Pacific railroad, has made his line one of the country's most prosperous, aided by the fact that its eight thousand miles of track are in seven Western states, comparatively free from competition. Russell quit Stanford University before graduation and has been working for the Southern Pacific ever since. He is a fanatic on using all technological advances to reduce costs and improve service, including computers and many other devices to cut down paper work. In five years, 1958–1962, he was able to eliminate forty per cent of his clerical workers—about 4,500 men—while traffic was increasing more than eleven per cent.

Naturally, the Brotherhood of Railway and Steamship Clerks, Freight Handlers, Express and Station Employees was unhappy, and said so. The protests were voiced by a tough union bargainer, James E. Weaver, general chairman for the Southern Pacific unit, backed by another tough bargainer, George M. Harrison, international president. The complaints became so loud that President Kennedy finally appointed a special investigating committee headed by Dr. Mann, who has been working in labor relations almost since he got his LL.B. from the University of Indiana in 1949. Mann was chairman of the Review and Appeals Committee for the Wage Stabilization Board during the Korean War, later worked on labor relations for the Atomic Energy Commission, was a member of the President's commission on the flight engineers' dispute with the airlines in 1961, and has been a negotiator in two railroad controversies.

His committee in the Southern Pacific dispute was set up in August, 1962, and brought in a report on December 31. It made some far-reaching suggestions that proved unacceptable to both sides. While investigations were in progress, Weaver set a date for a strike several times, and postponed it only at the last minute.

The union did not reject outright any reduction whatever of the work force because automation had eliminated jobs; the sticking point was how rapidly this should be done. The railroad, at least in theory, would have liked to see every position vacated as soon as it proved unnecessary; the union wanted to keep the reduction down to a fixed small percentage, perhaps one like the two per cent a year embodied in a separate agreement made two years earlier with the Order of Railroad Telegraphers.

By March of this year, agreement had been reached on some of the issues. President Kennedy now suggested that Professor Mann's committee have the power to arbitrate the remaining issues, with both sides agreeing in advance to accept the result. This was done, and a precedent-shattering final settlement was reached in ten days.

The most important principle set up was that job elimination should be held as close as possible to the rate of "natural attrition"—the normal reduction of the working force by resignation, retirement, promotion, ill health, dismissal for cause, or death; in the case of the Southern Pacific this rate is between five and six per cent a year. Very rarely in industry has any such proposal been made, and more rarely still has it been accepted.

Professor Mann's committee set another important precedent when it insisted that no union settlement can be allowed to endanger the financial health of the employer:

> This Board cannot sanction an approach which would inhibit the carrier's effort to remain competitive. Only if railroad management is free to introduce cost-saving innovations will this nation continue to enjoy an adequate and efficient transportation system. . . . Meaningful employment security cannot be achieved at the expense of change.

When a man's job is abolished, every effort will be made to retrain him to work in some other department. All appropriate agencies of government are being called in, beginning with the machinery of the Federal Manpower Development and Training Act, on the assumption that there is a public as well as a private obligation to help the victims of the economic storm that is created by technological advance.

If men are downgraded in their jobs, the gap in pay will be filled. Fringe benefits such as hospitalization are maintained at a level varying with length of service. If a man is asked to move from one town to another, he will be compensated for the expense, including any loss on the sale of his house. Many rigid union job classifications have been moderated to permit flexibility in moving men from one job to another.

The few employees actually displaced will receive furlough benefits coming partly from the Southern Pacific, partly from Railroad Unemployment Insurance funds. Depending on the length of service, the worker eliminated will receive seventy per cent of his earnings for a maximum of a year, followed by sixty per cent for a maximum of four years.

Don Russell has good reason to be pleased with the new contract. As far as the clerks are concerned, he can introduce as many laborsaving devices as are invented—and he keeps the Stanford Research Institute hopping to produce more. With the work force shrinking about five per cent a year, before long it will be as small as the railroad feels is safe. (The job eliminated need not be that of the person leaving the payroll, as long as the ratio of one to one is maintained.)

James Weaver and George Harrison also have solid grounds for satisfaction. Practically all the present members of their union working for the Southern Pacific now have job security, and the few who don't will get maximum help in finding new work.

Both sides should benefit from the new spirit of co-operation and good will—an intangible factor but one that can be of enormous importance.

THE GOLDEN GATE'S BRIDGES

The West Coast and Hawaiian waterfronts, both under the International Longshoremen's and Warehousemen's Union, have a long history of savage labor disputes. The longshoreman's work is—or used to be—almost entirely hard physical labor, requiring a rough, tough man to do it. The shipowners are also a hardy and individualistic breed, strong believers in personal initiative, despite the fact that the American merchant marine leans heavily on the Federal government for aid of various forms; they bitterly dislike taking orders from anybody, least of all a union representative. Over the years, work stoppages have been frequent; in 1934 a waterfront dispute turned into a San Francisco general strike in the course of which three men were killed and many injured.

While conditions became better than in the bad old days, the truculence on both sides continued for many years. There was so much trouble that, when possible, shippers began routing cargo to avoid using any of the ILWU ports.

The union continued to fight a rear-guard action against automation, trying to hold employment as high as possible even if featherbedding were required. Until the latest contract went into effect, it was common to see a gang on the dock with only half the men working at any one time. Goods taken from the hold of a ship on a flat container might sit on the wharf next to a waiting truck, but longshoremen had to move everything to the pier itself before loading could start. Though modern derricks can lift tremendous weights, any freight package of more than 2,100 pounds had to be broken down on the dock into smaller units. Petty grievances resulted in great numbers of quickie strikes.

The International Longshoremen's and Warehousemen's Union has been bossed for decades by Alfred Renton Bridges, who has renamed himself Harry. The government tried unsuccessfully for years to deport him to his native Australia on the ground that he was a Communist when he entered the country and his entry was therefore illegal. Harry, now a citizen, says deadpan that he is a Republican. Whatever his politics, he has proved himself one of the ablest and most farsighted union leaders in the United States.

Several years ago, Bridges began to doubt the policy of fighting automation. In spite of everything the union could do, advances were being made; when a dispute involving technology was arbitrated, the union often lost. Public sentiment was against featherbedding; further resistance was beginning to seem a mug's game. His views were reflected in a special report by a union committee. After demonstrating with a mass of facts and figures that automation did not cut the work force as much as most people thought, it continued:

> Our present policy can be described as one of intermittent guerrilla warfare directed against all changes which we anticipate will reduce the need for men. . . . Do we want to stick with [this plan] or do we want to adopt a more flexible policy in order to buy specific benefits in return?

The shipowners are represented by the Pacific Maritime Association, whose president is J. Paul St. Sure, meticulously courteous, faultlessly groomed, and tough. At a time when another work stoppage seemed imminent, legend has it that Bridges went to him and said, "A strike will cost you $70 million. Give us half that much as our share of the saving, and we'll agree to permit automation and not to strike for five years." (Like any sensible reporter, I have carefully avoided checking this story lest I find it false; in any case, the final contract came fairly close to these terms.)

Both Bridges and St. Sure had plenty of trouble, lasting for years, with diehards in their ranks. Technically, the longshoremen are usually employed by subcontractors working on a cost-plus basis. The shipowners really call the tune, however, and some of them were outraged at the notion of buying the right to improve dockside processes. Many union members sputtered at the idea of encouraging machines and cutting down the work force, and the Los Angeles local actually voted against the plan.

Finally, however, in 1961, the agreement was accepted. It provides for a total payment of $29 million over a period of five and a half years, to be deposited in a special fund under joint union-employer supervision. From it, every longshoreman is guaranteed pay equal to not less than a specified number of hours per week, whether there is work for him or not. At present, this number is thirty-five and the hourly rate is more than $4. Retirement is compulsory at sixty-five, at which time each man gets a lump sum of $7,920, without reference to any other pension rights. If he wishes, he may retire as early as sixty-two, in which case he gets his bonus in monthly payments of $220.

When the agreement was signed, it was expected that about four per cent of the longshoremen would retire each year, but in fact the rate has been twice as high. Though with unrestricted automation each worker accomplishes much more, a heavy rush of business has resulted in an actual shortage of labor. Bridges has lately been scolding his men for their reluctance to take in new members, and the union is being expanded by a thousand workers who have had some experience on the waterfront.

St. Sure and his shipowners have good reason to be pleased with the agreement. Much freight is now handled in huge sealed containers, so that a ship often need spend only twenty-four hours in port instead of a week, at a saving of thousands of dollars a day. The hundreds of small quickie strikes that formerly took place have been largely curbed; arbitrators are now kept continually on duty to come at once to the scene of any labor dispute and settle it on the spot. Pilferage, the curse of the waterfront the world over, has greatly diminished.

Labor costs are down; a reduction of only five per cent balances the annual payments into the special fund, and the cut has already gone far beyond that. If the work force can be reduced a third—a reasonable expectation as things are going—the shipowners should save about $40 million a year.

The union's advantages also seem substantial. Irregularity of employment is a thing of the past. Every man gets paid whether there is work for him or not, and retires at sixty-five or even sixty-two.

The new agreement at the Kaiser steel mill at Fontana, a few miles east of Los Angeles, is in some ways the most remarkable of the three. It owes its being to Edgar Kaiser, the amiable and hard-working fifty-five-year-old son of the fabulous Henry J. The elder Kaiser built ships so fast during the Second World War that it was said you had to watch your step at a launching not to be run over by the next ship coming down the same ways. Now, at eighty-one, he is romping around the Hawaiian Islands and leaving a big new hotel in almost every footprint. Edgar is in general charge of the Kaiser empire, which besides steel embraces engineering, automobiles, cement, gypsum, aluminum, chemicals, aircraft, electronics, and assorted sidelines. His father trained him in a hard school; he was working on a natural-gas line from Kansas to Texas when he was only twenty-two, and thereafter helped construct Boulder, Bonneville, and Grand Coulee Dams before he went into wartime ship production in Portland, Oregon.

THE FONTANA SETTLEMENT

The Fontana mill is an ultramodern three-million-ton plant. Despite its efficiency, it has usually operated in the red, being carried by the other Kaiser companies. This is partly because of foreign competition, partly because the typical order for fabricated steel in its sales area is small, with each requiring costly readjustment of machinery. Edgar's relations with his workers have always been good; in 1959, in the nationwide steel strike, he was the first to break away from the other companies and make an independent settlement with the United Steelworkers of America.

Over the years, like many another important executive, he had become more and more disgusted with exhausting day-and-night union bargaining under the threat of a strike. He called in a group of experts in labor relations, including representatives of the steel workers' union, to see what could be done. After many months of consideration, they proposed the present plan, which was finally accepted by the Fontana steelworkers on March 1, 1963. Explaining what he had in mind, Edgar says that he was seeking a scheme that would "offer the opportunity of completely eliminating contract deadlines on economic issues."

Under this new plan, savings in the cost of operations beyond the 1961 level are shared, the company getting two-thirds and the workers one-third. Since about half the company's profits—when there are any—go to taxes, Kaiser officials like to call this a three-way-split—management, workers, and public.

If a man's job is eliminated by automation, he goes into an Employment Reserve Pool. His standard hourly rate of pay is guaranteed for one year, and his employment is protected until he is reassigned. Like work on the waterfront, steelmaking is hard work even with today's techniques; the natural attrition at Fontana is eight per cent a year, and the management believes no one is likely to be in the Reserve Pool more than five or six months on the average. Kaiser also guarantees to maintain wage rates and fringe benefits substantially equivalent to those the Steelworkers may obtain at any time in the future through nationwide bargaining.

Like other steel mills, this one has had some of its men under special incentive pay, resulting in high remuneration. These workers were given a choice: they could remain under the old system or come into the new one on a majority vote of the members of each gang. If they decided to change, they got a "buy-out" lump sum, which could be as much as $5,000 per man.

There are several important advantages for management in the plan. The workers now have a very real incentive to try to think up shortcuts to save time and money. The likelihood of quickie strikes is reduced to a minimum, and so is the chance of a complete shutdown when the contract expires.

The advantages to the worker are also great. He has job security against anything except a severe economic depression, in which case very few are guaranteed their jobs in any industry. If he devises new techniques to help make steel more economically, his ingenuity is reflected in his pay envelope—and those of all his fellow workers. In the first two months of the plan, the total savings in cost of operation over the same period in 1961 amounted to $2,158,000, of which the workers' share was about $700,000, or twenty-five per cent of the payroll for those participating.

The Kaiser plan also has one decided advantage for the company's customers. Since they now have little reason to fear a shutdown, steel purchasers probably will not consider it necessary to stockpile large quantities, with the risk of deterioration.

"THE UNBORN"

These three agreements underscore some conclusions about labor-management relations that are steadily becoming more apparent in all industry throughout the country.

It seems clear that no union is likely to accept without a struggle any arrangement that involves the dismissal of a large proportion of its members without adequate safeguards for their future welfare. To resist this they will strike, unless forbidden by law, no matter how much the national economy may be affected. Indeed, if they are sufficiently bitter, they may find ways to circumvent a law; it is still true, as John L. Lewis used to say, that you can't dig coal with bayonets.

It is also clear that few employers will accept any substantial degree of featherbedding unless they are forced to. Public opinion, if it knows the facts, will be on their side.

With wages and working conditions becoming steadily less important, and with the new emphasis on job security and conditions of retirement, the area in which the interest of unions and management is parallel or identical is steadily expanding. In many cases, each side's thinking about the other is somewhat obsolete. Some unions overlook the fact that most businesses today are run by salaried employees who own little or none of the stock, many of them highly trained in industrial management, including labor relations. The employers are also slow to recognize a new breed of union representatives, men who know as much about economics and finance as those across the bargaining table, and who want the business—and the country—to prosper.

Agreements like the three described here cannot possibly be achieved in a crisis atmosphere, under pressure of a strike deadline. They therefore lend weight to the movement, now gaining momentum everywhere, for negotiations to continue the year round, with permanent machinery for constant contact.

More and more we may expect to see the introduction of neutral third parties into union bargaining, trained experts who can carry over into a new industry what they have learned in others.

Finally, it should be noted that contracts like these take care only of the existing union membership and those who may be hired for their immediate replacement. They do nothing for what labor experts call "the unborn," those who are now growing up who would have filled the ranks of the union in the future. Their problem remains, and it is serious.

The capitalist market system remains today in only a few nations. Professor Heilbroner analyzes why different economic systems have developed in different nations, and compares other systems with the American market economy.

Robert L. Heilbroner, a member of the faculty at the New School for Social Research, is a well-known free-lance writer.

88

The Drift of Modern Economic History

ROBERT L. HEILBRONER

In our last chapters we have followed the broad development of American capitalism down to present times. Now, as we turn back from America to the continents of the East, West, and South an extraordinary fact strikes us immediately. When we left the European scene, in the early 1800's, capitalism was fast becoming the dominant form of economic society. England, as we saw, was the very cradle of industrial capitalism itself; France was rousing herself to follow in England's footsteps; elsewhere on the continent, if capitalism was not already established, it was clearly waiting in the wings for the last remnants of feudalism to disappear. Had we looked abroad from America at any time in the nineteenth century, our expectations would have been fully justified. By then all of Europe was unquestionably capitalist in orientation. And not only Europe—by the end of the nineteenth century, capitalism had reached out to touch most of the other continents of the world. In Asia and Africa, the main European nations had established colonies or spheres of influence which projected the imprint of capitalism into societies, many of which had barely awakened from an age-long slumber of ancient ways. In South America, as well, capitalism was clearly the main fertilizing influence. Even in reactionary Russia—the last of the great European powers to abolish the legal fetters of feudalism—by the early 1900's, capitalism had succeeded in creating a small but active nucleus from which further growth seemed assured.

Yet what do we find today? To our astonishment, the seemingly unopposed evolution of the world into a capitalist market system has not taken

From Robert L. Heilbroner, *The Making of Economic Society;* copyright 1962 by R. L. Heilbroner. Reprinted by permission of Prentice-Hall, Inc., publisher.

place. In Europe, its original birthplace, capitalism continues to be the dominant economic system; and, yet we find that socialist parties either hold power or constitute the main opposition in England, France, Belgium, Netherlands, Italy, Sweden, Norway, Denmark, Germany, and Austria. In Russia, the nucleus of capitalism has been entirely swept away by a communist society. In the huge continents of the East and South—in Asia and Africa and South America—we find that the original organizing impetus of capitalism has given way, in many of the most important nations, to a noncapitalist framework of economic organization. China is more communist than communist Russia. India proclaims herself a socialist state. So do Indonesia, Burma, Ceylon, Egypt, Ghana, Guinea. Only in South America do we find socialism absent from the official ideologies of political economy, and even there, the example of Cuba and the rumblings elsewhere hardly make it possible to anticipate the kind of capitalist society which we would have expected fifty years ago.

What happened outside America to abort the seemingly assured development of capitalism? A full answer to such a question would require much more than a book in itself, but we can begin to grasp the main picture of evolutionary trends if we follow, first, the factors which caused capitalism in Europe to take on a form different from that in America. From Europe it is not so long a jump, geographically or historically, to Russia; and from Russia we can turn with increased understanding to the so-called "underdeveloped" world.

European Capitalism: Feudal Heritage and National Rivalry

What are the reasons behind the turn of events in Europe? They must be sought, to begin with, not in the economic tendencies of European capitalism but in the social and political background whence those tendencies emerged.

Certainly the social background was significantly different from that of America. In the New World, capitalism developed with a population which had, to a large degree, spiritually and physically shed the feudal encumbrances of the Old World; but in that Old World, many of the social outlooks and habitudes of the past lingered on. An awareness of class position—and more than that, an explicit recognition of class hostility—was as conspicuous by its presence in Europe as by its absence in America. In Vienna, in 1847, writes one social historian:

> At the top were the nobles who considered themselves the only group worth noticing. The human race starts with barons, said one of them. Then there were the big businessmen who wanted to buy their way into the human race; the little businessmen; the proud but poor intellectuals; the students who were still poorer and still prouder; and the workers who were poor and had always been very, very humble.

The result was a totally different climate for the development of an economic society. In America, building on a new and vigorous foundation, capitalism was, from the beginning, a system of social consensus; in Europe, building on a feudal base, it was deeply tinged with class conflict. While capitalism in America managed without any effort to embrace the aspirations of its "lower orders," in Europe, already by the time of the revolutions of 1848, those lower orders had turned their backs on capitalism as a vehicle for their hopes and beliefs.

Second and no less important in explaining the divergence of American and European economic evolution was the profound difference between the political complexion of the two continents. In America, save only for the terrible crisis of the Civil War, a single national purpose fused the continent; in Europe, an historic division of languages, customs, and mutually suspicious nationalities again and again prevented just such a fusion.

Accordingly, American capitalism came of age in an environment in which political unity permitted the unhindered growth of an enormous unobstructed market, while in Europe a jigsaw puzzle of national boundaries forced industrial growth to take place in cramped quarters and in an atmosphere of continued national rivalry. It is curious to note that whereas Europe was considered "wealthier" than America all through the nineteenth century, in point of fact, American productivity in many fields began to outstrip that of Europe from at least the 1850's, and perhaps much earlier. For instance, at the Paris Exposition of 1854, an American threshing machine was twice as productive as its nearest (English) rival and eleven times as productive as its least (Belgian) competitive model.

These advantages of geographic space, richness of resources, and political unity were widened by subsequent developments in European industry. Not surprisingly, European producers, like those in America, sought to limit the destructive impact of industrial competition, and for this purpose they turned to *cartels*—contractual (rather than merely voluntary) agreements to share markets or fix prices. Unlike the case in America, however, this self-protective movement received the blessing, overt or tacit, of European governments. Although "anti-cartel" laws existed in many European countries, in fact, these laws were almost never enforced: by 1914 there were over 100 international cartels, representing the most varied industries, in which most European nations participated.[1]

Cartelization was undoubtedly good for the profit statements of the cartelized firms, but it was hardly conducive to growth—either for those firms or new ones. By establishing carefully delineated and protected "preserves," the cartel system rewarded unaggressive behavior rather than economic daring; and together with the everpresent problem of cramping national frontiers, it drove European producers into a typical high-cost, high profit-margin, low-volume pattern rather than into the American pattern of very large plants with very high efficiencies. The difference in economic scale is dramatically illustrated by steel. In 1885, Great Britain led the world in the production of steel; fourteen years later her entire output was less than that of the Carnegie Steel Company alone.

As a result, by the early twentieth century, European productivity lagged very seriously behind American. A study by Professor Taussig in 1918 showed that the daily output of coal per underground worker was 4.68 tons in the United States, as contrasted with 1.9 tons in Great Britain, 1.4 tons in Prussia, and 0.91 tons in France. In 1905, the output of bricks per person was 141,000 in the United States and 40,000 in Germany; pig iron production was 84.5 tons per worker in 1909, compared with only 39 tons in Great Britain in 1907. As the twentieth century went on, United States production pulled steadily ahead.

The divergence was strikingly noticeable in per capita incomes. In 1911, for example, when per capita income in the United States was $368, the corresponding figure for Great Britain was $250, for Germany $178, for France $161, for Italy $108. By 1928, American per capita income was $541 (in unchanged dollar values), while that of the United Kingdom was only $293; of Germany, $199; of

---

[1] By 1939 an estimated 109 cartels also had American participation, since American companies were not prohibited by anti-trust laws from joining international restrictive agreements.

France, $188; and of Italy, $96. While American per capita incomes had grown by nearly 46 per cent, English and French per capita incomes had increased only a third as rapidly, German incomes rose only about a quarter as fast, and Italian per capita incomes had actually declined.[2]

The Breakdown of International Trade

Still another consequence followed from the division of European industry and agriculture into national compartments. To a far greater extent than in America, it made the development of European capitalism subject to the expansion of *international trade*.

It is significant that we have been able to describe the main lines of American economic growth without even mentioning international trade. American growth did depend, to a very important degree, on commodities and capital funds which it was able to obtain from other lands. In Colonial times, foreign trade was the very economic lifeline of the country; and even in 1850 it is estimated that 20 per cent of the goods we consumed were imported. By 1880, however, this was reduced to 10 per cent, and thereafter the trend was steadily downward. Imports as a per cent of GNP were never above five per cent in the twentieth century, and latterly, scarcely half of that. Similarly, exports, although of critical importance for certain industries (and for agriculture), never bulked as a major fraction of our total output. Thus international trade, taken as a whole, never dominated our economic picture.

In Europe, however, quite the contrary was the case. Here the division of the continent into many national units made international trade a continuous and critical preoccupation of economic life. For instance, a study has shown that in 1913, when manufactured imports provided but 3.6 per cent of United States' consumption of manufactured goods, they provided 9 per cent of Germany's, 14 per cent of England's, 21 per cent of Sweden's. Perhaps even more striking is the degree to which some nations in Europe depended on international trade for the foodstuffs on which they lived: in the five years preceding World War I, for instance, England produced less than 20 per cent of the wheat she consumed and barely over 55 per cent of the meat. We find the same dependence on foreign trade in the export side of the picture. Whereas the United States in 1913 exported a mere fifteenth of its national product, France and Germany exported a fifth, and Britain nearly a quarter of theirs.

To a far greater degree than America, Europe lived by foreign trade. The significance here needs underscoring, particularly for Americans. For we do not often appreciate that trade (with its semantic emphasis on "exchange") is, in fact, inextricably associated with production and *productivity*.

Why productivity? Because trade enables us to concentrate our effort and resources on the production of those things for which they are best suited. We could, for instance, at very considerable cost grow coffee in the United States. To do so, however, would use our land, labor, and capital in highly inefficient ways, instead of putting them to use where their productivity is high—say, in the production of cars. The fact that we can *trade* cars for coffee gives us the best of both worlds:

---

[2] We must be wary of placing too much faith in the translation of one income—say £500—into its "equivalent"—$1,400. Until we know the price levels, the living standards, and customs of the nations we are comparing, we make such translations strictly at our own risk. But changes *within* a country, from year to year, are, of course, as meaningful in one currency as in another.

we can have our coffee without sacrificing our productivity by producing a coffee crop. Ideally, the same advantages accrue to the coffee producer who would be sacrificing his productivity were he to devote his resources to the production of cars.[3] Trade makes possible a *division of labor* from which *all* gain.

Here we clearly see the advantage possessed by the enormous unbroken American market over the fragmented national markets of Europe. In America, the division of labor was permitted to attain whatever degree of efficiency technology made possible; for, in the end, virtually all products entered into a single vast market where they could be exchanged against one another. In Europe, where the need for, and the potential benefits of, a far-reaching division of labor were no less pressing, a tangle of national barriers prevented the optimal specialization of effort from taking place.

What was visible in Europe was a struggle between the need for international trade as a primary means for advancing productivity and the retarding hand of national suspicions, rivalries, and distrusts. A striking example was provided as recently as the early 1950's by the great cluster of European steel and coal industry near the German-Belgian-Luxembourg borders. Here, in a triangle, 250 miles on a side, was gathered 90 per cent of European steel-making capacity in a kind of European "Pittsburgh." But this natural geographic division of labor had to contend with political barriers which largely vitiated its physical productivity. Typically, German coal mines in the Ruhr sold their output to French steelmakers at prices 30 per cent higher than to German plants; while, in turn, French iron-ore producers charged far higher prices in Germany than at home. As a result, while American steel production soared 300 per cent between 1913 and 1950, the output of Europe's steel triangle rose but three per cent during the same period.

Our example, itself, poses a question, however. Prior to 1913, as we have seen, something like a great international division of labor did, in fact, characterize the European market, albeit to nothing like the extent seen in America. By 1913, we will remember, a very considerable flow of international trade was enhancing European productivity, despite the hindrances of cartels and national divisiveness. It was only the beginning of a truly free and unhampered international market, but at least it *was* a beginning.

What brought this promising achievement to an end? Initially, it was the shock of the First World War, with its violent sundering of European trade channels and its no less destructive aftermath of punitive reparations, war debts, and monetary troubles. In a sense, Europe never recovered from its World War I experience. The slow drift toward national economic separatism, at the expense of international economic cooperation, now accelerated fatefully. Tariffs and quotas multiplied to place new handicaps before the growth of international trade. Then, the Depression of 1929 came as the final blow. As the Depression spread "contagiously," nation after nation sought to quarantine itself by erecting still further barriers against economic contacts with other countries. Starting in 1929, an ever-tightening contraction of trade began to strangle economic life on the continent.[4] Between the late 1920's and the mid-1930's, manufactured imports (in

[3] As we shall later see, there are complications, with roots deep in history and politics, which prevent the full benefits of trade from manifesting themselves with many of the world's "coffee producers." The reasons for this will emerge in our discussion of the underdeveloped countries at the end of this chapter.

[4] It was not only European trade which declined, but *world* trade. For 53 grim months following January 1929, the volume of world trade was lower each month than the preceding.

constant prices) fell by a third in Germany, by nearly 40 per cent in Italy, by almost 50 per cent in France. As international trade collapsed, so did Europe's chance for economic growth. For two long decades there followed a period of stagnation which earned for Europe the name of the "tired continent."

European Socialism

Against this background of economic malfunction it is easier to understand the growing insecurity which afflicted European capitalism. During the 1930's serious rumblings were already heard. In England, the Socialist Labor Party had clearly displaced the middle-class Liberals as the Opposition. In France, a mildly socialist "Popular Front" government came to the fore, as it did in Austria. Even in Italy and Germany, the fascist dictators repeatedly declared their sympathy with "socialist" objectives—and whereas their declarations may have been no more than a sop to the masses, it was certainly indicative of the sentiments the masses wanted to hear.

What was the aim of European socialism?

We can sum it up in two words: *equality* and *planning*. By equality, socialism meant first, of course, greater economic equality—higher wages for the working class and more stringent taxation for the upper class. But the meaning of the word did not confine itself to economic privilege. It stood also for social and political equality, for an end to the privileges of hierarchical status which, as we have seen, were deeply entrenched in the European heritage. Thus European socialism was a movement closely associated with *political democracy,* a fact which earned for it the enmity of not only the Right, but of the Communist Left as well.[5]

Socialism was concerned with removing more than the existing injustices of the European capitalist order; it sought as well to remove the economic malfunction of that order by replacing it with a planned economy. This objective did not imply, as with the Communists, the total state control of all enterprise and agriculture. To most socialists, planning meant only that the strategic centers of production would be nationalized, while the remainder of the economy would be regulated by indirect controls, not too much unlike those we have seen developed in America, reinforced by appropriate actions taken by the nationalized sector itself.

By the end of World War II, socialist ideas were clearly in the ascendant throughout most of Europe. Even before the war was concluded, the Labor Party swept into office in England and rapidly nationalized the Bank of England, the coal and electricity industries, much of the transport and communications industry, and finally steel. As the first postwar governments were formed, it was evident that a socialist spectrum extended across Europe from Scandinavia through the Lowlands and France to Italy (where the Communists came within an ace of gaining power). To many observers, it seemed as if capitalism in Europe had come to the end of its rope.

THE RECOVERY OF EUROPEAN CAPITALISM

Yet, European capitalism did not come to an end. Instead, beginning in the late 1940's and early 1950's, it embarked on what is unquestionably its period of strongest economic growth. How could this have come about?

[5] Another very important difference between the Socialist and Communist movements was that the Socialists preached gradualism rather than revolution, and abhorred the use of violence.

The first reason was that the postwar Socialist governments were not revolutionary but reform administrations. Once in power, they quickly instituted a number of welfare and social planning measures, such as public health facilities, family benefits and allowances, improved social security and the like, but they did not engage in changes of a sweeping order. When many of the Socialist governments, facing the exigencies of the postwar period, were voted out again, they bequeathed to the conservatives the framework of a welfare state *which the conservatives accepted*. Consequently, we find today that in most European states, welfare expenditures form a considerably higher proportion of government expenditures than they do in the United States. We get some idea of this if we compare *nondefense* government expenditure among Western nations.

Government Nondefense Purchases of Goods
and Services as a Proportion of GNP

	Per cent
U.S. (1957)	9.7
West Germany (1953)	14.3
Belgium (1952)	11.0
United Kingdom (1953)	13.1
Sweden (1952	13.6

Sources: Francis Bator, *The Question of Government Spending* (New York: Harper & Row, Publishers, 1960), Table 14, p. 157.

Harkening back to one of the traditional weaknesses of European capitalism, we can say that this represents an attempt to create a social service state which will mend the historic antagonism of the lower classes.

The second reason was even more important. This was the rise of a movement *within* the conservative ranks to overcome a still more dangerous heritage of the past—the national division of markets. This great step toward creating a full-scale continental market for European producers is called the European Community—or more usually, the Common Market.

To some extent, the Common Market was born out of the vital impetus given to European production by the Marshall Plan. Despite Marshall aid, it soon became apparent that Europe's upward climb would necessarily be limited if production were once again restrained by cartels and national protectionism. To forestall a return to the stagnation of the pre-war period, a few far-sighted and courageous statesmen, primary among them Jean Monnet and Robert Schuman, proposed a truly daring plan for the abolition of Europe's traditional economic barriers.

The plan as it took shape called for the creation of a *supranational* (not merely an inter-national) organization to integrate the steel and coal production of France, Germany, Italy, Belgium, Luxembourg, and the Netherlands. The new Iron and Steel Community was to have a High Authority with power to eliminate all customs duties on coal and steel products among members of the Community, to outlaw all discriminatory pricing and trade practices, to approve or disapprove all mergers, to order the dissolution of cartels, and to provide social and welfare services for all Community miners and steelworkers. The Authority was to be given direct power to inspect books, levy fines, and enforce its decrees—and still more remarkable, it was to be responsible not to any single member government but to a multi-national Parliament and a multi-national Court, both to be created as part of the Community. A Council of Ministers was to act as a *national* advisory and permissory body, but even here action would be taken by majority vote, so that no single nation (or even two nations) could block a decision desired by the Community as a whole.

By the fall of 1952, the Coal and Steel Community was a reality, and it lost no time going about its business. At mid-1954, customs duties and discriminatory pricing within the coal and steel "triangle" had been virtually eliminated, and roughly 40 per cent more coal and steel was being shipped across national boundaries than had been shipped prior to the establishment of the Community.

The success of the Coal and Steel Community led, in 1956, to the next two organizations: Euratom, a supra-national atomic power agency, and the Common Market itself, an organization which was to do for commodities in general what the Coal and Steel Community had done for its products. Under the Common Market treaty, a definite schedule of tariff cuts was laid down, envisaging by 1969, at the latest, an entirely unimpeded continental market for Common Market members, with a single "external" tariff vis-à-vis the world. In addition, there were to be a single agricultural policy and, perhaps most imaginative, full freedom for the inter-member mobility of both capital and labor.

The Common Market is still in the process of achieving many of these goals, although it is well ahead of its timetable. Already, however, it has led to a remarkable increase in European production. By the early 1960's, industrial production has more than doubled, and agricultural output has risen by a third. Over the entire decade, Western Europe's rate of growth has exceeded by 50 per cent that of the United States, and most important of all, for the first time the standard of living for the middle and working classes of Europe has begun to resemble that of America.

The Rise of Conservative Planning

It is not merely in these prosperous statistics that the European situation reminds us of the general course of affairs in the United States. Looking deeper, we can see a more profound resemblance. Abroad, as in America, the market system has had to turn toward what we might call "conservative planning" in order to survive.

In Europe, the direction of public intervention has perforce concerned itself with international trade more than is the case with the United States. The underlying problems and philosophy of conservative planning are much the same nonetheless. A need to keep the market process within bounds, to insure its continued smooth operation, to stabilize and, if need be, to stimulate its operation, has resulted in a strengthening of the role of government in both market societies. A growing agreement on the role of government as the active guardian of social welfare marks European as well as American capitalism, and a consensus on the use of monetary and tax and budgetary powers of adjustment again testifies to a common avenue of approach to the solution of common problems on both sides of the Atlantic.

This does not mean that the European situation is entirely comparable to America. Although the economy of Europe is today more dynamic, more hopeful, than perhaps ever in the past, its political problems have not yet been fully overcome. An undercurrent of political dissension continues to threaten the stability of many European countries, not only from the extreme Left but from the far Right, bringing about a certain tension in political life from which the United States has been mercifully spared. Then, too, the continued presence of a strong "socialist" movement, no matter how cooled its ardor or how watered-down its program, indicates that capitalism as an *ideology* is not yet without substantial opposition.

Thus European capitalism remains, to a certain extent, on political trial, despite its economic recovery. Yet, if history teaches us anything, it is that economic success tends to breed political success. If the trend of the past decade can be continued—and the purely economic auguries are reasonably favorable—there is surely reason to hope for a strengthening of the European social consensus and for a further healing of its historic political wounds.

NONMARKET ECONOMIES: THE SOVIET UNION

In the recovery of European capitalism through its development of a conservative planning structure, we have seen one aspect of the slow evolution of the modern economic history. Clearly, however, this is not the most significant change of the past half-century or so. For this we must look to the emergence of a *totally planned, nonmarket* society as the dominant economic pattern for at least a quarter of the globe. Here the guiding impetus of change has been the Soviet Union.

Early Soviet Planning

We cannot here recount in detail the history of Soviet socialism. Let us, rather, begin by noting the extraordinarily difficult problem that faced the revolutionary leaders who had secured the victory of "socialism" in Russia in 1917. In the first place, Rusia was a semi-feudal society in which capitalism was restricted to a small industrial and commercial sector. Second, both production and distribution were highly disorganized in the chaotic situation following the civil war. Finally, there was little guidance in the official literature of the Communist movement as to how a socialist society should be run. Marx's *Das Kapital*, the great seminal work of communism, was entirely devoted to a study of capitalism; and in those few essays in which Marx looked to the future, his gaze rarely traveled beyond the watershed of the revolutionary act itself. With the achievement of the revolution, Marx thought, a temporary regime known as "the dictatorship of the proletariat" would take over the transition from capitalism to socialism, and thereafter a "planned socialist economy" would emerge as the first step towards a still less specified "communism." In the latter state—the final terminus of economic evolution according to Marx—there were hints that the necessary but humdrum tasks of production and distribution would take place by the voluntary cooperation of all citizens and that society would turn its serious attention to matters of cultural and humanistic importance.

In reality, the Revolution presented Lenin, Trotsky, and the other leaders of the new Soviet Union with problems far more complex than this utopian long-term design. Shortly after the initial success of the Revolution, Lenin nationalized the banks, the major factories, the railways, and canals. In the meantime, the peasants, themselves, had taken over the large landed estates on which they had been tenants and had carved them up into individual holdings. The central authorities then attempted for several years to run the economy by requisitioning food from the farms and allocating it to factory workers, while controlling the flow of output from the factories themselves by a system of direct controls from above.

This initial attempt to run the economy was a disastrous failure. Under inept management (and often cavalier disregard of "bourgeois" concerns with factory management), industrial output declined precipitously—by 1920 it had fallen to *14 per cent* of prewar levels. As goods available to the peasants became scarcer, the peasants, themselves, were less and less willing to acquiesce in giving up food to the cities. The result was a wild inflation followed by a degeneration into an economy of semi-barter. For a while, toward the end of 1920, the system threatened to break down completely.

To forestall the impending collapse, in 1921 Lenin instituted a New Economic Policy—the so-called NEP. This was a return toward a market system and a partial reconstitution of actual capitalism. Retail trade, for instance, was opened again to private ownership and operation. Small-scale industry also reverted to private direction. Most important, the farms were no longer requisitioned but operated as profit-making units. Only the "commanding heights" of industry and finance were retained in government hands.

There ensued for several years a bitter debate as to the course of action to follow next. While the basic aim of the Soviet government was still to industrialize and to socialize (i.e., to replace the private ownership of the means of production by state ownership), the question was how fast to move ahead—and, indeed, *how* to move ahead. The pace of industrialization hinged critically on one highly uncertain factor—the willingness of the large, private peasant sector to make food deliveries with which the city workers could be sustained in their tasks. To what extent, therefore, should the need for additional capital goods be sacrificed in order to turn out the consumption goods which could be used as an inducement for peasant cooperation?

The Drive to Total Planning

The student of Russian history—or, for that matter, of economic history—will find the record of that debate an engrossing subject. But the argument was never truly resolved. In 1927, Stalin moved into command, and the difficult question of how much to appease the unwilling peasant disappeared. Stalin simply made the ruthless decision to appease him not at all, but to *coerce* him by collectivizing his holdings.

The collectivization process solved in one swoop the problem of securing the essential transfer of food from the farm to the city, but it did so at frightful social (and economic) cost. Many peasants slaughtered their livestock rather than hand it over to the new collective farms; others waged outright war or practiced sabotage. In reprisal, the authorities acted with brutal force. An estimated five million "kulaks" (rich peasants) were executed or put in labor camps, while in the cities an equally relentless policy showed itself vis-à-vis labor. Workers were summarily ordered to the tasks required by the central authorities. The right to strike was forbidden, and the trade unions were reduced to impotence. Speed-ups were widely applied, and living conditions were allowed to deteriorate to very low levels.

The history of this period of forced industrialization is ugly and repellent, and it has left abiding scars on Russian society. It is well for us, nonetheless, to attempt to view it with some objectivity. If the extremes to which the Stalinist authorities went were extraordinary, often unpardonable, and perhaps self-defeating, we must bear in mind that industrialization on the grand scale has always been wrenching, always accompanied by economic sacrifice, and always carried out by the more or less authoritarian use of power. We have already seen what happened in the West at the time of the Industrial Revolution, with the forced emigration of the peasantry by enclosure and the heavy-handed exploitation of labor; and without "excusing" these acts, we have seen their function in paving the way for capital accumulation.

In much the same fashion, when the Soviet leaders deliberately held down consumption, regimented and transferred their labor forces into the new raw industrial centers, and ruthlessly collected the foodstuffs to feed their capital-building workers, they were, in fact, only enforcing the basic process of industrialization. What was new about the Soviet program was that totalitarian control over the citizenry enabled the planners to carry out this transformation at a much faster tempo than would have been possible had protests been permitted. Under Stalin's iron will, the planners did not scruple to exercise their industrializing power to the hilt.

Without seeking to justify the Russian effort, it is worth pondering one last question. Can rapid industrialization, with its inescapable price of low consumption, ever be a "popular" policy? [6] Will poor people willingly vote for an economic transformation which will not "pay out" for twenty or forty years? Does rapid and large-scale industrialization *necessitate* a large degree of authoritorian political control? We will return to these problems when we turn to underdevelopment, but we might well begin to think about them now.

*   *   *

[6] We might note in passing that universal male suffrage was not gained in England until the late 1860's and 1870's. Aneurin Bevan has written: "It is highly doubtful whether the achievements of the Industrial Revolution would have been permitted if the franchise had been universal. It is very doubtful because a great deal of the capital aggregations that we are at present enjoying are the results of the wages that our fathers went without." (From Gunnar Myrdal, *Rich Lands and Poor* [New York: Harper & Row, Publishers, 1957], p. 46.)

89

Questions
and Answers
on Soviet Life

What determines the standard of living
of the Soviet citizen? The Soviet
propaganda magazine, *U.S.S.R.*, provides
an idealized description of how wages
and consumption are distributed in the
Communist world.

U.S.S.R.

QUESTION: Can a Soviet worker quit his job of his own free will if he chooses to?
ANSWER: Certainly. The only requirement is that he give two weeks' notice. After the two weeks have expired, the management has no right to hold him if he wants to leave.

QUESTION: What is the old-age pension system in the Soviet Union?
ANSWER: Our pension system retires women at the age of 55 after 20 years of service and men at 60 after 25 years of service. Those working underground and in hot shops have more favorable retirement provisions.

The minimum payment is 30 rubles, and 120 rubles is the maximum. The amount is based on average earnings over a period of the last 12 months of employment or of any consecutive five years out of the last 10 employed. The pensioner may do two-months' paid work a year and still draw his full pension. Pensions are not taxable.

The pension granted to a worker who has reached retirement age but does not have the required 20 to 25 years of service is proportionate to his length of service, but in no case is it less than one-quarter of the full pension.

People on pension continue to get medical services and hospitalization free.

QUESTION: How is new housing distributed?
ANSWER: Every city in the USSR has a large-scale construction program. In 1961 some 119,000 Moscow families moved into new apartments. Available housing is distributed by the district Soviets strictly in order of need and without charge.

Excerpted from *U.S.S.R.*, January, 1962, and May, 1962.

550

Every district Soviet has a housing committee composed of deputies and representatives of the trade unions and other public organizations. Anyone living in the district—even though he works in another district—may submit an application for a new apartment. Applications are reviewed by the housing committee and approved or disapproved by the executive committee of the district Soviet.

Preference is given to disabled war veterans, to families of men who were killed in the war, to large families, newlyweds, and those suffering from tuberculosis or other chronic diseases. Rent averages about five per cent of earnings.

QUESTION: *Do Soviet college students pay tuition?*

ANSWER: They do not. Tuition is free in all colleges and professional schools. Moreover, students get maintenance scholarships ranging from 30 to 80 rubles a month, depending on years of study and grades. Out-of-town students pay very little for dormitory accommodations—one ruble a month for a room and 50 kopecks for linens.

QUESTION: *Will you describe the system of distribution of material benefits in the Soviet Union?*

ANSWER: Since all industrial enterprises and state farms are publicly owned, their income is public property. Add the income of the collective farms, and you have the total national income.

A quarter of the national income is spent to augment and develop the country's industry, transport, and agriculture and to expand and modernize existing enterprises and build new ones. This is paid for out of the accumulation fund.

The remaining three-quarters of the national income makes up the consumption fund. It is spent for the material and cultural needs of the citizen.

The consumption fund is subdivided into the wage fund and the public consumption fund.

QUESTION: *These, I gather, are two quite separate funds and go to pay for different things.*

ANSWER: Yes, the wage fund, as the name implies, covers the wages of people working in factories and offices, in what we call the areas of material production.

QUESTION: *How about the wages of workers in other spheres, say, in education, the arts, service industries, government?*

ANSWER: Their wages come out of the public consumption fund since this fund pays for the development of science and culture as well as the maintenance of the educational and public health systems and the various social insurance benefits.

QUESTION: *Does this mean that the public consumption fund is spent for a number of different things?*

ANSWER: Yes. Besides the wages of those working in the nonmaterial production areas I mentioned, the fund pays for pensions, student stipends, vacations, resort accommodations, temporary disability benefits, and the like. These are direct money payments to the individual citizen, direct additions to his income. There are also indirect additions to his income, the many necessary and valuable services provided by the kindergartens, schools, colleges, hospitals, research centers, and health and holiday resorts, all of which are financed by the public consumption fund.

QUESTION: *If you translate these various benefits and social services provided by the public consumption fund into monetary terms, how much would you say they increase the average Soviet worker's income?*

ANSWER: By a third, over and above wages.

QUESTION: It would be helpful if you could show us how the public consumption fund affects the budget of a typical Soviet family.

ANSWER: Well, the Suslins are as typical as any. They live in Shchelkovo, a small town about 25 miles from Moscow. The family has two bread-winners—Alexei Suslin, who worked at a chemical plant, and his wife Valentina, an assembler. Their joint annual earnings, after taxes, come to 2,118 rubles.

Alexei's father does not work. He gets an old age pension of 493 rubles 20 kopecks a year. Alexei is in his fifth year at a specialized secondary school, where he studies after work. His tuition, textbooks, and study aids are all free. He gets paid leave from his job—it amounts to 75 rubles 40 kopecks a year on the average —to take his school exams. That sum plus his father's pension adds up to 568 rubles 60 kopecks a year.

Alexei spent his regular summer vacation at a resort; 45 rubles 60 kopecks, or one third of the cost of his accommodations, was paid by his trade union. Add this to the sum above and you have 614 rubles 20 kopecks.

The youngest Suslin, two-year-old Valerik, goes to a kindergarten. The parents pay 10 rubles of the 34 rubles a month it cost the kindergarten to keep the child, so that in a year the state spends 288 rubles for this young citizen. Add this to the previous total of 614 rubles 20 kopecks and you have 902 rubles 20 kopecks.

In the shop where Alexei is employed, workers get a free lunch that would ordinarily cost 68 kopecks. This saves him about 200 rubles a year.

All told, the public consumption fund gives the Suslins 1,102 rubles 20 kopecks in the course of a year.

QUESTION: Since the public consumption fund serves as an indirect addition to wages, wouldn't it be simpler and better to raise wages directly?

ANSWER: Simpler perhaps, but not better. Our country operates on the principle of socialism—"From each according to his abilities, to each according to his work." This means that every able-bodied person receives equal pay for equal work, irrespective of sex, age, race, or nationality. A person's earnings depend on the quantity and quality of work he does.

People vary in stamina and skill. Some workers are stronger, capable of greater effort and endurance, and can therefore do more. Workers with more skill do a better job. Consequently their earnings are higher and they have more cash income to spend to satisfy whatever personal needs they have. Besides that, there is the difference in size of families, number of wage earners, and so on. All these things make for inequalities in material well-being which will be gradually ironed out as we move toward the communist principle of distribution—"From each according to his ability, to each according to his *needs.*"

When we come to the public consumption fund, this material inequality does not operate. Higher wages do not help a man to give his children a better education or to get more qualified medical attention, let us say. In Western countries the quality of these services depends entirely on the amount the family earns and can afford to spend. Our approach is altogether different. The public consumption fund is distributed by the communist principle—according to needs. If you have children, they go to school. If you are ill, you get free medical attention, hospitalization, surgery, or whatever else is indicated. When you grow old, you get an old age pension. The public consumption fund meets people's needs regardless of the quantity and quality of the work they do. It makes all Soviet citizens equal with regard to educational opportunity, medical care, and the other services the public consumption fund supplies.

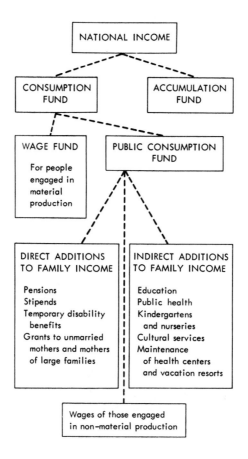

Fig. 1.

If you check back on the public consumption fund receipts of the Suslin family, you will see that they received, in monetary terms, a sum equal to more than half of their total earnings.

QUESTION: *Where does the money in the public consumption fund come from? Is the national budget its only source?*

ANSWER: The bulk of it is allocated in the national budget so that it can be distributed in a centralized fashion and with the interests of the whole society in mind.

The public consumption fund also includes enterprise funds—the money deducted from plant income and spent by management only with the approval of the trade union for the needs of its workers; and farm funds—cash or produce —that collective farms allocate for the same purpose.

90
Communist Economics: Reform vs. Orthodoxy

Soviet planning has apparently faced increasing difficulties as their system has grown more complex. This analysis reports the exploratory use of "profit" goals for managers since 1965, and points to some of the dilemmas this approach will pose for the Soviets if they expand it.

Alan A. Brown and Richard Yin are Research Associates of the Research Institute on Communist Strategy and Propaganda and Assistant Professors of Economics, University of Southern California.

ALAN A. BROWN

RICHARD Y. C. YIN

Communist countries have traditionally emphasized the goal of rapid growth of the economy, particularly of certain heavy industries, the maintenance of a strict central control over economic activities being another cardinal objective. To accomplish the basic goals, the Soviet-type economy, an economic system with its own methodology, was developed. The Soviet-type economy is not only a socialist (means of production publicly, i.e., government, owned) and a centrally planned economy, but it is also a command economy that tries to minimize its reliance on the market mechanism and indirect controls.

Because of their preoccupation with growth, as well as for purposes of control, the managers of the economy tend to overcommit the resources and emphasize the quantity rather than the quality of output. Detailed material allocation and taut planning, however, lead to bottlenecks, which are only partly alleviated by the unofficial, yet tacitly tolerated "informal activities" of the enterprises. Further corrective mechanisms for planning errors are provided by foreign trade (i.e., importation of essential goods in short supply) and by the domestic shock absorbers, which operate through a system of priorities. "The possible negative effects on economic growth of imbalances in supply plans are lessened because there are low priority

From *Communist Affairs*, January–February, 1965, pp. 3–9. (Bi-monthly publication of the Research Institute on Communist Strategy and Propaganda, School of International Relations, University of Southern California.) Reprinted by permission.

The authors wish to acknowledge their indebtedness to Harvard University Russian and East Asian Research Centers, to the Ford Foundation, and to the Social Science Research Council; and particularly to Professors Abram Bergson, Alexander Eckstein, Franklin L. Ho, and Egon Neuberger.

buffer sectors to absorb the shocks of these imbalances. The operation of the priority principle also lessens the negative effects of the interaction of imperfect supply planning and a not overly efficient supply bureaucracy."

The economic system of the Communist countries "is still evolving; in fact, it seems to have been more in flux lately than it had been for a long time." The past year has witnessed a proliferation of economic reorganizational measures throughout the Communist bloc. Out of lengthy public discussions emerged an increasing number of experimental projects, which are approaching an operational stage in most communist countries. The current wave of reforms promises to have a far more radical impact than reorganizational measures previously undertaken when "neither the basic methodology of planning nor the underlying philosophy [were] greatly affected." While the earlier reforms could be "better understood as part of the national campaign against excessive paperwork than as an attempt to influence managerial behavior," there is now a "widespread demand for more radical reforms and some of the proposals reach to the very foundations of traditional Soviet-type practices and theories."

REFORMS BORN OF ECONOMIC PRESSURES

The reformers are concerned with three types of interconnected shortcomings in the Soviet economic systems: (a) overcentralization in economic planning and control,[1] (b) the inadequacies of the system of material incentives, and (c) the irrationality of the price system.

Reasons for the reforms are not difficult to find. Surely, there are numerous sources of economic inefficiency, which have been thoroughly analyzed by Western scholars and are now admitted with increasing frankness in articles and letters printed in the Soviet press.[2] But reforms are usually the result of grievances. More basic questions of causality have to do with the timing of the reforms. Specifically, we should like to examine why the methodology of the Soviet economic system has begun to change.

It has often been stated that fundamental reforms or even "a free discussion of the problem had to await the post-Stalin 'thaw.' " Since the death of Stalin we have seen not an immediate but a gradual building-up of economic pressures. The old system that Stalin built became increasingly inadequate, not only because of certain new, or increased, requirements but also because the informal shock absorbers had worn thin.

For years, Stalin's heirs have attempted to find a new equilibrium without radically changing the underlying system and its basic methodology. But about a decade elapsed before the Central Committee of the CPSU decided to give a sympathetic hearing to the reform proposals, which now promise to change the fundamentals of the planning system. Eventually the need for these reforms would have become imperative even under Stalin, and the most that one can say

[1] The problem is not simply an overemphasis of the hierarchical chains of command, or rigid bureaucratization, but a plethora of commands and of planning agencies with overlapping authority.

[2] A "veritable flood of letters to the editor and articles, written by enterprise managers, engineers, workers, economists, and government officials, citing examples of irrational work organization and proposing changes in the existing structure of achievement indices and financial incentive rewards" appeared after an article in *Izvestiia*, November 22, 1961. (H. G. Shaffer, "What Price Economic Reforms? Ills and Remedies," *Problems of Communism*, Vol. XII, No. 3, May–June, 1963, p. 19.)

is that the process of self-reappraisal might have been delayed to some extent, but not indefinitely. Without denying the influence of individuals in historical development, we must look beyond personalities if we want to approach an understanding of important structural changes in an economic system.

GROWTH SLOWS AS PLANNING PROLIFERATES

The traditional Soviet planning apparatus has grown at a prodigious rate since its inception. In 25 years, after 1928, as estimated by Anatolii A. Dorodnitsyn, director of the computing center at the U.S.S.R. Academy of Sciences, planning became 1,600 times more complex. Victor M. Glushkov, mathematician and vice-president of the Ukrainian Academy of Science, expressed the phenomenal growth of the planning apparatus by means of a formula: "planning tends to increase as the square of output." Using the method of *reductio ad absurdum,* we see that Dr. Glushkov in fact proved that the planning system would have to be changed structurally, since by 1980—if the trend were to continue—every man and woman in the Soviet Union would be engaged in planning. Marx spoke of the increasing contradictions of capitalism; we may in turn stand Marx on his head and refer to the increasing contradictions of centralized, Soviet-type economies.

Planning becomes more complex as the economic interconnections grow and as a result of economic development (perhaps even as the square of output, as Glushkov calculated). It is easier to plan fewer and relatively homogeneous products, such as electricity, fuels, and steel, than more heterogeneous commodities, such as the output of the chemical industry. N. S. Khrushchëv compared "some officials" to blind horses, who "put on steel blinkers; they do everything as they were taught in their day. A material appears which is superior to steel and is cheaper, but they keep on shouting, 'steel, steel.'" The increasing complexity inherent in planning more numerous and more heterogeneous products goes a long way to explain the preoccupation with economic reforms in the U.S.S.R., where there has been a much-publicized slowing down of economic growth.

THE SITUATION IN SMALL OR BACKWARD COUNTRIES

We should not, however, conclude from the increasing difficulties experienced in the U.S.S.R. that either small economies, or primitive and poor countries are easier to plan and direct centrally. There are, in fact, reasons to believe that in small, as well as in backward countries, the contradictions of centralization tend to emerge *par excellence.* Not only are certain benefits of central planning and control denied to the small and to the backward countries, but also the costs of centralization (both what the economist calls explicit and implicit costs) tend to be magnified. In the smaller countries of the Soviet bloc, and—at the other end of the horizon—in China, the planners have experienced difficulties of greater intensity, or have felt them more keenly, judging by their earlier and more pervasive attempts to reform their systems. In the smaller communist countries the greater intensity of the problem is related to the important role that foreign trade plays in their economics. In the most backward countries, like China, the problem is related to poverty, the inadequacies of communications, and above all, the over-riding significance of agriculture.

Foreign trade and agriculture are the two sectors of the economy that are least suited to the traditional methods of a Soviet-type supercentralized command economy. In both of these sectors, it is very difficult (a) to predict conditions accurately, and (b) to supervise performance centrally. Without accurate predictions the need for frequent replanning is increased, and the more centralized the planning system, the more time-consuming and costly is replanning. At the same time, central planning, without effective supervision or control, offers little advantage, since the plan is then merely a paper plan.

Soviet-type economies, dedicated to rapid industrial growth—especially to the development of certain branches of heavy industry—have functioned traditionally by utilizing a rigid system of priorities. In general, the planners have favored investment at the expense of consumption, and more specifically, certain sectors of the economy at the expense of other sectors. Production of high-priority goods was emphasized, while planning errors were corrected by cutting back allocations to the low-priority sectors. Furthermore, the performance of the system, often measured by the spectacular growth of the high-priority industries, was predicated on the neglect or underemphasis of the low-priority economic branches, such as housing, consumers goods, agriculture, and foreign trade. As pointed out by numerous economists, this system resembled a war economy, and as such, it did fulfill certain needs. But in general, war economies have functioned only for relatively brief periods of time.

If such a system is operated for more prolonged periods, the shock-absorbing capacity of its low-priority sectors—because of their continued neglect—tends to be whittled away. This, coupled with the political necessity to provide more for the consumer, leads to an ironic situation—a farmer cannot indefinitely starve his draft animals and expect them to carry increasing loads.

The consequences of this process are evident enough in agriculture, the perennial problem sector of communist economies, but we can also identify similar developments in the foreign trade of these countries. The gains from foreign trade depend on the flexibility of the trader. Substantial reliance on imports, both to alleviate planning errors and to support rapid industrialization, coupled with the planners' traditional opposition to trade, set in motion several dynamic interactions. What evolved was not an increasing trend towards self-sufficiency, or a policy of autarky—as the communist trade policy has commonly been characterized—but an unstable equilibrium, which we may term *trade ambivalence*. The importance of foreign trade in Soviet-type economies has increased with a simultaneous tendency towards a decline of the gains from trade or a worsening of the terms of trade. There has been a paradoxical tendency to trade more and enjoy it less.

U.S.S.R. BELATEDLY STARTS REFORMS

In the U.S.S.R., the best-known economic reforms are associated with the name of Professor Yevsei G. Liberman, a Soviet economist, who in a series of articles outlined the need for "norms of profitability," which would provide "the greatest possible moral and material interest in making full use of reserves not only in plan fulfillment but also in the very compilation of plans. The goals of the proposal, according to Liberman, are the stimulation of enterprises towards increased outputs, better technology, and higher quality, as well as the elimination of bureaucratic excesses, or "petty tutelage," by superior agencies.

Liberman proposed to use profits as a single index for managerial bonuses, instead of numerous physical criteria. Also, he wanted to reduce the number of specific output targets set by the central planners, keeping only three: quantity, assortment, and delivery schedules. Liberman disclaimed that his proposal represented a departure from "the principle of central planning," which, he said, "should not only be maintained but should be strengthened by freeing the central agencies from unnecessary work and from tutelage over the enterprises." His argument was that the central planners would still specify the output plans of the enterprises, letting the enterprises decide only how to produce the required goods.

This mixed decentralization, however, would lead to a logical impasse. Since the outputs of one enterprise become the inputs for another (e.g., iron ore for steel), either the central planners will be unable to specify all outputs or the enterprise managers will have to use those semifinished commodities that are made available on the basis of central orders. If the "principle of central planning" is in fact to be strengthened, then the Liberman plan cannot prevent "some officials" from retaining their "steel blinkers" and "shouting, 'steel, steel,'" as Khrushchëv complained. Liberman either has failed to see the economic interrelationships or, what is more likely, prudently has chosen to ignore their existence. We must wait and see how the system is permitted to develop.

Although the Liberman proposal does represent a radical departure from the orthodox methodology of the Soviet system, it is essentially a one-sided approach to a multi-dimensional problem. As we have seen, Liberman took a contradictory stand on decentralization. He also brushed aside the arguments of his critics that the success of his profit scheme was dependent on a prior price reform. One can hardly reconcile, on the one hand, his ridiculing other economists' suggestions that rational prices were necessary to harmonize private and social interests, and on the other hand, his declaring: "What is profitable for the society, must also be profitable for each enterprise."

While Liberman confined his attention to the question of who should make decisions, other Soviet economists have delved into the problem of how to make correct decisions. Led by outstanding theoreticians, like L. V. Kantorovich, V. V. Novozhilov, and V. S. Nemchinov, an increasing number of Soviet economists have acknowledged that first the problem of meaningful valuation criteria must be solved, whether the purpose is to guide the activities of decentralized enterprise managers in reaching "rational" decisions, or [to implement] the choices of the central planners.

*   *   *

CHINA: FROM THE GREAT LEAP INTO A GREAT SLUMP

Events in China in recent years provide an interesting complement to the developments of the European Communist bloc. Although the cross-currents beneath the surface are not always easily distinguishable or categorized, the functioning of the Soviet model here seems to have had similar consequences. The planning and control of agriculture are an Achilles heel of any centralized economy; and, particularly in China, agriculture cannot be long ignored with impunity.

Agriculture in China is characterized by a large man-to-land ratio, low productivity per capita, and near-subsistence level of living. Compared to the U.S.S.R. of 1928, the margin of agricultural surplus that might be maneuvered to finance industrialization must have been much slimmer in China of the 1950's, if indeed such margin existed at all. Yet it was precisely the agricultural sector to which the least was given but from which the most was expected.

The stern constraint of agriculture on industrial growth became apparent to the Chinese authorities as early as 1955. The collectivization of agriculture, begun in earnest in the latter part of 1955, and virtually completed in 1956, brought with it a highly centralized system of direction and control of agricultural production and distribution. Judging from the retrenchment measures adopted soon afterward, the initial performance of this experiment was anything but an unqualified success. Two basic sources of the difficulties may be noted. On top of the formidable task of agricultural planning for a country as vast and varied as China, the hastily organized and largely untested collective farms had to be relied upon for the implementation of the plans. A step backward was taken in 1957, when the planned targets were simplified, the size of collective farms reduced, and price and market mechanisms briefly restored.

Thus the stress and strain generated by rapid industrialization and centralized planning and control reached another critical point in late 1957. Still persistent in the goal of rapid industrialization, the central authorities wanted to find some means to boost agriculture without sacrificing the emphasis on industrialization. The prescribed solution came in November 1957, in the form of a series of wide-ranging decentralization measures, designed partly to relieve the overloaded administrative system by giving more power to the provincial and local levels, and partly to encourage local initiative in the mobilization of local resources to aid agriculture as well as small industries. But coupled with the decentralization movement, there was a further tightening of political control over economic administration, which manifested itself in the ascendency of the role of Party cadres at all levels, at the expense of professional administrators and technical experts. "Expertness without redness" was considered not enough. In the country-side, a greater effort was to be made to capitalize on the vast human resources. Following a massive movement in "socialist education," the winter campaign for production (fertilizer collection and building of irrigation facilities) reached an unprecedented scale by the year-end. These developments ushered in the Great Leap Forward and the advent of the communes, which came to dominate the economic scene of China in 1958 and 1959.

During the Great Leap, with the emphasis on "politics in command" and "communist consciousness of the masses," individual initiative was played down, and the link of performance to material incentives all but disappeared. The piece-rate wage system was widely eliminated in industry; in agriculture, private plots were generally withdrawn, rural free markets abolished, and collective distribution of food and other essentials instituted. But it soon became evident that the dramatic reorganization, based on political enthusiasm in total disregard of material incentives and economic reality, could and did lead only to economic chaos and dislocation. The hoped-for improvement in production failed to materialize, and the Great Leap led into a Great Slump.

ORTHODOX PEKING SEEKS ALTERNATIVES

In 1960 and 1961, the deepening economic crisis brought about by the Great Leap was further aggravated by natural calamities. Necessity forced reversals of many of the measures adopted in the frenzy of the moment. Rural free markets reappeared, followed by the return and even expansion of private plots, a gradual transfer of ownership to the lower levels in the communes (first to the production brigades, then to the teams), and the rehabilitation of some form of piece-rate or wage-plus-bonus system. With the revival of economic incentives, there was a corresponding demotion of the role of Party cadres at all levels. But for our purpose the most notable development of all was the Party's decision, at the Ninth Plenum of its Central Committee in January 1961, *to give agriculture an overriding priority, which amounted to tampering with the hitherto sacrosanct goal of rapid industrialization.* The decision was subsequently endorsed by the 10th Plenum and has remained in force.

Taken as a whole, then, there appear to have been changes in the wind, which portend that either the planning system is to be loosened or the previously unrealistic sights lowered, or both. One wonders, however, in which direction the wind will blow, and for how long. At the First Session of the Third National People's Congress (Dec. 21–22, 1964) Premier Chou En-lai spoke of many of these liberalizing developments with apparent disfavor:

> From 1959 to 1962 . . . the class enemies at home launched renewed attacks on socialism, and consequently once again fierce class struggle ensued. In the domestic field, quite a few people actively advocated the extension of plots for private use and of free markets, the increase of small enterprise with sole responsibility for their own profits or losses, the fixing of output quotas based on the household, "going it alone" (i.e., the restoration of individual economy), "liberalization" . . .

WHY ARE THE REFORMS INEVITABLE?

As the dynamic pressures in the centrally planned Communist countries intensify, and their economies falter from one economic crisis to another, the economic medicine men are summoned and reform movements begin. At first they try to adopt partial improvements, i.e., suboptimization measures affecting only certain limited areas; then, the planning pendulum begins to swing, in search of a new equilibrium.[3] But reforms must be interrelated if they are to be effective: decentralization without incentives is meaningless; reforms in the payment system require rational valuation criteria, or prices. The implementation of the interrelated reforms, however, represents radical structural changes in economic philosophy and methodology.

Hungary and Poland have displayed the greatest degree of intellectual appreciation of the market mechanism and of the value of indirect controls, and Czechoslovakia and East Germany have followed fairly closely. Radical structural changes have been more tenaciously resisted in Bulgaria and Romania, as well as in the Soviet Union, but the reform movement even in these countries is approaching a critical point. In China, the economic system has been in a state of flux for years; although a wholesale reappraisal of the orthodox system is vehemently opposed on the official level, the logic of economic pressures remains very strong.[4]

[3] The basic economic lesson is the following: One may maximize a given goal, for a while even the output of a few high-priority sectors; many different goals, however, cannot be "maximized"—the problem is how to *optimize.* But the traditional model of Soviet-type economy is not a model of optimization. (E.g., the system of material balances is a method, which at best assures consistency, not optimality.) The reform movements are to be interpreted, therefore, as attempts to find a methodology of economic optimization.

[4] As Professor Peter Wiles stated, "Rationality is not less important because an economy is poorer. On the contrary, it is much more important. . . . It is only the rich who can afford to waste things, and it is a really amazing reversal of common sense to suggest that the marginal rules can be safely neglected in, say, China or India. . . ." (Peter J. D. Wiles, "Rationality, the Market, Decentralization, and the Territorial Principle," in Gregory Grossman, ed., *Value and Plan, op. cit.,* 1960, p. 184.)

The economists, and even the top leadership of the respective Communist parties, have shown in numerous statements that they are becoming aware of the long-run incompatibility of their traditional system and the goal of sustained, ambitious heavy industrial growth. As they lose their economic innocence, the planners at first try to find some fig leaves, such as the Liberman Plan. But since limited and isolated measures fail to provide lasting relief, it now remains to be seen to what extent the leadership of the individual countries will be willing to compromise the goal of economic growth to preserve the system, which, from the Danube to the Yellow Sea has outlived its usefulness.

Red China has become a significant
world force in a remarkably short period of
time. It is difficult to evaluate objectively
the economic accomplishments of the
Communist regime, but this reporter
presents his personal observations of some
of their achievements and failures.

Mark Gayn is an editorial writer for
The Toronto Daily Star *and author of a*
book on China to be published in 1966
by Delacorte Press.

91

China Today

MARK GAYN

CHINA TODAY: AN EGALITARIAN POVERTY

This is the first of a series of articles by Mark Gayn, author and editorial
writer for The Toronto Daily Star, *who has just completed a visit to*
Communist China. Mr. Gayn, who was born in China in 1909, is a
Canadian citizen. He has lived in or toured virtually all Communist
countries.

CANTON, China—At 6 in the morning, sounds of a familiar song are
heard. School children are singing: "Where is the Lin Yan River? It's in
Hunan and near it Chairman Mao Tse-tung was born. He is for us bright
sun. He brought us happiness."

A little later a column of about 800 men and women goes by. Their
wide straw hats are covered with green branches for camouflage. This is
the militia on its way to military exercises in the hills. Some are carrrying
tommy guns; others have sticks. The older women in the ranks look wilted
under the bright sun.

On the outskirts of the city smoke rises from the chimneys of new factories. In streets, billboards show Chairman Mao with Marx, Engels, and
Lenin. Red streamers urge the public to be self-reliant, to crush American
aggressors. Newsboys are peddling the latest from Peking. The Communist
party newspaper, *Jenmin Jih Pao,* has again denounced leaders in Moscow.

These are among my last sights and sounds as I leave China. Behind me are two months and close to 8,000 miles of travel. I have seen the north, south, and west of China, the ports of the Yellow and China Seas and the grasslands of Mongolia.

The places and the men to see are limited by official restriction. But I talked with farmers in remote areas, toured the large steel works at Anshan in the northeast and dined at the Great Hall, of the People in Peking, with the nation's leaders and about 5,000 other guests. I talked with living heroes and saw the shrines of dead ones. I visited kindergartens, hospitals, universities, cattle breeding stations, jade factories, and village communes. I spoke with housewives, army officers, movie stars, miners, writers, Buddhist lamas, and members of the élite.

I lived and worked in this land for many years and in many ways it has changed beyond recognition. Yet I was struck by the fact that so much has changed so little.

Perhaps the most striking change has been psychological, and nowhere has it been more obvious than in Shanghai. I worked here in the nineteen-thirties and again on the eve of the Communist triumph of 1949. I remember clearly the wicked and cruel city that was.

For a year I lived on the bank of a canal, facing a huge textile mill. At six each morning, thousands of girls, aged 12 and 13, streamed into its gates, not to come out until six at night.

Twice I found dead infants wrapped in newspapers and tossed under my car parked on the Bund, within a few hundred yards of the richest banks in the world. Each morning municipal trucks picked up as many as 30 bodies of men and women who had died of starvation. Yet each night the city came ablaze with neon lights, and honky tonks and night clubs were jammed with the well-fed and well-groomed.

The city was run first by a gangster named Tu, whom the Chinese Who's Who identified as "a leading philanthropist," and run later by a man named Hyang. They were kings of the underworld that made the Mafia look innocent.

They brought shiploads of opium from Szechuan, controlled crime and prostitution, and were neck-deep in national politics. A visitor, pushing his way past teenage prostitutes in Nanking Road, the main thoroughfare, or at the Great World Amusement Center, could hardly know that behind the heavily made-up youngsters loomed a mighty gangster-politician.

Swept by Spiritual Revolution

Shanghai then had 3 million inhabitants. Today it has 10 million, crammed into not much more space, but one could hardly recognize its citizens. The spiritual revolution that has swept China has changed Shanghai's soul and ways.

General poverty remains, but there are no beggars displaying their sores to passers-by and no starving children with distended bellies. Labor laws keep the children out of the factories and mill hands work only eight hours six days a week. Prostitutes have been "re-educated," and instead of girlie shows, the Great World now serves operas on the sufferings and triumphs of the revolutionary heroes.

Obscene contrasts between rich and poor have vanished, for here there are no more rich people. This has become an egalitarian society. Even managers of huge factories wear badly worn uniforms. They are never paid more than three times the average pay of their workers.

Because China was hungry its people were servile. Now the servility is gone.

Instead, those I met displayed inordinate pride in their country and its achievements. They have become thin-skinned and even innocent jokes may be taken as a slight to China's glory.

In old Shanghai thieves were like locusts. Today, honesty is commonplace.

Not once in my two months in China have I had to lock my hotel doors. Not once did I have to watch my luggage on trains, at airports, or in hotel lobbies; a Westerner who throws a pair of torn socks into a wastepaper basket is likely to have them returned in the next city.

Posters Stress Hygiene

All these—the new pride in China, the puritanism, the confidence, the dedication, the honesty—form the texture of the spiritual revolution. But there are at least two more elements—public health and education.

Notions of hygiene here may cause a visitor to shudder, but China has become conscious of the rudiments of public sanitation and cleanliness.

At movie houses a film is preceded with an appeal to the public not to spit or throw rubbish on the floor. Some hotels may not have running water or indoor plumbing, but they now have spittoons inside the rooms. Posters explaining hygiene have become part of the landscape.

On a new Viscount airliner, a stewardess, serving me tea, suddenly withdrew the glass and dashed away. I watched in amazement as she picked up a fly swatter and stalked the fly. Eventually the fly was dispatched and the girl carefully polished the spot with a rag. This may sound ludicrous, but it occurs on a national scale.

Public education has become a national obsession. Literacy is not yet universal, and schools cannot admit all those hungering for knowledge. Nevertheless, it is startling to come to Harbin, once a sleepy town in Manchuria, and find it has 11 universities and institutes.

To confine this report to achievements, however, would be to distort the picture. There is another side, just as important and far more disturbing.

Mainland China is seemingly involved in a perpetual demonstration. It is a rare day that people aren't called out to march in protest against something or other, to shout defiance, to listen to words of hate and anger.

The man produced by this is militant, intense, humorless. He is taught to accept exaggeration as normal, to use barnyard language, to see the complex panorama of world events in only two colors, white and black. How can an individual do otherwise when President Johnson is customarily called "gangster" and "bandit." Britain is described as "pimp," and the authoritative *Jenmin Jih Pao* employes four letter words?

To a much greater degree than in the Soviet Union of the nineteen-twenties, personal lives in China are subordinated to the needs of the state and Communist party.

Youths who desire university education may have it only if the five-year plans call for more university-trained specialists. A healthy man of 27 told me he is not yet married. "If I get married now, I would be distracted," he said, "and I won't be able to perform my duty to the nation."

Families Separated

Again and again I ran into married men and women, separated for months or even years, because the state demands their services in different places. Thousands of industrial workers and youngsters are ordered out of cities to the countryside, which is reluctant to have them because it does not need more manpower. But the party has set its policy and there is no room for personal dissent.

The free flow of ideas has ended, after a brief fling into the famous campaign of "Let a hundred flowers bloom, let a hundred schools of thought contend." Instead there are party pronouncements on everything—on the present and future, on morals and sex life, on books, films, and the arts, on politics and personal life.

When asked their opinion, most persons now reply in stilted propaganda phrases. A discourse with a Chinese usually follows a formula, with appropriate quotations from Mao Tse-tung's essays and with the final: "We have shortcomings, and we should appreciate your advice." But if one asks what these shortcomings are, he is certain to produce consternation.

This is not a war-minded nation. Despite the fierce talk of "the paper tiger of American imperialism," there are no war preparations to be seen. Yet from kindergarten on, the Chinese are injected with militancy, with a sense of self-righteousness, and with conviction that the leaders in Peking have found the wave of the future.

Perhaps most disturbing of all is the fact that people know nothing of the outside world except the unbelievably distorted image painted for them day in and day out.

The press talks of the "toiling masses" of North America who are going to oust the "bandit Government of President Johnson." Canada and Britain are described as lackeys of Washington. Soviet leaders are pictured as fat bourgeois plotting with American imperialists to destroy the world revolutionary movement. And all comment on the United Nations is saturated with contempt.

The picture is neither all black nor all white. Maoism has brought vast reforms to China. But it has also made China's millions march, carry rifles, throw grenades, and shout slogans of violence.

Nothing seems to delight the Chinese quite so much as taking a foreign visitor on a tour of their young and bustling industry.

The pride the hosts exhibit is both childish and touching, but they have good reason for it. The white hot steel pouring out of blast furnaces, the rails clanging at rolling mills, the new boilers, lathes, gauges, dies and ball bearings are proof that China is entering the industrial age.

There is also a hint of a coming industrial revolution that should eventually dwarf the miracle of Japan. Today China is where Japan was about 40 years ago. Barring a nuclear war, the Chinese should be able to do more in less time. For the men who govern in Peking, industrialization is an obsession, the key to China's future greatness and military might.

Great Leap Backward

These leaders first tried their hand at industrialization with the Great Leap Forward in 1957 and 1958. That was a half-baked venture for which the Chinese had neither the knowhow nor the resources. It collapsed with the first ill winds.

So disastrous was the impact of the lean years of 1959 to 1962 that it took Peking until now to recover. No new five-year plan was attempted. Statistics were no longer made public. All energy was put into the job of survival.

This bleak period is now all but over. Lights are burning late over planning boards and at the eight machine-building ministries, where men are toiling on the third five-year plan due to start next year. No targets are being made public but there are signs that this will be a common sense plan with no dreams of great leaps.

Evidence of modest intent is ample. At none of the plants I visited was there any talk of expansion. Technical schools are planning to turn out no more engineers than they did last year. Nor is there any hint of plans for greatly expanded purchases of raw materials or machinery. The Chinese may want to do no more than exploit the unused capacity of the plants they already have.

Big Factories Visited

In my two months in China I visited some of the nation's proudest factories—the great Anshan steel complex with its 40 plants and 100,000 workers, a truck plant in Manchuria, a tractor works in Loyang.

What I saw was impressive, if only because it did not exist when Mao Tse-tung rode into power in 1949. In old China there were some industries the Japanese had built in Manchuria and there were some industries, mainly textile, in the large ports of China.

A few weeks ago I stood at a window of my hotel in Taiyuan, once a sleepy preserve of a minor warlord, and counted 58 factory chimneys.

Nagging Doubts Raised

Two months of looking, however, raise some nagging doubts about the quality of things observed.

All the big plants I saw were designed, built, and equipped by the Russians.

When the Russians walked out in the summer of 1960, their action set back Chinese industry by as much as two years. At the largest machine building plant in China I saw enormous Soviet lathes standing idle. After five years the Chinese still had not mastered them.

By and large, however, the Chinese have learned how to run the Soviet machinery and how to replace undelivered equipment with their own. At Nanchang airport I saw four MIG-19's roar off into the skies. They came from a plant that long stood idle after Soviet experts walked out, but the Chinese have now resumed production.

Chinese exhibitions proudly display a new family of sophisticated machines. They are enough to gladden the heart of any patriot. They appear to be only exhibition pieces, however. I certainly saw nothing like them in any of the plants I visited.

What the Chinese do produce in quantity is copies of machines acquired from the Soviet bloc. At Anshan they show the visitor blast furnace No. 10 "designed and built entirely by us." It is nothing but a slightly larger version of nine other furnaces installed by the Russians in the early fifties, built in the late forties and probably designed in the thirties.

Even more striking was a visit to a huge cable plant in Shanghai. When the Communists marched into the city in 1950 they found a small cable factory with a few prewar General Electric machines. Now they have rows of Chinese copies of what are really museum pieces.

30 Years Behind Times

Here and at Anshan, as in so many other places, the Chinese are building obsolescence into their new factories. Their new industry begins by being 30 years behind times. This industry is still very useful, but sooner or later the Chinese will have to realize that the world is pulling away from them and they will have to start anew.

Chinese industry is woefully inefficient. Its management by civil war veterans is zealous but technically ignorant, its labor force is far too large and it has too many people pushing pens in offices.

In a typical plant, with its numerous banners and posters bearing appeals to work harder, one is struck by the number of workers clustered about each machine. A lathe built for one may have four or five persons about it. Sometimes it is explained that these are young hands being trained, but a couple of times, in bursts of candor, factory managers said it was redundant labor.

Factory Pay Is Low

The state compensates for the resulting low productivity by paying low wages. The average factory pay now runs to around $22 a month. The top pay of a skilled worker is just under $45. This is low pay even for China, but it is all that low productivity will justify.

While some managers talk of unneeded hands, they will not lay them off. This is a land in which no one is unemployed.

Before the Chinese industrial revolution moves far ahead, the Communist party will have to change its attitude toward intellectuals. Factories are now run by political appointees who know little of modern industry. Men who completed five years of engineering studies are often employed as common laborers. They may become technicians after a year or two and may attain the status and pay of engineers in three to five years more, depending on their political soundness.

Not all engineers and scientists are treated with such disdain. The kernel of China's nuclear establishment, for instance, is provided by nearly 1,000 specialists trained at Dubna near Moscow. Some significant research is being done. But most of it appears to be focused on military projects.

A look at China's industry thus leaves one with mixed feelings. What is being done is often done with startling inefficiency. There is an obsession with such industrial status symbols as the Red Banner passenger car, of which 100 will be made this year for the governing élite. China would have saved a great deal of money by importing Rolls-Royces instead.

Yet what is being done is a vast advance on anything this country ever had before. Men who serve the young industry do it with zeal and pride. Industry does turn out needed essentials, as well as nuclear devices.

This industry cannot be regarded lightly. Sooner or later it will adapt itself to the times. Beyond doubt what one sees here is the beginning of a great industrial revolution.

Of all the battles being fought by Peking, however, none is so crucial as its drive to bring the revolution to rural China. Agriculturally, China is in the Dark Ages.

Blunders made during the period of the Great Leap Forward and natural disasters afterwards caused an agricultural crisis. China averted famine only by going into the world market to shop for grain.

This year the Chinese are counting on a good harvest. In Peking, senior Government officials told me the harvest will be better than last year's and possibly even than the record harvest of 1957.

Personal observations offer some support to this claim. The northeast and the west are showing the effects of drought, but in the Yangtse River valley I saw a bountiful crop of wheat being harvested.

Promising crops can also be seen from the great plain of North China to the lush green paddies in the south.

Good Crop Is Vital

A good crop is vitally important to China. It will enable her to add to the present grain ration—one pound a day for office help and intellectuals and as much as two pounds for workers in mines, transport, and heavy industry.

A good crop would also help boost morale of the half billion people who live and work in China's 74,000 communes.

92

Lessons from the West German Miracle

The author analyzes the rapid post-war
economic growth in West Germany, and
identifies the selective government
policies which helped make it possible.
He suggests that we consider similar
policies for the American economy.

Karl W. Roskamp is a member of the
Economics Faculty at Wayne State
University.

KARL W. ROSKAMP

What lessons does West Germany's remarkable postwar economic growth offer to the American economy today with its five million unemployed, gold outflow and "growth gap"? One comforting deduction is that a capitalist economy is still capable of achieving rates of growth comparable to the best that the socialist countries can offer.

But what type of capitalist economy has achieved these growth rates? Was the German "miracle" the result mainly of an orthodox monetary policy and the restoration of the free market that together galvanized private initiative?

This popular view is at best a half-truth. Some of the reasons for calling it a half-truth are reasonably obvious. West Germany had most of the basic ingredients for rapid growth. Its labor force was highly skilled and its physical plant was only partially demolished. Until 1955 it had a labor surplus (which stemmed largely from the inflow of refugees from the east). Its trade unions were rather weak, partly because of this labor surplus. The cost to Germany of the Allied occupation was low; the U.S. provided special economic aid in the early postwar years, and the military burden has only in the past two or three years begun to approximate that of other European countries.

Less obvious, however, has been the major positive role of the government. It has fostered capital formation through large budgetary surpluses and has done much to influence the volume and direction of private investment. These actions, though little noted, shed a rather different light

Reprinted from Challenge, The Magazine of Economic Affairs, 475 Fifth Avenue, New York, N. Y., 10017, July 1, 1961, pp. 10–14.

on the German "miracle" and on the mixed character of the postwar German economy. Far from being a paragon of McKinleyite rectitude, West Germany's economic policy is close enough to ours to provide us with some guidance on the effective use of selective fiscal measures to promote economic growth without inflation.

A few words of caution are, however, needed. In this article, I do not attempt to "explain" West Germany's growth. This was a complex process for which no simple explanation can be given. It was not solely due to a return to "free competition"—there is much oligopoly (domination of a market by a few firms) and monopoly in West Germany. Nor was the currency reform in 1948 the only cause. Likewise it cannot be attributed chiefly to general monetary and fiscal policy, trade union behavior, or the influx of refugees.

Each of these factors had an important influence, but none of them, taken alone, can furnish an explanation of why the country progressed as fast as it did. The same is true of the important role of public authorities in this process; it is not *the* explanation of why growth rates were high. Nevertheless, governmental influence was a very important ingredient, and it is certainly worthwhile to take a closer look at it.

PROPER PERSPECTIVE

To get the impact of governmental action upon the West German growth into the right perspective, and to understand its nature and extent, we must first outline the situation of the economy in 1948.

When Germany was divided after the war, West Germany was separated from agricultural districts in the east and highly developed light industries in central Germany. This forced severe readjustments on the West German economy. Its need for food imports increased, and new light industry had to be constructed. Swept into a country devastated by the war were, between 1945 and 1948, about seven million refugees, many of them initially without employment. Through this influx the housing situation, which was already bad enough, became catastrophic. The lack of raw materials for industry handicapped production in early postwar years, but more important than this, perhaps, was the general lack of incentives.

There was a severe food shortage, which would have been disastrous if Allied supplies had not been available. There were black markets all over the country. Those who could still produce often preferred to hoard products rather than to sell them. In many cases, the reason for this was the fear that no new raw materials could be obtained except by barter.

An extremely severe inflation prevailed. The Allies excluded West Germany from direct international trade and limited its production of steel and other important items. In addition, they had raised income tax rates to such a high level that these alone would have probably been sufficient to strangle a good deal of all incentives.

The West German currency reform in 1948 marked a turning point in the country's history. This measure stimulated business strongly. But it also had many inequitable features. In brief, holders of old Reichsmarks were allowed to convert only a limited amount of them into Deutsche marks, the new currency. Most personal savings, certainly all small savings, the national debt, and nearly all business cash reserves were thereby wiped out. But confidence that the new currency would retain its value caused businessmen to offer goods for sale that previously they had hoarded or bartered. Trade revived and the economy started on its upward course.

Accompanying the reform was the abolition of price controls over all but a few important commodities. Allied control of international trade was relaxed. The currency reform, however, discouraged saving by individuals for some time, since small savers had just had virtually all the fruit of their thrift confiscated.

At the time of the currency reform, there were industrial capacity, industrial skills, and a powerful backlog of demand for all sorts of consumer goods—plus excess labor that kept wages down. As a result, profits were initially extremely high. In brief, the currency reform was a hard reform. It was an "efficiency" solution geared to create incentives rather than to promote social justice. It caused a lot of social hardship, but it got the economic machine started.

After 1950 the German "miracle" began; gross national product in constant 1954 prices rose from 113.1 billion DM in 1950 to 233.8 billion DM in 1960. (Four Deutsche marks equalled $1 during this period.) In 1950 West Germany suffered from substantial unemployment and a large balance of payments deficit; today it has a serious labor shortage, rising prices, and a large balance of payments surplus.

An outstanding feature of West Germany's economic growth was the astonishingly high rate of investment. That this was needed was recognized by many West Germans at an early date. Debates in the country's parliament in 1949 indicate that the government was keenly aware of this necessity.

West Germany needed new plants to meet domestic demand and to make its exports competitive in the world market. Big investments were also required to house and provide productive employment for the refugees. Thus the need for rapid capital formation was obvious to all. The problem was how to generate the necessary savings.

However, the Germans were disinclined to save; after both World Wars they had seen their savings wiped out by currency reforms. Thus, voluntary savings could be scarcely relied upon to supply enough funds for capital formation—at least not in the crucial years between 1950 and 1955. Even if interest rates had been extremely high, they would have scarcely induced a sufficient volume of savings, for incomes were rather low.

In these circumstances the government took a hand in the process of saving and investment. Had it not done so, and left saving and investment to the private decisions of a free market, what would have happened? There would have been too few funds seeking investment, and these would have flowed into sectors of the economy, such as trade, where high profits could be made quickly.

SOCIAL CONSIDERATIONS AND GROWTH

Sectors of the economy vital to sustained growth would have been starved of funds. For instance, mining and basic industries such as steel could scarcely have attracted enough savings—dividends from investments in them would not have been high enough to do so. The fact that the remaining price controls applied largely to basic industries would have kept profit expectations down in this sector. Residential construction would also have been neglected as rent controls would have kept profits down. Not to supply cheap housing for destitute refugees was, however, socially unacceptable. Not to invest in sectors temporarily unprofitable but vital for future economic growth would have been shortsighted.

Therefore, for social reasons and to ensure future economic growth, the government intervened to supply and direct the flow of funds for investment. This government action was carried out on the federal, state, and local level. A tight orthodox monetary policy kept interest rates high. With this was combined a complex and ingenious fiscal policy, largely implemented by tax exemptions. The often-heard argument that the high interest rates maintained by the Central Bank were the key to West Germany's growth is an oversimplification. It ignores the role of fiscal policy.

Thus, though West Germany had high *nominal* interest rates and high nominal tax rates, the selective tax measures softened their impact. One result of this was that for a long time bank rates were high but capital market rates were low. This was made possible by tax subsidies. Those sectors which were considered important for the country's economic growth or in which investments were necessary for social reasons could obtain low-cost capital market funds. Other sectors had to pay stiff bank rates if they decided to finance investment externally.

How did it happen that the West Germans resorted to an extensive selective use of fiscal policy to further economic growth? The Allied occupational powers immediately after the war had substantially increased many tax rates, particularly on income, in the vain hope of stopping the mounting inflation. After the currency reform the West German government feared that the high tax rates would have a strong adverse effect on the economic incentives of capital and labor. The Allies, however, refused to allow a general tax cut, arguing that high tax revenues were essential to prevent inflation. In fact, they prohibited budget deficits by law.

As a result, the high tax rates, together with a broadening of the tax base due to rising incomes, generated large tax revenues. Moreover, "defense expenditures" (in the form of occupation costs) were relatively small, and as the national debt had been wiped off the slate in 1948, there were no interest charges on it. Thus, the public sector became an important supplier of funds for investment. If the West Germans did not save voluntarily, they certainly saved heavily through taxes.

Budgetary surpluses were used both for large direct government investments and for substantial loans and subsidies to private investors. What the precise criteria were for the allocation of these funds is not known, but the government clearly had a very effective means for selectively aiding various sectors of the economy and industries. In the period 1948–57, between 35 billion and 40 billion DM were used in this way. Residential construction, agriculture, and industry all benefited from these public capital funds.

The tradition of public ownership in Germany facilitated this public capital formation. Government enterprises are much more numerous in West Germany than in the United States. Railroads and the telephone and telegraph systems are operated by the government, as are radio and TV stations. In addition, the government owns completely or in part numerous coal mines, power plants, and manufacturing plants. For instance, the much discussed Volkswagen plant is partly public property. A recent study indicates that more than 14 per cent of all corporations are government-owned.

INFLUENCE ON INVESTMENT

But the role of government in supplying funds for investment went much beyond supporting public enterprises. Subsidies to housing under the "Social Residential Construction" program totaled about 21 billion DM between 1950 and 1957.

Under the "Green Plan" low-cost credits were extended to agriculture. Under the "Investment Aid Law" in effect from 1952 to 1956 business in general was forced (not induced) to provide 1.1 billion DM for "bottleneck" sectors in industry. All of these programs provided low-cost funds for the private investments that helped to eliminate crucial shortages of capacity.

The influence of public authorities on investment was not limited to direct expenditures. After 1949 a large tax exemption program came into existence to promote investment. For, although West German tax authorities during the Allied occupation had no power to change the high personal and corporate income tax rates, they could grant tax exemptions. At a time when monetary policy was tight and tax rates high, tax exemptions proved to be a very effective means of directing private investments into areas preferred by public authorities.

The tax exemptions granted under this program amounted to about 28 billion DM between 1949 and 1957. Below is a brief summary of the more important of these exemptions.

ACCELERATED DEPRECIATION

Under paragraph 7A of the income tax law introduced in 1948, capital goods (plant, equipment, etc.) acquired after January 1, 1949 could be depreciated up to 50 per cent in the first two years up to a limit of 100,000 DM per firm. Business made extensive use of this accelerated depreciation and applied tax savings to augment working capital. This measure probably cost the government about 1.3 billion DM between 1950 and 1957.

Paragraph 7B of the income tax law provided tax incentives for residential construction. In the first two years after the completion of a house, 20 per cent of its value could be deducted as depreciation. For subsequent years the annual depreciation allowance was three per cent. Thus in 12 years one could deduct 50 per cent as depreciation. The amounts deducted under this provision were substantial. They increased from 38 million DM during 1949 to an estimated 900 million DM in 1957.

Housing was favored not only by paragraph 7B but also by paragraph 7C. This provided that interest-free loans given for house building could be deducted as a business cost in the year in which the loan was granted. Later, when such loans were repaid in equal installments, the creditor had to report each repayment as taxable income. Between 1949 and 1957 about 3.5 billion DM were deducted in this way. This provision of the law was widely used to shift payment of taxes from years of extremely high profits to years with low profits or lower tax rates.

Under paragraph 7D, funds loaned for ship building could be declared as a business cost in the year in which they were granted. These loans were to be given free of interest and to be repaid after a stipulated time. After repayment the funds became taxable.

This provision seems to have provided a golden opportunity for corporations to avoid the tax collector and to establish an influence in shipping at the same time. A clever man could do a lot of things under this paragraph. West Germany was surprised in 1957 that a manufacturer of baking powder, through skillful use of this and other tax exemptions, had managed to build up a whole fleet of freighters. Probably 1.5 billion DM were made available under these provisions between 1949 and 1957. This helped, naturally, to rebuild West Germany's merchant marine.

Paragraph 10 of the German Income Tax Law had always allowed certain deductions for payments made to insurance and building and loan associations. Contributions to these institutions were considered socially desirable and therefore tax-favored. Only individuals could receive these tax benefits. After 1949 the categories of personal savings which were considered socially desirable were considerably broadened. New forms of tax-exempt savings were introduced. Tax privileges were also granted if specific kinds of tax-exempt securities were bought. The provisions were complicated and changed from year to year. Banks would publish small booklets by tax experts that gave their customers advice on how to lower tax bills. Deductions made under these provisions constituted the largest budget losses. Between 1949 and 1957 they probably amounted to over 12 billion DM.

Finally, mention should be made of the "Investment Aid Law," the "Law to Favor Exports," and the "Capital Market Law." Deductions made under these laws between 1949 and 1957 probably amounted to 5.5 billion DM.

OVERALL PICTURE

Let us summarize the government influence on investment in order to get an overall picture. Total West German net investment, domestic and foreign, between 1948 and 1957 was approximately 213.5 billion DM; of this, 92.8 billion DM, or 43.5 per cent, was directly supplied by the government. In addition, about 28 billion DM was "influenced" by government, through tax exemption. Thus, about 56 per cent of all net investment between 1948 and 1957 was influenced in one way or another by public preferences. This surely constituted a considerable interference with West Germany's alleged "competitive free market economy."

During the crucial first years of economic revival and growth, the necessary framework was re-established in which the market mechanism could function efficiently. The West Germans made sure that through public interference and guidance the allocation of resources into areas of shortage was facilitated. By 1955 the rapidly expanding West German economy was much nearer to a "free market economy" than it was in 1950.

But while government intervention rapidly increased the efficiency of the economy, the effects on income distribution were probably adverse. We have little precise information on personal income and property distribution during the postwar period. We do know, however, that profits were extremely high and that tax incentives benefited mainly those in the upper-income brackets.

There were, it is true, some factors making for a more equal distribution. The comprehensive West German Social Security System put a floor under low-income groups. In addition, a large program of partial compensation for war losses may have favored some of the low-income groups. There is good reason to assume that, on balance, the distribution became more unequal. Today, despite the general rise in incomes of all classes, income distribution in West Germany is probably more unequal than in Great Britain or the United States. If this is actually so—and it should be stressed that a lot of research is still necessary to throw more light on this subject—the social cost of the German "miracle" was not inconsiderable.

Of course, the West German economy, economic institutions, and social environment are in many respects different from ours. Nevertheless, I believe that some of our problems have a marked family resemblance to West German ones. What lessons, then, can we learn from the West German experience?

Perhaps the most interesting lesson concerns the efficacy and use of *selective* economic policy measures. To the extent that many of our present economic troubles are of a structural nature which cannot be successfully tackled through general economic policy measures, this lesson has particular relevance for us.

Severe bottleneck problems exist or could come into existence here, as in West Germany—for instance, in education, research, housing, specific industries, and urban redevelopment. Selective government expenditures or taxation measures may be the most effective means of eliminating them speedily. Their elimination through the working of the market mechanism may be too slow and may cause an undesirable degree of inflation.

The social cost of relying solely on the market mechanism could be forbidding. To illustrate, in West Germany the provision of housing for refugees was an essential first step toward rehabilitation. This could not be left to the market unless it was decided to exclude low-income receivers for a long time from decent housing. In addition providing housing in areas where labor was short facilitated the recruitment of a stable labor force. The problem was attacked and largely solved through selective government loans. (Between 1950 and 1957, 34 per cent of all funds used for residential construction were directly supplied by public authorities.)

To the extent that substantial shifts in the location of the U.S. labor force are necessary—and they may now be needed as a consequence of changes in the production or consumption pattern—they could be facilitated through selective government aid. This could take the form of providing retraining facilities, transportation, and, if necessary, housing. (The Swedes, in their attempts to maintain a high level of employment, seem to have learned quite a bit from the West Germans in this respect.)

If we wish to increase capital formation to accelerate economic growth, we may think of using tax incentives for investments as the West Germans did. Accelerated depreciation and tax-exempt investment loans may be the answer. In West Germany these had a powerful boosting effect. However, if the U.S. granted such incentives, care should be taken that the right sectors of the economy get the benefits. (This problem seems to have caused the West Germans some headaches.) Actually, it is difficult to be certain about the extent to which such selective tax measures could be applied in the U.S. Opposition to them could be quite strong on the ground that they were inequitable.

DESIRABLE BALANCE

If we wish to obtain a desirable balance between the needs of the public and the private sector, it may be necessary to increase public revenues by taxing less essential private expenditures. In West Germany there have been few complaints that the public sector has been neglected; rather the business community has complained that the public sector was too much favored and, in general, too large. Direct investments by public authorities have been very heavy, and there is no sign that this sector is going to decline in importance. There is also no indication that the large public sector in West Germany retarded the country's growth.

Finally, to increase our exports, we may well consider the package of West German measures—discounting of bills for exports at low rates, tax rebates on exports, and tax exemptions on investments in export industries. Some of these measures may be distasteful. Others may provide useful hints.

There is a growing consensus that many of our present economic problems require selective treatment. Such treatment was applied during the most crucial period of West Germany's economic growth. Further investigation of the selective measures employed by the government may throw some new light on the German "miracle"—which was, in fact, no miracle at all but the result of hard work, wise policy, and a substantial amount of good luck. Moreover, such an investigation may provide us with new insights. There can be no doubt that the West Germans were and are strong believers in a free market system. But they were quick to recognize that there are many situations in which the free market forces must be aided and guided in order to facilitate structural adjustments and to generate a satisfactory rate of economic growth.